Readings in Perception

THE UNIVERSITY SERIES IN PSYCHOLOGY

Editor

DAVID C. McCLELLAND

Harvard University

Readings in Perception

SELECTED AND EDITED BY

DAVID C. BEARDSLEE

Professor of Psychology
Oakland University of Michigan State University

AND

MICHAEL WERTHEIMER

Professor of Psychology
University of Colorado

D. VAN NOSTRAND COMPANY, INC.

PRINCETON, NEW JERSEY

TORONTO　　　　　　　　　　　LONDON

NEW YORK

D. VAN NOSTRAND COMPANY, INC.
120 Alexander St., Princeton, New Jersey (*Principal office*)
24 West 40th Street, New York 18, New York

D. VAN NOSTRAND COMPANY, LTD.
358, Kensington High Street, London, W.14, England

D. VAN NOSTRAND COMPANY (Canada), LTD.
25 Hollinger Road, Toronto 16, Canada

First Published April 1958
Reprinted, June 1960,
August 1963, October 1964,
August 1965

Preface

PERCEPTION IS one of the oldest areas of research in experimental psychology. Since before Aristotle it has been a substantial part of general psychology. Less than a hundred years ago sensation and perception *were* experimental psychology, and today perception is still regarded as one of the three fundamental research topics, along with motivation and learning. Yet the contemporary student has to look in many different books and journals if he wants to get an understanding of this field, and much of the material is in foreign languages.

There are, it is true, several recent excellent texts on sensory psychology and handbook chapters on human sensation and perception, but these do not include sufficient treatment of perception for even a one-semester course. None of them, for example, covers more than a fraction of the topics suggested for a "core course" in perception by Buxton *et al.* in *Improving Undergraduate Instruction in Psychology.*

In bringing material together in this book, we have tried to select some important papers and arrange them in a sequence which presents the contemporary understanding of "why things look as they do." In such a form these readings are intended to serve as a supplement to or in lieu of a text for a one- or two-semester course in the psychology of perception. Admittedly, work in perception has not yet yielded as organized and quantitative a set of laws as is available in sensory psychology. Yet the number of principles of perceptual processes which emerge from such a collection is encouraging, even though in many ways they are incomplete.

We have selected studies that we feel represent the core of the experimental psychology of perception upon which so much current personality, motivation, and social psychological research builds. But even though the resurgence of interest in perception today is partly due to the more personological fields of psychology, we have restricted our selection of perceptual work in related fields such as personality, comparative psychology, and applied psychology to ar-

v

143351

ticles that made contributions to fundamental problems in perception. That there has also been much recent work in "general perceptual" psychology is shown in the large proportion of recent articles which we found desirable to include. Papers that have become classic in the field have been included where they have not been substantially superseded or amended by newer work.

Some psychologists may be surprised not to find a section devoted to sensory sensitivities. Several considerations influenced the decision not to try to cover this topic by means of readings. First, there are readily available texts whose presentations are more complete and integrated than readings can be. Second, few if any of the papers reprinted, or the alternate papers considered for inclusion, make any reference to or use of the extensive body of highly systematized quantitative knowledge available in sensory psychology. While it may be that ultimately the understanding of perception will be an outgrowth of studies of sensitivity to various modalities of stimulation, such explanation seems to be at present potential rather than actual. Third, the highly developed and quantified status of sensory psychology makes most current studies exceedingly specialized and technical. Older studies, on the other hand, no longer adequately represent the kinds of research methods and theoretical interpretations of current interest. This book, therefore, attempts to present a sequence of papers reporting empirical studies of perceptual processes from physiological and methodological foundations through the experiences created by simple stimuli to complex perceptual categorizing.

ACKNOWLEDGMENTS

This book is a joint product. It has profited from the advice and assistance of many people. We wish to acknowledge with thanks the willingness of authors and publishers to have their contributions reprinted here. Dr. David C. McClelland encouraged us from the start and assisted in many ways. Mrs. Helen Ehlinger gave invaluable aid in preparation of the manuscript. Ultimately, it is our students' active interest in perception which has motivated us to provide this collection.

D.C.B.
M.W.

Middletown, Connecticut
Boulder, Colorado

Table of Contents

Contents

Contents

Contents

Introduction

THE PAPERS in Part I of this book discuss recent knowledge about the physiological mechanisms involved in perceptual processes. They extend the coverage of the general characteristics of organismic sensitivity and the basic information on special senses available in all standard introductory texts. The nature of the sense receptors and the psychological implications of the ways in which they are connected to the central nervous system provide the framework for the understanding of complex perceptual phenomena. Later, Köhler's paper on relational determination in perception offers an alternative interpretation of the neural substrate of perception.

The active work now in progress on the effects of drugs on perceptual phenomena has not yet jelled into general principles, but the selection by Hoffer, Osmond, and Smythies points up the variety of perceptual processes affected by drugs, and the large individual differences in reactions of two subjects suggest the dangers of overgeneralization. Hoagland's paper on time perception returns to body chemistry as a perceptual determinant, and Bruner's paper on perceptual readiness again attempts to integrate physiological and psychological understanding of perceptual processes.

Part II presents a brief history of the development of research methods for the study of perception. Hirsh points out that the classical psychophysical methods are not now interpreted as ways of measuring subjective events but as means for studying responses to stimulation. Nonetheless, analysis of thresholds is a central method of study of the organism's handling of stimulus input, in studies of thresholds for perception of words or sensitivity to food objects as well as in research on sensory events.

The papers in Part III deal with problems of perception of areas, figures, events, and space. This is the area in which perceptual research has been focused, the world of objects in space. An attempt has been made to present the selections in a sequence from "undifferentiated" percepts to the phenomena and laws of the highly organized percepts of space and time. This section begins with a report of the experiences aroused by undifferentiated stimulus input and proceeds through the effects of introducing minimal differentiation to the organism's capacity to handle differentiated stimulation regarded as information input. Next a series of papers introduce the concepts of organization, grouping, and figure-ground articulation of stimuli. Studies of figural "goodness" and its stimulus correlates are included here.

In this connection, considerable interest has attached to studies of the role of "experience" in organizing perception. Several papers treat the consequences of limited perceptual experiences during development or the effects of exposing adult organisms for periods of time to altered or limited stimuli. Hochberg's paper on the Gestalt revolution and Hess' in the section on space perception contain additional information on this problem. Perception of the brightness, hue, and form properties of areas is discussed. Then sequential effects of exposure to stimuli upon perception of later stimuli are discussed both in terms of the effects upon judgments of properties of later stimuli and the specific spatial aftereffects.

The relation between perceptual fields which follow each other in time may lead not only to changed perceptions of new stationary stimuli but, under appropriate conditions, to experiences of movement. The dependence of movement phenomena on relations between stimuli is analyzed in several papers. Finally, perception of the time dimension itself, the experience of duration, is studied. Additional observations on time perception were noted in the study on the effects of drugs and in the observations on subjects subjected to limited stimulation.

The favorite single topic of the perception psychologist has for some time been the perception of space. Strictly speaking, space perception is a definition of a topic in terms of the *results* of psychological processes instead of the nature of the processes involved. However, the experimental findings seemed to fit together better as a group than if distributed through the preceding sections on perceptual consequences of relations between stimuli. The possible role of past experience is again discussed here, the classical cues are reported and reinterpreted, and the problems associated with orientation in auditory space are discussed. Finally, two papers report research on the vertical dimension of space and its interrelationships with other perceptual functions.

The first paper of Part IV indicates the lack of a sharp empirical dividing line between percepts and images, and the remaining papers deal with imagery as an aspect of the total perceptual processes of the organism.

Part V introduces the perceptual problems of "meaningful" stimuli. The first section contains studies on word and symbol recognition, the determinants of recognition, and the interpretation of situations in which recognition is apparently interfered with. The second section contains two studies on the special perceptual consequences of ambiguous or conflicting stimulus input. The results of additional studies and their implications for general perceptual categorizing are developed in Bruner's paper.

···

PART ONE

*Biological Factors
in Perception*

■■

Some Structural Factors in Perception*

CLIFFORD T. MORGAN

PERCEPTION HAS its substrate in structure. We can only see and feel what our sense organs and nervous system let us sense. It is natural, therefore, that this chapter should deal with anatomical and structural factors in perception. It will provide a background of the facts and present conception of·how physiological structures function in perception.

In setting out on this task there is obviously no point in repeating the many details of anatomy, physiology, and psychology that can be found in the various textbooks. In fact, acquaintance with the basic physics of stimuli, the anatomy of our sense organs, and the neurology of sensory systems must be assumed. Having these fundamentals in mind, however, it is possible to work toward two goals in this chapter.

One is to bring the discussion up to date on the results of recent research. Many of these results really upset our old ideas and make us take new views of the anatomy of perception.

The second goal will be to look at perceptual mechanisms as a whole. When we study some one part of a sensory system, say the retina, we often "cannot see the woods for the trees." If we stand off a bit, however, and look at all the senses together, we begin to be able to make some general rules and principles about the mechanisms of perception.

That will be attempted in this chapter—at the risk sometimes of suggesting ideas that not everyone will agree with.

---

* From Morgan, C. T., Some structural factors in perception, in Blake, R. R., and Ramsey, G. V. (Eds.), *Perception—an approach to personality*. New York: The Ronald Press Co., 1951. Reprinted by permission of the author and the publisher.

THE QUALITIES OF EXPERIENCE

We see with our eyes, hear with our ears, and feel with our skins, and it is obvious in each case that the structure of the sense organ has a lot to do with what we perceive through it. More than a hundred years ago, however, Müller carried the anatomical approach far beyond the obvious and gave us his now famous doctrine of specific nerve energies. We see red or blue, hear high tones or low tones, feel pain or heat, he said, only because each of these perceptions involves different sensory paths. Thus he gave us an anatomical explanation for qualities of experience.

Hardly any suggestion could have been taken so seriously by so many persons for so many years. Even today some physiologists take it as an axiom, rather than a hypothesis, and try to prove other notions by it. Many specific theories of sensory functions have been based upon it, and a good many of them have been wrong. Müller's general idea, however, still looks like a good one. We have simply had to revise again and again our specific notions of how the idea works in practice.

The Shape of Receptors. Take the question of structure of receptors. It would have been very handy not only for Müller's doctrine to prove right but for every receptor to have some unusual shape or color that would let us tell it from other receptors for other experiences. Our wishful thinking on this score has made us waste a lot of research time and peddle some bad notions. They tell us in the elementary textbooks, for example, that we have two kinds of receptors in our eyes, one for twilight vision and the other for color vision. We have been taught, too, that there are different kinds of receptors for skin perception—Meissner corpuscles for touch, Krause end-bulbs for cold, Ruffini cylinders for warmth, and free nerve endings for pain (2, pp. 489-501). It would indeed be nice if anatomy were that good to us—if each receptor had its trade-mark of experience on it—but we are gradually learning to be wary of such notions.

VISUAL RECEPTORS. Take as an example the matter of visual receptors. In Figure 1 you see drawings of the photoreceptors of four different vertebrate animals (46). In *A* are those of the frog, and they divide themselves fairly well into cones and rods, just as the classical doctrine says they should. In *B* are the rods and cones of the house sparrow. Again they look somewhat as they are supposed to, but the

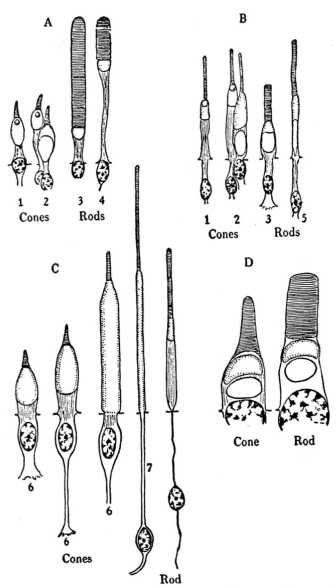

FIG. 1. Rods and cones found in the eyes of different vertebrates. *A*, the leopard frog; *B*, the house sparrow; *C*, man; and *D*, the mud puppy. 1, typical cones; 2, so-called twin cone; 3, typical red rod; 4, green rod; 5, rod from the central area; 6, cones from different regions of the periphery of the retina; and 7, cone from the fovea. (Based on work of L. B. Arey and G. L. Walls. From Willmer, E. N., *Retinal structure and colour vision*. Cambridge: Cambridge University Press, 1946, p. 2. By permission of the publisher.)

5

rods look something like cones and the cones look like rods. In *C* we meet a disturbing situation, for these are the receptors of man. Many of the cones from the peripheral retina look like cones and the rods look like rods, but notice what is supposed to be a cone from the fovea centralis—the all-cone area of our fovea. It outdoes the rods in being long, cylindrical, and rodlike. The best excuse for calling it a cone is that our theory of duplicity says that it should be a cone. Anatomy certainly does not justify the label.

These are just a few examples of the problem. There are other animals in which it is hard to make out rods and cones. In some cases, like that of the lizard *Gecko,* the animal seems to have all rods in its eye, yet reacts to visual objects as though it had only cones (7). In other cases, histologists have a hard time deciding whether there are any cones in an animal's eye, when electrical records of the eye's behavior make it quite certain that "cones" are there (15, 46). Finally, some vision scientists have reason to believe that our perception of the color blue may rest not upon the cones, as we have so long thought, but rather upon some kind of rod (19, 46).

So the duplicity theory seems to be passing on toward its death. It gave us a kind of anatomical explanation for one aspect of perception which would have been very nice if true. Indeed, we may even go on teaching students this theory for years to come as a sort of teaching device that may be partly true. It is not true enough, however, to depend on to make correct guesses about perception. We cannot tell about the color perception of an animal by the looks of the receptors in its eyes.

SKIN RECEPTORS. We are being even more rudely disappointed by the skin senses. In Figure 2 are some of the receptors that the histologists have found in the skin (9, p. 3). The physiologists and psychologists used to assign these receptors to different experiences. Some in fact still do. The common scheme is to assign the Meissner corpuscle to the experience of touch or pressure, the Krause end-bulb to cold, the Ruffini cylinder to warmth, and the free nerve ending to pain. The reason for this kind of scheme is that one kind of receptor seems to be in greater numbers in regions of the skin where one experience may be more prominent. Other arguments can and have been made with great vigor.

The only trouble—and the big trouble—is that these receptors are not always present where they ought to be (13). It is, of course, a simple matter to make a map of the skin, marking just where we feel various experiences. When a spot seems to give one experience much more than another, we can do a biopsy on the spot, that is, cut out a piece of skin and see what receptors we have been able to trap. Such experiments have often been done in the last seventy years, and the result all too often is that the receptors our anatomical scheme calls for are missing. We do not always find Meissner corpuscles under pressure spots, Krause end-bulbs under cold spots, and so on. We can swear in fact that they very often are not there (13, 22).

What scientists always do find when they make biopsies is a network of nerve fibers and blood vessels (13). This is not strange, of course, because our skin needs blood and so do the nerve fibers. Nerve fibers are also needed to control the dilation and contraction of blood vessels. More than that, however, these networks obviously supply the skin with a good many free nerve endings. These endings, in fact, are about the only possible receptors in many areas of the

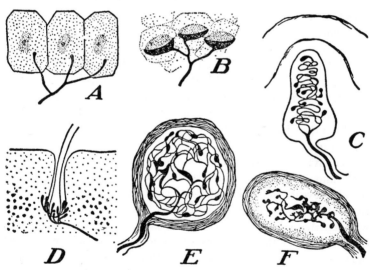

FIG. 2. Principal cutaneous receptors. *A*, free nerve endings from the cornea of the eye; *B*, Merkel's cells from the snout of the pig; *C*, Meissner's tactile corpuscle; *D*, basket ending at the base of a hair follicle; *E*, Krause end-bulb from the human conjunctiva; *F*, Golgi-Mazzoni corpuscle from the human skin. (From Fulton, J. F., *Physiology of the nervous system* [2d ed.]. New York: Oxford University Press, 1943. Copyright 1943 by Oxford University Press, Inc. By permission of the publishers.)

skin. We can be very sure that they serve as pain receptors and as pressure receptors. The experiments leave little doubt about that. They strongly suggest, too, even if they do not prove, that we can experience cold and warmth with free nerve endings. Perhaps some of the fancier corpuscles also get involved in our experiences of touch and temperature, but they are certainly not the sole receptors.

We should not get into too many details here. The upshot of the matter is that one cannot tell much about perception from the anatomy of receptors in the skin. A free nerve ending is just as likely to give one kind of experience as another. The beautifully designed corpuscles such as the Meissner or Krause bodies do not stand for a particular experience. It would have been very nice—in fact, it would often be very helpful—if each receptor in the skin had a different function. Alas, it is not so.

The Receptors as Analyzers. Even though the receptors do not wear uniforms that tell us their duties, Müller could still be right. Which receptor gets stimulated could still decide what we perceive. The differences in receptors might be chemical or electrical rather than anatomical. There may very well be a receptor in the eye for red, another for blue, and so on without our being able to tell it by looking at them. So, too, with the skin receptors. All the receptors have to do is respond differently to different stimuli, and then make the proper connections in the sensory pathways so that the brain can keep their identities straight. If they do that, then Müller's theory is right.

SPECIFICITY VS. PATTERN. As we know, research workers have divided into two camps on this issue. Natanson, Helmholtz, Von Frey, Hecht, Stevens, and Dallenbach—to mention but a few—have stood by Müller. Lotze, Hering, Goldscheider, Wever, and Nafe are some who departed a little or a lot from the anatomical point of view (4). They have held that receptors can send in to the nervous system different kinds of messages and that these messages, and not just the receptors that sent them, affect our experiences. Wever (45) used to say, for example, that the frequency of impulses in the auditory nerve had something to do with whether we hear a high tone or a low tone. Hering believed that the same receptor could make us see red acting in one way and, sending in another kind of message, could make us see green. Nafe (33) has been saying that what receptors *do,* not just which ones they are, determines our perception.

When people argue long and loud about something, there is a fair chance that both sides are partly right, partly wrong. So it seems to be in this case. Research has been telling us enough lately to let us make some decisions about these issues, and it looks more and more as though both camps are partly right. With very small electrodes and the right electrical systems, physiologists have been finding out just what receptors do when they are stimulated (10, 11, 15). Many facts of great interest have come out of their work. Let us spend just a little time hitting their high points.

KINDS OF RECEPTORS. It looks as though we have two kinds of receptors in all the senses. One kind responds in about the same way as does the sense organ as a whole. The eye, for example, can see wave lengths of light as long as 760 mμ and as short as 380 mμ. Some of the individual receptors in the eye do exactly the same thing. When plotted on a graph, their response looks about the same as the over-all response of the eye (15). In hearing, too, some of the

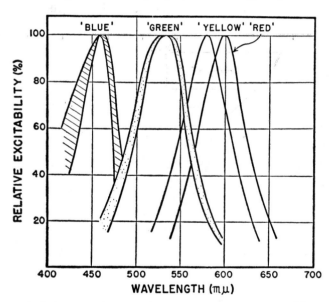

FIG. 3. Relative excitability of four types of receptors found by Granit in different mammalian eyes. The cross-hatched and stippled portions of the "blue" and "green" receptors indicate variability in the exact forms of these curves. (From Morgan, C. T., and Stellar, E., *Physiological psychology* [2d ed.]. New York: McGraw-Hill Book Co., Inc., 1950. By permission of the publisher.)

receptors of the ear are aroused by about the same range of stimuli as is the whole ear, namely, 20 cps to 20 kcps (10). In taste, too, there are receptors that give impulses to almost any kind of chemical stimulus, whether it be sour, salt, or bitter (35). Receptors such as these may be very good for telling us about the intensity of a stimulus and are thus of help in perception. They cannot tell us much, however, about the nature of a stimulus. A receptor that reacts just as does the eye as a whole, or the ear, or the tongue, is not good for quality of perception. It does not let us perceive different colors or pitches or tastes.

Besides these broad-band receptors, however, we have some narrow-band receptors—cells that pick out only some of the spectrum of stimuli that hit the receptors. Granit (15), for example, has put his electrodes in the retinas of various animals and gotten the records shown in Figure 3. Some of the nerve cells he records from have peak responses at 600 mμ, and he calls them red elements. Some have peaks at 530 mμ in the green, 580 mμ in the yellow, and 450

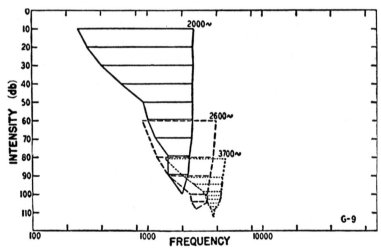

Fig. 4. Thresholds of response at different frequencies for individual auditory neurons. Data for three different elements are shown: a 2,000 cycle element, a 2,600-cycle element, and a 3,700-cycle element. Each element is named by the frequency at which its threshold is lowest. Scale of intensity is in decibels below a reference level, and hence the larger the number the lower the threshold. (From Galambos, R., and Davis, H., The response of single auditory-nerve fibers to acoustic stimulation. *J. Neurophysiol.*, 1943, **6**, 39-57. By permission of the authors and the publisher.)

mμ in the blue. Galambos (10), making the same kind of experiments in a cat, finds nerve cells that react to a small part of the acoustic spectrum. The examples in Figure 4 are of receptors with peaks at 2,000 cps, 2,600 cps, and 3,700 cps. And from the cat's tongue, Pfaffmann (35) has picked up cells that respond more to bitter than to salt or more to salt than to bitter. Those are the only experiments we have now, but we shall probably hear before long of similar results in smell or the skin senses.

Physiology is now giving us an answer to the long debated question whether receptors are at the root of the different qualities of experience we have. Müller was at least partly right. Receptors are analyzers. One receptor picks out some stimuli to respond to more than others, and they somehow or other keep themselves identified upstream in the nervous system. We can perceive different colors, tones, tastes, and probably odors because different anatomical receptors send in messages. There is little doubt about that.

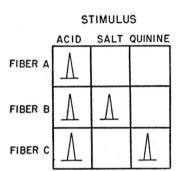

FIG. 5.   Pfaffmann's results with individual fibers from the taste nerve of the cat. *A*, type of fiber that responds only to acid; *B*, type of fiber that responds both to acid and salt; and *C*, a type of fiber that responds to acid and quinine.

PATTERNS FOR MESSAGES. The story, however, is not as simple as it might seem at first glance. We do not have receptor *A* sending in its private message over line *A*, and receptor *B* talking to the nervous system over line *B*. The notion of private lines from receptors to the brain is simple and attractive. Unfortunately, however, it is not true. Instead, receptors get hooked up with each other, so different receptors are talking to the nervous system at the same time. Their talk makes a complex pattern that must be uncoded by the nervous system before we can perceive their meaning.

To make this point clear, let us turn to some examples. Take first Pfaffmann's study of the taste receptors of the cat (35). What he found makes the pattern shown in Figure 5. All the fibers that he got under his microelectrodes would respond to acids. They were, one might say, sour receptors. Some of the fibers would respond only to acid. Another type of fiber, however, responded to both acid and bitter stimuli. Still a third class reacted to acid and salt. So there are at least three classes of taste receptors in the cat. They let the cat perceive different tastes, but not in the simple way we might expect. Instead, the cat tastes "salt" when fiber *A* is sending in messages, "bitter" when fiber *B* is signaling, but "sour" when all three fibers—*A*, *B*, and *C*—are firing. Thus it is a pattern of impulses that comes into the nervous system and that makes the basis for perceiving different tastes.

COUPLING OF RECEPTORS. Pfaffmann's records of taste receptors come from fibers heading into the nervous system which have not yet made synapses. At the first synapse, there are a lot of possibilities for matters to get more mixed up. Perhaps the different classes of taste fibers—*A*, *B*, and *C*—make connections at these synapses that make the pattern much more complicated. Certainly that happens in the eye and the ear. For example, the records of Galambos (10) and of Granit (15), referred to above, probably come from nerve cells that have had synapse since the messages left the eye and ear (12).

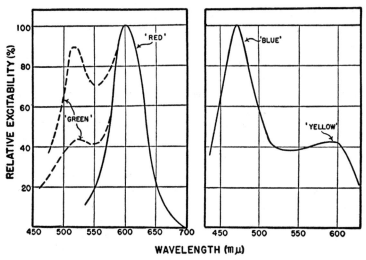

FIG. 6.   Coupling of "red" and "green" receptors in the eye of the snake (left) and coupling of "blue" and "yellow" components in the eye of the frog (right). Both graphs are based on the work of Granit with microelectrodes. (From Morgan, C. T., and Stellar, E., *Physiological psychology* [2d ed.]. New York: McGraw-Hill Book Co., Inc., 1950. By permission of the publisher.)

Granit's records probably come from the third order ganglion cells of the eye, and Galambos' from second order neurons of the cochlear nucleus. Both scientists report complex patterns of response in the nerve cells that gave them their records.

In the eye we see receptors getting coupled together in various ways. Receptors, each responding to a narrow band of the spectrum, hook into the same neurons after one or two synapses are passed. Just to make this point, Figure 6 shows a few of the records that Granit got from hundreds of experiments with all sorts of animals, including the frog, snake, and cat. Sometimes a green and a blue receptor are coupled together, sometimes a blue and a yellow, and sometimes there are other combinations. There are certainly cases in which many are ganged together in different ways. That can be proved by bleaching out some receptors with one wave length of light and then seeing what records the remaining receptors give. Some

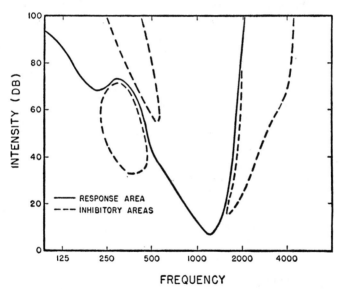

FREQUENCY

Fig. 7. Composite schematic diagram of inhibitory and response areas of individual elements of the cat's auditory system. Probably no single element ever gives results exactly like those in the diagram. It shows, however, that inhibitory areas may occur at frequencies above, below, and the same as those involved in the response area of an element. (Based on Galambos and Davis, 1944. From Morgan, C. T., and Stellar, E., *Physiological psychology* [2d ed.]. New York: McGraw-Hill Book Co., Inc., 1950. By permission of the publisher.)

day, with the right facts in hand, we may be able to say exactly how the coupling of receptors makes us see different colors. So far we know only that the receptors are coupled in many ways.

INHIBITION BY RECEPTORS. Life would be simple if receptors were coupled together in only one way, so that their responses added up. Thus it would be nice if a red and a green receptor were so hooked onto the same bipolar or ganglion cell that their responses simply added together. Sadly enough, though, receptors not only add together, they also subtract from each other's effects. That is to say, when receptors are coupled together, one receptor sometimes inhibits or stops the effects of the other. We have examples of that in both hearing and seeing.

Figure 7, for example, is from Galambos' experiments (11). Probably no one experiment ever gave exactly the picture seen there, but it permits the right conclusion. It shows that one receptor sometimes inhibits another. In the graph, there is a nerve cell that reacts to a narrow range of frequencies and best of all to 1,200 cps. By sounding tones at the same time as one at 1,200 cps, we see that the nerve cell can be inhibited. There is a region around 300 cps, another near 500 cps, and one at 1,800 cps that will give this inhibition. We do not entirely understand this kind of picture, but we are reasonably certain that the record comes from a nerve cell upon which several fibers from the cochlea end. It seems, too, that certain of the receptors when stimulated are stopping the impulses that were set off by other receptors.

We find this sort of coupling turning up in other kinds of experiments with the eye. From electrodes in the optic nerve or in the ganglion cells of the retina, we can see several kinds of reactions to light (14, 18). As is shown in Figure 8, some nerve cells "go on," that is, give impulses, when a light comes on. Some are in spontaneous activity while the eye is in the dark and stop firing when a

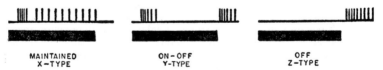

| MAINTAINED
X–TYPE | ON–OFF
Y–TYPE | OFF
Z–TYPE |

FIG. 8. Activity of three types of ganglion cells distinguished in the vertebrate eye by Hartline. (From Bartley, S. H., Some factors in brightness discrimination. *Psychol. Rev.*, 1939, **46**, 340. By permission of the author and the publisher.)

light comes on. Still others go on when the light goes on, then stop while the light is on, and finally start firing again when the light goes off. The main point is that turning on a light can inhibit or stop impulses that have been started by other lights or in some other way. Thus we are led to believe that receptors are coupled not only by adding but also by subtracting, that is, by inhibiting arrangements of various sorts.

We do not understand just how the receptors add and subtract in perception. We are starting to get the general idea though, and we are making progress year by year. As matters now stand, we know this much: One cannot tell what a receptor does by the way it is built or how it looks. Receptors have different features that do not meet the eye. Some act like the sense organ as a whole, but others pick out only part of the sensory gamut of stimuli to react to. We can perceive different tones, colors, and tastes by what receptors signal that they are responding to. The signals, however, are not simple. In the synapses between the receptors and the brain, receptors get coupled to the same nerve cells. Sometimes this coupling adds up signals from different receptors. Sometimes it causes a nerve cell to be inhibited by a receptor. Our perception thus rests on very complex patterns of signals coming from receptors.

PERCEPTION OF SPACE

We not only perceive amounts and kinds of stimuli, but we perceive the size, shape, and form of various stimuli in the world outside us. In talking about anatomy and perception, we therefore need a device of some sort for the perception of space. Offhand, of course, a mechanism like a camera might do. That is to say, if one spot on a sense organ connects with a spot up in the sensory centers of the brain, it would let the brain see, hear, or feel the picture of the world that the sense organ is getting. That is the idea that people have had about perception for a long time. Let us see what there is to it.

Overlapping of Receptors. In Figure 9 we see an experiment that Bishop (3) has carried out fairly recently. He got a machine that let him prick the skin with an electric spark. Naturally such a spark was painful. With sparks flying, he mapped an area on the arm of a man so that he could tell where the nerve serving the skin was located. Having found nerve twigs in this way, he shot the skin with local anesthetic to deaden the nerve twigs. Then by deadening the right set of nerve fibers, he could produce an island on the skin which was still sensitive to pain. Around it, however, was a ring of skin where the subject could feel no pain. By doing this kind of experiment over and over again, Bishop managed to map the area that each nerve fiber of the skin served. This map, it turns out, is very much like that gotten in other experiments by other scientists using only anatomical methods (41, pp. 16-43).

There are three important points about the map. One is the rather large area that each nerve fiber serves. It may be a half-inch across. In some areas of the body, in fact, it is much wider than that. Another point is that nerves overlap a lot in the areas that they serve. Indeed, a prick in almost any part of the arm arouses not just one free nerve receptor but two or three. The same is true of receptors in other parts of the body. A third point, the most important of all, is that our ability to tell what point on our arm is pricked, or to tell the space between two points, is much less than the area served by

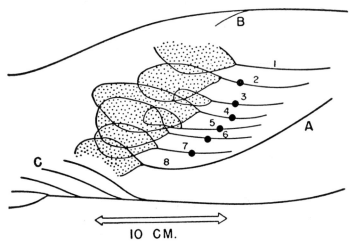

FIG. 9. Pain units mapped in an experiment by Bishop. The dotted areas are the endings of nerve fibers 1, 2, etc., which are branches of the group of nerve fibers A. B and C are other groups. The black dots show the spots that were anesthetized. By blocking nerve twigs in different combinations and mapping the areas of remaining sensibility for pain, these maps of the areas served by each twig could be constructed. (After Bishop, 1944. From Morgan, C. T., and Stellar, E., *Physiological psychology* [2d ed.]. New York: McGraw-Hill Book Co., Inc., 1950. By permission of the publisher.)

any one receptor. The reason, however, is almost obvious. It is that we never perceive the signal from just one receptor but always from two or three receptors. The set of signals from two receptors—which two they are and how strongly they signal—tells us much more certainly where a prick is than we could know from just one receptor. Thus we have a sort of anatomical triangulation to help us in our perception of space.

Pricks on the skin just happen to be the method by which the map in Figure 9 was produced. We have a right to think that the same principle applies to other kinds of receptors. It certainly must work for the pressure receptors of the skin. In the eye, receptors do not sprawl about in the retina in the way that free nerve endings do in the skin, but they are coupled together with bipolar and lateral cells in a way that has about the same effect. In many regions of the retina, one ganglion cell gets impulses from several receptors, and the regions that ganglion cells serve overlap each other. So we do not have the simple mosaic we might expect, but instead we find overlapping of the areas of service of receptors.

Summation in Sensory Pathways. Even after we leave the sense organs we do not find sensory pathways making clear tracks into the brain. At each synapse in the pathway, nerve cells connect with a good many other cells. This fact is plain in the nerve cells of almost every sense that we have observed. Thus a nice simple possibility goes by the board—that the way neurons connect with each other

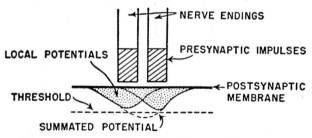

Fig. 10.   Synaptic summation. Two impulses come down nerve endings to the cell body of another neuron at about the same time. Each arouses a local potential in the cell body that is too small to evoke an impulse. The two local potentials add together, however, to make a potential above the threshold of the neuron. Thus a postsynaptic impulse gets started only through summation at the synapse. (From Morgan, C. T., and Stellar, E., *Physiological psychology* [2d ed.]. New York: McGraw-Hill Book Co., Inc., 1950. By permission of the publisher.)

explains our perception of space. It does not, and the fact has been slowly dawning on physiologists for the last few years. It is something in the way neurons function, not their anatomy, that is at the root of space perception.

We have already talked about the effects of receptors in adding and subtracting. In saying that, we mean what the neurophysiologist means when he speaks of "summation" and "inhibition." Both these factors seem to be at work in the sensory pathways to let the brain see space in the world in about the same way that the sense organ does. We have no direct proof yet of the way summation and inhibition enter into spatial mechanisms, but we know that they take place in the sensory pathways, and we have enough other physiological experiments and theories to give us a general picture of the way things must be.

Take addition or summation first. It is illustrated in Figure 10. Physiologists learned some time ago that nerve cells in the nervous system usually need more than one impulse to set them off (28, 32).

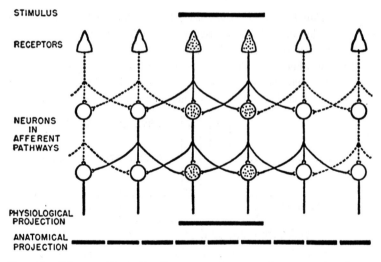

STIMULUS

RECEPTORS

NEURONS IN AFFERENT PATHWAYS

PHYSIOLOGICAL PROJECTION

ANATOMICAL PROJECTION

FIG. 11. Diagram illustrating how synaptic connections at various levels of the visual system give relatively diffuse anatomical projection and how, by means of the synaptic summation required in transmission, there can be a point-to-point physiological projection of images on the cerebral cortex. (After Lorente de Nó. From Morgan, C. T., and Stellar, E., *Physiological psychology* [2d ed.]. New York: McGraw-Hill Book Co., Inc., 1950. By permission of the publisher.)

When just one impulse comes to a synapse, the neuron on the other side is excited, but only locally, and it does not get an impulse started down its fibers. Much of the time what seems to be needed is two impulses arriving at just about the same time. This we call *synaptic summation*.

Figure 11 shows how such summation helps keep impulses in the right neurons of a sensory pathway to preserve the shape of the original stimulus in the picture that gets to the brain (31, p. 166). Assume that the stimulus hits only two receptors. These receptors connect with several neurons at their first synapse, and the second-order neurons in turn connect with several more. Thus impulses could get widely spread in the sensory pathway if it were not for the fact that neurons need summed impulses in order to be fired. The two receptors first aroused can add to each other's effects on two second-order neurons. The net result is as represented in Figure 11; that is to say, the pattern of the stimulus out in the world can get sent up to the brain even though neurons connect much too promiscuously.

In this connection, two points about the eye are interesting. Even though receptors in the eye do not ramify but are lined up like soldiers, the eye as an optic instrument spreads images on the retina so that a pin-point stimulus always excites more than one receptor. The other point is that the scientists who have taken up the question of how much energy is necessary for us to see light under the best of conditions have come out with a minimum figure of two quanta (21). They say we must have at least two quanta in order for us to see. So everything hangs together. Adding impulses is basic in the sensory pathways. We have to have it to perceive anything and we must have it to perceive space.

Inhibition in Sensory Pathways. As we said above, impulses must not only add but also subtract at the synapses of the sensory pathways. This means that inhibition is going on. We cannot prove just how the inhibition works, but some ideas about it occur to the present writer from seeing what physiologists are doing these days.

All through their history, physiologists have been discovering and distinguishing different types of inhibition: Wedenski inhibition, successive inhibition, spatial inhibition, reciprocal inhibition, and so on. Just a while back "direct inhibition" was added to the list (27). This is the plain and simple case where a stimulus stops impulses that otherwise would be going on. Direct inhibition, although discovered last, probably is more basic to our understanding of what goes on in normal events in the nervous system than any other sort of inhibition. Moreover, right on the heels of its discovery, physiologists had reached the point in their knowledge of how nerve cells get excited and conduct that they could give us a good theory of how and why direct inhibition occurs. It is an anatomical theory.

Figure 12 is a diagram that helps explain both the fact and the theory of direct inhibition (5). The fact is that impulses coming in over neuron E can "pass" the synapse and fire impulses off in neuron A, but impulses coming in over neuron I stop neuron A from firing. The theory is that the short neuron A is the cause of the inhibition. It is supposed to be the cause both because it is short and because it

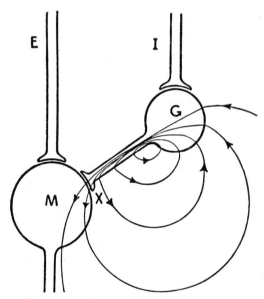

FIG. 12.   Schematic diagram of the electrical theory of direct inhibition. Impulses coming in over axon E excite neuron M and those coming from axon I inhibit neuron M. G stands for a small internuncial neuron (Golgi type II), which is locally excited by axon I but does not get excited enough to give a propagated spike-potential. Instead, only a local flow of current, indicated by the lines with arrows on them, is set up. Because the focal currents are inflowing for the membrane of neuron M, they are inhibitory. (From Brooks, C. McC., and Eccles, J. C., An electrical hypothesis of central inhibition. *Nature,* Lond., 1947, **159**, 761. By permission of the authors and the publisher.)

does not get enough summation of impulses from neuron I to fire. As a result, all that happens in the short neuron is that a local potential and current are set up. The current is depicted by the lines and arrows in the diagram. Currents at the bottom end of the short neuron make a loop through the neuron. They go in a focus at the foot of neuron A and come out some distance away. Physiologists now have good reason to believe that inflowing currents inhibit neurons and that outflowing currents excite them. The short neuron makes a focus of inflowing current and this inhibits neurons. That, in a nutshell, is the story. The short neuron, because it does not fire and because it is short, puts an inhibiting current on neuron A and stops it from firing.

With this notion of inhibition in mind, an anatomist—and the psychologist too—can have a heyday looking at the sensory pathways. There are lots of short neurons in the nervous system, and inhibition might be taking place wherever they are. In the retina, for example, we have long known the amacrine and horizontal cells as short lateral neurons. Now, in fact, we have good reason to believe they are there to inhibit things. Certainly many experiments, and the last of them microelectrode experiments, prove that there is inhibition in the retina. In some of the way stations, too, there are many short neurons, and the cerebral cortex, of course, has millions of them. It is too early to say just when and how inhibition may be at work in all these places, but we may expect the physiologists to bring us news of it in the years just ahead.

Spatial Projection on the Cerebral Cortex. These comments have taken us a little off our main subject—that is, the anatomy of space perception. We have seen so far that the spatial layout of receptors and summation and inhibition all have something to do with preserving a spatial picture of the outside world in our sensory pathways. Let us come now to the projection of the sensory pathways on the cerebral cortex.

We have known for some time that there is a somewhat faithful projection of visual affairs on the occipital cortex of the brain. The spatial arrangement of the auditory and cutaneous pathways has, however, been a matter for debate and research. Fortunately, the research has been coming through with new and valuable answers. With a relatively new technique—the technique of mapping electrical potentials in the cortex during various kinds of sensory stimulation

—we have come to a new conception of how the sensory cortex is spatially arranged. This is illustrated in Figures 13 and 14.

Figure 13 is for skin perception (47). It tells what parts of the cortex give electrical waves for different parts of the body. There is a clear spatial arrangement, a homunculus, so to speak, in which each part of the body has a place on the cortex. Most interesting, however, is the fact that there is not simply one area for skin perception, but rather there are two. We call them areas I and II to be neutral about them until we understand better what their jobs are. Area I, it will be noted, is about where anatomists always say the primary area for

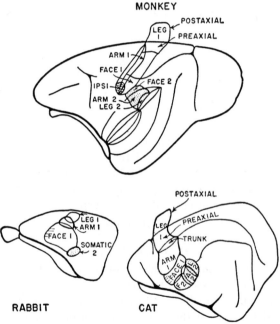

FIG. 13. Somatic areas of the cortex in the rabbit, cat, and monkey. In each diagram, the dotted area is somatic area II. In every case, area II can be subdivided roughly into face, arm, and leg areas, but the diagram for the rabbit is too small to show that fact. There is a certain amount of overlapping of face, arm, and leg sub-divisions in both areas I and II. The cross-hatched part of the face area I in each diagram is the part that has ipsilateral representation of the face. Note that somatic area II is located laterally toward the temporal lobe, not in the posterior parietal lobule. (After Woolsey, 1947. From Morgan, C. T., and Stellar, E., *Physiological psychology* [2d ed.]. New York: McGraw-Hill Book Co., Inc., 1950. By permission of the publisher.)

skin perception is, but area II turns up in a somewhat unexpected place on the lateral part of the cortex. It too has a spatial arrangement in which its different parts represent different parts of the body. So we have two homunculi—two little men—in our cerebral cortex.

As is indicated in Figure 14, we have also learned recently that the auditory system preserves a spatial picture up through its sensory pathways (42, 43). This picture has little to do with space in the outside world but rather makes a mechanism for telling the cortex about the frequency of auditory stimuli. In Figure 14, the letter *B* stands for the basal part of the cochlea, *M* for the middle, and *A* for the apical end of the cochlea. These letters are, therefore, crude ways of showing how the cochlea projects on the cortex. Notice, too, in Figure 14, that there is more than one auditory area. In all the animals so far used in this kind of experiment there are at least two areas—we call them areas I and II—and in the dog there seem to be three areas. Maybe there is a third area in other animals too, and investigators just have not found it yet.

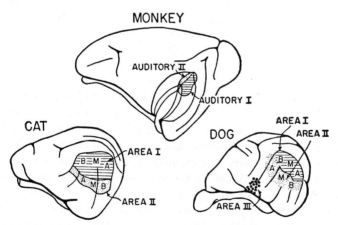

Fig. 14.   Auditory areas of the monkey, cat, and dog. All diagrams are left lateral views of the cortex. Because the auditory area of the monkey is buried partly in the lateral fissure, it is represented as it would be seen with the lateral fissure spread apart. Tonotopic organization is shown by the letters *B*, *M*, and *A*, which stand for the basal, middle, and apical parts of the cochlea respectively. The diagram for the dog is more approximate than the others. (After Woolsey, 1947, and Tunturi, 1945. From Morgan, C. T., and Stellar, E., *Physiological psychology* [2d ed.]. New York: McGraw-Hill Book Co., Inc., 1950. By permission of the publisher.)

These areas of the cortex for auditory and skin perception are of interest for our purposes not because they have any obvious bearing on the anatomy of perception—we do not yet know what they mean —but because we now have a much better chance than we have had in the past to find out what the cortex has to do with perception. It is obvious now why we made so little progress for so long—we did not know what areas of the cortex to study. Now we do know, and it would not be surprising if we soon make some very great strides forward in the cortical anatomy of perception. Some members of the Hopkins laboratory, using such maps as those in Figures 13 and 14, are already at work on the psychological functions of these sensory areas.

The Embryology of Spatial Arrangements. There is just one other point to make in connection with anatomy and space perception. It may have occurred to the reader, as we have gone along, that the sensory pathways are laid out in a very refined spatial pattern. The visual, auditory, and somatic systems—indeed, all the senses—seem to maintain a spatial projection from the surface of the body up to the cortex. Moreover, connections in each system must be very precise for the signals from the various receptors to be kept straight as they pass up the system. The precision of arrangement is remarkable.

It should be in order to ask how such an arrangement came about. What factors are at work as the organism develops to make all the connections come out right? To this question we now have an answer. First, Weiss (44), then L. S. Stone (40), and more recently Sperry (38, 39) have gone through a series of ingenious experiments to pin down the factors that control how connections are formed in the nervous system. Sperry, for example, has crossed the sensory and motor nerves in the legs of the rat, and from that has picked up some clues. He has also cut the optic nerve, rotated the eyeballs in various degrees, allowed the nerves to regenerate and then tested animals for the return of spatial vision. There are many details to his experiments, and they prove somewhat confusing, but the upshot of them all is this: *Nerve fibers grow back to make the same connections that they made in the first place.* To put the matter in another way, the nerve cells along the sensory pathways have some sort of biochemical tags that keep them straight when connections are being laid down. One might say that each nerve cell has a name and that other nerve cells know what that name is. It is still a mystery what these names are and how the cells know each other's names, and that will be a subject for future research. At any rate, nerves can be badly cut, mangled, and twisted, but somehow or other nerve fibers get back where they belong. For us, it is interesting to know that biochemical factors are at work in laying out the spatial arrangements of the nervous pathways.

ANATOMY AND COGNITION

We have discussed so far the qualitative and spatial aspects of our experience. Both are basic, more or less unlearned features of perception. Let us turn now to cognitions, that is, to such matters as recognizing a familiar situation, knowing the names of objects, acquiring sensory discriminations, and using sensory cues in learned behavior. Both the clinician and the experimentalist have given such perceptions a good deal of attention in order to discover what anatomical features of the brain may have to do with them. The question is where we stand at present.

Arrangement of the Cortex. The anatomists and physiologists for their part have been making good headway. As we saw just a moment ago, they have given us new facts about the primary and secondary areas of the brain. Even more than that, however, they have come forth with a wealth of information about the arrangement of the cerebral cortex. By using drugs and electrical methods of recording, they have set up a disturbance in one area of the cortex, then recorded the effects in various other areas of the cortex. From such methods they have been able to tell us in great detail how various parts of the cortex are interrelated. Moreover, to everyone's surprise, they have discovered that some areas of the cortex are inhibitory— they suppress activity in other areas—and other areas are excitatory in function (29).

First, a few words about suppressor areas. This is no place to name all the suppressor areas or to go into the details of their relations. Two of these areas, however, are in the sensory sphere of things. One of them, Brodmann's area 2, lies right alongside somatic area 1 that we were just looking at. Another is Brodmann's area 19, long known to be some sort of "visual association area." The interesting thing about both of these sensory areas is that they can suppress activity in many other areas of the cerebral cortex, both sensory and motor. The areas which they suppress are diagrammed in Figure 15.

The somesthetic suppressor area, for example, can suppress somatic area I and the parietal association areas 40 and 39 (Brodmann's numbers), as well as many of the motor areas in the frontal part of the cortex. The visual suppressor area, Brodmann's 19, similarly can block activity in many sensory, motor, and associative areas of the cortex.

If we continue to look at Figure 15, we see that it shows not only suppressor but also excitatory connections between different areas of the cortex. The somatic area (Brodmann's 39), for example, has connections with the motor area and with areas 5 and 39 in the parietal lobe. Motor areas have connections with the somatic and parietal areas. There are many such relations depicted in Figure 16, but we need not go into them now. In fact, we do not know what all these connections mean. We can be glad, however, that physiologists have now been able to tell us about them. With this as background information, psychologists can now devise experiments to find out more about events going on in various cortical areas in perception. That is why they are brought to the reader's attention at this time.

THE CORTEX AND AGNOSIA. Although we are learning a good deal about cortical anatomy, we must admit, I think, that we have been

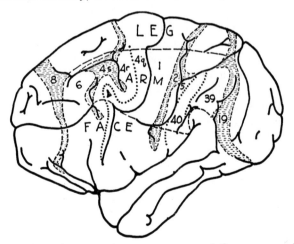

FIG. 15. Main excitatory and suppressor areas of the sensory and motor cortex of the chimpanzee. The shaded areas are the suppressor areas. Figure 16 shows in detail how they are interrelated with excitatory areas. (From McCulloch, W. S., Cortico-cortical connections, in Bucy, P. C. (Ed.), *The precentral motor cortex* [2d ed.]. Urbana, Ill.: University of Illinois Press, 1949, p. 233. By permission of the publisher.)

making very little progress with the anatomy of cognitive functions. The facts stand very much as they did ten years ago (23, 24). At that time Lashley's work with animals had posed the mystery that is still with us, to wit, that the primary sensory areas of the cortex are involved in learning a sensory cognition but are not really necessary for it. We may recall his case of the rats that completely lost their memory for a brightness discrimination when he took out their striate cortical areas, yet they were perfectly able to learn the discrimination again. Many a research worker has confirmed Lashley (32), not only

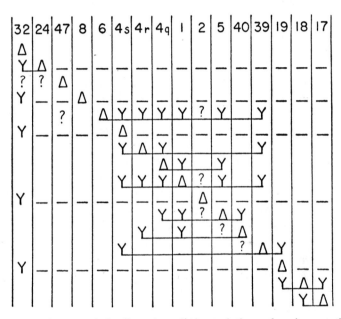

FIG. 16. Diagram of the (homolateral) interrelations of various cortical areas of the chimpanzee as mapped by the method of strychninization. Triangles (△) indicate the area to which strychnine is applied. Any other areas that also show electrical activity when the strychnine is applied are indicated in the same row by the open angle (Y). Areas whose electrical activity is suppressed are represented by dashed lines. Areas whose activity is questionable have a question mark (?) in the appropriate box. Where there is no mark in a box, there is no response for that area to the strychninization of the other areas indicated in the same row. The column marked 32 refers to areas 32 and 31, which respond together as a unit. (Based on McCulloch, 1944. From Morgan, C. T., and Stellar, E., *Physiological psychology* [2d ed.]. New York: McGraw-Hill Book Co., Inc., 1950. By permission of the publisher.)

in the matter of visual habits but also in auditory and somatic habits as well. When almost any animal—say the rat, cat, dog, or monkey—learns almost any sensory habit and then loses the appropriate sensory area of its cortex at the hand of an experimenter, it will lose the habit. Given another chance, however, it will learn the habit again.

This problem of forgetting a sensory habit after injury to the cortex is an important problem both to the pure scientist and the practicing neurologist. Neurologists could ply their trade much better if they knew just why such things happen and could tell in advance when they would and would not happen. Those of us who are pure scientists would understand learning and what goes on in the brain much better if we knew why this sort of agnosia with recovery takes place.

Some of us think that the mystery has something to do with perception, that an animal appears to lose a habit after cortical destruction because it has lost a way of looking at its world and must learn a new one. Helping out this viewpoint a little is Harlow's experiment with monkeys (17). He took out only one side of their visual cortices after teaching them a visual discrimination. If he left them in the dark after operation, they were very disturbed and took some time to relearn. If, however, he gave them plenty of postoperative experience in the light before bringing them to the test, he found them to perform very well. Apparently they had to learn to see their world in a new way to compensate for the great change made in their visual perception by the loss of part of their brains.

We have some other recent reports that point the finger at perception, rather than memory, as the causes of the agnosia following cortical lesions. Ades (1) did a very interesting experiment with some of the visual "associations" areas (Brodmann's 18 and 19). He trained some monkeys to discriminate sizes and shapes, then took the areas out. If both sides were removed, they gave the classical phenomenon of completely forgetting the habits and then relearning them anew after enough training. If, however, he took out only one side, as he did in one monkey, then gave the monkeys some practice on the habits, and finally took out the other side, there was no loss of memory. In other words, what the monkeys completely forgot when subjected to a one-stage bilateral operation they remembered without trouble when operated upon in two stages and given some training in between.

Lashley (26), for reasons we need not go into now, gives us some reason to question Ades' experiment. Perhaps there is something wrong with this particular experiment, but even if that is the case, his point is probably right. Raab (36), in fact, has done the same kind of experiment with hearing in the dog. He conditioned dogs, then took out one auditory cortex, gave them some retraining, and finally took out the other auditory cortex. His animals remembered the auditory habit all through the procedure. Other animals which had both cortices removed at once, however, gave the classical picture. Recently the present writer has been doing some work along this line with rats. In this case, the rats have learned a visual brightness discrimination and have then been subjected to removal of the striate areas in two successive unilateral stages. Between the two stages of operation, however, there has intervened a short period of "refresher" training. Animals put through this procedure do not forget the visual discrimination they have learned, as they do forget it when they have only a one-stage bilateral operation after original learning.

There must be several ways to interpret experiments like these, and the reader may already have thought of some. To this writer, however, perception looms up as the key to understanding them. In the classical, bilateral experiments in which both sensory areas are removed at the same time, we know that we make a big change in an animal's sensory capacity (32). It would seem that we make such a big change that the animal can no longer make use of the cues it has been leaning on for its discrimination. If we make the removal in stages, however, we give the animal a bridge. We let it have part of its old normal perceptual equipment, while introducing it to the new. With a little exercise in the habit and with both new and old perceptions available, it makes the switch and is able to continue when the cortical damage is made complete.

This is just a hypothesis, but the present writer is willing to make it a general one. The hypothesis is that changes in perception—that is, in the way the world looks, sounds, and feels to people and animals —account for many of the agnosias, amnesias, and apparent losses in memory that we see in both our clinical reports and animal experiments after areas of the cerebral cortex are damaged. There are many details of the hypothesis to be made specific for different kinds of habits, but it offers a challenge to research that may change our view of learning processes in the brain and put a much greater emphasis on perception.

ASSOCIATIVE AREAS OF THE HUMAN CORTEX. Still on this matter of anatomy and cognition, we come finally to the role of the primary and secondary sensory areas of the brain in complex perceptions. Many years ago neurologists were inclined to make elaborate, detailed maps of the brain and to stake out different functions in different areas. Many speak of these days gone by as the era of the "map makers." We gradually got away from these maps because there were many human cases of cerebral injury that did not give the symptoms that the maps called for, and also because animal experiments gave the maps no support. So the maps of cognitive areas of the cortex, and the general idea of localization of cognitive function in the cortex, have not been too popular of late.

No doubt the map makers went much too far. They certainly gave us some impossible ideas, and the present writer would not be one to uphold them. However, these maps have never been given a fair

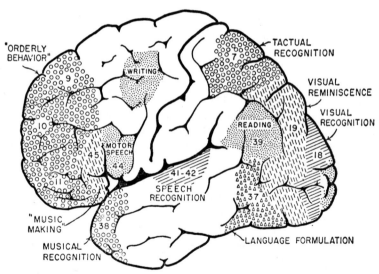

FIG. 17. Composite diagram of the supposed "association" areas of the human cerebral cortex. Many neurologists believe that the cortex functions in some such way as is indicated here; some do not. The scheme is worth while mainly to provide hypotheses for further research and to help in thinking about the role of the cortex in learning and memory. (From Morgan, C. T., and Stellar, E., *Physiological psychology* [2d ed.]. New York: McGraw-Hill Book Co., Inc., 1950. By permission of the publisher.)

chance either in the clinic or in the laboratory, and it is worth our while to find out why. In Figure 17 is a map of the cerebral cortex of man, giving various cognitive functions for each of the many sensory areas. This map is one made up recently by the present writer (32) to represent many different opinions about localization in the human brain, but it comes rather close to what Nielson (34), the latest neurologist to make his view explicit, has to say. None of us may find it easy to take this map very seriously, yet is presents us with a hypothesis—indeed, many hypotheses—that have not been tested.

In the first place, hardly any of our experiments with animals have tested this kind of map. For that there has been good reason. We have no end of trouble, of course, devising methods that will get at some of the more complex learned perceptions implied in such a map. On the psychological side, therefore, our experiments have often been inadequate. Our anatomy, too, has been lacking. We have not, in fact, been able to tell just which areas in the rat or cat or monkey correspond to the areas you see marked out on the human brain. From the maps which were presented earlier, we know where to look in the brains of animals for the areas like these in man.

Lateral dominance has also been a serious problem in getting at the anatomical basis of cognition. That one of our hands or feet or eyes is the major one and the other the minor one is a fact not easily disputed. We know, too, that in some affairs one side of the brain is dominant; that is to say, it plays a major role in perception or action, while the other side is minor. Although people have often argued about how important lateral dominance is and how many of the world's ills it accounts for, few deny altogether that it exists. We must, in fact, believe that some parts of the brain, like the speech area, show very strong one-sidedness and that, in the case of others, the sides share about equally in the functions that concern them. If that be true, how can we tell where to look for a particular function? If one kind of cognition belongs to one side of the brain and we make a lesion in the other side, we will completely miss the point. Or if a type of cognition shares equally corresponding areas on both sides, it takes a perfect bilateral lesion in the areas to make the localization known.

We ought to consider, too, the matter of individual differences. We find it natural to say that people are different in the measurements of personality, intelligence, or some other aspect of behavior, but we often seem to assume that brains are standard products turned out on an assembly line so that they look as much alike as new cars. The fact is that brains vary a lot in their size and shape. Lashley (25) has been going into that matter lately, and he assures us that there are individual differences in brain anatomy. If that be true, why are there not individual differences in which areas of the brain get involved in different functions? And how can our conventional techniques let us know beforehand which brain is which and thus tell us the answers to our questions about localization?

All these are reasons why we have not been making more progress with the question of localization of learned perceptions. There are more that we could go into in a more extended discussion. They do not answer our problem, however, and they do not tell us whether the map in Figure 17 is all right, partly right, or all wrong. There are many neurologists who would accept a good deal of it, and, if a choice were necessary, the present writer certainly would choose it before nothing at all.

If we had to end by saying *only* that we do not yet know what kinds of cognitive maps of the brain to construct, our time would be wasted; but there is a bright prospect in the progress we have made. We now know much more than we did ten years ago about the anatomical organization of the brain. We know what areas go with each sense, how they are arranged spatially, how they connect with each other, and even which areas they inhibit and excite. Moreover, we now know something of the homologues in animals, that is, what areas in animals correspond with those in man. All these, together with our previous failures and our improved techniques, let us understand clearly, probably for the first time, how we must proceed if we are to learn how the anatomy of the brain takes part in our perceptions.

COMMENT

The reader may wonder why some topics have received little or no discussion in this chapter on structural determinants of perception. The present writer would like in closing to make a few comments about them.

Aging. One such topic might be age. We know that structures of the sense organs and nervous system take time to develop in the embryo and in infancy and that they may also deteriorate later in life when aging processes take their toll. There is much to be said, and also much yet to be learned, about aging and perception. In general we know that sense organs and sensory systems mature at different rates in different animals, depending upon their embryonic environment and later way of living (6). In general, however, we know that these organs and systems tend to mature about the time they are needed for the behavioral repertoire of the animal. We do not know very well, however, just how maturation affects the rate at which numerous complex perceptions develop in the young animal or child. We have anatomical evidence (32) that neural maturation goes on long after birth, certainly up to two years and perhaps much longer, but the established correlations between developing structure and perception are few.

The effect of later aging upon perception is a subject that has only recently been getting much needed attention (37). And it is probably too early to tell the general trend of conclusions from research in the area. What studies we have tend to suggest that changes in perception, at least the basic aspects of perception with which we have been dealing in this chapter, are caused by disease, injury, or retrogression of sensory structures. Visual perception fails, for example, when certain conditions develop in the retina. Apparently there are degenerative changes in the ear that cause losses and changes in auditory perception. In other words, once knowing the general structural basis of perception and knowing how structures may be affected in aging, we can piece together and predict some of the effects of aging on perception.

Brain Injury. I have said relatively little about the numerous studies of brain injuries and their effects upon perception in clinical subjects. Freeman and Watts (8), for example, report many perceptual changes in their patients suffering frontal lobotomy. Halstead, too, has an excellent report (16) of the aspects of attention and perception that are affected in cases of brain injury. Hebb (20), in his series of research reports and in his monograph, emphasizes particularly the way in which early versus late learning is involved in the perceptual deficits found in cases of brain injury. But for a fuller discussion of these points the reader should turn to the original sources. One should also keep in mind the tentative and somewhat conflicting nature of the evidence in these clinical studies. For a thorough study that explodes many of the clinical conclusions about frontal lobotomy, for example, one may turn to the recent Columbia-Greystone study on this subject (30).

Body Chemistry. We have been coming to realize more and more in recent years that the sense organs and the nervous system are not completely self-sufficient structures. They function in a milieu of factors, such as circulation, enzymes, and hormones, that continually play upon them. These factors greatly modify the perceptions which they subserve. No attempt has been made to discuss them here.

REFERENCES

1. ADES, H. W. Effect of extirpation of parastriate cortex on learned visual discriminations in monkeys. *J. Neuropath. exp. Neurol.*, 1946, **5**, 60-65.
2. BAZETT, H. C. Temperature sense in man. In American Institute of Physics, *Temperature: its measurement and control in science and industry.* New York: Reinhold Publishing Corp., 1941.
3. BISHOP, G. H. The peripheral unit of pain. *J. Neurophysiol.*, 1944, **1**, 71-80.
4. BORING, E. G. *Sensation and perception in the history of experimental psychology.* New York: Appleton-Century-Crofts, Inc., 1942.
5. BROOKS, C. McC., and ECCLES, J. C. An electrical hypothesis of central inhibition. *Nature,* 1947, **159**, 1-12.
6. CARMICHAEL, L. Experimental embryology of mind. *Psychol. Bull.*, 1941, **38**, 1-28.
7. CROZIER, W. J., and WOLF, E. The flicker response contour for the Gecko (rod retina). *J. gen. Physiol.*, 1939, **22**, 555-66.
8. FREEMAN, W., and WATTS, J. W. *Psychosurgery.* Springfield: Charles C. Thomas, Publisher, 1942.
9. FULTON, J. F. *Physiology of the nervous system* (2d ed.). New York: Oxford University Press, 1943.
10. GALAMBOS, R., and DAVIS, H. The response of single auditory-nerve fibers to acoustic stimulation. *J. Neurophysiol.*, 1943, **6**, 39-58.
11. GALAMBOS, R., and DAVIS, H. Inhibition of activity in simple auditory nerve fibers by acoustic stimulation. *J. Neurophysiol.*, 1944, **7**, 287-304.
12. GALAMBOS, R., and DAVIS, H. Action potentials from single auditory-nerve fibers? *Science,* 1943, **108**, 513.
13. GILMER, B. V. H. The glomus body as a receptor of cutaneous pressure and vibration. *Psychol. Bull.*, 1942, **39**, 73-93.
14. GRANIT, R. The distribution of excitation and inhibition in single-fibre responses from a polarized retina. *J. Physiol.*, 1946, **105**, 45-53.
15. GRANIT, R. *Sensory mechanisms of the retina.* New York: Oxford University Press, 1947.

16. HALSTEAD, W. C. *Brain and intelligence.* Chicago: University of Chicago Press, 1947.
17. HARLOW, H. F. Recovery of pattern discrimination in monkeys following unilateral occipital lobectomy. *J. comp. Psychol.*, 1939, **27**, 467-89.
18. HARTLINE, H. K. The response of single optic nerve fibers of the vertebrate eye to illumination of the retina. *Amer. J. Physiol.*, 1938, **121**, 400-15.
19. HARTRIDGE, H. The visual perception of fine detail. *Phil. Trans. roy. Soc. Lond.*, Series B, 1947, **232**, 519-671.
20. HEBB, D. O. *Organization of behavior.* New York: John Wiley and Sons, Inc., 1949.
21. HECHT, S., SHLAER, S., and PIRENNE, M. H. Energy, quanta and vision. *J. gen. Physiol.*, 1942, **25**, 819-40.
22. JENKINS, W. L., and STONE, L. J. I. Recent research in cutaneous sensitivity. II. Touch and the neural basis of the skin senses. *Psychol. Bull.*, 1941, **38**, 69-91.
23. LASHLEY, K. S. Factors limiting recovery after central nervous lesions. *J. nerv. ment. Dis.*, 1938, **88**, 733-55.
24. LASHLEY, K. S. The problem of cerebral organization in vision. In H. Klüver (Ed.), Visual mechanisms. *Biol. Symp.*, 1942, **7**, 301-22.
25. LASHLEY, K. S. Structural variation in the nervous system in relation to behavior. *Psychol. Rev.*, 1947, **54**, 325-34.
26. LASHLEY, K. S. The mechanism of vision. XVIII. Effects of destroying the visual "associative areas" of the monkey. *Genet. Psychol. Monogr.*, 1948, **37**, 107-66.
27. LLOYD, D. P. C. Facilitation and inhibition of spinal motoneurons. *J. Neurophysiol.*, 1946, **9**, 421-38.
28. McCULLOCH, W. S. Irreversibility of conduction in the reflex arc. *Science*, 1938, **87**, 65-66.
29. McCULLOCH, W. S. Cortico-cortical connections. In P. C. Bucy (Ed.), *The precentral motor cortex* (2d ed.). Urbana, Ill.: University of Illinois Press, 1949.
30. METTLER, F. A. (Ed.). *Selective partial ablation of the frontal cortex.* New York: Harper and Bros., 1949.
31. MORGAN, C. T. *Physiological psychology.* New York: McGraw-Hill Book Co., Inc., 1943.
32. MORGAN, C. T., and STELLAR, E. *Physiological psychology* (2d ed.). New York: McGraw-Hill Book Co., Inc., 1950.
33. NAFE, J. P. Toward the quantification of psychology. *Psychol. Rev.*, 1942, **49**, 1-18.
34. NIELSON, J. M. *Agnosia, apraxia, aphasia: their value in cerebral localization.* New York: Paul B. Hoeber, Inc., Medical Book Department of Harper and Bros., 1946.

35. PFAFFMANN, C. Gustatory afferent impulses. *J. cell comp. Physiol.*, 1941, **17**, 243-58.

36. RAAB, D. H., and ADES, H. W. Temporal and frontal contributions to an auditory conditioned response. *Amer. Psychol.*, 1948, **3**, 370.

37. SHOCK, N. W. Older people and their potentialities for gainful employment. *J. Geront.*, 1947, **2**, 93-102.

38. SPERRY, R. W. Restoration of vision after crossing of optic nerves and after contralateral transplantation of the eye. *J. Neurophysiol.*, 1945, **8**, 15-28.

39. SPERRY, R. W. The problem of central nervous reorganization after nerve regeneration and muscle transposition. *Quart. Rev. Biol.*, 1945, **20**, 311-69.

40. STONE, L. S., and ELLISON, F. S. Return of vision in eyes exchanged between adult salamanders of different species. *J. exp. Zool.*, 1946, **100**, 217-27.

41. TOWER, S. S. Pain: definition and properties of the unit for sensory reception. In Association for Research in Nervous and Mental Disease, *Pain*. Baltimore: The Williams and Wilkins Co., 1943.

42. TUNTURI, A. R. Further afferent connections to the acoustic cortex of the dog. *Amer. J. Physiol.*, 1945, **144**, 389-95.

43. WALZL, E. M., and WOOLSEY, C. N. Effects of cochlear lesions on click responses in the auditory cortex of the cat. *Bull. Johns Hopkins Hosp.*, 1946, **79**, 309-19.

44. WEISS, P. Self-differentiation of the basic patterns of coordination. *Comp. Psychol. Monogr.*, 1941, **17**, No. 88.

45. WEVER, E. G. The electrical responses of the ear. *Psychol. Bull.*, 1939, **36**, 143-87.

46. WILLMER, E. N. *Retinal structure and colour vision.* Cambridge: Cambridge University Press, 1946.

47. WOOLSEY, C. N. Patterns of sensory representation in the cerebral cortex. *Fed. Proc.*, 1947, **6**, 437-41.

....

Some Psychological Effects
of Adrenochrome*

ABRAM HOFFER, HUMPHREY OSMOND, AND JOHN SMYTHIES

ONCE THE TOXICITY of adrenochrome had been established in animals it was possible to begin trials in humans. It was uncertain how such an unstable substance should be given or what sort of dose would prove to have any psychological properties. On 9.x.52 it was therefore decided to start using very small doses to begin with. Unfortunately, we later discovered that there was some doubt about the quantity of adrenochrome used in these first experiments because it was weighed out in a new and unfamiliar balance.

The first subject (A. B.) received what we supposed was .1 mgm. in 1 c.c. of water subcutaneously. This makes a fine port-wine coloured liquid. The injection was accompanied by a sharp and persistent pain at the site of injection. There were no recognizable psychological changes. Blood pressure and pulse readings taken every five minutes for half an hour showed no change.

The second subject (C. D.) was given what we believed was 0.5 mgm. Again there were no pressor effects but there were marked psychological changes (see below).

Further experiments on two wives and one subject (A. B.) using 1 mgm. subcutaneously produced some minor results, but by this time it seemed that our adrenochrome, which is very unstable, was beginning to deteriorate. On 16.x.52 5 mgm. of this deteriorating solution was given to C. D. and produced a response which was unpleasantly prolonged.

Since the subcutaneous injections were so painful, the first intravenous injection was given to a volunteer, Mr. E. F. It was

---

* From Schizophrenia: a new approach. II. Result of a year's research. *J ment. Sci.,* 1954, **100**, 29-45. Pp. 38-42 reprinted by permission of the authors and the publisher.

Minor changes have been made in the manner of identifying subjects. (Eds.)

believed that adrenochrome given by this route would be much less painful. 1.0 mgm. of adrenochrome was, therefore, diluted with two 3 c.c. of sterile physiological saline and injected into the left ante-cubital vein. Almost immediately after the injection E. F. experienced a very severe pain which travelled up his left arm to the praecordium. This lasted about 10 minutes and was accompanied by pallor and sweating. There were no obvious psychological effects apart from alarm and dismay in the experimenters. It was later discovered that, if the adrenochrome solution is mixed with blood from the patient's vein, pain can usually be completely avoided.

Later A. B. and his wife both took 10 mgm. doses intravenously and had marked changes particularly in affect and behaviour. A. B. became overactive, showed poor judgment and lack of insight. G. B., his wife, became deeply depressed for four days and endured a condition which was indistinguishable from an endogenous depression. This unpleasant experience was aggravated by lack of insight, for she was unable to relate her depression to the injection of adreno-chrome, although her change of mood came on immediately after it. An acute piece of observation by Dr. Roland Fischer, Ph.D.,[1] suggests that this prolonged effect of adrenochrome was probably due to an attack of infectious hepatitis some years ago. It would therefore be prudent to enquire about previous liver disease before injecting adrenochrome or other toxic substances into an experimental subject.

To those who are familiar with mescal and lysergic acid we would emphasize that judging from the little experience which we have, it does seem that adrenochrome is more insidious than these two hallu-cinogens, its effects last longer and possibly in consequence of this its administration is accompanied by a loss of insight. Since this may have serious results experimenters should guard their subjects very carefully.

Summary of an Account of an Adrenochrome Trial 9.x.52, 20-30 hours approx. (Condensed from notes made at the time by the subject (C. D.).) After the purple red liquid was injected into my right forearm I had a good deal of pain. I did not expect that the experimenters would get any results from a preliminary trial and so was not, as far as I can judge, in a state of heightened expectancy.

---

[1] Fischer, R., Georgi, F., Weber, R., Piaget, R. H. *Schweiz. Med. Wehnschr.*, 1950, **80**, 129.

The fact that my blood pressure did not rise suggests that I was not unduly tense. After about 10 minutes, while I was lying on a couch looking up at the ceiling, I found that it had changed colour. It seemed that the lighting had become brighter. I asked Abe and Neil [2] if they had noticed anything, but they had not. I looked across the room and it seemed to have changed in some not easily definable way. I wondered if I could have suggested these things to myself. I closed my eyes and a brightly coloured pattern of dots appeared. The colours were not as brilliant as those which I have seen under mescal, but were of the same type. The patterns of dots gradually resolved themselves into fish-like shapes. I felt that I was at the bottom of the sea or in an aquarium among a shoal of brilliant fishes. At one moment I concluded that I was a sea anemone in this pool. Abe and Neil kept pestering me to tell them what was happening, which annoyed me. They brought me a Van Gogh self-portrait to look at. I have never seen a picture so plastic and alive. Van Gogh gazed at me from the paper, crop headed, with hurt, mad eyes and seemed to be three dimensional. I felt that I could stroke the cloth of his coat and that he might turn around in his frame. Neil showed me the Rorschach cards. Their texture, their bas relief appearance, and the strange and amusing shapes which I had never before seen in the cards were extraordinary.

My experiences in the laboratory were, on the whole, pleasant, but when I left I found the corridors outside sinister and unfriendly. I wondered what the cracks in the floor meant and why there were so many of them. Once we got out of doors the hospital buildings, which I know well, seemed sharp and unfamiliar. As we drove through the streets the houses appeared to have some special meaning, but I couldn't tell what it was. In one window I saw a lamp burning and I was astonished by its grace and brilliance. I drew the experimenters' attention to it but they were unimpressed.

We reached Abe's home where I felt cut off from people but not unhappy. I knew that I should be discussing the experience with Abe and his wife but could not be bothered to do so. I felt no special interest in the experiment and had no satisfaction at its success, although I told myself that it was very important. Before I got to sleep I noticed that the coloured visions returned when I shut my eyes. (Normally I have hypnagogic visions after several minutes in a darkened room when I am tired.) I slept well.

---

[2] The subject was an acquaintance of the experimenters.

Next morning, although I had only slept a few hours, life seemed good. Colours were bright and my appetite keen. I was completely aware of the possibilities arising from the experiment. Colour had extra meaning for me. Voices, typewriting, any sound was very clear. With those whom I felt did not appreciate the importance of the new discovery I could have easily become irritable, but I was able to control myself.

C. D.'s Second Adrenochrome Experience 16.x.53 (p.m.). I had 5 mgm. of adrenochrome this time because it was thought that it was probably deteriorating.

I saw only a few visual patterns with my eyes closed. I had the feeling that there was something wonderful waiting to be seen but somehow I couldn't see it. However, in the outside world everything seemed sharper and the Van Gogh was three dimensional. I began to feel that I was losing touch with everything. My sister telephoned and, although I am usually glad to hear her voice, I couldn't feel any warmth or happiness. I watched a group of patients dancing and, although I enjoy watching dancing with the envious interest of one who is clumsy on his feet, I didn't have a flicker of feeling.

As we drove back to Abe's house a pedestrian walked across the road in front of us. I thought we might run him down, and I watched with detached curiosity. I had no concern for the victim. We did not knock him down.

I began to wonder whether I was a person any more and to think that I might be a plant or a stone. As my feeling for these inanimate objects increased my feeling for and my interest in humans diminished. I felt indifferent towards humans and had to curb myself from making unpleasant personal remarks about them. I had no inclination to say more or less than I observed. If I was asked if I liked a picture I said what I felt and disregarded the owner's feeling.

I did not wish to talk and found it most comfortable to gaze at the floor or a lamp. Time seemed to be of no importance. I slept well that night and awoke feeling lively, but although I had to attend a meeting that morning, I did not hurry myself. Eventually I had to be more or less dragged out of the house by Abe. I had to get my car from a garage where it was being repaired. There was some trouble about finding it in the garage. When at last I was seated in the driver's seat I realized that I couldn't drive it through traffic, although quite able to do so usually. I did not, however, feel anxious or distressed by this but persuaded the garage proprietor to drive me to my destination. I would, I believe, have normally found this a humiliating situation. I did not feel humiliated.

I attended the scientific meeting, and during it I wrote this note: "Abe, this damn stuff is still working. The odd thing is that stress brings it on, after about 15 minutes. I have this 'glass wall other side of the barrier' feeling. It is fluctuant, almost intangible, but I know it is there. It wasn't there three quarters of an hour ago; the stress was the minor one of getting the car. I have a feeling that I don't know anyone here; absurd but unpleasant. Also some slight ideas of reference arising from my sensation of oddness. I have just begun to wonder if my hands are writing this, crazy of course."

I fluctuated for the rest of the day. While being driven home by a psychologist colleague I discovered that I could not relate distance and time. I would see a vehicle far away on the long, straight prairie roads, but would be uncertain whether we might not be about to collide with it. We had coffee at a wayside halt and here I became disturbed by the covert glances of a sinister looking man. I could not be sure whether he was "really" doing this or not. I went out to look at two wrecked cars which had been brought in to a nearby garage. I became deeply preoccupied with them and the fate of their occupants. I could only tear myself away from them with an effort. I seemed in some way to be involved in them.

Later in the day when I reached home the telephone rang. I took no notice of it and allowed it to ring itself out. Normally, no matter how tired I am, I respond to it.

By the morning of 19.x.52 I felt that I was my usual self again.

Subject's Comment. I shall make no attempt to elaborate or discuss these two experiences. I am satisfied that they represent a model psychosis, but each reader must decide for himself on the evidence of what I have written and what the experimenters report.

Observations by A. H. and N. A. on Subject C. D.'s Reaction to Adrenochrome. Within 15 to 25 minutes of receiving the adrenochrome injection C. D. was preoccupied with the distasteful colour of the laboratory. He had never before made any comment concerning this although he had often seen it. After he had described some of his experiences to us we showed him a reproduction of a Van Gogh painting which he observed very carefully for a long time. It was difficult to divert his attention toward some Rorschach cards we wished him to see. He stated they were not nearly as interesting. But when he did consent to examine these cards he refused to change cards until ordered to do so. Continual persuasion was needed to get a response. For this reason no complete evaluation of the protocol was obtained. However, in response to upper centre D section of card No. 10 he gave the response, "these are shrimps, no they are statesmen—they are shrimp statesmen." This tendency toward contamination or the process of loosely combining two associations is not typical of C. D., who normally tends toward high F plus per cent. On the other hand, in word association tests under normal conditions, C. D. does give above average distant responses but is able to report the path of the associative process with no difficulty.

The change in C. D., marked by strong preoccupation with inanimate objects, by a marked refusal to communicate with us, and by strong resistance to our requests, was in striking contrast with C. D.'s normal social behaviour.

On the occasion of C. D.'s second trial the most noticeable objective change was his withdrawal from people. After the laboratory session we drove to the home of A. H. C. D. entered, found a chair where he sat for approximately one hour intently examining the rug. He did not greet the group of people who were at the house nor enter into the discussion.

C. D. was anxious and fearful on retiring and once was found wandering about. In the morning he was easily distracted. He required two hours to dress.

Briefly, the changes noted were preoccupation with inanimate objects, negativism, loosening of the associative process, anxiety, and distractibility.

PART TWO

....

Psychophysical Measurement

SELECTION 3

....

Sensation and Measurement*

Ira J. Hirsh

THE MEANING OF MEASUREMENT

WHAT KINDS OF EVENTS or things can we measure? The mathematician's formal definition of measurement tells us that we measure something whenever we assign numerals to things according to any specified rules (Stevens, 1951). These rules are always arbitrary and sometimes may be very simple. In other words, whenever we say that we are going to measure something, we mean merely that we are about to label something with numbers. For example, I may decide to assign numbers to the three chairs in my office. I may call the swivel chair "24," the straight chair "13," and the stool "6." But having done this, I have only named the chairs with numerals. The swivel chair is not *more* than the stool in any sense, because the *rule* for assigning the numerals was only a *naming* one.

If, however, you are told that the swivel chair weighs 24 lb, the straight chair 13 lb, and the stool 6 lb, then the rules by which the numbers have been assigned are specified in terms of formal properties that establish a relation between these measurements and others of weight. Furthermore, there are invoked relations among the numbers themselves that have been agreed upon by the makers of similar measurements. We learned about these rules when we were first exposed to arithmetic and algebra, but there is nothing sacred about them. The rule that 9 represents something greater than 8, or that 20 is twice as great as 10, or that whenever we reach a multiple of 10 in counting, we add a number to the second column from the right and then begin over is arbitrary but generally agreed upon. The most precise measurement is made by assigning numerals in accordance with rules that are rigorously defined in arithmetic or

* From Hirsh, I. J., *The measurement of hearing.* New York: McGraw-Hill Book Co., Inc., 1952. Pp. 5-17 reprinted by permission of the author and the publisher.

algebra. If we use less rigorous rules, like simple naming, our measurements lose various degrees of meaningful information.

Sensations and Responses. Our definition of measurement tells us that we must assign numerals to events. Having determined the rules for assignment, we must now proceed to determine what are the observable events in hearing. Since we cannot observe the sensation that exists in another individual's world of experience, it would seem indeed that we cannot measure sensation. On the other hand, we can twist the meaning slightly and define the sensation in terms of events that we can measure. When a man says, "I see red," we cannot measure the redness of his visual sensation, nor even be sure that he has one, but we can observe his verbal behavior—"I see red." The phenomena of audition may be studied in the same way. We cannot measure auditory sensations that are private, but we can measure sensations that are defined in terms of behavior or observable responses.

The man who studies hearing—be he audiologist, psychologist, physiologist, otologist, physicist, or engineer—must know the capacities of the auditory system. He must know something about the smallest energies that he must present to the ear in order to observe a measurable response. He wants to know what are the highest and lowest frequencies to which the auditory system will respond. Beyond these so-called *absolute thresholds,* he may be interested in the smallest detectable change, whether the change be of frequency, of energy, or of any other physical dimension in which a change can be made. Then there are all the problems about interference, the effect of the presence of one signal on the detectability of another, the judgments of psychological magnitudes like *loudness* and *pitch,* and the intelligibility of spoken language. We define all these in terms of relations between measures of the physical stimulus and responses of the system that we are studying.

One worker may be interested in the over-all auditory system of man or animal, or he may be interested in only a small part of the auditory system, *e.g.,* the *middle ear* or parts of the *central nervous system.* In any case, the worker is faced with the problem of measuring the input-output characteristics of the system in which he is interested. That is to say, he must be able to put in some signal that is physically specifiable and then must provide himself with means for specifying the output of the system in terms of a measurable response.

The general procedures that he will use do not differ very much from those that the engineer uses in the measurement of similar characteristics of a radio or an engine. He does not need to know anything about what is inside the system but rather needs only to specify the input and be able to measure the output. The essential difference between measurements made on the auditory system and those made on a radio lies in the method of measuring the output. In the case of the radio, we measure both input and output with voltmeters and oscilloscopes. The output of the auditory system of a living organism, however, must be measured in terms of other, arbitrarily defined responses—responses that vary in a much more troublesome way than do the voltage responses of a radio or the horse-power responses of an engine. Responses of the over-all auditory system in man may be verbal, or the raising of a finger, or the pressing of a button. Study of a smaller part may involve only a relation between the stimulus and the kinetic response of an *ossicle* or the electrical response of the *cochlea*.

The measurement of hearing or of any sensory process involves the establishment of relations between the responses of individuals and the stimuli that give rise to such responses. It is generally agreed nowadays that we can measure—that is, assign numbers to, according to certain rules—both the dimensions of a physical stimulus that is presented to an observer and the responses of the observer. We can specify relations between two such measurable quantities, but we cannot, scientifically, make these relations extend to private sensations or events in the mind, because we cannot invent operations for getting at such events. The operational definition of the sensation has become the specification of a response.

Psychophysical Measurement. The measurement of observers' responses to measurable stimuli grew up in what is called *psychophysics,* the study of the relations between sensations and the stimuli that produce them. Psychophysics came into being during the middle of the nineteenth century when *experimental psychology* was first becoming experimental. Early investigators in this area were concerned with the study of the average, normal, adult human being. This study was statistical in the sense that investigations sought to describe an average person. Measurements obtained on different people yielded different results, and the main concern was with an average or some other representative measure of central tendency among the results for a particular group of observers.

Differences among people constituted a bother for the early psychophysicists. They would have preferred to throw away this variability or, better yet, to have none in a population where all persons were exactly equal to the average in all respects. Soon after the study of the psychophysics of the average man got under way, however, a group of psychologists broke off from the earlier traditions through an interest in individual differences. Whereas the early psychophysicists were interested in the *average* man and ignored the way in which real persons deviated from this average, the *differential psychologists* ignored the mean (average) almost completely and concentrated on the differences among people.

Today a similar difference exists between the man who seeks experimental results that describe a population of individuals and the clinically oriented worker who, like the differential psychologist, assumes the experimenter's average figure and focuses his interest on the amounts by which different individuals deviate from this average. An experimental average, for example, is incorporated in the audiometer, and the clinician uses the difference between the hearing of an individual and this average to obtain a measure of Hearing Loss. There are certain principles and operations that are basic to *both* the experimental and the clinical approaches to the measurement of hearing. One of the premises is that the essential differences between experimental and clinical audiometry can be understood only after their common factors have become clear.

HISTORY

Philosophy is concerned with human knowledge. In particular, that part of early philosophy that was known as psychology was concerned with how the human mind acquires knowledge. We find explicit in the writings of philosophers from Aristotle[1] through the British empiricists of the nineteenth century the notion that knowledge comes to the mind by way of the senses. This empirical view of the source of human knowledge fostered, in the early philosophical psychologists, a great interest in sensation and the sensory mechanisms.

In the early part of the nineteenth century, things were happening in physiology that were to set the stage for rapid advances in

---

[1] No references will be found in the bibliography for most of the names in this section on History. For original sources, the reader is referred to Boring

the psychology and physiology of sensation. Early in the nineteenth century Sir Charles Bell and François Magendie discovered that the ventral and dorsal roots of the spinal cord had different functions; the ventral roots served motor functions, while the dorsal roots had to do with sensory functions. This discovery made possible a physiology of sensation that commanded the interest of many important physiologists of the day.

One of them, Johannes Müller, was responsible for the *doctrine of specific nerve energies,* the notion that the kind or nature of a sensation (*e.g.,* visual, auditory, tactual, etc.) is determined by the specific nerve fibers that are stimulated. No matter how the auditory nerve is stimulated, the stimulation gives rise to an auditory sensation. This theory seemed to Helmholtz to be no more valid for the whole system than for parts—*e.g.,* vision and audition. He held not only that auditory nerve fibers were responsible for auditory experience but also that the quality of a given auditory sensation depended on which of the auditory fibers were stimulated. If we could find the fibers for red in the optic nerve, then no matter how we might stimulate them, a visual sensation of red would be produced.

Still another discovery in nineteenth-century physiology was to have a profound effect on the philosophy or psychology of sensation. In 1850, Helmholtz measured the velocity of transmission of the electrical impulse in a nerve. Although the details need not concern us here, we must note that the measured velocity was not that of light but one of a much lower order of magnitude. It was barely conceivable at that time that a measurable amount of time intervened between the occurrence of a stimulus and the experienced sensation. It was humiliating to think that first you willed to move your finger and then, only after the message got to the finger, the finger moved. The worlds of sensation and stimulus were distinctly separate, at least in time.

By the middle of the nineteenth century, then, the way had been opened for experiments on the physiology of sensation. But what about the philosophical psychologists? How far had they come on the problems of sensation and the sensory mechanisms? The thinking of this period was dominated by a dualism that had been made explicit by Descartes in 1650. There were the mind and the body. The brain, that part of the body that had most to do with the mind, interacted with the mind. This notion of interaction was changed by succeeding writers, but the dualism remained. The doctrine that the mind and body are parallel in their respective processes was made explicit by Leibnitz and by Hartley, the British philosopher. It was this parallelism between the experienced world and processes in the body, presumably in the nervous system, that led G. T. Fechner to seek a mathematical expression that would unite the two realms.

Fechner, the physicist, could measure the stimulus. Aware of the difficulty of measuring introspected sensations, he began to measure responses, and, by relating responses to physical changes, he hoped to attach meaningful numbers to sensory qualities. Actually Fechner was concerned with two kinds of relations. First, there was the relation between events in the physical world and the processes of the nervous and sensory systems. Second, there was the relation between these nervous processes and events in the psychological or experienced world. Apparently the physiological processes were assumed to be closely related to those of the physical world, so that the main problem was to establish a relation between experience and the physical world. Specifically, Fechner presented a scheme in his *Elemente der Psychophysik* (1860) whereby the magnitude of a sensation could be computed from objective measurements of physical stimuli and responses. Stimuli and responses could be measured directly, whereas the sensations could not.

The foundation of Fechner's science was what we now know as *Weber's Law*. E. H. Weber had observed (1834) that in order for a stimulus to appear just noticeably different from a preceding stimulus, the necessary increment had always to be a constant fraction of the original stimulus. Let us consider an example.

Suppose we have a weight resting on an observer's hand. We want to find out how much we must add to that weight in order that the observer will just be able to notice that the weight is different. The *just noticeable difference,* or *jnd,* is a difference that is noticed 50 per cent of the time. According to Weber's Law, the amount of increase divided by the weight that was increased should yield a constant ratio. If we have a weight of 30 oz to begin with and if we find that we must add just 1 oz for our observer to just notice the difference, then to a weight of 30 half-ounces (15 ounces) we should have to add only 1 half-ounce. Also, to a weight of 30 dr we should have to add 1 dr. The constant ratio for weights would be, then, 1:30.

FECHNER'S LAW AND SENSORY MAGNITUDE

Fechner reasoned that if one were to count up just noticeable differences from the absolute threshold on upwards, one would actually be counting up equal sensory units along a psychological scale. Cumulating, for example, successive thirtieths of weight units, beginning with the smallest weight that could just be felt, one would obtain successive sensory units along the psychological scale of "weightiness." One pound does not necessarily seem to be twice as "weighty" as $\frac{1}{2}$ lb, but a weight 20 jnd's above threshold would feel twice as "weighty" as a weight 10 jnd's above threshold.

We probably do not need to mention the tremendous impact made on psychology and physiology by Fechner's Law. The mathematical transposition that is involved in going from Weber's Law to Fechner's Law led to the notion—which subsequently became general—that the responses of human organisms to stimuli vary as the logarithms of those stimuli. Weber's Law stated that a just noticeable difference in any stimulus dimension was obtained from constant increments in the stimulus when those increments were expressed as ratios of the magnitude of change to the absolute magnitude from which the change was made.

$$\frac{\Delta I}{I} = K \text{ (for a jnd)}$$

Fechner now proposed that we cumulate such just noticeable differences to calculate a sensory magnitude. Hence a sensory magnitude could be measured by counting up measurable $\Delta I/I$'s.

The specific relation that Fechner finally proposed, and that we know as Fechner's Law, was

$$S = K \log I$$

where S is the magnitude of sensation, I is a dimension of the stimulus, and K is a constant of proportionality that varies with sense modality.

It is usually held nowadays that Weber's Law is only approximately true and that the Weber fraction is constant over a very small range of the stimulus magnitude. As a matter of fact, with only slight correction Weber's Law is true for hearing over a considerable part of the intensity range.

The more serious objection to Fechner's Law and its application to sensory magnitudes is that the jnd is not necessarily the unit of such magnitude. For example, if one is just able to detect a difference between two intensities that are low and another difference between two intensities that are high, it is not necessarily true that these two differences would constitute equal magnitudes in the judged loudness of a sound. Although an observer may not be able to say directly whether one jnd is greater or less than another, still the difference can become obvious with larger magnitudes when an observer may note that one pair of stimuli 20 jnd's apart seems farther apart than another pair that are also 20 jnd's apart. Neither Fechner nor any of the very early psychophysicists carried out the operations that were necessary to validate the assumption of subjective equality among jnd's. There have been, since Fechner's time, independent operations established for the direct measurement of sensory magnitudes, for example, of loudness.

<h3>THE CLASSIC PSYCHOPHYSICAL METHODS</h3>

Although we may not agree on how successful Fechner was in supplying a mathematical device for measuring psychological dimensions in terms of the physical dimensions of the stimulus, we cannot but agree that the methods that he worked out and formalized for the measurement of the differential threshold, the basic unit of measurement in his argument, represent very valuable tools. It is clear that the methods were first conceived for the purpose of measuring the differential threshold, because this was the important datum to be used in the formula that related sensation to the stimulus. The methods have been extended, however, to the measurement of the absolute threshold and other more complicated psychophysical phenomena. Let us outline very briefly the methods as they would be formulated for the measurement of the difference limen (DL), or differential threshold.

One of the simplest ways of determining the magnitude of a change in the stimulus that is required for an observer to just detect the change is to give the observer control of the stimulus so that he can adjust the magnitude to satisfy his criterion of detectability. Leaving all auditory examples, let us suppose that we have two lengths, one that is fixed and one that can be adjusted by the observer. We ask the observer to adjust the variable length until it appears equal to the fixed length. Since the organism is not a very precise measuring device, a series of such adjustments will show some deviations from physical equality. If we subtract the fixed length from each of the adjusted lengths that the observer has made, we have a series of errors. The difference limen (DL) is defined in this case as the average of these errors calculated arithmetically— *i.e.*, we ignore the sign of direction of the error. Sometimes the standard deviation[1] (σ) is used as the measure of the DL. The reasoning behind such a computational procedure is simply this: if we are to estimate how much of a change is necessary for an observer to detect a difference, we can just as well use a statistic that indicates how poorly he can determine equality. We have computed, therefore, not the just noticeable difference, but rather the just *not* noticeable difference. The computation involved in the method of adjustment for determining the DL has provided another name for this method, namely, the *method of average error*.

The Method of Limits. This method is sometimes called the *method of serial exploration* or the *method of the just noticeable difference*. In this case the observer simply observes, and the experimenter has control of the stimulus. Continuing with our example of the DL for length, we present both the fixed and the variable lengths to the observer. We begin with both lengths physically equal. We gradually increase the variable length until the observer first reports that it looks different from (in this case longer than) the fixed length. We record the physical difference between the variable and the fixed lengths at the time the observer makes this report. We then set both lengths at equality again and gradually decrease the variable length until the observer again reports that it is different (this time shorter). We repeat this procedure a number of times and get several estimates of the mean difference that is required for the observer to just detect a difference. It may be that the DL for increasing length is systematically different from the DL for decreasing length; such a constant error may be noted in the tabulation

---

[1] The standard deviation of a set of scores is a measure of the dispersion of the set about the average, or mean, score and is defined as the square root of the sum of the squares of the deviations (*i.e.*, differences between particular scores and the mean score) divided by the number of scores:

$$\sigma = \sqrt{\frac{\Sigma(\overline{X} - X)^2}{N}}$$

where σ is the standard deviation, Σ the symbol for "sum of," $\overline{X}$ the mean, X the individual score, and N the number of scores in the set. The reader who has no background in statistics should consult any good text on elementary statistics.

of the data. The *method of gradual limits* involves a gradual change from equality that is continued until the observer reports a difference and the subsequent computation of a measure of central tendency (mean or median) with a series of such measurements.

The Method of Constant Stimuli. This method was referred to in the earlier years of psychophysics as the *method of right and wrong cases.* What we do is to get a percentage or ratio measure of judgments of "right" and "wrong" or of "equal," "greater," or "less" for several constant stimulus differences, constant in the sense that they do not change in time. We would, for example, present our fixed length of n cm along with the variable-length set at n, $n-1$, $n+1$, $n-2$, $n+2$ . . . cm and ask the observer each time whether the two lengths were the same, or whether the second was greater or less than the first. Normally we would expect the frequency with which

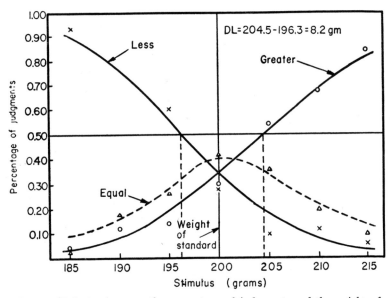

FIG. 1. Relation between the percentage of judgments and the weight of a stimulus that is compared with a standard weight of 200 gm. The curves show, for example, that a stimulus weight of 195 gm is judged to be "less" than the standard weight (200 gm) 60 per cent of the time, "greater" 14 per cent of the time, and "equal" 26 per cent of the time. (From Guilford, J. P., *Psychometric methods.* New York: McGraw-Hill Book Co., Inc., 1936. By permission of the publisher.)

the observer responded "same" to decrease as the difference between the two physical lengths becomes greater.

Guilford has used data from an experiment on lifted weights to obtain the curves shown in Fig. 1. Here we see that the frequency with which the variable stimulus is reported to be larger than the standard increases as the variable becomes larger, and the converse is also true. Judgments of "equal" reach a maximum where the judgments of "less" and "greater" appear about equally often. In this case of three categories of judgments, it is usual to define the DL as the interval of uncertainty (or half of it) between the 50-per-cent point on the "less" and the 50-per-cent point on the "greater" curve.

Another variation of this procedure is to force the observer to use only two categories of judgment, *e.g.*, "greater" and "less" instead

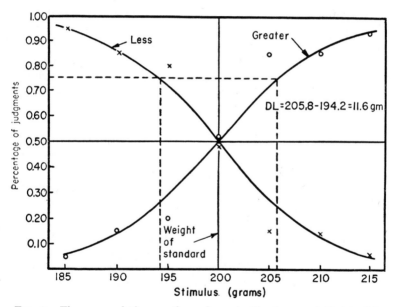

FIG. 2. The same relations as those shown in Fig. 1., except that in this case the observer is forced to choose between two judgment categories only. Judgments of "less" and "greater" appear equally often when the variable stimulus is equal to the standard. The *interval of uncertainty* is defined as the range of stimulus weights between the two 75-per-cent crossings. The upper or lower DL is defined in terms of the difference between the appropriate 75-per-cent crossing and the point of indifference. (From Guilford, J. P., *Psychometric methods*. New York: McGraw-Hill Book Co., Inc., 1936. By permission of the publisher.)

of "greater," "less," and "equal." If there is no constant error in this case, then when the variable and the standard are approximately equal physically, the judgments of "less" and "greater" will be made about equally often. As a matter of fact the cumulative curves would cross each other at 50 per cent. In order to compute a DL in this second case, it is usual to use as an *interval of uncertainty* the range of stimuli between 75 per cent on the "less" curve and 75 per cent on the "greater" (see Fig. 2).

The methods of adjustment, limits, and constant stimuli are the three so-called *classic psychophysical methods* that were used in the determination of the theoretically important DL.

PSYCHOPHYSICS TODAY

Some psychophysicists of the present day are concerned with methods for computing or measuring psychological dimensions of sensations. Much progress has been made in hearing, vision, space perception, and taste. Many experimenters have denied the necessity for using the jnd as the basic unit for sensory magnitude and have proceeded to use independent operations for the establishment of sensory scales. They may, for example, ask an observer to adjust the physical magnitude of a stimulus until it appears half as loud or half as bright or half as sweet as another, fixed stimulus. Judgments of twice, ten times, etc., have been demanded and recorded reliably. Use of an older technique, the judgment of sense distances, has also figured large in these attempts.

The development of sensory scales represents, however, only a part of contemporary psychophysics. Broadly speaking, psychophysics has become the study of the relations between the responses of organisms and the stimuli that are presented to such organisms. This sounds almost like a definition of modern experimental psychology, and indeed, it is difficult to separate the two. The influence of behaviorism in American psychology is easily seen in modern psychophysics. We no longer look for relations between stimuli and sensations but rather relations between stimuli and responses. We can observe responses, the elements of behavior, and measure them, whereas the private sensation, which remains as untouchable as it was in Fechner's day, does not concern us. We do not ask whether or not a man hears a tone. We seek only to find whether or not he responds in a specified way to a tone. We can have measurement, then, on both sides of the psychophysical relation. The "psycho" part refers merely to behavior.

We shall have more to say about specific responses when we come to discuss conditioning and its relation to psychophysical measurement. We should note here, nevertheless, that there are very few observable innate responses to sound. Different components of the startle response may be observed when a very loud sudden sound is presented. Most of the stimuli to hearing that will concern us, however, are of lower intensities than those required to elicit the startle response. We resort, therefore, to training or conditioning techniques in order to elicit the responses that we wish to observe. The audiometrist *tells the patient to raise a finger or press a button* when he hears a tone. Here is an example of a very complicated kind of conditioned or substitute stimulus, and the results of such measurement are valid only in so far as we have faith in the effectiveness of such conditioning.

Responses may be measured in many different ways. Sometimes we use an all-or-none criterion; the response is either made or it is not made. We may, however, go on to record the number of responses that have been made after a given number of stimuli have been presented. The measure of the response then becomes one of frequency of response. Other techniques involve a measure of the amplitude of a single response.

SUMMARY

To apply numbers to phenomena of experience must have been inconceivable to the early philosophical psychologists. The measurement of sensation has come about only as a result of several gradual transitions, primarily in respect of the way the problem was stated. The dualism that began with Descartes and became the psychophysical parallelism of the nineteenth century made the problem quite clear: there were physical events in the world that gave rise to the sensations of experience; how were the two kinds of events related?

Fechner thought that if he could relate changes in the physical stimulus to changes in the response of an observer, he might be able to write an equation that would relate the physical world with the world of sensation. His basic thesis appears now to have been right, although an apparent mistake was made when he chose the jnd as the crucial response. Perhaps the development of sensory scales as such does not excite us very much, but the fact that they can be and were developed means that we now have a systematic body of method for performing experiments that is based on these apparently dead issues. So far as sensory theory is concerned, the main problems seem to have been distilled into a problem of the appropriate specification of the *real* stimulus and response.

Many of our basic problems have been solved for us. We can approach the measurement of hearing from an operational, behavioristic point of view without worrying about philosophical points concerning experience and the real world. To measure hearing is to establish a relation between a measure of a stimulus (physical) and a measure of an appropriate response (psychological). Our first job is to examine the nature of the auditory stimulus and to learn something about its production, control, and measurement.

REFERENCES

Boring, E. G. *Sensation and perception in the history of experimental psychology.* New York: Appleton-Century-Crofts, 1942.

Guilford, J. P. *Psychometric methods.* New York: McGraw-Hill, 1936.

Stevens, S. S. Sensation and psychological measurement. Chap. 11 in E. G. Boring, H. S. Langfeld, and H. P. Weld (Eds.), *Foundations of psychology.* New York: Wiley, 1948.

Stevens, S. S. Mathematics, measurement and psychophysics. Chap. 1 in S. S. Stevens (Ed.), *Handbook of experimental psychology.* New York: Wiley, 1951.

....

PART THREE

Perception of Objects and Events

A. *The Stimulus Field and Its Differentiation*

SELECTION 4

••

Color Adaptation Under Conditions of Homogeneous Visual Stimulation (Ganzfeld)*

JULIAN E. HOCHBERG, WILLIAM TRIEBEL, AND GIDEON SEAMAN

GESTALT THEORY assumes that the arousal of articulated perceptual processes depends upon inhomogeneous stimulus distributions on the sensory surface (4, 5). Thus, to Koffka (4, p. 110), the "simplest" visual percepts are occasioned, not by punctiform stimulation of a single rod or cone, but by distributions of retinal stimulation which approach complete uniformity. Although investigations of the effects of such homogeneous distributions would seem important in understanding organization under more complex circumstances (and in approaching such problems as the formation of three-dimensional perceptual space, the segregation of the "Ego," etc.), the research done in these areas since the pioneer investigations of Metzger (6) has been meager. This paper describes a comparatively simple method for approximating the required visual stimulus conditions, and reports the perceptual responses obtained in exploratory experimentation on the effects of spatially homogeneous chromogenic stimulation.

Metzger had his observers sit 1.25 m. from a whitewashed wall equipped with wings attached at all four edges with a minimum of inhomogeneity so as to fill the S's field of view. When the intensity of illumination was sufficiently low, imperfect accommodation blurred the slight textural inhomogeneities of the wall so that the stimulus distribution was so homogeneous that the Ss perceived a space-filling, surfaceless fog. This finding offers support for Koff-

* From the *J. exp. Psychol.* 1951, **41**, 153-159. Reprinted by permission of the authors and the publisher.

ka's hypothesis that homogeneous illumination of the retina does not provide the differentiation necessary to maintain a surface as a structure in the visual field (4, p. 117). With increased illumination and, presumably, improved accommodation, the texture of the wall provided sufficient inhomogeneity to institute the perception of a surface through an interesting and significant series of transition stages.

Koffka makes a further prediction, which has not yet been tested, concerning the response to homogeneous visual stimulation. Since the Gestalt explanation of color constancy (and of "framework" phenomena in general) requires that the "general background . . . will appear as neutral as the conditions will allow" (4, p. 256), Koffka predicts (4, p. 121) that a perfectly homogeneous field of colored light will appear neutral rather than colored as soon as the S relinquishes the "framework" carried over from his previous environment.[1] Since the Hering theory of color vision predicts that continued stimulation of color receptors should ultimately result in sensations of middle gray, there have been a number of studies of color adaptation under prolonged stimulation; their results, as reviewed by Helson and Judd (3), indicate that disappearance of color takes place only under very special circumstances. Thus, Helson and Judd had their Ss place their heads in a 36-in.-diameter sphere lined with Hering orange-red paper under "very intense" illumination (to hasten any adaptation effects as might occur). They report that "at no time, not even after 75 min. adaptation, did the color of the surface viewed completely and permanently disappear. The equilibrium condition with its associated neutral gray demanded by the Hering theory under conditions of constant retinal stimulation failed to appear" (3, p. 386). They were, however, able to get "fairly good grays" maintained for very short periods of time with fixation of the eyes, and concluded that *eye-movements alone, even with homogeneity of retinal stimulation,* will destroy adaptation. It should be noted, however, that these color adaptation studies (and the more recent investigations of Wright [8]) were not performed under conditions of complete homogeneity of stimulation over the entire retina. Even the conditions used by Helson and Judd un-

---

[1] In fact, with ideal homogeneity (involving uniform distributions in all modalities) perhaps the S will perceive *nothing at all* (4, p. 120), although, due to the status of the "Ego" in the Gestalt conception of the perceptual field (4, p. 113), Koffka expects (4, p. 121) that the disappearance of color may be attended by a change in the "mood" of the S.

doubtedly retained sufficient textural inhomogeneity to allow the perception of a surface color, since the distance of the surface allowed fixation and accommodation. They do not constitute adequate test of Koffka's hypothesis, therefore, and repetition under more homogeneous stimulus conditions is in order.

The experiments here reported constitute an exploratory study of the percepts obtained under spatially homogeneous colored illumination over the entire visual field.[2] Specifically investigated were (1) whether fields of colored illumination of sufficient homogeneity to be perceived as surfaceless fog will lose their color and become chromatically neutral and whether the effects upon any such chromatic adaptation of (2) separate adaptation of each eye, (3) the introduction of an inhomogeneity (here, a shadow) into the field, (4) eye movements, and (5) interruption of the illumination after adaptation, are in accordance with what would be expected from Koffka's hypothesis and/or with the results obtained by Helson and Judd under conditions of less complete homogeneity.

APPARATUS

The apparatus used consisted of two eyecaps, made from halved table-tennis balls of heavy material and good diffusing power, carved to fit over the eyes and eyelids with snug contact around the edges. In these experiments, a light coating of a nonirritating, easily removed, latex-based surgical adhesive applied around the eye socket and to the edges of the eyecaps assured a strong support and light-seal. Since in most cases the S's eyelashes are so long as to disturb both the homogeneity of stimulation and his own comfort, the upper eyelashes were temporarily fastened to the upper eyelids with a small quantity of the same adhesive before applying the eyecaps.

This apparatus was designed and constructed in preference to that used by Metzger (2, 6) because of what the authors believe to be inherently superior characteristics:[3] (1) The nose and cheekbones, etc., are not included in the visual field, yet there is no narrowing of the field of view. (2) The diffusing surfaces of the eyecaps are within the mini-

---

[2] Other work with modified forms of this device is under way at Cornell University in connection with a research project on the effective stimuli for space perception supported by the United States Air Force and directed by Prof. J. J. Gibson; with further studies in color adaptation; and with an investigation of the personality-determined aspects of perception under homogeneous stimulation.

[3] The expedient of using the halves of a table tennis ball for this purpose had apparently been developed independently by Dr. R. S. Harper of Knox College.

mum accommodation distance for all Ss used. (3) The intensity of the incident light can be varied at will without introducing the textural cues of illumination. (4) The eyecaps in no way encumber the S, and there is complete flexibility with respect to movement (a consideration of no weight in this study, but vital to several projected studies). (5) The savings in construction expense and laboratory space are considerable.

The light was projected from 100-w. Kodaslide Model 2a projectors, either through a red Wratten filter No. 70 in B glass, or through a green filter, No. 54. The distance between projector lens and eyecaps of the S was 9 ft. 3 in. and S's head was held in a headrest with attached side reflectors of white cardboard in order to attain approximately equal illumination on the front and sides of the eyecaps.

RESULTS

Experiment A. The purpose of this experiment was to determine whether a homogeneous field of either red or green light will become chromatically neutral after prolonged inspection. Eleven Ss who were instructed to report continuously on shape, distance, color, texture, and any changes which might occur were divided into two groups.

In Group A1 ($N = 6$), light was projected through the red filter upon both eyecaps. An arbitrary limit of 20 min. was set as the time within which color disappearance was to be obtained. Five of the six Ss initially reported a red-colored surfaceless field followed by the total disappearance of the color within the first 3 min. The remaining S reported a cone-shaped three-dimensional surface, concave towards himself, whose color even after prolonged adaptation (20 min.) remained a "very dark, brownish magenta." This was accompanied by considerable anxiety and a strong desire to "put his hands into" the extended form he saw before him.[4] Of the other five Ss, one reported a dull ivory as the stable adapted field, and the description of the adapted field by the remaining four Ss varied from a deep black (or a feeling of having gone blind) to that of a dark gray sensation. The course of adaptation consisted of a darkening of the field, both by a desaturation of the red by admixture of

---

[4] Whether any relationships exist between personality factors, the mode in which the *Ganzfeld* is perceived, and the course of color adaptation, is yet to be investigated. However, the indeterminacy and the true lack of structure in the situation, the individual differences in hallucinatory objects and patterns perceived during the course of adaptation, and the intense fear and feelings of "going blind" expressed by some of the Ss suggest a possible method for investigation of personality structure.

black or dark gray, and by encroaching regions of black or dark gray, frequently taking the form of fanciful or threatening shapes.

In Group A2 ($N = 5$), light was projected through the green filter upon both eyecaps, the procedure otherwise being the same as for Group A1. In Group A2, all five Ss initially reported a green surfaceless field followed within a maximum of 6 min. by total disappearance of green. In this group, the adapted field ranged from black (or "nothingness") to dark gray. One of the Ss reported a flight of colors before the final state of adaptation (here, dark gray) appeared. The other Ss reported desaturation of the green by gray and blue before the final disappearance of color.

Three Ss in Group A1 and two Ss in Group A2 reported the appearance of "hallucinatory" shapes or objects at some time during the course of adaptation, and two of the Ss in Group A1 were hard to convince afterwards that such shapes had not actually been introduced as part of the experimental procedure. All Ss were firm in their belief that the illumination had at least been changed in some manner during the session.

Only one of the 11 Ss in Groups A1 and A2 reported a surface. The remainder of the Ss reported what may be subsumed under the term "fog" or "cloud." All of the Ss who did not see a surface experienced a stable, well-defined disappearance of the color, and many of these were unwilling to believe that the lights had not been changed or shut off. These results are more in accordance with Koffka's prediction than were those obtained in the situation employed by Helson and Judd. In agreement with the findings of Helson and Judd, and against what would be expected from Hering's theory, the color reported after adaptation was not mid-gray, but was generally inclined towards dark gray or black.

Experiment B. The purpose of this experiment was to determine the effects of separate adaptation by each eye. In Group B1 ($N = 5$), the right eyecap was covered by a shield mounted on the table between the projector and the S, and the left eyecap was exposed to red light until the S reported all color gone from the field. After this, the shield was removed without interrupting the light reaching the left eyecap, and the right eyecap was thus also illuminated. All five Ss reported a red sensation appearing as the right (unadapted) eye was first stimulated. Three of the Ss localized the red sensation as coming from the *right eye alone, the left eye remaining black.*

In Group B2 ($N = 5$), in which the same procedure was used

with green light rather than red, the results obtained were of the same nature as those found in Group B1: when the right eye was exposed to the same light to which the left eye had already been adapted, all five *S*s reported a strong green sensation, and four of them identified it as appearing in the *right eye alone, the left eye remaining black.*

In general, the results of adaptation of the left eye in Groups B1 and B2 supported the findings of Experiment A. One *S* in Group B1 reported deep brown as the final adaptation state, and one *S* in Group B2 reported varicolored spots in the final adapted field; the remaining eight *S*s reported "nothingness," complete blackness, dark gray, or a suspicion that the lights had been turned off. In both groups, B1 and B2, disappearance of color was finally achieved in the right eye as well, although not as satisfactorily as it was with simultaneous adaptation of both eyes, or of one eye alone.

If such an adaptation process (or, in terms of Koffka's hypothesis, the disappearance of color because of its becoming what might be termed the "chromatic neutral point") took place at any neurological level past that at which binocular fusion occurs, the adaptation state should hold for the visual field in general, and not be confined to the eye which had been exposed to the light. The results of Experiment B suggests, on the contrary, that the adaptation process is restricted to the exposed eye, a finding more indicative of relatively peripheral than central processes.

Experiment C. The purpose of this experiment was to determine the effects of introducing a shadow into a homogeneous field after adaptation. After the *S*s in Groups A1 and A2 had reported disappearance of the color, the shadow of a finger was cast vertically upon the central region of their eyecaps in such fashion as to provide a shadowed portion in the adapted field, but not to shadow the entire field. In Group A1, in which the incident light was red, all five *S*s reported a black shadow surrounded by a red halo, and both the shadow and the halo quickly disappeared with the removal of the finger. In Group A2, in which the incident light was green, four of the five *S*s reported a black shadow against a green background or halo. The remaining *S* in this group reported a purple shadow against a green halo.

No new reference point has been provided in the *chromatic* series with the introduction of a shadow into the homogeneous adapted field. We would expect, according to the hypothesis of a "chromatic neutral point," that if the shadow were seen, it would be black against an achromatic, lighter background. The only way in which the shadow would seem capable of providing a chromatic reference point would be by the appearance of the complementary color in the shadowed region, a phenomenon obtained with only one S out of ten.

Experiment D. The purpose of this experiment was to determine the effects of eye movements on the adapted field. After the Ss of Group A1 had reported the results of Experiment C and after the Ss of Group B1 had reported the disappearance of color from their left eyes, they were asked to move their eyes briskly from left to right, then back again. This was done eight times. Of the ten Ss achieving complete color disappearance in Groups A1 and B1, five reported no re-appearance of color due to deliberate eye movements. The other five Ss reported a quickly-fading flash of red. In four of the Ss the flash of red was preceded by a flash of blue-green while the eye was in motion, and the intensity and duration of the red flash decreased with each repetition of the eye movements. After the fourth eye movement, two of these Ss reported no further recurrence of color after eye movement for that or for the four subsequent eye movements. Furthermore, it seems reasonable to assume that at least minor eye movements were continuously occurring even in the absence of instructions calling for deliberate eye movements, since there was no possible fixation upon any point in the field; nevertheless, most of the Ss in Experiments A and B reported disappearance of color.

Thus, eye movements here had only a limited ability to restore the vanished color, as contrasted with the important part they played in the situation reported by Helson and Judd. Because of four Ss' report of the complementary color during eye movements, it would appear possible that the effects of such movements are a special case of the effect discussed below and are due to a change of retinal illumination accompanying eye movement.

Experiment E. The purpose of this experiment was to determine the effect of interrupting the homogeneous chromogenic stimulation to which the S has become adapted. After Groups A1 and B1 had reported the results of Experiment D, the ten Ss who had achieved complete disappearance of color were subjected to interruption of the red light for intervals of approximately 2 sec. and were asked to report whether any change in sensation had occurred. While brief blinking during and after adaptation had no apparent effects (even under instructions to pay attention to the blinking), closing the eyes or interrupting the red light at its source for intervals of approximately 2 sec. elicited the complementary color, blue-green, for nine of the Ss. Re-establishment of the stimulation resulted in a very brief flash of red for these Ss. Only one of the Ss in Group A1 reported no effect consequent either to interruption or restoration of the illumination, continuing to report "nothingness."

These findings are in contradiction to those obtained by Helson and Judd (3, p. 393), who report that continued stimulation with saturated "colored" light (their Ss here wore spectacles which, it should be noted, permitted articulated spatial perception) did not result in the arousal of the complementary color as afterimage if the retina was kept in total darkness. The appearance of the complementary color when *homogeneous* stimulation is interrupted, as occurred in the experiment here reported, would seem to contraindicate attempts to explain the disappearance of color by assuming that the adapted receptors simply stop responding to the impinging chromogenic light. If the latter were the case, the Ss should also report the complementary color while the lights are still on, because the response occasioned by the failure of the adapted receptors to react to light should not be different, by this explanation, from the response occasioned by cessation of illumination of those receptors. Attempts at explanation might be made either by assuming that continued stimulation with light of a given color somehow *inhibits* neural impulses from receptors sensitive to the complementary wave lengths (1), *even though the receptors* (or *ganglia*) *sensitive to the impinging light may not themselves be responding any longer,* or by assuming that the receptors sensitive to the impinging light are exhausted until they reach an equilibrium condition of activity which *just balances* (7) the entoptic level of the other, relatively unaffected, receptors. Any attempt at the purely retinal explanation would, however, leave unexplained the fact that most Ss in Experiment C reported that the shadow, introduced into the field after color had disappeared, was seen as "black," not as the complementary color. The complementary appeared only when the entire retina ceased receiving chromogenic stimulation, as in Experiment E.

SUMMARY

A technique is described whereby spatially homogeneous illumina-
cion may be presented to the eye, and the results of some exploratory
experiments, using homogeneous colored light, are presented. Koffka's
hypothesis that a colored *Ganzfeld* would lose its color was tested
with red and with green light. Complete disappearance of color was
obtained, in most cases, despite considerable individual differences
in the course of the adaptation process and in the phenomenal content during adaptation. However, the results of presenting colored
light to one eye after the other eye had been adapted to light of the
same color, and of introducing a shadow into the field, make it
difficult to ascribe the disappearance of the color to its adoption as
a general "chromatic neutral point" for the entire visual field.

REFERENCES

1. GOSTELIN, G. E. Inhibitory processes underlying color vision and
   their bearing on three-component theories. *Amer. J. Psychol.*, 1943,
   56, 536-550.
2. ENGEL, W. Optische Untersuchungen am Ganzfeld: I. Die Ganzfeld-
   ordnung. *Psychol. Forsch.*, 1930, **13**, 1-15.
3. HELSON, H., and JUDD, D. B. A study of photopic adaptation. *J. exp.
   Psychol.*, 1932, **15**, 380-398.
4. KOFFKA, K. *Principles of Gestalt psychology*. New York: Harcourt,
   Brace, 1935.
5. KÖHLER, W. *Physische Gestalten in Ruhe und im stationären Zustand.*
   Braunschweig: Vieweg, 1920.
6. METZGER, W. Untersuchungen am Ganzfeld: II. Zur Phänomenologie
   des homogenen Ganzfelds. *Psychol. Forsch.*, 1930, **13**, 6-29.
7. TROLAND, L. T. The colors produced by equilibrium photopic adaptation. *J. exp. Psychol.*, 1921, **4**, 344-390.
8. WRIGHT, W. D. *Researches on normal and defective color vision.*
   St. Louis: Mosby, 1947.

SELECTION 5

....

Points and Lines as Stimuli*

KURT KOFFKA

POINTS

WE SHALL NOW APPLY our principles to some other cases, such
as abound in our normal experience. We begin by modifying our last
condition, one area of uniform stimulation enclosed in another, without alteration of its character, by reducing the size of the enclosed
area, first in one, then in both, dimensions. The first procedure leads
us to lines, straight or curved, the second to mere points. The last
is that condition which older theories have taken as the simplest
case. It appears now as a special case, a case which would have been
a bad case to start from; for a seen point, though geometrically it
may be a very small circle or square, has phenomenally no shape at
all. It is just a point. Therefore, in using the point as our standard
case we should have overlooked the rôle of shape in perception, as
traditional psychology has done. In considering the point as a special
case of a more general condition, we do not only, however, avoid this
mistake, we also gain a new positive insight into the processes of
organization. Single points are unstable structures which tend to
disappear.

Attitudes. Moreover, frequently enough their appearance requires
definite attitudes on the part of the observer. One may look at a
white sheet of paper for a long time unaware of a point on it, and
only when one becomes suspicious and examines the paper carefully
will one discover it. What does this mean? Without a critical attitude
the inhomogeneity of stimulation corresponding to the point was not
sufficient to break the homogeneity of the well-defined unit in the
visual environment. It required a new factor, an attitude, to bring
the point into existence. Had the inhomogeneity been greater in size

---

* From *Principles of Gestalt Psychology* by Kurt Koffka, copyright, 1935, by
Harcourt, Brace and Co., Inc.

it would have enforced the appearance of a visible object without a special attitude. Thus we learn two new facts. In the first place, we find the field organization under certain circumstances dependent upon attitudes, i.e., forces which have their origin not in the surrounding field at all, but in the Ego of the observer, a new indication that our task of investigating the surrounding field alone is somewhat artificial, and that we shall understand its organization completely only when we study the total field which includes the Ego within its environment.

Why Points Are Unstable. In the second place we must raise the question why single points are so unstable, why they may remain invisible. Formulated in this way, the question can meet only spurious answers, like those given by an older generation of psychologists who would have explained this fact by the hypothesis of the non-noticed sensations. But the inadequacy of this explanation is quite evident in our case. When we fail to see the point, we see a homogeneous surface instead, i.e., if it is a black point on a white surface we see white when we fail to notice the point. This, the hypothesis of the non-noticed sensations fails to explain, for *not* to notice something black is not equivalent to noticing something white. We said just now that our question was badly formulated. Our last proposition gives us a clue as to how to formulate it better. Instead of asking why we do *not* see something, viz., the point, we should ask why we see something else, viz., the homogeneous surface, instead. We can fall back for our answer on the Wertheimer-Benussi contrast experiment, which shows how a strongly unified whole resists forces which would make it inhomogeneous as to color.* In our present case there exists a force to break the uniformity of the

---

* In this experiment a ring is cut out of a uniform medium-grey sheet of paper. The ring is about 1 inch wide and has a diameter of about 6 inches. The ring is placed in the center of a large, rectangular cardboard background whose left half is black and whose right half is white. By simultaneous brightness contrast, one would expect the left half of the ring, which is on the black background, to look lighter than the right half of the ring, which is on the white background. But the "cohesive forces" holding the ring together as a unit are so strong that the ring is seen as a uniform medium-grey. If the ring's unity is decreased, as by placing a long strip of paper 1 inch wide over it (along the vertical line where the black meets the white background), the simultaneous contrast effect occurs, and the left half of the ring (on black) does indeed look lighter than the right half (on white). Removing the strip, and thereby once more obtaining a strongly unified whole ring, produces a return of the uniformity of the grey color of the entire ring. (Eds.)

surface, and if it does not accomplish this result, this failure must be due to other and stronger forces, those which make the uni*fied* area also uni*form*. These latter forces have their origin in the homogeneous coloration of the entire unitary surface in which the point is the only inhomogeneity. Around the point homogeneous processes occur in close proximity, all over the rest of the surface in contiguity. As we shall see very soon, proximity of equal processes produces the same kind of forces as contiguity. Therefore the unifying forces must be very strong in our case, and the single inhomogeneity will often not be strong enough to overcome them without an added force.

One conclusion of our discussion is that to see a point is not a primitive but a high grade achievement. Only in specially developed systems will such a slight inhomogeneity be capable of producing articulation; in others it will give rise to a simple homogeneous field.

LINES

We turn now to the consideration of lines. Ordinary lines, whether straight or curved, appear as lines and not as areas. They have shape, but they lack the difference between an inside and an outside and are in that respect another special case of our general one. Geometrically, each straight line that we draw is a rectangle; psychologically, it is not. Shape, on the other hand, is a very important characteristic of lines, an assertion which we shall prove by experimental evidence a little later.

Closed Contour Figures. The consideration of lines, however, introduces a new point of view. If a line forms a closed, or almost closed, figure, we see no longer merely a line on a homogeneous background, but a surface figure bounded by the line. This fact is so familiar that unfortunately it has, to my knowledge, never been made the subject of a special investigation. And yet it is a very startling fact, once we strip it of its familiarity. Therefore, we want a functional proof for our claim that a figure surrounded by contours is an entity different from the field outside the contours, which in all other respects produces the same stimulation. We possess methods by which a difference between a contour figure and its surroundings could be established, but these methods have not been applied to our problem. We might measure the threshold of a small figure produced either inside or outside the contour of our original figure, e.g., by projecting such a figure on the contoured surface and having an episcotister between the lantern and the surface, an apparatus like that employed by Hempstead. If then the little figure required a greater episcotister opening in order to become visible inside than outside the contour, we should have proved a greater cohesiveness of the enclosed area as compared with its surroundings, which would make it more difficult to produce a new figure on it. Unfortunately this experiment has never been made, although from two similar experiments, one by Gelb and Granit and the other by Granit, our assumed result seems predictable.

The Dynamic Causes of Contour Figures. But our main problem appears when we accept this difference as a real one. For we want to know the causes which separate not only the contour from the rest of the field but at the same time the enclosed figure from its surroundings. Our principle of discontinuity certainly does not explain it. For the discontinuity between the contour and the surface on which it is drawn is the same in either direction, towards the inside and the outside. From our old principle we can only explain why we see lines as lines, i.e., as units segregated from the rest, but not the case which concerns us now, viz., when we see the area enclosed by a line, or a pattern of lines, segregated from the rest of the field and not in the same way segregated from the contour. Although discontinuity of stimulation still has a segregating effect and in so far is in harmony with our law, this segregation is asymmetrical. What is the reason of this asymmetry?

FACTOR OF CLOSURE. Unfortunately this question has not been treated. But since a mere profession of ignorance might raise some doubt in the minds of the readers as to the validity of our general principle, we shall try to point out some factors which might possibly explain the phenomenon. The first point we would raise is the fact that closed, or almost closed, lines or patterns of lines have this peculiarity, whereas it is lacking in unclosed ones. This seems to indicate that the process of organization depends upon the properties of its result, in strict accordance with the general law of prägnanz. Closed areas seem to be self-sustaining, stable organizations, a conclusion which will be reached independently later on the basis of special experiments.

FACTOR OF GOOD SHAPE. Secondly, we might try to find out whether there are closed lines or patterns of lines which will more readily be seen as mere lines than others. Although no experiments have been made to decide this point, I am inclined to believe that such differences exist, and that, e.g., a circle will be more easily seen as a mere line than a triangle, the latter appearing as a triangular surface rather than as three lines meeting each other at their terminal points. If this is true, we might attempt to connect this fact with our law of good shape. The circle is a perfectly good figure as a line. Each piece of it contains the principle of the whole. Not so the triangle, where no small piece demands to be continued in such a way that a triangle results. On the contrary, each part of each side will by itself demand a continuation in its own direction, the three corners being breaks in this mode of continuation. As lines, then, the contours of a triangle are not "simple," and therefore, we may tentatively conclude, not stable. Contrariwise the surface of a triangle, particularly if it is an isosceles or an equilateral one, is simple, possesses symmetry, and the reason for the segregation of the whole area may well be this symmetry, which should be accompanied by stability.

Briefly, then, we propose as a tentative hypothesis that the contour bounds a figure rather than segregates itself as a line from the rest of the surface, because this is the better, the more stable organization.

With this explanation we do not introduce a new principle. For we have seen before how factors of shape, as factors of stability, will organize a field against the mere effects of discontinuity of stimulation. Nevertheless I should be the last to be satisfied with my hypothesis. Not only does it, as yet, lack experimental evidence, but it is not explicit enough, it contains no statement about the actual forces along the contour line and their asymmetrical function.

Organizations Produced by Line Patterns. But we must let the matter rest at that. The fact remains that areas can be unified and segregated from the rest of a homogeneous field by mere closed lines. And this fact helps us to study the factor of shape in new ways. We shall now consider the specific principles according to which line patterns produce organization, line patterns which are still special cases of our general one: the field divided up into two different parts, each in itself homogeneous or practically homogeneous. Any one of the patterns to be discussed now fulfills this condition; the field consists of a continuous white part, the ground of the page, and a continuous black part, the lines. All these patterns might be produced by first making a large black spot and then removing some of the black.

Our question is: Given a certain line pattern, what figures shall we see? What are the general principles that govern this relation? Two papers from the Berlin laboratory contain a wealth of material, one as an integral part of a study devoted to a different problem by Gottschaldt (1926), the other, directly concerned with our problem, by Kopfermann. We shall choose our examples from the latter.

When our line pattern is such that it simply separates one part of the surface from the rest, no new problem arises. We shall now consider patterns such in which the separated area itself contains lines which divide it geometrically into two or more smaller areas. What shall we see? We have come across this same problem already under simpler conditions, when we dealt not with line-, but with surface-figures. If the enclosed homogeneous area had a special shape, it would appear not as one figure but as two overlapping ones.

PROBLEM OF UNUM AND DUO. Taking this case as a starting point we can ask the question: When will an outline figure be seen as one, with lines in its interior, and when as two or more? Figs. 1 and 2

FIG. 1.   FIG. 2.

give examples for either case; in the first, one sees a rectangle with a line passing through it, in the second two adjoining hexagons. The reason is clear: in the first the total figure is a better figure than either of the two part figures, whereas the opposite is true in the second. Moreover, in the first figure, the upper and lower side of the rectangle are continuous straight lines, while these same straight lines have to be broken up if the two irregular quadrangles are to be seen.

GOOD CONTINUATION. The first factor we have already encountered; the second would mean that, as we have also pointed out previously, a straight line is a more stable structure than a broken one, and that therefore organization will, *ceteris paribus*, occur in such a way that a straight line will continue as a straight line. We may generalize thus: any curve will proceed in its own natural way, a circle as a circle, an ellipse as an ellipse, and so forth. This aspect of organization has been called the law of good continuation by Wertheimer (1923).* We shall meet with many examples of it in actual organizations. Here we add another one, in Fig. 3, taken from Bühler (1913),

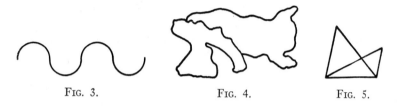

FIG. 3.   FIG. 4.   FIG. 5.

in which the external forces prevent the good continuation. The result is an esthetically unpleasant impression, because the proper continuation of the four semicircles is interrupted.

If in a line pattern the "unum" and the "duo" organization are equally good with regard to shape of the areas and continuation of the lines, is there a preference for either of these? Kopfermann thinks there is, in favour of the unum, a preference for a single all-enclosed figure, for an all-enclosing contour. However, her figures are all such that the other factors, notably that of good continuation, enter in favouring the unum, so that she has not proved her claim. As a matter of fact it is at least extremely difficult, if not impossible, to produce such patterns as will fulfill our conditions (see Fig. 4), and the result with the best of them is very ambigious. I am, therefore, not sure whether such a factor exists or not.

DUO-ORGANIZATION. Our distinction of unum- and duo-organization, even if we include within the latter the cases where more than two figures are seen, does not do full justice to the variety of actual organizations. On the one hand, most duo-formations have at the same time a unum-quality, and on the other the duo-formation may be of various kinds. The duo-figure of the two adjoining hexagons (Fig. 2), e.g., has at the same time a definite whole-character; so has Fig. 5, although it appears as two partially overlapping triangles. The unum and the duo of an organization may be in perfect harmony with each other, indeed such a harmony can be achieved in an in-

---

* See Selection 8. (Eds.)

definite variety of ways. At the one extreme we have dominance of the unum, the duo being perfect parts of the whole. At the other extreme we have strong dominance of the duo, the unum being the more or less fortuitous combination of the parts as in Fig. 6, our two preceding examples (Figs. 2 and 5) lying somewhere between them. The duo itself can be of various kinds. We distinguish two notable cases: (a) exemplified by Fig. 2, in which the two parts are co-ordinated, and (b) exemplified by Fig. 7, where one figure lies

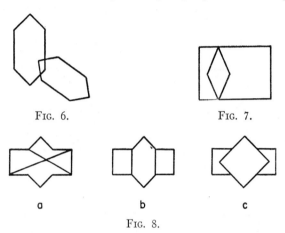

FIG. 6.   FIG. 7.

a   b   c

FIG. 8.

"on top" of another. Fig. 8 shows how one and the same outline pattern can be made by internal lines to appear either as unum (Fig. 8a); or as duo-(a), (Fig. 8b); or finally as duo-(b), (Fig. 8c). Good shape and continuation explain all these cases.

THE EMPIRICIST'S OBJECTION. We could consider our experimental proof of the effectiveness of our organizing factors as amply sufficient, had we not to contend with the vested interests of an old theory which claims to explain all our facts as well as we do, but without the assumption of all these different organizing forces. I mean the empiristic theory which would say: We see in an individual case such figures as we have frequently seen before; the stimulus conditions of our present cases are sufficiently similar to the stimulus conditions of previous and frequently repeated cases to produce the same results. Perfectly true, if two alternative theories are proposed for one and the same effect, a decision between them must be reached by weighing their relative merits against each other and, if possible, by crucial experiments.

Let us then weigh the claims of the empiristic theory with regard to our problems of perceptual organization. Look at the series of three figures, Fig. 8. An empiricist would have to say: "We see in *a* the decagon with two lines in its interior because we have seen such a figure more frequently than the four other irregular small figures; in *b* we see two oblongs with a hexagon between them because they have been seen more frequently than the decagon, which was seen in the first figure; and finally in *c* both square and oblong have been seen more frequently than the decagon and are therefore seen now." The explanation seems plausible. But in 1923 Wertheimer met such an objection by constructing figures like Fig. 9, in which the initials

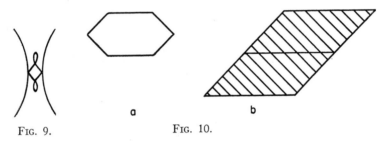

FIG. 9.   FIG. 10.

of his name, M W, are concealed, and Köhler has published a number of other figures (1925 and 1929).

EXPERIMENTAL DISPROOF OF THE EMPIRISTIC THEORY. More systematic proof was furnished by Gottschaldt (1926). In his experiments the subjects were presented with 5 simple line patterns (*a* patterns) which were projected on a screen for 1 second each, with an interval of 3 seconds between two exposures. They were told to learn these figures as best they could, so that when tested later they would remember them and be able to draw them on paper. After a certain number of presentations, different for two groups of subjects, new patterns (*b* patterns) were shown for 2 seconds each; the subjects were told that the learning experiments were to be continued later, meanwhile they were being shown a new set of pictures which they were merely to describe, mentioning if anything particular struck them about these pictures. Now each *b* picture was so constructed that geometrically it contained an *a* picture, but that under normal circumstances the *b* picture would not be seen as containing the shape of the *a* pattern. Fig. 10 gives one example, the most difficult one in the series. To each *a* figure there corresponded six or seven b figures; e.g., to the a figure of our last diagram also the much easier b, Fig. 11. Now if the empiristic theory were right, practice in seeing the a figure should make the b figure look like a plus something else. In order to test this assumption three subjects were shown the a figure three times only and eight subjects 520 times. Of the 3 subjects in the first group 2 saw the b figures as new figures on all 30 occasions, and of the 8 subjects of the second group 5 gave the same result. The outcome of this experiment is not changed if one lumps all the subjects of one group together.

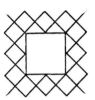

FIG. 11.

To do this one has to distinguish a number of different possibilities. (1) The a figure would be seen at once when the b figure was presented. This happened only once in the 92 experiments of the first group and 4 times in the 242 experiments of the second. (2) It was discovered later either at the end of the exposure or afterwards in the image. 5 such cases occurred in the first and 3 in the second group. (3) The subjects did not really see the a but they guessed correctly that it was there, no case in the first group, 5 in the second. There is a (4) in which the subjects guessed at an a figure but made a wrong guess, and finally a (5), in which they only saw the b figure.

In Table 1 we give in percentages of the total number of cases the combined number of cases 1-3 in which some influence of the a figure can be traced and those of cases (4) and (5) where no such influence was apparent.

TABLE 1. (FROM GOTTSCHALDT)

	3 repet. 92 cases	520 repet. 242 cases
a has some influence	6.6	5.0
a has no influence	93.4	95.0

The assumption has been disproved. There is absolutely no significant difference between the two groups. The very few cases, moreover, in which an influence of the a figure was apparent, cannot be due to mere experience either; first of all they do not increase with an increase of experience, and secondly the subjects who showed that influence were not in an entirely neutral attitude, but expected to

find the old figures again, as is evidenced by the wrong guesses made
by two of the four subjects concerned.

The conclusion is that experience does not explain why we see a
line pattern in the shape in which we see it, but that direct forces of
organization, such as we have analyzed, must be the real cause.
To this conclusion I have heard the following objections made.
The first I owe to one of my students. It says, consistent with the
empiristic principles, that we see the *b* figures in their *b* shapes and
not as *a* shapes because some of their parts are very familiar figures,
more familiar than the *a* figures. Thus the square in the second and
the "grill" in the first example have a greater experience behind
them than the hexagon of the *a* figure. The first answer to this objection is that it does not explain why the difference between 3 and 520
repetitions of the *a* figure should have made no difference whatsoever
for the result. A second point is that not in all cases were shapes of
b figures more familiar than the shapes of *a* figures as demonstrated
by Fig. 12. True enough the simple shapes are as a rule the familiar

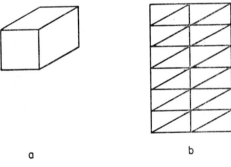

a   b

FIG. 12.

shapes, a coincidence which makes the empiristic theory so plausible,
a coincidence which is, moreover, by no means fortuitous. Naturally
if the laws of organization are true laws, we must expect the products
of human activity to be simple, since they owe their existence to
organized processes; and therefore the simple will be the frequent.
Because of this connection between simplicity and familiarity it was
of such fundamental importance when Fuchs proved that not the
familiarity but the simplicity of certain figures was the cause of their
completion. We can add a third point to our answer: Gottschaldt

devised an ingenious method for measuring the degree of difficulty which each *b* figure offered to the finding of its *a* figure. Now if the objection were right, those *b* figures which contained the most familiar parts should be the most difficult ones. Nothing of the kind is true. Fig. 11 is much easier than Fig. 10, and yet the square is much more familiar than the grill. And one of the three easiest of Gottschaldt's *b* figures has the shape of a well-known pattern. This objection, clever as it is, cannot, therefore, stand the test of the facts.

The other objection runs like this: there was no experience of *b* figures, the *a* figures when experienced were always in a different setting and one must of course include the "total situation."

THE "TOTAL SITUATION." This argument has the semblance of plausibility because of the term "total situation," which in reality means nothing. For in each "total" situation there are always parts that are relevant to the particular effect we are studying, and some that are not. And thus the term "total situation" obscures the problem. Turn back to our series of figures, Fig. 8, to which we applied the empiristic theory. In this application there was no mention made of total situation, and indeed we could not have seen the decagon, the oblongs, the hexagon and square very often, if at all, in those particular "total situations." The argument rested entirely on the fact that we had seen these figures *per se* more frequently than the other figures whose shape did not appear in those patterns. And the empiristic argument would have to be this, for otherwise it would beg the question. If, for instance, it claimed that we saw the decagon with its internal lines in the first pattern of our series because we had seen this, or similar, patterns before, then we should ask, *Why* have we under these stimulus conditions seen just this shape and not the others? In other words, if the empiricist were to argue like this, he would commit what we have called the experience error.

Finally, it is quite easy to produce total situations which are entirely new and which will not in the least interfere with the recognition of the *a* figure. Köhler has given a very good demonstration of this fact in his book (1929, p. 210). Fig. 13 demonstrates the same with a pattern we have frequently used before. If, then, some "total situations" do not (or very little) interfere with the shape of a special part, while others obliterate it completely, there must be some specific factors in those "total situations" responsible for this difference. These factors we have singled out in our laws of spontaneous organization.

Tri-dimensional Organization of Line Patterns. These laws explain even more than the two-dimensional shape we have so far considered. Of the three patterns of Fig. 14, *a,* when presented without *b* and *c,* is a plane figure, a hexagon with diagonals, or a sort of cross or star-like figure; Fig. *c,* on the other hand, appears tridimensionally as a cube, and *b* can appear either bi- or tri-dimensional: in the former case one sees the pattern of Fig. 15 lying on top of a hexagon, in the

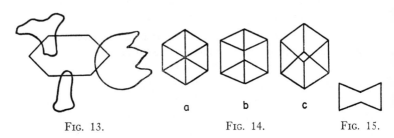

	a	b	c	

FIG. 13.　　　　　　FIG. 14.　　　　　　FIG. 15.

latter, it is a cube. All three figures are projections of one and the same wire-edged cube, either of them could therefore be the retinal image of such a cube. A simple application of our laws will show why these different projections have such different effects. On account of both good shape and continuation, *a* as a plane figure is perfectly simple and symmetrical, whereas as a cube the long straight lines are broken up. The opposite is true of *c* where the plane figure is very irregular, without any simple plan, and therefore very hard to see. In *b* the forces are more balanced, both the bi- and the tri-dimensional aspect being regular. The greater symmetry of the cube is in favour of tri-dimensionality, while the continuation of the central vertical line favours bi-dimensionality. For this reason *b* is more ambiguous than either *a* or *c.* Kopfermann has developed these ideas with a number of other figures; I have tried to show why an empiristic explanation is false, using arguments similar to the last employed in the refutation of the empiristic theory of tri-dimensional shape (1930).

SELECTION 6

....

The Modes of Appearance
of Colours*

David Katz

FILM COLOURS AND SURFACE COLOURS

IT HAS ALWAYS BEEN clear to me that when one looks through the
eyepiece of a spectroscope, the colours one sees in it have an entirely
different mode of appearance from that of other colours, *e.g.*, the
colours of the coloured papers which we use so frequently.

The spectral colour of the usual apparatus is generally not localized so precisely at an exactly definable distance as is the colour of
a paper. The latter usually appears wherever we see the surface of
the paper. The distance of the spectral colour from the eye of the
observer can be gauged only with some degree of uncertainty. The
absolute distance at which the spectral colour is presented is not to
be held responsible for its peculiar mode of appearance. In the apparatus which I used (Asher's spectrometer) the distance at which
the colours appeared varied according to the observer's estimate
from 50 cm. to 80 cm. Now coloured papers can be presented at
smaller or at greater distances without being thereby made to look
like spectral colours. The variation which we observe in spectral
colours with respect to ease of localization is connected in general
with a certain spongy texture which they evince, whereas in the case
of the colour of a paper we can speak of a greater compactness of
the colour base. The paper has a surface in which the colour lies. The
plane in which the spectral colour is extended in space before the observer does not in the same sense possess a surface. One feels that one
can penetrate more or less deeply *into* the spectral colour, whereas
when one looks at the colour of a paper the surface presents a barrier beyond which the eye cannot pass. It is as though the colour of

* From Katz, D., *The world of colour*. London: Kegan Paul, 1935 (translated by R. B. MacLeod and C. W. Fox). Pp. 7-15 reprinted by permission of
the publisher.

the paper offered resistance to the eye. We have here a phenomenon of visual resistance which in its way contributes to the structure of the perceptual world as something existing in actuality.[1] The spongy texture of the spectral colour is not of such a nature that it could be referred to as a *voluminousness* or as a colour-*transparency*. Rather, a spectral colour has this much in common with the colour of a paper, that *it is extended through space in the form of a bidimensional plane, and functions as a rear boundary for it.* The delimitation of space takes place differently for the two types of colour. A spectral colour never loses an essentially *frontal-parallel* character. When the colour fixated is directly before the eyes and projected on the fovea, the plane in which it is seen always presents an orientation essentially perpendicular to the direction of vision. The colour of a paper, on the other hand, can assume *any orientation whatsoever with reference to the direction of vision,* for its plane is always that of the surface of the coloured paper. If it appears in frontal-parallel orientation, this is to be considered simply as a special case. We shall distinguish between these two opposed types of colour-impression on the basis of their common and differentiating factors by characterizing spectral colours, and all the colours which share their mode of appearance, as *film colours* and the opposite type as *surface colours.* Surface colours are seen almost solely on objects, so that it might not be out of place to speak of them as "object colours."[2] In some cases, however, this term might be misleading. Thus we tend to consider the redness of a red glass or of a red liquid as an object colour, belonging to the object, whereas this red does not possess the character of a surface colour, but presents rather the mode of appearance which we shall characterize below as *voluminousness.*[3] On the other hand, surface colours do not appear only on objects; they may be seen, for instance, on clouds of smoke or steam which stand out in clear relief, and we should be doing

---

[1] *Cf.* in this connection W. Dilthey, "Ueber die Gründe unseres Glaubens an die Existenz der Aussenwelt," *Berichte d. preuss. Akad. d. Wiss.,* 1890.

[2] Whittmann has drawn attention to the fact that the colours of objects which are seen as reversed may present a decidedly surfacy character without actually being seen as object colours. J. Whittmann, *Arch. f. d. ges. Psychol.,* 1919, 39. Some further observations of surface, film and volume colours under similar conditions are reported by E. v. Hornbostel, *Psychol. Forsch.,* 1921, 1.

[3] "Thus we see that colour-impressions can constitute object colours of differing spatial mode of appearance." A. Gelb, "Ueber den Wegfall der Wahrnehmung von 'Oberflächenfarben,'" *Zsch. f. Psychol.,* 1920, 84, p. 245.

violence to common usage if we were to refer to these clouds of smoke or steam as objects.

Most naturally or artificially coloured objects, such as wood, paper, stone or cloth, awaken under ordinary conditions the impression of surface colour. By far the most common setting for this type of impression is when light is reflected diffusely from dull-surfaced objects, for as a rule it is only solidly structured objects which possess a clear-cut surface character. The relationship between the physical origin of a light-ray and the mode of appearance of the corresponding impression is not in accordance with any simple law. All possible intermediate stages are to be found between surface colours and film colours.[1] Monocular observation instead of the customary binocular observation results in a recession of surface colour. Lack of sharpness in accommodation can have the same effect. The surface colour-impression normally given by an object can easily be supplanted by the impression of film colour if a screen, containing a single aperture, is so placed before the object as to conceal it completely, except for the part appearing through the aperture, and at the same time to prevent the recognition of any surface structure in the object. Colour-impressions do not, however, change their modes of appearance only in response to changes in the external conditions. There are also more or less controllable inner sets which can bring about transformations of colour-appearance. Some observations made by v. Allesch[2] are worth quoting in this connection. "It often happened that the same colour appeared at one time as surface colour, at another as film, and at yet another as volume colour. . . . The purposeful set of the observer [was] in this connection of great significance." It is noteworthy that the transformation from surface colour to film colour is more easily induced than is the reverse change. Even the transformation of film

---

[1] G. E. Müller has drawn attention to the fact that a visual phenomenon tends of its own accord to approximate more closely the mode of appearance of film and volume colours the more closely its intensity approximates that of the intrinsic visual grey. *Zsch. f. Sinnesphysiol.*, 1923, 54, p. 140. "Reds and yellows certainly possess the property of being more strongly condensed, whereas the colours on the right half of the spectrum are blurred." Sophie Belajew-Exemplarsky, *Zsch. f. Psychol.*, 1925, 96, p. 424. Mabel F. Martin has made a special study of transitional stages between film, surface and volume colours "Film, Surface and Bulky Colours and their Intermediates," *Amer. J. Psychol.*, 1922, 33.

[2] G. J. v. Allesch, *Die ästhetische Erscheinungsweise der Farben.* Berlin, 1925, p. 22.

colour into volume colour "was not altogether as obvious and as easy as the opposite." We chose spectral colours as our original example of film colours; nevertheless any physical light-ray can produce the impresion of film colour. A blue or uniformly beclouded grey sky presents an opportunity for the observation of film colours. If one wishes to limit oneself to a relatively small section of the sky one can use an aperture screen. If one lies on one's back in a large open meadow and looks upward, the sky produces the impression of a very extended film colour. For me the intrinsic visual grey also approximates the film-colour appearance. According to my experiments this proves to be the case for other individuals as well, but a number of people have classified it rather as a volume colour. The intensity of illumination within a given space can be so reduced that it becomes impossible, even with a completely adapted eye, to recognize either the structure or the orientation of the surfaces of objects. What can still be distinguished are merely the outlines of objects and those of their surfaces which stand out as distinct from each other on the basis of brightness differences. The grey colours perceived under these conditions resemble film colours.

The "indefinite localization" of a film colour implies for us a positive statement about its localization. The expression is used in a purely descriptive sense. The category of indefiniteness seems to deserve greater consideration in the psychology of perception (and in other fields as well) than it has as yet been accorded. Rubin deserves credit for having drawn attention to impressions of indefinite size and of indefinite configuration.[1]

We have seen that film colour always possesses an essentially frontal-parallel character. In contrast with this, surface colours *may* have an afrontal orientation, since they always lie in the surface of the object in which they are seen. Resulting from this peculiarity is a new factor which distinguishes surface colour further from film colour. The surface of an object can be either smooth or wrinkled, and according as it is the one or the other the surface colour, too, will be either smooth or wrinkled. Surface colour follows all the wrinkles of the surface of the object, and presents, too, its finest structure and texture. Film colour, on the other hand, is always localized in a smooth plane. Pronounced wrinkles never appear in film colours. One might assume from this that greater pronounced-

---

[1] E. Rubin, *Visuell wahrgenommene Figuren.* Gyldendalske Boghandel, 1921, § 8. [See also Selection 13. Eds.]

ness of structure or texture would in itself be enough to stamp certain colour-impressions as surface colours; where structure or texture is absent we should then have film colours. The distinction between surface and film cannot, however, be made as easily as this. If we stretch a sheet of exceedingly smooth paper, which is not shiny, across a pane of glass, and view it from a sufficiently great distance, we shall have a surface colour from which all texture is completely absent.

Not all colours which we see as colour-qualities of objects possess the character of surface colour, but it seems to hold fairly generally that all surface colours are seen as attributes of objects. Contrariwise it is not our custom in the same sense to associate with film colour the impression that it refers beyond to some sort of object. It appears simply as a "smooth or space-filling *quale*," as Hering[1] expressed it on one occasion when he had this particular mode of appearance in mind.

Some brief reference must be made to the different *æsthetic* effects of these two modes of appearance of colour. For most of the observers whom I have questioned in this connection the film colours have a certain delicacy about them, and for this reason are characterized as æsthetically more pleasing than the surface colours.[2]

This is the proper place for a discussion of a few observations reported by Gelb in that valuable article on the disappearance of the perception of surface colours, in which my distinction between the different modes of appearance of colour received its first application to questions in the pathology of perception.

The study is of two cases of disturbance of colour-vision, brought about by cerebral lesion.[3] In each case the lesion was occipital. In the case of one of the patients, who because of his greater intelligence and reliability proved to be a particularly fruitful subject, the

---

[1] Hering, VI, p. 12. Matthaei occasionally refers to film colour as "free colour." R. Matthaei, *Die Welt der Farbe*. Bonn, 1927. Free colour becomes condensed into surface colour or diffuses itself into volume colour.

[2] "Numerous special experiments . . . indicated that the specifically æsthetic appearance of colour is the film colour, a factor which comes into operation, too, when a coloured object is judged as far as possible on the basis of its colour alone (as is nowadays being attempted in impressionistic painting)." v. Allesch, *op. cit.*, p. 22.

[3] A. Gelb, "Ueber den Wegfall der Wahrnehmung von 'Oberflächenfarben,'" *Zsch. f. Psychol.*, 1920, 84. Gelb refers to a similar case described by O. Pötzl, Die optisch-gnostischen Störungen, *Handbuch der Psychiatrie*, ed. by Aschaffenburg, Spez. Teil, Abt. 3, 2 Hälfte, 2 Teil, 1 Band. Leipzig and Vienna, 1928, pp. 158 and 238.

diagnosis was of a wound-scar "which indicated an original wound on the left side in the region of the inferior parietal lobe and of the lateral part of the occipital lobe." At the time of the investigation there was a total colour-blindness involving the whole visual field (but no central scotoma). Within approximately four months colour-sensitivity was almost completely restored. The brightness distribution in the spectrum corresponded exactly to that of the normal eye. At a certain stage in the course of recovery the patient proved on examination to be trichromatic for very large areas, dichromatic for areas of medium size, and monochromatic for very small areas. In the achromatic stage the patient was not capable of voluntarily recalling memory images of previously seen colours, but apart from this colour-amnesia there was also at the beginning of the recovery period an amnesia for colour-names. We have thus a case of the loss of "memory colour." "We observed this lack of ability to recall colours, previously perceived in the normal state, in all of the patients with colour-disturbances resulting from a lesion at the cortical end of the optic tract." Gelb speaks here of an apperceptive mental blindness.

Now that we have presented the general facts of the case, we may proceed to a more detailed discussion of its significance for the present investigation. "A more careful analysis of the perceptual process revealed the fact that the colours of visual objects assumed for the patient the character of film colours, having almost the appearance of volume colours." It was discovered that "the colours of all visual objects had for the patient lost their surfacy character, in the sense that as far as localization and spatiality were concerned they had in part assumed the character of film colours which came very close to being volume colours." The patient was unable to localize the colours of objects as definitely at a precisely reportable distance as a normal person could. Colours failed to lie flat on the surfaces of objects. The distance between the actual position of the surface of a paper and the position at which the patient localized it varied with the type of colour, being in general greater with bright than with dark colours. Colours appeared to the patient to have a spongy texture; everything appeared "fuzzy and soft." The patient had to reach *into* the colour in order to touch the surface of a coloured object. He had to plunge farthest in when the paper was black and least when the paper was white. A coloured plate was "always apprehended in the frontal-parallel plane, whether its orientation was perpendicular or oblique to the direction of vision." According to Gelb "there can be no doubt that our patient had lost the ability to perceive surfaces." "All the spatial criteria which Katz sets up as being especially characteristic of film colours apply directly to the way in which the colours of objects in space appeared to our patient." Gelb observes that even his patient's filmy colour-impressions possess a relatively definite localization with reference to each other. As surface colour-perception was restored, it was the bright colours which first recovered their surface character.

Because of their theoretical significance, I should like to report here some further observations of Gelb's in connection with the same case. If the patient was presented with a series of greys, ranging from very dark to very light in steps approximating a normal scale of just noticeable differences, and was asked to indicate the number of brightness differences which he recognized in the whole series, he would point out only four steps. "He reported spontaneously that these four brightness steps represented *sharp breaks in continuity*." Thus the patient saw not a kind of regular, steeply mounting series, corresponding to the increase in brightness, but rather four distinct steps. Gelb points out that the different "thicknesses" of the colours are not intelligible solely on the basis of their different degrees of insistence, since a white in weak illumination appeared thinner than a black which through a reduction screen would appear the same as the white. As long as the ability to see surface colours continued to be absent, the patient in characterizing his impressions always used the expressions "bright" and "dark," never the expressions "black" and "white."

There is also evidence to indicate the existence of numerous relationships between the differences which I have demonstrated among the various modes of appearance of colour and Rubin's well-known analyses of the figure-ground relationship. Rubin found that "the colour of the ground approaches more closely the appearance of film colour than does the colour of that part of the field which is apprehended as figure."

SELECTION 7

●●

The Magical Number Seven, Plus or Minus Two: Some Limits on Our Capacity for Processing Information*,[1]

GEORGE A. MILLER

MY PROBLEM IS that I have been persecuted by an integer. For seven years this number has followed me around, has intruded in my most private data, and has assaulted me from the pages of our most public journals. This number assumes a variety of disguises, being sometimes a little larger and sometimes a little smaller than usual, but never changing so much as to be unrecognizable. The persistence with which this number plagues me is far more than a random accident. There is, to quote a famous senator, a design behind it, some pattern governing its appearances. Either there really is something unusual about the number or else I am suffering from delusions of persecution.

I shall begin my case history by telling you about some experiments that tested how accurately people can assign numbers to the magnitudes of various aspects of a stimulus. In the traditional language of psychology these would be called experiments in absolute judgment. Historical accident, however, has decreed that they should have another name. We now call them experiments on the capacity of people to transmit information. Since these experiments would not have been done without the appearance of information theory on the psychological scene, and since the results are analyzed in terms

* From *Psychol. Rev.*, 1956, **63**, 81-97. Reprinted by permission of author and the publisher.

[1] This paper was first read as an Invited Address before the Eastern Psychological Association in Philadelphia on April 15, 1955. Preparation of the paper was supported by the Harvard Psycho-Acoustic Laboratory under Contract N5ori-76 between Harvard University and the Office of Naval Research, U. S. Navy (Project NR142-201, Report PNR-174). Reproduction for any purpose of the U. S. Government is permitted.

of the concepts of information theory, I shall have to preface my discussion with a few remarks about this theory.

INFORMATION MEASUREMENT

The "amount of information" is exactly the same concept that we have talked about for years under the name of "variance." The equations are different, but if we hold tight to the idea that anything that increases the variance also increases the amount of information, we cannot go far astray.

The advantages of this new way of talking about variance are simple enough. Variance is always stated in terms of the unit of measurement—inches, pounds, volts, etc.—whereas the amount of information is a dimensionless quantity. Since the information in a discrete statistical distribution does not depend upon the unit of measurement, we can extend the concept to situations where we have no metric and we would not ordinarily think of using the variance. And it also enables us to compare results obtained in quite different experimental situations where it would be meaningless to compare variances based on different metrics. So there are some good reasons for adopting the newer concept.

The similarity of variance and amount of information might be explained this way: When we have a large variance, we are very ignorant about what is going to happen. If we are very ignorant, then when we make the observation it gives us a lot of information. On the other hand, if the variance is very small, we know in advance how our observation must come out, so we get little information from making the observation.

If you will now imagine a communication system, you will realize that there is a great deal of variability about what goes into the system and also a great deal of variability about what comes out. The input and the output can therefore be described in terms of their variance (or their information). If it is a good communication system, however, there must be some systematic relation between what goes in and what comes out. That is to say, the output will depend upon the input, or will be correlated with the input. If we measure this correlation, then we can say how much of the output variance is attributable to the input and how much is due to random fluctuations or "noise" introduced by the system during transmission. So we see that the measure of transmitted information is simply a measure of the input-output correlation.

There are two simple rules to follow. Whenever I refer to "amount of information," you will understand "variance." And whenever I refer to "amount of transmitted information," you will understand "covariance" or "correlation."

The situation can be described graphically by two partially overlapping circles. Then the left circle can be taken to represent the variance of the input, the right circle the variance of the output, and the overlap the covariance of input and output. I shall speak of the left circle as the amount of input information, the right circle as the amount of output information, and the overlap as the amount of transmitted information.

In the experiments on absolute judgment, the observer is considered to be a communication channel. Then the left circle would represent the amount of information in the stimuli, the right circle the amount of information in his responses, and the overlap the stimulus-response correlation as measured by the amount of transmitted information. The experimental problem is to increase the amount of input information and to measure the amount of transmitted information. If the observer's absolute judgments are quite accurate, then nearly all of the input information will be transmitted and will be recoverable from his responses. If he makes errors, then the transmitted information may be considerably less than the input. We expect that, as we increase the amount of input information, the observer will begin to make more and more errors; we can test the limits of accuracy of his absolute judgments. If the human observer is a reasonable kind of communication system, then when we increase the amount of input information, the transmitted information will increase at first and will eventually level off at some asymptotic value. This asymptotic value we take to be the *channel capacity* of the observer: it represents the greatest amount of information that he can give us about the stimulus on the basis of an absolute judgment. The channel capacity is the upper limit on the extent to which the observer can match his responses to the stimuli we give him.

Now just a brief word about the *bit* and we can begin to look at some data. One *bit* of information is the amount of information that we need to make a decision between two equally likely alternatives. If we must decide whether a man is less than six feet tall or more than six feet tall and if we know that the chances are 50-50, then we need one bit of information. Notice that this unit of information does not refer in any way to the unit of length that we use—feet, inches, centimeters, etc. However you measure the man's height, we still need just one bit of information.

Two bits of information enable us to decide among four equally likely alternatives. Three bits of information enable us to decide among eight equally likely alternatives. Four bits of information decide among 16 alternatives, five among 32, and so on. That is to say, if there are 32 equally likely alternatives, we must make five successive binary decisions, worth one bit each, before we know which alternative is correct. So the general rule is simple: every time the number of alternatives is increased by a factor of two, one bit of information is added.

There are two ways we might increase the amount of input information. We could increase the rate at which we give information to the observer, so that the amount of information per unit time would increase. Or we could ignore the time variable completely and increase the amount of input information by increasing the number of alternative stimuli. In the absolute judgment experiment we are interested in the second alternative. We give the observer as much time as he wants to make his response; we simply increase the number of alternative stimuli among which he must discriminate and look to see where confusions begin to occur. Confusions will appear near the point that we are calling his "channel capacity."

ABSOLUTE JUDGMENTS OF UNI-DIMENSIONAL STIMULI

Now let us consider what happens when we make absolute judgments of tones. Pollack (17) asked listeners to identify tones by assigning numerals to them. The tones were different with respect to frequency, and covered the range from 100 to 8000 cps in equal logarithmic steps. A tone was sounded and the listener responded by giving a numeral. After the listener had made his response he was told the correct identification of the tone.

When only two or three tones were used, the listeners never confused them. With four different tones confusions were quite rare, but with five or more tones confusions were frequent. With fourteen different tones the listeners made many mistakes.

These data are plotted in Fig. 1. Along the bottom is the amount of input information in bits per stimulus. As the number of alternative tones was increased from 2 to 14, the input information increased from 1 to 3.8 bits. On the ordinate is plotted the amount of transmitted information. The amount of transmitted information behaves in much the way we would expect a communication channel to behave; the transmitted information increases linearly up to about 2 bits and then bends off toward an asymptote at about 2.5 bits. This value, 2.5 bits, therefore, is what we are calling the channel capacity of the listener for absolute judgments of pitch.

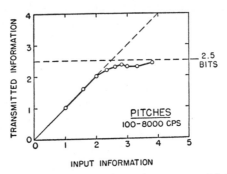

FIG. 1. Data from Pollack (17, 18) on the amount of information that is transmitted by listeners who make absolute judgments of auditory pitch. As the amount of input information is increased by increasing from 2 to 14 the number of different pitches to be judged, the amount of transmitted information approaches as its upper limit a channel capacity of about 2.5 bits per judgment.

So now we have the number 2.5 bits. What does it mean? First, note that 2.5 bits corresponds to about six equally likely alternatives. The result means that we cannot pick more than six different pitches that the listener will never confuse. Or, stated slightly differently, no matter how many alternative tones we ask him to judge, the best we can expect him to do is to assign them to about six different classes without error. Or, again, if we know that there were N alternative stimuli, then his judgment enables us to narrow down the particular stimulus to one out of $N/6$.

Most people are surprised that the number is as small as six. Of course, there is evidence that a musically sophisticated person with absolute pitch can identify accurately any one of 50 or 60 different pitches. Fortunately, I do not have time to discuss these remarkable exceptions. I say it is fortunate because I do not know how to explain their superior performance. So I shall stick to the more pedestrian fact that most of us can identify about one out of only five or six pitches before we begin to get confused.

It is interesting to consider that psychologists have been using seven-point rating scales for a long time, on the intuitive basis that trying to rate into finer categories does not really add much to the usefulness of the ratings. Pollack's results indicate that, at least for pitches, this intuition is fairly sound.

Next you can ask how reproducible this result is. Does it depend on the spacing of the tones or the various conditions of judgment? Pollack varied these conditions in a number of ways. The range of frequencies can be changed by a factor of about 20 without changing the amount of information transmitted more than a small percentage. Different groupings of the pitches decreased the transmission, but the loss was small. For example, if you can discriminate five high-pitched tones in one series and five low-pitched tones in another series, it is reasonable to expect that you could combine all ten into a single series and still tell them all apart without error. When you try it, however, it does not work. The channel capacity for pitch seems to be about six and that is the best you can do.

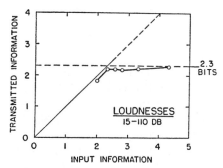

Fig. 2.   Data from Garner (7) on the channel capacity for absolute judgments of auditory loudness.

While we are on tones, let us look next at Garner's (7) work on loudness. Garner's data for loudness are summarized in Fig. 2. Garner went to some trouble to get the best possible spacing of his tones over the intensity range from 15 to 110 db. He used 4, 5, 6, 7, 10, and 20 different stimulus intensities. The results shown in Fig. 2 take into account the differences among subjects and the sequential influence of the immediately preceding judgment. Again we find that there seems to be a limit. The channel capacity for absolute judgments of loudness is 2.3 bits, or about five perfectly discriminable alternatives.

Since these two studies were done in different laboratories with slightly different techniques and methods of analysis, we are not in a good position to argue whether five loudnesses is significantly different from six pitches. Probably the difference is in the right direction, and absolute judgments of pitch are slightly more accurate than absolute judgments of loudness. The important point, however, is that the two answers are of the same order of magnitude.

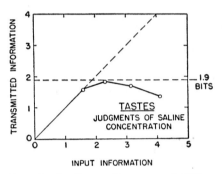

Fig. 3.   Data from Beebe-Center, Rogers, and O'Connell (1) on the channel capacity for absolute judgments of saltiness.

The experiment has also been done for taste intensities. In Fig. 3 are the results obtained by Beebe-Center, Rogers, and O'Connell (1) for absolute judgments of the concentration of salt solutions. The concentrations ranged from 0.3 to 34.7 gm. NaCl per 100 cc. tap water in equal subjective steps. They used 3, 5, 9, and 17 different concentrations. The channel capacity is 1.9 bits, which is about four distinct concentrations. Thus taste intensities seem a little less distinctive than auditory stimuli, but again the order of magnitude is not far off.

On the other hand, the channel capacity for judgments of visual position seems to be significantly larger. Hake and Garner (8) asked observers to interpolate visually between two scale markers. Their results are shown in Fig. 4. They did the experiment in two ways. In one version they let the observer use any number between zero and 100 to describe the position, although they presented stimuli at only 5, 10, 20, or 50 different positions. The results with this unlimited response technique are shown by the filled circles on the graph. In the other version the observers were limited in their responses to reporting just those stimulus values that were possible.

That is to say, in the second version the number of different responses that the observer could make was exactly the same as the number of different stimuli that the experimenter might present. The results with this limited response technique are shown by the open circles on the graph. The two functions are so similar that it seems fair to conclude that the number of responses available to the observer had nothing to do with the channel capacity of 3.25 bits.

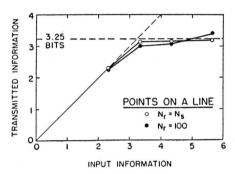

FIG. 4.   Data from Hake and Garner (8) on the channel capacity for absolute judgments of the position of a pointer in a linear interval.

The Hake-Garner experiment has been repeated by Coonan and Klemmer. Although they have not yet published their results, they have given me permission to say that they obtained channel capacities ranging from 3.2 bits for very short exposures of the pointer position to 3.9 bits for longer exposures. These values are slightly higher than Hake and Garner's, so we must conclude that there are between 10 and 15 distinct positions along a linear interval. This is the largest channel capacity that has been measured for any unidimensional variable.

At the present time these four experiments on absolute judgments of simple, unidimensional stimuli are all that have appeared in the psychological journals. However, a great deal of work on other stimulus variables has not yet appeared in the journals. For example, Eriksen and Hake (6) have found that the channel capacity for judging the sizes of squares is 2.2 bits, or about five categories, under a wide range of experimental conditions. In a separate experiment Eriksen (5) found 2.8 bits for size, 3.1 bits for hue, and 2.3 bits for brightness. Geldard has measured the channel capacity for the skin by placing vibrators on the chest region. A good observer can identify about four intensities, about five durations, and about seven locations.

One of the most active groups in this area has been the Air Force Operational Applications Laboratory. Pollack has been kind enough to furnish me with the results of their measurements for several aspects of visual displays. They made measurements for area and for the curvature, length, and direction of lines. In one set of experiments they used a very short exposure of the stimulus—$\frac{1}{40}$ second —and then they repeated the measurements with a 5-second exposure. For area they got 2.6 bits with the short exposure and 2.7 bits with the long explosure. For the length of a line they got about 2.6 bits with the short exposure and about 3.0 bits with the long exposure. Direction, or angle of inclination, gave 2.8 bits for the short exposure and 3.3 bits for the long exposure. Curvature was apparently harder to judge. When the length of the arc was constant, the result at the short exposure duration was 2.2 bits, but when the length of the chord was constant, the result was only 1.6 bits. This last value is the lowest that anyone has measured to date. I should add, however, that these values are apt to be slightly too low because the data from all subjects were pooled before the transmitted information was computed.

Now let us see where we are. First, the channel capacity does seem to be a valid notion for describing human observers. Second, the channel capacities measured for these unidimensional variables range from 1.6 bits for curvature to 3.9 bits for positions in an interval. Although there is no question that the differences among the variables are real and meaningful, the more impressive fact to me is their considerable similarity. If I take the best estimates I can get of the channel capacities for all the stimulus variables I have mentioned, the mean is 2.6 bits and the standard deviation is only 0.6 bit. In terms of distinguishable alternatives, this mean corresponds to about 6.5 categories, one standard deviation includes from 4 to 10 categories, and the total range is from 3 to 15 categories. Considering the wide variety of different variables that have been studied, I find this to be a remarkable narrow range.

There seems to be some limitation built into us either by learning or by the design of our nervous systems, a limit that keeps our channel capacities in this general range. On the basis of the present evidence it seems safe to say that we possess a finite and rather small capacity for making such unidimensional judgments and that this ca-

pacity does not vary a great deal from one simple sensory attribute
to another.

You may have noticed that I have been careful to say that this
magical number seven applies to one-dimensional judgments. Everyday experience teaches us that we can identify accurately any one
of several hundred faces, any one of several thousand words, any one
of several thousand objects, etc. The story certainly would not be
complete if we stopped at this point. We must have some understanding of why the one-dimensional variables we judge in the laboratory
give results so far out of line with what we do constantly in our
behavior outside the laboratory. A possible explanation lies in the
number of independently variable attributes of the stimuli that are
being judged. Objects, faces, words, and the like differ from one
another in many ways, whereas the simple stimuli we have considered
thus far differ from one an-
other in only one respect.

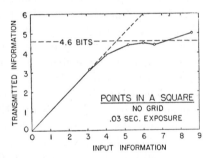

Fortunately, there are a few
data on what happens when
we make absolute judgments
of stimuli that differ from one
another in several ways. Let
us look first at the results
Klemmer and Frick (13) have
reported for the absolute judgment of the position of a dot
in a square. In Fig. 5 we see
their results. Now the channel
capacity seems to have increased to 4.6 bits, which

Fig. 5. Data from Klemmer and
Frick (13) on the channel capacity
for absolute judgments of the position
of a dot in a square.

means that people can identify accurately any one of 24 positions in
the square.

The position of a dot in a square is clearly a two-dimensional
proposition. Both its horizontal and its vertical position must be
identified. Thus it seems natural to compare the 4.6-bit capacity for
a square with the 3.25-bit capacity for the position of a point in an
interval. The point in the square requires two judgments of the
interval type. If we have a capacity of 3.25 bits for estimating inter-

vals and we do this twice, we should get 6.5 bits as our capacity for locating points in a square. Adding the second independent dimension gives us an increase from 3.25 to 4.6, but it falls short of the perfect addition that would give 6.5 bits.

Another example is provided by Beebe-Center, Rogers, and O'Connell. When they asked people to identify both the saltiness and the sweetness of solutions containing various concentrations of salt and sucrose, they found that the channel capacity was 2.3 bits. Since the capacity for salt alone was 1.9, we might expect about 3.8 bits if the two aspects of the compound stimuli were judged independently. As with spatial locations, the second dimension adds a little to the capacity but not as much as it conceivably might.

A third example is provided by Pollack (18), who asked listeners to judge both the loudness and the pitch of pure tones. Since pitch gives 2.5 bits and loudness gives 2.3 bits, we might hope to get as much as 4.8 bits for pitch and loudness together. Pollack obtained 3.1 bits, which again indicates that the second dimension augments the channel capacity but not so much as it might.

A fourth example can be drawn from the work of Halsey and Chapanis (9) on confusions among colors of equal luminance. Although they did not analyze their results in informational terms, they estimate that there are about 11 to 15 identifiable colors, or, in our terms, about 3.6 bits. Since these colors varied in both hue and saturation, it is probably correct to regard this as a two-dimensional judgment. If we compare this with Eriksen's 3.1 bits for hue (which is a questionable comparison to draw), we again have something less than perfect addition when a second dimension is added.

It is still a long way, however, from these two-dimensional examples to the multidimensional stimuli provided by faces, words, etc. To fill this gap we have only one experiment, an auditory study done by Pollack and Ficks (19). They managed to get six different acoustic variables that they could change: frequency, intensity, rate of interruption, on-time fraction, total duration, and spatial location. Each one of these six variables could assume any one of five different values, so altogether there were 5^6, or 15,625 different tones that they could present. The listeners made a separate rating for each one of these six dimensions. Under these conditions the transmitted information was 7.2 bits, which corresponds to about 150 different categories that could be absolutely identified without error. Now we are beginning to get up into the range that ordinary experience would lead us to expect.

Suppose that we plot these data, fragmentary as they are, and make a guess about how the channel capacity changes with the dimensionality of the stimuli. The result is given in Fig. 6. In a moment of considerable daring I sketched the dotted line to indicate roughly the trend that the data seemed to be taking.

Clearly, the addition of independently variable attributes to the stimulus increases the channel capacity, but at a decreasing rate. It is interesting to note that the channel capacity is increased even when the several variables are not independent. Eriksen (5) reports that, when size, brightness, and hue all vary together in perfect correlation, the transmitted information is 4.1 bits as compared with an average of about 2.7 bits when these attributes are varied one at a time. By confounding three attributes, Eriksen increased the dimensionality of the input without increasing the amount of input information; the result was an increase in channel capacity of about the amount that the dotted function in Fig. 6 would lead us to expect.

The point seems to be that, as we add more variables to the display, we increase the total capacity, but we decrease the accuracy for any particular variable. In other words, we can make relatively crude judgments of several things simultaneously.

We might argue that in the course of evolution those organisms were most successful that were responsive to the widest

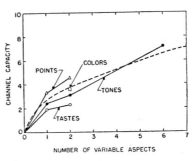

Fig. 6. The general form of the relation between channel capacity and the number of independently variable attributes of the stimuli.

range of stimulus energies in their environment. In order to survive in a constantly fluctuating world, it was better to have a little information about a lot of things than to have a lot of information about a small segment of the environment. If a compromise was necessary, the one we seem to have made is clearly the more adaptive.

Pollack and Ficks's results are very strongly suggestive of an argument that linguists and phoneticians have been making for some time (11). According to the linguistic analysis of the sounds of human speech, there are about eight or ten dimensions—the linguists call them *distinctive features*—that distinguish one phoneme from another. These distinctive features are usually binary, or at most ternary, in nature. For example, a binary distinction is made between vowels and consonants, a binary decision is made between oral and nasal consonants, a ternary decision is made among front, middle, and back phonemes, etc. This approach gives us quite a different picture of speech perception than we might otherwise obtain from our studies of the speech spectrum and of the ear's ability to discriminate relative differences among pure tones. I am personally much interested in this new approach (15), and I regret that there is not time to discuss it here.

It was probably with this linguistic theory in mind that Pollack and Ficks conducted a test on a set of tonal stimuli that varied in eight dimensions, but required only a binary decision on each dimension. With these tones they measured the transmitted information at 6.9 bits, or about 120 recognizable kinds of sounds. It is an intriguing question, as yet unexplored, whether one can go on adding dimensions indefinitely in this way.

In human speech there is clearly a limit to the number of dimensions that we use. In this instance, however, it is not known whether the limit is imposed by the nature of the perceptual machinery that must recognize the sounds or by the nature of the speech machinery that must produce them. Somebody will have to do the experiment to find out. There is a limit, however, of about eight or nine distinctive features in every language that has been studied, and so when we talk we must resort to still another trick for increasing our channel capacity. Language uses sequences of phonemes, so we make several judgments successively when we listen to words and sentences. That is to say, we use both simultaneous and successive discriminations in order to expand the rather rigid limits imposed by the inaccuracy of our absolute judgments of simple magnitudes.

These multidimensional judgments are strongly reminiscent of the abstraction experiment of Külpe (14). As you may remember, Külpe showed that observers report more accurately on an attribute for which they are set than on attributes for which they are not set. For example, Chapman (4) used three different attributes and compared the results obtained when the observers were instructed before the tachistoscopic presentation with the results obtained when they were not told until after the presentation which one of the three attributes was to be reported. When the instruction was given in advance, the judgments were more accurate. When the instruction was given afterwards, the subjects presumably had to judge all three attributes in order to report on any one of them and the accuracy was correspondingly lower. This is in complete accord with the results we have just been considering, where the accuracy of judgment on each attribute decreased as more dimensions were added. The point is probably obvious, but I shall make it anyhow, that the abstraction experiments did *not* demonstrate that people can judge only one attribute at a time. They merely showed what seems quite reasonable, that people are less accurate if they must judge more than one attribute simultaneously.

SUBITIZING

I cannot leave this general area without mentioning, however briefly, the experiments conducted at Mount Holyoke College on the discrimination of number (12). In experiments by Kaufman, Lord, Reese, and Volkmann random patterns of dots were flashed on a screen for $\frac{1}{5}$ of a second. Anywhere from 1 to more than 200 dots could appear in the pattern. The subject's task was to report how many dots there were.

The first point to note is that on patterns containing up to five or six dots the subjects simply did not make errors. The performance on these small numbers of dots was so different from the performance with more dots that it was given a special name. Below seven the subjects were said to *subitize;* above seven they were said to *estimate.* This is, as you will recognize, what we once optimistically called "the span of attention."

This discontinuity at seven is, of course, suggestive. Is this the same basic process that limits our unidimensional judgments to about seven categories? The generalization is tempting but not sound in my opinion. The data on number estimates have not been analyzed in informational terms; but on the basis of the published data I would guess that the subjects transmitted something more than four bits of information about the number of dots. Using the same arguments as before, we would conclude that there are about 20 or 30 distinguishable categories of numerousness. This is considerably more information than we would expect to get from a unidimensional display. It is, as a matter of fact, very much like a two-dimensional display. Although the dimensionality of the random dot patterns is not entirely clear, these results are in the same range as Klemmer and Frick's for their two-dimensional display of dots in a square. Perhaps the two dimensions of numerousness are area and density. When the subject can subitize, area and density may not be the significant variables; but when the subject must estimate, perhaps they are significant. In any event, the comparison is not so simple as it might seem at first thought.

This is one of the ways in which the magical number seven has persecuted me. Here we have two closely related kinds of experiments, both of which point to the significance of the number seven as a limit on our capacities. And yet when we examine the matter more closely, there seems to be a reasonable suspicion that it is nothing more than a coincidence.

THE SPAN OF IMMEDIATE MEMORY

Let me summarize the situation in this way. There is a clear and definite limit to the accuracy with which we can identify absolutely the magnitude of a unidimensional stimulus variable. I would propose to call this limit the *span of absolute judgment,* and I maintain that for unidimensional judgments this span is usually somewhere in the neighborhood of seven. We are not completely at the mercy of this limited span, however, because we have a variety of techniques for getting around it and increasing the accuracy of our judgments. The three most important of these devices are (*a*) to make relative rather than absolute judgments; or, if that is not possible, (*b*) to increase the number of dimensions along which the stimuli can differ; or (*c*) to arrange the task in such a way that we make a sequence of several absolute judgments in a row.

The study of relative judgments is one of the oldest topics in experimental psychology, and I will not pause to review it now. The second device, increasing the dimensionality, we have just considered. It seems that by adding more dimensions and requiring crude, binary, yes-no judgments on each attribute we can extend the span of absolute judgment from seven to at least 150. Judging from our everyday behavior, the limit is probably in the thousands, if indeed there is a limit. In my opinion, we cannot go on compounding dimensions indefinitely. I suspect that there is also a *span of perceptual dimensionality* and that this span is somewhere in the neighborhood of ten, but I must add at once that there is no objective evidence to support this suspicion. This is a question sadly needing experimental exploration.

Concerning the third device, the use of successive judgments, I have quite a bit to say because this device introduces memory as the handmaiden of discrimination. And, since mnemonic processes are at least as complex as are perceptual processes, we can anticipate that their interactions will not be easily disentangled.

Suppose that we start by simply extending slightly the experimental procedure that we have been using. Up to this point we have presented a single stimulus and asked the observer to name it immediately thereafter. We can extend this procedure by requiring the observer to withhold his response until we have given him several stimuli in succession. At the end of the sequence of stimuli he then makes his response. We still have the same sort of input-output situation that is required for the measurement of transmitted information. But now we have passed from an experiment on absolute judgment to what is traditionally called an experiment on immediate memory.

Before we look at any data on this topic, I feel I must give you a word of warning to help you avoid some obvious associations that can be confusing. Everybody knows that there is a finite span of immediate memory and that for a lot of different kinds of test materials this span is about seven items in length. I have just shown you that there is a span of absolute judgment that can distinguish about seven categories and that there is a span of attention that will encompass about six objects at a glance. What is more natural than to think that all three of these spans are different aspects of a single underlying process? And that is a fundamental mistake, as I shall be at some pains to demonstrate. This mistake is one of the malicious persecutions that the magical number seven has subjected me to.

My mistake went something like this. We have seen that the invariant feature in the span of absolute judgment is the amount of information that the observer can transmit. There is a real operational similarity between the absolute judgment experiment and the immediate memory experiment. If immediate memory is like absolute judgment, then it should follow that the invariant feature in the span of immediate memory is also the amount of information that an observer can retain. If the amount of information in the span of immediate memory is a constant, then the span should be short when the individual items contain a lot of information and the span should be long when the items contain little information. For example, decimal digits are worth 3.3 bits apiece. We can recall about seven of them, for a total of 23 bits of information. Isolated English words are worth about 10 bits apiece. If the total amount of information is to remain constant at 23 bits, then we should be able to remember only two or three words chosen at random. In this way I generated a theory about how the span of immediate memory should vary as a function of the amount of information per item in the test materials.

The measurements of memory span in the literature are suggestive on this question, but not definitive. And so it was necessary to do the experiment to see. Hayes (10) tried it out with five different kinds of test materials: binary digits, decimal digits, letters of the alphabet, letters plus decimal digits, and with 1,000 monosyllabic words. The lists were read aloud at the rate of one item per second and the subjects had as much time as they needed to give their responses. A procedure described by Woodworth (20) was used to score the responses.

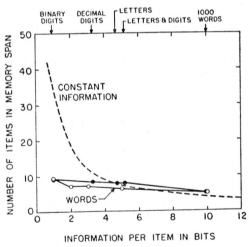

Fig. 7. Data from Hayes (10) on the span of immediate memory plotted as a function of the amount of information per item in the test materials.

The results are shown by the filled circles in Fig. 7. Here the dotted line indicates what the span should have been if the amount of information in the span was constant. The solid curves represent the data. Hayes repeated the experiment using test vocabularies of different sizes but all containing only English monosyllables (open circles in Fig. 7). This more homogeneous test material did not change the picture significantly. With binary items the span is about nine and, although it drops to about five with monosyllabic English words, the difference is far less than the hypothesis of constant information would require.

There is nothing wrong with Hayes's experiment, because Pollack (16) repeated it much more elaborately and got essentially the same result. Pollack took pains to measure the amount of information transmitted and did not rely on the traditional procedure for scoring the responses. His results are plotted in Fig. 8. Here it is clear that

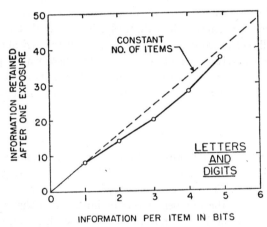

Fig. 8. Data from Pollack (16) on the amount of information retained after one presentation plotted as a function of the amount of information per item in the test materials.

the amount of information transmitted is not a constant but increases almost linearly as the amount of information per item in the input is increased.

And so the outcome is perfectly clear. In spite of the coincidence that the magical number seven appears in both places, the span of absolute judgment and the span of immediate memory are quite different kinds of limitations that are imposed on our ability to process information. Absolute judgment is limited by the amount of information. Immediate memory is limited by the number of items. In order to capture this distinction in somewhat picturesque terms, I have fallen into the custom of distinguishing between *bits* of information and *chunks* of information. Then I can say that the number of bits of information is constant for absolute judgment and the number of chunks of information is constant for immediate memory. The span of immediate memory seems to be almost independent of the number of bits per chunk, at least over the range that has been examined to date.

The contrast of the terms *bit* and *chunk* also serves to highlight the fact that we are not very definite about what constitutes a chunk of information. For example, the memory span of five words that Hayes obtained when each word was drawn at random from a set of 1000 English monosyllables might just as appropriately have been called a memory span of 15 phonemes, since each word had about three phonemes in it. Intuitively, it is clear that the subjects were recalling five words, not 15 phonemes, but the logical distinction is not immediately apparent. We are dealing here with a process of organizing or grouping the input into familiar units or chunks, and a great deal of learning has gone into the formation of these familiar units.

RECODING

In order to speak more precisely, therefore, we must recognize the importance of grouping or organizing the input sequence into units or chunks. Since the memory span is a fixed number of chunks, we can increase the number of bits of information that it contains simply by building larger and larger chunks, each chunk containing more information than before.

A man just beginning to learn radio-telegraphic code hears each *dit* and *dah* as a separate chunk. Soon he is able to organize these sounds into letters and then he can deal with the letters as chunks. Then the letters organize themselves as words, which are still larger chunks, and he begins to hear whole phrases. I do not mean that each step is a discrete process, or that plateaus must appear in his learning curve, for surely the levels of organization are achieved at different rates and overlap each other during the learning process. I am simply pointing to the obvious fact that the dits and dahs are organized by learning into patterns and that as these larger chunks emerge, the amount of message that the operator can remember increases correspondingly. In the terms I am proposing to use, the operator learns to increase the bits per chunk.

In the jargon of communication theory, this process would be called *recoding*. The input is given in a code that contains many chunks with few bits per chunk. The operator recodes the input into another code that contains fewer chunks with more bits per chunk. There are many ways to do this recoding, but probably the simplest is to group the input events, apply a new name to the group, and then remember the new name rather than the original input events.

Since I am convinced that this process is a very general and important one for psychology, I want to tell you about a demonstration experiment that should make perfectly explicit what I am talking about. This experiment was conducted by Sidney Smith and was reported by him before the Eastern Psychological Association in 1954.

Begin with the observed fact that people can repeat back eight decimal digits, but only nine binary digits. Since there is a large discrepancy in the amount of information recalled in these two cases, we suspect at once that a recoding procedure could be used to increase the span of immediate memory for binary digits. In Table 1 a method for grouping and renaming is illustrated. Along the top is a sequence of 18 binary digits, far more than any subject was able to recall after a single presentation. In the next line these same binary digits are grouped by pairs. Four possible pairs can occur: 00 is renamed 0, 01 is renamed 1, 10 is renamed 2, and 11 is

TABLE 1. WAYS OF RECODING SEQUENCES OF BINARY DIGITS

Binary Digits (Bits)		1	0	1	0	0	0	1	0	0	1	1	1	0	0	1	1	1	0
2:1	Chunks	10		10		00		10		01		11		00		11		10	
	Recoding	2		2		0		2		1		3		0		3		2	
3:1	Chunks	101			000			100			111			001			110		
	Recoding	5			0			4			7			1			6		
4:1	Chunks	1010				0010				0111				0011				10		
	Recoding	10				2				7				3						
5:1	Chunks	10100					01001					11001					110			
	Recoding	20					9					25								

renamed 3. That is to say, we recode from a base-two arithmetic to a base-four arithmetic. In the recoded sequence there are now just nine digits to remember, and this is almost within the span of immediate memory. In the next line the same sequence of binary digits is regrouped into chunks of three. There are eight possible sequences of three, so we give each sequence a new name between 0 and 7. Now we have recoded from a sequence of 18 binary digits into a sequence of 6 octal digits, and this is well within the span of immediate memory. In the last two lines the binary digits are grouped by fours and by fives and are given decimal-digit names from 0 to 15 and from 0 to 31.

It is reasonably obvious that this kind of recoding increases the bits per chunk, and packages the binary sequence into a form that can be retained within the span of immediate memory. So Smith assembled 20 subjects and measured their spans for binary and octal digits. The spans were 9 for binaries and 7 for octals. Then he gave each recoding scheme to five of the subjects. They studied the recoding until they said they understood it—for about 5 or 10 minutes. Then he tested their span for binary digits again while they tried to use the recoding schemes they had studied.

The recoding schemes increased their span for binary digits in every case. But the increase was not as large as we had expected on the basis of their span for octal digits. Since the discrepancy increased as the recoding ratio increased, we reasoned that the few minutes the subjects had spent learning the recoding schemes had not been sufficient. Apparently the translation from one code to the other must be almost automatic or the subject will lose part of the next group while he is trying to remember the translation of the last group.

Since the 4:1 and 5:1 ratios require considerable study, Smith decided to imitate Ebbinghaus and do the experiment on himself. With Germanic patience he drilled himself on each recoding successively and obtained the results shown in Fig. 9. Here the data follow along rather nicely with the results you would predict on the basis of his span for octal digits. He could remember 12 octal digits. With the 2:1 recoding, these 12 chunks were worth 24 binary digits. With the 3:1 recoding, they were worth 36 binary digits. With the 4:1 and 5:1 recodings, they were worth about 40 binary digits.

It is a little dramatic to watch a person get 40 binary digits in a row and then repeat them back without error. However, if you think of this merely as a mnemonic trick for extending the memory span, you will miss the more important point that is implicit in nearly all such mnemonic devices. The point is that recoding is an extremely powerful weapon for increasing the amount of information that we can deal with. In one form or another we use recoding constantly in our daily behavior.

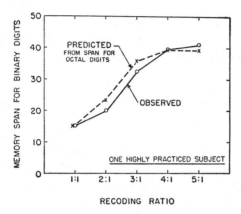

FIG. 9. The span of immediate memory for binary digits is plotted as a function of the recoding procedure used. The predicted function is obtained by multiplying the span for octals by 2, 3, and 3.3 for recoding into base 4, base 8, and base 10, respectively.

In my opinion the most customary kind of recoding that we do all the time is to translate into a verbal code. When there is a story or an argument or an idea that we want to remember, we usually try to rephrase it "in our own words." When we witness some event we want to remember, we make a verbal description of the event and then remember our verbalization. Upon recall we recreate by secondary elaboration the details that seem consistent with the particular verbal recoding we happen to have made. The well-known experiment by Carmichael, Hogan, and Walter (3) on the influence that names have on the recall of visual figures is one demonstration of the process.

The inaccuracy of the testimony of eyewitnesses is well known in legal psychology, but the distortions of testimony are not random— they follow naturally from the particular recoding that the witness used, and the particular recoding he used depends upon his whole life history. Our language is tremendously useful for repackaging

material into a few chunks rich in information. I suspect that imagery is a form of recoding, too, but images seem much harder to
get at operationally and to study experimentally than the more symbolic kinds of recoding.

It seems probable that even memorization can be studied in these
terms. The process of memorizing may be simply the formation of
chunks, or groups of items that go together, until there are few
enough chunks so that we can recall all the items. The work by Bousfield and Cohen (2) on the occurrence of clustering in the recall of
words is especially interesting in this respect.

SUMMARY

I have come to the end of the data that I wanted to present, so
I would like now to make some summarizing remarks.

First, the span of absolute judgment and the span of immediate
memory impose severe limitations on the amount of information that
we are able to receive, process, and remember. By organizing the
stimulus input simultaneously into several dimensions and successively into a sequence of chunks, we manage to break (or at least
stretch) this informational bottleneck.

Second, the process of recoding is a very important one in human
psychology and deserves much more explicit attention than it has
received. In particular, the kind of linguistic recoding that people
do seems to me to be the very lifeblood of the thought processes.
Recoding procedures are a constant concern to clinicians, social psychologists, linguists, and anthropologists; and yet, probably because
recoding is less accessible to experimental manipulation than nonsense syllables or T mazes, the traditional experimental psychologist
has contributed little or nothing to their analysis. Nevertheless, experimental techniques can be used, methods of recoding can be specified, behavioral indicants can be found. And I anticipate that we will
find a very orderly set of relations describing what now seems an
uncharted wilderness of individual differences.

Third, the concepts and measures provided by the theory of information provide a quantitative way of getting at some of these
questions. The theory provides us with a yardstick for calibrating
our stimulus materials and for measuring the performance of our
subjects. In the interests of communication I have suppressed the
technical details of information measurement and have tried to express the ideas in more familiar terms; I hope this paraphrase will

not lead you to think they are not useful in research. Informational concepts have already proved valuable in the study of discrimination and of language; they promise a great deal in the study of learning and memory; and it has even been proposed that they can be useful in the study of concept formation. A lot of questions that seemed fruitless twenty or thirty years ago may now be worth another look. In fact, I feel that my story here must stop just as it begins to get really interesting.

And finally, what about the magical number seven? What about the seven wonders of the world, the seven seas, the seven deadly sins, the seven daughters of Atlas in the Pleiades, the seven ages of man, the seven levels of hell, the seven primary colors, the seven notes of the musical scale, and the seven days of the week? What about the seven-point rating scale, the seven categories for absolute judgment, the seven objects in the span of attention, and the seven digits in the span of immediate memory? For the present I propose to withhold judgment. Perhaps there is something deep and profound behind all these sevens, something just calling out for us to discover it. But I suspect that it is only a pernicious, Pythagorean coincidence.

REFERENCES

1. BEEBE-CENTER, J. G., ROGERS, M. S., and O'CONNELL, D. N. Transmission of information about sucrose and saline solutions through the sense of taste. *J. Psychol.*, 1955, **39**, 157-160.
2. BOUSFIELD, W. A., and COHEN, B. H. The occurrence of clustering in the recall of randomly arranged words of different frequencies-of-usage. *J. gen. Psychol.*, 1955, **52**, 83-95.
3. CARMICHAEL, L., HOGAN, H. P., and WALTER, A. A. An experimental study of the effect of language on the reproduction of visually perceived form. *J. exp. Psychol.*, 1932, **15**, 73-86.
4. CHAPMAN, D. W. Relative effects of determinate and indeterminate *Aufgaben*. *Amer. J. Psychol.*, 1932, **44**, 163-174.
5. ERIKSEN, C. W. Multidimensional stimulus differences and accuracy of discrimination. *USAF, WADC Tech. Rep.*, 1954, No. 54-165.
6. ERIKSEN, C. W., and HAKE, H. W. Absolute judgments as a function of the stimulus range and the number of stimulus and response categories. *J. exp. Psychol.*, 1955, **49**, 323-332.
7. GARNER, W. R. An informational analysis of absolute judgments of loudness. *J. exp. Psychol.*, 1953, **46**, 373-380.
8. HAKE, H. W., and GARNER, W. R. The effect of presenting various

numbers of discrete steps on scale reading accuracy. *J. exp. Psychol.,* 1951, **42,** 358-366.

9. HALSEY, R. M., and CHAPANIS, A. Chromaticity-confusion contours in a complex viewing situation. *J. Opt. Soc. Amer.,* 1954, **44,** 442-454.

10. HAYES, J. R. M. Memory span for several vocabularies as a function of vocabulary size. In *Quarterly Progress Report,* Cambridge, Mass.: Acoustics Laboratory, Massachusetts Institute of Technology, Jan.–June, 1952.

11. JAKOBSON, R., FANT, C. G. M., and HALLE, M. *Preliminaries to speech analysis.* Cambridge, Mass.: Acoustics Laboratory, Massachusetts Institute of Technology, 1952. (Tech. Rep. No. 13.)

12. KAUFMAN, E. L., LORD, M. W., REESE, T. W., and VOLKMANN, J. The discrimination of visual number. *Amer. J. Psychol.,* 1949, **62,** 498-525.

13. KLEMMER, E. T., and FRICK, F. C. Assimilation of information from dot and matrix patterns. *J. exp. Psychol.,* 1953, **45,** 15-19.

14. KÜLPE, O. Versuche über Abstraktion. *Ber. ü. d. I Kongr. f. exper. Psychol.,* 1904, 56-68.

15. MILLER, G. A., and NICELY, P. E. An analysis of perceptual confusions among some English consonants. *J. Acoust. Soc. Amer.,* 1955, **27,** 338-352.

16. POLLACK, I. The assimilation of sequentially encoded information. *Amer. J. Psychol.,* 1953, **66,** 421-435.

17. POLLACK, I. The information of elementary auditory displays. *J. Acoust. Soc. Amer.,* 1952, **24,** 745-749.

18. POLLACK, I. The information of elementary auditory displays. II. *J. Acoust. Soc. Amer.,* 1953, **25,** 765-769.

19. POLLACK, I., and FICKS, L. Information of elementary multi-dimensional auditory displays. *J. Acoust. Soc. Amer.,* 1954, **26,** 155-158.

20. WOODWORTH, R. S. *Experimental psychology.* New York: Holt, 1938.

SELECTION 8

....

Principles of Perceptual Organization*

MAX WERTHEIMER

I STAND AT THE WINDOW and see a house, trees, sky. Now on theoretical grounds I could try to count and say: "here there are . . . 327 brightnesses and hues." Do I *have* "327"? No, I see sky, house, trees; and no one can really have these "327" as such. Furthermore, if in this strange calculation the house should have, say, 120 and the trees 90 and the sky 117, I have in any event *this* combination, this segregation, and not, say, 127 and 100 and 100; or 150 and 177. I *see* it in this particular combination, this particular segregation; and the sort of combination or segregation in which I see it is not simply up to my choice: it is almost impossible for me to see it in any desired combination that I may happen to choose. When I succeed in seeing some unusual combination, what a strange process it is. What surprise results, when, after looking at it a long time, after many attempts, I *discover*—under the influence of a very unrealistic set—that over there parts of the window frame make an *N* with a smooth branch . . .

As another example, take two faces, cheek to cheek. I see the one (with, if you like, "57" brightnesses) and the other (with its "49"), but not in the division 66 plus 40 or 6 plus 100. Again, I hear a melody (17 notes) with its accompaniment (32 notes). I hear melody and accompaniment, not just "49"; or at least not 20 and 29.

This is true even when there is no question at all of stimulus continua; for instance if the melody and its accompaniment is played by an old music box, in short, separate little tones; or in the visual

---

* An abridged translation by Michael Wertheimer of *Untersuchungen zur Lehre von der Gestalt*, II. *Psychol. Forsch.*, 1923, **4**, 301-350. Translated and printed by permission of the publisher, Springer, Berlin.

area, when figures composed of discontinuous parts (e.g., dots) become segregated on an otherwise quite homogeneous ground. Even though alternative organizations may be easier here than in the preceding cases, it is still true that a spontaneous, natural, normally expected combination and segregation occurs; and other organizations can be achieved only rarely, under particular conditions and usually with special effort and some difficulty.

In general, if a number of stimuli are presented together, a correspondingly large number of separate "givens" do not generally occur for the human; rather there are more comprehensive givens, in a particular segregation, combination, separation.

Are there principles for this resulting organization? What are they? One can try to determine and isolate the factors operating here experimentally, but a simpler procedure can be used in the presentation of the most critical factors: demonstration with a few simple, characteristic cases. The following is limited to the exposition of some essentials.

1. Given, in an otherwise homogeneous field, a row of dots with alternating distances, e.g., $d_1 = 3$ mm, $d_2 = 12$ mm.

● ●   ● ●   ● ●   ● ●   ● ●   ● ●   ● ●

Normally such a row of dots is spontaneously seen as a row of small groups of points, in the arrangement ab/cd, and not, say, in the arrangement a/bc/de. . . . Really to see this arrangement (a/bc/de . . .) simultaneously in the entire series is quite impossible for most people. (If the constellation is composed of *few* dots, the opposing organization is easier to achieve and the result is more ambiguous. The situation is in general more labile. For instance, if the series above is decreased to ● ●   ● ●   ● ● , the grouping a/bc/de/f is readily achieved.)

Of course a real *seeing* is meant here, not just conceiving some arbitrary combination; perhaps this will be clearer in dot series like the following:

●˙   ●˙   ●˙   ●˙   ●˙   ●˙   ●˙

You see a row of slanted groups (●˙ ●˙), slanting from lower left to upper right, with the arrangement ab/cd/ef . . . ; the opposite arrangement, a/bc/de . . . , with long slanted groups (●   ˙●) is much more difficult to achieve. For most people it is impossible to achieve *simultaneously throughout the entire series* in such a constellation. It is difficult to achieve and when it does occur, it is much less certain—much more labile than the first, in relation to eye movements and changes in attention.

In other examples, such as

You see a row of small slanted groups $\left(_{\bullet}{\bullet}^{\bullet}\right)$, going from lower left to upper right. That is, if we label the dots as follows, you see

$$
\begin{array}{cccc}
 & c & f & i & l \\
b & & e & h & k \quad \text{etc.,} \\
a & & d & g & j
\end{array}
$$

the form abc/def/ghi/. . . . The opposite organization,

ceg/fhj/. . . , is not seen, and is impossible to achieve simultaneously in the entire series for most people.

Or, further, in

you see the triads abc/def/ . . . and not one of many other theoretically possible groupings.

I   II

And in I, you typically see the verticals, in II the horizontals.

In all of these cases, a first simple principle emerges. The naturally resulting organization is the grouping together of the dots with small separation. The organization of the dots with greater separation into groups either does not occur at all or occurs only with difficulty and artificially, and is more labile. As a tentative formulation: other things being equal, *grouping occurs on the basis of small distance* (the factor of nearness).*

This principle has wider applications. It holds not only in vision and in spatial relations. Tapping continuously in the rhythm of our first example (● ●   ● ●   ● ●   ● ●   ● ● etc.) or the next to the last one (● ● ●   ● ● ●   ● ● ●   ● ● ●   ● ● ●) demonstrates this effect in a very convincing way.

2. Given a constellation of dots with equal distances, with successive pairs different colors, in a homogeneous field—e.g., white and black in a gray field, in the following schema:

    a.   o o ● ● o o ● ● o o ● ● o o ● ● o o ● ●

Or better, a surface filled as follows:

b.   o ● o ● o ● o ● o ● o ●   *c.*   o o o o o o o o o o o o
     o ● o ● o ● o ● o ● o ●   ● ● ● ● ● ● ● ● ● ● ● ●
     o ● o ● o ● o ● o ● o ●   o o o o o o o o o o o o
     o ● o ● o ● o ● o ● o ●   ● ● ● ● ● ● ● ● ● ● ● ●
     o ● o ● o ● o ● o ● o ●   o o o o o o o o o o o o
     o ● o ● o ● o ● o ● o ●   ● ● ● ● ● ● ● ● ● ● ● ●
     o ● o ● o ● o ● o ● o ●   o o o o o o o o o o o o
     o ● o ● o ● o ● o ● o ●   ● ● ● ● ● ● ● ● ● ● ● ●
     o ● o ● o ● o ● o ● o ●   o o o o o o o o o o o o
     o ● o ● o ● o ● o ● o ●   ● ● ● ● ● ● ● ● ● ● ● ●

Or:

d.   o o o ● ● ● o o o ● ● ● o o o ● ● ● o o o ● ● ● etc.

One sees the groups that are determined by similarity. In *a*, ab/cd/ . . . ; in *b*, verticals; in *c*, horizontals; in *d*, abc/def/ . . . ; to see the opposite organization clearly and simultaneously in the entire figure is usually impossible: *a*, a/bc/de/ . . . ; *b*, the horizontals; *c*, the verticals; *d*, any of the arrangements, like cde/fgh/ . . . etc.

---

* Omitted from this translation is a detailed discussion (pp. 337-347) of quantitative experimental techniques for the study of the strength of the factor of nearness. (Eds.)

If the number of stimuli is decreased, the other organizations also become possible, as in the first example of nearness as a factor; but generally they are still more difficult and more labile.

This leads to a second principle, which could tentatively be formulated this way: other things being equal, if several stimuli are presented together, there is a tendency to see the form in such a way that the similar items are grouped together (*factor of similarity*).

As before, the same holds true in continuous (not too slow) tapping rhythms in which loud and soft tapping are alternated. Analogous to *a*: . . ! ! . . ! ! . . ! ! . . ! ! etc.; analogous to *d*: . . . ! ! ! . . . ! ! ! . . . etc. In the first, you hear ab/cd/ef/ . . . ; in the second, abc/def/ghi/. . . . To try consistently to maintain a different grouping is a task which requires considerable effort. Usually the natural (first) arrangement results soon all by itself, with the grouping as it were "tipping over."

Pitch operates the same way: analogous to *a* is, for example, c c g g c c g g c c g g c c g g; analogous to *b*, c c c g g g c c c g g g c c c.

In cases 2*a* and 2*d* just above, the conditions for the opposite organizations are not quite equivalent: aside from "leftovers," the rarer, or impossible, organization involves a change within the groups, a change in direction.

In 2*a*, o o ● ● o o ● ● o o ● ● o o ● ● o o ● ●, the b-c group is o ●, but the d-e group ● o . Or in the rhythm . . ! ! . . ! ! . . ! ! . . ! ! , b-c is weak → strong, but d-e strong → weak.

One can decrease this complication, e.g., by a continuation of the gradient: in the series of knocks, by following the first two weak ones by a stronger pair, these by a still stronger, etc., in the schema:

a.   or *b.*

(with the ordinate indicating intensity).

Analogously, in vision is the series (on a green background) white,

white, light grey, light grey, medium grey, medium grey, dark grey, dark grey, black, black. Or with notes: a—c, c, e♭, e♭, f♯, f♯, a, a, c, c . . . or b—c, c, c, e♭, e♭, e♭, f♯, f♯, f♯, a, a, a, c, c, c . . .

The regularity indicated up to this point constitutes only a special case. Not only similarity or dissimilarity, but also *greater* and *lesser* *dissimilarity* operate in the same way, at least over a certain range. The note series a—c, c♯, e, f, g♯, a, c, c♯ . . . ; b—b, c, d, d♯, f, f♯, g♯, a, b ,c . . . ; and c—c, c♯, d, e, f, f♯, g♯, a, a♯ . . . normally produce the organizations a—ab/cd/ . . . , b—ab/cd/e . . . , and c—abc/def/ . . . ; that is, they follow grouping according to minimal distances.

Analogous to corresponding simultaneous brightness and color series are the schemas:

d.   *e.*

If one confronts this principle of the size of the stepwise differences with that of nearness, there seems to arise the possibility of a more general principle which encompasses both of these and which would, in a certain sense, include spatial, temporal, *and* qualitative characteristics. If it should turn out that intensive and qualitative distance can be coordinated to a general spatio-temporal lawfulness, the instances discussed above could be considered instances of the principle of nearness. This must be carefully tested, but it *can* be experimentally studied.

Fields which were, previously, psychologically separate and heterogeneous could then be compared quantitatively in respect to the applicability of the same laws.

3. What happens, when *two* such factors are present together in such a constellation?

One can let the factors work together or against one another; for example, if the first produces the organization ab/cd/ . . . , the other can be set so as to enhance the same organization or to go in the other direction (. ./bc/de/ . . .). One can weaken or strengthen an already present tendency by changing distance relations as much as one can within the law of nearness.

For example, in series *a* (● ● ● ● ● ● ● ●) the factor of nearness produces ab/cd/ . . . ; with this diminished number of stimuli this is not as unequivocally compelling as in a longer series; the organization a/bc/de/ . . . , which occurs spontaneously very rarely, can yet be achieved by some, even though more difficult.

In series *b* (● ● o o ● ● o o) the factor of similarity also operates in the direction of the organization ab/cd/ . . . ; achievement of the opposing arrangement, a/bc/de/ . . . , is much more difficult than in *a* and is impossible for most people.

In series *c* (● o o ● ● o o ●) the factor of similarity operates in a direction opposite to that of the factor of nearness; in spontaneous perception, a/bc/de . . . occurs more often than ab/cd/ . . . ; aside from this, the series often looks typically "confused." The artificial achievement of the organization ab/cd/ . . . , simultaneously in the entire series, is relatively difficult.

More clearly unequivocal relations, as in the following examples, may help to clarify this issue. However they must be exposed to observation one by one.

d. ● ●   ●   ●   ●   ●   ●
        ●   ●   ●   ●   ●   ●   ●

e. ● ●   o   ●   o   ●   o   ●
        ●   o   ●   o   ●   o   ●

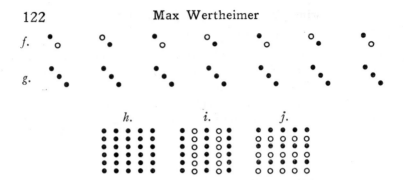

In the initial series, *d*, the distance relations are such that the factor of nearness operates to some extent in the direction ab/cd . . . , but not as strongly as it would if the differences in distance were greater. As a rule, the short slanted lines • • , from upper left to lower right, result. The opposite organization (the long slanted lines •   • , from lower left to upper right) is clearly more difficult, less certain, and rarer.

In *e*, where nearness and similarity work in the same direction, the short slanted form is more unequivocal and more certain, and the opposite organization is in general impossible (or, at best, leads to confusion).

In *f*, where nearness and similarity are opposed, the factor of similarity is often victorious: one can see the long slanted forms •   • ; however, grouping into the short slanted forms is possible for most people.

Series *g* shows the same thing as *d*.

In *i*, the verticals result (nearness and similarity cooperate); in *j*, the horizontals (the opposing factor of similarity is victorious).

Through a systematic variation of the distance relations in the initial series one could attempt to determine the region in which similarity wins out when it is added but works in an opposing direction. In this way one could also begin testing the strength of these grouping tendencies.

What has been demonstrated here in vision can also readily be shown in tones, varying time intervals and pitch appropriately.

Further, the same relations with respect to the factors of nearness and similarity can be shown in experiments with stroboscopic movement. In both *a* and *b*, movement is typically perceived as occurring within the group,

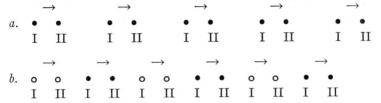

determined in *a* by nearness and in *b* by similarity. Here again one could try to determine the relative strength of the two factors.

4. Given the following constellation, with its grouping clearly determined by nearness,

● ● ●   ● ● ●   ● ● ●   ● ● ●

a b c   d e f   g h i   j k l

if, before his eyes, but without the subject expecting it, a change in the parts occurs, as, e.g., a sudden, small, vertical displacement of several of the dots upwards, two kinds of events are clearly distinguishable:

I. *Structurally reasonable* alterations, such as affect the groups already organized on the basis of nearness; e.g., shifting d, e, f upwards (or d, e, f and j, k, l).

II. *Structurally contrary* alterations, in which the common fate of the changed dots does *not* go along with the grouping that is already present; e.g., moving c, d, e upwards simultaneously (or c, d, e and i, j, k, or h, i, j).

Changes of this second kind do not go as smoothly as those of the first; while the first kind is readily taken in stride, the second usually produces a characteristic process. It is as if a special (much stronger) resistance existed against changes of this kind; there is a hesitation, sometimes a bewilderment, often a tipping over. The component parts affected by a common fate result in a grouping (in opposition to the influence of the factor of nearness). When c, d, e, i, j, k are displaced, the series is no longer in the form abc/def/ . . . but is seen in the form ab/cde/fgh/ijk/l. (The threshold for the perception of such alterations also seems different in I and II.) We might designate this factor tentatively as that of "common fate"; the above cases are only special cases of its effects.

It is important to note that it is not only a question of *equal* alterations; similar things happen in changes that are, piecemeal, very different. For example, a slanting displacement of three of the dots in either the I or the II manner, or in "turning" c, f, i, l down and b, e, h, k upwards. (Qualitative changes operate similarly.) This principle also has a wide field of operation; how wide remains to be ascertained.

5. Imagine a series of rows, starting perhaps with the following row:

• •	• •	• •	• •	• •
a b	c d	e f	g h	i j

Let the distance between a and b, between c and d, etc. (S_1) be 2 mm, and the distance between b and c, between d and e, etc. (S_2) be 20 mm; now construct a series of further rows, holding the position of a, c, e, g, i constant, and thus keeping $S_1 + S_2$ constant, but systematically varying the position of b relative to a and c (and the position of d relative to c and e, etc.). For example:

Row	$S_1 = 2$ mm	$S_2 = 20$ mm	$S_1 + S_2 = 22$ mm
A	2	20	22
B	5	17	22
C	8	14	22
D	11	11	22
E	14	8	22
F	17	5	22
G	20	2	22

This is schematic; one must use a larger number of rows (with smaller steps of change). The number of dots (or groups) in a row can be varied as required.

Once one has constructed a larger number of such rows, one can now present them separately. The result is that one is not dealing with a multitude of psychologically equal steps. Three primary, distinct impressions emerge: the ab/cd/ . . . form, clearest and most certain in the first rows; the /bc/de . . . form, equally clear in the last rows; and a third characteristic form, which is equally distinct from the other two forms and is produced by the middlemost row (row D in our example), giving an impression of uniformity, a "regular row."

Intermediate rows, lying outside these distinctive regions, often are ambiguous, not quite as precise; they easily appear more indeterminate, less clearly distinct, and can often be seen more easily in different ways.

Each of the three kinds of impressions are most distinct for certain ranges of stimulus values. Each has its field of application, thus, intermediate rows near D are typically seen as not quite regular, even when the distance differences are clearly supraliminal.

Another example can illustrate what is meant here: the series of angles from 30° through 150° (holding one side horizontal) is not simply a multitude of equals with a particular number of psychologically equal steps, as perhaps provided by just noticeable differences; but there are distinct primaries: the sharp angle, the right angle, the blunt angle. These three "qualities" emerge as more or less pure. The right angle, for example, has its "field": an angle of 93° appears typically as a more or less inadequate right angle. Intermediate steps have a characteristic lack of nicety or precision and can easily be seen as deviants from one or another of the original distinct steps; the number of significant steps—initially three—can increase with further experience with the forms, and new (intermediate) distinct steps can develop.

Significant here is that a form which is near a distinct step looks primarily like a "worse" form of the step; the 93° angle is not, above all, *that particular* angle (what a major change of the material would be necessary, to see such a form *as* characteristic in itself!), but is, psychologically, a "poor" right angle. That this is so can be shown clearly in an experiment, which shows the striking regularity of the tendency to the clear form. In tachistoscopic exposures, the subject just sees a right angle, an assimilation to the standard form, even when the stimulus is objectively quite deviant from a right angle. Other results indicate the same thing: with such forms near the particular step, one often gets the impression that the standard form is not quite right, somehow bad, "out of kilter," wrong, without being able to indicate in what direction the error lies.

In general, if one systematically varies materials in a stepwise manner—as in our example, the position of b between a and c—the resulting impressions are not psychologically equivalent, with each step having its own individual characteristics. Rather specific distinct steps occur, each with its range; the series shows discontinuities; intermediate forms typically appear as deviants from the category steps nearest to them. The same is true of the sequence from white to black and especially in the series of chromatic colors.

6. If one views the series of rows in Section 5 successively, one after the other in order, a new factor soon becomes clear: the factor of *stimulus-determined set*. If one begins with A and proceeds successively through G (or inversely from G to A), the original form character (ab/cd/ . . . in the former case, bc/de . . . in the latter), persists, often past the middle of the series, until finally, often not until the last rows, it "tips over" into the opposite organization. (In experienced subjects, and under good experimental conditions, this tipping over can be a useful quantitative index.) Thus a constellation, row C for example, appears different if preceded by A, B, than if preceded by G, F, E, and D. In short, if such a row is a part of a *sequence* (in general, part of a *whole*), the sequence plays a determining role. A constellation which in one sequence appears one way looks specifiably different in a different sequence. In other words, a constellation which, taken by itself, would not give unequivocal results and would be less clear and less distinct achieves a lawfully determined form when placed in a sequence.

This factor of stimulus-determined set is very strong: even constellations which, by themselves, typically result in unequivocal or-

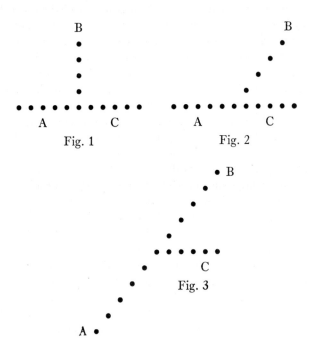

Fig. 1   Fig. 2

Fig. 3

ganizations can be turned into a different form by this factor. It should be noted that, in addition to such a successive stimulus-determined set, simultaneous stimulus sets can also operate; and, more generally, certain field conditions play an essential contributory role.

7. If one computes the distances among all dots (relative to every single dot), theoretically Fig. 1 would result in the following according to the factor of nearness: the dots of the left half of the horizontal line (group A) are in any case closer to the dots of the vertical line (B) than to those of the right half of the horizontal line (C); similarly, the dots of C are geometrically nearer those of B than those of A. As a rule the result is "a straight line with a vertical standing on it," that is, (AC)B. The theoretical situation is not simple in Fig. 1; according to the distances among the dots, (AB) and (BC) are equally favored relative to (AC); but in Fig. 2, without a doubt (BC) is favored, relative to (AC) as well as to (AB); in spite of this, the spontaneous organization is as a rule not A(BC), but (AC)B—horizontal with slanting line.

Similarly favored according to nearness is the organization (BC) in Fig. 3, yet typically (AB) C occurs—a long slanting line with a short horizontal.

This is stronger and still more distinct in constellations like Fig. 4. Geometrical consideration of the separate distances among the dots

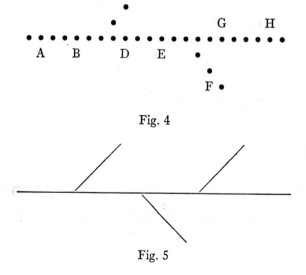

Fig. 4

Fig. 5

would result, here in (CD) as favored above (BD), (FG), above (EG), etc.; yet typically one sees (ABDEGH . . .) and C and F, and not (DC), (FG), etc.; a long straight line with short slanting lines.

We could also substitute an objectively continuous line for the dot constellations. This does not alter the theoretical issue (Fig. 5).

What is involved in these cases? The continuous straight line is favored, the *group with a direction*. But is it just a continuous *straight* line that is favored in this way? No; one can replace a straight course with many others:

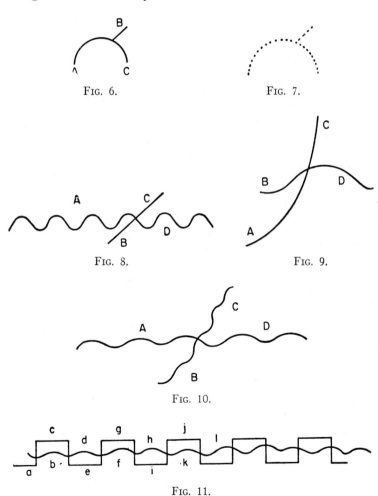

FIG. 6.

FIG. 7.

FIG. 8.

FIG. 9.

FIG. 10.

FIG. 11.

Figs. 6 and 7 typically are organized (AC)B, not (AB)C or A(BC); Fig. 8 is organized (AD)(BC), not (AB)(CD); Fig. 9 (AC)(BD), not (AB)(CD); Fig. 10 (AD)(BC), not (AB)(CD); in Fig. 11, try to *see* the organization (abefik . . .)(cdghjl . . .) as against the natural one (acegij . . .)(bdfhk . . .)!

One might think that angle relations at the critical place of crossing are all that is involved: 180° is more favorable than an acute or obtuse angle; certainly such an "angle" often appears as an inhomogeneity in the course of the line, but this factor also still misses the essential point, as the following figures indicate:

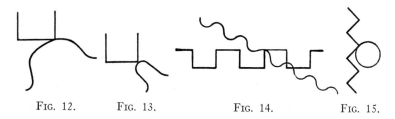

FIG. 12.   FIG. 13.   FIG. 14.   FIG. 15.

All kinds of experimental possibilities arise here; one could systematically vary the parts of such figures and see under what conditions one organization occurs, under what conditions another. In such variations, certain cases stand out as distinctive steps which are especially clear; there are other, intermediate cases which produce less clearcut results. For example:

FIG. 16.   FIG. 17.   FIG. 18.   FIG. 19.

In constructing such designs, it soon becomes clear what is involved. One might tentatively formulate it this way: what is crucial is a good continuation, an appropriateness of the curve, an *inner belongingness,* a resulting in a *good whole* or *good configuration* which exhibits its own definite inner requirements. Clearly this is but a very tentative formulation. As will be seen below, several techniques are available for increasing the precision of this statement so that it comes closer to a truly scientific form. I might remark at this juncture that this principle does not imply a mathematical "simplicity" in every sense of the term; it does not include just *any* arbitrary piecemeal regularity. The mathematical formula defining the figure can be quite complex; it is much less a matter of the simplicity of the smallest parts than of a simplicity relative to the larger parts (subwholes), in relation to the qualities of the whole. Such qualities of wholes play an extremely significant role here, characteristics like closure, symmetry, and inner balance. Further study is necessary to increase the precision of these formulations; it is clear that certain purely mathematical problems must be considered, especially the problem of characteristics of the whole as against mere piecemeal regularity.

The following cases illustrate a further factor, that of closure.

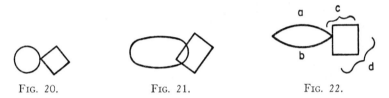

FIG. 20.   FIG. 21.   FIG. 22.

Given A, B, C, D, if AB/CD provide two closed processes and AC/BD two open ones, AB/CD is favored. As further examples:

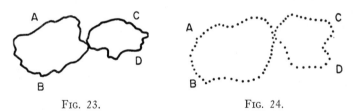

FIG. 23.   FIG. 24.

This factor of closure can be isolated from that of the good curve or of the good whole. Figs. 25 and 26 are each typically not seen as three closed forms, but rather are determined by the factor of the good curve; the factor of the good curve wins over that of closure. This victory is still more decisive if the lines and curves are continued beyond the places where they meet one another at the ends.

FIG. 25.   FIG. 26.

It is instructive to try to determine, in this connection, which constellations of two line figures produce an impression of the *duality* of the figures, which do not, and which result typically in something entirely different, a kind of new unity. Comparing Fig. 27 with

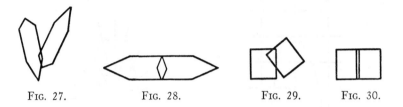

FIG. 27.   FIG. 28.   FIG. 29.   FIG. 30.

Fig. 28, and Fig. 29 with Fig. 30 clearly shows the tendency to the good whole configuration. The following provide further examples of this tendency; in general, it is instructive to determine what additions are capable of altering the configuration. It soon becomes clear that the way to achieve such alterations is to complete subparts of the figure into good subwholes, preferably using a structurally contrary, poor division of the subparts. And this is central, for other additions (whether, in a piecemeal sense, quantitatively larger or smaller) do *not* have this consequence. A part (Fig. 31) appears different (in Figs. 32-36) when it is included in one constellation than

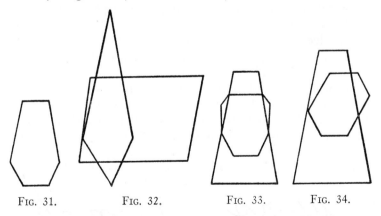

FIG. 31.   FIG. 32.   FIG. 33.   FIG. 34.

when it is included in a different one. Subjected to this technique, a person, thoroughly familiar with a given constellation presented alone, can be made quite blind to it. This implies consequences for recognition and for perception in general.

One might object that what has been meant by "good curve" in
the last paragraphs could be readily apparent in the relations among
the separate pieces ("elements") of the constellation. But this is not
the case; variations quickly show that the exact position of in-

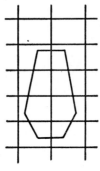

FIG. 35.   FIG. 36.

dividual dots or points is not essential. The sweeping course of
events, characteristics of the constellation seen from above, from the
whole, main directionalities, characteristics of the whole, are crucial
—even when the details, the form of the lowest parts is irregular
and haphazard.

8. A further factor which produces certain integrations and divisions is *habit,* or *experience.* The principle, in simplest formulation,
states that if AB is habitual, and C is habitual, but BC is not
(perhaps due to still other associations such as names), or, again, if
AB/C fits with past experience but A/BC does not, there is a
tendency, given ABC, to see AB/C, the frequently repeated, learned,
trained arrangement. It is characteristic of this principle that, in
contrast to the principles in the preceding paragraphs, there is no
involvement of the contents of the constellation, of their relations,
of their characteristics. The resulting organization depends principally only on external, extrinsic, arbitrary habit or drill.

For example, Fig. 37 will not be organized as in Fig. 38, but as

jump   *ju m p*

FIG. 37.   FIG. 38.

jump. 314 cm is organized abc/de, not ab/cde or abcd/e; that is, 314 cm, not 31/4 cm or 314 c/m.

Doubtless this happens; to a great extent (how great, is an interesting question), arbitrary materials can be organized in arbitrary ways through a sufficient amount of drill. Whether, even in these cases, the process actually is simply due to arbitrary things happening to have occurred together or to have been seen together is still a question. Some scientists, with very strong theoretical orientations, will be inclined to view all the preceding, and especially the material in Section 7, as simply due to a factor of "past experience," and think they have solved all of the problems by the glib use of this magic word.

One might say, for instance: Are not organizations to which we have become accustomed the ones that are favored? Are not the straight line, the right angle, the smooth curve, the square, all familiar from past experience? Are we not accustomed to seeing divisions between units? Consider that words in print are close together, while there are spaces between words, thousands of trials in one's past experience. Does not past experience drill into us to see equal colored areas as belonging together?

All of this sounds, on the surface, quite obvious. But it by no means solves the problems. It is the duty of the doctrine of past experience to demonstrate concretely for each of these cases and for each of the factors the actual past experiences and times of drill that are involved. It must be shown concretely that the less appropriate organizations actually had not been previously experienced or had been experienced less frequently, and that for the acquisition of experience the assumed "arbitrariness" is actually valid. As soon as one examines this problem seriously, it becomes clear that it is nowhere near as simple and smooth as the answer first seems to suggest. This is even true in areas which at first seem quite clear. To mention but one example: the right angle. Does not the child, in thousands of instances, experience it—think but of tables, cupboards, windows, corners of rooms, houses? This seems self-evident; and yet, is the child's environment filled only with such man-made objects? Are there not in nature many—and very different—other "angles," in tree branches for example, which certainly are very frequent in one's experience (and these relative frequencies would of course have to be quantitatively estimated)? But still more important: is it really *true* that, in the sense of piecemeal experience, the cupboards, table, etc. present thousands of right angles to the child? In terms of retinal stimulation, no. Only in the extremely rare case of a direct frontal-parallel orientation is there a right angle on the retina. In the remaining, far more frequent cases, when the child looks at the table or the cupboard, the stimulus-experience is not that of a right angle at all. If one does not want to consider the literal stimulus situations, but phenomenal percepts, the problem simply repeats itself.

But whether or not one views the factors as somehow based on experience, the question still remains: in these factors, *are there or are there not some basic regularities, some basic principles? And if there are, what are they?* Precisely what are these principles, these regularities? These are the research problems that cannot be solved through the word "experience." As an example, take a case where, on the basis of past experience, we would see abc and def; placing these together, into abcdef, do we *always* see abc/def? To make this concrete, I will choose an area in which we have a tremendous amount of past experience (Fig. 39).

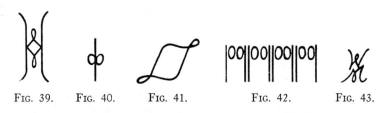

FIG. 39.   FIG. 40.   FIG. 41.   FIG. 42.   FIG. 43.

This is nothing but a familiar M and a familiar W placed together; yet typically it is seen as a quite unfamiliar form: a curved unit between two symmetircal curves on the right and left. If the W is composed of parts abc and the M of def, one typically sees not abc/def but ad/be/cf, with /be/ between /ad/ and /cf/. Or, further, Fig. 40 is composed of a "b" and a "q" (or a "d" and a "p"), Fig. 41 of a written capital L and capital J, Fig. 42 of p's and q's.

One might object that in the case of Fig. 39, we are not familiar with a placement of one above the other, even though we may be familiar with the M and the W separately. But we could place them in the arrangement of Fig. 43, quite as unfamiliar as the arrangement in Fig. 39, and yet the M and the W emerge clearly.

9. To summarize, all of these factors and principles point in a single direction: perceptual organization occurs from above to below:

the way in which parts are seen, in which subwholes emerge, in which grouping occurs, is not an arbitrary, piecemeal and-summation of elements, but is a process in which characteristics of the whole play a major determining role.

SELECTION 9

■■

An Experimental Study of the Phenomenon of Closure as a Threshold Function[*][1]

JOSEPH M. BOBBITT

THE CONCEPT OF CLOSURE

THE CONCEPT OF CLOSURE is one which was originally developed by members of the Gestalt school. However, the term is one which has been used rather widely both by Gestalt writers and by those outside this group; and the meaning of the term has not been invariable. In his 1922 article Koffka (10) makes reference to the concept of closure in the following manner: "A good figure is always a 'closed' figure, which the boundary line has the function of closing" (p. 557). Wertheimer (22) a year later refers to closure as a tendency for closed organization of stimuli to be preferred to open organizations. Later writers have, however, extended these early and relatively simple applications of the term. Helson (8), in his review of Gestalt psychology, relates closure to the reasoning process when he says, "The concept of closure can be applied to thinking. Questions demanding thought arouse configurational processes which are incomplete and which call for closure" (p. 54). Reiser (18) has also related closure and reasoning in the following words: "A problem presents itself as an open Gestalt which 'yearns' for solution, and it is the function of thought to find the solution by transforming the open Gestalt into a closed one" (p. 361). He adds, "Such 'closure' or insight reasoning is really reasoning by analogy . . ." (p. 362). Ogden (16) in a reply to a query from G. W. Hartmann (7) relates closure and insight by saying that all insight implies closure but

* From *J. exp. Psychol.*, 1942, 30, 273-294. Reprinted by permission of the author and the publisher.
[1] From the Psychological Laboratory at Northwestern University. The writer wishes to express his appreciation of the help of Dr. A. R. Gilliland who directed this study.

that closure does not always involve insight. Ogden (17) also presents a definition of perception in terms of closure: "Therefore, instead of defining perception as a complex of sensory experience and associated imagery, we have defined it more broadly as the experience of a *closed circuit* of events. Indeed it is because of this 'closure' that we give heed to a series of events and thus *perceive* it" (pp. 126-127). Koffka (11, p. 151) gives closure systematic orientation by identifying it as a special case of the law of Prägnanz. In other words, Koffka considers closure as a manifestation of the tendency of the energies involved in perception to resolve toward a state of equilibrium. If the purpose of the above review were critical rather than expository, one might well express misgivings over the general and loose uses to which the term has been put.

The foregoing review of the uses of the term does not make a definition of closure simple. However, it may be said that the term has been applied to any psychological phenomenon in which a condition of incompleteness, either in the stimulus field or in some phase of the organism's activities, creates a tendency to overcome this incompleteness by perceptual reorganization, by a combination of two or more different experiences, or by some overt activity of the organism. As applied to perception, the term may be defined as a tendency on the part of the organism perceptually to complete stimulus presentations which are physically incomplete. This statement does not mean that the missing parts of, say, a geometrical form, are actually seen, but merely that the parts are organized as belonging to a complete figure and that they represent, as such, a more nearly stable organization than they would represent if separately organized.

HISTORY

There has been very little experimental work directly on the problem of closure. In 1929 Rosenbloom (19) demonstrated a relationship between the tactual two point space threshold and configurational influences in tactual perception. Street (20) in 1931 published a Gestalt completion test designed to measure the ability to perceive incomplete pictures. Tiernan (21) has recently measured the relative recall and recognition value of open and closed forms in the case of children 7 to 14 years old. In addition to these studies there are many other experiments, some of them of the pre-Gestalt era, which are relevant. In the field of visual perception, the studies of Hempstead (9), Meakin (15), Zigler (23), and Liebmann (13) are notable. The work of Gibson (4) on the progressive changes in the reproduction of visually perceived forms is also significant. Zigler and Northup (25) demonstrated what may well be called closure effects in the case of tactual perception. Finally, the work of Fuchs (3) with completion effects in the case of hemianoptic patients cannot be ignored in any consideration of closure.

FORMULATION OF PROBLEM

The purpose of the present investigation was that of systematically studying closure in its most simple realm of phenomenal expression, the field of form perception. Specifically, the investigation concerned itself with the question of the perception of physically incomplete triangles, and answers were sought to the following definite questions:

1. Is it possible, in the case of triangles, psychophysically to demonstrate a threshold of closure, defined in terms of the percentage of the perimeter of the figure necessary for the occurrence of the phenomenon?

2. Is the threshold of closure, in the case of triangles, partially a function of the angular characteristics of the figures?

3. Is the threshold of closure, in the case of triangles, partially a function of the absolute size of the figures?

4. Is the tendency toward perceptual completion of physically incomplete presentations to be explained primarily in terms of the experience of the subject with the complete figure and its various incomplete stages?

5. Is the threshold a stable one, dependent in main part upon a relatively permanent relationship between the organism and the stimulus, or is it primarily determined by the subject's attitude of the movement?

6. Does the measurement of the closure phenomenon give any indication concerning its psychological nature and of the processes underlying it?

THE EXPERIMENT

A. The Stimulus Forms. 1. GENERAL DESCRIPTION AND LINEAR RELATIONSHIPS OF THE STIMULUS FORMS. Each of the stimulus forms, drawn in black India ink on white paper, consisted of two angles representing incomplete portions of the opposite sides of a triangle (Figs. 1 and 2).

The degree of completeness of any one figure was determined, of course, by the length of the lines forming these opposed angles. There were four separate series of triangles. First, there was an equilateral triangle series, which will be designated hereafter as series T-I (Figs. 1 and 2). The

Fig. 1.

dimensions of the complete form of this series were $3\frac{1}{2}'' \times 3\frac{1}{2}'' \times 3\frac{1}{2}''$. Second, there was a large apex isosceles triangle series, which will be indicated hereafter as series T-II. The dimensions of the complete form of this series was $3\frac{1}{2}'' \times 3\frac{1}{2}'' \times 4\frac{2}{3}''$. Third, there was a small apex isosceles triangle series, which will be designated hereafter as series T-III. The dimensions of the complete form of this series were $3\frac{1}{2}'' \times 3\frac{1}{2}'' \times 2\frac{1}{8}''$. Fourth, there was a large apex isosceles triangle series, the angular characteristics of whose forms were the same as those of series T-II and the area and perimeter of whose complete form were equal to those of the complete form of series T-III. The dimensions of the complete form of this fourth series were $2\frac{4}{5}'' \times 2\frac{4}{5}'' \times 3\frac{11}{15}''$. This series will be indicated hereafter as series T-IIR. All lines were $\frac{3}{64}''$ wide. Attention is called to the fact that the base lines in series T-II were twice as long as the base lines in series T-III. Furthermore, the difference between the lengths of the base lines of series T-I ($3\frac{1}{2}''$) and those of series T-II ($4\frac{2}{3}''$) was $1\frac{1}{6}''$, the same as the difference between the length of the base lines of series T-I ($3\frac{1}{2}''$) and those of series T-III ($2\frac{1}{3}''$).

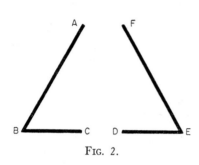

FIG. 2.

A complete set of each series of triangles consisted of 28 forms, the most incomplete of which represented only 3.57 percent of the perimeter of the entire figure and was designated as number 1 in the series. The opposite extreme of the series was, of course, a complete figure and was designated as number 28 in the series. Actually, only form 3 and forms 10 to 27 inclusive for each series was used.[2] This method of numbering the forms makes it possible to identify any form by indicating the series to which it belongs and its place in the series from 1 to 28. Thus, the form represented in Fig. 2 may be indicated as T-I-21.

The way in which the individual forms were constructed deserves detailed description. For the sake of clearness, reference is made to Fig. 2. This figure represents form T-I-21, and there is 75 percent of the total perimeter of the figure present. In this figure, the distance AB represents 75 percent of the side of the triangle of which it is a part. The same statement is true of the distance FE. The distance BC represents 75 percent of half of the base line, and the distance DE bears a similar relationship to the other half of the base line. Hence, there is the same percentage of each side of the triangle present as there is of the whole perimeter of the figure. It should be obvious from the foregoing description that forms belonging to different series but having the same location in the series from 1 to 28 were matched in percentage of perimeter both for the whole figure and for each of the parts of the form.

2. THE AREAL RELATIONSHIPS OF THE STIMULUS FORMS. The way in which the percentage of perimeter present in equivalent forms of the four triangle series was matched has just been described. It is significant that the percentage of area represented in equivalent forms was also matched. Referring to Fig. 2, let the percentage which the combined areas of tri-

---

[2] Form 3 was not drawn for series T-IIR.

angles ABC and FDE (each having one imaginary side) represent of the area of the complete triangle be called r_2. Further, let the percentage which is present of the total perimeter of the figure be represented as r_1. It can be shown mathematically that

$$r_2 = r_1^2.$$

Hence, the relationship is independent of the angular characteristics of the triangle. Therefore, the equivalent forms of the four triangle series were matched in terms of area represented as well as in terms of the percentage of the perimeter present. It should be noted, however, that this method of determining the percentage of area represented in a given figure is purely arbitrary and that, from the standpoint of the subject's phenomenological experience, the actual amount of area indicated in a given form of the series might not correspond to the amount represented according to any arbitrary way of determining the percentage present.

B. Apparatus. The apparatus used in this experiment was a modification of the mirror tachistoscope devised by Dodge (2). The pre-exposure and exposure fields were carefully equated for brightness. The fixation point of the pre-exposure field corresponded in position to the center of the figure on the exposure field. The exposure interval of a tenth of a second was controlled by means of a Bergström chronoscope.

C. Subjects. Twenty-five subjects were used in the investigation. Of these observers, twenty-two were undergraduates, chiefly college freshmen and sophomores; one was a first year graduate student in psychology; one was a second year graduate student in psychology; and one was a trained psychologist. For the purpose of this experiment, all of the undergraduate subjects may be considered as naïve. None of the other three subjects had complete knowledge of the nature of the experiment, but each of them knew the general character of the study.

D. Procedure. Before describing the specific procedure, it is necessary to describe the kind of discrimination that was required of the subjects. The more incomplete forms of each of the series of triangles had what may be termed a quality of *twoness*. That is, the two angles did not appear as necessarily related in any one definite way. They could easily be seen as parts of a triangle, as parts of two separate complex figures, as parts of two triangles, as parts of a trapezoid, or as related in any one of several other ways. In short, while the two angles were recognized as related, they were separately perceived; they did not form one figure. On the other hand, the more complete forms of each series were characterized by a quality of *oneness*. That is, the two angles, while discriminably separate, were spontaneously perceived as being closely related, as belonging to one figure. Obviously, since the forms at one extreme of the series had the quality of oneness and since the forms at the other extreme of the series had the quality of twoness, at some point in the series of intermediate forms there was a transition point between the forms having predominantly the latter quality and those having predominantly the former quality.

Using a variation of the method of minimal changes, the threshold for closure (defined as the point in the series representing the transition between the forms having the quality of twoness and those having the quality of oneness) was separately determined for each subject for series T-I, T-II, and T-III. The threshold was always stated in terms of the percentage of the total perimeter of the figure present at the point in the series representing the transition between the forms having the quality of twoness and those having the quality of oneness. There are only six different orders in which these series of triangles just mentioned may be presented. One of the orders of presentation was used with five subjects; the other five orders of presentation were used with four subjects each. Hence, each series preceded each other series and was followed by each other series an equal number of times. Therefore, any influence which one triangle series might have on the other series is cancelled in the average results for the whole group.[3] When series T-IIR was used, it was always presented last. Except for the first four subjects, the presentation of the different series of triangles was separated in each instance by at least one day. This provision tended to minimize the influence of one series on the other two series. In the case of eleven subjects, the regular set of tests was followed with the presentation of series T-IIR. Since series T-IIR was given for the purpose of comparing the results obtained by its use with those obtained with series T-II, no subjects were used in this case for whom the first series seen was series T-II. This precaution was taken upon the assumption that the threshold determination for the first series with which a subject was tested might not be quite as reliable as the thresholds obtained with the succeeding series.

The instructions which were read to the subject before presenting the first test series offer the best detailed description of the procedure followed in the actual determination of a threshold.

Instructions to Subjects. Here are two incomplete figures (Forms 3 and 27). The one on your right is nearly a complete figure, while the one on your left is very incomplete. Do these two figures look markedly different to you? Would you agree to the statement that the two angles on the right appear to belong together as parts of the same figure, while

---

[3] The fact that one of the orders of presentation was used one more time than were the other orders makes this statement slightly inaccurate, but this slight lack of balance does not defeat the purpose for rotating the presentation orders.

those on the left do not appear to be closely related to each other in any one definite way; that, in other words, the right-hand angles have a quality of oneness, while the left-hand angles have a quality of twoness?

Obviously, if I should slowly increase the length of the lines forming the left-hand angles by adding small amounts to them, they would at some point lose their quality of twoness and acquire the quality of oneness possessed by the right-hand angles. Here is just such a set of forms, which will be presented in this exposure apparatus. In some of the series, I shall start with a relatively incomplete form and present successive forms which are relatively more complete than the first one. In these cases, your job will be that of determining at what point in the series the angles lose their quality of twoness and acquire the quality of oneness. The series ends at this point. In the other series, I shall start with a relatively complete form and present successive forms which are relatively less complete than the first one. In these cases, your job will be that of determining at what point in the series the angles lose their quality of oneness and acquire the quality of twoness. The series ends at this point. These ascending and descending series will be alternated. These two forms (Forms 10 and 27) represent the most complete and least complete figures that will be used. Remember, however, that, while I shall always start with a form that is relatively complete or one that is relatively incomplete, I shall not always start at one of the extremes of the series. That is, I shall sometimes start with a form that is one or more steps removed from these two forms which represent the extremes of the series that will be used.

In order to give you a more clear idea of what the transition from oneness to twoness is, I am going to show you the whole series outside of the exposure device. Indicate the point at which any decided difference in the angles becomes apparent to you. (After this one preliminary trial, subject was placed before tachistoscope.)

Preliminary to the real experiment, I shall show you the same card two or three times in order that you may become adapted to the apparatus. You should sit in a comfortable position and look through this eyepiece. You will see a rectangular white field, upon which there are two gray circles which overlap, forming a small, vertical, black oval in the center of the field. Adjust your eyes so that the oval is as nearly as possible in the center of the rectangle. When you have made this adjustment, let me know. Before each presentation, I shall give you a ready signal, and very shortly thereafter I shall expose the figure. These trials will be the preliminary ones of which I spoke.

Now we are ready for the real experiment. After each presentation, reply as quickly as possible, that is, without deliberation, with the word *two* if the angles have the quality of twoness; with the word *one* if the angles have the quality of oneness. Please remember that there are no right or wrong answers. This experiment is not in any sense a test of your ability.

There will be rest periods at appropriate intervals. Have you any questions?

It is true that the instructions could be criticized due to the fact that they make suggestions concerning the *oneness* and *twoness* qualities. The answer to this charge is the fact that preliminary work showed these qualities to exist. The suggestions rather than biasing the subjects merely made clear the basis of discrimination which was involved. Also, any such suggestions would not affect the location of the threshold. Further, this influence would not explain the similarity of the thresholds for the different subjects or other characteristics of the data secured.

Attention should be called to several additional points. The parenthetical material in the instructions is explanatory and was not, of course, read to the subject. Form 3 was used as a basis for establishing the subject's criterion of *twoness;* form 27, for establishing his criterion of *oneness.* Form 3, of course, was never used in the actual threshold determination series. A complete test for one triangle involved twenty separate threshold determinations, consisting of ten ascending series and of ten descending series, arranged in the counterbalanced order for the purpose of equalizing as much as possible such factors as fatigue and practice. With thirteen of the twenty-five subjects the order of ascending and descending series was adada dadad dadad adada; with the other twelve subjects the order of presentation was dadad adada adada dadad. This arrangement prevented the average results for all subjects from being biased as a result of the influence of the initial presentation (either ascending or descending) upon the results of subsequent presentations. The first two presentations of the stimuli included all eighteen forms (forms 10 to 27 in the series). On the basis of the results of these two presentations, a series of fourteen forms was chosen so that the subject's threshold was approximately at the middle of the series. After the range of forms was chosen for a subject, the same range was used for all the series of triangles with which he was tested. All exposure times were a tenth of a second.

Presentations of stimuli were made at the average rate of three or four forms a minute, including the time used for rest periods and for recording the data. Hence, the determination of a subject's threshold for one triangle series, involving between 140 and 150 stimulus presentations, took between forty and fifty minutes. The time necessary to record the data and to rearrange the stimulus cards after each series of ascending or descending presentation of stimuli provided short rest periods. A rest interval of three or four minutes was given upon the completion of the first half of the test.

RESULTS

A. Results for Individual Subjects. As mentioned in the previous section, the results for any one subject consisted of twenty separate determinations of the threshold of closure for each of the triangle series T-I, T-II, and T-III. For eleven subjects, the procedure also

TABLE I. RESULTS OF INDIVIDUAL SUBJECTS FOR SERIES T-I AND T-II

Subject	Mean Closure Threshold in Percent of Perimeter		S.D. of Distribution in Percent of Perimeter	
	T-I	T-II	T-I	T-II
1	77.86 ± 1.25*	85.00 ± 0.46	5.43 ± 0.86	2.00 ± 0.32
2	73.03 ± 1.07	71.43 ± 1.04	4.71 ± 0.75	4.57 ± 0.71
3	74.82 ± 1.04	77.32 ± 0.86	4.57 ± 0.71	3.79 ± 0.60
4	64.46 ± 1.14	68.21 ± 1.07	5.00 ± 0.79	4.71 ± 0.75
5	75.71 ± 0.68	85.00 ± 0.54	3.00 ± 0.46	2.29 ± 0.36
6	59.46 ± 0.61	63.21 ± 0.50	2.61 ± 0.43	2.14 ± 0.32
7	63.57 ± 1.39	64.11 ± 0.93	6.00 ± 0.96	4.00 ± 0.64
8	62.68 ± 0.68	66.25 ± 0.54	2.89 ± 0.46	2.39 ± 0.39
9	80.71 ± 0.50	82.86 ± 0.54	2.21 ± 0.36	2.29 ± 0.36
10	74.29 ± 0.79	78.39 ± 0.54	3.39 ± 0.54	2.39 ± 0.39
11	69.46 ± 0.75	79.11 ± 0.46	3.21 ± 0.50	2.04 ± 0.32
12	71.79 ± 0.54	76.79 ± 0.68	2.36 ± 0.36	3.00 ± 0.46
13	55.18 ± 1.07	54.82 ± 0.54	4.71 ± 0.75	2.36 ± 0.36
14	78.57 ± 0.39	84.64 ± 0.32	1.79 ± 0.29	1.43 ± 0.21
15	68.57 ± 0.75	67.14 ± 0.82	3.21 ± 0.50	3.57 ± 0.57
16	84.46 ± 0.36	83.57 ± 0.89	1.50 ± 0.25	3.89 ± 0.61
17	88.57 ± 0.39	90.54 ± 0.46	1.64 ± 0.25	2.04 ± 0.32
18	73.57 ± 0.64	73.93 ± 1.14	2.75 ± 0.43	5.00 ± 0.79
19	60.54 ± 0.82	63.75 ± 1.00	3.64 ± 0.57	4.29 ± 0.68
20	74.64 ± 0.61	81.61 ± 0.61	2.61 ± 0.43	2.61 ± 0.43
21	66.07 ± 0.57	73.75 ± 0.46	2.43 ± 0.39	2.04 ± 0.32
22	76.43 ± 1.00	75.18 ± 1.21	4.36 ± 0.68	5.25 ± 0.82
23	83.21 ± 0.61	83.39 ± 0.54	2.68 ± 0.43	2.36 ± 0.36
24	65.00 ± 0.79	68.57 ± 0.64	3.39 ± 0.54	2.79 ± 0.43
25	76.61 ± 0.75	78.04 ± 0.68	3.29 ± 0.54	3.04 ± 0.46

* In this table and all succeeding ones, variability measures of means and of standard deviations are in terms of the standard error.

TABLE I *(Continued)*. RESULTS OF INDIVIDUAL SUBJECTS FOR SERIES T-III AND T-IIR

Subject	Mean Closure Threshold in Percent of Perimeter		S.D. of Distribution in Percent of Perimeter	
	T-III	T-IIR	T-III	T-IIR
1	78.39 ± 0.39		1.79 ± 0.28	
2	74.64 ± 0.64		2.86 ± 0.46	
3	75.89 ± 0.86	76.43 ± 0.64	3.71 ± 0.57	2.75 ± 0.43
4	63.57 ± 1.18		5.07 ± 0.79	
5	70.18 ± 0.54	83.39 ± 0.39	2.36 ± 0.36	1.71 ± 0.29
6	57.68 ± 0.54		2.36 ± 0.36	
7	60.18 ± 0.68	65.71 ± 1.36	3.03 ± 0.46	5.96 ± 0.93
8	56.25 ± 0.86	67.50 ± 0.46	3.71 ± 0.57	2.07 ± 0.32
9	80.71 ± 0.68		2.96 ± 0.46	
10	71.25 ± 0.93		4.00 ± 0.64	
11	61.61 ± 0.64	75.89 ± 0.43	2.75 ± 0.43	1.93 ± 0.32
12	62.50 ± 0.64	75.71 ± 0.39	2.86 ± 0.46	1.64 ± 0.25
13	47.50 ± 0.68		2.89 ± 0.46	
14	77.14 ± 0.43	77.14 ± 0.43	1.93 ± 0.32	1.93 ± 0.32
15	55.89 ± 0.68		3.04 ± 0.46	
16	83.39 ± 0.54		2.36 ± 0.36	
17	77.50 ± 0.79	87.14 ± 0.43	3.50 ± 0.57	1.93 ± 0.32
18	50.71 ± 1.21		5.25 ± 0.82	
19	57.32 ± 0.93	58.21 ± 0.71	4.00 ± 0.64	3.11 ± 0.50
20	74.64 ± 0.75	79.82 ± 0.54	3.29 ± 0.54	2.36 ± 0.36
21	64.64 ± 0.46		2.07 ± 0.32	
22	72.50 ± 1.00		4.32 ± 0.68	
23	77.32 ± 0.39		1.71 ± 0.29	
24	59.11 ± 0.75	62.86 ± 0.64	3.29 ± 0.54	2.75 ± 0.43
25	78.03 ± 0.75		3.25 ± 0.50	

included the use of triangle series T-IIR. For a given determination, the threshold of closure was assumed to fall halfway between the two forms representing the change from the quality of twoness, to the quality of oneness. For example, if, on an ascending series in which the forms were becoming progressively more complete, the subject reported a quality of twoness for form 20 in the series and a quality of oneness for form 21, the closure threshold for that determination was assumed to fall at a point in the series halfway between the two forms. It will be remembered that the threshold is always stated in terms of the percentage of the total perimeter of the figure present at this point in the series. Using the twenty separate thresholds thus secured, the mean closure threshold and the standard deviation were determined for each subject. Also, the standard error of each of these measures was computed. Table I summarizes these values for each subject.

B. Results for Entire Group of Subjects. 1. GROUP MEAN CLOSURE THRESHOLDS. The group results were based in each case upon the mean thresholds for individual subjects. Using these values, the group's mean closure threshold, the standard deviation, and the standard error of each of these measures were computed for each triangle series. Table II summarizes these values for triangle series T-I, T-II, and T-III.

TABLE II. SUMMARY OF GROUP RESULTS
(SERIES T-I, T-II, AND T-III), $N = 25$

Series	Mean Closure Threshold in Percent of Perimeter	S.D. of Distribution in Percent of Perimeter
T-I	72.00 ± 1.68	8.18 ± 1.14
T-II	75.06 ± 1.75	8.64 ± 1.21
T-III	67.63 ± 2.04	10.00 ± 1.43

2. DIFFERENCE BETWEEN GROUP MEAN THRESHOLDS FOR THE THREE MAIN TRIANGLE SERIES. The differences between the group's mean closure thresholds for these three triangle series are shown in Table III on page 148. It is to be noted, too, that the standard error of the difference (σ diff.) and the critical ratio are also given in each case.

3. INTER-CORRELATIONS OF THE THREE MAIN TRIANGLE SERIES AND THE RELIABILITIES OF THE SEPARATE SERIES. Table IV shows the three possible coefficients of correlation between the performance of the subjects on the three triangle series, T-I, T-II, and T-III. The coefficients were computed by the method of rank differences. The correlations indicate the degree to which a subject's mean threshold tended to occupy the same relative position on each of the three series of triangles with regard to the distribution of thresholds of the various members of the group. Also, these correlations between

TABLE III. SUMMARY OF DIFFERENCES BETWEEN GROUP MEAN
THRESHOLDS (SERIES T-I, T-II, AND T-III), $N = 25$

Mean Threshold in Percent of Perimeter	Mean Threshold in Percent of Perimeter	Diff. in Percent of Perimeter	σdiff. in Percent of Perimeter	C.R.σ
Mean, T-II 75.06 ± 1.75	Mean, T-I 72.00 ± 1.68	3.06	0.68	4.50
Mean, T-I 72.00 ± 1.68	Mean, T-III 67.63 ± 2.04	4.37	1.07	4.08
Mean, T-II 75.06 ± 1.75	Mean, T-III 67.63 ± 2.04	7.43	1.18	6.30

different triangle series indirectly indicate the coefficient of reliability
for the separate triangle series.

TABLE IV. RANK ORDER COEFFICIENTS OF CORRELATION (RHO)
(SERIES T-I, T-II, AND T-III), $N = 25$

	T-I	T-II	T-III
T-I	—	+.908 ± .023*	+.877 ± .033
T-II		—	+.816 ± .047
T-III			—

* Probable errors.

4. FIRST HALF-SECOND HALF ANALYSIS OF THE DATA. In order to
ascertain whether or not there was a tendency for the closure
threshold to shift significantly in either direction during the course
of the experiment, two separate closure thresholds were determined
for each subject for each of the three triangle series, T-I, T-II, and
T-III. One of these measures represented the subject's mean
threshold on the first half of the twenty separate threshold determinations; the other measure represented the subject's mean threshold in
the last half of the test. Using these individual results, the group's
mean closure threshold and the standard error of the mean for the
first and second halves of the test were separately determined for

each of the three series of triangles. Table V summarizes these results for the group. The table also shows the differences between the first

TABLE V. Comparison of Group Results for First Half and Second Half of the Threshold Determinations (Series T-I, T-II, and T-III), $N = 25$

	T-I	T-II	T-III
Group Mean Threshold for First 10 Trials in Percent of Perimeter............	71.91 ± 1.64	74.57 ± 1.75	67.50 ± 1.96
S.D. of Distrib. for First 10 Trials in Percent of Perimeter.................	8.04 ± 1.14	8.61 ± 1.21	9.54 ± 1.36
Group Mean Threshold for Second 10 Trials in Percent of Perimeter........	72.08 ± 1.71	75.56 ± 1.82	67.76 ± 2.18
S.D. of Distrib. for Second 10 Trials in Percent of Perimeter..............	8.46 ± 1.21	8.82 ± 1.25	10.61 ± 1.50
Diff. Between Means in Percent of Perimeter........	−0.17	−0.99	−0.26
σdiff. in Percent of Perimeter	0.46	0.39	0.50
C.R.σ..................	0.37	2.54	0.52

and second half group mean thresholds, the standard errors of these differences, and the corresponding critical ratios.

C. Results for the Area Control Group. Attention should be called to the fact that the three triangle series, T-I, T-II, and T-III, differ from each other not only in terms of their angular characteristics but also in terms of their areas and of their perimeters. Of the three series of triangles, the complete form of series T-III had the smallest area (3.85 sq. in.); that of series T-II, the largest area (6.09 sq. in.). In order to determine whether or not part of the significant differences between the mean group thresholds of the three series of triangles was the result of differences in the areas and perimeters, triangle series T-IIR was used with eleven subjects. It will be remembered that the angular characteristics of the forms of this series were the same as those of series T-II and that its complete form had the

TABLE VI. SUMMARY OF RESULTS FOR AREA CONTROL GROUP
(SERIES T-I, T-II, T-III, AND T-IIR), $N = 11$

Series	Mean Closure Threshold in Percent of Perimeter	S.D. of Distribution in Percent of Perimeter
T-I	71.40 ± 2.64	7.89 ± 1.68
T-II	76.15 ± 2.93	8.79 ± 1.86
T-III	66.77 ± 2.68	8.07 ± 1.71
T-IIR	73.62 ± 2.82	8.50 ± 1.82

same area and perimeter as did the complete form of series T-III.
Hence, the results obtained with triangle series T-IIR give a basis
for determining the influence upon the closure threshold of differences
of absolute size. In order to facilitate discussion the eleven subjects
with whom series T-IIR was used will be called the area control
group.

1. GROUP MEAN CLOSURE THRESHOLDS. Table VI summarizes the
area control group results for triangle series T-I, T-II, T-III, and
T-IIR. The table indicates for each triangle series the group's mean
closure threshold, the standard deviation, and the standard error of
each of these measures.

2. DIFFERENCES BETWEEN GROUP MEAN THRESHOLDS FOR THE FOUR
TRIANGLE SERIES. The differences between the mean closure thresholds for the group for these four triangle series are shown in Table
VII on page 151. It is to be noted, too, that the standard error of
the difference (σ diff.) and the critical ratio are also given in each
case.

DISCUSSION

*A. Comparison of the Present Experiment and Traditional Thresh-
old Studies.* The present experiment represents the application of the
threshold concept to a fairly complex perceptual process. The method
followed is strictly analogous to that used in traditional threshold
measurements. It should be noted that the data secured in this study
are similar to those secured in measurements of simple sensory
thresholds. By reference to Table I it may be seen that the separate
threshold determinations for each subject varied within a small range
around a very definite central tendency. Table V indicates that there
is relatively little tendency for the threshold to shift during the

TABLE VII. SUMMARY OF DIFFERENCES BETWEEN MEAN THRESHOLDS FOR AREA CONTROL GROUP (SERIES T-I, T-II, T-III, AND T-IIR), $N = 11$

Mean Threshold in Percent of Perimeter	Mean Threshold in Percent of Perimeter	Diff. in Percent of Perimeter	σdiff. in Percent of Perimeter	C.R.σ
Mean, T-IIR 73.62 ± 2.82	Mean, T-I 71.40 ± 2.64	2.22	1.14	1.95
Mean, T-II 76.15 ± 2.93	Mean, T-IIR 73.62 ± 2.82	2.53	0.93	2.72
Mean, T-IIR 73.62 ± 2.82	Mean, T-III 66.77 ± 2.68	6.85	1.68	4.08
Mean, T-II 76.15 ± 2.93	Mean, T-I 71.40 ± 2.64	4.75	0.93	5.11
Mean, T-I 71.40 + 2.64	Mean, T-III 66.77 ± 2.68	4.63	1.14	4.06
Mean, T-II 76.15 ± 2.93	Mean, T-III 66.77 ± 2.68	9.38	1.53	6.13

course of the measurement. These observations justify the statement that the present investigation involves the measurement of a true threshold function.

B. The Main Experimental Finding. 1. ANALYSIS OF THE MAIN EXPERIMENTAL FINDING. There are obviously many factors which may influence the closure threshold. They may be legitimately divided, however, into two classes: (1) intrinsic factors, which are those connected with the figure as such, and (2) extrinsic factors, which are those external to the figure itself. In this latter group are, for example, such determinants as exposure time, intensity of illumination, and all other strictly methodological variables. The intrinsic factors, on the other hand, are those dependent upon the internal relationships of the figure and upon the general phenomenological characteristics of the form. In the present study, all extrinsic variables were, as far as possible, held constant, and the only differential influences upon the closure threshold in the various triangle series were the intrinsic ones. In the light of this statement, then, *the main experimental finding of the present study is the fact that there are statistically significant differences between the thresholds of closure of different triangles (See Table III) which can be explained only in terms of the influence which the intrinsic factors involved have upon the size of the threshold.* The specific nature of these variables in the present case is indicated in the analysis of the two ways in which the three main series of triangles, series T-I, T-II, and T-III, differed from each other. (1) Their angular characteristics were different, which means that the proportional relationships of their sides to each other were also different. (2) Their absolute sizes (areas) were different, which means that their perimeters (specifically, in this case, their base lines) were of different absolute lengths. These two variables are also functions of each other. The observed threshold differences must, then, be explained in terms of the effect of one or of both of these two factors upon the location of the closure threshold.

The data obtained with triangle series T-IIR give some information concerning the influence which these two factors, the angular characteristics of the forms and their area, had on the closure threshold. The forms of this series differed from those of series T-III only in terms of their angular characteristics; that is, these two series were equated in terms of absolute size. Table VII shows that even when this factor is equated, the threshold difference between the two series of triangles does not disappear. This difference, as the table shows, is statistically significant as expressed by a critical ratio of 4.08 in terms of the standard error of the difference. Moreover, series T-IIR and series T-II differed from each other only in terms of their size; that is, these two series were equated in terms of their angular characteristics. In this case, a small measure difference is obtained which fails to meet the conventional standard of statistical significance (See Table VII). However, the critical ratio of 2.72 in terms of the standard error of the difference is large enough to suggest that the difference is possibly a real one and that a greater number of cases would demonstrate its statistical significance. In this connection, it is interesting to note that Fuchs (3) found that completion effects on the blind half of the retina in the case of hemianoptic patients are largely but not absolutely independent of the absolute size of the figures used. He also found that in most cases about 75 percent of the figure had to be represented on the good half of the retina in order for completion effects to occur. The group mean closure thresholds obtained in the present study for the three main series of triangles range between 67.63 percent to 75.08 percent of the total perimeter. It is possibly significant that the present writer's results with normal subjects and those obtained by Fuchs with hemianoptic cases are as similar as they are. In recapitulation, then, the main experimental finding of this study shows that factors other than the mere percentage of the figure present influence the threshold of closure. On the basis of the experimental results, two statements concerning these other factors may be made. (1) The data conclusively show that the angular characteristics of the forms are important determinants of the closure threshold. (2) The factor of absolute size appears slightly to modify the threshold of closure, but the measured difference does not meet the conventional test of statistical significance; and there is the further possibility that this observed difference may be a reflection of the fact that the smaller forms (those of series T-IIR) had a different relationship to the constant size exposure field than did the larger forms (those of series T-II).

2. SIGNIFICANCE OF THE MAIN EXPERIMENTAL FINDING. *a*. The Main Experimental Finding in the Light of Empirical Concepts. While there is in the literature no formal consideration of closure by traditional psychologists upon which to base the statement, it appears patent to the writer that an explanation of this phenomenon from the existential, functional, or behavioristic point of view would have to be stated in terms of the influence of experience upon perceptual responses. Specifically, an explanation stated in such terms would have to assume that a person's experience with a complete figure and its various incomplete forms would result in his recognition of the relationship of the incomplete representation to the complete figure. Such a theory would have to assume that after sufficient experience of this kind a person would be able to recognize a partial representation of a figure as belonging to a complete form. The amount of experience would, of course, determine the facility with which the recognition process takes place. Stated in its most simple terms, then, closure would become, in terms of this explanation, a phenomenon dependent upon perceptual habits.

In the writer's opinion, this explanation is unable to account for the fact that there are statistically significant differences between the closure thresholds of different kinds of triangles. In the first place, the existence of the differences necessitates the assumption that one figure has an experience advantage over the other one. It is conceivable that such a difference in the experience with different kinds of triangles might exist for any one subject, but this possibility offers no explanation of why the same triangle enjoys this superiority for nearly all subjects. Incidentally, the equilateral triangle which might plausibly be expected to be the one with which a person normally has the most experience has neither the highest nor the lowest threshold of the three kinds of triangles used in this study. In the second place, it will be remembered that in the case of each triangle series the group mean closure threshold based upon the second half of the separate determinations for each subject was slightly higher than was the threshold based upon the first half of the determinations for each subject (See Table V). None of these differences is, however, statistically significant. Hence, while the subject had some experience with the various incomplete forms of each triangle series during the course of the experiment, it did not significantly influence his closure threshold. Any empirical explanation of closure would, of course, have to assume that this experience would result in a lowering of the threshold. As a matter of fact, the obtained differences between the first and second half mean thresholds indicate that any changes which did occur during the experiment were in the direction of higher thresholds rather than in the direction of lower ones. There are, of course, two obvious objections to this last criticism of the empirical explanation of closure. First, it is possible that the subjects had already had so much experience with partial representations of triangles that the small amount of experience gained during the experiment was ineffective in causing any difference in the closure threshold. In other words, the process of learning to recognize complete figures upon the basis of perception of their parts had possibly already reached a final level. While this contention is very reasonable, it leaves to be explained the fact that this final level was reached at different points in the case of different triangles. Second, the slight increase in the closure threshold during the experiment might be explained on the basis of fatigue. This claim is not very tenable in view of the fact that only one triangle series was presented during one experimental session (except for four subjects), that the subject had a short rest interval after each six to ten stimulus presentations, that a rest of three or four minutes was given at the end of the first half of the test. In summary, then, an explanation of closure in terms of traditional psychological concepts would have to be stated in empirical terms. It is difficult to offer an interpretation of the results of the present study on the basis of such an explanation because its use in this connection necessitates the assumption that nearly all of the subjects used had had significantly different amounts of experience with the different kinds of triangles. The present writer feels that this assumption is unjustified. Also, the fact that the closure thresholds did not change significantly during the experiment and that what change did occur was in a direction opposite to what one would anticipate on the basis of empirical principles militates against the acceptance of any explanation of closure involving the effects of experience as the primary determinant of its occurrence.

    b. The Main Experimental Findings in the Light of Gestalt Concepts. The Gestalt writers have been no more definite than have the empiricists in giving a detailed explanation of what happens when closure occurs. The present study does not supply this information, but it does demonstrate that progressive changes in the degree of completeness of a figure result in a rather sudden change in the way the presentation is organized. It is possible to suggest the basis of this change in the light of the principles of brain activity supported by the Gestalt writers. These writers speak of perception as being the result of potential differentials in the cortex (12, pp. 185-188) and then further suggests that the potential patterns set up internal organizational forces which tend to resolve themselves to a simple stable pattern (11, pp. 138-176). Such an hypothesis of brain activity during perception may be applied to the present situation. The primary assumption involved in such an explanation is that each part of the figure (say, the two angles of the figures used in the present study) is represented cortically by an area having a potential level different from that of the rest of the cortex. A secondary assumption is that two areas of potential difference will be subject to organizational forces and that this organization will tend to be as simple and well balanced as possible. There are, however, two fundamentally different ways in which the two angles of the forms used here may be organized. That is, they may be organized in a dual manner as two separate figures having a balanced relationship to the whole visual field, or they may be organized in a unitary manner as parts of one figure. Obviously, the relative strength of the forces acting toward dual and unitary structurization of the field is a function of the percentage of the figure present. When the figure is very incomplete the tendency to perceive each angle separately is stronger than is that to see the angles in a unitary manner. With the slow increase of the percentage of the perimeter present, a critical point is reached at which the tendency toward a unitary organization becomes stronger than the tendency toward a dual structuring of the field. Phenomenologically, this point corresponds to the experience of closure. In terms of the present study this point represents the place in the series at which occurred the shift from the quality of twoness to the quality of oneness.

The different thresholds for the different kinds of triangles, from this point of view, merely seems to indicate that the organization forces are affected not only by the completeness of the figure, but also by the kind of figure it is (*i.e.*, by the angular characteristics of the forms, in this case). Attention may be called to the fact that there is a perfect correspondence between the size of the indicated apex angle and the threshold of closure. That is, the small apex triangle series (T-III) had the lowest threshold; the large apex triangle series (T-II) had the largest one. There are other experimental data which may be considered consistent with this finding. Zigler (23) found that the apex of a visually perceived triangle has the greatest attributive significance. Collier (1) found acute angle forms to be easier to recognize in peripheral vision than are obtuse angle forms. Zigler and Barrett (24) found acute angle forms (and specifically triangles) are easier to perceive tactually than are obtuse angle forms, and Lindemann (14) showed the gamma movement to be correlated with the shape characteristics of the figure. In the case of triangles having horizontal base lines, a violent gamma movement occurred at the apex. Hence, angular forms are shown to be highly organized. Further, acute angle forms appear to have a superiority in this respect over obtuse angle forms. Finally, in the case of triangles, the apex appears to be the point of the highest expression of organizational dynamics. In summary, then, two statements may be made. (1) Closure may be considered as an expression of organizational dynamics. (2) The differences between the closure thresholds of the three main series of triangles appears to be largely due to the fact that the tendency toward unitary organization of the field is partially a function of the angular characteristics of the figure and possibly, but to a lesser extent, of the absolute size of the forms.

C. *Secondary Experimental Findings.* 1. THE SIGNIFICANCE OF THE
FIRST HALF-SECOND HALF ANALYSIS OF THE DATA. It has already been
noted that the group's mean closure threshold for each triangle series
computed upon the basis of each subject's first ten threshold determinations was not significantly different from the group's mean
threshold computed upon the basis of each subject's last ten
determinations. It has already been suggested, since fatigue does not
appear to be a very likely explanation of the small increase in the
threshold during the experiment, that experience within the limits of
that given in this experiment does not appear to influence the closure
threshold. Further elaboration of this point is not necessary, but the
writer wishes to call attention to the similarity between this finding
and Gottschaldt's (5, 6) demonstration that the amount of experience which his subjects had with simple geometrical forms did not
appreciably change the degree to which they spontaneously recognized these forms when they were embedded in complex figures. Apparently, in both the present investigation and in Gottschaldt's, the
primary importance of the configurational influences is demonstrated.

2. THE IMPLICATIONS OF THE HIGH POSITIVE CORRELATIONS. It is
highly significant that the performance of the subjects on any one of
the main series of triangles correlated highly with their performance
on either of the other two series of forms (See Table IV). As already
stated, these correlations show the degree to which a subject's mean
threshold tended to occupy on each of the three series of triangles
the same relative position with regard to the distribution of individual thresholds of the various members of the group. The importance
of these high positive correlations lies in the fact then that the subjects' general attitude (resulting from physiological condition, immediately preceding experience, and the like) at the time of taking
the test was not very important in determining the location of the
closure threshold. If the subject's attitude, as just defined, had been
of great importance in determining the location of his closure threshold, it would have resulted in variations from one test series to the
next, which, not being correlated with variations caused by similar
factors in the case of the other subjects, would have greatly reduced
the measured coefficients of correlation. The fact that these positive
correlations are high indicates that the threshold for each series of
triangles was dominantly determined by a relatively permanent or-
ganism-stimulus field relationship.

REFERENCES

1. COLLIER, R. M. An experimental study of form perception in indirect vision. *J. comp. Psychol.*, 1931, **11**, 281-290.
2. DODGE, R. An improved exposure apparatus. *Psychol. Bull.*, 1907, **4**, 10-13.
3. FUCHS, W. Untersuchungen über das Sehen der Hemianopiker und Hemiamblyopiker. II: Die totalisierende Gestaltauffassung. *Zsch. f. Psychol.*, 1921, **86**, 1-143.
4. GIBSON, J. J. The reproduction of visually perceived forms. *J. exp. Psychol.*, 1929, **12**, 1-39.
5. GOTTSCHALDT, K. Über den Einfluss der Erfahrung auf die Wahrnehmung von Figuren. I. Über den Einfluss gehäufter Einprägung von Figuren auf ihre Sichtbarkeit in umfassenden Konfigurationen. *Psychol. Forsch.*, 1926, **8**, 261-317.
6. GOTTSCHALDT, K. Über den Einfluss der Erfahrung auf die Wahrnehmung von Figuren. II. Vergleichende Untersuchungen über die Wirkung figuraler Einprägung und den Einfluss spezifischer Geschehensverläufe auf die Auffassung optischer Komplexe. *Psychol. Forsch.*, 1929, **12**, 1-87.
7. HARTMANN, G. W. The concept and criteria of insight. *Psychol. Rev.*, 1931, **38**, 242-253.
8. HELSON, H. The psychology of *Gestalt. Amer. J. Psychol.*, 1926, **37**, 25-62.
9. HEMPSTEAD, L. The perception of visual form. *Amer. J. Psychol.*, 1900, **12**, 185-192.
10. KOFFKA, K. *Perception:* an introduction to the *Gestalt-Theorie. Psychol. Bull.*, 1922, **19**, 531-581.
11. KOFFKA, K. *Principles of Gestalt psychology.* New York: Harcourt, Brace and Co., 1935.
12. KÖHLER, W. An aspect of Gestalt psychology. In Carl Murchison (Ed.), *Psychologies of 1925.* Worcester, Mass.: Clark Univ. Press, 1928, 163-195.
13. LIEBMANN, S. Über das Verhalten farbiger Formen bei Helligkeitsgleichheit von Figur und Grund. *Psychol. Forsch.*, 1927, **9**, 300-353.
14. LINDEMANN, E. Experimentelle Untersuchungen über das Entsehen und Vergehen von Gestalten. *Psychol. Forsch.*, 1922, **2**, 5-60.
15. MEAKIN, F. Mutual inhibition of memory images. *Psychol. Monog.*, 1903, **4**, 235-275.
16. OGDEN, R. M. Insight. *Amer. J. Psychol.*, 1932, **44**, 350-356.
17. OGDEN, R. M. *Psychology and education.* New York: Harcourt, Brace and Co., 1932.

18. REISER, O. L. The logic of Gestalt psychology. *Psychol. Rev.*, 1931, **38**, 359-368.
19. ROSENBLOOM, B. L. Configurational perception of tactual stimuli. *Amer. J. Psychol.*, 1929, **41**, 87-90.
20. STREET, R. F. A gestalt completion test. A study of a cross section of intellect. *Teach. Coll. Contrib. Educ.*, 1931, No. 481.
21. TIERNAN, J. J. The principle of closure in terms of recall and recognition. *Amer. J. Psychol.*, 1938, **51**, 97-108.
22. WERTHEIMER, M. Untersuchungen zur Lehre von der Gestalt. II. *Psychol. Forsch.*, 1923, **4**, 301-350.
23. ZIGLER, M. J. An experimental study of visual form. *Amer. J. Psychol.*, 1920, **31**, 273-300.
24. ZIGLER, M. J., and BARRETT, R. A further contribution to the tactual perception of form. *J. exp. Psychol.*, 1927, **10**, 184-195.
25. ZIGLER, M. J., and NORTHUP, K. M. The tactual perception of form. *Amer. J. Psychol.*, 1926, **37**, 391-397.

....

A Cross-Cultural Investigation of Closure*,1

Donald N. Michael

ACCORDING to Gestalt theory, to quote Köhler, "sensory organization . . . appears as a primary fact which arises from the elementary
dynamics of the nervous system" (4, p. 199). To be sure, the Gestaltists have indicated that perceptual organization is the product of
both internal and external organizing forces: those "within the
process in distribution itself which will tend to impress on this distribution the simplest possible shape" and those "between this distribution and the stimulus pattern which constrain the stress toward
simplification" (5, p. 138). But while the Gestaltists concede the
effects of external stimulus constraints on the organization of perceptions, it seems safe to say that they have not considered in detail
the effects of previous experience and learned responses on the so-
called internal organizing forces. That is, given the same external
stimuli, will Ss with different previous experience with those stimuli
organize their perceptions similarly? The problem is not whether
perceptual organization is or is not completely independent of neural
processes, since obviously it must be dependent on them at some
level. Rather, the problem is how far along a perceptual organization
continuum, so to speak, do such processes determine perception in-

* From *J. abnorm. soc. Psychol.*, 1953, **48**, 225-230. Reprinted by permission
of the author and the publisher.

¹ This research was facilitated by the Laboratory of Social Relations, Harvard University, in conjunction with the research project on the Comparative
Study of Values. The research was undertaken with funds provided by the
Social Science Division of the Rockefeller Foundation. The writer wishes to
thank Professor Jerome Bruner for suggestions on the design of this experiment and Professors Clyde Kluckhohn and Evon Vogt for advice and assistance
in the field. He also wishes to thank Dr. Eleanor Maccoby and Professor
Nathan Maccoby for suggestions on the analysis and interpretation of these
data.

dependently of the particular experience context of the individual.[2] It may be that some of the so-called "sensory organizations . . . which arise from the elementary dynamics of the nervous system" are instead universally *learned* types of sensory organization within a given culture. If this is so, then it is possible that such learned responses are masked by their cultural universality and thereby are taken for innate. Therefore, it was the purpose of this study to determine whether the process of closure is such a learned response or whether the Gestalt contention that closure is a general law of innate perceptual organization tends to be substantiated.

In order to determine whether or not the tendency to closure is dependent on culturally determined perceptual organization, it was necessary to compare response patterns of two cultures, one of which stressed closure and one of which stressed nonclosure, both in terms of the actual stimulus patterns (e.g., ornamental designs) prevalent in the culture and in terms of the values (i.e., directives for behavior) stressed in the cultures. The two cultures used in this experiment were Anglo-Saxon American and Navaho Indian.

It seems safe to propose that Western European culture in general and American culture in particular stress the concept of closure. In the area of asthetics and design, unbroken continuity (e.g., streamlining) and symmetry are emphasized. And among the ideal behavior patterns favored are those stressing task completion, both materially and temporally.

On the other hand, students of the Navaho have long remarked on the Navaho "fear of completing anything" (7, p. 226). "As a spirit outlet the basketmaker leaves an opening in the design; the weaver leaves a small slit between the threads . . ." (7, p. 226) and so on. In Navaho values there is a "need to have no completely enclosing frame around any of the works so that the evil inside can have an opening through which to leave" (8, p. 12). In discussing the dimension of generality in value systems, Kluckhohn says: "a negative value in Navaho culture is fear of closure" (6, p. 413). Not only is emphasis on nonclosure primary in the Navaho value system, but, as indicated above, it pervades their designs. For example, on pottery an ornamental band around the pot is left incomplete. There is an

---

[2] See, e.g., Bruner, J. S. Personality dynamics and the process of perceiving. In G. Ramsey and R. Blake (Eds.), *Perception: an approach to personality.* New York: Ronald Press, 1951. Ch. V.

opening on the average of 1 to 5 degrees in the band. Thus, while the Navaho exposure to circles is by no means limited to those with openings, it is probable that they are systematically exposed to more experiences stressing nonclosure than would be ascribed to white Americans.

It was presumed that if Navaho experiences of the sort described above contribute to a differential capacity, compared to whites, to respond to nonclosure, there should be unacculturated Navaho Indians who reflect this differential capacity.

The stimuli selected for testing the Ss' responses were a series of circles and double concentric circles with and without breaks in their periphery. Circles were selected as the stimuli because the Gestalt experiments on closure had been performed using circles and because the circle is a familiar visual pattern in the Navaho culture. Furthermore, in many of its occurrences in Navaho culture, the circle is deliberately not completed, i.e., a small opening is left in the periphery. The double concentric circle was also utilized because it is similar to both a common pattern used in Navaho sandpaintings and to many design patterns in white American culture.

Therefore, the null hypothesis to be tested was: there is no significant difference in the response behavior (i.e., tendency to closure) to a set of open and closed circles between samples of white Americans and Navaho Indians.

METHOD

Subjects. The sample of 20 white Americans consisted of male and female members from the very small farming community of Homestead, New Mexico, located in the same region as that from which the Navaho sample was obtained.[3] These Ss were exposed to the stimuli in a darkened warehouse.

The Navaho sample of 20 Ss consisted of male and female members of the surrounding Navaho reservation.[4] They were exposed to their stimuli in a darkened building attached to a local trading store.

Apparatus. The experimental situation consisted of exposing the Ss to

---

[3] Various research projects involving this community are still under way. It is therefore necessary to preserve the anonymity of the community by giving it a fictitious name in order that there be no possibility that information of the results of research on the community can affect its attitude toward the present researchers, thereby distorting future research findings.

[4] It is the judgment of Professors Evon Z. Vogt and Clyde Kluckhohn that the Navahos used in this experiment can be considered as unacculturated representatives.

a series of circles, with varying degrees of incompleteness, for .1 second. The stimuli were projected on 2 x 2" slides through a translucent plastic screen (the screen being between the projector and the subjects) and appeared on the screen as 12 inches in diameter.[5] The Ss sat four to six feet from the screen. Thus the circle subtended a visual angle of 7.1 to 5.6 degrees.

The size of incompletion of the stimulus circle ranged from zero to eight degrees in one-degree steps. A double concentric circle with a break in the outer circle of 0, 1, or 7 degrees was also used. Further, it was possible to control the light intensity of the projected image (the Variac was patched into the light circuit) and the Ilex No. 3—Acme shutter screwed to the front of the projection lens allowed variations in time of exposure. The use made of these extra facilities and additional stimuli will be discussed later.

Procedure. Each S had a pencil, pad of paper, and writing board on which to record what each thought he or she saw.[6] There was sufficient light projected through the screen between stimuli projections to make this procedure entirely feasible. The Ss were treated in groups of from 3 to 6 persons per group.

Directions were given orally by the experimenter to the white group and orally through a Navaho interpreter to the Navaho group.[7] The instructions were as follows:

I want to know what you see on my screen when I show a picture to you for a very little time. The pictures are simple designs. Each time I show a picture you draw what you see on the screen on a page of the pad of paper you have. Draw one picture on each page, using one page after the other. If you don't see anything on the screen, leave that page empty and turn over to the next page. Because I want to know what you yourself first see, please don't look at what the other people are drawing and don't talk about it. I will tell you when I am going to show each picture. Then I will show the picture. Then you draw what you see. Then I will tell you to turn the page. Then I will tell you that I am going to show another picture, and so on. Are there any questions? . . . Now we will start. Here is a picture.

---

[5] The projector was a 35-mm commercial model manufactured by the Three Dimensional Corporation of Chicago, Illinois under the designation, "TDC Vivid." The 300-watt projection lamp was driven by 110 volts at 60 cycles and blower cooled. Light intensity was adjusted through a Variac (General Radio Co. type V-5MT) set at a scale reading of 40.

[6] It should be noted that all Navahos are able to use a pencil and paper as means for representing what they see.

[7] Professor Clyde Kluckhohn checked the Navaho interpretation of the directions and was of the opinion that it adequately expressed the purposes and directives of the English version.

After the recording was completed, each pad of pictures was checked while S was still present so that any drawings which might be misinterpreted could be discussed with him. Finally the Ss were requested not to discuss their experience with others because it would spoil them for the experiment.[8]

RESULTS

The four measures used for determining differential capacity to perceive the openings in the circles were (a) the total number of openings seen, (b) the number of persons seeing the openings regardless of size, (c) the mean number of openings seen per person, and (d) the median size of openings seen.

TABLE I. RESPONSES TO CIRCLE STIMULI

Subjects	Number of Circles Seen			Number of Persons Seeing Any Circles		
	Open	Closed	Totals	Open	Closed	Totals
Navaho	43	137	180	16	4	20
White	55	125	180	18	2	20
Totals	98	262	360	34	6	40

The distribution of the number of circles seen as open and as closed by the whites and the Navahos appears in Table 1. Note that since, conceivably, the truly closed circle could have been seen as open, responses to it are included in this distribution. A $p = .20$, obtained by Fisher's exact method for chi square (3, pp. 96-197), indicates that there is no significant difference between the total number of openings seen by the whites and Navahos.

Reference to Table 2 gives the number of persons seeing *an* opening. Here $p = .66$ as obtained by Fisher's exact method for chi square, indicating no significant difference between the total number of whites and Navahos seeing any opening at all.

---

[8] Because of the nature of the relationship between the researchers and the natives, both white and Indian, which has been developed over many years, it is most likely that this request was carefully honored. At any rate, all Ss were asked preliminary to the experiment if they knew what it was about, and none indicated that they did.

The mean number of openings seen per person for the Navahos was 2.69; for the whites it was 3.06. The standard t test gives a $t = .555$ which is a p of approximately .5. This too is clearly not a significant difference. Further, since the data are considerably skewed, and since one would expect such a distribution of the mean number of openings to be skewed toward the lower end, it was felt advisable to use Festinger's F test (2). Here an F of 1.22 was obtained which is less than the F of 1.83 required for significance at the .05 level.

The final test for significance was on the median size openings seen by whites and Navahos. These medians may be regarded as a measure of that size opening for which the probabilities of a "closed" response and an "open" response are equal. The median size opening for Navahos was 6 degrees and for the whites 5.4 degrees. This gives a $t = .718$ or a p of approximately .45. As such, there is no significant difference between the median size opening seen by whites and Navahos.

Thus the null hypothesis to the effect that there are no significant differences in the tendencies of whites and Navahos to perceive open circles as closed is not disproved.

DISCUSSION

The fact that this is a cross-cultural study requires that several other conditions must be considered which might conceivably lead to the same results as those indicated above, but for reasons having little to do with the presence or absence of innate neurological processes such as closure. Some of these factors which possibly are culturally controlled follow.

Visual Acuity. If the Navaho's ability to make fine visual discriminations is less than that of the white sample, then we would hardly expect them to see openings when they are physically incapable of doing so under the best of seeing conditions. The possibility that Navahos simply cannot see as well as whites was controlled as follows. In all cases where S recorded no openings during the exposure, a circle with a 1° opening was projected for an unlimited time and S was then asked again to report on what he saw. In the very few cases where S was unable to report the opening the data were discarded. (This procedure was also used for the white sample.)

TABLE 2. NUMBER OF PEOPLE SEEING 7° OPENING IN CIRCLE
AT VARIOUS LIGHT INTENSITIES

Light Intensity*	Number of People Seeing Opening		Cumulative Number of People Seeing Opening	
	White	Navaho	White	Navaho
15	1	1	1	1
20	5	1	5	2
25	6	2	7	4
30	10	2	11	5
35	14	8	15	9
40	12	8	15	11
45	11	9	16	11
50	12	7	16	12

* The numbers indicating the light intensity settings are the same as those on the indicator dial on the Variac. The larger the number, the brighter the image.

Light Intensity. Do Navahos require more light to discriminate as well as whites? Since E had control over light intensity, some pre-testing was done in order to find an intensity level "acceptable" to both whites and Navahos. Setting the Variac at a scale value of 40 seemed to be a good working value. However, each S was also exposed to a 7° opening at a variety of light intensities so that more precise comparisons could be made later. The data are given in Table 2.

While there is a difference in the number of Ss seeing an opening of 7° at a light setting of 40, the difference is not significant, either in terms of the actual percentage of the population seeing the opening or the cumulative percentage of the population seeing the opening. The p's are .34 and .36, respectively. They are based on the difference between proportions, corrected for continuity, between uncorrelated samples (1, pp. 76-83). It is true that for values rather lower than 40, the whites consistently see better than the Navahos (except at the lowest intensity of 15), but it is clear that at the light intensity used in obtaining the results reported above, no significant difference existed in the tendency of either group to see the opening. Further, essentially the same results obtain when the double concentric circle with the 7°opening in the outer one is presented under

TABLE 3. NUMBER OF PEOPLE SEEING 7° OPENING IN DOUBLE
CONCENTRIC CIRCLE COMPARED TO LIGHT INTENSITY

Light Intensity*	Number of People Seeing Opening		Cumulative Number of People Seeing Opening	
	White	Navaho	White	Navaho
15	0	2	0	2
20	3	2	3	3
25	10	3	10	5
30	10	2	10	5
40	11	8	13	9
50	9	10	13	11

* See footnote under Table 2.

varying light intensities (see Table 3). Thus, at the light intensity used, there is no reason to believe that the Navahos cannot discriminate as well as do the whites.

"Set" Tendencies. The Navaho tendency to "sit tight" has often been commented on by anthropologists. "When in a new and dangerous situation do nothing. If a threat is not to be dealt with by ritual canons, it is safest to remain inactive. If a Navaho finds himself in a secular situation where custom does not tell him how to behave, he is usually ill at ease and worried. . . . The American tradition says, 'When danger threatens, do something.' The Navaho tradition says: 'Sit tight and perhaps in that way you may escape evil' " (7, p. 226). Is this tendency operating here to a greater extent than it is on the white sample? If it is assumed, for example, that the initial exposure is seen as a closed circle, will there be a greater tendency on the part of the Navaho to be set to continue to see them as closed? In an effort to test for "set," E did the following experiment. One set of Ss was exposed to circles with openings of 8°, 5°, and 1°, exposed in sequence from the largest to the smallest, and each of the circles was exposed for 5, 1, 1/2, 1/5, 1/10, and 1/25 of a second in that order. Each opening was presented through all time exposures before the next size opening was presented. Another set of Ss was exposed to precisely the same variables, only in their case the order was ascending: i.e., the smallest opening was exposed first and for the

shortest time interval. Unfortunately, the only available white and Navaho samples were too small to be statistically stable. However, analysis of the data would seem to indicate that, trendwise at least, perceptual set tendencies for this sort of stimulus are not importantly different between the two groups.

Unfamiliarity with the Experimental Situation. Certainly one feels that the total experimental situation is likely to be less familiar to the Navaho than to the whites even if the whites do live in a small farming community. As such, one might expect this to have some effects on Navaho behavior. However, it is difficult to see how unfamiliarity can account for tendencies to see figures as closed or as open unless one hypothesizes which type of response is more "natural" in an unfamiliar situation. But it is the problem of determining, so to speak, which type of response is the more natural that is the subject of this research. Thus, while unfamiliarity may affect the perception of open or closed circles, we cannot say which way the effect would work without begging the question.

Effect of Context. It is possible that, because the experimental context is probably relatively meaningless for the Navaho, openings were not perceived, whereas *in* context they would have been perceived. In other words, fewer breaks are seen precisely because, unless the context is important, no careful visual discrimination of the breaks occurs: i.e., everything that is not explicitly (contextually) broken is *ipso facto* closed.[9] This would be in keeping with Kluckhohn's description of the Navaho characteristic of describing experience in terms of events rather than by attributes, especially when it is remembered that nonclosure in Navaho culture usually occurs in specific contexts (e.g., sand paintings, pottery, and basket ornamentation).

It is difficult to verify this point experimentally. For one thing, there was no way of determining whether a nonclosure response, in a context, was by association with the rest of the context or independent of the context. Or to state the point in more Gestaltist terms, it would be difficult in complex stimulus situations to predict the relative degree of dominance and interaction of various tendencies

---

[9] Note, however, that if one accepts this argument, one also accepts the implication that the capacity to discriminate breaks as such is learned and that nonperception of breaks is not due to autochthonous processes, which, as an argument in this experimental situation, seems to beg the question.

to prägnanz. Moreover, there do not seem to be any contextually equivalent white and Navaho stimulus situations.[10]

Thus within the range of considerations discussed above, the results of this experiment do not disprove the null hypothesis which was that there is no significant difference in the response behavior (i.e., tendency to closure) to a set of open and closed circles between samples of white Americans and Navaho Indians. This finding does not refute the Gestalt contention that closure is an innate and not a learned process. It does not prove, however, that closure is not a learned process since it is still possible that closure is a consequence of culture-bound learning which is not detectable by the methods used herein. The results of this research would be critical only if there were differences in the data. Then it could be stated that the ability to perceive closure is learned.

It may thus be argued that these results are, possibly, consequences of unspecified or indeterminate cultural characteristics which may override any "real" differences in perceptual response, learned or innate. That such may indeed be the case argues well for more cross-cultural research. Until more such research is undertaken, there will be considerable indeterminancy about the contributions to behavior, in the laboratory situation, of innate or pan-cultural processes, compared to the contributions of culture-bound learning, which may underlie the whole repertory of behavior that the S (and E) brings to the laboratory situation.

SUMMARY

The purpose of this experiment was to determine the effect of differences in cultural conditioning on the perception of closure. One sample of Ss was Navaho Indians living in a culture stressing nonclosure, both in values and in ornamental design. The other sample

---

[10] In an effort to expose the Navaho to a stimulus of at least potential contextual significance, the 20 white and 20 Navaho subjects used in the main experiment described above were also exposed to a double concentric circle with an opening of 0, 1, or 7 degrees in the outer one. This design abstractly corresponds to the basic design of many sand paintings. Using the same analysis procedures described above, the results were (a) for the total number of openings seen, $p = .52$; (b) for the total number of persons seeing the openings, $p = .74$; (c) for the mean number of openings seen per person, $t = .82$ or $p = .4$. Because only three different sized openings were used, no useful estimate of the median size opening is available.

However, the three measures reported indicate clearly no significant difference in behavior of whites and Navahos to this stimulus.

of Ss was white Americans who stressed closure both in values and design. Closure was investigated by determining the differential capacity of the two samples of Ss to detect small openings in tachistoscopically presented circular stimuli. If the perception of closure is innate, as proposed by the Gestaltists, then culturally determined learning should have no effect on the perception of closure. If closure is primarily a learned perception, the differences in cultural experiences of the two samples might result in differences in ability to detect closure. The Ss were presented with circles with different size openings for various lengths of time. The measures used for determining differential capacity to perceive the openings in the circles were (a) the total number of openings seen, (b) the number of persons seeing the openings regardless of size, (c) the mean number of openings seen per person, and (d) the median size of openings seen. The results, for all conditions, gave p's which indicated no significant differences in the perception of closure between the two cultures. A number of factors involving culture differences which may have contributed to the results are discussed. The point is emphasized that considerable cross-cultural research will be necessary in order to eliminate the indeterminateness of these factors.

REFERENCES

1. EDWARDS, A. L. Experimental design in psychological research. New York: Rinehart, 1950.
2. FESTINGER, L. Statistical test for means of samples from skew populations. Psychometrika, 1942, 8, 205-210.
3. FISHER, R. A. Statistical methods for research workers. New York: Hafner, 1948.
4. KÖHLER, W. Gestalt psychology. New York: Liveright, 1947.
5. KOFFKA, K. Principles of Gestalt psychology. New York: Harcourt, Brace, 1935.
6. KLUCKHOHN, C. Values and value orientation in the theory of action. In T. Parsons and E. Shils (Eds.), Toward a general theory of action. Cambridge: Harvard Univer. Press, 1951. Pp. 388-433.
7. KLUCKHOHN, C., and LEIGHTON, DORTHEA. The Navaho. Cambridge: Harvard Univer. Press, 1946.
8. LEE, DORTHEA D. Religious perspectives of college teaching in anthropology. New Haven: The Edward W. Hazen Foundation, 1951.

....

Configurational Properties Considered 'Good' by Naïve Subjects*, †

MARIAN HUBBELL MOWATT

THE CONCEPT of the "good" configuration has been widely used since Wertheimer proposed it as a descriptive term to indicate the tendency of certain types of grouping to appear more spontaneously than others.[1] Experimenters have noted that in apparent movement, memory changes, and forms at threshold values, configurations tend toward symmetry, closure, and simplicity, and they have implied that these properties characterize all good configurations wherever found.[2] But to answer the question as to what constitute good configurations for the *subjects*, a new approach to the problem should be made, namely, an approach in which the Ss try to produce good configurations. Analysis of the configurations created by a large number of Ss should reveal whether or not the properties regarded as good by the configurational experimenters also characterize the productions of Ss given free rein to make as good configurations as possible.

---

*From *Amer. J. Psychol.*, 1940, **53**, 46-69. Reprinted by permission of the author and the publisher.

† This article is an abridgement of a dissertation presented to the faculty of Bryn Mawr College in partial fulfillment of the requirements for the degree of Doctor of Philosophy. The complete dissertation is on file in the library at Byrn Mawr College, Bryn Mawr, Pa. I am indebted to Professor Harry Helson of Bryn Mawr College for suggesting the problem and method, and for advice in writing the report, and to Professor Max Wertheimer of the New School for Social Research for aid in methods of treating the results.

[1] M. Wertheimer, Untersuchungen zur Lehre von der Gestalt, II, *Psychol. Forsch.*, 1923, **4**, 301-350.

[2] These experiments may be found in H. Helson, The Psychology of *Gestalt*, *Amer. J. Psychol.* 1925, **36**, 342-370, 494-526; 1926, **37**, 25-62, 189-223; and in K. Koffka, *Principles of Gestalt Psychology*, 1935, 129-132, 139-147, 493-506.

MATERIALS AND PROCEDURE

Method. The method of production, in which the *S*s are free to change given material in any way, was used in order to give the widest range of possibilities in the results. Thus a great variety of changes were produced, exemplifying goodness of form in many different ways.

Materials. The material consisted of forty geometrical figures, which appear in Fig. 1. A few were adapted from Fehrer's material,[3] and a few from Wulf's,[4] while the large majority were improvised in accordance with the following principles. One half of the figures were symmetrical on one or more axes, and one half were asymmetrical. Eight figures consisting of dots were used, and 32 consisting of lines. Of the latter, half had a closed or continuous outline, the other half consisting of unconnected lines or of one line with one or more changes of direction. While the figures contain a varying number of lines or dots, no figure is so chaotic that it may not be perceived in one glance. The figures were drawn in pencil (in order to allow for erasures) on separate sheets of white paper, 5½ x 8½ in., the longer dimension representing the horizontal as the sheets were presented. The figures were no larger than 2 in. in any dimension. This left adequate space on all sides for additions if desired. The *S*s were provided with pencils and erasers so that deletions as well as additions could be made.

Subjects. The *S*s were 50 young women students at Bryn Mawr College, having an average age of 19 yr. All but two were in the first semester of their first course in psychology. The other two had not taken more than an elementary course in psychology. All were ignorant of the problem under investigation.

Procedure. Every *S* was presented individually with a set of the 40 figures in random order, the order differing for each *S*. The sheets were placed face down on the table, with mimeographed instructions, as follows.

This is an experiment to find out what kinds of figures are most pleasing. When you have finished reading the directions, turn over the pages one at a time. Look at each figure. If you do not think it is as "good" a figure as it might be in any respect, change it in any way, adding or erasing as much as you like. There is no right or wrong in this experiment. When you have finished the first figure, place it face down before taking up the next. Once you have placed a figure down, do not refer to it again.

---

[3] E. V. Fehrer, An investigation of the learning of visually perceived forms, *Amer. J. Psychol.*, 1935, **47**, 187-221.

[4] F. Wulf, Beiträge zur Psychologie der Gestalt: VI. Über die Veränderung von Vorstellungen (Gedächtnis und Gestalt), *Psychol. Forsch.*, 1922, **1**, 333-373.

You may have as much as 55 min. for the experiment if necessary. But do not pause too long over any of the figures, since we want your first impression.

Please do not talk to anyone about the experiment until after it is over.

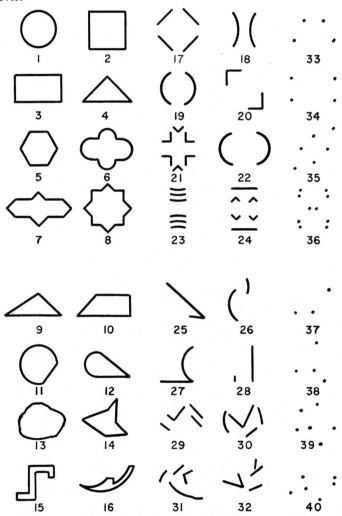

FIG. 1. The original figures. Figs. 1-8 are the closed symmetrical ones; 9-16, the closed asymmetrical ones; 17-24, the open symmetrical line figures; 25-32, the open asymmetrical line figures; 33-36, the open symmetrical dot figures; and 37-40, the open asymmetrical dot figures.

The Ss were also told that if they liked a figure the way it was given, or thought it good, they were to leave it that way and were not to feel that they must change all the figures. On the last page appeared the following directions.

On this page give your reasons for changing the figures as you did. Do not try to give a reason for each separate figure, but give any general principles which you may have followed. Do not refer back to the figures for this.

The Ss finished the experiment in varying lengths of time, ranging from 15 to 60 min. Some showed a disposition to change most of the figures painstakingly; others made very few or very slight changes.[5]

RESULTS

(A) Frequency of Changes in Various Types of Figures. Since the instructions allowed the Ss to make no changes if they so desired, those figures which remained unchanged can be considered good, for the Ss, in their original form. Each figure was presented to each of the 50 Ss, and of the total of 2000 figures, 1560, or 78% were in some way changed. A consideration of the frequency of changes in the various types of figure reveals striking differences pointing to certain properties considered good and poor.

(1) FIGURES. The individual figures least frequently altered are given in Table I, where it is found that the isosceles triangle and the circle were left unchanged by the largest percentage of Ss, 72% and 70% respectively, paralleling the finding of Helson and Fehrer[6] that the triangle tended to be seen as a form more frequently than other forms under reduced illumination, and the contention of Köhler[7] that the circle is the best *Gestalt*. The other figures frequently left unchanged—the hexagon, rectangle, and square—are likewise closed, symmetrical, simple, and regular forms; and these results confirm the high aesthetic ratings given these figures by Birkhoff's[8] formula for aesthetic measure.

---

[5] Another experiment in which a similar method was used is that of F. H. Lund and A. Anastasi, Aesthetic experience, *Amer. J. Psychol.*, 1928, **40**, 434-448. Their Ss were asked to complete unfinished figures. But their purpose was to find "the most aesthetic effect," and they do not present their results quantitatively.

[6] H. Helson and E. V. Fehrer, The rôle of form in perception, *Amer. J. Psychol.*, 1932, **44**, 79-102.

[7] W. Köhler, The problem of form in perception, *Brit. J. Psychol.*, 1923, **14**, 262-268.

[8] G. W. Birkhoff, *Aesthetic Measure*, 1933, 16-48.

TABLE I. FIGURES LEAST FREQUENTLY CHANGED BY THE Ss

No.	Figure	% Unchanged
4	Isosceles triangle	72
1	Circle	70
5	Hexagon	62
3	Rectangle	62
2	Square	60

At the opposite extreme are figures 28, 29, 37, 38 and 39 (Fig. 1), which were most frequently changed, changed by all but one of the Ss.[9] These figures are seen to be open, asymmetrical, and irregular figures. These properties must therefore be considered poor.

TABLE II. PERCENTAGE OF ALL TYPES OF FIGURES CHANGED

Type of Figure	Total Number*	Percentage Changed
Open asymmetrical dot figures	200	98
Open asymmetrical line figures	400	95
Av.	600	96
Open symmetrical dot figures	200	92
Open symmetrical line figures	400	88
Av.	600	89
Closed asymmetrical figures	400	73
Closed symmetrical figures	400	40
All open figures	1200	92
All closed figures	800	56
All asymmetrical figures	1000	87
All symmetrical figures	1000	70
All figures	2000	78

* These values are the product of number of figures by number of Ss (50).

(2) TYPES. In Table II the percentages of change are given by types for the various figures. The type of figure showing the highest percentage of changes is the group of open asymmetrical dot figures, of which 98% were changed. Combining this group with the open asymmetrical line figures, of which 95% were changed, we find that 96% of all open asym-

---

[9] The same S was responsible for the one unchanged figure in all these cases. This S changed none of the figures. One might ask if she really entered into the spirit of the experiment, or if she was totally lacking in aesthetic sensibility. In any case, her results were kept.

metrical figures were changed. This indicates clearly that this type of figure is not considered good. While open symmetrical figures are changed in 89% of all cases, this percentage is significantly below (Table III) that for open asymmetrical figures (96%). The figures embodying opposite characteristics, *i.e.* the closed symmetrical figures, are changed least frequently or in only 40% of the cases, while closed asymmetrical figures are changed in 73% of all cases, as is shown in Table II. The difference between these two types of figure is evident from the critical ratio of 9.8 (Table III).

TABLE III. CRITICAL RATIOS OF THE DIFFERENCES BETWEEN THE
PERCENTAGES OF CHANGE IN VARIOUS TYPES OF FIGURE

Type of Figure	Critical Ratio (Diff./σdiff.)
Open asymmetrical dot *vs.* open asymmetrical line figures	1.8
Open symmetrical dot *vs.* open symmetrical line figures	1.4
Open asymmetrical figures *vs.* open symmetrical figures	4.3
Closed asymmetrical figures *vs.* closed symmetrical figures	9.8
All open figures *vs.* all closed figures	18.8
All asymmetrical figures *vs.* all symmetrical figures	9.4

Comparing all closed with all open figures, 56% of the former as against 92% of the latter were changed, a difference of enormous significance, (C.R. 18.8, Table III) both statistically and psychologically. The difference of 17% between the symmetrical and the asymmetrical groups, while not as large, is still a significant one. A consideration of Table II reveals the steadily decreasing proportion of figures changed with an increase in the symmetry and closure of the figures. That the differences in *configurational* properties are significant and not the differences in *components* is shown by the fact that the critical ratios holding between the dot and the line figures are *not* statistically significant (1.8 and 1.4 in Table III).

The results so far show that symmetry and, even more strongly, closure are considered good properties, as judged by the relatively few changes in these groups. The significance of these properties will be discussed below in connection with the types of changes made.

(*B*) *Consistency and Variety in the Changes Made.* In observing the extent to which the Ss agreed in their changes, we find that in no case were all the changes for a given figure exactly alike. Some of the simple dot figures in which many of the Ss simply connected the dots with lines showed the greatest consistency, *e.g.* No. 33 (Fig. 1), in which 21 of the Ss did exactly the same thing. On the other hand, No. 26 (Fig. 1) was changed by 48 of the Ss in 48 different ways, some of the changes being similar but in no case exactly alike. Though the majority of figures were changed in identical ways only by small groups of Ss, and in individual ways by the rest, nevertheless clear-cut principles are found to govern most of the changes. This fact is remarkable in view of the great variety of individual differences, and shows that changes which seem different from an atomistic point of view are actually in the same direction from the viewpoint of configurational properties.

(C) *Types of Changes Made.* We have next to answer the question: Are there any common properties or principles underlying the changes made in the 40 figures by the 50 Ss? The principles found to govern the changes form the most significant results of the experiment.

(1) GREATER DIFFERENTIATION AND SIMPLIFICATION. An important question for the problem of goodness of form is the relative importance of simplicity and complexity. That a good configuration is simple, and that our perceptual and memorial processes tend toward simplification of forms, has been frequently observed, for example, by Lindemann,[10] Allport,[11] and Perkins.[12] On the other hand such findings as Fehrer's point to complication of forms under certain conditions.[13] Our results may offer evidence toward a reconciliation of these seemingly opposed facts.

TABLE IV. PERCENTAGES OF FIGURES CHANGED BY THE
ADDITION AND BY THE SUBTRACTION OF LINES AND DOTS

Type of Change	Percentage
Addition of lines or dots	94
Subtraction of lines or dots	3
Number of lines or dots not affected	3

One approach to the problem is the purely atomistic method of considering the extent to which lines or dots were added to the original figures or subtracted by erasing. The proportions of figures

---

[10] E. Lindemann, Experimentelle, Untersuchungen über das Entstehen und Vergehen von Gestalten, *Psychol. Forsch.*, 1922, 2, 5-60.
[11] G. W. Allport, *Brit. J. Psychol.*, 1930, 21, 133-148.
[12] F. Perkins, Symmetry in visual recall, *Amer. J. Psychol.*, 1932, 44, 473-490.
[13] *Op. cit.*

to which parts were added, those from which parts were removed, and those in which the changes did not affect the number of lines or dots appear in Table IV. The large majority (94%) of all changes consist in the addition of lines or dots to the given figure, while parts are removed in only 3% of the changes.[14]

The addition of lines and dots, however, does not prove that the figures are made more complicated in such cases. For only a very atomistic view of complication would hold it to be the result of the mere presence of a larger number of parts. A figure of many parts arranged in an orderly manner may give an impression of less complexity than a figure with a smaller number of parts arranged in a haphazard manner, as Fig. 2 well shows. In Fig. 2, eight added lines

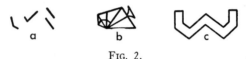

FIG. 2.

result in a more complex figure than eleven lines added in c. Certainly c is simpler in appearance than b. The difference seems to depend upon the orderly symmetrical arrangement of parts in c, which gives a unitary appearance. The lines of b, on the other hand, result in so many subdivisions that the figure possesses little unity. Indeed b appears like several figures merely "hitched" together. Thus the *organization* of the added lines may be more important than mere number in determining simplicity or complexity.

(2) CLOSURE. We have already observed (*supra*, Table II) that the open figures are changed much more frequently than the closed. This evidence in favor of closure as a good quality is fully supported by the nature of the changes themselves.

The proportions of such changes in the various classes of figure appear in Table V. The last row indicates that the tendency toward increasing and emphasizing closure is overwhelmingly greater than that toward decreasing or destroying it. Considering the two general trends toward and away from closure, we find that 61% of all changes enhance closure, while only 2% detract from it. Still more

---

[14] In explanation of this difference, it has been suggested that it is less trouble to add lines than to erase them. The fact that none of the original figures was extremely chaotic may also account for the small percentage of subtractions.

striking is the case of the open figures, where 87% of the open symmetrical, and 76% of the open asymmetrical group were changed in the direction of closure. The average of 81% is in striking contrast with the mere 5% of decreased and destroyed closure in closed figures. For theoretically the S was just as free to open a closed figure as he was to close an open one, yet he did the latter *sixteen* times more frequently than the former.

TABLE V. PERCENTAGES OF CHANGES INVOLVING CLOSURE IN THE VARIOUS TYPES OF FIGURE (An asterisk [*] means that occurrence is impossible by definition, whereas 00 indicates that the Ss might have made a change which was never made.)

| | Closure | | | | |
Type of Figure	In- creased	Empha- sized	De- creased	De- stroyed	Not Affected
Closed symmetrical	*	12	4	1	83
Closed asymmetrical	*	8	4	1	87
Open symmetrical	87	*	00	*	13
Open asymmetrical	76	*	00	*	24
All open	81		00		19
All closed	9		5		86
All	58	3	1	1	37
	61		2		

Thus the fact that open figures are most frequently changed, and the extent to which these figures are closed by the Ss both indicate the importance of closure as a factor in the good configuration. Rosenbloom found that with tactual stimulation, using metal outline figures, open figures were perceived as closed.[15] Similarly hemianopsic patients, reported by Fuchs saw a complete figure when only half or three-quarters of it was in their normal field of vision.[16] Gibson found a similar tendency in his work on memory,[17] *i.e.* fewer and smaller gaps appeared in the memory trace of forms than in the original figures. Closure thus operates both at the lower, automatic

---

[15] B. Rosenbloom, Configurational perception of tactual stimuli, *Amer. J. Psychol.*, 1929, **41**, 87-90.

[16] Koffka, *op. cit.*, 146.

[17] J. J. Gibson, The reproduction of visually perceived forms, *J. Exper. Psychol.*, 1929, **12**, 1-39.

level of memory trace and sensory processes, and at the level of conscious activity in the creation of good configurations.

(3) SYMMETRY. Symmetry is another property frequently mentioned as characteristic of a good configuration. Our results already give evidence that symmetry is an operative factor in that symmetrical figures were left unchanged more frequently than asymmetrical (Table II).

The percentages for each type of change in the four main classes of figures appear in Table VI. An outstanding result is that more than twice as many of the changes are in the direction of increased

TABLE VI. PERCENTAGES OF CHANGES INVOLVING SYMMETRY IN THE VARIOUS CLASSES OF FIGURE (An asterisk [*] means that occurrence is impossible by definition, whereas 00 indicates that the Ss might have made a change which was never made.)

Symmetry

Type of Figure	In-creased	Empha-sized	De-creased	De-stroyed	Not Affected
Closed symmetrical	9	38	38	1	14
Closed asymmetrical	50	12	10	*	28
Open symmetrical	17	5	21	2	55
Open asymmetrical	39	00	8	*	53
All symmetrical	15	13	25	1	46
	28		26		
All asymmetrical	43	4	9	*	45
	47		9		
All	30	8	16	1	45
	38		17		

or emphasized symmetry (38%) as in the direction of decreased or destroyed symmetry (17%). It is notable also that only 1% of all changes completely destroy the symmetry. The closed asymmetrical figures were changed toward increased symmetry more frequently than any other type—50% of all cases in this group, with the open asymmetrical group second—39% of all changes. One would expect the asymmetrical figures to have symmetry increased more frequently than symmetrical ones, and the table shows that this is true. But the difference between the open and the closed figures may probably be explained by the fact that Ss tend to close the open figures. Within the frame of reference of the given figure, closure represents a degree of improvement for an originally open figure, and further improvement in the form of symmetry does not seem to be demanded. With a closed asymmetrical figure, however, the possibility for increased closure is not present, and a change toward increased symmetry is therefore more frequently made. Each improvement is carried out with relation to the frame of reference of the original figure, rather than of the finished product. That the closed symmetrical group shows the highest percentage of emphasized symmetry corroborates the finding that this group had the highest percentage of differentiations, for the drawing of lines to emphasize symmetry constituted one form of differentiation. Taking all asymmetrical figures, we find 47% of all changes increase or emphasize this property. This result, together with the small percentages of decreased and destroyed symmetry, shows that this property, while not absolutely necessary for a good configuration, is nevertheless definitely preferred in a figure.

(4) "GOOD CONTINUATION" AND DYNAMIC PROPERTIES. Among the dynamic tendencies operating in the productions of the Ss, that known as "good continuation" frequently appeared.[18] Good continuation in a configuration means that one part of the pattern follows out the direction of another part, fulfilling the implications inherent in the latter. Thus figures in which the added lines continue the direction of given lines in the original figure were classified as cases of good continuation.

TABLE VII. PERCENTAGE OF CHANGES IN THE DIRECTION OF
GOOD CONTINUATION IN EACH TYPE OF FIGURE

Type of Figure	Good Continuation
Closed figures	23
Open figures (except dot figures)	27
Symmetrical figures	20
Asymmetrical figures	30
All figures	25

The percentage of changes showing the factor of good continua-

---

[18] Wertheimer, *op. cit.*

tion for each main type of figure appears in Table VII.[19] 25% of all changes are in the direction of good continuation. But this should by no means be interpreted as indicating that the remaining 75% of changes exemplified "poor continuation." It was impossible to count the cases of poor continuation, since no objective criterion for it could be set up, but very few cases which would strike the observer as definitely poor were noted. Rather, the other cases were changes in the direction of symmetry, differentiation, etc. In short, the absence of good continuation does not necessarily imply the presence of its opposite. Had a less strict interpretation of good continuation been used, the percentage of cases falling in this category would be much higher than 25%.

The difference between the classes of figures is worth noting, especially that between symmetrical and asymmetrical figures, which is statistically significant (C.R., 5.0). Since asymmetrical figures already lack balance, it is not surprising that the added lines sometimes accentuate this lack, often giving a feeling of motion to the figure.

(5) ACCENTUATION AND LEVELLING. In his study of memory for forms, Wulf stressed the fact that all changes in the memory trace were in accordance with the law of *Prägnanz*,[20] in that they brought about either an accentuation or a levelling of the characteristics of the figure. These two tendencies were found to govern some of the changes toward good configuration in our experiment. Since it was difficult to set up an objective criterion for these changes which did not yield many doubtful cases, no numerical count was made.

(6) FAMILIAR FORMS. In any experiment involving forms and their changes, the question most frequently raised is: Are these changes in the direction of more familiar figures? The answer to this question in this experiment is that 31% of all changes created familiar objects (*e.g.* houses, people, animals), familiar designs (such as flower patterns) or familiar geometrical figures. The latter include the circle, square, triangle, rectangle, ellipse and parallelogram. But to find the relative importance of structural properties versus the factor of familiarity in determining the changes, several possibilities must be considered.

---

[19] Dot figures were not included in the count, since it was difficult to consider the direction of lines in figures which did not originally possess lines.

[20] *Op. cit.*

First, there are cases in which a figure with properties found to be good, such as symmetry and closure, is changed into a more familiar form at the expense of good structural properties. We assume that in such cases familiarity, rather than goodness of form is the chief determinant of the change. At the opposite extreme are found cases in which a figure originally familiar in form is changed to have good characteristics at the expense of its familiarity. In these two types of change, either the factor of familiarity or that of good form is clearly predominant. But in addition, there is a great group of cases in which changes toward good properties also make the figure more familiar. Such equivocal cases cannot be taken as evidence either for or against the factor of familiarity as the cause of the change. Some of the figures left unchanged are likewise ambiguous, for example, the circle and the square, which are both familiar and good according to the results of the experiment.

TABLE VIII. CHANGES DETERMINED BY SYMMETRY OR
CLOSURE ALONE, AND BY FAMILIARITY ALONE

Type of Change	Number of Changes
Symmetry or closure but *not* familiar forms	867
Familiar forms but *not* symmetry or closure	167
Ratio	5 :1

In comparing the extent to which good configurational properties and the factor of familiarity governed the changes, only closure and symmetry were regarded as good properties, since they are more objectively determined than most of the others, and since the inclusion of differentiation and simplification would comprise the great majority of figures. Limiting goodness of form to symmetry and closure make the odds all the more strongly in favor of the factor of familiarity by cutting down the number of figures which possess good characteristics. In Table VIII the changes which increase the familiarity but do not in any way increase the symmetry or the closure of the figures, 167 in all, have been compared with the changes which increase or emphasize symmetry or closure, but do not increase the familiarity. Of the latter there are 867, making the ratio of changes determined entirely by these two good properties to those determined by familiarity (to the exclusion of these two factors) 5 to 1. This indicates that these structural factors account for five times as many of the changes as are accounted for on the basis of past experience alone.

The numbers given above do not include the figures left unchanged which must have been considered good, so we may now consider the results for *all* figures. The categories into which the figures were classified may be briefly summarized as follows. (1) Cases of familiar forms in which neither symmetry nor closure was present. (2) Cases of symmetry or closure which were not familiar forms. (3) Cases of forms both familiar and closed or symmetrical. (4) Cases of forms neither familiar nor closed nor symmetrical.

The numbers and percentages of figures falling in each category appear in Table IX. Closure and symmetry, in the absence of familiar forms, appear in 57% of all cases, while familiar forms lacking symmetry and closure appear in only 8% of all cases, showing that these two structural properties govern the Ss' preferences seven times as frequently as does the factor of familiarity of the figure. The remaining cases comprising 27% of all figures, in which both familiarity and good properties were present, and 7% in which neither occurred, cannot be used as evidence for the importance of either factor.

Thus the evidence from all figures, even more strongly than that from changed figures alone, is in favor of the structural properties as against past experience with the figures as determiners of good configurations. Our results are in line with those of Gottschaldt whose well-known experiment demonstrated the importance of structural properties over past experience in determining our perception.[21]

TABLE IX. OCCURRENCE OF FAMILIARITY VS. SYMMETRY AND CLOSURE

Classification	No.	Percentage of All Cases
(1) Familiar forms, no symmetry or closure	167	8
(2) Symmetry or closure, no familiar forms	1137	57
(3) Both familiar forms and symmetry or closure	548	27
(4) Neither familiar forms nor symmetry nor closure	148	8
Total	2000	100

A second question often raised in connection with the factor of familiarity is: Are such properties as closure, symmetry, etc., produced because they are good properties or merely because they are familiar qualities? Since they do occur more frequently in daily life than do their opposites (asymmetry, openness, etc.), were the Ss simply trying to produce patterns more familiar to them than the given forms? This question of the familiarity of *general properties* has not been attacked in this study, and other experiments must be designed to answer it. However, the overwhelming predominance of the structural properties over past experience with the figures, as

---

[21] K. Gottschaldt, Über den Einfluss der Erfahrung auf die Wahrnehmung von Figuren I., *Psychol. Forsch.*, 1926, **8**, 261-317.

shown by the ratios given above, points to the view that symmetry, closure, and such factors appear in the world of man-made objects because they are good and not because they are frequently experienced. It may be that we make things in these forms because they are physically stable and result in economy of behavior and perception, in short, because they are good: later, because we have made them, they become familiar.

(*D*) *Simultaneous Operation of Several Principles.* While the various types of changes were treated separately, one is not to suppose that in each figure only one principle underlies the change made by each *S*. Rather it was the rule that several of the principles operated together in determining a change.

TABLE X. REASONS GIVEN FOR CHANGES COMPARED WITH CHANGES

Reasons	Percentage	
	of all reasons	of all changes
Symmetry and balance	22	38
Closure, connection, and completion	20	60
Familiar forms:	26	31
objects	13	21
geometrical designs and figures	13	10
Simplicity, regularity and uniformity	9	37
Elaboration (differentiation)	6	68
Motion (good continuation)	4	25
Miscellaneous individual reasons	13	

(*E*) *Reasons for Changes.* We may next consider the reasons given by the *S*s for their changes in relation to the changes themselves. The reasons given show, on the whole, that the *S*s were often conscious of the principles they were employing in making their changes. The various types of reason are compared with the changes in Table X. Balance and symmetry were classified together, as were all terms conveying closure, such as connection and completion. The various reasons, though mirroring many of the tendencies found in the results, do not correspond numerically to the changes actually produced. The latter usually occur more frequently than the former. The two reasons most frequently mentioned, symmetry and closure, occur in about equal numbers, whereas changes toward closure far outnumber those toward symmetry. Familiar objects and simplicity were also created more frequently than they were mentioned by the *S*s. Elaboration (the reason most comparable to differentiation) is not mentioned nearly as frequently as it occurred. This discrepancy may indicate that the differentiation was not made for the sake of mere elaboration, but to accomplish some of the other aims of which the *S*s were conscious, *e.g.*, symmetry, connection, uniformity, and motion. This corroborates the finding already discussed, that the added lines were almost always in accord with the whole-properties of the figure. The fact that simplification is mentioned as a reason more frequently than elaboration is significant in showing that the *S*s preferred to regularize the figures rather than to complicate them. But even when they had no clearly formulated rule in mind, their productions reveal the operation of the principles we have discussed.

SUMMARY AND CONCLUSIONS

In this study we have attempted to find the principles governing the productions of naïve *S*s in attempts to produce good visual configurations by making changes in a wide variety of figures. A consideration of the types of figures changed shows that there is a steady increase in the chances that a change of some sort will take place as the figures go from the most closed and symmetrical to the most open and asymmetrical (Table II). We may conclude that closure and symmetry are considered good properties of a figure.

While lines or dots were added to the figures in 88% of all changes, this result is meaningless without a consideration of the ways in which they were added. The change occurring most frequently, in 68% of all changes, is that toward greater differentiation, a factor which must henceforth be reckoned as significant for goodness of form. The differentiation was found to exemplify configurational principles by enhancing the unity, simplicity or symmetry of the original figure and by emphasizing its natural subdivisions and regularities.

That the good configuration tends to be simple (unified and coherent) is shown by 38% of changes which were in this direction. That this number is not larger indicates that a good figure must not be too simple, or lacking in structuration.

Closure occurs in 61% of all changes, while the opposite tendency toward opening occurs in only 2%, showing again that the need for closure is strong in the good configuration.

Symmetry is increased in 47% of asymmetrical figures, and decreased in only 27% of symmetrical figures. Of all the changes, 38% are toward increased symmetry, showing that while not as important as closure, symmetry is nevertheless a preferred property.

That symmetry occurred less frequently than in other studies is partially explained by the tendency of the Ss to produce an effect of movement, incompatible with exact symmetry. This was frequently accomplished (25% of all changes) by continuing lines already present in the given figure.

Sharpening and levelling of the characteristics of the given figure also occurred to some extent.

Although 31% of the changes brought about familiar forms, good configurational properties often were operating in the same cases. Considering all figures, both changed and unchanged, we find that the two factors of symmetry and closure alone (without familiar forms) govern almost seven times as many cases as does the factor of familiarity in the absence of symmetry and closure. Thus configurational properties, rather than familiarity with the figures, determined the Ss' judgments.

Working with an entirely different method from other investigators, we find that many of the factors commonly interpreted as good are considered good by naïve Ss. Our Ss, although free to do as they chose, and with plenty of time at their disposal, still were guided by the principles found to govern the good configuration in more primitive psychological functions. These factors operate as well in the fields of art and aesthetics. Since the continuity with respect to these principles between the various levels of mental activity is so clear, we may minimize culture as the determinant of the changes in the experiment. The tendencies toward closure, symmetry, good continuation, simplicity and differentiation operate in the short exposure of forms, vision in the blind spot, and tactual perception of forms, where the factor of culture could scarcely enter into the almost automatic reaction of the S. The prevalence of these properties in such natural events as crystal formation, plant structures, etc., attests their fundamental nature.

....

A Quantitative Approach to Figural "Goodness"*

Julian E. Hochberg and Edward McAlister

E MPIRICAL STUDY of the Gestalt principles of perceptual organization is, despite their great heuristic value, frequently made difficult by their subjective and qualitative formulation. We wish to
suggest here that it may be possible to achieve *parallels* to these
"laws" of organization through analysis of the objective stimulus
pattern. This approach differs from similar ones (1, 6) in the orient-
ing hypothesis that, other things being equal, the probabilities of
occurrence of alternative perceptual responses to a given stimulus
(i.e., their "goodness") are inversely proportional to the amount of
information required to define such alternatives differentially; i.e.,
*the less the amount of information needed to define a given organ-
ization as compared to the other alternatives, the more likely that
the figure will be so perceived.*[1] However, to make this hypothesis
meaningful, it is necessary to determine empirically the stimulus
dimensions in which such "information" is to be measured. Therefore, we are concerned here mainly with so-called ambiguous stimuli
(which evoke no single response with a probability of 1.0), although
we will consider a possible theoretical bridge to the conditions of
what Gibson and Waddell (2) call "determining stimuli."

An objective definition of perceptual "goodness" requires some
measure of Ss' responses to stimulus figures. One such index might

---

* From *J. exp. Psychol.*, 1953, **46**, 361-364. Reprinted by permission of the
author and of the publisher.

[1] After preparation of this paper, we have been privileged to see the manuscript of a paper by Dr. F. Attneave, which contains a much more detailed
theoretical discussion of the tendency of the organism to perceive in terms of
"maximum redundancy"; although this formulation is probably not precisely
equivalent to the one proposed here, and the experimental techniques employed
are quite different in method and assumptions, we are agreed as to the basic
similarity of our general approaches.

be the *threshold* (illumination, tachistoscopic, etc.), the "best" pattern having the lowest limen; however, this measure is too laborious for any really extensive survey of stimuli, and restricts the variety of stimuli which can be tested, being highly sensitive to recognition effects. Instead, we propose to use as a measure of "goodness" the response frequency or the relative span of time devoted by S to each of the possible perceptual responses which may be elicited by the same stimulus. This seems close to the intuitive meaning of "goodness" (3), and its probabilistic nature may permit rapprochement between perceptual laws on the one hand, and "information theory" (and, eventually, behavior theory) on the other (5).

That the concept of "information" (here meaning the number of different items we must be given, in order to specify or reproduce a given pattern or "figure," along some one or more dimensions which may be abstracted from that pattern, such as the number of different angles, number of different line segments of unequal length, etc.) may be useful in approximating figural "goodness" is suggested by almost any random selection of Gestalt demonstrations. The illusion of transparency obtains in Fig. 1a when less information is required to specify the pattern as *two* overlapping rectangles (number of different line segments: 8, plus one for notation of locus of intersection; number of angles to be specified: either 8, plus one for notation of angle of intersection or, more simply, one right angle plus the repetition implied in the notation of rectangularity, plus one for notation of angle of intersection; etc.) than, alternatively, as

a

b

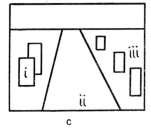

c

Fig. 1. Transparency, symmetry, and depth.

five irregular shapes (number of different line segments: 16; number of angles: 16; etc.). In Fig. 1b, less information is necessary to specify the symmetrical central black area as figure (number of different angles or points of inflection: 10, plus notation of duplication by bilateral symmetry) than the irregular white areas (number of different angles: 17). Listing the organizational "laws," from "good continuation" and "proximity" to the more general "simplicity" or "homogeneity," one finds translation impressively easy; the eventual utility of such translation depends, however, upon empirical determination of the dimensions of abstraction along which "information" is to be scored (shall we use "number of angles," "number of line segments," a weighted combination of these, or entirely different dimensions?), and upon the demonstration of a quantitative dependence of response frequency on the "information scores."

But can we approach the study of *determinate* (2) perception in this manner? Consider the task of representing spatial depth in two dimensions (Fig. 1c). Stimulus part *i* requires less specification as two overlapping rectangles than as L and rectangle; part *ii* requires less specification as a rectangle at a given slant (say 45°) than as trapezoid at other slants; finally, in one way part *iii* requires less specification as three identical rectangles at the appropriate distances than as different sized rectangles at other distances (although here rather involved assumptions are necessary about a size-distance relationship "built in" to the specifying coordinate system, etc.). Now, although each part is ambiguous, if we take all the parts together and if the slant and depth relationships associated with the "best" response to each stimulus part should coincide, the probability of obtaining just these slants and depths will be reinforced. As we add more such "cues," the probability of obtaining alternative depth responses approaches zero, and we may therefore consider *determinate* perception as different from the ambiguous variety, with which we are concerned at present, not in kind, but in degree.

METHOD

The approach outlined above is of little use unless it is possible to select dimensions for scoring "information" which are in correspondence with empirically obtained response-probabilities. The relative durations of alternate classes of response may be obtained by the usual method of pressing telegraph keys for each phase, but with this procedure Ss often report that the act of key-pressing altered the percept, which often fluctuated too rapidly to record; moreover, only one S can be used at a time. For these reasons, a sampling method was devised in which signal tones were presented by tape recording at "random" intervals and Ss indicated the phase they had perceived at the time each signal tone sounded. The frequency with which a given response is obtained is assumed to be proportional to the amount of time that response would have been obtained by "ideal" continuous recording.

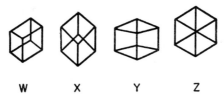

W X Y Z

FIG. 2. The Kopfermann "cubes."

The problem here was to apply this method to the case of Kopfermann cubes (Fig. 2) which may all be seen either as bidimensional patterned hexagons, or as tridimensional cubes (4). Drawings of each cube were presented in balanced order for 100 sec. each to 80 college students, providing a pool of over 2,600 responses for each stimulus; Ss indicated by pencil code marks which phase they had experienced just prior to each of the 33 signal tones presented at random intervals during the 100 sec.

RESULTS AND DISCUSSION

The results obtained correspond roughly to Kopfermann's more subjective findings: that figure which possesses the best phenomenal symmetry as a two-dimensional pattern was obtained least often as a cube (see Table 1). In terms of Gestalt theory, we would expect that the likelihood of seeing a figure in two dimensions would not only vary directly with its "goodness" in two dimensions, but, in addition, would vary inversely with its "goodness" in three dimensions. However, in this study, we may consider the "goodness" of the bidimensional patterns alone, since the tridimensional phase of each figure is more or less the same cube, the only appreciable difference being the apparent angle with respect to S. That is, we take the relative duration of two-dimensional responses to be proportional to the "goodness" of the two-dimensional patterns, the "goodness" of the tridimensional phases being approximately constant.

The bidimensional patterns may be analyzed for a large number of stimulus properties whose values will yield a relationship similar to that of the four points of bidimensional "goodness" response measures (Table 1), and the relationships fit quite well if these properties are differentially weighted. However, data are still needed on many other stimulus figures before a general system of factors and weights can be attempted, so that we are probably safer, at this stage, in merely noting stimulus variables which match the response relationships without employing differential weights. Two such stimulus dimensions fit the responses quite well, namely the number of angles and the number of line segments (Table 1). (Note that with the present figures, both dimensions represent the same geometrical fact.) Another dimension is the number of points of intersection required to define each bounded shape in the flat patterns. Any of

TABLE 1. BIDIMENSIONAL RESPONSES TO THE KOPFERMANN "CUBES" AND SOME TWO-DIMENSIONAL STIMULUS CHARACTERISTICS OF THE CUBES

"Cubes"	Bidimensional Responses (%)	Stimulus Characteristics		
		Line Segments	Angles	Points of Intersection
W	1.3	16	25	10
X	0.7	16	25	10
Y	49.0	13	19	8
Z	60.0	12	17	7

these scores would be consistent with an inverse relationship between response probability and the amount of "information," as discussed above, required to *specify* a given pattern; it is simple, however, to construct other figures whose relative strengths in alternate response phases may appear, at least intuitively, to be poorly handled by these dimensions, and we will need quantitative data from a wide sample of such figures before general stimulus dimensions can be chosen.

SUMMARY

Probability of alternate perceptual responses is suggested as an approximate quantitative index of "goodness" of figure, and a group technique is presented by which this score can be obtained for ambiguous stimuli. Using the technique to obtain group scores for relative duration of tri- and bidimensional phases of four Kopfermann cube figures, the resulting responses are not inconsistent with the working hypothesis, namely that the probability of a given perceptual response to a stimulus is an inverse function of the amount of information required to define that pattern.

REFERENCES

1. BROWN, J. F., and VOTH, A. C. The path of seen movement as a function of the vector-field. *Amer. J. Psychol.*, 1937, **49**, 543-563.
2. GIBSON, J. J., and WADDELL, D. Homogeneous retinal stimulation and visual perception. *Amer. J. Psychol.*, 1952, **65**, 263-270.
3. KOFFKA, K. *Principles of Gestalt psychology.* New York: Harcourt Brace, 1935.
4. KOPFERMANN, H. Psychologische Untersuchungen über die Wirkung zweidimensionaler Darstellungen körperlicher Gebilde. *Psychol. Forsch.*, 1930, **13**, 293-364.
5. MILLER, G. A. *Language and communication.* New York: McGraw-Hill, 1951.
6. ORBISON, W. D. Shape as a function of the vector-field. *Amer. J. Psychol.*, 1939, **52**, 31-45.

••

*Figure and Ground**

EDGAR RUBIN

The Fundamental Difference between Figure and Ground. We shall here attempt to clarify the difference in the appearance of an area when it is seen as figure and when it is seen as ground.

This difference has several aspects. The most important of these is that what is perceived as figure and what is perceived as ground do not have shape in the same way. In a certain sense, the ground has no shape. A field which had previously been experienced as ground can function in a surprising way when experienced as figure. This effect depends on the new shape, which had not previously been in awareness, and which is now experienced for the first time.

In several cases, in which the change from seeing an area as ground to seeing it as figure occurred rather slowly, I experienced how the ground gradually took on a certain shape and became figure. In German, there is an expression which is perhaps strikingly appropriate: "wie der Grund gestaltet wird" ("How the ground becomes structured"). Something happens to the ground when it goes over into figure. Especially when it proceeds slowly, it seems that there is something new added to the area which was ground and is becoming figure. The experienced object becomes enriched while changing. This impression is also clear when the reversal of figure and ground occurs suddenly.

To characterize the fundamental difference between figure and ground it is useful to consider the contour, which is defined as the common boundary of the two fields. One can then state as a fundamental principle: when two fields have a common border, and one is seen as figure and the other as ground, the immediate perceptual

---

* An abridged translation by Michael Wertheimer of pp. 35-101 of Rubin, E., *Visuell wahrgenommene Figuren* (translated by Peter Collett into German from the Danish *Synsoplevede Figurer,* Copenhagen: Gyldendalske, 1915). Copenhagen: Gyldendalske, 1921. Translated and printed by permission of the publishers.

experience is characterized by a shaping effect which emerges from the common border of the fields and which operates only on one field, or operates more strongly on one than on the other.

The field which is most affected by this shaping process is figure; the other field is ground. In principle, two limiting cases are possible: both fields may become figure simultaneously (in which case both are equally affected by the shaping process of the contour), or neither field may be affected by this shaping process, and therefore neither becomes figure.

It must be emphasized that one does not sense this shaping process as such, but only its effect, the emergence of a shaped surface. Therefore, it might be more correct to say, instead of "a shaping effect emerges from the contour," that it is *as though* a shaping effect emerges from the contour. Then the expression "the shaping effect of the contour" is regarded as figurative. Whatever one chooses, it is certain that the contour can have a completely different significance for the two fields. It often happened that when the subjects were asked to describe the ground, they said that they had the impression that it extended behind the figure.

With the help of Fig. 1, the reader can make observations along these lines. One can experience alternately a radially marked or concentrically marked cross. If the concentric cross is seen as figure after the radial one, it is possible to note a characteristic change in the concentric markings which depends on whether they belong to the figure or the ground. When they are part of the ground, they do not appear interrupted. On the contrary, one has the impression that concentric circles continue behind the figure. Nothing of this kind is noticed when the concentrically marked sectors compose that which is seen as figure.

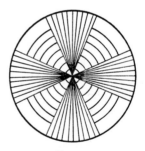

FIG. 1.

By cutting a nonsense figure out of cardboard and placing it at a slant in front of a frontal-parallel homogeneously colored wall, a very clear example is obtained of both how a common border can only affect the shape of one surface, and how the other surface seems to extend behind it. If one observes such a piece of cardboard, it will clearly emerge as figure, and it hides a part of the wall. It is, so to speak, obvious that the wall continues behind the cardboard. An interesting task is to try to determine how the visible portion of the wall, which is not covered by the cardboard, would look if *it* were seen as figure. If one tries this, one will discover that the task is very difficult. Furthermore, it is extremely foreign and "unnatural," which proves that it does not occur in everyday life. It almost seems impossible to get the contour that wall and cardboard have in common to exert its shaping effect on the wall surface.

Observations of this kind on the continuous extension of the ground behind the figure can easily be made on almost any object—preferably not too regular—which stands in front of a wall or surface. In effect, the common contour indicates this is the end of the object, and seems to concern the ground to such a small degree that the ground can quietly continue on past behind the figure. Subjects have frequently pointed this out.

It must be noted that the impression that the ground extends behind the border, or that the figure ends at the border, is not a matter of an abstract knowing or an abstract assumption, but of an immediate impression which occurs *in spite of* knowledge. If an irregular black area, e.g., a piece of black paper, is placed on the center of a piece of white paper lying on the floor and the white area emerges as figure, it is easy to get the impression that the black is a dark hole which continues behind the opening. Under these conditions, when I wanted to alter the figure in such a way as to get stronger white "tongues" extending into the "hole," I had to pull myself together to pick up the black piece of paper in order to cut it. In spite of my knowledge of the stimulus, the impression that the border common to the black and the white was the end of the white object was so striking that it seemed to me as though my behavior were absurd: to cut a hole smaller, in order to make the white field in which the hole was, larger. The peculiar conflict which one can experience here between what one knows, and what one sees with one's own eyes, is so interesting that it is recommended that the reader try the experiment himself. Further, if one places the white paper on a patterned rug and reduces the illumination to a very low level, one can experience something very remarkable: the rug pattern is seen in the hole—through the black and the white paper! The awareness that the experienced object is a hole, and that one can look through holes, is responsible for the result, but only in a suggestive way. I must add that I have only had this experience under exceptional conditions, and it occurred only rarely in my subjects. I have a strong recollection of having read a treatise in which something similar was described, but I have been unable to locate it again.

The "Thing-Character" of the Figure and the "Substance-Character" of the Ground. When a reversal of figure and ground occurs, one can observe that the area affected by the shape-giving function of the contour at the same time obtains a characteristic which is similar to that which leads one to call objects "things." The experienced shape is essential to the object, and the contour is the edge of this object. When we talk of the thing-character of the figure, we do not intend to say that the particular figure is similar to a particular thing like a hairbrush. Even when the figure does not look like any known thing, it can still have this thing-character. By "thing-character" we mean a similarity to what is common in all experienced objects to which can legitimately be attached the predicate, "thing."

In contrast with this characteristic of the figure, the ground—or the background—which is unaffected by the shape-giving function of the contour, has a characteristic which is more like a "substance," like flour, sand, iron, etc. This does not mean that the substance of which the ground is composed, e.g., the paper, comes clearly into awareness, but that the experienced ground, as such, has a characteristic in common with all the referents of the word "substance."

The function of the individual character of the figure shows a close relation to the principle that the difference between two fields is essentially greater when the experienced objects are both figures than when they are both grounds. A field experienced as figure is a richer, more differentiated structure than the same field experienced as ground.

Subjective Color Differences between Figure and Ground. I have noticed in many different situations that the color seems more substantial and more compact in the figure than in the ground. Dr. Katz had the same impression in several experiments. One subject, in some experiments in which she was asked to describe the difference between figure and ground, confirmed these findings. (She had read Katz's work, and was herself engaged in research on color.) She clearly expressed in her description of the ground the indefinite localization which is characteristic of film colors according to Katz.[1]

---

[1] Die Erscheinungsweisen der Farben, etc. *Zeitschr. f. Psychologie,* Ergänz. Band 7. [See also Katz, Selection 6. Eds.]

That this impression was also present in other subjects, but did not enter their protocols because they were unaware of the concepts and descriptions, can be surmised from their uncertain statements when asked about the localization of the ground.

That excellent observer, Hering, has described an experiment[2] in which an open-topped box with a blackened inside and covered by a piece of white cardboard with a ragged-edged hole cut in it, can be seen in two ways. Either one sees a hole in the cardboard and, behind the plane of the hole, a dark space, or one sees a black spot, the shape of the hole, on top of the white cardboard. The percept in the two cases is entirely different. In the first case the percept of the dark stimulus is a space-filling one, spread out in depth. In the second, the dark stimulus appears surface-like, and is squeezed into a surface, and looks like the color of a surface. When the experiment succeeds, the difference is very striking.

FIG. 2.

A good procedure for making observations similar to Hering's is the following. I sketched an octagon in the middle of a large piece of white cardboard, cut out one of the systems of sectors (as in Fig. 2), and stood the cardboard in an open window so that the dark night could be seen through the openings. If I viewed the white sector-systems as figure, the dark or black areas had the character of a weak, space-filling film color behind the piece of cardboard. If I viewed the dark system as figure, I saw a pitch-black surface, lying on the cardboard. Not only did the film color become more compact and substantial, but at the same time it became more decidedly black. There was a weak light from a lamp in the room.

At this point we can also refer back to the experiment mentioned above, in which a black field was surrounded by a white. When the white field is seen as figure, the black piece of paper stops looking like a black surface. Usually it is seen as a dark, weak, space-filling color. One can say briefly, though not quite precisely, that in this case something which actually is the surface color of an object is experienced as a space-filling color, while in Hering's experiment something which actually is a space-filling color is experienced as a surface color.

It appears as though the greater structural solidity of the color of

[2] Hermanns Handbuch der Physiologie, Vol. 3, Part 1, pp. 574 f.

a field when seen as figure can be noticed not only in direct perception but also in after-images and in visual images.

Difference between Figure and Ground in Apparent Localization. It has already been indicated that a difference can appear in the localization of figure and ground in the third dimension, in that the ground is often less clearly localized than the figure. In addition to this relatively qualitative difference, a non-objective but more quantitative difference is very frequently noticed. This difference is based on the strong tendency to localize the area seen as figure closer than that seen as ground. Since often only very uncertain estimates are obtained of the greater distance of the ground, one can only speak of a certain order of magnitude of this difference in distance, and this order of magnitude can vary widely between one meter and one mm. Often the difference is only that the figure lies on the ground, without any real difference in distance.

In Relation to the Ground, the Figure Is More Impressive and More Dominant. Everything about the figure is remembered better, and the figure brings forth more associations than the ground. As a rule there is a further difference when an area is seen as figure or as ground, in that when it is experienced as figure it is in general more impressive than when it is experienced as ground. It dominates consciousness; consequently in descriptions, the figure is usually mentioned before the ground.

If one has sufficient practice in observations of this kind, the following conditions demonstrate effectively that a figure is more impressive and dominant than the ground. First look simply and naturally at a piece of rectangular white paper, and then quickly place a small black figure in its center. You can then observe, almost directly, how the white surface recedes from the center of consciousness, while the black figure takes over. The form of the white surface, determined by the contour it has in common with the table-top, is no longer as clear. This last effect surely contributes to the phenomenon that the experienced white area loses some of its thing-character even though you fully realize that it is a piece of white paper that is before you.

Another illustration of the dominance of the figure is that if a subject is asked to make judgments about the familiarity or unfamiliarity of a series of figures of the same color, on a uniformly colored ground, he speaks about the figure and not the ground. This fact could be explained in that the grounds on which the figures lie are less different, since they are less affected by the influence of the contour they have in common with the figure. The ground seems to merge into the general environment, a circumstance which is hardly taken into account in judgments about familiarity or unfamiliarity.

It seems to be relatively unimportant for the recognition of a figure whether it is seen on one or another ground. In this connection, there is a kind of figural autonomy. In experiments in which the ground was yellow with strong black parallel stripes, recognition of the figures was 58% when the stripes were similarly oriented during training and test (either vertical both times or horizontal both times), and was 46.5% when their orientation was different in training and test. Probably the small difference in these numbers can be accounted for by an indirect effect (emphasized by special instructions) of the stripes in the ground on the character of the perceived figure.

In comparison judgments between two fields, each of which contains figure and ground, subjects report that the figures are similar or different; they do not talk about the grounds. This is true of judgments of differences. A natural explanation of why this is also true of judgments of similarity (in addition to the factor that figures in general are more impressive than grounds) is that the grounds in general do not seem as different as the figures. In consequence, statements of similarity between two grounds are practically meaningless.

That the figure is as a whole more impressive and dominates consciousness also implies that everything about the figure is recalled better than characteristics of the ground. When I held a separate nonsense figure in my hand, I often caught myself noticing, in the moment after I had looked at it, that I did not have the slightest notion over which ground I had held the figure. In the experiments just mentioned, with figures on yellow, striped grounds, the subjects did not mention that in half the figures the stripes had been turned 90°, an indication that the direction of the stripes had not been strongly learned during training.

The rule that more is remembered about the figure than about the ground holds for immediate, natural attitudes; this does not suggest that under special conditions one cannot set oneself to remember more about the ground.

For that matter, it is not easy to decide whether the fact that details about the ground are difficult to reproduce later is due to nothing about such details ever having been in consciousness or to something having been there but forgotten. Even if one assumes that something *was* there, it can be difficult to decide what this "something" was.

In experiments with nonsense figures subjects often "read into" the figures. This can involve known objects, birds, animals, and people, flowers, or coffee-cans, crochet hooks, etc., but sometimes also more abstract forces, tendencies, directions, and movements. In addition, verbal naming as well as loosely connected conceptions are sometimes used in thinking about the figure. It must be emphasized that in experiments with nonsense figures there was not a single instance in which such associations occurred in regard to the part of the field that was seen as ground. . . .

FIG. 3.

When something is read into a figure, this process is based on a similarity in shape between the figure and the particular thing. This explains why things are not read into the ground. Since the contour's shaping effect is absent or less strong on the ground than the figure, no particular shape similarity exists between the ground and the particular thing. In Fig. 3 the reader has the opportunity not only to convince himself that the ground is perceived as shapeless but also to see that a meaning read into a field when it is figure is not read in when the field is seen as ground.

The Relation between Figure and Ground with Regard to Affect. In experiments on figure and ground the opportunity sometimes arose to observe relations connected with affective experience. Some of these are not special to these experiments, such as that the subjects get tired of the experiments, or that they feel satisfied when they think they have accomplished the task set for them by the instructions, etc. Other affective relations are more closely related to the special conditions of these experiments. This holds of feelings associated with what is read into the figure. This is a function of the fact that feelings are attached to figures and not to grounds, and these feelings are an aspect of the relation implied in the statement that the figure dominates in consciousness. In the first place, the remarkable or unexpected that the subjects see in the figures can amuse them. In the second place, the particulars that they read into the figure can arouse certain feelings related to what is read in. If a figure looks like a beloved and admired professor from the homeland, this may remind the subject of the pleasure in having met him again as he stopped by on the way to Göttingen. If a figure looks like a beautiful female torso, this also indubitably calls forth certain feelings.

In addition to feelings of this kind, feelings of an æsthetic character can also occur. The autonomy of the figure relative to the ground has the consequence that, independently of the ground on which it lies, a figure can arouse an æsthetic impression. In contrast, the objective figure which constitutes the ground is usually æsthetically indifferent. This is obvious as long as it is not experienced as figure, but is worth mentioning since it plays no small role in art. When one succeeds in experiencing as figure areas which are intended as ground, one can sometimes see that they constitute æsthetically displeasing forms. If one has the misfortune in pictures of the Sistine Madonna to see the background as figure, one will see a remarkable lobster claw grasping Saint Barbara, and another odd pincer-like instrument seizing the holy sexton. These figures are hardly beautiful. Ornaments frequently become æsthetically displeasing when the part intended as ground is seen as figure. . . .

Rules for the Probability That a Surface Is Seen as Figure. When two fields adjoin one another, what are the characteristic qualities of these fields which make it probable that one will be seen as figure and the other as ground? The following principle is fundamental: if one of the two homogeneous, different colored fields is larger than and encloses the other, there is a great likelihood that the small, surrounded field will be seen as figure. . . .

Conscious intent can also play an important role. . . .

Further, there is a certain tendency to uniformity. In a design in which the same motifs are repeated, there is a tendency to see the repetition in the same way. There is a tendency to experience a cohesive, homogeneously colored field either entirely as figure or entirely as ground. . . .

In experiments with reciprocal cross figures (as Fig. 2) presented squarely to the subject, the cross whose sectors are horizontal and vertical is more easily seen as figure than is the other cross. In general, it is easiest to see as figure that sector system which appears "straightest."

The Effect of "Punishment" (Electric Shock) on Figure-Ground Perception[*][1]

Donald E. P. Smith and Julian E. Hochberg

THE PROBLEM

THE EFFECT of reward and punishment on perception as reported by Schafer and Murphy (6) has been contested both on empirical and on theoretical grounds (4, 5, 7).

Their study used two sets of two half-moon "faces," the two faces of each set forming a circular reversible figure-ground when joined at the profile (6, p. 336). Subjects won four pennies when each of two of the single faces was projected tachistoscopically, and lost two pennies when each of their companion faces were presented. In a test series, the two faces of each set were combined so that either could be seen as figure. Rewarded faces were reported more often than punished ones, suggesting the operation of autism (and of pre-perceptual recognition, 1) since autism as obtained here logically seems to require that, *at some level prior to figure-ground formation*, both faces are "perceived" and reacted to in terms of the rewards and punishment of the training series.

Wallach (7), assuming that an area must be organized into figure and ground before trace arousal and recognition can occur, suggests a possible explanation: the *outline* figures used by Schafer and

---

[*] From *J. Psychol.*, 1954, **38**, 83-87. Reprinted by permission of the authors and the publisher.

[1] These present findings are *not* believed to support any hypothesis of "subception" or "pre-perceptual trace-connection." The results of the first experiment cannot be considered without reference to those of the second. Furthermore, the experimental design and statistical analyses were aimed at testing two restricted, rather technical assertions, and the probability statements obtained should not be considered as indices either of populational or of ecological generality. [Authors' Note.]

Murphy permitted recognition of "line" rather than of figural form, and the form of such a profile "line" may remain recognizable in both figures, unlike the *contour* of a solid figure; he suggested, therefore, that repetition with *solid* figures, would not yield "autism." Rock and Fleck (5), attempting replication of the Schafer and Murphy procedure, using *outline* figures, found no consistent results, but (3) the rewards used (two and four cents) may not have been motivationally equivalent in 1943 and 1950.

The first problem is whether, with electric shock as punishment rather than questionable monetary rewards, "perceptual defense" can be obtained with *solid* figures. The problem is similar to that of McLeary and Lazarus (2) although "faces," rather than nonsense syllables, were used.

EXPERIMENT I

Method. Two solid white (B, D) and two solid black (A, C) "faces" identical in contour to those of Schafer and Murphy (6, p. 336) but with no "outlines," were reproduced on 2″ x 2″ slides, singly, for the training series and in two combination (A-B, C-D) on a gray ground for the test series, and projected to 15 inches in diameter. Two groups of 10 subjects each were seated at a table, five at a time, separated by cardboard blinds; their distance from the screen varied from 84 inches to 96 inches. Electrodes were attached to their hands and to induction coils and 6-volt dry cells in single series to a telegraph key operated by E.

Fifteen 1/3 second exposures were made of each of the four faces in random order. Electrical shock accompanied one member of each pair each time it was presented. Before each presentation during the first 12 trials, attention was directed to the appropriate one of four cardboard "help" faces mounted on the wall (non-reversible, "improved" figures), and the name (A, B, C, or D) was given. To aid learning, Ss called out the name of each figure after presentation for the remainder of the series.

Group I was shocked simultaneously with the presentation of Figure A and with presentation of D, Group II, with B and C, in order to control possible structural, positional, or color dominance. Thus, if both groups subsequently displayed a significantly greater perception of unshocked than shocked faces, or one group showed this effect significantly while the other group did not differ from it significantly in the *opposite* direction, such results could not be attributed to structural, positional, etc., factors, and the effects would be assumed as due to the shock procedure.

A learning check test of eight presentations, two of each single face, followed the training series.

TABLE 1. NUMBER OF CORRECT RESPONSES TO POST-TRAINING
TEST FIGURES

Group	No. of Subjects	NS	S	P	B
		Experiment I			
I	10	116	128		1
II	10	146	54	<.01	0
Sum:		262	182	<.01	1
		Experiment II			
III	5	41	33		75
IV	5	28	26		32
Sum:		69	59		107

Note: NS, S list the number of correct responses to the non-shocked and shocked figures, respectively; *B* is the number of correct identifications of both faces; *P* is the probability of obtaining such proportions by chance.

As in previous studies, a post-training series consisted of 63 presentations (1/3 sec. each): 16 of each of the two reversible drawings (*A-B, C-D*) and 31 of two extraneous "set breaking" figures, irreversible faces pointing right or left. After each test figure, the extraneous figure pointing in the direction opposite to that of the non-shocked face was presented.[2] Subjects wrote the name of the face seen, "X" for extraneous figures and "?" if the face could not be identified.

Results. For Group I, the difference between responses of shocked

---

[2] This procedure differs from the previous studies in which the extraneous figure was determined by the preceding response of the subject (impossible with groups of subjects); however, the results showed no directional effects following the setbreaking figures (P > .10).

and non-shocked faces is not significant (Table 1); that for Group II *is* (P < .01), as are the pooled results (P < .01).[3]

Analyzing each set, *A-B* and *C-D*, alone, Rock and Fleck reported a significant tendency for *S*s to report punished faces in the *A-B* situation and to report rewarded faces in the *C-D* situation. In the present case, 164 unshocked and 101 shocked faces were reported for the *A-B* figure, and 98 unshocked and 81 shocked for the *C-D* figure, i.e., the same direction in both cases. In short, while purely "figural" factors were of importance, the shock procedure clearly had effect.[4]

However, although something which may be called "perceptual defense," was obtained, this still does not necessarily imply pre-perceptual (or even pre-figural) recognition. Despite Wallach's belief that with solid figures *S*s would not be able simultaneously to recognize both "faces," this may be just what occurred. Hence, the next problem is to determine whether, with appropriate instructions, *S*s are capable of identifying both faces (if this is the case, of course, we would also expect an attendant decrease in or absence of "autism" in these circumstances).

EXPERIMENT II

Method. Ten *S*s were trained as in Experiment I, five in Group III and five in Group IV. To determine whether it is possible to identify *both* figures in a given 1/3 sec. test presentation, *S*s received written directions prior to the post-training series to the effect that two faces would appear in juxtaposition at each presentation and that they should attempt to identify both.

Results. Nearly half (107) of all correct reports (235) identified both stimulus figures (Table 1). Here the difference between shocked and unshocked faces is not significant, but the increase in correct reports of *both* faces, as compared to Experiment I, is (P < .01).

---

[3] Rock and Fleck discarded the results of subjects who failed to recognize all faces in a check test administered after the experiment proper; we here retained all subjects. No significant differences (P > .10) in "autism" were found between those subjects who made one or more errors on the check list and those with perfect scores.

[4] It seems unlikely, moreover, that the "autism" (at least, that obtained in this experiment) is due to inhibition of the verbal "naming" response, since the errors in identification did not contain significantly more shocked than unshocked responses (P > .10).

DISCUSSION

The results of the first experiment do not contradict the original findings of Schafer and Murphy. Wallach's expectation that "autism" would not appear with solid figures was not fulfilled. Apparently the "punishment" (shock) procedure did affect the selection of the figure perceived.

But does the individual first perceive (albeit unconsciously) the painful stimulus so that he may avoid perceiving it? Actually, we need not assume that figure-ground organization springs into all-or-none dichotomy, even in 1/3 second. If, during the *early* stages of differentiation, before perceptual integration is complete (cf. Murphy and Hochberg, 3), *one portion of a given boundary may serve as contour for the black region while in another segment, the white is "figure,"* two not-necessarily exclusive explanations suggest themselves:

1. Wallach's objection to the use of outline figures may be a more general one, and may apply to solid figures as well, since it appears from the second experiment that it is possible to identify aspects of both figures, and, thereby, a "choice" between them based upon Effect is at least conceivable.

2. Shock may be a "distracting" deterrent to perceptual learning (or "integration"). The unshocked figure, perhaps with briefer latency, might be favored in the integration of the final figure-ground organization; several Ss reported that the shock "made it harder to learn the faces" or "took my attention away from the faces."

SUMMARY

The contested "autism" effect of Schafer and Murphy was tested with solid (rather than outline) figures and with electrical shock as "punishment." With 20 Ss a significant difference favoring non-shocked figures was obtained, against Wallach's prediction; however, his objection to outline figures may actually hold here as well since a second experiment with 10 Ss indicated that with the proper set the identification of *both* phases of a reversible figure-ground configuration can be increased, suggesting explanations which do not invoke pre-recognition processes such as "subception" (2).

REFERENCES

1. HOCHBERG, J., and GLEITMAN, H. Toward a reformulation of the perception-motivation dichotomy. *J. Pers.*, 1949, **18**, 180-191.

2. McCleary, R. A., and Lazarus, R. S. Autonomic discrimination without awareness: an interim report. *J. Pers.*, 1949, **18**, 171-179.

3. Murphy, G., and Hochberg, J. Perceptual development: some tentative hypotheses. *Psychol. Rev.*, 1951, **58**, 332-349.

4. Pastore, N. Need as a determinant of perception. *J. of Psychol.*, 1949, **28**, 457-475.

5. Rock, I., and Fleck, F. S. A re-examination of the effect of monetary reward and punishment on figure-ground perception. *J. exp. Psychol.*, 1950, **40**, 766-776.

6. Schafer, R., and Murphy, G. The rôle of autism in a visual figure-ground relationship. *J. exp. Psychol.*, 1943, **32**, 335-343.

7. Wallach, H. Some considerations concerning the relationship between perception and cognition. *J. Pers.*, 1949, **18**, 6-13.

SELECTION 15

....

Configuration and Brightness Contrast*

WILLIAM H. MIKESELL AND MADISON BENTLEY

IT IS A COMMONPLACE in psychology that a local gray area set in a general visual field depends for its phenomenal quality both upon the character of the local light stimulus and upon the filling of the general field. The most obvious demonstration of this dependence is made by placing two like gray papers right and left, the one upon white paper and the other upon black. The gray-on-white looks darker than the gray-on-black. This phenomenal difference has commonly been regarded as brightness contrast, to be explained by a mutual excitatory influence of neighboring retinal areas. But Gestalt psychologists,[1] using certain more complicated visual patterns, have recently contended that visual contrast does not adequately account for the observed change in local grays when the grays are inserted in geometrical designs. Wertheimer cut out a heavy black cross and exposed it upon a white background. Two small triangles of like size and shape were then cut from the same piece of gray paper. One triangle was placed upon a limb of the black cross and the other just outside the cross but within an angle

* From *J. exp. Psychol.*, 1930, **13**, 1-23. An abridged version printed by permission of the senior author and the publisher.
[1] W. Benary, Beobachtungen zu einem Experiment über Helligkeitskontrast, *Psychol. Forsch.*, 1924, **5**, 131-142; M. Eberhardt, Untersuchungen über Farbschwellen und Farbenkontrast, *ibid.*, 1924, **5**, 85-130; W. Fuchs, Experimentelle Untersuchungen über die Änderung von Farben unter dem Einfluss von Gestalten, *Zsch. f. Psychol.*, 1923, **92**, 298 ff; A. Gelb, Über den Wegfall von 'Oberflächen Farben,' *ibid.*, 1920, **84**, 193; A. Gelb and R. Granit, Die Bedeutung von 'Figur' und 'Grund' für die Farbenschwelle, *ibid.*, 1923, **93**, 83; E. Rubin, Visuell wahrgenommene Figuren, Berlin, 1921; M. Wertheimer, Untersuchungen zur Lehre von der Gestalt, *Psychol. Forsch.*, 1921, **1**, 47-58; 1923, **4**, 301-350; 1925, **7**, 81-136; K. Koffka, Über Feldbegrenzung und Felderfüllung, *ibid.*, 1923, **4**, 176-203; W. Köhler, Die physischen Gestalten in Ruhe und im stationären Zustand, 1920; H. Werner, Studien über Strukturgesetze, *Zsch. f. Psychol.*, 1924, **94**, 252 ff.

formed by two adjacent limbs. Contrast, which moves in the direction of 'opposition,' would lead one to expect the gray which is adjacent to most white to be darker and the gray which is adjacent to most black to be lighter; but Wertheimer saw exactly the opposite. The gray on the black design (G_i, inside gray) looked lighter than the outside gray (G_o), although more white actually surrounded it. Aherents of the doctrine of *Gestalt* have interpreted this effect as due to the fact that G_i was in the *Gestalt* or *configuration* while G_o was outside. G_i was a part of the 'figure' and G_o was not. G_i belonged-to or inhered-in the figure while G_o did not. It was for some the figural inherence (*Zugehörigkeit*) which determined the quality of the first gray. This was in line with the contention of the *Gestalttheorie* that the whole determines the parts. Benary, who repeated Wertheimer's observation, also used a cross-and-triangle figure, a thick 'H' and 'I' and a heavy C-figure. The general outcome was the same in all, and it was to some extent confirmed when colored patches replaced the 'critical' grays. We have repeated and extended Benary's experiments.

Preliminary Observations. We repeated his observations under the following conditions. The designs were copied as well as they could be from Benary's descriptions. They were pasted on large black or white sheets of cardboard (22 in. x 28 in.). Holes of the size and form of the critical grays were cut in the black or white designs. Behind them were placed homogeneous sheets of the critical gray. The whole was evenly illuminated by a 400-watt artificial (Corning) day-light bulb. This exposure field was covered by black when O entered the room. O was seated behind a hooded screen, with a head-rest, and the exposure was governed by raising a shutter before his eyes. The cards were exposed 1 to 15 sec, after which O was asked to report.

The instruction was as follows:

"At the signal 'ready' fixate. At the signal 'now' compare in quality the patches of gray in the total field. Be prepared at the signal 'now' to observe plane designs of black, white and gray. Report your comparison in one of the four degrees of assurance: high (4), moderate (3), small (2), and wanting (1). Do not fixate any point of an object and be prepared for a brief exposure."

The preliminary trials generally confirm Benary's result. This method of Benary can, however, be improved. We have every reason to believe that the gray qualities compared were determined in part by the variable excitations of the retina as the designs were examined. Two photometrically equated lights would naturally be reported as 'different' when foveal vision passed to one of them from a black surface and to the other from a white surface. It is obvious that such a research as ours must control the state of the entire retina throughout the entire period of excitation.

To this end a camera shutter was secured with a calibrated exposure-range of $3\,\sigma$ to $1000\,\sigma$. We used an exposure time of approx. $25\,\sigma$, in order to fall below the limits for eye-movement. The shutter was placed in the front wall of a light-box before the 400-watt lamp, with a water-cell to prevent damage to the shutter by heat. The light was reduced by ground-glass plates to eliminate after-images. Except for the flash upon the exposure field, the room was dark. A faint fixation-light was arranged near the middle of the field and O held this in steady foveal vision just before the flash revealed the objects in the field. The field was 3 meters distant from the eyes. As the critical grays were to be differently oriented in the various patterns and objects to be presented, O had to be prepared each time for the approximate placing of the impending grays. This was arranged by a brief pre-exposure (in the direction of the field) of an outline sketch of the two critical grays oriented as they were about to appear. This sketch was weakly illumined in a frame set before the front opening of the hood and was removed just before the 'ready' for the main exposure of the field.

Five minutes were allowed for partial dark-adaptation. Observations fell within an hour, care being taken to prevent fatigue and to provide sufficient intervals between exposures.

THE MAIN EXPERIMENTS

Cards were made by pasting designs, together with the critical grays, on various backgrounds. The critical grays were observed to be phenomenally equal before being pasted in place. Each card was presented in four positions; straight up, inverted, and on its right and left.

The instructions follow.

"Before the main exposure-field is presented, you will be shown a sketch to indicate the relative positions of the fixation point and two gray areas. Simply note these relations.

After the sketch is removed, take a comfortable observing position at the caution 'prepare.' When the fixation light appears, *hold* it. After a short interval will appear the two gray areas in the places indicated by the sketch. Compare the grays with respect to *quality* only.

Report 'same' or 'right darker' ('lighter') or 'left lighter' ('darker') or 'upper darker' ('lighter') or 'lower darker' ('lighter'). If a report is not formulated, simply say 'no report.'

Always add to your report the degree of assurance.

4 means high assurance (virtual certainty)
3 " moderate assurance (moderate certainty)
2 " small assurance (moderate uncertainty)
1 " lack of assurance (virtual uncertainty)

Note well the following cautions:

(1) Make sure of steady fixation. Comment upon any slip. Be prepared to answer inquiries upon steadiness during the appearance of the fixation-light.

(2) The exposures will be brief; be prepared.

(3) Remember that 'no report,' 'small assurance' or 'same' has the same psychological value as reports of clear difference and of high certainty.

(4) Be on your guard against self-instruction, bias, and reflective judgments. Report photographically and promptly.

(5) Do not complicate your task, which is *only* to observe the grays with respect to likeness or difference of quality.

(6) Avoid discussion of this problem with the experimenter."

Series I: Benary Designs and Variants of Them. Eighteen patterns (numbered 1-18 below) of the Benary type were used. Twelve of them were repetitions of Benary's actual designs with variation in size, brightness, design and background. They are described as follows.

(*a*) Four variations of the cross design in *black upon white* background (dimensions in cm).

	Horiz.	Vert.	Crit. Grays (Qual.)	Crit. Grays (Size)
(1) Cross..........	6	8	Medium	1.5 x 3.6 x 4.0
(2) "	6	8	Medium	4.0 x 8.0 x 10.0
(3) "	6	8	Dark	4.0 x 7.0 x 7.0
(4) "	3	4	Medium	0.8 x 1.8 x 2.0

(*b*) Two variations of the cross design in *white upon black* background.

	Horiz.	Vert.	Crit. Grays	Crit. Grays
(5) Cross..........	6	8	Medium	1.5 x 3.6 x 4.0
(6) "	3	4	Dark	0.8 x 1.8 x 2.0

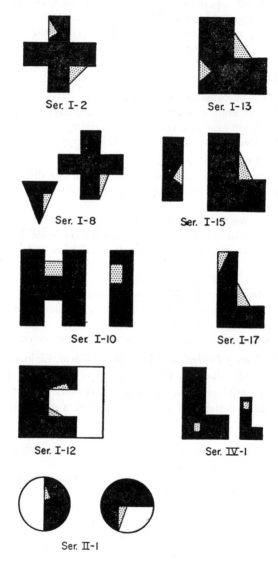

FIG. 1. Samples of the geometrical and literal designs used. (The gray patches are represented here by stippled areas.)

(*c*) One dark gray cross upon white background with medium gray critical fields.

(7) Same size as (6)[2]

(*d*) Two triangle-cross patterns: one *black on white* (See Fig. 1, Ser. I-8), the other *white on black*.

	Triangle	Cross Horiz.	Vert.	Crit. Grays
(8, 9)	6 x 7.9 x 7.7	3	4	0.8 x 1.8 x 2.0

(*e*) Two H-I patterns: one *black on white*, the other *white on black* (Fig. 1, Ser. I-10).

	The "H" Vert. Beams	Crossbeams	The "I" Crit. Grays (rect.)	
(10, 11)	3 x 10	3 x 3	3 x 10	2.0 x 3.0

(*f*) Two equally weighted patterns which are so made up that a left black design is mortised on the right side and in to this opening fits a corresponding tenon of a white design. The patterns balance each other. G_i (inside gray) is placed in the black and G_o (outside gray) in the white design.

(12)

(*g*) The first departure from Benary's design, but preserving the type (Fig. 1, Ser. I-13). Two large broad "L's": 13, *black on white;* 14, *white on black*. The critical fields were so arranged that G_i and G_o had equal areas of adjacent black. We sought here and in the succeeding patterns to devise less complicated objects than Benary's.

	Length	Width	Width of Horiz.	Crit. Grays
(13, 14)	12	12	6	3 x 4 x 5

(*h*) Two I-L designs: one *black on white*, the other *white on black*. The critical field in the "I" was adjacent to very little black or white in comparison with the G_o gray. The letters were more widely separated than the cut (Fig. 1, Ser. I-15) shows.

	"I"	Length of "L"	Width of "L"	Crit. Grays
(15, 16)	2.8 x 9	11	4 (top)	2 x 3
			6 (bottom)	8 x 4.2

(*i*) A slight departure from the Benary type. G_i has one black (design) border and G_o has two. Should G_i be reported as lighter, this fact would indicate that an area into which a gray is inserted would have a greater effect upon it than a much larger area would have upon

---

[2] All the critical fields of the designs following No. 6 were medium gray.

the outside gray. No. 17 was *black on white* (Fig. 1, Ser. I-17); No. 18 was *white on black*.

	Length	Width	Width of Horiz.	Crit. Grays
(17, 18)	14.5	4 (top) 10 (bottom)	4.5	3.2 x 5 x 5.7

The observers had an interval of at least a day between observations. One of the four orientations of the cards was given at each sitting. A position was not repeated under two weeks.

The order of orientation throughout the series was as follows:

1st set	First position............... Designs 1-18
	Second position............ " 1-18
	Third position............... " 3, 2, 1, 5, 4, 12-18, 6-11
	Fourth position............ " ditto
2d set	First position............... Designs 17, 18, 1-16
	Second position............ " ditto
	Third position............... " 12-18, 6-11, 1-5

The results of Series I are presented in Tables I and II, the first giving design by design and the last summarizing the entire series. Our 10 observers made 700 reports upon the black-and-gray pat-

TABLE I. SERIES I: THE BENARY DESIGNS AND VARIANTS
Black and Dark Gray Designs on White Ground

	Lighter		Darker			No	
	G_i	G_o	G_i	G_o	Equal	Report	Totals
Crosses							
(1) Large black......	7	1	2	42	1	11	64
(2) Large black......	10	2	1	41	5	5	64
(3) Large black......	14	1	1	45	0	3	64
(4) Small black......	9	2	0	45	2	6	64
(7) Large dark gray..	1	1	1	12	13	36	64
(8) Triangle-Cross ...	9	3	6	27	11	8	64
(10) H-I Design......	16	1	6	25	6	10	64
(12) Double Design...	8	0	7	30	5	14	64
(13) Large L.........	13	1	5	36	3	5	63
(15) I-L Design.......	12	0	4	31	10	6	63
(17) Small L.........	6	6	12	27	9	2	62
Totals.........	105	18	45	361	65	106	700

White Designs on Black Ground

	Lighter		Darker			No	
	G_i	G_o	G_i	G_o	Equal	Report	Totals
Crosses							
(5) Large White.....	11	7	28	3	2	13	64
(6) Small white......	2	4	45	3	3	7	64
(9) Triangle-Cross ...	5	0	27	3	7	22	64
(11) H-I Design......	2	2	30	4	8	18	64
(14) Large L.........	4	7	39	3	7	4	64
(16) I-L Design......	3	5	38	1	10	6	63
(18) Small L.........	5	3	22	15	12	4	61
Totals.........	32	28	229	32	49	74	444

terns. If we subtract the 106 'no-reports' (Table I, above), we find that 465 of the remaining 594 reports suggest that the *outside*[3] critical gray (G_o) is phenomenally *darker* (361 DG_o + 105 LG_i = 466) than the inside critical gray (G_i). Only 63 (18 + 45) take the contrary direction. The corresponding results from the white-on-black objects stand 257 (229 + 28) for a *lighter outside* critical gray (G_o) against only 64 (32 + 32) in the contrary direction.

TABLE II

REPORTS FOR 10 OBSERVERS FROM 11 BLACK DESIGNS ON WHITE

Obs.	G_oD	G_iL	G_oL	G_iD	Equal	No Report	Totals
C...................	8	36	11	1	9	12	77
F...................	51	0	1	8	7	10	77
G...................	49	4	1	8	6	9	77
Hi..................	3	31	1	0	7	2	44
M...................	49	5	0	8	9	6	77
S...................	60	1	0	5	5	6	77
Su..................	27	25	3	4	14	4	77
T...................	58	3	0	6	3	7	77
Y...................	24	0	0	3	2	44	73
Z...................	31	0	1	2	2	8	44
Totals...........	360	105	18	45	64	108	700
		465		63			

[3] For the present, 'outside' will merely mean 'spatially outside.' It will not imply that the pattern is configured is the sense of the *Gestalt*.

REPORTS FOR 10 OBSERVERS FROM 7 WHITE DESIGNS ON BLACK

C...................	0	15	6	18	8	2	49
F...................	6	0	1	34	5	3	49
G...................	5	3	4	30	4	3	49
Hi..................	0	2	5	10	7	4	28
M...................	4	2	2	30	4	7	49
S...................	0	2	0	41	3	3	49
Su..................	5	6	8	18	8	4	49
T...................	10	0	0	30	3	6	49
Y...................	1	1	0	6	5	32	45
Z...................	1	1	2	12	2	10	28
Totals...........	32	32	28	229	49	74	444
		64		257			

The difference of the phenomenal (critical) grays appears with all ten observers and with the white as well as with the black designs on highly contrastive ground. The above results run contrary to what might be expected according to the ordinary effect of contrast.

Whether the relative difference from the black and the white designs (66 percent and 58 percent) is significant is by no means certain.

Summary of Series I. (1) Where we have one gray within and another without a geometrical design, with more black around one gray than the other, we obtain results which are not wholly explained according to the ordinary summational effects of contrasting brightnesses, although the latter are in evidence.

(2) The above conclusion also holds for designs where the relative amount of border upon the design-areas is the same for the two grays.

(3) If the contrastive borders of the design are decreased, so that the G_o gray has two while G_i has but one, then there is a decrease in the number of reports which run contrary to simple contrast.

To make sure that the critical grays were not themselves phenomenally different in their various positions they were observed as in the preceding series *but without the designs.*

They were presented in their four orientations (up, down, right and left) upon plain black and plain white backgrounds. Shape, size and relative positions were the same as before. The grays were from the large cross and the H-I figures.

Eleven Os made 208 observations on the black background and 203 observations on the white background. Of these grays, 121 (on black) and 134 (on white) were pronounced equal. Some Os reported 'different' more often than others and there was a general tendency to report 'darker' oftener than 'lighter'; but none of the gray pairs showed a difference between lighter and darker in any spatial arrangement, for any gray form, or with any of the four placements by rotation.

It appears therefore that the reported difference in the grays in Series I rests upon the presence of the designs and not upon position or orientation in the black and white fields.

Series II: Mutilated Designs. An attempt was here made to eliminate the Benary patterns but to retain the black and white borders of the grays. This was accomplished by including in a circular area the spatial context of the grays of Series I (Fig. 1, Ser. II-1).

For example, the G_i gray of Benary's cross was transferred, with its immediate surroundings of black and white, to a circular disc and the G_o gray to another of the same size. The relative amount of black and white borders of both grays was preserved for all the excerpts. These circular patches were too small to include the entire cross or any other original pattern. They were exposed upon the large white background. Five sets of designs were used. We were still left with a (circular) design, of course. In the excerpt from the cross, *e.g.*, G_i and its black and white borders were seen at times as a disc-shaped pattern with black, white and gray parts, and G_o with its context as a somewhat similar design. But at least the original geometrical and lettered patterns, assumed by the Gestalt psychologists to be configured with or without a given gray, were eliminated.

There were also four non-circular sets of excerpts from Benary's designs used merely because they were more feasible to construct than circular designs.

The Os were now asked to report not only upon the gray qualities but also upon the nature of their 'inclusion' or 'exclusion.' The gray-quality reports are presented in Table III. Of 290 reports (nine black excerpts on white), 191 (about $\frac{2}{3}$ of all) give the spatially inside gray as lighter. Out of a total of 346 descriptive reports, 275 show G_i as phenomenally 'inside'; while G_o was perceived as phenomenally within the borders only 45 times, and 23 of these 45 cases were from two excerpts which were so cut as virtually to set G_o within the boundaries of the new design.

TABLE III. SERIES II: MUTILATED FIGURES

All Reports of 11 Os from 9 Black Designs on White

Os	G_oD	G_iL	G_oL	G_iD	Equal	No Report	Totals
C.................	0	19	5	0	2	6	32
F.................	20	1	0	4	3	4	32
G.................	12	2	1	1	11	4	31
H.................	18	11	4	5	1	3	42
Hi................	2	9	2	1	4	2	20
M.................	26	0	0	4	4	1	35
S.................	10	8	4	3	3	4	32
Su................	7	18	1	0	9	3	38
T.................	19	0	0	4	8	3	34
Y.................	4	0	0	2	2	24	32
Z.................	1	4	1	1	9	2	18
Totals...........	119	72	18	25	56	56	346
	191		43				

Summary of Series II. (1) The grays of the excerpts of Benary's geometrical and literal patterns were frequently perceived as one *within* and the other *without* these excerpts.

(2) The *inside* gray (G_i) is commonly lighter and the outside gray (G_o) darker, as in Benary's complete designs. But since Benary's patterns were obliterated, they cannot be held responsible, as he contends, for the observed difference in the grays.

(3) 'Nonsense' designs reproduce Benary's results when the inclusion and exclusion of the grays and their immediate context are maintained.

(4) The descriptive reports indicate that the gray was seen as 'inside' or 'outside' only in a spatial and local way, not belonging to it or appearing as a member in a unitary whole.

Series III: Cross Effects of Design and Background. Benary's chief interest in his 'figures' seems to lie only in the effect of the patterns upon his 'inside' grays. He has not considered the possible effect here of the background, as well as the influence of the main pattern upon his 'outside' gray. The purpose of the present series lies just in this direction, *i.e.* it is to test the effect of the background upon the 'inside' gray and the effect of the design-area upon the 'outside' gray.

To this end seven patterns were prepared, each showing side by side duplicate designs with an inserted gray (G_i) or an adjacent gray (G_o). In one design (right or left in the pair) contrast from figure or ground was diminished (1) by pasting a similar gray alongside G_i or G_o upon the background, (2) by making one design of a gray similar to G_o and the other of black, or (3) by making both designs slightly unlike an *inserted* gray (the left design) and an outside gray (right design). The designs were thick rectangular Is and Ls. The Os then reported the lighter (darker) of the two critical grays of the twin designs as these were presented side by side.

Our results make it evident that the effect of the background upon G_i and of the design upon G_o was greatly reduced when the critical gray was separated from background or design by a very similar gray strip. This rule held both for black on white and for white on black. The ratios in the reports were 25 : 4, 22 : 5 and 21 : 7 ('equal' and 'no-report' thrown out) for our designs 1, 2, and 3. Pair 4 (gray and black twin-designs) showed again that the brightness of the design has a decided effect on G_o as well as on G_i. Ratio 24 : 3. It appeared, however, that when a high brightness difference was removed between design and the critical grays—two gray designs compared, one with (a slightly different) G_i and the other with (a slightly different) G_o—the background (whether white or black) exerted a greater effect upon the G_o than upon G_i. (Ratios 9 : 0 and 3 : 0, with 19 and 25 'equals.') This suggests that when the distinction between design and the critical grays is almost eliminated, the background exerts a greater effect upon G_o than upon G_i. The 11 Os were highly consistent in all these results.

When 4 Os, subsequently to this series, directly compared designs, one of which showed the *effect of the background upon G_i* and the other the *effect of the design upon G_o*, the two cross-effects appeared to be sensibly equal. This is a nice matter which deserves further study.

Summary of Series III. (1) The design-area has a decided contrast effect upon an *outside* gray.

(2) The ground has a decided contrast effect upon an *inside* gray.

(3) There appears to be a pronounced effect from all of the inducing fields surrounding each critical gray, whether the latter is spatially within or without the main pattern.

Series IV: Submerged G_i with Variable Amounts of Design and *of Critical Gray.* This series was designed to verify the contrast effect of the patterned area upon an internal gray member *which has no border on the background,* in order to see whether this member received the contrast effect according to the summational theory or whether a configurational or some other perceptive factor also was required.

Eight black designs (Ls, triangles and squares) were made with gray inserts (also Ls, triangles and squares) which were entirely surrounded by the design. Each type of design was presented in 2s, 3s or 4s, showing a difference in (1) size of design, (2) size of gray insert, or (3) position of insert within the design. A variation in relative size or in position would seem to lead to a variable contrastive effect which might come out in the comparative reports upon gray quality.

Summary of Series IV. (1) There is no clear difference in the quality of the grays as observed in abstraction from the main design and with the whole 'figure' integrated. This result is concordant with our results with mutilated designs (Series II).

(2) A gray which is set wholly within the spatial limits of a design is amenable to the summational effects of contrast.

Series V: 'Inhering' Grays Spatially Outside the Design. Benary states that if a gray is 'included' within a design it is subject to a configurational influence. This influence must mean more, then, than mere physical or spatial insertion of the gray within a geometrical or lettered boundary. May the gray not actually stand apart from the pattern and still 'inhere'? We have tried in the present series to complete a configuration with the critical gray falling outside the spatial boundaries of the main pattern.

Our designs may be called *completion designs.* The horizontal bar of an L (*e.g.*) completes the literal character, while a like bar attached part way down on one side of a like vertical may not complete anything but only add another line. These two grays may, then, functionally correspond with the G_i and the G_o of our earlier series. Since we are dealing with an inherent membership instead of with a physical inclusion, however, we shall have to designate these grays as G_c (a completing gray) and G_n (a non-completing gray).

Let us see whether the quality of such an 'integrated' gray is explained according to the ordinary rules of contrast or requires the configurational or other comparable factor. The 11 patterns were always presented in pairs. On one member of each pair was a gray strip attached to black and *completing* the black design. The other member also had a like gray strip attached; but the black and gray together made (at least for the experimenter) no integral figure. Our completed designs were L, H, E, T, a sharp triangle set squarely upon its base, a round disc and a hat with its gray band. There were several variants of the literal designs.

We found it necessary, of course, to discover by way of the O's report what 'figure' was *actually perceived* and just *how it was integrated*. In displaying our gray comparisons, then, we shall distinguish the *conventional* designs from the *actual phenomenal* integrations of the observers.

We obtained 662 observations from our 11 Os. Of these a little over half (341) showed one of the two compared designs as actually completed by the gray, *i.e.* as phenomenally integrated. Of these 94 were 'equals' and 'no-reports.' This left 247 reports divided between 'lighter' and 'darker' in the ratio 189L : 58D (about 3.3 times as many L as D reports). This would seem to support the *Gestalt* doctrine that an incorporated gray tends to lighten, as in Benary's cross.

DISCUSSION AND CONCLUSION

In our experiments we have repeated and extended, under stricter control, the observations of Benary and others. We have also tried to maintain a sharp distinction between geometrical designs and spatial arrangements, on the one hand, and inherence and configuration, on the other.

The more significant of our experimental results may be now set down.

In the original Benary designs, a gray patch (G_i) spatially included within the contours of the black (or white) design tended to be reported as lighter (or darker) than a photometrically similar gray (G_o) set just outside these contours. This is in agreement with Benary.

By comparing the grays on a common field but without the black (or white) design, we made sure that the above outcome was not due to placement, distance or orientation of the grays, for under these conditions they tended to be the same in quality.

When we destroyed Benary's designs (Series II) by limiting the compared areas to the grays and their immediate surroundings (method of mutilated excerpts) we obtained the same result as before. Furthermore, G_i was reported as 'lighter' when the black, white and gray were apprehended as *juxtaposed patches* and not *configured* in Benary's sense, when G_i was within the black (or white) in a *spatial* way but not integral to, or *membered* with, it.

We next discovered cross-effects (Series III). The design qualitatively affected G_o, and the background affected G_i.

When we wholly submerged G_i in the design (Series IV), we found it to be amenable to brightness contrast; but we also found the gray quality to be the same whether 'membered' with the design or observed in abstraction from it.

When we succeeded in completing a design (Series V) by a gray that was spatially outside it, this completing gray tended to be lighter than a photometrically similar gray which failed to complete. But the lightening appeared practically the same with and without configuration.

Brightness Constancy and the Nature of Achromatic Colors*

HANS WALLACH

PART I

THE PROBLEM of brightness constancy arises through the following circumstances. The amount of light which is reflected by an opaque object and which stimulates the eye depends not only upon the color of the object but just as much upon the amount of light which falls on the object, that is upon the illumination in which the object is seen. When in spite of this, the seen colors are in agreement with the object colors, when a given object appears to have the same color in various illuminations, we speak of brightness constancy.

The majority of investigators who aim at all at functional explanations understand this problem to mean: How is illumination registered and in what way is it taken into account so that the experienced colors remain constant when the illumination is varied? In this version the problem is a difficult one at the outset, for illumination is never directly or independently given but is represented in stimulation only in as much as it affects the amount of light which is reflected by the objects. To be sure, we perceive illumination as well as surface color; a spot of light here, a shadow there, a brightly lighted region near the window or the dim light of dusk on everything. But the fact remains that both variables, object color and objective illumination, affect the eye through the same medium, the varying amount of reflected light. If the seen illumination were found to be in agreement with the objective illumination, in principle the same problem would arise which we face regarding the surface colors. There is only one stimulus variable to represent two objective variables each of which seems to have its counterpart in experience. Under these circumstances investigation has largely consisted in the

---

* From *J. exp. Psychol.*, 1948, **38**, 310-324. Reprinted by permission of the author and the publisher.

study of factors by which illumination could be recognized and in the demonstration of their effectiveness in bringing about constancy.

The following observations suggested a radically different approach to the writer. They concern some variations of an experiment by A. Gelb which demonstrated brightness constancy in a most impressive way. Gelb's experiment[1] is most conveniently performed by opening the door of a dimly lighted room and by suspending in the frame a piece of black paper. This paper is illuminated by a strong projection lantern which stands on the floor or on a low table and is tilted upwards so that the part of its beam which is not intercepted by the black paper passes through the open door onto the ceiling of the adjacent room where it is invisible to the observer. In the light of the strong lantern the paper may look white instead of black. When a white piece of paper is held up in front of the black paper so that it too reflects the strong light of the lantern, the black paper assumes a black color. According to the usual interpretation it looks first white because no cues for the special strong illumination are available when this illumination affects only one visible surface. With the introduction of the white paper into the beam a special brilliant illumination becomes visible and constancy is restored: the two papers are perceived with their real color.

The arrangement of Gelb's experiment lends itself to a still more impressive demonstration. When the black paper is presented alone, reducing the intensity of the lantern light by small steps to zero causes the perceived color of the paper to vary all the way from white through gray to black. Every change in illumination is accompanied by a corresponding change in the perceived color. However, when a larger white paper is fastened behind the black paper so that the latter is seen surrounded by white, the same changes in illumination do not at all affect the seen colors which remain white and black throughout. Paired in this way the colors are immune to changes in illumination and remain 'constant.' It is rather a change in the perceived illumination which now accompanies the change in the objective illumination.

The question arises: what determines the color with which the black paper is seen at a given intensity of the lantern light when the paper is presented alone? Do we deal in this situation with an

---

[1] Described in W. D. Ellis, *A source book of gestalt psychology.* New York: Harcourt, Brace, 1939, p. 207.

absolute relation between the intensity of the light which stimulates a portion of the retina and the resulting perceived color? In considering this question we have to remember that there is another variable in the situation, the dim general illumination of the room. When this is varied it becomes immediately clear that this general illumination also affects the color of the black paper. When, with a high intensity of the lantern light, the general illumination is raised, the color of the black paper changes from white to gray, and this in spite of the fact that the paper too now reflects light of a somewhat higher intensity than before. Only *relatively*, that is in relation to the light which comes from other surfaces, has the light reflected by the black paper become less intense.

Such dependence of the perceived color on the *relative* intensity of the perceived light should be demonstrable in a much simpler form, and this is the case.

In a dark room a white screen is illuminated by the light of two slide projectors. In one of the projectors an opaque card with a circular hole of ½ in. diameter is inserted, and the bright image of the hole is focused on the screen. The slide for the other projector consists of a blank glass covered with an opaque card with a circular hole of one in. diameter and with a ½ in. cardboard disk which is pasted concentrically into the hole. Focused on the screen this slide produces a bright ring. The two projectors are so adjusted that this ring surrounds the image of the ½ in. hole so that the edge of the latter coincides with the inner edge of the ring. The light intensity of the projectors can be changed by running them on variable transformers or by letting their beams pass through episcotisters.

We have then on the screen a circular region (disk) and surrounding it a ringshaped region which reflect light intensities that can be separately controlled. When the intensity of the disk is kept constant and that of the ring is widely varied, the color of the disk may change all the way from white to dark gray. The disk looks dark gray when the light reflected from the ring is of high intensity and it becomes white when the brightness of the ring is greatly lowered. When the light intensity of the disk is varied and that of the ring is kept constant, the color of the disk, of course, undergoes similar changes. Again it is quite clear that the color which appears in one region, namely in that of the disk, depends on the relation of the light intensity of this region to that of its surroundings. This is true also of the ring. It can be shown in corresponding fashion that its color depends on the relation of the intensity of the ring to that of the disk.

When the ring is altogether omitted so that the disk is seen in completely dark surroundings, it ceases to look white or gray and assumes instead a luminous appearance similar to that of the moon at dusk. Lowering the intensity of the disk greatly does not change this mode of appearance, provided the rest of the room is really dark; the disk looks merely dimmer. The same observation can be made with the ring when it is presented without the disk, or with both the ring and the disk when they are placed far from each other on the screen. Opaque colors which deserve to be called white or gray, in other words 'surface colors,' will make their appearance only when two regions of different light intensity are in contact with each other, for instance when the ring surrounds the disk or when two oblongs have the longer edges as their common border.

The importance of a close contact for the emergence of surface colors becomes strikingly clear in the following observation. The intensity of the disk is adjusted to be one quarter that of the ring, which makes the color of the disk a medium gray. An opaque object is moved from the side into the beam of the lantern which projects the ring so that part of it is blotted out by the shadow of that object. When this happens the gray color disappears almost simultaneously from that part of the disk which is adjacent to the shadow. It looks as if the dense gray there were dissolving leaving the screen transparent to let a light behind it shine through. Brought about in this fashion, the change from surface color to a luminous appearance is quite impressive. That side of the disk which is still well surrounded by a brighter ring continues to show the gray color, and between it and the luminous side the disk shows a steady gradient in the density of the gray.

These observations make it clear that, at least under these conditions, surface colors occur in our experience when regions of different light intensity are in contact with each other and that the particular surface colors which come about depend on the relation of these light intensities. They are apparently the product of nervous processes of limited scope, for close spatial contact between the regions of different light intensity is required for their emergence. Moreover, the degree to which surface color is present in a certain region depends on the intimacy of the contact between this region and its partner. This is easily demonstrated by the following observations.

No matter what the brightness relation between ring and disk be, the ring will always show a less dense surface color and have more of a luminous appearance than the disk. This becomes quite clear when two pairs of such regions are presented for comparison which are so chosen that the intensity of the ring in one pair equals that of the disk in the other one, and vice versa. Even the region of lower light intensity in each pair, which is perceived as a gray, has a more luminous appearance where it occurs in the ring than where it occurs in the disk. The most obvious explanation for this difference in the mode of appearance is that the disk is more under the influence of the ring than vice versa, in as much as the disk is completely surrounded by the ring, whereas the ring is in contact with the disk only on one side. This explanation agrees well with the observation reported earlier that the elimination of part of the ring rendered that part of the disk more luminous which was then no longer enclosed by a region of different light intensity.

This influence under which surface colors emerge is clearly a mutual one. Though less so, the ring does display surface color. There is a great difference in the mode of appearance between a ring which surrounds, for instance, an area of higher intensity and an equal ring presented in an otherwise dark field. Whereas the latter looks merely luminous, the former shows in addition to some luminosity a distinct gray.

The mutual influence on which the emergence of surface colors depends must also account for the fact that the particular colors which come about depend on the relation of the stimulating light intensities. It is probably best conceived of as some kind of interaction which takes place as part of the nervous process which underlies color perception.

It will be remembered that the dependence of the perceived colors on the relative intensities of the stimulating light was also evident in the variations of Gelb's experiment which were first reported. It remains to be added that the transition from surface color to a luminous mode of appearance can be demonstrated with Gelb's set-up in the following way. At first the special illumination of the black paper and the general illumination of the room are so adjusted that the black paper looks white. When now the general illumination is further reduced, the paper becomes more and more luminous, and it ceases altogether to look white when the rest of the room is completely dark. Luminosity of the paper can also be produced by excluding the general illumination from its immediate neighborhood. By such measures a rather luminous gray, not unlike that appearing in the ring, may also be achieved. Thus it is not only in projected rings and disks that luminosity appears as an alternative to surface colors when adequate differences in intensity are lacking or when the contact between those regions is diminished. Clearly discernible segregated objects as for instance a suspended piece of black paper function in the same fashion.

PART II

So far, we have become acquainted with the way in which surface colors come into existence and with the manner in which they depend on the stimulus situation. They depend on the relation of stimulus intensities on the retina which are so located with regard to each other that the subsequent nervous processes interact. Now the question arises what bearing this has on the problem of brightness constancy.

In order to answer this question, some clarification of the nature of brightness constancy is needed. One may say that brightness constancy prevails when a perceived color is in agreement with the corresponding object color. Object color is a persistent physical characteristic of a surface, the property to reflect a certain proportion of the light which falls on that surface. For instance, a surface which looks black under constancy conditions reflects about four percent of the illuminating light, and a white one about 80 percent. This property, called reflectance, is not conveyed to the eye as such. It is rather represented to the eye by light of a given intensity. This fact constitutes the problem of brightness constancy, for the intensity of the reflected light depends to the same degree on the color of the reflecting surface as on the strength of the illumination. If in our environment illumination were always and everywhere the same, the fact that our visual sense is not directly affected by reflectances but only by the reflected light intensities would not raise a problem in perception, for the reflected light could represent the object colors unequivocally. But illumination varies widely, even between different parts of the same visual field, and often very different light intensities come to represent the same reflectance to the eye and, in constancy, produce the same color in the observer's experience. When, for instance, a medium gray which reflects 20 percent of the illuminating light is presented once in an illumination of an intensity 100 and again under light of an intensity 300, the intensities of the reflected light are 20 and 60 respectively; if complete constancy prevails, both stimulus intensities lead to perception of the same medium gray. Similarly the white background on which the gray samples are shown will reflect light of the intensity 80 in the weaker illumination and of the intensity 240 where it is in the stronger illumination, and the two differently illuminated parts of the background will probably both be judged as white. At first glance no orderly connection between stimulus intensity and perceived color seems to exist.

There is, however, one feature in the stimulus situation which remains the same when the illumination is varied. The intensity of the light reflected by the gray in the weaker illumination (20) stands in a ratio of 1 : 4 to that reflected by the white in the weaker illumination (80), and the same ratio exists between the intensities reflected by the gray and the white in the stronger illumination (60 and 240). It is easy to see that in the case of any given set of object colors the *ratios* of the intensities of the reflected light remain the same for any change in illumination which affects all of them.[2] Thus, if the perceived colors were to depend on the *ratios* of the intensities of the reflected lights, they would remain unchanged when a given set of object colors were presented in changed illumination, and constancy would be assured. A medium gray may serve again as an example. Although it affects the eye with different light intensities when the illumination is changed, it would be perceived as the same color because the ratio of the intensity that it reflects to the intensity of the light reflected by the surrounding white would remain the same, for a change in illumination affects the latter in the same proportion.

At this point we have to consider the observations reported in Part I. They suggested that the perceived surface colors depend on the relation, not yet quantitatively defined, of the light intensities in interacting regions. But we now find that constancy would result,

---

[2] This is a simple consequence of the fact already mentioned that object colors reflect a constant *fraction* of the illumination.

if our visual perception functioned in such a fashion that the perceived colors depended on the *ratios* of the intensities of the reflected light.

Thus, we merely have to make the assumption that the relation on which surface colors depend is one of simple proportionality to give the observations of Part I a direct bearing on the problem of brightness constancy. If this assumption were correct brightness constancy would find its explanation in the very process by which surface colors come about.

This assumption can be tested by simple experiments. If it is correct, the particular colors which are perceived in a pair of ring and disk should depend on the ratio of the intensities of the two regions, and only on that ratio. In other words, no matter what the absolute intensities of ring and disk may be, the same colors should be seen in the case of any pair of intensities which happen to stand in the same ratio to each other. This is, in close approximation, the case, as the following report of quantitative experiments[3] shows.

Two pairs of ring and disk were used, in order to permit simultaneous comparison. The intensity of each of these four regions could be varied independently.

Four identical projections lanterns equipped with 500 watt bulbs were used for this purpose. They were arranged in two groups and each group produced on the screen a pair of ring and disk as described in Part I. They were all so adjusted that they gave their respective regions the same light intensity. This was done in the following way. First a pair of ring and disk was formed with one lantern from group I and one from group II, and the intensity of one of them was varied until the contour between the ring and the disk disappeared because of brightness equality. Then these two lanterns were restored to their respective groups and similar adjustments were made within each group by varying the light intensities of the not yet equated lanterns.

The intensity variations required by the experiments were brought about with the help of episcotisters through which the lantern beams had to pass before reaching the screen. This technique has the advantage that the episcotister apertures are a direct measure of the relative intensities in the various regions.

Measurements were made by the method of limits. Ring and disk of one pair and the ring of the other pair were kept at constant intensities,

---

[3] These experiments were performed by the students of various seminars in Perception and classes in Experimental Psychology at Swarthmore College under the author's supervision.

and the intensity of the remaining disk was varied in suitable steps until the S judged the colors of the two disks as equal.

In the first experiment one of the rings was given the full illumination of its lantern and the disk inside it received half of the intensity, for its light beam passed through an episcotister of 180 degrees aperture. The light for the ring of the other pair was cut down to one-eighth of full intensity by passing it through an episcotister of 45 degrees aperture. The aperture for the disk of the latter pair was varied in steps of two degrees. The following are the means of one upper and one lower limit for each of five Ss: 24, 26, 24, 23, 24 degrees with a total mean of 24.2 degrees. This result means that, on the average, a light intensity in a disk corresponding to an episcotister aperture of 24.2 degrees when it is surrounded by a ring of an intensity of 45 degrees aperture brings about in the S's experience the same gray as does a disk of an intensity of 180 degrees aperture inside a ring of an intensity of 360 degrees aperture. There is only a small deviation from the value of 22.5 degrees which with 45 degrees forms the same ratio as does 180 degrees with 360 degrees. Comparing the grays in the two disks was not difficult for the Ss. The great difference in absolute intensity between the two pairs of ring and disk (8 : 1) made the less intense pair look much dimmer, but that did not affect the distinctness of the disks' color. However, it made the rings look very different; though both were white, the more intense one was by far more luminous. This latter observation which was also made in most of the following experiments seems to be important, for it corresponds to a fact which can be observed in real constancy situations. When identical sets of object colors are placed in different illuminations and appear approximately the same, the set in the stronger objective illumination is often also *seen* to be more strongly illuminated. Perceived illumination and the different degree of luminous appearance which was frequently observed in our experiments seem, functionally speaking, to be closely related experiences.

In another experiment a disk of 90 degrees intensity was shown in a ring of 360 degrees intensity. This combination which forms an intensity ratio of 4 : 1 brings about a much darker gray in the disk. In the other pair, the disk whose intensity was varied was surrounded by a ring of 180 degrees intensity. The proportionate value for the disk is here 45 degrees. The averages of two upper and two lower limits for each of four Ss were 46, 52, 45, 44 degrees with a mean of 47 degrees.

In the following experiment the disk of the brighter pair was varied and a ratio of 3 : 1 between ring and disk was used. In the darker pair, the ring had an intensity of 180 degrees and the ring one of 60 degrees, and the variable disk was surrounded by a ring of 360 degrees intensity. Five upper and five lower limits were determined for each of three Ss. The means were 113, 115, 121 degrees. The proportionate value is here 120 degrees.

It will be noted that so far all deviations from the proportionate values were in one direction. They all imply that, where they occur, a disk of proportionate intensity in the dimmer pair looks darker than the disk in the pair of higher intensity; *viz.*, in the first two experiments the disk in the less intense pair had to be given a slightly higher than proportionate intensity to give a color match and in the last experiment the disk in the more intense pair had to be made objectively darker. Thus, although these deviations are small, they deserve our attention. Experiments with an improved technique were made to find out how significant they are.

To facilitate measuring a variable episcotister[4] was used for the determination of the limits. This device permits changing the aperture by definite amounts while it is spinning. Only when the Ss had given a judgment of equality was the episcotister stopped and its angle measured with a protractor.

It has been described above how the intensities of the four lanterns were equated at the outset of the experiments. These equations are likely to contain subliminal errors which could affect our measurements. In the experiments which follow the episcotisters were interchanged between the groups of lanterns after half the number of limits had been determined for a given S, so that the group which during the first half of an experiment produced the brighter pair of ring and disk were made to produce the dimmer pair during the second half, and vice versa. Thus, any error in the original lantern adjustment which would affect the measurements during the first half of the experiment in one direction would in the second half affect it in the opposite direction. In this manner such an error will appear in the scatter of the limit values but will not affect their mean.

The first experiment (I) done with this improved technique was one with a small difference between the brighter and the dimmer pair.

---

[4] Designed and built by R. Gerbrands, Emerson Hall, Cambridge, Mass.

The former had a ring of 360 degrees intensity and a disk of 180 degrees, and the other pair had a variable disk in a ring of 180 degrees. Four Ss took part in the experiment. For each one four upper and four lower limits were determined. Table I presents the means of these limits. The proportionate value is here 90 degrees. It will be noted that the small deviations from this value are in a direction opposite to those previously reported, for they would imply that a disk of proportionate intensity in the dimmer pair is perceived as a slightly lighter gray than the disk in the more intense pair.

TABLE I. EPISCOTISTER SETTINGS IN DEGREES FOR DISK WITHIN RING OF 180 DEGREES IN COMPARISON WITH DISK OF 180 DEGREES WITHIN RING OF 360 DEGREES

Subjects	Ad.	McN.	Ba.	Cl.	
Upper limit	88	86	85.5	90	
Lower limit	84	84	79.5	84.5	
Mean	86	85	82	86	Grand mean: 85

TABLE II. EPISCOTISTER SETTINGS IN DEGREES FOR DISK WITHIN RING OF 90 DEGREES IN COMPARISON WITH DISK OF 240 DEGREES WITHIN RING OF 360 DEGREES

Subjects	Mo.	Cr.	Ke.	Cy.	
Upper limit	61	62	73	74	
Lower limit	62	64	68	67	
Mean	61.5	63	70.5	70.5	Grand mean: 66.4

This is not so with the results of the following experiment (II) in which a still lighter gray was produced and in which the intensity of the dimmer ring was only one quarter of that of the brighter one. In the dimmer pair the ring had an intensity of 90 degrees and the disk was variable, while in the brighter pair the ring had 360 degrees and the disk 240 degrees of light. The results are given in Table II. With the Ss Mo. and Cr., 10 upper and 10 lower limits were determined, with Ke. and Cy. only six. Individual differences are larger in this experiment. For two of the Ss there was a marked deviation from the proportionate value of 60 degrees, which implied that for them a disk of 60 degrees intensity in the dimmer pair showed a slightly darker gray than the disk in the brighter pair.

Ten Ss were employed in an experiment (III) in which the variable disk was surrounded by a ring of 360 degrees of light and the dimmer pair consisted of a ring of 90 degrees and a disk of 30 degrees intensity. Six upper and lower limits were determined for each S, except for Ss Mo. and Cr., who again supplied 10 pairs of limits each. The average of the individual means as shown in Table III was 106 degrees, a clear deviation from the proportionate value of 120 degrees. It implies that the gray in the disk of low intensity looks somewhat darker than a disk of proportionate value in the brighter pair.

TABLE III. EPISCOTISTER SETTINGS IN DEGREES FOR DISK WITHIN
RING OF 360 DEGREES IN COMPARISON WITH DISK OF
30 DEGREES WITHIN RING OF 90 DEGREES

Subjects	Ca.	Ga.	Hs.	Ht.	Lu.	Ro.	Mo.	Cr.	Ke.	Cy.	
Upper limit	104.5	91	117.5	116.5	113	130	128	107.5	105	113	
Lower limit	92.5	91	99.5	98.5	103	112	100	103	97	95	
Mean	98.5	91	108.5	107.5	108	121	114	105	101	104	Grand mean: 106

The direction of the deviations from proportionate values encountered in the last two experiments was such that they could be regarded as the effect of a slight influence of the absolute stimulus intensities on the color process which otherwise could be conceived as functioning according to a proportional law. The question arose whether these deviations reflected intrinsic properties of the color process or whether they were introduced by incidental experimental conditions. An answer cannot yet be given and must be left to further detailed investigation. However, an experiment which was performed with this question in mind will be reported below, because it will add the data of still another combination of intensities.

It was suspected that the presence of the brighter pair of ring and disk in the visual field when the gray in the disk of the dimmer pair developed was responsible for the fact that this gray looked a trifle too dark. If the high intensities of the brighter pair had an influence across the spatial interval on the colors which emerged in the dimmer pair, this is what should have happened. Such an influence can be avoided by presenting the pairs successively. This was done in the following experiment (IV). The intensities in the brighter pair were 360 and 180 degrees, the ring in the dimmer pair was 90 degrees and the disk was varied. Table IV shows for four Ss the means of four upper and four lower limits. Ordinarily, with an intensity ratio of 4 : 1 between the rings the deviation under discussion was to be expected. It did not appear. The slight deviation from the proportionate value of 45 degrees was in the opposite direction.

In another experiment, however, successive presentation failed to eliminate completely the deviation under discussion. Experiment III was repeated with three further Ss who did the experiment twice, once with successive and once with simultaneous presentation. The limits listed in Table V are the averages of four determinations each. Although successive presentation reduces the deviation from the proportionate value of 120 degrees, it does not eliminate it.

TABLE IV. EPISCOTISTER SETTINGS IN DEGREES FOR DISK WITHIN RING OF 90 DEGREES IN COMPARISON WITH DISK OF 180 DEGREES WITHIN RING OF 360 DEGREES

Subjects	Ad.	McN.	Ba.	Cl.	
Upper limit	43	42	41	44	
Lower limit	41	40	42	44	
Mean	42	41	41.5	44	Grand mean: 42

TABLE V. EPISCOTISTER SETTINGS IN DEGREES FOR DISK WITHIN RING OF 360 DEGREES IN COMPARISON WITH DISK OF 30 DEGREES WITHIN RING OF 90 DEGREES

Subjects	Cl.		He.		Be.	
Presentation	Sim.	Succ.	Sim.	Succ.	Sim.	Succ.
Upper limit	110.5	121	99	108.5	104	112
Lower limit	99.5	99	97.5	99	94	104
Mean	105	110	98	104	99	108

These deviations from proportionate values appear rather insignificant when one compares them with the remaining effect of the proportional law. For example, in Experiment III which showed the largest deviation, a disk of an intensity of 30 degrees aperture had on the average the same color as one of an intensity of 106 degrees aperture, that is, an intensity 3.5 times as high. The deviation from the proportionate value of 120 degrees amounts only to 12 percent.

It should be mentioned at this point that such experiments can also be done with a less elaborate set-up. Two color mixers and one projection lantern suffice for a crude demonstration of the proportional law. With the help of a large color wheel of black and white disks and a small one fastened on top of it to the same mixer one can obtain a ring-shaped and a circular region in which the intensities of the reflected light can be varied independently. On one mixer, e.g., the large wheel can be set to show a sector of 90 degrees white and the small one a sector of 45 degrees white. To the other mixer are fastened a small wheel with a white sector of 180 degrees and a large wheel of 360 degrees white. When the mixers spin in general room illumination, one sees a dark gray disk surrounded by a medium gray ring on one mixer and a light gray disk in a white ring on the other one. However, when the mixers are placed in separate strictly local illumination they look quite different. That illumination can be provided by a lantern equipped with an opaque slide which has two circular holes a good distance apart. It projects two narrow beams of light of equal intensity. When the mixers are placed each in one of the beams at such a distance from the projector that their wheels are covered by the light almost to the outer rim and the rest of the room is entirely dark, both color mixers show a white ring and a light gray disk much alike in color. The reason for this change is easy to understand. Under local illumination the two color mixers provide exactly the same pattern of stimulus intensities as the set-up in Experiment IV, and thus the same colors develop as in that experiment. In general illumination, on the other hand, the pairs of ring and disk are surrounded by regions of other intensity, e.g., the light reflected by the wall of the room, which cooperate in determining the colors which come about in the pairs. If, for instance, light reflected by a white wall forms the stimulus intensity of the surrounding region, that intensity stands to the intensity of the dimmer ring in a ratio of 4 : 1, and in this relation the ring should assume a medium gray color, as indeed it did.

It was explained above how the assumption that the achromatic colors depend on the ratios of the pertinent stimulus intensities accounts for brightness constancy. On that occasion complete constancy was shown to follow from this assumption. However, complete constancy has hardly ever been demonstrated experimentally. An object color presented in reduced illumination usually looks somewhat darker than another sample of that color in full illumination, though not as much darker as the difference of the reflected light intensities would warrant if there were no constancy. Yet complete constancy would follow from a direct application of the proportional law. Deviations from proportionality which occurred in our experiments are by far too small to account for the usual lag in constancy. The difficulty resolves itself when it is realized that the proportional law cannot be applied so simply to this situation. Here the two pairs of regions, the sample and its background in full illumination and the other sample with background in reduced illumination, are not as completely separated from each other as the corresponding regions in our experiments, for the regions of different illumination are in contact with each other and the brighter one can have an influence on the dimmer one. In other words, we have here a case where three or more regions of different intensity interact. Such processes have not yet been sufficiently investigated, and no report can be made at this time. It seems, however, quite likely that a full investigation will furnish the rules for the prediction of the lag in constancy in individual experiments.

This report may so far have given the impression that, apart from the small deviations discussed, the proportional law permits prediction of color equations if the pertinent stimulus intensities are known. However, this is so only with important qualifications. To a certain extent also the geometrical arrangement of the regions of different intensity has an influence on what colors come about in these regions. Some brief experiments which permit a first appraisal of the importance of these conditions will be reported below.

In the measuring experiments so far reported the width of the ring was ⅝ of the diameter of the disk so that the area of the ring was four times as large as the area of the disk. A reduction of the width of the ring to ¼ of the diameter of the disk so that its area was about the same as that of the disk did not affect the color in the disk as the following experiment shows, in which the colors in two disks were compared which were surrounded by rings of different width. Both rings were given the same intensity of 120 degrees aperture; the disk in the narrow ring had an intensity of 15 degrees and appeared as a very dark gray; the disk in the ring of standard width was variable. The mean of two upper and two lower limits for a single S was also 15 degrees. A number of other observers were satisfied with that equation.

The width of the narrow ring was further reduced so that it amounted to only $\frac{1}{16}$ of the diameter of the disk. The same constant intensities as in the last experiment were used. The averages of two upper and two lower limits for each of two Ss were 37 and 37 degrees. This result means that a disk of 15 degrees intensity inside the very narrow ring looked as light as a disk of 37 degrees intensity inside a ring of standard width. The outcome of this experiment was so striking that we repeated it with another combination of intensities. The intensity of the two rings remained the same, but the disk in the very narrow ring had an intensity of 60 degrees. Again a higher intensity was needed for an equation in the disk inside the standard ring. The averages of two upper and two lower limits for the same two Ss were 87 and 86 degrees. However, with this intensity ratio of 120 : 60, which produces a light gray, the effect of making the ring very narrow was not so great. It amounted only to 45 percent, whereas in the case of a ratio of 120 : 15 which normally produces a very dark gray the disk in the standard ring had to be made 145 percent more intense. On the whole it looks as if the very narrow ring which has only one-quarter of the area of the disk cannot make the disk color as dark as does a ring of sufficient width.

As just reported, no difference in the effect of a ring which has about the same area as the disk and of one which has four times the area of the disk has been found. Two further measurements were made with a much wider ring. Its width was 1.5 the diameter of the disk and its area 15 times that of the disk. In one experiment the intensity ratio between the wide ring and its disk was again 120 : 15. In the disk of the standard pair the averages of four upper and four lower limits for the two Ss were 17 and 16 degrees. When a ratio of 120 : 60 was used, averages for two pairs of limits were 66 and 63 degrees. The deviations from 15 and 60 degrees respectively are probably incidental. At any rate, they are not in the direction which would indicate an enhancement in the effectiveness of the ring with increased width. It seems that, once the ring has an area equal to that of the disk, any further increase in its width does not affect the resulting color of the disk.

It was reported in Part I that a ring looks more luminous than a disk of the same intensity in another pair in which the intensities of ring and disk are the same as in the first pair but interchanged. The question arises whether such a reversal of intensities also causes a color difference in the regions of equal intensity. Two pairs of disk and ring in which the area of the ring was the same as that of the disk were presented and the lights were so arranged that in one pair the lower intensity was in the ring and in the other pair in the disk. The two higher intensities in the two pairs amounted both to 360 degrees, the ring of lower intensity was kept at 45 degrees, and the disk of lower intensity was variable. Measurements were made with four *S*s. The means of three upper and three lower limits were 54, 71, 83, 86 degrees. These figures indicate that for the same intensity ratio the lower intensity appears as a lighter gray when it is given in the ring than when it is given in the disk. A rather dark gray results from a ratio of 360 : 45 degrees. In the case of smaller ratios which give rise to lighter grays the differences in color which result when the intensities of ring and disk are interchanged are very much smaller. For an intensity ratio of 2 : 1 only a difference in luminosity can be discerned.

SUMMARY

It was found that opaque achromatic surface colors are perceived when light of different intensity stimulates adjacent areas on the retina. The achromatic color which is seen in a particular region must be regarded as the result of stimulation received from that region *and* of stimulation from neighboring regions. Although these colors are qualities which are perceived in a given region, they are products of an interaction process, which depends on difference in stimulation in at least two areas. In the absence of a suitable difference in stimulation a color of an entirely different mode of appearance is seen. A single bright region in an otherwise dark field, for instance, looks luminous instead of white, and reducing the light intensity in that region fails to make it look gray; it continues to appear luminous and merely becomes dimmer.

The first steps were taken to investigate quantitatively the rules of this dependence in the simplest case, that of two regions of different intensities of stimulation where one region surrounds the other. The colors which come about under these circumstances depend in close approximation on the *ratios* of the intensities involved and seem independent of the absolute intensity of local stimulation. The region of higher intensity will assume the color white and that of lower intensity will show a gray (or a black) which depends on the intensity ratio of the two regions. The greater the difference in intensity the darker will be the gray which appears in the region of the lower intensity.

It can be shown that a dependence of perceived colors on the ratios of stimulus intensities accounts for the constancy of achromatic colors under varying illumination. Complete constancy would follow from this rule of interaction of two intensities. The fact that measurements of brightness constancy rarely give results which denote complete constancy presents no difficulty for this explanation. These experiments involve interaction between more than two regions of different stimulus intensity.

■■■

Some Factors and Implications of Color Constancy*, †

HARRY HELSON

PROBLEMS OF COLOR CONSTANCY

THAT COLORS AND FORMS tend within limits to remain constant in spite of changes in illumination and orientation is well-known from common experience. It was recognized by both Hering and Helmholtz who saw in it problems for visual science and formulated explanations to account for questions it raised. According to Helmholtz[11] we learn to judge how objects should look in white illumination and see them accordingly under different lighting conditions. While we are not conscious of the basis of our inferences learning operates to restore colors as they should be in daylight. Helmholtz emphasized the fact that colors interest us mainly as properties of objects and not in their own right. Hence the approximate constancy. Hering put it thus: "Approximate constancy of the color of objects in spite of large qualitative and quantitative changes in general illumination of the visual field is one of the most striking and important facts in the domain of physiological optics. Without this approximate constancy a piece of chalk on an overcast day would appear as dark as a piece of coal on a sunny day and in the course of one day would take on all possible lightnesses between white and black." [15] Whereas Helmholtz attributed constancy to learning and judgment, Hering sought more tangible physiological mechanisms as the cause such as pupillary changes, adaptation, and contrast. But Hering felt obliged to invoke psychological factors in addition because he believed that "All the things which are known to us from past experience . . . in respect to color are seen through the spectacle of 'memory colors.' "

* From *J. opt. Soc. Amer.*, 1943, **33**, 555-567. Reprinted by permission of the author and the publisher.

† Paper presented at the Symposium on Vision at the Optical Society Meeting in New York City, March 5-6, 1943.

Katz at first[21] accepted the Hering concept of memory color but later[22] in the second edition of his book admitted that the evidence against was greater than the evidence for memory color.

It is now seen that the problem of color constancy involves not one but many aspects of color vision as well as the spatial functions of the eye. Among the questions to be clarified before the problems of constancy can be satisfactorily explained the following seem most important: (1) Conditions and modes of colors; (2) Dimensions of colors in the various modes; (3) Tolerance to changes in amount and composition of the illumination; (4) Relations of contrast, constancy, adaptation, assimilation, and other visual processes; (5) Effects of neighboring colors, surroundings, distance, and special conditions of vision such as tubular and lens vision; (6) Spatial effects on colors and effects of color on spatial attributes of vision; and (7) Role of retinal *versus* central mechanisms. The problems of color constancy are thus seen to be neither simple nor univocal.

CONDITIONS AND CHARACTERISTICS OF FILM AND SURFACE COLORS

We are indebted to David Katz for bringing the problems of constancy into the laboratory and for devising a way by which they can be controlled and measured. Katz used several methods for investigating constancy, the most striking being the cast shadow set-up as shown in Fig. 1. Two color mixers are placed before a homogeneous background and a screen is placed between them. Light coming from one side fully illumines one mixer and is partly cut off from the other. An observer is asked to obtain a match between various mixtures of white and black on the shadowed side and the fully illuminated mixer. Starting with 360° W on the shadowed mixer it is found that although 360° W on the illuminated side is too light for a match the disk mixture which does match is not as dark as would be expected from the reduction in illumination on the shadowed side. After a match is obtained if the two disks are viewed through small holes in a neutral screen placed before the observer it is found that the shadowed disk is much darker than the illuminated one. If the two disks are again matched as "hole" or aperture colors they will not be equal in unrestricted vision. Matches made under the one set of conditions do not hold for the other. A photograph of the disks when matched in free observation shows the shadowed disk as too dark or as if the camera sees the disks in aperture vision. Anything done to narrow the field of view to the disks themselves tends toward the aperture appearance: squinting, monocular vision, small visual angle, and "analytical attitude." Peripheral vision also tends to approximate aperture viewing.

The changes in lightness just described as one views colors in free and in aperture conditions are not the only effects observable. Whereas the two disks match very well as aperture colors, in free observation observers find it hard to obtain equality between all characteristics of the colors simultaneously: when the disks are equal in one respect they still appear different in others. At this point it should be noted that while the term constancy has been extensively used in the literature, nothing like complete preservation of all color dimensions is found under changing conditions. At best

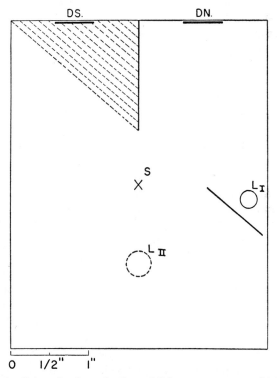

FIG. 1. Conditions for investigation of lightness constancy. Light source L_I illuminates the normal color mixer DN and casts a shadow by means of a screen on shadowed mixer DS. The observer sits at S. L_{II} is an optional room light.

only one or two dimensions remain stable while others change. Recognition of this fact led Katz to postulate additional dimensions for the achromatic series which can no longer be regarded as unidimensional. The other changes which follow change in what Katz called "mode of color appearance" concern aspects of color which are not usually regarded as pure color qualities. Aperture colors lack surface texture and tend toward a common soft, filmy appearance. They have no definite localization behind the aperture in which they are seen but do tend to stay in the frontal-parallel plane with respect to the observer. Colors in free observation are characterized by surface texture or "micro-structure," are hard and resist the gaze, and take whatever plane the object is in since they belong to objects. Surface colors approximate various degrees of constancy while aperture colors tend to maintain closer correspondence with the actual stimulus impinging on the retina. We now know that aperture colors are no less subject to influence from the aperture screen than surface colors are to their surroundings.

Still other modes and their conditions were described by Katz: volume or bulky colors, transparent surface and transparent film colors, mirrored, glossy, and lustrous modes. Different modes may require different descriptive terms or dimensions. All modes of appearance may be reduced to the film mode by viewing the color through the reduction screen technique described above. This mode Katz regarded as the most primitive in color vision. The Viennese group under the leadership of Bühler has identified the film mode with rod function and the surface mode with cone action. It does not appear that sharply defined mechanisms are necessary for the various modes of color which Katz has described.

ROLE OF THE ILLUMINANT

It is natural that in the first accounts of constancy the role of the illumination should have been singled out for attention since the problem first arose in connection with preservation of object color in spite of change in illumination. Accordingly Katz[21] ascribed color constancy in chromatic illumination to "noticing" the abnormal lighting so that object colors are transformed back to their "normal" appearance. Jaensch[16] asserted, on the contrary, that transformation occurs because object color is abstracted from illumination or at least the illumination is not noticed. Bühler,[4] followed by his students, Bocksch,[2] Krauss,[27] Kardos[19] and others, stressed the differences between rod and cone functioning and separation of general illumination from object color by means of stray light from dust particles in the air and in the media of the eye. Thouless,[37] interested in the constancy of form, points out that perception gives neither perfect constancy nor one-to-one correspondence with stimulus variables, but rather presents us with a compromise between the two which represents a regression toward the real.

Psychological terms like noticing or discounting the changes in illumination, transformation, and regresison toward the real, imply some standard set of conditions in which object colors were seen and toward which they tend to revert under new conditions. Several findings indicate that, while the net effect may be constancy in many cases, these expressions give no indication of the mechanisms by which the result is achieved and may give a wrong steer to thinking. Thus when observers are asked to report on colors in deep shadow or in strongly chromatic illumination they do so without knowledge of what the "normal" colors should be and without reference to external standards if none is provided. On the other hand, even if observers are made fully aware of the nature of the illumination conditions and how they differ from so-called normal, knowledge does not affect the striking phenomena previously reported.[13] Finally, experiments with animals preclude the possibility that higher psychological functions are involved in the phenomena of constancy unless we are willing to grant much more to infra-human organisms "mentally" than is possible on many other grounds. Animals below man show tendencies toward constancy as strong as he. Thus Köhler[25] found that chimpanzees chose food from containers of high (low) reflectance after the illumination was changed so that the absolute amount of light was less (more) than from food boxes nearby of low (high) reflectance. Locke[29] reports that humans showed degrees of approach to constancy ranging from 0.10 to 0.23 (1.00 representing perfect constancy) whereas rhesus monkeys had values ranging from 0.47 to 0.65. Katz and Révész[23] trained hens to discriminate rice grains which were white in daylight from grains colored yellow and found that the hens subsequently continued to pick the "white" grains in strongly yellow illumination. Burkamp[5] testing fishes (Cyprinides) found strong tendencies toward both lightness and chromatic constancy with changes in amount and quality of illumination.

With this evidence from animals below man it does not seem

necessary to postulate higher cortical activity to explain the facts of color constancy. The concept of "normal illumination" is one of the concepts implying that constancy springs from more or less complicated learning mechanisms and it has therefore been subjected to criticism. There are some senses in which it may be legitimate to speak of "normal" illumination even though it may be misleading in other respects. Katz suggested [21] that details of surface structure are best seen in normal illumination and from these details texture and other object properties are identified. This criterion depends upon the resolving power of the eye which is usually regarded as a spatial function rather than a color function, although resolution is known to be affected by wave-length as we shall see below. Judd and the writer[17] attempted to synthesize an illuminant in which it was believed all non-selective samples would appear achromatic. This criterion of normal illumination is based on chromatic properties of the illuminant. Preliminary attempts at synthesis were not successful but the possibility is not thereby ruled out that such an illuminant may be found. If achromaticity of non-selective samples of all reflectances proves to be too stringent a requirement for normal illumination, Illuminant C of the I.C.I. might be referred to as normal and the colors seen under it might be taken as the normal colors of objects. But this raises the difficulty that what is normal for one purpose may not be for another, hence relevancy to purpose at hand may be the deciding factor in the choice of a normal illuminant. If this is true then there may be more than one normal illuminant.

While the concept of normal illumination has been subjected to criticism and has undergone revision as a result, it has served to focus attention on the role of the illumination as one of the general conditions of vision. The part played by the illumination will be further discussed in succeeding sections.

TOLERANCE FOR CHANGES IN ILLUMINATION
AND IN THE DIMENSIONS OF COLORS

We have just seen that animals far below man compensate for changes in amount and composition of illumination by responding to objects as if their colors retained their daylight appearance. Does this mean that changes in general illumination pass unnoticed as Jaensch asserted or is there some means by which object color is distinguished from the illumination in which it appears? Perception of illumination is, as Katz has insisted, as immediate as awareness of object color and in many cases the composition of the illuminant must be exactly right for matching and grading objects. We come here to the limits of compensation which have important consequences which we must now discuss.

Reverting to the cast-shadow experiment we find that two white disks in different illuminations may be equated for lightness but the one in shadow is seen as "white-in-dim-illumination," that is, as a less pronounced white. Were the two disks alike in every respect it would mean that we cannot distinguish between bright and dim illuminations. The failure in this case to achieve complete constancy serves as a cue to the fact that the illuminations are different. Similarly decrease in illumination makes red and yellow less pronounced as chromas while green and blue become more pronounced (Sinemus[35]). Increase in amount of illumination causes opposite effects on pronouncedness of these hues. Sinemus has found that artificial production of micropsia through the use of concave lenses has the same effect as increase in illumination on the pronouncedness of colors.[35] White and black also behave differently in high and low illuminations and in micropsia, the former gaining in pronouncedness in strong light, the latter losing under the same conditions. Pronouncedness thus furnishes a direct clue to conditions of illumination in the case of both cromatic and achromatic colors.

When the composition of the illumination is changed radically from daylight, as in spectrally homogeneous illuminants, the usual relations between the fundamental dimensions of color are greatly altered. Thus highly reflecting samples in spectrally homogeneous illumination cannot be matched by any mixture of daylight colors because the former are both lighter and more saturated than any possible daylight colors (Helson and Jeffers;[13] Krauss[27]). From experience with daylight colors it seems like a contradiction in terms to assert that colors can be both whiter and redder at the same time since increase in the one means decrease in the other under "normal" viewing. Breakdown in constancy also occurs when objects are viewed at a distance and the results are quite surprising, as Schmeckebeier[34] has described them. Thus yellow appears red, then orange, and lastly yellow with decreasing distance; violet appears blue, then brown, then black, and lastly violet. Once the limits of compensation have been reached color changes from common experience are many and at first sight baffling.

The differential responses to complex viewing situations are largely responsible for whatever constancy exists and help explain other facts as well, once it is recognized that the visual mechanism behaves as if it had different sensitivities for different dimensions. The eye is least sensitive to change in general illumination. Krüger[28] found that thresholds for general changes are 2.2-5.0 times greater than thresholds for lightness of grays on Maxwell disks. The same fact is noted by Marzynski[31] who distinguishes between partial and total changes in the visual field, the latter having less effect on lightness than the former. Gates[7] found the "qualitative" limen (for lightness?) to be about 12 percent higher than the limen for "intensitive" changes (for brightness?) using Maxwell disks, a fact confirmed by Henneman.[14] Approaching the matter from a somewhat different angle, Miss Martha DeWitt at Bryn Mawr College determined the range of reflectances of non-selective samples on non-selective backgrounds which were called white, gray, and black, by more or less naïve observers. Table I shows that a wide range of reflectances can yield black, gray, or white, depending upon reflectance of background (cf. Judd [18]).

In this section we have distinguished three differential responses of the visual mechanism: (1) to changes in general illumination; (2) to white-gray-black quality; and (3) to bright-dim quality of either objects or illumination. These three discriminatory responses enable the eyes to perform multiple functions simultaneously: to apprehend the general level and quality of illumination, and to distinguish between objects and their surroundings. These functions include chromatic as well as achromatic qualities. Because we have spoken of different discriminatory responses with different thesholds of response it should not be inferred that we therefore regard the visual mechanism as composed of several mechanisms. Rather, we regard the visual apparatus as a unitary mechanism with extraordinary lability in function. Re-interpretation of such terms as adaptation, contrast, assimilation, and induction makes possible a unitary view of how the eyes can perform these multiple functions. Already highly successful physiological theories have been elaborated by Hecht and his co-workers[9] and mathematical theories by Judd [17] and Spencer[36] have resulted in successful predictions of color conversions. The known properties of such retinal substances as visual purple and similar properties of bleaching and regeneration which other retinal pigments undoubtedly possess[10] make such terms as adaptation, contrast, and assimilation more than descriptive of color phenomena for they apply to the underlying physiological processes at the basis of vision as well. In the remainder of this paper the attempt will be made to show how these processes can be made to explain the chief facts of constancy* and related phenomena by means of a single theory.

TABLE I. REFLECTANCES OF NON-SELECTIVE SAMPLES ON NON-SELECTIVE GROUNDS FOUND TO APPEAR BLACK, GRAY, AND WHITE

Background Reflectance	Black	Lightness Quality Gray	White
0.037	0.037	0.037-0.377	0.377-0.803
0.230	0.037-0.042	0.042-0.430	0.430-0.803
0.803	0.037-0.084	0.084-0.630	0.630-0.803

EFFECTS OF BRIGHTNESS OF STIMULUS, REFLECTANCE OF BACKGROUND, AND DEPTH OF SHADOW ON LIGHTNESS COMPENSATION

I propose now to discuss some experiments on lightness constancy carried on by Mr. R. W. Bornemeier at Bryn Mawr College, which were designed to determine whether our theory would account for certain experimental results reported in the literature. The bearing of these experiments on some of the striking cases of constancy will be stressed.

Using an experimental situation similar to the cast-shadow set-up of Katz (Fig. 1), observers were required to match a black-white Maxwell disk in bright illumination with one in shadow for various mixtures of the latter. The reduction screen technique of Katz was unnecessary since we could measure the luminances of the disks with

---

* In the remainder of this paper the term "constancy" will be used as little as possible and the term "compensation" will be used instead. The change in terms is desirable because constancy is only approximate and never applies to all the dimensions of color, even when perfect. The term compensation implies that the visual mechanism compensates for changes in conditions of viewing up to certain limits beyond which approximations to constancy are absent. According to the terminology employed by the writer, when the limits of compensation have been reached colors change and "color conversion" is said to have occurred. Discussion of color conversion will be found in previous publications by the writer (references 12, 13).

a Macbeth illuminometer. Instead of using any of the formulae for constancy couched in terms of degrees white of disks in free and reduced observation we have used the ratio of luminances in apparent footcandles of the two disks as measures of compensation. The larger this ratio is the greater the compensation since the eye has had to compensate for greater differences in illumination. While the main variable of interest to us was reflectance of background, since this factor has either been overlooked or too casually dismissed, reflectance of shadowed disk, and depth of shadow were also investigated. The interrelations of these three variables seemed to us to be of paramount importance in the explanation of phenomena of visual compensation.

Turning first to effect of reflectance of the shadowed disk we note that as reflectance changes from 0.80 to 0.03 the color of the disk

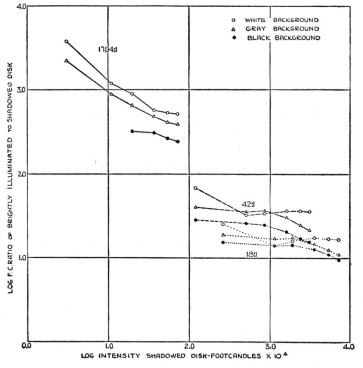

FIG. 2.   Effects of background, brightness of disks, and depth of shadow on lightness compensation.

changes from white to gray and finally becomes black. Hence three compensations are involved as reflectance of disk is lowered: with high reflectances the compensation consists in a lightening of the shadowed disk while with low reflectances the effect consists of a darkening of the brightly illuminated disk. In Table II it is seen

TABLE II. EFFECT OF INTENSITY OF STIMULUS, REFLECTANCE OF BACKGROUND, AND DEPTH OF SHADOW ON LIGHTNESS COMPENSATION

($W°$, degrees white in shadowed disk; $S°$, degrees white in brightly illuminated disk; F.C., apparent footcandles; Ratio, brightly illuminated to shadowed F.C.) Reflectance of white used for background and in disks = 0.80. Reflectance of black used for background and in disks = 0.03. Reflectance of gray background = 0.26.

$W°$	F.C.	White Background			Gray Background			Black Background		
		$S°$	F.C.	Ratio	$S°$	F.C.	Ratio	$S°$	F.C.	Ratio
				A						
			Bright illuminance	= 16.15 ft.-c						
			Shadowed illuminance =	0.879 ft.-c						
360	0.703	322.7	11.63	16.54	208.7	7.75	11.02	184.0	6.78	9.46
270	.536	252.0	9.20	17.16	177.3	6.62	12.35	152.3	5.81	10.84
180	.360	168.3	6.30	17.50	142.0	5.33	14.80	123.7	4.68	13.00
90	.193	74.3	3.07	15.91	84.3	3.39	17.56	60.3	2.58	13.37
45	.114	33.3	1.61	14.12	43.5	1.94	17.02	31.3	1.61	14.12
0 or 15	.026	3.5	0.65	25.00	1.0	0.48	18.46	10.8	0.81	15.58
				B						
			Bright illuminance	= 16.15 ft.-c						
			Shadowed illuminance =	0.388 ft.-c						
360	0.310	302.7	10.98	35.42	178.3	6.62	21.35	126.7	4.84	15.61
270	.237	236.3	8.56	36.19	155.3	5.81	24.51	104.3	4.04	17.05
180	.160	156.3	5.81	36.31	126.0	4.84	30.25	85.0	3.39	21.19
90	.085	70.0	2.91	34.23	74.0	3.07	36.12	47.7	2.10	24.71
45	.050	31.0	1.61	32.20	38.3	1.78	35.60	22.0	1.29	25.80
0 or 15	.012	8.2	0.81	67.50	0.5	0.48	40.00	7.2	0.65	28.26
				C						
			Bright illuminance	= 16.15 ft.-c						
			Shadowed illuminance =	0.009 ft.-c						
360	0.0072	92.3	3.71	515.3	67.7	2.74	380.5	36.7	1.78	247.2
270	.0055	71.7	2.91	529.1	53.3	2.26	410.9	26.2	1.45	263.6
180	.0037	47.3	2.10	567.6	37.0	1.78	481.1	16.8	1.13	305.4
90	.0020	35.5	1.78	890.0	24.7	1.29	645.0	7.2	0.65	325.0
45	.0011	25.7	1.29	1172.7	12.8	0.97	881.8			
0	.0003	17.3	1.13	3766.7	5.0	0.65	2166.7			

that the apparent footcandle ratios increase with decreasing reflectance of shadowed disk, except for the white background where there is an increase, then a decrease, and then a sudden increase again. Greatest luminance ratios are found with lowest reflectance or black disk where we find that with deepest shadow the ratio of luminances is 3766 to 1, an enormous difference for two disks said to be equally black! It appears that black endures more light while remaining black than white endures shadow while remaining white as a comparison of ratios for white and black shows in Table II. Since the maximum and minimum ratios are found with black and white respectively, the intermediate values for the grays show that they stand between white and black in degree of compensation.

Reflectance of background which had been previously found to be of decisive importance in determining hue, lightness, and saturation of samples in chromatic illuminations[12] is of equal importance for the achromatic colors in "white" light. As shown by Fig. 2, highest degrees of compensation are found with white background and least with black background, gray background occupying an intermediate position. The use of backgrounds of different reflectances demonstrates that visual compensation is not an unilateral effect springing only from the so-called "abnormal" illumination. Compensation is just as much darkening of surfaces of low reflectances in high illuminances as it is lightening of surfaces of high reflectance in low illuminances although the latter has received more acclaim. The most striking effects of background are found when a divided background is used white on one side and black on the other. Using illuminances having a ratio of 18 : 1 observations were made with white background on illuminated side and black background on shadowed side and then with these backgrounds interchanged. The results are startling and help to explain some of the paradoxes in the literature without recourse to psychological processes as such. The plot of the luminance ratios as a function of reflectance of disks in Fig. 3 reveals that with white background on shadowed side and black on illuminated side, compensation is even less than with uniform black ground (cf. Tables II and III) which gives the lowest degree of compensation of the three backgrounds. Reversal of backgrounds results in higher degrees of compensation than those found with white background. Moreover, reflectance of disk has different results in the three cases: with uniform background decreasing reflectance of disk gives increasing luminance ratios; with shadowed white and brightly illuminated black grounds the luminance ratios decrease with decreasing reflectance of disk; but with shadowed black and bright white grounds these ratios increase with decreasing reflectance and there is no secondary maximum in the light gray disks as in the case with uniform white ground.

Results with the three backgrounds explain the difference in constancy effects reported by Katz and later by Gelb.[8] In the experiments of Katz the observer always sat in a brightly illuminated portion of the room when making his color matches whereas in Gelb's experiments the observers were placed in the shadowed portion. In both cases aperture matches did not match in free observation but the inequalities were different: for Katz the shadowed disk appeared too white while the illuminated disk retained its aperture character but in the Gelb conditions the shadowed disk retained its aperture appearance but the illuminated disk appeared far too black. According to Bornemeier[2] who used aperture matches for these observations as well as free vision:

"With the black background the shadowed disk appears as far too light in free vision and the illuminated disk retains its aperture appearance. This is the effect described by Katz.

"With the white background the shadowed disk retains its aperture appearance and the illuminated disk appears as far too dark. This is the effect described by Gelb.

"With the gray background the shadowed disk lightens considerably and the illuminated disk darkens. A splitting effect occurs. This

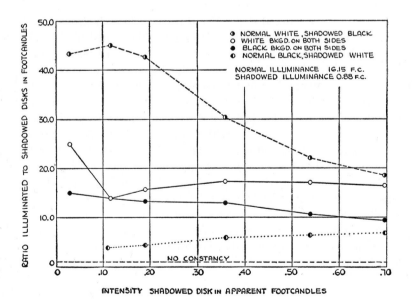

FIG. 3.

latter is neither the Katz nor the Gelb effect. These relations hold
regardless of the illumination conditions, for repeated efforts to obtain the Gelb effect with black background or the Katz effect with
white in both illuminations used by them were unsuccessful."

The third variable, depth of shadow, also proves to have definite
and important effects for compensation. Using ratios of illuminances
ranging from 18 : 1 to 1794 : 1, Bornemeier found, as shown in
Table II and Fig. 2, that the deeper the shadow the greater the
compensation on all backgrounds. Increasing the shadow 100-fold
was compensated for in roughly the same ratio as shown by the ft.-c
ratios in Table II. Lowered reflectance of disk and darker shadow
both work in the same direction since compensation is greater in
the case of darker disks whether caused by one means or the other.
The surprising thing about compensation for such dark shadows is
not that objects seen in them retain their lightness character because
equally great changes in general level of illumination show the same
effects. The surprising aspect of compensation under these conditions is that two objects which stand in such greatly different illuminations and are compared simultaneously are said to match in lightness. The preservation of lightness quality under these conditions is
striking.

It has been asserted [30] if photometric equality obtains between
a shadowed white background and brightly illuminated black background that compensation for a disk in the shadowed region occurs
so that it matches a disk in bright illumination sending more light
to the eyes. Bornemeier found, however, that under these conditions
no compensation occurs and the disk in bright illumination must be
darkened to match the shadowed disk in brightness before they are
judged as equal in lightness. With as little as 0.22 ft.-c difference in
luminance of the backgrounds, compensation was again found with
its tendency toward constancy. It appears that the results reported
with "photometrically" equal backgrounds of different reflectance
were due to small inequalities in brightness. Faulty measurement and
failure to realize how much very small differences in brightness of
background count were responsible for this erroneous view. Compensation occurs only when the backgrounds in the two regions differ
in brightness.

A THEORY OF COLOR CONVERSION
AND COMPENSATION

We are now in a position to see if physiological principles can explain the fundamental facts of visual compensation without recourse to psychic factors. As a result of work with non-selective samples in chromatic illuminations on various backgrounds the following principle of color conversion was formulated which applies equally well to phenomena of compensation: in every viewing situation there is established an adaptation level such that samples having reflectances above adaptation reflectance take the hue of the illuminant while samples below take the hue of the after-image complementary to the illuminant; samples near adaptation reflectance are either achromatic or very low in saturation. Background reflectance, by virtue of the large area of background and because background furnishes the border for all samples in the field, is the most important single factor in the visual field determining adaptation reflectance which is to be regarded as a weighted mean reflectance of all parts of the visual scene. This formulation embraces adaptation phenomena and contrast, the former as phnomena of level and the latter as matters of gradients from level. It requires recognition of adaptive processes much faster than those usually envisaged. Since Katz found some compensation with exposures as short as 0.0017 sec. we are justified in concluding that there is an almost instantaneous adaptive process as well as the longer, durative process commonly called adaptation. Contrast must be regarded as the establishment of gradients not with respect to reflectances of contiguous surfaces but with respect to adaptation level which tends rather to be intermediate between these reflectances.

The principle just enunciated has the advantage of providing a unitary explanation for phenomena formerly attributed to different mechanisms or mechanisms supposed to be more or less independent. It gives a reasonable explanation of the interdependence of adaptation, contrast, and compensation and the many questions raised by them. On this basis compensation occurs for very different reasons but all springing from a single source. Compensation thus may be the result of visual tolerance through shifts in adaptation level, as when a daylight blue sample is blue in green light having a blue component because the green though physically stronger is weakened by adaptation. Or compensation may arise through gradient processes, as in the case of a non-selective surface of low reflectance which is seen as black in strong achromatic illumination against a white ground or when a daylight green of low reflectance is seen as green in red illumination—in both cases the compensation is due to the fact that the samples are below adaptation reflectance and the complementary to the illuminant hue happens to coincide with day-

TABLE III. EFFECT OF A DIVIDED BACKGROUND

Illuminance on brightly illuminated side = 16.15 app. ft.-c. Illuminance on shadowed side = 0.879 app. ft.-c. Reflectance of white background = 0.80. Reflectance of black background = 0.03. ($W°$, degrees white in shadowed disk; $S°$, degrees white in illuminated disk matching the shadowed disk; App. ft.-c, apparent footcandles; Ratio, luminance of illuminated disk to luminance of shadowed disk.)

A
Shadowed White Background and Illuminated Black Background

	Shadowed White Background		Illuminated Black Background	
$W°$	App. ft.-c	$S°$	App. ft.-c	Ratio
360	0.703	127.7	4.84	6.88
270	.536	88.0	3.55	6.62
180	.360	51.0	2.26	6.28
90	.193	11.8	0.81	4.20
45	.114	2.5	0.48	4.21

B
Shadowed Black Background and Illuminated White Background

	Shadowed Black Background		Illuminated White Background	
$W°$	App. ft.-c	$S°$	App. ft.-c	Ratio
360	0.703	360.0	12.92	18.38
270	.536	334.3	11.95	22.29
180	.360	299.0	10.82	30.05
90	.193	223.3	8.24	42.69
45	.114	135.0	5.17	45.35
0	.026	21.3	1.13	43.46

light hue. Other cases equally common yield no compensation because the complementary happens not to coincide with the daylight hue. The change in color which actually does take place is called color conversion.[12] The effects of background, reflectance of disks, and amount and quality of illumination fit together in accordance with the above-stated principle of color conversion. Background of low reflectance induces illuminant hue and in achromatic light samples on this ground are lighter; background of high reflectance induces complementary to the illuminant and in achromatic light its effect is to darken samples. This explains why greatest compensation ratios are found with white ground provided we recognize that the illuminated region is no less important than the shadowed for compensatory effects. Increased degrees of compensation with greater depth of shadow point to the lightening effect of low illuminations. This is in accordance with the long-established principle of opposite-sightedness in bright and dim illuminations and follows from our principle of gradient-level.

The theory proposed here implies that colors arise as gradient phenomena taken with respect to adaptation level. Reports on colors in strongly chromatic illuminants indicate that adaptation reflectance is always below the average reflectance of all objects in the field (Judd;[17] Helson[12]). For this reason a chromatic color is seen when one views a perfectly uniform surface reflecting spectrally homogeneous light. Thus on this theory there is a gradient between adaptation reflectance and reflectance of the surface even in the case of uniform fields. We have recently found that observers see a uniform, non-selective highly reflecting surface illuminated with daylight as white even in the dimmest illumination. On this theory it may be asked: How is it possible to see black with uniform, non-selective low reflecting surfaces since the surface is above adaptation reflectance and should therefore yield a "white"? However, a strictly uniform surface cannot be perceived as a surface and approximations to such a surface do not yield as good a black as the blacks which are aided by gradient effect or contrast, as is well known. Irregularities in approximately uniform surfaces furnish the negative gradients by which such surfaces appear black. This brings us to the role of gradients in the visual field.

It has been customary by some workers in vision to regard only the colors associated with positive gradients, those above adaptation level, as "real" and to assign those arising from negative gradients to the eye or the mind. If, as the facts of compensation and color conversion imply, all colors must be regarded as gradient effects within the visual mechanism, the distinction need not be made. It is commonly thought that "black" is the color *par excellence* due wholly to the eye. As a matter of fact any hue, in all saturations, can be evoked either from positive or negative gradients: in spectrally homogeneous yellow illumination samples of high reflectance are yellow while those of low reflectance are reddish-blue, the former a result of positive gradient, the latter of negative gradient; but in spectrally homogeneous blue illumination samples of high reflectance are blue and those of low reflectance are reddish-yellow as a result of reversal of gradients in the two illuminants. The colors arising from either positive or negative gradients are equally good, the latter often appearing more saturated in strongly chromatic illumination than the former.

CONTOURS, BOUNDARIES, AND TRI-DIMENSIONAL EFFECTS

So far we have dealt mostly with cases that seem to offer less difficulty for physiological explanations than certain crucial phenomena which have been offered as requiring other types of explanation. Let us see what we can do with them. A black disk illuminated by a spotlight appears as a white, luminous object until a small piece of white paper is brought near when it turns black with startling rapidity (Gelb[8]). The converse effect can be demonstrated by shadowing a white disk and leaving the rest of the surroundings brilliantly illuminated. The disk appears black until displacement of the shadow so that its penumbra becomes visible causes the disk to appear as "white-in-shadow" (Kardos[20]). It has been denied (MacLeod [30]) that contrast mechanisms could account for these effects because of the great difference in size between the areas involved. But triggering effects are not unknown in the domain of physics and chemistry. The inequality in magnitudes of the terminal members of the gradients and the rapidity of the changes imply that the visual mechanism is capable of triggering effects. This assumption is consonant with what is known about retinal interaction, the rapid establishment of initial adaptation level, and the great importance of borders and contours.

The effects of boundaries on colors were noted in compensation phenomena as well as long before on contrast. Hering pointed out that a shadow may be seen on one's sleeve as either a stain (surface color) or as a shadow thrown on the cloth (modification of the illumination). If a dark line is drawn around the shadow it becomes a thing and, apparently contrary to contrast effect, darkens. Change from one to the other appearance is accompanied by changes in texture, transparency, and tri-dimensional localization of the color. Here we touch upon the relations between spatial and color effects. Katz[21] found that as he approached a white disk behind a rotating sectored disk, the white disk grew lighter and retreated in the third dimension. MacLeod [30] also found greater compensation with space-filling shadows than with cast or bi-dimensional shadows.

Some suggestions toward including these spatial effects within the general framework of retinal processes may be ventured as follows. Along with gradient processes which accentuate differences within the visual field go assimilative or inductive color processes which tend to obliterate differences through spread. Contours and bound-aries tend to restrict spread within a figure but often boundaries are nullified as induction forces its way across lines of demarcation. Spread within an object is seen in Fig. 4 wherein the lowest gray bar, *A*, shows little or no contrastive lightening or darkening effect from the black and white surrounds respectively. Some contrast effect

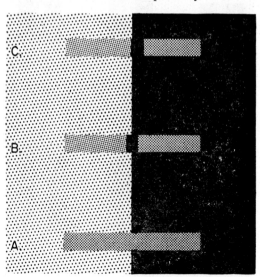

Fig. 4.   Effects of boundaries in preventing spread and aiding contrast gradient.

is seen in the middle bar, *B*, with one boundary and more is apparent in bar *C* with the double boundary which better segregates the two parts of the figure so that spread within the figure is prevented and each part is more amenable to gradient influence from the surround.

Inductive effects across boundaries giving rise to assimilation are found in Fig. 5. While examining these figures for the levelling effects of color induction Newhall's reversal of contrast effect[32] was found. Here grays surrounded by larger areas of black are *darker* than those with smaller black surrounds. Furthermore, assimilative effects appear also within the grays since little or no lightening gradient is visible at the black borders. We thus find inductive, assimilative, and gradient effects coincident with contour and boundary phenomena which are important in bi-dimensional organization of visual fields. We turn now to tri-dimensional problems.

In what way can processes of spread, assimilation, and induction help clarify tri-dimensional color effects? Contrast gradients, especially of brightness-differences, establish the boundaries between

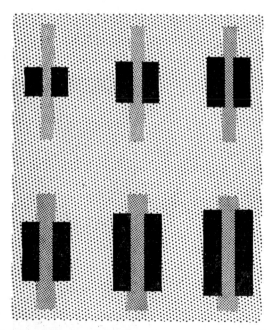

FIG. 5. Relative absence of contrast due to assimilation within central gray strips and Newhall's reversal of contrast effect due to induction from black surround.

objects and their surroundings. To see objects in the third dimension requires separation of planes and formation of borders. Gradients help in separating objects from surrounds and spread within figures makes for figural unity since similar parts tend to form units as Wertheimer has shown.[38] It was pointed out that drawing a border around a shadow changes its localization from in front of the surface to "within" the surface. Here the presence of well-defined contour is accompanied by change in tri-dimensional localization as well as by change in lightness of the shadow. So long as the shadow has the fuzzy, indefinite edges characteristic of its penumbra it is localized in front of the surface and appears transparent; when the penumbra is replaced by a well-defined border the shadow takes the plane of the surface and becomes part of it. But these are not the only ways in which brightness and chroma differences contribute to tri-dimensional spatiality in vision.

Colors also possess inherent spatial properties inseparable from contour and boundary effects and just as important for organization of the visual field. Ames[1] has generalized these properties as follows: (1) cold colors appear more distant than warm; (2) weak chromas appear more distant than intense chromas; (3) values near background value are more distant than high or low; (4) soft edges appear more distant than hard edges; (5) depth effect may be achieved by overlay (interposition); (6) depth may be obtained by accent; (7) dark objects with blue edges appear more distant than those with red edges. Substantiating the distinction between warm and soft colors, Koffka and Harrower[24] refer to red and yellow (warm colors) as advancing and to green and blue (cold colors) as retreating. These writers show that the hard colors, red, yellow, and white, have greater organizing power than the soft colors, green, blue, and black. The former give evidence of greater visual acuity than the latter because of their hard boundaries which enable observers to separate them more easily. Hard colors on hard grounds give greater acuity than soft colors on soft ground, according to the same investigators.

The inseparability of chromatic and spatial effects in vision needs no argument for vision serves to acquaint us not only with color but with form, size, distance, and tri-dimensionality of objects as well. Assimilation within a figure tends to give it internal unity and gradient between it and its ground serves to demarcate it from other objects. The processes of adaptation, contrast, induction, and assimilation which have usually been regarded as contributory only to color effects are thus seen to be no less important for the spatial characteristics of vision. The preservation of lightness serves to demarcate the object from its surround and to make it a thing just as much as it tends to "color constancy." It is thus seen that color processes play a double role in the color-space functions of vision: they contribute the matter or stuff of the visual field and at the same time determine the way in which the field is organized both bi-dimensionally and tri-dimensionally. Which is to be regarded as primary, color or space, it is too early to decide but the evidence now at hand points to the increasing recognition of the importance of color for spatial discriminations. Color compensation by yielding approximate color constancy thus aids in the production of a stable visual world not only through preservation of color as such but just as much through preservation of spatial organization which is largely due to the color processes of the eye.

REFERENCES

For more extended bibliographies consult Helson,[12] Judd,[17] and Mac-Leod.[30]

1. AMES, A. Depth in pictorial art. The Art Bulletin, 1925, 8, No. 1 The College Art Assoc., New York University, Washington Square, New York.

2. BOCKSCH, H., and KRAUSS, S. Bunte Farben in bunter Beleuchtung. Zeits. f. Psychol., 1926, 99, 202.

3. BORNEMEIER, R. W. The inter-relating conditions determining lightness constancy. Unpublished manuscript.

4. BÜHLER, K. Die Erscheinungsweisen der Farben. Jena: 1922.

5. BURKAMP, W. Versuche über das Wiedererkennen der Fische, Zeits. f. Sinnesphysiol., 1923, 55, 307.

6. FIELDER, K. Das Schwarz-Weiss-Problem. Neue Psychol. Stud., 1926, 2, 347.

7. GATES, E. J. On intensive and qualitative judgments of light sensation. Am. J. Psychol., 1915, 26, 296.

8. GELB, A. Die "Farbenkonstanz" der Sehdinge, Handb. d. norm. u. pathol. Physiol., XII/1, Receptionsorgane, 594. Berlin: 1929.

9. HECHT, S. The nature of the photoreceptor process. In Murchison's Handbook of General Experimental Psychology. Worcester, Massachusetts: Clark University Press, 1934.

10. HECHT, S. The chemistry of visual substances. *Ann. Rev. Biochem.*, 1942, **11**, 465.
11. VON HELMHOLTZ, H. *A Treatise on Physiological Optics*. Optical Society of America, 1924.
12. HELSON, H. Fundamental problems in color vision. 1. The principle governing changes in hue, saturation, and lightness of non-selective samples in chromatic illumination. *J. exp. Psychol.*, 1938, **23**, 439.
13. HELSON, H., and JEFFERS, V. B. Hue, lightness, and saturation of selective samples in chromatic illumination. *J. exp. Psychol.*, 1940, **26**, 1.
14. HENNEMAN, R. H. A photometric study of the perception of object color. *Arch. Psychol.*, 1935, **27**, 5.
15. HERING, E. *Grundzüge der Lehre vom Lichtsinn.* Berlin: Springer, 1920.
16. JAENSCH, E. R. Ueber den Farbenkonstanz and die sogennante Berücksichtigung der farbigen Beleuchtung. *Zeits. f. Sinnesphysiol.*, 1921, **52**, 165.
17. JUDD, D. B. Hue, saturation and lightness of surface colors with chromatic illumination. *J. Opt. Soc. Am.*, 1940, **30**, 2.
18. JUDD, D. B. The definition of black and white. *Am. J. Psychol.*, 1941, **54**, 294.
19. KARDOS, L. Dingfarbenwahrnehmung und Duplizitätstheorie. *Zeits. f. Psychol.*, 1928, **108**, 240.
20. KARDOS, L. Ding und Schatten. *Zeits. f. Psychol.*, 1934, Ergbd. 23.
21. KATZ, D. Die Erscheinungsweisen der Farben und ihrer Beeinflussung durch die individuelle Erfahrung. *Zeits. f. Psychol.*, 1911, Ergbd. 7.
22. KATZ, D. *Der Aufbau der Farbwelt*, revised edition of *Erscheinungsweisen der Farben*. Leipzig: Barth, 1930; English translation, *The World of Color*, R. B. MacLeod and C. W. Fox. London: Kegan, Paul, Trench, and Trubner, 1935.
23. KATZ, D., and RÉVÉSZ, G. Experimentelle Studien zur vergleichenden Psychologie (Versuch mit Hühnern). *Zeits. f. angew. Psychol.*, 1921, **18**, 307.
24. KOFFKA, K., and HARROWER, M. R. Colour and organization. *Psychol. Forsch.*, 1931, **15**, 193.
25. KÖHLER, W. Optische Untersuchungen am Schimpansen und am Haushuhn. Abh. d. preuss. Akad. d. Wiss., Math.-Phys. Abt. 1915.
26. KOHLRAUSCH, A. *Allgemeines über Umstimmung und 'Farbenkonstanz der Sehdinge,'* Handb. d. norm. u. pathol. Physiol., X11/2, Receptionsorgane II. Berlin: 1931.
27. KRAUSS, S. Das Farbensehen in bunter Beleuchtung und die Farbenkonstanz der Sehdinge. *Zeits. f. Psychol.*, 1926, **100**, 50.
28. KRÜGER, H. Ueber die Unterschiedsempfindlichkeit für Beleuchtungseindrücke. *Zeits. f. Psychol.*, 1925, **96**, 58.

29. LOCKE, N. M. Color constancy in the rhesus monkey and in man. *Arch. Psychol.*, 1935, No. 193.

30. MACLEOD, R. B. An experimental investigation of brightness constancy. *Arch. Psychol.*, 1932, No. 135.

31. MARZYNSKI, G. Studien zur centralen Transformation der Farben. *Zeits. f. Psychol.*, 1921, **87,** 45.

32. NEWHALL, S. M. The reversal of simultaneous brightness contrast. *J. exp. Psychol.*, 1942, **31,** 393.

33. ROSENAU, F. Gesetzmässigkeiten des Farbensehens bei streng monochromatischer Beleuchtung. *Arch. f. d. ges. Psychol.*, 1938, **100,** 22.

34. SCHMECKEBEIER, L. Die Erscheinungsweisen kleinflächiger Farben. *Arch. f. d. ges. Psychol.*, 1932, **85,** 1.

35. SINEMUS, A. Untersuchungen über 'Beleuchtung' und 'Körperfarbe' bei Mikropsie. *Zeits. f. Psychol.*, 1932, **125,** 1.

36. SPENCER, D. E. Adaptation in color space. *J. Opt. Soc. Am.*, 1943, **33,** 10.

37. THOULESS, R. H. Phenomenal regression to the real object. *Brit. J. Psychol.*, 1931, **21,** 339.

38. WERTHEIMER, M. Untersuchungen zur Lehre von der Gestalt, I. *Psychol. Forsch.*, 1922, **1,** 47; II *ibid.*, 1923, **2,** 301.

....

Expectation and the Perception of Color*†

JEROME S. BRUNER, LEO POSTMAN, AND JOHN RODRIGUES

THE PRESENT EXPERIMENT TESTS a proposition derived from a general theory of perception. Although the general theory has been stated in tentative terms elsewhere, a brief outline of it is necessary here as an introduction to our theme.[1]

We shall assume that perceiving can be analyzed as a three-step process. First, the organism gets set or prepared in a certain way, selectively 'tuned' toward some class of stimuli or events in the environment. When the organism is thus set or tuned, it is said to have an *hypothesis*. The second step consists of the *input of stimulus information*. By using the term 'stimulus-information,' or simply 'information,' we seek to indicate that we are dealing with the cue characteristics of the stimulus rather than with the energy characteristics of stimulation.[2] In the third step of the cycle the hypothesis is *confirmed* or *infirmed*. Given a certain quantity and kind of information, an hypothesis will be confirmed and lead to a stable perception. If the critical quantity of 'cue' information is not present, the hypothesis will be infirmed partially or fully. Under these circumstances, an unstable perceptual field will result and an altera-

---

* From *Amer. J. Psychol.*, 1951, **64**, 216-227. Reprinted by permission of the authors and the publisher.

† This research was supported by a grant from the Laboratory of Social Relations, Harvard University.

[1] J. S. Bruner, Personality and the process of perceiving, in *Perception: An Approach to Personality,* edited by R. R. Blake and G. V. Ramsey, 1951; Leo Postman, Toward a general theory of cognition, in *Social Psychology at the Crossroads,* edited by J. H. Rohrer and M. Sherif, 1951. In our development of the concept of hypothesis we have, of course, leaned on the work of E. C. Tolman and I. Krechevsky, Means-end-readiness and hypothesis—a contribution to comparative psychology, *Psychol. Rev.,* 1933, **40**, 60-70.

[2] R. S. Harper and E. G. Boring, Cues, *Amer. J. Psychol.,* 1948, **61**, 119-123.

tion in hypothesis will follow, that will, in turn, be 'tested' against incoming information. The cycle of checking altered hypotheses against incoming information will continue until there is a stabilized perception. The range of information or of 'cues' which is known by independent test to be potentially confirming or infirming of an hypotheses, we shall call *appropriate* or *relevant* to that hypothesis. Thus, for example, an hypothesis about the size of an object can be confirmed by a variety of cues to magnitude, distance, and so on. The appropriateness of these cues can be determined independently by traditional cue-reduction experiments familiar in the study of the constancies. Note particularly that appropriate information is necessary either to confirm *or* infirm an hypothesis.

The hypothesis with which an organism faces a situation at the moment of initial stimulus-input we shall refer to as the *initial hypothesis*. The hypotheses which develop when an initial hypothesis is not confirmed we shall refer to as *consequent hypotheses*. The difference is an heuristic one and does not connote a qualitative distinction in the operation of initial and consequent hypotheses.

An hypothesis may vary in strength. *The greater the strength of an hypothesis, the less the amount of appropriate information necessary to confirm it.* One may vary the amount of appropriate information given to the organism in numerous ways: by changing the amount of time a stimulus is available, by altering the illumination of the stimulus-field, by changing the extent to which a stimulus-field is in focus, and the like. The strength of an hypothesis (and, therefore, the amount of appropriate information necessary to confirm it) varies as a function of its past use, past success, the degree to which it competes with other hypotheses and many other conditions which need not concern us here.

In the present experiment, we shall not be concerned with varying the strength of hypotheses. We shall assume it to be constant. Our concern is rather with the rôle of *appropriateness of information* as it affects the confirming of initial hypotheses of equal strength. The specific proposition which we seek to test is the following: the smaller the quantity of appropriate information, the greater the probability of an established initial hypothesis being confirmed, even if environmental events fail to agree with such hypotheses. An inverse way of restating this proposition is to say that the greater the quantity of appropriate information present, the greater the opportunity for infirming an initial hypothesis where necessary and developing 'fitting' consequent hypotheses.

THE EXPERIMENT

The basic task of all *S*s was to make a color match between a stimulus-patch and a variable color-mixer. Conditions of judgment and the color and shape of the stimulus-patch varied systematically in the four experimental conditions to be described.

Stimuli. The stimuli used consisted of eight patches cut from paper to represent the following objects:

Ovaloid Objects: shaped to represent (and designated as)
Tomato (5.0 cm. horizontal axis, 3.0 cm. vertical axis)
Tangerine (5.1 cm. horizontal, 3.0 cm. vertical)
Lemon (5.1 cm. horizontal, 2.9 cm. vertical)
Neutral oval (5.1 cm. horizontal, 3.0 cm. vertical)

Elongated Ellipsoid Objects:
Boiled lobster claw (7.6 cm. horizontal, 2.4 cm. vertical)
Carrot (7.7 cm. horizontal, 2.2 cm. vertical)
Banana (7.7 cm. horizontal, 2.0 cm. vertical)
Neutral elongated ellipse (7.6 cm. horizontal, 2.3 cm. vertical)

The Matching Task. It was the task of *S* to match these patches, shaped and designated as specified, to a variable color-wheel (20 cm. in diameter) made up of yellow and red segments. The color-mixer could be shifted in hue from a well saturated red through the oranges to a well saturated yellow without stopping the wheel. A modified method of adjustment was used, *E* altering the color-wheel at the instruction of *S*. In all four conditions to be discussed, a group of 8 *S*s being allocated to each condition, the color-wheel was at a distance of 150 cm. from *S*, at approximate eye-level.

Order of presentation of the eight stimulus-patches was controlled in the same way throughout. Every object-patch appeared in each of the eight positions and, therefore, every serial position contained all of the eight objects for each of the four groups. Upon the presentation of an object-patch, *S* made two successive matches, one with the initial position of the color-wheel at red, the other with the initial position at yellow. Whether initial yellow or initial red came first for a given match was randomly determined.

The Four Experimental Conditions. The four groups of eight *S*s were treated as follows.

Group I. Induced Color Group (Uninformed). A stimulus-patch was placed on a table before *S*, illuminated by a 150-w. GE Reflector Spot sealed-beam in a shielded alcove 60 cm. above the table, shining directly on the patch. Each patch (tomato, tangerine, etc.) was cut from neutral gray paper (Stoelting #19), and placed on a blue-green sheet of paper (Stoelting #10) of the dimensions 15 x 15 cm. Gray figure and blue-green background were covered by a finely ground glass, also 15 x 15 cm. All these operations were performed behind a cardboard screen which had been dropped between *S* and the field. When the screen was lifted, *S* saw before him on the brown table a poorly saturated blue-green square on which could be seen a brownish orange figure. The color-wheel and the rest of the field were illuminated by four 40-w. fluorescent lamps overhead.

S was instructed that his task was to match the color-wheel to the object before him on the table. Between the stimulus-patch and the color-wheel there was approximately 80° of visual arc so that the comparison was perforce successive rather than simultaneous. As each object-patch was presented for matching, *S* was told what it was, *e.g.* "This is a tangerine. Make the color-wheel the same color as it." As already indicated, two matches were made for each object-patch, one from the yellow and one from the red initial positions of the color-wheel. *S*s experienced some difficulty in making the match since the induced color was not sufficiently pronounced in hue to provide a good basis for judging. It was also impossible to reproduce a color on the wheel which was alike in surface and saturation to the stimulus-patch. Finally, the hue-match was only approximate, since no combination of the yellow and red sectors would yield a hue identical to the induced orange brown.

After making two matches to each of the eight stimulus-patches, *S* was given a 5-min. rest-period. Following this, he repeated the identical procedure. Then came a rest-period of 10 min., following which *S* was asked to make *from memory* settings on the color-wheel for each of the eight patches already seen. Again, two settings were made for each patch. In all, the first procedure required about an hour of *S*'s time.

Group II. Induced Color Group (Informed). This group received the same treatment as the preceding group, with one exception. At the end of the first judging-period and during the 5-min. rest, *S* was given a brief lecture on induced color and shown how the color was produced in the stimulus-patches judged. In short, their second series of judgments and their memory-matches were made with knowledge of the 'illusory' quality of the colors before them. A judging session required about an hour.

The second condition was designed, of course, to provide additional information to our *S*s about the hue of the stimulus-patches which they were being asked to judge. The third and fourth groups, as we shall see, were provided with still more information.

Group III. Stable Color Group. The judging procedure for this group was exactly the same as for Group I, save that in place of induced color, a 'real' color was used for the stimulus-patches. This was a well saturated orange-color which matched very closely the middle region of the red-yellow mixture on the color-wheel both with respect to hue and to saturation. The stimulus-patches were pasted on glossy white cardboard plaques, again 15 x 15 cm. in dimension. As in the first two conditions, the cards bearing the stimuli were so placed before *S* on the table that about 80° of visual arc intervened between the stimulus and the color-wheel, thus necessitating successive comparison. The color-wheel and the stimulus-patch were illuminated by 150-w. sealed-beams of the type previously described at a distance of 60 cm. Judgments required about an hour.

Group IV. Optimal Matching Group. An effort was made in designing the procedure for this group to provide *S*s with a maximum of appropriate information for making their matches with a minimum of irrelevant information in the situation. Put in communications-engineering terms, we sought to establish a judging condition in which the signal-to-noise ratio was at a maximum. A box was constructed, 150 cm. in length, 61 cm. in width, and 50 cm. in height. At one end of the box an eyepiece was inserted, approximately 3.5 x 11 cm. in size. At the far end of the box, the wheel of the color-mixer and the stimulus-patch appeared side by side. The inside floor, ceiling and the walls of the box were painted a homogeneous medium gray (matching Hering gray #15). Set in concealed alcoves on either side of the box were two spotlights (150 w., GE sealed-beams) which were trained from a distance of 60 cm. on the color-wheel and on the stimulus-patch. The appearance of the field, viewed from the eye-piece, was of a homogeneous, gray, well-lighted, closed tunnel, at the far end of which were the wheel of the color-mixer and a stimulus-patch in the same frontal parallel plane. Stimulus-patches were cut of orange paper of identical hue and saturation with those used in the immediately preceding condition and mounted on cardboard. The cardboard, 17.5 x 30.5 cm. in dimension, was inserted into the box through a slide opening. When the cardboard was thus inserted, there was a distance of 10 cm. from the edge of the stimulus-patch to the edge of the color-wheel. Such a separation of patch and wheel at a distance of 150 cm. from the eye made the task of simultaneous comparison quite easy. Group IV, then, was the only one which could make matches by simultaneous comparison. It should be remarked, finally, that Group IV had the very minimum of extraneous stimulus-input, competing cues from the room and general background of the room being eliminated by the use of the 'reduction' tunnel. Because of the easier judging conditions, *S*s required but three-quarters of an hour to complete this procedure.

RESULTS

Recall the proposition advanced for testing. The smaller the quantity of appropriate information, the greater the probability of an initial hypothesis being confirmed even if environmental events fail to agree with such hypotheses. In proportion to the deficiency of stimulus-information, established initial hypotheses will determine the color match. The results, generally, confirm this prediction.

Table I contains a summary of the judgments made by the four groups during the first matching series. In order to estimate the effect of initial hypotheses in the matches, we computed first a grand mean in degrees of yellow on the wheel of all the matches made by a group in this series, regardless of the patch which was being matched. We then computed the difference between this grand mean and the mean match made for each kind of stimulus patch: 'red' objects, 'orange' objects, 'yellow' objects, and neutral objects. The final row of Table I also contains the standard deviation of all the judgments of a group. The latter may be taken as a rough approximation of sensitivity to hue differences under the particular judging conditions imposed upon each group.

Consider first the matches made for 'red,' 'yellow,' and 'orange'

TABLE I. AVERAGE SETTINGS OF COLOR-WHEEL FOR VARIOUS OBJECTS
DURING FIRST SERIES OF MATCHES

Settings are expressed as deviations in degrees of yellow from the average of settings made for all objects by a given group. Positive sign denotes more yellow; negative sign, less yellow.

Stimulus-objects	Group I (Induced color, *S*s uninformed)	Group II (Induced color, *S*s informed)	Group III (Stable color)	Group IV (Stable color, optimal cond.)
Red	−14.2°	−12.1°	−3.6°	+2.9°
Orange	−0.6°	−0.2°	+3.4°	−4.5°
Yellow	+19.2°	+10.6°	−0.8°	+4.5°
Neutral	−5.6°	+1.7°	+1.2°	−2.4°
Mean (yellow)	121.4°	118.5°	141.1°	191.6°
SD	39.9°	37.0°	23.4°	15.6°

objects. In both Groups I and II (the groups which worked with contrast-induced colors), normally red objects were judged considerably redder, normally yellow objects, considerably yellower than the average level. In both groups, moreover, the 'orange' objects were matched to a color almost exactly at average level. It is interesting to remark in passing that Ss in these groups proffered the information that they believed all their matches to be the same. Nevertheless there is between the setting made for 'red' objects and those made for 'yellow' objects for Group I an average difference of 33.4° of yellow segment on the wheel. The difference for Group II is 22.7°. Both of these color-differences are grossly supraliminal, the difference between a yellowish orange and a reddish orange.

With improvement of judging conditions as provided in the procedures applied to Groups III and IV, the effect is first reduced and finally washed out. Sufficiently stable stimulus-information is provided to alter the initial hypothesis established by such instructions as "This is a lemon," or "This is a carrot." Note too in these groups a striking reduction in the standard deviation of all judgments which results from the increase in appropriate stimulus-information. Both 'orange' and neutral objects yield matches which fluctuate closely about the grand mean.

Table II contains a summary of matching in the second series—a second series of judgments of the eight patches after a 5-min. rest.

TABLE II. AVERAGE SETTINGS OF COLOR-WHEEL FOR VARIOUS OBJECTS DURING SECOND SERIES OF MATCHES

Settings are expressed as deviations in degrees of yellow from the average of settings made for all objects by a given group. Positive sign denotes more yellow; negative sign, less yellow.

Stimulus-objects	Group I (Induced color, Ss uninformed)	Group II (Induced color, Ss informed)	Group III (Stable color)	Group IV (Stable color, optimal cond.)
Red	−9.9°	−15.9°	−5.4°	+3.6°
Orange	+3.7°	+0.5°	−0.2°	−2.8°
Yellow	+13.9°	+12.8°	+5.8°	−0.3°
Neutral	+2.2°	+2.5°	+0.4°	−0.3°
Mean (yellow)	113.3°	113.1°	142.1°	184.7°
SD	41.0°	35.5°	23.4°	15.9°

Save in Group II, this second series may be regarded simply as a replication of the first series. Recall that Group II received a brief lecture on, and demonstration of, color contrast before embarking on these judgments. The results were substantially the same as before. Note that the lecture and demonstration seemed to have no effect on Group II. Where before the color-distance between 'yellow' and 'red' object matches was slightly less than 23° of yellow segment, now it is somewhat more than 28°. In this second series, Group III seems to succumb more to the effect of the labeling or meaning of the objects judged than in the first series. Note again that for Groups I, II, and III, 'orange' and neutral objects fall close to the grand mean.

Group IV, working with simultaneous comparison under optimal conditions of illumination and surround, shows no systematic effect at all and continues to exhibit a strikingly high sensitivity as one may infer from the size of the standard deviation of their judging distribution.

TABLE III. AVERAGE SETTINGS OF COLOR-WHEEL FOR
VARIOUS OBJECTS DURING MEMORY MATCHES

Settings are expressed as deviations in degrees of yellow from the average of settings made for all objects by a given group. Positive sign denotes more yellow; negative sign, less yellow.

Stimulus-objects	Group I (Induced color, Ss uninformed)	Group II (Induced color, Ss informed)	Group III (Stable color)	Group IV (Stable color, optimal cond.)
Red	−25.9°	−13.0°	−13.4°	−1.9°
Orange	+4.5°	+3.9°	+0.4°	−1.9°
Yellow	+22.3°	+11.5°	+11.3°	+5.5°
Neutral	−0.4°	−2.5°	+1.6°	−1.1°
Mean (yellow)	109.3°	103.0°	141.2°	187.3°
SD	44.7°	27.2°	20.2°	21.7°

When we come to the third series of matches—matches made from memory—a striking effect is obtained. These results are summarized in Table III. Differences for the first three groups are of great magnitude. Between the 'yellow' and 'red' matches of Group I, there is a separation of 48.2° of yellow segment; for Group II it is 24.5°;

and for Group III, 24.7°. Under memory-matching conditions, Group IV begins to exhibit a systematic judging tendency, although it is not great; a separation of 7.4° of yellow segment between 'red' and 'yellow' object matches, the meaning of which is rendered somewhat dubious by the lack of distinction between matches for 'red' and 'orange' objects.

INTERPRETATION

We have reported an experiment which is at once as old as Hering's conception of memory-color[3] and at the same time is presented as supporting evidence for a contemporary theory of perception. Perhaps we should first come to terms with history. Hering, of course, introduced the conception of memory-color to account for certain phenomena of color-constancy.

Duncker showed that a notion such as memory-color or trace-color could be used in the interpretation of the mode of appearance of meaningful objects under constancy conditions using hidden illumination.[4] Duncker demonstrated, for example, that a leaf cut from green felt and bathed in a hidden red illumination was judged greener by his Ss than a donkey cut from identical material in identical illumination. Indeed, it is patent that the rôle of 'memory' as a determinant of attributive judgment has long been recognized as important in the field of perception.

A more recent and more systematic attempt to describe the effects of past experience with colors upon present judgments of them has been undertaken by Helson in a provocative paper on adaptation-level.[5] In very brief summary, adaptation-level theory would hold that, within limits, the judgment of an attribute will depend upon the relation of the stimulus judged at any one moment to the weighted geometric mean of the series of stimuli presented previously in the judging situation. It is difficult to apply Helson's conception to our own data for one quite obvious reason. Each of our judging groups judged only one color. The difference in the stimuli was not in their photometric colors, but in their designation as objects implying certain normal colors. The effect of the designation, however, may be referred not to the situational adaptation-

[3] E. Hering, *Grundzüge der Lehre vom Lichtsinn*, 1905, 1-80. See also G. K. Adams, An experimental study of memory color and related phenomenon, *Amer. J. Psychol.* 1923, **34**, 359-407.

[4] K. Duncker, The influence of past experience upon perceptual properties, *Amer. J. Psychol.* 1939, **52**, 255-265.

[5] H. Helson, Adaptation-level as a basis for a quantitative theory of frames of reference, *Psychol. Rev.,* 1948, **55**, 297-313. [See also selection 24. Eds.]

level but to the adaptation-levels for various types of objects built up in the course of past commerce with tomatoes, tangerines, lemons, and other like objects. However clarifying such a statement may be, we should like to go beyond it to a consideration of the cognitive processes involved in the type of our own judging situations.

We turn accordingly to the theoretical framework presented in general terms in our introductory paragraphs. Let us interpret the behavior of our Ss in terms of the three-cycle conception of 'hypothesis-information-confirmation.' Assume the following sequence of events to be occurring, for example, in Group I. S is given the initial hypothesis by instruction that the poorly saturated patch before him represents a tomato, an hypothesis readily confirmed by shape cues from the stimulus-patch. The hypothesis 'tomato' is not, however, fully confirmed by the color cues provided. Because of the poorness or instability of the color-information, the initial hypothesis is not, however, completely infirmed. That this initial hypothesis plays a large part in determining the final color match, in short is not fully replaced by a consequent 'corrected' hypothesis, is indicated by the systematic tendency of Ss to make a redder match to objects designated as tomatoes and boiled lobster claws than to objects not normally red. Given an input of inadequate information, the initial hypothesis plays a proportionately greater rôle by virtue of not having been infirmed.

Nor are initial hypotheses infirmed appreciably by providing Group II with added verbal information about the nature of the contrast-color which is used in the stimulus-patch. From the first to the second matching situation, there is no discernible change. As in the case of verbal efforts to dispel such classical illusions as the Müller-Lyer, here too our instructions seemed to provide no effective perceptual information. Perhaps verbal instruction does not basically alter the *stimulus* information given S.

The only difference between Groups I and II appears to be in the tendency of the second group to show a decreasing variability of judgment with more experience in the judging situation (Tables I-II). We do not know why this occurred.

In Group III, stimulus-information is better, serves more adequately to infirm the initial hypothesis which links the various stimulus-patches with certain 'normal' object-colors. In consequence, the matches made by this group show less of a tendency to redden objects designated as 'normally red' and to yellow objects designated as 'normally yellow.' Yet the information, somewhat contaminated as it is by extraneous information in the perceptual field, is not sufficiently appropriate to infirm the initial hypothesis altogether. In this group, moreover, as in the preceding groups, judgments are made under conditions of successive comparison. What does this imply? Essentially, it means that there is a moment intervening between looking at the stimulus-patch—the relevant stimulus-information—and making an adjustment on the color-wheel to match the patch. Granted, the intervals consumed in turning successively through the 80° separating patch and color are not great in duration, yet separation may serve to reinforce the systematic judging tendency by introducing reliance on memory-information. We shall return to this point shortly in discussing the results of the memory series.

Group IV, making its judgments under optimal conditions with a minimum of competing information in the situation and with opportunity for simultaneous comparison shows no systematic effect at all. Stimulus-information is sufficiently stable and adequate to infirm the initial hypothesis, and the matches which are made reflect not the color of objects designated by the E but rather the photometric color of the patches themselves.

We turn finally to the results of the memory series. Note that under all conditions represented by our four groups, some systematic effects were found; e.g. in memory, orange-colored tomatoes are redder than orange-colored lemons. The greatest effect was exhibited by the naïve groups operating with induced contrast-color (Group I). For them, there were 48.2° of yellow separating their matches for red and yellow designated objects. Note the marked difference, however, between Groups I and II. The only distinction between the two groups was that the second was given information about color-contrast. Whether for this, or for some other reason, the memory effect of object-color designation was markedly reduced in spite of an equality of the effect in the second perceptual matching situation.

How may we account for the heightened effect of the initial hypothesis on memory matches? We should like to propose the following approach, one which recommends itself for the continuity it suggests between phenomena usually called perceptual and phenomena conventionally designated as memory. In any given situation, the individual may depend upon input stimulus-information for the confirmation of hypotheses or, lacking such perceptual input, upon memory-information as represented by traces. We suggest, furthermore, that trace-information is less stable, or less appropriate information, or both, for confirming or infirming initial hypotheses of the kind built into our Ss. This being the case, initial hypotheses should have a determinative effect upon memory-matches in much the same way that the initial hypotheses of Groups I and II had a determinative effect upon the perceptual matches because of poor stimulus-information provided.

CONCLUSION

Given less than optimal stimulus-conditions, certain factors of past experience may play a determinative part in perceptual organization. For past experience is normally among the determinants of initial hypotheses.

Insofar as we may adopt the above as a general conclusion, it is also possible to draw a methodological lesson from our results. When an experiment demonstrates under certain conditions an effect of needs or past experience on perception, that experiment is not necessarily invalidated by another done under other conditions and showing that the alleged effect has not appeared. The basic question is under what conditions of stimulus-information does the effect occur and by what improvement in stimulus-information can it be destroyed.

Further Studies in the Perception of a Changing Shape*

F. J. LANGDON

INTRODUCTION

A PREVIOUS PAPER (Langdon, 1951) described some phenomenal relationships noted in the course of investigating the general problem of shape constancy. The present paper deals more fully with certain other aspects of this question, in particular with the theory of invariance between tilt and perceived shape. This theory, originally proposed by Koffka (1935), has been the subject of considerable speculation and experiment.

It is now some twenty years since the work of Eissler (1933), and more since that of Thouless (1931), aroused the original controversy. More recently, interest in perceptual phenomena has veered away from the particular problems which gave rise to it, and a survey of present day literature reveals little in the form of experimental investigation which is likely to resolve the issue. As Vernon (1953a) has pointed out, the general trend of evidence from experimental studies has been to stress the divergencies rather than the similarities between the different perceptual phenomena. This has had the effect of displaying the Gestalt theories as oversimple formulations of complex problems. The tendency towards independent lines of development in perceptual theory, noted by the same writer (Vernon 1953b), has had the effect of diminishing the precise significance of detailed arguments about shape constancy and the shape-tilt relation, and of giving such discussions an air of outdated scholasticism.

Nonetheless, whatever may have been the fate of the general theories in which these problems were set, the problems themselves remain. Neither has more recent experimental and theoretical work

---

* From *Quart. J. exp. Psychol.*, 1953, **5**, 89-107. Reprinted by permission of the author and publisher.

suggested any plausible solutions. The abandonment of Gestalt propositions in favour of later formulations as regards general perceptual theory does not of itself result in the appearance of shapetilt formulae as an inevitable corollary. Neither does it show that the shape-tilt relation is a pseudo-problem arising only from an incorrect theory. And this is hardly likely, since this relationship is a fact of experience based upon properties of the physical and visual world.

THEORETICAL CONSIDERATIONS

The postulation of a direct relationship between perceived size and distance for the case of size constancy has continued to receive confirmation. Thus the work of Holway and Boring (1941) has been confirmed by later studies and theoretical analysis by Gilinsky (1951), and by the work of Gibson (1947) and Ittleson (1951). Despite various disagreements by these authors on the significance of their work (cf. Brunswik, 1944; Joynson, 1949) and, particularly, on the order of importance of different perceptual cues, the general principle of the direct relation between distance and perceived size seems generally agreed upon.

Acceptance of this principle would, not surprisingly, lead to the expectation of an analogous relation between tilt and perceived shape. Such an application is entirely comprehensible since shape is defined in terms of size, and is considered as an extension of it. Thus the Oxford English Dictionary (1914) defines shape as "That quality of a material object or a geometrical figure which depends on constant relations of position and proportionate distance among all the points composing its outline or external surface."

Koffka, in discussing shape constancy, assumes the application of the size-distance relation, and he develops these assumptions in his theory of the "invariant relation." This theory he states in the course of criticising the work of Thouless and Eissler. Thouless, as is well-known, had found variations in shape constancy over the arc of possible tilt (line of regard to frontal parallel), calculating constancy as a standard index by means of the formula Log P-Log S/Log R-Log S; the indices for various angles to the line of regard were as follows:

7°	10°	20°	30°	45°	65°	90°
.28	.41	.33	.32	.16	.1	/

Thus here, constancy is variable, being greatest when the angle is smallest. Eissler, employing a slightly different technique, had also obtained varying amounts of constancy through the arc of tilt, though his results appear to conflict with those of Thouless. The variation, which he termed "relative constancy," was in the opposite direction to that observed by Thouless. But the "absolute constancy," that is, relative constancy treated by a "transformation function" increased with angle of tilt. The transformation ratio

(Verarbeits Funktion) $= A = \dfrac{S\text{-}P}{P}$.

Thouless had accounted for the variations in constancy by the hypothesis of "phenomenal regression," which stated that, where the perceptual indications were in conflict, there was a tendency for the resultant perception to "regress" to the character of the real object. Eissler, for his part, suggested that variations arose out of the subjects' attempts to compensate for the growing disparity visible between the "real" and the "apparent" shape through the increasing tilt-angle. An increase in constancy is the outcome of "overcompensation" by the subject. The same suggestion is made by Stavrianos (1945) and, in the case of whiteness constancy, by Hsia (1943). It will be seen that although they express it differently, Thouless and Eissler are saying very much the same thing, since both look upon variations as outcomes of conflict between different perceptual cues.

Koffka commences his discussion (pp. 227 ff.) by suggesting that the true cause of variations in scores is an outcome of the formula. For, says Koffka, the formula assumes that the tilted shape (a circle) is always seen as such, so that the range of constancies is always calculated in terms of the frontal-parallel as the reference plane. But if this assumption failed to hold, variations in constancy could arise from subjects perceiving the shape not as a circle, but as an ellipse with a minor axis somewhere between the axis of the standard figure and that of the tilted comparison circle.

The assumption of an invariant relation between tilt and perceived shape demands as a corollary that a measure of shape constancy for an object perceived under constant conditions should remain the same through the arc of tilt. Moreover, such a measure must be "unique," i.e., it must refer only to constancy of a given shape at a given orientation, and it must show that the true shape was perceived with a given degree of perceptual constancy. This, it is submitted, the constancy formula fails to do. Koffka gives a suppositious example of an ellipse with minor axis 15 cm., major axis 20 cm., seen at an angle of 45° from the line of regard. The retinal image of such a shape equals that produced by a frontal-parallel ellipse with a minor axis of 10.7 cm. But it also equals the retinal image of a circle seen at an angle of 15° 13 in. to the line of regard. The formula ignores shapes lying between these two, though there is no *a priori* reason why it should do so.

Since it is already laid down that "two proximal stimuli, if more than liminally different, cannot produce exactly the same effect" (p. 228), then the two ellipses which appear to be of similar shape must be examples of "pure orientation," and variations in shape constancy through the orientational arc are due to shortcomings in the formula which conceal the tilt-shape relationship.

This is a much condensed statement of the gist of Koffka's argument, and it appears to be the main one on which his adducement of an invariant shape tilt relation appears to rest, together with the assumed analogy of the size/distance relation. At the same time it should, in fairness to Koffka, be said that he qualifies this expectation with the proviso (p. 233) that the invariant may depend upon total sets of conditions and need not be identical under all conditions.

It is first of all necessary to note two points arising from this argument before passing on to consider any scientific evidence in support of it. A careful study of the text will reveal that Koffka is arguing by means of an undemonstrated converse. Thus it can be a valid premise that there are unexplained variations in shape constancy computed by means of the Brunswik-Thouless formula, and that the formula fails to state explicitly the determinants (in their respective terms of shape and inclination) governing the perceptual process. But this is not sufficient to demonstrate that such variations are due solely to the shortcomings of the formula, and hence the converse, that a correct formula would disclose an invariant relation. Such a relation is not the logical product of the discussion, but an entirely new postulate, independent of it.

Secondly, from having demonstrated by means of a suppositious case the possibility of the two different shapes having been perceived as similar, or conversely, of the standard being perceived as other than it is, Koffka proceeds as if this example were a real one. For the only evidence offered in support of this contention is isolated instances from Thouless's and Eissler's studies. And these, as shown above, do not prove what they are assumed to prove.

For if the subject saw the "real" shape as other than it was, or other than he saw it at another time, this would not in any way afford evidence of an "invariant relation" between perceived shape and inclination. The only evidence which could suggest such a relation would be that which showed that a different constancy value was associated with a different perception of tilt. Nowhere, however, does Koffka offer such evidence.

It would seem then, that on logical grounds alone the argument for this relationship, as presented by Koffka, is not very convincing; nor is the case much helped when experimental evidence is examined.

The main study prompted by this hypothesis was that of Stavrianos (1945). Her subjects attempted to estimate the degree of tilt by their perception of shape. Her results are unfortunately not in a form convenient for direct presentation. In summary, subjects attempted both estimates of shape and explicit judgments of inclination at four selected angles of tilt (15°, 30°, 45°, 55°). This occurred under conditions of binocular normal vision, binocular reduction-tube vision, monocular vision, and monocular reduction-tube vision. Paired judgments for shape and tilt failed to show any significant correlation. At the same time, the comparison of mean standard error under decreasingly favourable conditions through reduced orientation cues showed a corresponding decrease in accuracy of estimated tilt. This was not accompanied, however, by a corresponding decrease in accuracy of estimated shape. The *accuracy* of estimated shape remained surprisingly high for all conditions, whilst variations in the Brunswik-Thouless ratio did not occur systematically as a function of presented angle. On the other hand, an approximate relation of invariance for perceived shape and angle of tilt was found, under the monocular condition, for some observers.

From these experiments Stavrianos concluded that failure to demonstrate a shape-tilt relation was due to the difference between the observer's adjustment of tilt (or shape) and the tilt (or shape) which he "took into account" or "registered" when making this adjustment. Hence the implication remains that a different attitude or reaction is involved in perception of tilt, as distinct from the perception of shape.

It might perhaps be thought that since perception of shape and perception of tilt involve different reactions (the subject directing his attention to different ends) an invariant relation between these factors is somewhat improbable. This would be an unwarranted conclusion, however, since, although the experiments aim at correlating such factors and fail to do so, Koffka's hypothesis does not in fact require such a correlation for its confirmation. The hypothesis of invariance merely states that an invariant relation exists between the perception of a shape and of its degree of tilt, not between the perception of a shape and an *estimate* of its degree of tilt. And Stavrianos is herself clearly aware of the superogatory nature of the task before her demonstration, since she states that in failing to uphold the hypothesis of invariant relation the experiments may have offered too severe a test of it.

Although the elusive concept put forward by Koffka appears to have escaped the grasp of Stavrianos' investigation, it is not impossible to conceive of techniques which might go some way to confirm or confute it. And at least two ways of doing this are suggested by Koffka's original discussion.

In the first place, his suppositious case may be treated as an actual one. Two shapes, one a circle, the other an ellipse, must be matched with some third shape such as another ellipse. They must yield similar constancies and simultaneously appear similar in order to confirm his criticism of Thouless's formula. In the second place, the fate of constancy needs to be investigated throughout the arc of inclination, under conditions which make it a reasonable assumption that the shape undergoing tilt *continues* to be perceived as physically unchanged.

Under these circumstances, if constancy throughout the arc of tilt were to remain constant, the formula might be said to disclose an invariant relation. Alternatively, if changes in constancy occurred corresponding to some simple function of the tilt-arc (i.e. a geometrical function such as the sine of the angle), such a relation might be said to be exhibited by a suitably amplified formula. But if it were not found possible to assign any simple function whatever to calculate a standard constancy, the likelihood of an invariant relation would appear remote.

Before concluding this discussion a final point must be noted. The technique employed in all these studies of shape constancy is one which necessarily precludes the attainment of complete constancy, and which, moreover, cannot preserve absolutely identical conditions throughout the arc of tilt. For in all such experiments the comparison shape is not physically changed; a flat surface is simply rotated upon an axis. The more remote implications of this fact are discussed below. For the moment it is sufficient to note one obvious outcome. If a shape such as the circle is compared with an ellipse which is a projection of the circle tilted 10° from the frontal-parallel plane, the possible range of constancy is some 80°, whereas a similar disc turned for comparison with an 80° ellipse can only be turned another 10° before disappearing altogether. Thus the actual conditions of constancy are in part dependent upon the degree of tilt. And neither treatment with nonlinear functions, nor the employment of "transformation functions" in the manner of Eissler can overcome these difficulties. For this reason, if for no other, it would seem that any attempt to develop a general function for shape constancy analogous to the size/distance relation can only be of limited value, *even were the hypothesis of invariance upheld.*

EXPERIMENT I: METHOD OF INVESTIGATION

In the above discussion two possible lines of investigation were suggested, the first of which aimed at reproducing in actuality the suppositious example given by Koffka. The means of achieving this were extremely simple.

Three flat shapes were mounted upon a platform by means of vertical rods, these last forming the axes of the shapes, their lower ends passing through the base of the platform. Within the base protractor scales were mounted, and pointers attached to the rods travelled over their surfaces. When the pointers were moved, the shapes rotated on their vertical axes.

These shapes were a circle and two ellipses. The circle was 20 cm. in diameter and was placed on the left-hand side of the platform. The centrally placed ellipse was 10.7 cm. in minor axis, whilst the ellipse on the right-hand side had a minor axis of 15 cm. All the shapes were made from matt card optically blacked to minimize the total range of albedo and thus lessen the surface cues to tilt-angle. The three shapes were separated by a distance of 30 cm. between their centers, and the apparatus was covered by a screen which could be slid from side to side, revealing in turn either the centre and left-hand shapes, or the centre and right-hand ones.

The subject was seated in a chair equipped with head and chin rest, directly before the central shape. All shapes were placed at eye-level. He viewed the apparatus from three different distances in turn, namely 6, 4, and 2 metres, in a large room lit evenly throughout by means of six 120-watt fluorescent lamps.

DESCRIPTION OF EXPERIMENT I

Part I. Whilst the subject was being seated, the apparatus remained covered with the screen, upon which was a large central fixation X to enable the chair to be adjusted to the correct position. When the subject was ready, the screen was moved to one side, revealing the circle (left) and the small ellipse (centre, appearing right), but covering the third ellipse. Under the subject's instructions the experimenter adjusted the movable circle, step by step, until the subject indicated a match between the two shapes. After noting the angle of inclination shown by the pointer, the experimenter turned the circle to the extreme position (line of regard) and worked back step by step until the subject once more declared the two shapes to be most similar.

The circle was returned to the original frontal-parallel position, and the screen moved to reveal the ellipse on the right-hand side and the central standard ellipse, which now appeared on the left whilst the screen covered the circle. The procedure described was then repeated. Finally, the experiment was repeated at the other distances.

Part II. After these observations had been made, the screen was moved to cover the entire set-up. The experimenter then removed the standard ellipse from the central position and brought the two outer rotatable shapes to positions corresponding to the means of their former settings. The screen was removed and the subject asked whether the shapes appeared similar, if they matched one another. Finally the standard ellipse was replaced and the subject asked to comment on the appearance of the entire collection. Were the shapes similar in appearance, did they match, etc.? In conclusion, subjects were asked for general introspective comments and reflections.

Part III. With the three shapes in their final positions the lights were extinguished, a small light source was exposed behind the platform and a white screen raised behind the apparatus. This had the effect of exhibiting the shapes as silhouettes against a dimly illuminated ground in an almost totally dark room. The subject was then asked if the shapes appeared to match one another. If the answer was no, then the two variable shapes were rotated step by step until subjects declared them most similar.

For the observations of Part I six subjects were used, none of them psychologists and all having perfect sight without spectacles. Some subjects may have read of constancy phenomena, but none knew any formal psychology or the purpose of the experiment. All were warned against feeling that they were "on trial" or that test results depended upon or implicated their mental powers or abilities. In Parts II and III only one

distance was used for each subject in order to shorten a rather fatiguing
session, the range being covered by different subjects. Subjects were told
they might arrive at their estimation of the appearance of the forms by
any means they chose, but not to attempt to move their heads or try
squinting or screwing up their eyes. For all observations full binocular
vision was used.

EXPERIMENT I: RESULTS

Table I gives the scores recorded by six subjects for the circle and
variable ellipse, together with constancy values rendered by the
simple Thouless formula. In the case of Part III, the settings arrived
at varied so little from the calculated values for retinal image (projective values) that it is hardly worth while to record them in detail.

TABLE I

Sex	Subject	Shapes	Distance			Mean Thouless Values		
			6M	4M	2M	6M	4M	2M
F.	A.M.	Circle	54.3	56.6	60.0	.2	.26	.34
		Ellipse	39.2	39.0	40.2	.1	.1	.13
M.	L.M.	Circle	53.0	55.5	44.7	.18	.23	—
		Ellipse	49.0	53.0	54.3	.28	.35	.37
M.	E.L.	Circle	61.0	63.3	66.0	.36	.4	.47
		Ellipse	51.5	53.3	58.0	.32	.36	.44
M.	G.H.	Circle	56.0	55.5	55.5	.25	.23	.23
		Ellipse	53.0	47.0	51.0	.35	.25	.31
F.	H.B.	Circle	57.5	66.0	65.0	.28	.34	.44
		Ellipse	52.5	53.0	60.0	.34	.35	.47
M.	D.M.	Circle	55.0	56.5	58.2	.25	.29	.35
		Ellipse	46.0	50.0	54.3	.22	.26	.29
Pooled Mean:		Circle	56.1	58.0	58.2	.25	.29	.35
		Ellipse	48.5	49.2	53.0	.26	.29	.35

Subjects—6. N = 228.

Under these conditions all subjects recorded stimulus matches and showed little personal variation.

Match scores for two shapes are recorded at three distances. Angles and Thouless ratios are each the mean of three trials for each subject.

In Part II, subjects inspected the shapes set at the positions in which they had already been separately matched, but with the central standard ellipse removed. All subjects denied any resemblance between the appearance of the two shapes. Most thought the circle appeared wider than the ellipse. When the central standard ellipse was replaced, all declared none of the shapes similar, but most thought the standard narrower than the other two shapes, rating them in order of circle (widest), variable ellipse, standard ellipse (narrowest). All subjects were definite that the widest appearing shape was actually a circle. Two subjects stated that they saw the shapes as different but could not specify clearly what the differences appeared to be.

In Part III, all subjects declared that the set positions did not constitute a matched set of shapes. The positions at which they agreed on a genuine match of shapes were, as reported, a distribution about the point of stimulus equality.

EXPERIMENT I: DISCUSSION

The results of this experiment are not by themselves conclusive, since, although the pooled mean given in terms of Thouless ratio shows similar constancies for two different shapes (thus appearing to support the formula as against Koffka), the effect is purely adventitious. Thus, if the modified Brunswik formula is employed, or the pooled mean constancy is calculated direct from the pooled mean scores, differences in these constancy values arise. Moreover, inspection of individual scores in terms of angular setting and the mean Thouless values for each subject shows great differences in the way the two shapes were perceived. In addition, although a rough estimate of significance carried out by the writer failed to show significant differences, this is mainly because of the wide differences between individuals rather than because of any uncertainty of estimates.

But results from Parts II and III, as also comments and introspections of subjects, showed clearly a recognition of differences in the appearance of the two shapes, although their implicit registration of this in terms of angular placing of the shapes seems wayward and variable. If the results of Part I are contrasted with those of Parts II and III it would seem that each shape is regarded as a form "in its own right," the constancy value recording the reaction to this particular situation. Thus another shape may (in isolation) be matched in such a way as to make the second choice appear incompatible with the first when these two are brought into juxtaposition.

As Stavrianos found in attempting to relate implicit orientation of tilted shapes, it is very difficult to try to guess what a particular match of "apparent shape" represents in terms of the notion of "tilt" or orientation possessed by the subject at that moment. Yet there does seem some degree of reliability in subject's choices; again and again the subject makes the same setting. Variations in subsequent settings are very small (order of $30'' - 1.0°$) and space error is small (around $2°$).

In introspection, subjects are far from sure of themselves. Their apparent reliability in accuracy of setting (measured by repeated observation) contrasts strangely with their diffidence in discussion. Most stated they were not sure about the correctness of their estimates, though giving confident commands of "stop" "that's enough" to the experimenter in the actual course of observations.

To summarize briefly the results of this experiment, it would seem that, whilst far from conclusive, they are not those required to support Koffka's criticisms of Thouless and Eissler. Whereas his argument demands that the formula give different constancy values whilst the subjects see similar phenomena, production of the example appears to indicate that subjects see different phenomena (and become aware of this) whilst constancy values vary in an unsystematic fashion. Insofar as there are differences in constancy, it is not beyond possibility that different shapes have different potentialities in evoking perceptual reactions on the part of the observer.

An incidental outcome of the experiment is the systematic variation of constancy with distance in the direction of greater constancy with shorter distance. The effect may be due to a number of causes such as increased perception of microstructure when nearer the object, increased angular separation (cf. Joynson, 1949b) or increasing disparity of the two uniocular stimulus patterns. All or any of these factors tend to produce more effective criteria for the perception of the true shape of the object.

AIM OF EXPERIMENT II

In taking up the second of the two lines of enquiry suggested in the theoretical discussion, the shortcomings of this first test of Koffka's hypothesis will, it is hoped, be overcome. It should be clear that the first experiment represented only a rough "realization" of what remained purely hypothetical in the original discussion and cannot be taken very seriously as evidence.

When a shape is turned so that its full projective outline may not be seen by an observer (i.e. away from his frontal-parallel plane), then what does the seen shape relate to? It is Koffka's contention that perceived shape, under optimal perceptual conditions, relates to the frontal-parallel shape, i.e. to a shape seen at full constancy. A departure from full constancy is only possible through the failure to achieve optimal conditions of perception. For a given level of perceptual conditions, the constancy should remain constant throughout the arc of tilt for a given shape.

However, there has so far been no way of clearly establishing that there is some definitive shape which continues its, so to say, perceptual existence unchanged so that, at whatever angle it be viewed, it is a reasonable assumption that it relates to the shape it presents when turned to frontal-parallel. Thus in Experiment I there is no way of establishing unequivocally that matches of subjects did relate to the specific circle and ellipse presented. The simple constancy formula—the only means suggested so far, whereby perceptual judgments of different things may be compared among one another—does not give a definite answer.

So far then, despite contrary indications, Koffka may yet be correct in maintaining that variations are due to the tilted shape being seen as other than it in fact is, without the formula being able to indicate what this difference amounts to.

Thus what is required is a means of ensuring that the experimenter knows what actual shape the subject is perceiving throughout its various changes, and guaranteeing that this "notion" remains constant.

In the normal type of constancy experiment, the comparison of a pair of shapes is carried out step by step. Between each presentation there may be concealment of the stimuli. Whether or not this is done, there will occur some forty or fifty adjustments during which there is no return to the initial frontal-parallel position, whilst the whole operation may take considerable time.

It might well be argued that the final estimate has a direct relation only to the shape then seen and little relation to the object producing it. That is, it might be produced by some other object. In this case the estimated constancy is not inherently unique, and it is a matter of dubious theory that it is so.

It is therefore essential that the technique employed should endeavour to preserve the "object character" of the changing stimulus whilst at the same time it ensures that only present conditions of perception are the immediate cues on which the subject can base his estimate. It could then be assumed that the subject perceives the "true shape" and not the shape as "other than it is."

A second point which may be noted in passing is the tendency for the subject's estimate to be affected by extraneous factors such as the time taken by the experiment. Evidence from earlier experiments suggests that step by step setting of the stimulus can result in significantly different outcomes according to whether adjustments are made regular and frequent, or irregular and infrequent. The effect may be generalized in the direction of raised constancy for regular and frequent setting of the stimulus, and vice versa. Hence it was thought that the technique to be described would result in the lessening of variations from these causes.

The main aim of the experiment is, then, to explore the fate of constancy through the arc of tilt under closely controlled conditions, whilst ensuring that the continuity, substantiality or "object character" of the changing stimulus is stressed by rotating the standard shape continuously and having the subject record his estimates "en passant."

METHOD OF EXPERIMENT II

A small D.C. electric motor was mounted on a platform together with relay switching mechanism. The relays enabled the motor to be reversed automatically at any desired point during the revolution of its shaft. On the final shaft of the motor, which protruded vertically from the platform, was mounted a circular card 25 cm. in diameter with a matt-black surface. By means of the mechanism described, this object would rotate from frontal-parallel to the line of regard and return to its initial position. The rate of sweep for one excursion was 10 secs.

Beneath the platform a moving pointer arm which actuated the reversing mechanism held at its extremity a small solenoid relay in which was mounted the element of a ball-point pen. Immediately beneath the pen point lay the perimeter of a large perspex protractor. The solenoid was connected to a battery and a push button held by the subject. When the button was pressed the solenoid caused the pen to descend, thus touching the surface of the protractor. At the completion of each 90° arc the solenoid assembly was caused automatically to move ⅛ in. along the radial arm. In this way successive scores could not fall one on the other, but extended radially across the scale of the protractor.

The apparatus was located 6 metres distant from the subject and at the same distance was a similar looking platform carrying the comparison shape. The two stimuli were separated by an included angle of 10° and on a great arc. Thus both were exactly "straight ahead" for the subject, yet could not be fixated simultaneously.

The comparison shapes were eight ellipses, each of which was a projection of the circle in steps of 10°, from 10° to 80° through the arc of tilt. Thus constancy judgments might be obtained for the range of possible tilt from frontal-parallel to line of regard. The subject sat comfortably in a chair with the objects at eye-level. No provision was made for securing his head. When the subject's button was pressed, a small red lamp (invisible to the subject) glowed, thus informing the experimenter that the subject had made a response. The apparatus was arranged so that four possible movements of the shape could be studied, tilting from centre to extreme left, left to centre, centre to extreme right, and right to centre.

DESCRIPTION OF EXPERIMENT II

Part I. New subjects who had not taken part in Experiment I were used in this experiment. The subject was brought into the room whilst the apparatus remained covered with a screen. When the screen was removed two black matt shapes, one a circle the other an ellipse, were visible against a neutral buff background. Without giving any instructions or mentioning the purpose of the experiment, the experimenter set the mechanism in motion, introducing it merely as a phenomenon which the subject was invited to watch and comment upon.

After the subject had watched the rotating shape for some moments, he was asked for any observations upon what he had seen. These having been noted, the subject was given the small hand push-button and told what to do, namely, press it when he felt the two shapes to be most similar.

He was warned against attempting to make every possible match whenever the point of similarity appeared, but only to do so if and when he felt sure of himself. The subject was asked not to make head movements, nor to squint, close or screw up his eyes in order to make matches, but to use his normal vision. After recording four attempted matches in each direction of tilt, the apparatus was stopped with the shape at frontal-parallel, the scores were noted, the perspex scale was wiped clean, and the fixed ellipse was removed and replaced by another.

The series of ellipses was presented in randomized order with a fixed succession, and beginning with a different ellipse for each subject. Thus for each subject there was a different shape as his "first experience," and from this set of "first experiences" a set of values could be obtained and compared with the pooled mean for the group. No significant difference was detected by comparison of such scores.

Upon the conclusion of this experiment (taking about 45 mins.) the series of shapes was explored once more, step by step, using hand setting. This time each subject took four shapes (20°, 40°, 60°, 80°) (10°, 30°, 50°, 70°), partly due to the lesser importance of this part of the experiment, but also because the latter procedure was lengthy and fatiguing for the subject.

Part II. In the second part of the experiment the black matt cards were replaced by wire outlines, thus removing possible illumination and textural cues to perception of tilt. The experiment was repeated identically with that described above, excepting that the experience was of necessity no longer a novel one.

All subjects taking part in these experiments had perfect vision or suitable correction by spectacles. In the case of these latter, only those suffering from simple visual defects (no astigmatics) were admitted. Only two subjects had taken part before in psychological experiments. Of the ten subjects selected five were women and five were men. None were psychology students. Six were university students, four were workers or housewives.

RESULTS

These are listed below (Tables II-VI and Graph I). Before discussing these, the general comments of the subjects will be dealt with. It must be remembered that subjects never saw the apparatus at close hand on first entering the room. When they did see it, it was some 6 metres distant, at eye-level and on a great arc of their saggital line. It will therefore be appreciated that the sole experience, in terms of sensory stimulation, was that of an ellipse (left) and a circle (right) which declined through various elliptical shapes to a straight line and returned once more to its original form.

F. J. Langdon

TABLE II(a). SOLID SHAPES MECHANICALLY ROTATED

| 80° | | 70° | | 60° | | 50° | | 40° | | 30° | | 20° | | 10° | | Subject |
In	Out	In	Out	In	Out	In	Out	In	Out	In	Out	In	Out	In	Out	
.55	.5	.1	.05	.03	.03	.08	.08	.22	.16	.13	.14	.14	.11	.12	.19	1
.7	.7	.45	.57	.27	.3	.33	.35	.2	.32	.22	.32	.33	.33	.31	.35	2
.7	.7	.37	.55	.2	.4	.22	.37	.24	.26	.23	.18	.24	.21	.24	.22	3
.4	.35	.2	.35	.11	.33	.14	.35	.06	.34	.06	.33	.1	.1	.15	.23	4
.7	.7	.2	.25	.26	.26	.4	.4	.34	.22	.3	.23	.12	.16	.09	.08	5
.75	.8	.35	.2	.28	.25	.17	.25	.22	.29	.1	.1	.11	.08	.25	.25	6
.6	.7	.3	.2	.3	.33	.2	.12	.1	.22	.19	.28	.2	.2	.14	.15	7
.7	.7	.55	.5	.27	.34	.17	.32	.26	.28	.28	.23	.24	.24	.22	.2	8
.6	.6	.4	.45	.3	.28	.35	.37	.26	.24	.2	.22	.24	.29	.27	.29	9
.7	.75	.45	.47	.26	.32	.34	.35	.3	.27	.22	.25	.18	.2	.15	.17	10
.65	.65	.34	.33	.23	.28	.24	.3	.22	.26	.19	.23	.19	.19	.2	.22	Mean (In–Out)
.65		.335		.255		.27		.24		.21		.19		.21		Mean (Combined)

Constancies given in Thouless values for every 10° of arc, moving in two directions.
Subjects—10. N = 1280.

Scanty though this sensory information was, all subjects stated that they "*saw* a circle turning round." At a later stage an attempt was made to draw subjects into a discussion of their experience. All efforts to encourage them to entertain doubts as to the unambiguous character of their perception were unavailing. It was eventually pointed out to them that they could not "see" this but only infer it (it should be self-evident that the appearance may be produced without any rotatory motion, as in the case of Lissajous figures), but the general reaction was that the experimenter was indulging in a linguistic quibble. On the other hand, at a later stage in the experiment proper, almost all subjects stated that suddenly they no longer saw a "circle going round" but a two dimensional changing shape.

During the preliminaries most subjects described the phenomenon as interesting to watch but commonplace and unremarkable. Most expressed preference for watching the wire outline rather than the solid form. During the course of the experiment there would always come a point at which the subject would declare that he now saw a new appearance. Various terms were used to describe this: "A circle being squeezed in and out"; "A football bladder"; "The sort of thing a dentist uses when he gives you gas"; "An orange being squashed," etc. All subjects resorted to metaphorical terms of visual imagery. One subject, after giving responses for some time, suddenly described such an alternation of experience and then stated that she "could not do the experiment properly unless I see the shape being squeezed." Seeing the circle turning round then appeared to "make

TABLE II(b). SOLID SHAPES MECHANICALLY ROTATED

80°	70°	60°	50°	40°	30°	20°	10°
1.0	1.66	2.23	1.62	2.1	2.55	3.03	3.5
1.0	2.42	2.12	4.6	4.2	3.16	2.87	2.55
0	2.7	3.42	4.1	2.55	3.27	2.94	1.9
1.9	2.5	3.87	5.1	7.35	8.54	2.22	3.87
1.0	2.06	2.12	1.32	4.43	4.12	2.92	3.16
1.0	2.5	2.45	2.22	3.0	4.31	5.1	3.2
1.62	2.64	1.18	3.24	4.18	3.32	5.66	3.0
1.0	1.27	1.63	3.32	2.0	2.56	2.23	1.8
1.0	1.8	2.16	3.11	3.5	4.23	2.7	2.88
1.0	2.2	2.8	2.32	3.76	4.54	3.74	3.33
1.05	2.18	2.4	3.1	3.71	4.05	3.35	2.92

σ of mean space errors for each subject. Pooled mean for group.

TABLE III(a). WIRE OUTLINE SHAPES MECHANICALLY ROTATED

80° In	80° Out	70° In	70° Out	60° In	60° Out	50° In	50° Out	40° In	40° Out	30° In	30° Out	20° In	20° Out	10° In	10° Out	Subject
.7	.65	.35	.42	.14	.22	.21	.25	.34	.37	.27	.29	.19	.15	.13	.17	1
.75	.75	.57	.6	.42	.47	.25	.27	.4	.42	.33	.39	.27	.27	.2	.24	2
.42	.4	.27	.33	.21	.27	.19	.17	.25	.27	.26	.29	.15	.22	.15	.19	3
.75	.75	.44	.48	.29	.37	.22	.25	.21	.27	.2	.23	.21	.18	.19	.2	4
.8	.8	.3	.37	.28	.27	.4	.47	.32	.3	.32	.27	.12	.18	.1	.11	5
.75	.8	.42	.31	.3	.27	.22	.29	.25	.31	.18	.14	.11	.14	.25	.27	6
.7	.7	.44	.32	.37	.39	.27	.22	.17	.2	.2	.27	.22	.23	.16	.17	7
.7	.7	.57	.62	.33	.37	.28	.35	.3	.32	.29	.3	.25	.25	.26	.25	8
.7	.7	.5	.52	.37	.3	.35	.35	.27	.28	.24	.25	.24	.21	.26	.28	9
.7	.7	.5	.55	.3	.33	.4	.41	.33	.32	.25	.28	.2	.22	.19	.19	10
.69	.7	.44	.45	.30	.33	.28	.3	.28	.31	.25	.27	.2	.21	.19	.21	Mean (In–Out)
.7		.45		.32		.29		.3		.26		.21		.20		Mean (Combined)

Constancies given in Thouless values for every 10° of arc, moving in two directions.
Subjects—10. N = 1280.

her go wrong." Inspection of her scores, however, failed to reveal any systematic differences in response to either type of phenomenon, and this may be generalized for all subjects in that variations of experience do not appear to affect their matchings of the shapes, neither do their volunteered opinions on how they think they are responding: (typical excerpts:—(subject) "don't take any notice of that one (a score), I was a bit late then," or "I'm not doing so

TABLE III(b). WIRE OUTLINE SHAPES MECHANICALLY ROTATED

80°	70°	60°	50°	40°	30°	20°	10°
1.0	1.42	1.66	1.84	2.24	2.33	2.87	2.9
1.0	1.84	1.9	3.33	3.2	3.0	2.74	2.65
1.0	2.24	2.83	4.0	3.09	2.24	2.45	1.73
0	1.41	2.12	3.32	4.12	4.06	2.34	2.12
0	2.55	2.24	2.45	3.0	3.09	4.0	2.35
1.0	2.12	2.24	1.87	2.92	3.16	3.87	3.0
1.0	1.41	1.73	2.83	2.12	2.34	2.23	1.58
1.0	1.22	1.58	3.08	1.73	1.58	2.0	1.41
1.0	1.22	2.0	1.87	2.23	2.73	2.45	2.12
.7	1.3	2.12	2.32	3.08	3.87	3.87	2.34
.77	1.55	2.04	2.69	2.77	2.83	2.88	2.22

σ of mean space errors for each subject. Pooled mean for group.

TABLE IV. MECHANICALLY ROTATED SHAPES, WIRE OUTLINE AND SOLID FORMS

	80°	70°	60°	50°	40°	30°	20°	10°
Binoc. vision—								
Wire outline	.75	.44	.27	.29	.25	.23	.2	.22
σ S.E.	1.0	1.5	2.12	2.23	2.2	1.88	1.87	2.04
Monoc. vision—								
Wire outline	.45	.2	.21	.23	.1	.15	.11	.12
σ S.E.	2.23	2.64	3.08	4.79	4.47	4.69	3.87	4.12
Binoc. vision—								
Solid shape	.6	.44	.25	.29	.23	.2	.19	.2
σ S.E.	1.0	1.8	2.15	2.87	2.23	2.0	2.12	1.87
Monoc. vision—								
Solid shape	.37	.2	.19	.24	.11	.14	.1	.09
σ S.E.	3.0	4.47	2.73	5.29	4.58	3.05	8.66	4.47

Comparison of binocular and monocular vision for two subjects. N = 256.
First line of data gives Constancy Values.
Second line of data gives Space Error Dispersions.

well now," or "the narrow ellipses were easiest, these (oblate) are harder," etc., etc.).

There may be perceptual differences in these subjective states of mind, but they do not seem to correspond in any systematic way with accuracy, variations in space error or degree of constancy. This latter appears to be determined solely by the point around the arc of tilt occupied by the shape and the actual cues available to its perception. In the case of moving shapes (at this velocity) subjective variations in attitude seem incidental to the external objective situation.

Most comments after the experiment were similar to those recorded above. Most subjects thought the experiment interesting, and perhaps strangely, "rather difficult to do well" (no one could be disabused entirely of the idea that some test of ability was involved), though no amount of discussion could make quite clear what "well" or "badly" related to in terms of objective performance.

Turning to the recorded data, in the case of Tables II(a) and III(a) each constancy recorded is the mean of eight actual trials of one subject, covering his responses for both directions of tilt (waxing and waning). The calculations of dispersion have been made direct from the angular settings. Thus the working units are degrees of angle and the constancy tables are calculated from them. For the purpose of the experiment a complete set of Thouless constancies was calculated for all possible declinations of the circle with any one comparison shape. Hence constancy ratios could be read off direct.

It will be appreciated that dispersion shown in the tables is wider than that obtained for any one direction, since it incorporates the space error. It might be thought that such a procedure is unjustified, but in practice it was found that dispersions for subsequent matches in a given direction were extremely small. In obtaining the eight matches, the first response in each direction was ignored.

A characteristic of the results is the extreme similarity, subject for subject, between the solid shapes and the wire outlines. It would seem that under these conditions the wire outline is a superior object to perception, whilst the results for hand-setting (Table V) show the opposite.

However, the most interesting result is the marked and consistent nature of the curve of constancy through the arc of tilt. Table V for step by step setting gives similar results to those obtained by Thouless and the reverse of those obtained by Eissler, in showing a

TABLE V. WIRE OUTLINE AND SOLID SHAPES MATCHED BY
HAND SETTING (STEP BY STEP)

	80°	70°	60°	50°	40°	30°	20°	10°
Wire outline	.25	.22	.17	.18	.11	.08	.06	—
σ S.E.	2.4	4.05	5.5	6.76	4.24	4.12	4.06	—
Solid shape	.29	.25	.19	.19	.1	.07	.05	—
σ S.E.	2.12	2.23	3.08	3.16	4.0	4.06	3.87	—

For 10 subjects, two trials in each direction. N = 320.
First line of data gives Constancy Values.
Second line of data gives Space Error Dispersions.

TABLE VI. CONSTANCY VALUES FOR WIRE OUTLINES AND
SOLID SHAPES (POOLED MEANS)

	80°	70°	60°	50°	40°	30°	20°	10°
Wire outlines	.118	.154	.16	.186	.23	.22	.199	.197
Solid shapes	.113	.115	.128	.174	.184	.182	.187	.207

Treated by formula (P-S/R-S), Cos. S.

progressive decline in constancy toward the frontal-parallel plane. The curves from the experiment involving continuous motion all show an extremely high constancy toward the line of regard falling to a low point around 60°-50°, rising slightly thereafter and then declining once more as the frontal-parallel plane is approached. The phasic character of the contour persists in the records of every subject and is present under conditions of monocular vision (Table IV).

Fig. 1 shows the records for the pooled mean through the arc of tilt placed, for comparison, adjacent to the curve of a simple *sine* function. This curve is obtained by taking an arbitrary constancy value and calculating plot points from the product of that value and the sine of the angle.

A surprising feature of the results was the stability and precision of recorded matches. Space error remained small and was almost always "overestimation" or "late response." Anticipating responses were rarely obtained (i.e. negative space error). It might be asked to what extent the speed of the moving shape influences the subject, so that his response is never a pure "space error" but a time error. Although it is believed by the present writer that so-called "space errors" in traditional comparison experiments cannot be taken as such at their face value, since the rate at which fresh estimates are called for can influence the score, there seems no reason to suppose that, at the velocity used here, any special temporal factor is in evidence more than in ordinary paired comparisons. Results from experiments already reported (Langdon, 1951), and others to be described later, appear to confirm this over a wide range of speeds.

DISCUSSION

It can be granted that the experiment has succeeded in one particular, if in no other, in that subjects retain a clear and un-

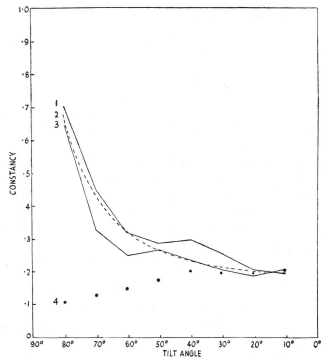

Fig. 1.   Constancy/Tilt Angle. From Tables II(a), III(a), & VI.
1. Table III(a).   2. Sine Function.
3. Table II(a).   4. Results treated by formula: (P-S/ R-S) COS.S.

changing notion of the "real object" throughout its vicissitudes. The continuing identity, the regular motion, together with certitude in belief as to what they were experiencing, together with the accuracy and consistency of their responses, appear convincing on this point. At the same time it is recognized that these phenomena may constitute a special class of experiences from which it may be illegitimate to generalize to those of the traditional type of experiment.

If the continuing identity of the shape is retained unchanged, what bearing do these results have upon Koffka's argument? Here the results are not quite so clear. It is obvious that the measure of constancy, as calculated from the Thouless formula, undergoes variations—though for reasons, it seems, other than those advanced by Koffka—but are such variations truly alterations in the character of the *percept* through the arc of tilt, or are they products of an over-simple method of treatment?

The basic formula developed by Thouless and Brunswik takes the form P-S/R-S where P is the percept or phenomenal match, S is the stimulus value and R the real object. Thouless replaced the numerical values by Log. values and Brunswik (1933) has shown that such notations may be used to make the formula independent of the absolute values in any situation. In the present case the arc of tilt involves a decrease in minor axis of the circle, seen projectively, by the *cosine* of the tilt-angle. Change of apparent shape will increase throughout the arc, angle for angle, according to this function. But replacement of the simple formula by such a function (i.e. Cos.P-Cos.S./Cos.R-Cos.S) does not alter matters, since this procedure affects both sides of the ratio equation and the non-linearity of the scale is not counteracted. As a rough approximation a non-linear angular scale can be achieved by plotting constancy values according to a sine function, viz. (P-S/R-S)Cos.S. Mean values for solids and wire outlines treated this way are given in Table VI and appear as plotted points in the graph.

The aim of such a procedure is to query the appropriateness of the simple constancy formula applied through the arc of tilt, and also to see whether the straight-line contour implied by the hypothesis of an invariant shape/tilt relation can be produced by some simple function.

Whilst the resultant contour may be approximated to a straight line, the mere fact of equal constancy values does not amount to very much. For in the untreated contour there may be seen repeated variations, clear rises and falls in the middle of the arc which cannot be ignored. Some of these variations are significant in the conventional sense, others are not. But this sense of significance has to be extended when small variations are ceaselessly repeated—as is found here—and there is no one function which can produce a uniform constancy with such data.

Apart from these considerations, it must be realized that the total set of perceptual conditions through the phases of the tilt arc are varying. Thus there is better "anchorage" for estimates of shape near the reference planes (line of regard, frontal-parallel). At the same time, these reference planes are non-equivalent since shapes orientated to line of regard may be sharply differentiated from one another and from the circle, whilst when orientated toward the frontal parallel, far less easily. And Stavrianos has pointed out in her study that there is poorer anchorage to the accepted reference planes at intermediate tilt-angles, and cites Hsia's work on whiteness constancy as providing analogous confirmation of this. His suggestions are reminiscent of the argument developed by Eissler and reported above.

But in the context of present experiments this argument does not appear very convincing. If the increase in constancy is due, as Stavrianos, Eissler and Hsia suggest, to "over-compensation" by the subject attempting to counteract the loss of a strong plane of reference, why should there occur a great increase in constancy at the line of regard when such a reference plane is being approached? It might be objected that loss of the plane of reference must involve a fall in accuracy of judgments, and the fact that this does not take place is evidence that there is no such loss of "anchorage." But this cannot be accepted since Stavrianos has herself pointed out that "Accuracy of judgment of *tilt* was found to decrease significantly at the intermediate angles of inclination . . . (but) the accuracy of *shape* perception was not found to vary systematically as a function of the angle at which the Standard was presented" (p. 92). Thus it would seem premature to entertain with any degree of confidence such speculations on the rôle of planes of reference, solely on the basis of evidence so far obtained.

The assumption of an invariant relation between shape and tilt carries the implication that the data may be fitted to a smooth curve of a simple function, and it is possible to find an expected theoretical value at any point along the contour, using the existing parameters. If this is done for the data of Table III(a) by the method of least squares, then for observations of the 40° range (where the rise in constancy takes place) the expected value is .26 and the observed value is .3.

It would be convenient to apply the χ^2 test to the data at this point and try to find the goodness of fit of such a calculated curve corresponding to this simple function. This is hardly possible to obtain from pooled data however, since there is no reason why a pooled mean of constancy values should tend to a normal, or any cumulative distribution. Each subject has his own constancy level (cf. Sheehan, 1938) and all that a group show in common are changes in relative values with changes of perceptual conditions. It is therefore necessary to apply a cruder test to the pooled data.

If it is assumed that the drawn point of the functional curve is approximately correct, it might be expected that the distribution of observed scores about its mean should indicate the likelihood of coincidence with the observed mean. An examination of raw scores, however, shows that of a population of 160 observations only 42 would lie on the further side of this theoretical mean, with the remaining 118 on its upper half.

Thus it would seem that although the variation from expected values is small, the recurrence of this variation in a large population gives it importance. A calculation from two sets of data for subjects 1 and 6 Table III(a) at 40° and the same subjects for Table II(a) at 50° (where a similar rise in the contour for solid forms occurs) gives values of "P" taken from Fisher's Table of χ^2 (1932) as .2 and .16 respectively which indicate only medium to poor fit. Subsequent experiments have, however, confirmed these tendencies to phasic shifts within the arc of tilt under extremely varied conditions. This has made the task of demonstrating statistically the precise degree of improbability of a simple functional curve seem superfluous, since the constant variations may be seen by inspection.

To summarize the results from these experiments the following points may be noted:

1. Mechanically rotated shapes seen in continuous movement exhibit constancy of shape similarly to stationary forms.

2. Supplementary cues from surface texture and illumination do not appear to play an important rôle in maintaining constancy, whereas they do appear to do so in the case of stationary shapes.

3. The contour of constancy over the arc of tilt differs markedly from that obtained with stationary shapes.

4. This contour appears composite and irregular, and the probability of its corresponding to any simple function appears small.

5. Koffka's hypothesis of an invariant shape/tilt relation appears to derive little support from these experiments, although they are not absolutely conclusive.

6. It is possible that some non-linear function is involved in interpreting the results, but there is no reason to assume that one element determines the whole of the contour. Subjective factors may well enter as secondary determinants.

7. The situation created by mechanically rotated shapes is stable and clearly perceptible to the subject.

8. The subject's reactions appear to be independent of his conscious attitude and opinions: he is "drawn into" the situation, and makes estimates corresponding to the "synthetic attitude" described by Brunswik.

REFERENCES

BRUNSWIK, E. Die Zugänglichkeit von Gegenständen für die Wahrnemungen und deren orientative Bestimmung. *Arch. ges. Psychol.*, 1933, **88**, 377-419.

BRUNSWIK, E. Distal focusing of perception; size constancy in a representative sample of situations. *Psychol. Monogr.*, 1944, **56**, 254.

EISSLER, K. Gestaltkonstanz der Sehdinge bei Variation der Objekte und ihre Einwirkungsweise auf den Wahrnemenden. *Arch. ges. Psychol.*, 1933, **88**, 487-551.

GIBSON, J. J., and GLAZER, N. M. (Ed.). Motion picture testing and research. Report No. 7, A.A.F. Aviation Psychology Research Reports, Washington, D. C., 1947.

GILINSKY, A. S. The problem of size and distance. *Psychol. Rev.*, 1951, **58**, 460-82.

HOLWAY, A. H., and BORING, E. G. Determinants of apparent visual size with distance variant. *Amer. J. Psychol.*, 1941, **54**, 21.

ITTELSON, W. H. Size as a cue to distance. *Amer. J. Psychol.*, 1951, **64**, 54-67; 188-202.

JOYNSON, R. B. An examination of some problems in the visual perception of size. Unpublished thesis, Oxford, 1949a.

JOYNSON, R. B. The problem of size and distance. *Quart. J. exp. Psychol.*, 1949b, **1**, 119-135.

KOFFKA, K. *Principles of Gestalt Psychology.* London, 1935.

LANGDON, J. The perception of a changing shape. *Quart. J. exp. Psychol.*, 1951, **3**, 157-65.

SHEEHAN, M. R. A study of individual consistency in phenomenal constancy. *Arch. Psychol.*, 1938, No. 222, 1-95. Columbia.

STAVRIANOS, B. K. The relation of shape perception to explicit judgments of inclination. *Arch. Psychol.*, 1945, No. 296, 1-94. Columbia.

THOULESS, R. H. Phenomenal regression to the real object. *Brit. J. Psychol.*, 1931, **21**, 339-359; **22**, 1-29.

VERNON, M. D. Vision. *Ann. Rev. Psychol.*, 1953a, **4**, 59-88.

VERNON, M. D. *Further studies in visual perception.* Cambridge, 1953b.

C. *Effects of Learning and Special
or Limited Experience*

SELECTION 20

■■

Arrested Vision[*]

Austin H. Riesen

MANY PRIMITIVE ORGANISMS show immediate and highly uniform reactions to light from the moment of birth. In man vision is a much more complex skill that develops gradually through the years of infancy and childhood. How much of this capacity is innate and how much is acquired by learning or through the natural maturation of the eyes during the child's early years? What are the factors that determine visual perception? If we knew the answers to these questions we could do a great deal more than we can now to improve defective vision.

The task of separating the hereditary factors from the effects of experience in human vision obviously is not easy. For example, a newborn infant at first shows no clear indication of any response to a bright disk presented before its eyes. Only after several weeks does the growing infant begin to look at the disk. Is this the result of growth, of experience or of both? Does the change in response come about through practice in the use of the eyes, or through a natural maturation that occurs, quite independently of use, in the retina of the eye, in the eye or neck muscles, in fiber tracts of the central nervous system or in several of these parts combined?

Scientific studies of the growth of behavior have shown that certain abilities do develop without use as animals mature. Thus tadpoles raised under anesthesia to prevent swimming movements nevertheless improve in swimming ability. Chicks and rats kept in darkness for a time show some progress in vision-controlled behavior. Children also demonstrate a basic rate of maturation in some capacities: there is a limit to the degree of retardation or accelera-

[*] From *Scientific American*, 1950, **183**, 16-19. Reprinted by permission of the author and the publisher.

tion of these abilities that can be effected by restricting or expanding their training.

But some of these studies have revealed curious contradictions. Wendell Cruze at North Carolina State College found that after newly hatched chicks had been kept in darkness for five days, they were generally able to peck at and hit 24 of the first 25 grains presented to them; this score was 12 per cent better than the average of hits by chicks immediately after hatching. On the other hand, S. G. Padilla at the University of Michigan showed that if the period of darkness was extended to 14 days, the pecking response failed to appear, presumably because the instinct to peck at spots on the ground died out through disuse. The chicks began to starve in the midst of plenty. So it appears that lack of practice, at least if sufficiently prolonged, can interfere with the development of behavior which is basically instinctive or reflex in nature.

In human beings the most nearly pertinent evidence on this problem has come from studies of patients operated upon at advanced ages for congenital cataracts. These patients, who have passed all their lives in near-blindness, ranging from the bare ability to tell day from night to some ability to distinguish colors and localize light, invariably report an immediate awareness of a change after a successful operation. They begin at once to distinguish differences in the parts of the visual field, although they cannot identify an object or describe its shape. After a few days' practice they can name colors. From this point on progress is slow, often highly discouraging, and some patients never get beyond the ability to distinguish brightness and color. Others, over a period of months and even years, develop the ability to identify simple geometric figures, read letters and numbers and, in rare cases, to identify complex patterns such as words, outline drawings and faces. During their efforts to improve their visual skill the patients go through a long period of picking out elements in an object and inferring the nature of the object from these elements—often erroneously. For example, a child of 12, some months after her operation, is reported by her doctor to have pointed to a picture and called it "a camel, because it has a hump." What she identified as a hump was the dorsal fin of a fish.

But such cases of congenital cataract do not give us very satisfactory evidence on the elementary problem of how disuse affects the development of visual behavior. There are too many other variables; we must take into account (1) the degree of the patient's previous blindness, since he was not in total darkness, (2) the limit that is imposed on his potentialities for improvement by the fact that the eye operated on lacks a lens, and (3) the circumstance that in all these cases there appears to be another visual handicap—jerky movements of the eyeballs known as spontaneous nystagmus. The effects of these combined difficulties are not readily calculable. For a more meaningful study it is highly desirable to eliminate these variables by setting up a controlled experiment that will determine the effects of disuse on normal eyes. Obviously such an experiment cannot be risked in human beings; no one would wish to impose permanent reading difficulties on any person having to adjust himself to a civilized society. The most logical subject for the experiment is another higher primate. The chimpanzee was chosen, because its behavior, like man's, is dominated by vision, and because it is intelligent and tractable.

In 1942 at the Yerkes Laboratories of Primate Biology in Orange Park, Fla., an infant male chimpanzee was separated from its mother on the day of birth and blindfolded with a gauze bandage and adhesive tape. This animal defeated the experimenters by loosening the tape at the side of his left nostril and habitually peeking down his nose with his left eye. By the age of 16 weeks he gained full freedom from facial bandages. Although he did not recognize his feeding bottle at this time, nor show fixation of persons or objects, he developed fairly adequate visual behavior within a few weeks.

In 1945 the experimenters tried again. This time two newborn chimpanzee infants, a male and a female respectively named Snark and Alfalfa, were housed in a completely darkened room. During the first 16 months the only light these infants experienced was an electric lamp turned on for intervals of 45 seconds several times daily for their routine care and feeding. When they were first tested for visual perception at the age of 16 months, both chimpanzees showed extreme incompetence. Their reflex responses indicated that their eyes were sensitive to light—the pupils constricted; sudden changes of illumination startled the animals; they responded to a slowly waving flashlight with jerky pursuit movements of the eyes and side to side following motions of the head. But both chimpanzees failed to show any visual responses to complex patterns of light until after they had spent many hours in illuminated surroundings. They did not respond to play objects or their feeding bottles unless these touched some part of the body. They did not blink at a threatening motion toward the face. When an object was advanced slowly toward the face, there was no reaction until the object actually touched the face, and then the animal gave a startled jump.

After the 16-month period of darkness, Alfalfa was placed on a limited light schedule until the age of 21 months and Snark until 33 months. When Alfalfa was later moved into a normal daylight environment, in the course of many months she developed normal recognition of objects, began to blink in response to threats and ceased to be startled by a touch. Snark was much more retarded. Between the ages of 20 and 27 months, while he was still on rationed light, he learned after many hundreds of trials to tell the difference between contrasting signs, differing in color or pattern, which indicated either food or a mild electric shock. His visual acuity, as measured by ability to discriminate between horizontal and vertical lines, was well below that of normally raised animals. At the end of 33 months he began to live in the normally lighted chimpanzee nursery and later out of doors with chimpanzees of his own age. It was expected that he would rapidly acquire normal visual behavior. He did improve slightly at first, but after this small initial improvement he actually lost ground in visual responsiveness, until even reflex activity began to die away.

What is the explanation of this deterioration? Had the development of his eyes been permanently arrested by the absence of light? There had been no previous evidence that stimulation by light is essential for the normal growth of the primate retina or optic nerve. It was a surprise to find that, while the eyes of these chimpanzees remained sensitive to light after 16 months in darkness, the retina and optic disk in both animals did not reflect as much light as normal chimpanzee eyes do. Snark later developed a marked pallor of the optic disk in both eyes. There is other evidence suggesting that fish and amphibians, at least, need light-stimulation for normal eye development. So the physiological effects of the lack of light may be part of the explanation for Snark's loss of visual function. But it is not the whole explanation for all the visual abnormalities in these two chimpanzees, nor does it explain the visual difficulties of the cataract patients. These patients have excellent color discrimination, and, incidentally, do not show pallor of the optic disk. Moreover, we now have clear evidence from further experiments with chimpanzees that not merely light itself but stimulation by visual patterns is essential to normal visual development.

In these experiments three other newborn chimpanzees, two females and a male, were put into the darkroom. Debi was raised for seven months in complete darkness, even during her feedings and other care. Kora was raised for the same period on a ration of an average of one and a half hours of light daily, but the light, admitted through a white Plexiglas mask, was diffuse and unpatterned. Lad was given one and a half hours of patterned light daily: he could observe the edges of his crib, the variations in pattern introduced by movements of his own body and appendages, and all the accompaniments of bottle-feeding, including the moving about of persons in the moderately lighted room.

At seven months, when the three subjects were removed to normal daylight surroundings, Lad's visual performance was indistinguishable from that of chimpanzees raised normally. Kora and Debi, however, showed the same kinds of retardation as had Snark and Alfalfa, with some minor exceptions. Kora did not develop the blink response to a moving object until six days after her removal from darkness, and Debi not until 15 days. It took Kora 13 days and Debi 30 days to acquire the ability to pursue a moving person with the eyes, and they did this by a series of refixations instead of following smoothly as normal animals of comparable age do; it took Kora 20 days and Debi 16 days to pursue visually a moving feeding bottle; Kora 13 days and Debi 30 days to fixate the image of a stationary person.

These differences between Debi and Kora may lie within the range of variation that would occur in a group of animals treated exactly the same as either Debi or Kora. This question could be checked only by repeating the experiment many times.

Between seven and 10 months of age Debi and Kora both showed a moderate and intermittent outward (wall-eyed) deviation of the eyes. This gradually was overcome. Both infants also showed an initial spontaneous nystagmus, i.e., jerky eye movements. It appeared only sporadically, and was more pronounced under general excitement than when the animals were well relaxed.

Normal animals of seven months learn to avoid a large yellow and black striped disk after receiving one or two mild electric shocks from it. Debi and Kora, however, were shocked by the disk twice a day for six and nine days, respectively, before they so much as whimpered when it was shown. Only after 13 days in Kora's case and 15 days in Debi's did they consistently indicate by some sort of avoidance response that they saw the disk within five seconds of the time that it was raised in front of their eyes.

In still another study an infant chimpanzee named Kandy was put in the darkroom for only the first three months of life. After she was removed to daylight surroundings, her progress on the same tests was approximately paralled to that of Debi and Kora. There were three interesting differences: 1) Kandy showed a convergent squint (cross-eyes), which cleared up in a little less than two months; 2) she did not have spontaneous nystagmus; 3) she required 24 days, as compared with 13 or 15, to develop consistent avoidance of the black and yellow shock-disk. The last difference suggests that Kandy learned more slowly because of her younger age; in other words, that the development of visual discrimination was a matter of maturity as well as learning. This conclusion was strongly supported by the finding that an infant chimpanzee started through the same training at the age of two days failed to show avoidance in a month's time.

All these observations demonstrate that vision must be put to use if it is to develop normally, but they also indicate that during the first few months of an infant's life visual development is advanced by growth factors which are entirely independent of practice. Normally reared animals, for example, do not blink in response to the movement of objects across the visual field until they have reached the age of two months; the older darkroom animals, despite previous lack of experience, began to show this response within about two weeks after they were transferred to daylight surroundings.

The development and maintenance of normal visual functions in higher primates depends on a whole complex of interrelated factors, hereditary and environmental, and it can readily be disturbed at any stage of the individual's growth. This was shown in an experiment with a chimpanzee named Faik. Faik was raised in the normal light of the laboratory's nursery until the age of seven months. At that time the standard series of tests described above showed that he had excellent use of vision. Then from the age of eight to 24 months he was kept in the darkroom. He lived an active life filled with tactile, auditory, olfactory, gustatory and kinesthetic stimulation. He invited rough-house play from his caretakers at feeding times, and his general state of health remained entirely satisfactory.

When Faik was returned to daylight living quarters at 24 months, he had lost all ability to utilize vision in his interplay with the environment. He no longer recognized the feeding bottle, and failed to look at objects or persons, either stationary or moving. More than this, he possessed a strong spontaneous nystagmus and was even unable to follow a moving light in a darkroom until the fifth day after he was put back into a lighted environment. His first visual following movements, like those of all the darkroom-raised subjects, were not smooth but a series of jerky refixations, made even more jerky by the pronounced spontaneous nystagmus.

Even in direct sunlight Faik failed to grimace or close his eyelids; he gave no indication of the slightest discomfort when the sun shone in his eyes. (The chimpanzees raised in the darkroom from birth did close their lids in intense light.) Faik showed pallor similar to that of Snark and Alfalfa in his optic disks. His recovery of vision has been slow and is still only partial. Explanation of his case, and that of Snark, remains a challenge to further research.

These chimpanzee studies have established several fundamental points. They show that newborn animals, and older infants that have been kept in darkness for a time, exhibit visual reflexes when they are first subjected to light. Some responses that bear a close resemblance to reflex behavior, such as blinking at something rapidly approaching the face, become automatic only after considerable practice. Visual pursuit of moving objects, the coordination of the two eyes and convergent fixation, and the first recognition of objects come only after many hours or weeks of experience in use of the eyes. It takes the chimpanzee hundreds of hours of active utilization of the eyes to develop its vision to the stage where it can adequately guide locomotion and complex manipulations. The findings in the cases of two subjects that were kept in darkness for long periods indicate that the postponement of light exposure for too long can result in making the development of normal visual mechanisms extremely difficult if not impossible.

SELECTION 21

....

Effects of Early Experience on Social Behaviour[*][1]

RONALD MELZACK AND WILLIAM R. THOMPSON

PERCEPTUAL EXPERIENCE acquired early in life has been shown in many recent studies to have a profound influence on the intellectual (9, 10), perceptual (8), and emotional (7) behaviour of the mature organism. There is one area of mammalian behaviour, however, which is relatively unexplored: social behaviour. Reviews of animal studies by Beach and Jaynes (1) and Hebb and Thompson (5) point out the paucity of evidence on the effects of early perceptual and social experience on adult social behaviour.

Fredricson (3) has provided experimental evidence that mice raised with experience in competitive social situations show more aggressive behaviour at maturity than litter-mates raised without such experience. Similarly, a preliminary investigation by Clarke et al. (2) has shown that dogs deprived of normal social and perceptual experience during development are later consistently submissive to their normally reared litter-mates. Part of the present study, then, is an attempt to investigate more systematically the effects of early experience on dominance behaviour in the dog.

Clarke et al. (2) have also reported that normally reared dogs eagerly accept friendly approaches by humans while restricted dogs repeatedly withdraw from human attention. A method for analysing complex social and emotional behaviour of one species toward an-

---

[*] From Canad. J. Psychol., 1956, 10, 82-90. Reprinted by permission of the authors and the Univ. of Toronto Press.

[1] This investigation was done at the McGill University Psychology Laboratory, and supported by grants from the Dominion-Provincial Mental Health Program, the Rockefeller Foundation, and the Foundations Fund for Research in Psychiatry. The authors gratefully acknowledge the advice and guidance of Dr. D. O. Hebb throughout this study, and the assistance of Drs. Woodburn Heron, Helen Mahut, and Harry Scott in carrying out some of the experiments.

other has been described by Hebb (4). The wide range of emotional behaviour manifested by dogs (7) thus also permits an attempt to investigate the effects of early experience on the social and emotional responses made by dogs to experimenters acting in a "friendly," "bold," or "timid" manner toward them.

METHOD

Subjects. Nine litters of purebred Scottish terriers, all descendants of one litter of the Bar Harbor strain, were used. Each litter was randomly divided into two groups. One group, containing a total of 21 dogs (14 males and 7 females), was placed in restriction cages. The 16 dogs (8 males and 8 females) which comprised the "free environment" or control group were raised normally as pets in private homes and in the laboratory.

Rearing. Three different methods of restriction, described elsewhere in detail (9, 10), were used during this study. (*a*) Four dogs were reared separately in ordinary metal dog cages, and were able to look out at the other kennel cages and dogs. But, apart from a monthly 15-minute grooming period, they were never removed from their cages. (*b*) Seven dogs were reared in cages which were covered with heavy cardboard. The only part of the laboratory room that these dogs could see was the ceiling directly above an air- and light-vent at the top of each cage. Two or three dogs were kept in a single cage; but the only contacts they had with human beings until maturity occurred briefly during the daily feeding and cleaning period. (*c*) Ten dogs were reared in complete social isolation in cages like those used in (*b*). Only one dog was kept in a cage, and contact with human beings was eliminated. Each cage contained two compartments, and when the sliding partition between them was opened once a day, the dog was allowed to enter a freshly-cleaned compartment containing a pan of food. By means of these three methods, then, 21 dogs were deprived of a normal social and sensory experience from the time when weaning was completed at the age of four weeks until they were removed from their cages at from seven to ten months of age.

After the restricted dogs were released from their cages, they received the same opportunities for social and sensory stimulation as their normally reared litter-mates. They had long walks and play periods outdoors and in the laboratory, and had frequent contacts with other dogs and with human beings. Testing began about three weeks after the restricted dogs were released and was completed within six months. Since the litters used in this study were born at different times over a five-year period, it was not possible to use each litter for all of the tests.

EXPERIMENT I: SOCIAL RELATIONS
WITH DOGS (DOMINANCE)

Subjects. Twenty-one restricted and 15 free-environment dogs were used.

Procedure. To test for dominance behaviour (6), a restricted and a normally reared dog, both food-deprived for 24 hours, were held at two opposite corners of the testing room by two experimenters. Either a large bone or a dish of food was located at the centre of the floor. Both dogs were brought up to the food and allowed to smell it. They were then returned to their corners and released at the same time.

The results for each contest, which lasted for five minutes, were classified as a *win* for one of the dogs, or a *tie*. A dog scored a *win* when he drove the second dog away from the food by growling or barking, and remained in control of the food for all or most of the time. A *tie* was recorded when the contest did not yield manifest dominance on the part of either dog.

In order to test only dogs of like ages, dominance contests were held within each of four groups of restricted and free-environment dogs. The number of dogs in each group is shown in Table I. There

TABLE I. NUMBER OF WINS MADE BY FREE-ENVIRONMENT (F) AND
RESTRICTED (R) DOGS IN DOMINANCE TESTS

	N		No. of Contests	Wins		Ties
	F	R		F	R	
Group 1	4	5	20	15	5	0
Group 2	2	5	10	7	1	2
Group 3	7	8	43*	35	1	7
Group 4	2	3	6	0	0	6
Totals	15	21	79	57	7	15

$$\chi^2 = 41.62$$
$$p = .001$$

* Some dogs were not tested because of the possibility of serious fights and the fact that some of the females were in heat at the time of testing.

were approximately the same number of males and females among the restricted and free-environment dogs of each group.

RESULTS

Table I shows that the normally reared dogs made 57 "wins," as against 7 made by the restricted dogs. It is interesting to note that the highest number of wins made by restricted dogs occurred in Group I, in which two or three dogs were reared in a single restriction cage. The five wins made by these dogs were all scored against the same female control dog. However, no consistent sex differences could be discerned in the results. The difference in number of wins between restricted and control dogs for the four groups is significant at the .001 level.

The behaviour of the restricted dogs was such that the results cannot be attributed to their submissiveness alone; the dogs seemed also to be highly confused by the situation. Growling or snapping by the normally reared dogs, whose responses always seemed oriented toward the food and the competing dog, rarely elicited any comparable, organized, competitive behaviour in the restricted dogs. Indeed, most of them appeared unaware that there was any "contest." They tended to sit and watch the other dog eat, or to move off and explore the room. At times they went to the food when the dominant dog was present, but most often they were easily pushed out of the way. Only occasionally did they compete by actually fighting.

Supplementary observations. The observations of sharing among restricted dogs reported by Clarke *et al.* (2) were confirmed in the present study. A number of contests were held between pairs of restricted dogs and between pairs of normally reared dogs. It was observed that when two restricted dogs were pitted against each other, they frequently shared the bone or food dish. Such sharing of food was only rarely observed among the normally reared dogs. Further evidence of the ineptitude of the restricted dogs in competitive situations was observed when they were tested against normally reared dogs which were six months younger. The restricted dogs consistently lost the bone or food to the younger control animals.

EXPERIMENT II: RELATIONS AMONG DOGS (SOCIAL CURIOSITY)

Subjects. Sixteen restricted and 11 normally reared dogs were used.

Procedure. Each dog was led into a testing room containing two dogs which were kept separately behind two wire-mesh barriers. Chalk lines were drawn 1½ feet in front of each barrier, and the amount of time during a 10-minute period which each dog spent across the chalk lines near the two other dogs was recorded. This test was repeated next day with the same dogs behind the barriers.

RESULTS

On the first testing day, the normally reared dogs ran almost immediately to the dogs in the room. They sniffed and looked at them, sometimes growled and barked, and usually followed them closely on the other side of the barrier. They spent a mean of 97.7 seconds in such social investigation. During the remaining time they tended to explore the room or sit at a distance from the other dogs. On the second day, 9 of the 11 normally reared dogs spent less time near the two dogs than they did on the first (mean: 64.6 seconds): this suggests a diminution in "social curiosity" (10).

The restricted dogs, in comparison, showed a high degree of excitement in the presence of the dogs behind the barriers, but rarely followed them closely, or showed behaviour which seemed oriented with respect to these dogs. Indeed, a restricted dog would often wander close to one of the pens and urinate on it without taking any notice of the dog inside. At times the restricted dogs explored quietly around the room, then suddenly dashed toward one of the dogs in the barriers and spent considerable time running around in circles and moving rapidly back and forth, with gross, excited body movements, suggesting a diffuse emotional excitement. They spent a mean of 64.5 seconds across the chalk lines close to the two dogs. This type of behaviour increased on the second day, without the emergence of more sustained, socially-organized curiosity behaviour. Eleven of the 16 restricted dogs spent more time across the line than they did on the previous day, giving a mean of 72.9 seconds. The difference in shift of means (Day 1 to Day 2) between the restricted and the normally reared dogs is significant at the .01 level of confidence ($\chi^2 = 6.68$).

EXPERIMENT III: SOCIAL RELATIONS WITH MAN

Subjects. Fourteen restricted and 14 free environment dogs were used.

Procedure. Three social roles, representing "typical" human behaviour toward animals (4), were played by an experimenter in the presence of each dog. (1) *Friendly man: E* tried to pat the dog and gently stroke his head and back. (2) *Timid man: E* retreated and tended to "cringe" after every approach that the dog made toward him. (3) *Bold man: E* moved directly and continually toward the dog with short, rapid, stamping steps. Each role was played for a period of two minutes, with about a five-minute interval between roles for recording the dog's behaviour.

Every attempt was made to present identical testing conditions to all dogs of both groups. *E* first walked slowly around the room for two minutes to make sure that no dog avoided him in advance of testing. The same *E* subsequently played all three roles, in the above sequence, to both the restricted and the normally reared dogs of any given litter. He was not told, prior to testing, whether a dog had been reared normally or in restriction, although this could sometimes be inferred from its behaviour.

The recorded observations of each dog's behaviour toward the "friendly man" and the "timid man" were tabulated under one of four categories of socio-emotional response: *friendly behaviour, avoidance, diffuse emotional excitement,* and *aggressive stalking.* The responses made to the "bold man" were classified as *avoidance* or *escape.*

RESULTS

(1) *Behaviour to the "friendly man."* Thirteen of the 14 normally reared dogs showed *friendly behaviour* to the "friendly man" (Table II). They permitted *E* to pat them and play with them throughout the period; they approached at *E*'s call, and remained at his side, frequently turning onto their sides or backs while *E* stroked them. None of the restricted dogs showed this type of behaviour.

Ten of the 14 restricted dogs made responses which were classified as *diffuse emotional excitement.* They moved excitedly and rapidly near and around *E,* with short, jerky, to-and-fro movements. Whenever they tried to lick or "nuzzle" any part of *E*'s body, however, they assumed a characteristic bodily posture: the front part of the dog's body lay close to the floor, with the neck, head and forelegs stretched far forward; the hindquarters were at walking height, with the hind legs pushed back slightly, so that the dogs always appeared to be in a "springing" or "stalking" position. Rudimentary forms of friendly behaviour, avoidance, and aggressive stalking

TABLE II. FREQUENCY OF EACH TYPE OF EMOTIONAL RESPONSE BY
RESTRICTED (R) AND FREE-ENVIRONMENT (F) DOGS TO
3 SOCIAL ROLES PORTRAYED BY EXPERIMENTER

Categories of Emotional Behaviour	Type of Social Role					
	Friendly		Timid		Bold	
	R	F	R	F	R	F
Friendly behaviour	—	13	—	1	—	—
Diffuse excitement	10	—	2	2	—	—
Aggressive stalking	—	—	8	9	—	—
Avoidance	4	1	1	—	2	8
Escape	—	—	—	—	12	6
No emotional response	—	—	3	2	—	—
N	14	14	14	14	14	14
χ^2	24.79		2.28		3.89	
p	.001		.70		.05	

could sometimes be discerned in their profoundly excited behaviour, but its most striking feature was that no consistent, organized, adient social responses to the "friendly man" ever emerged from it. Any attempt by E to pat or touch the dogs produced only jerky withdrawal movements with a marked concomitant increase in excitement. This tended to be followed by rapid, circular, prancing motions, until they resumed their excited licking behaviour, usually in the characteristic "stalking" stance.

One normally reared and four restricted dogs showed *avoidance* of the "friendly man"; they continually withdrew from E and always maintained a distance of at least two feet between E and themselves. These differences in behaviour between the restricted and the free-environment dogs are significant at the .001 level.

(2) *Behaviour to the "timid man."* Of the 14 dogs in each group, 8 restricted and 9 normally reared dogs displayed a type of behaviour which appears closely related to diffuse emotional excitement, but is much better described as *aggressive stalking*. These dogs moved excitedly and rapidly to and fro in the characteristic "stalking" position, making short, jerky jumps, and constantly facing E. As

the "timid man" retreated, however, this behaviour became a progressive, excited, forward approach, often with vigorous stamping movements of the forelegs in fitful starts and stops. And, as they moved nearer to E, they began to bark, growl, and snap their jaws with increasing frequency. However, the dogs rarely came within two feet of E.

This *aggressive stalking* gave the impression that the dogs were trying to "tease" a response out of E. They maintained the "stalking" posture almost continually in the presence of the "timid man," executing forward and backward movements with equal facility. Although they tended to spring forward toward E, they were also poised to spring backwards, and any sudden movement by E, even though in retreat, often elicited a sudden, short jump backwards by the dog.

The remaining responses to the "timid man" are shown in Table II. There is no statistical difference between the responses of the two groups of dogs, but, for the combined groups, the probability of such a high proportion of *aggressive stalking* occurring by chance in response to the "timid man" is .001 ($\chi^2 = 31.28$).

(3) *Behaviour to the "bold man."* The responses of the dogs to the "bold man" were classified as *avoidance* or *escape*. Of the 14 dogs in each group, 8 normally reared and 2 restricted dogs showed *avoidance*: they would usually stand quietly as the "bold man" approached, and then suddenly dash out of his way, never getting caught in a corner or against the wall. The remaining dogs (12 restricted, 6 free-environment) showed *escape behaviour*: they ran out of the way of the "bold man" only after they were nudged or pushed by his foot during his aggressive approach. Many of them got caught in corners or against the wall; others simply did not move and would have been stepped on by E had he not stopped. These differences between the two groups are significant at the .05 level of confidence.

(4) *Supplementary observations.* Seven restricted dogs, which had been reared two or three in a cage, were tested a year after their release along with four of their normally reared litter-mates. The restricted dogs still showed more diffuse emotional excitement to the "friendly man," and more escape behaviour to the "bold man," than did the free-environment dogs. But four restricted dogs showed friendly approach to the "friendly man," and two of them showed

avoidance behaviour to the "bold man." Thus there were no longer any statistical differences between the two groups in their behaviour toward these two roles.

DISCUSSION

The outstanding feature of the behaviour of the restricted dogs in these tests was their obvious ineptitude in coping with the social situations presented to them. The dominance tests showed clearly that they were incapable of responding adequately in a competitive social situation with other dogs, confirming the earlier observations of Clarke *et al.* (2). Indeed, most of the restricted dogs appeared not even to know how to *try* to be dominant, thus putting themselves at the very bottom of the dominance hierarchy in their canine society. They also differed markedly from the control animals in their capacity to perform responses which would be instrumental in satisfying such a basic need as curiosity toward other dogs. They showed a general excitement in the presence of other dogs, but did not exhibit sustained, well-oriented curiosity toward them.

A similar lack of adequate social behaviour was observed in the responses of the restricted dogs to the three roles portrayed by the experimenter. They did not know how to accept and reciprocate the friendly approaches of the "friendly man." Nor were they able, in the threatening social situation presented by the "bold man," to avoid physical contact in the unexcited, organized manner typical of the normally reared dogs. After a year of living in a normal environment, however, there was a decrease in the high level of emotional excitement which characterized their earlier responses, and several of them exhibited friendly behaviour to the "friendly man" and avoidance of the "bold man."

It may be concluded, then, that restriction of early social and perceptual experience has a definite retarding effect on the emergence of normal, adult social behaviour in dogs, whether toward members of their own or other species. With opportunities to gain such experience, however, dogs reared in moderate isolation, at least, can overcome to a significant degree the adverse effects of restriction on their social responses to man.

SUMMARY

Twenty-one Scottish terriers were raised for the first seven to ten months of life with their social and perceptual experience re-

Effects of Early Experience on Social Behaviour 321

stricted in varying degrees. Their 16 litter-mates, serving as normal controls, were raised as pets in homes or in the laboratory.

After the restricted dogs were released, all dogs were given a series of tests of social behaviour. Tests for dominance showed that the restricted dogs were strikingly inept in a competitive situation, as compared with the high degree of dominance behaviour displayed by the normal controls. Similarly, the restricted dogs did not exhibit the sustained, well-oriented curiosity toward other dogs that was observed in the control dogs. The restricted dogs were also unable to accept and reciprocate the friendly approaches of a "friendly man," or avoid physical contact with a "bold man" in the unexcited, well-organized manner typical of the normally reared dogs.

It was concluded that restriction of early social and perceptual experience has a definite retarding effect on the emergence of normal, adult social behaviour in dogs.

REFERENCES

1. BEACH, F. A., and JAYNES, J. Effects of early experience upon the behavior of animals. *Psychol. Bull.*, 1954, 51, 239-263.
2. CLARKE, R. S., HERON, W., FETHERSTONHAUGH, M. L., FORGAYS, D. C., and HEBB, D. O. Individual differences in dogs: preliminary reports on the effects of early experience. *Canad. J. Psychol.* 1951, 5, 150-156.
3. FREDRICSON, E. Competition: the effects of infantile experience upon adult behavior. *J. abnorm. soc. Psychol.*, 1951, 46, 406-409.
4. HEBB, D. O. Temperament in chimpanzees: I. Method of analysis. *J. comp. physiol. Psychol.*, 1949, 42, 192-206.
5. HEBB, D. O., and THOMPSON, W. R. The social significance of animal studies. In G. LINDZEY (Ed.), *Handbook of social Psychology.* Cambridge: Addison-Wesley, 1954.
6. *Manual of dog testing techniques.* Bar Harbor, Me.: Jackson Memorial Laboratory, 1950.
7. MELZACK, R. The genesis of emotional behavior: an experimental study of the dog. *J. comp. physiol. Psychol.*, 1954, 47, 166-168.
8. NISSEN, H. W., CHOW, K. L., and SEMMES, J. Effects of restricted opportunity for tactual, kinesthetic, and manipulative experience on the behavior of a chimpanzee. *Amer. J. Psychol.*, 1951, 64, 485-507.
9. THOMPSON, W. R., and HERON, W. Effects of restriction early in life on problem-solving ability in dogs. *Canad. J. Psychol.*, 1954, 8, 17-31.
10. THOMPSON, W. R., and HERON, W. Exploratory behavior in normal and restricted dogs. *J. comp. physiol. Psychol.*, 1954, 47, 77-82.

....

Effects of Decreased Variation
in the Sensory Environment[*,1]

W. HAROLD BEXTON, WOODBURN HERON,
AND THOMAS H. SCOTT

THIS STUDY began with a practical problem: the lapses of attention that may occur when a man must give close and prolonged attention to some aspect of an environment in which nothing is happening, or in which the changes are very regular. Watching a radar screen hour after hour is a prime example. As Mackworth (5) and others have shown, when at last something *does* happen in such circumstances the watcher may fail to respond. Such monotonous conditions exist in civilian occupations as well as in military ones (marine pilotage by radar, piloting aircraft on long flights), and here too lapses of attention may have extremely serious consequences. For example, such lapses may explain some otherwise inexplicable railroad and highway accidents.

Besides its practical significance this problem has theoretical implications of great interest. There is much evidence from recent neurophysiological studies to indicate that the normal functioning of the waking brain depends on its being constantly exposed to sensory bombardment, which produces a continuing "arousal reaction." Work now being done by S. K. Sharpless at McGill indicates, further, that when stimulation does not change it rapidly loses its power to cause the arousal reaction. Thus, although one function of a stimulus is to evoke or guide a specific bit of behaviour, it also has a non-specific function, that of maintaining "arousal."

In other words, the maintenance of normal, intelligent, adaptive behaviour probably requires a continually varied sensory input. The

* From *Canad. J. Psychol.*, 1954, **8**, 70-76. Reprinted by permission of the author and the Univ. of Toronto Press.

[1] D. R. B. Project No. D 77-94-85-01. The advice and assistance of Dr. D. O. Hebb are gratefully acknowledged.

brain is not like a calculating machine operated by an electric motor which is able to respond at once to specific cues after lying idle indefinitely. Instead it is like one that must be kept warmed up and working. It seemed, therefore, worth while to examine cognitive functioning during prolonged perceptual isolation, as far as this was practicable. Bremer (2) has achieved such isolation by cutting the brain stem; college students, however, are reluctant to undergo brain operations for experimental purposes, so we had to be satisfied with less extreme isolation from the environment.

PROCEDURE

The subjects, 22 male college students, were paid to lie on a comfortable bed in a lighted cubicle 24 hours a day, with time out for eating and going to the toilet. During the whole experimental period they wore translucent goggles which transmitted diffuse light but prevented pattern vision. Except when eating or at the toilet, the subject wore gloves and cardboard cuffs, the latter extending from below the elbow to beyond the fingertips. These permitted free joint movement but limited tactual perception. Communication between subject and experimenters was provided by a small speaker system, and was kept to a minimum. Auditory stimulation was limited by the partially sound-proof cubicle and by a U-shaped foam-rubber pillow in which the subject kept his head while in the cubicle. Moreover, the continuous hum provided by fans, air-conditioner, and the amplifier leading to earphones in the pillow produced fairly efficient masking noise.

GENERAL EFFECTS

As might be expected from the evidence reviewed by Kleitman (3) for onset of sleep following reduced stimulation in man and other animals, the subjects tended to spend the earlier part of the experimental session in sleep. Later they slept less, became bored, and appeared eager for stimulation. They would sing, whistle, talk to themselves, tap the cuffs together, or explore the cubicle with them. This boredom seemed to be partly due to deterioration in the capacity to think systematically and productively—an effect described below. The subjects also became very restless, displaying constant random movement, and they described the restlessness as unpleasant. Hence it was difficult to keep subjects for more than two or three days, despite the fact that the pay ($20 for a 24-hour day) was more than double what they could normally earn. Some subjects, in fact, left before testing could be completed. There seemed to be unusual emotional lability during the experimental period. When doing tests, for instance, the subjects would seem very pleased when they did well, and upset if they had difficulty. They commented more freely about test items than when they were tested outside. While many reported that they felt elated during the first part of their stay in the cubicle, there was a marked increase in irritability toward the end of the experimental period.

On coming out of the cubicle after the experimental session, when goggles, cuffs, and gloves had been removed, the subjects seemed at first dazed. There also appeared to be some disturbance in visual perception, usually lasting no longer than one or two minutes. Subjects reported difficulty in focussing; objects appeared fuzzy and did not stand out from their backgrounds. There was a tendency for the environment to appear two-dimensional and colours seemed more saturated than usual. The subjects also reported feelings of confusion, headaches, a mild nausea, and fatigue; these conditions persisted in some cases for 24 hours after the session.

EFFECTS ON COGNITIVE PROCESSES

Our present concern is primarily with cognitive disturbances during the period of isolation and immediately afterwards. The subjects reported that they were unable to concentrate on any topic for long while in the cubicle. Those who tried to review their studies or solve self-initiated intellectual problems found it difficult to do so. As a result they lapsed into day-dreaming, abandoned attempts at organized thinking, and let their thoughts wander. There were also reports of "blank periods," during which they seemed unable to think of anything at all.

In an attempt to measure some of the effects on cognitive processes, various tests were given to the subjects before, during, and after the period of isolation.

First, the tests given during isolation. Twelve subjects were given the following types of problem to do in their heads: multiplying two- and three-digit numbers; arithmetical problems (such as "how many times greater is twice 2½ than one-half 2½?"); completion of number series; making a word from jumbled letters; making as many words as possible from the letters of a given word. Each subject was tested on problems of this type before going into the cubicle, after he had been in for 12, 24, and 48 hours, and three days after coming out of the cubicle. Twelve control subjects were given the same series of tasks at the same intervals. The average performance of the experimental subjects was inferior to that of the controls on all tests performed during the cubicle session.

Secondly, tests given before entering the cubicle and immediately after leaving it. On the Kohs Block Test and the Wechsler Digit Symbol Test the experimental subjects were inferior to the controls on leaving the cubicle ($p = .01$). They also tended to be slower in copying a prose paragraph ($p = .10$).

HALLUCINATORY ACTIVITY

Finally there were the hallucinations reported by the subjects while in the experimental apparatus. Among our early subjects there were several references, rather puzzling at first, to what one of them called "having a dream while awake." Then one of us, while serving as a subject, observed the phenomenon and realized its peculiarity and extent.

The visual phenomena were actually quite similar to what have been described for mescal intoxication, and to what Grey Walter (6) has recently produced by exposure to flickering light. There have also been rare cases of hallucinations in aged persons without psychosis (1), which, like ours, involved no special chemical or visual stimulation. As we did not ask our first subjects specifically about these phenomena we do not know the frequency among them. The last 14 subjects, however, were asked to report any "visual imagery" they observed, and our report is based on them. In general, where more "formed" (i.e., more complex) hallucinations occurred they were usually preceded by simpler forms of the phenomenon. Levels of complexity could be differentiated as follows: In the simplest form the visual field, with the eyes closed, changed from dark to light colour; next in complexity were dots of light, lines, or simple geometrical patterns. All 14 subjects reported such imagery, and said it was a new experience to them. Still more complex forms consisted in "wall-paper patterns," reported by 11 subjects, and isolated figures or objects, without background (e.g., a row of little yellow men with black caps on and their mouths open; a German helmet), reported by seven subjects. Finally, there were integrated scenes (e.g., a procession of squirrels with sacks over their shoulders marching "purposefully" across a snow field and out of the field of "vision"; prehistoric animals walking about in a jungle). Three of the 14 subjects reported such scenes, frequently including dreamlike distortions, with the figures often being described as "like cartoons." One curious fact is that some of the hallucinations were reported as being inverted or tilted at an angle.

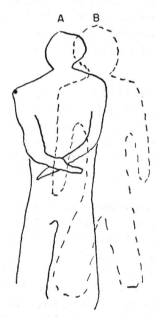

FIG. 1. Drawing made by a subject to show how he felt at one period in the cubicle. He reported that it was as if "there were two of me," and was momentarily unable to decide whether he was A or B.

In general, the subjects were first surprised by these phenomena, and then amused or interested, waiting for what they would see next. Later, some subjects found them irritating, and complained that their vividness interfered with sleep. There was some control over content; by "trying," the subject might see certain objects suggested by the experimenter, but not always as he intended. Thus one subject, trying to "get" a pen, saw first an inkblot, then a pencil, a green horse, and finally a pen; trying to "get" a shoe, he saw first a ski boot, then a moccasin. The imagery usually disappeared when the subject was doing a complex task, such as multiplying three-place numbers in his head, but not if he did physical exercises, or talked to the experimenter.

There were also reports of hallucinations involving other senses. One subject could hear the people speaking in his visual hallucinations, and another repeatedly heard the playing of a music box. Four subjects described kinesthetic and somesthetic phenomena. One reported seeing a miniature rocket ship discharging pellets that kept striking his arm, and one reported reaching out to touch a doorknob he saw before him and feeling an electric shock. The other two subjects reported a phenomenon which they found difficult to describe. They said it was as if there were two bodies side by side in the cubicle; in one case the two bodies overlapped, partly occupying the same space. Figure 1 shows this subject's subsequent drawing, made in an attempt to show what he meant.

In addition, there were reports of feelings of "otherness" and bodily "strangeness" in which it was hard to know exactly what the subject meant. One subject said "my mind seemed to be a ball of cotton-wool floating above my body"; another reported that his head felt detached from his body. These are familiar phenomena in certain cases of migraine, as described recently by Lippman (4), and earlier by Lewis Carroll in *Alice in Wonderland*. As Lippman points out, Lewis Carroll was a sufferer from migraine, and it is suggested that Alice's bodily distortions are actually descriptions of Carroll's (i.e., Charles Dodgson's) own experiences.

REFERENCES

1. BARTLETT, J. E. A. A case of organized visual hallucinations in an old man with cataract and their relation to the phenomena of the phantom limb. *Brain*, 1951, **74**, 363-373.
2. BREMER, F. and TERZUOLO, C. Nouvelles recherches sur le processus physiologique de réveil. *Arch. internat. de Physiol.*, 1953, **61**, 86-90.
3. KLEITMAN, N. *Sleep and wakefulness*. Chicago: Univer. of Chicago Press, 1939.
4. LIPPMAN, CARO. Certain hallucinations peculiar to migraine. *J. nerv. ment. Dis.*, 1952, **116**, 346-351.
5. MACKWORTH, N. H. *Researches on the measurement of human performance*. Med. Res. Council, Spec. Rep. Ser., 1950, No. 268. London.
6. WALTER, W. GREY. *The living brain*. New York: Norton, 1953.

Visual Disturbances after Prolonged Perceptual Isolation*,

Woodburn Heron, B. K. Doane, and Thomas H. Scott

This report has its origins in the studies by Bexton, Heron, and Scott (1) of the effects on behaviour of prolonged and drastic reduction in the variation of the sensory environment. These conditions produced impairment of intellectual ability and disturbance of motivation, both during and after the period of isolation. Pronounced hallucinatory activity (primarily visual) also occurred during isolation.

In addition, remarks made by the subjects on returning to a normal environment indicated some disturbance of visual perception. Comments such as "things looked curved," "near things looked large and far things looked small," and "things rushed at me," were typical. Since the vagueness of such statements made them difficult to interpret, we thought it advisable, before undertaking a systematic study of the visual effects of isolation, that we ourselves should serve as subjects. We hoped thereby to gain some inkling of what aspects of perception it might be most fruitful to investigate.

The disturbances in visual perception which were observed after six days in isolation were unexpectedly profound and prolonged, and were in general the same for all three observers. Since this was so, and since many of the effects did not appear amenable to quantitative study, the observations of the three experimenter-subjects are here reported.

METHOD

The experimental conditions have been previously described (1). Briefly, they were as follows: the subjects lay on a bed in a small cubicle

* From *Canad. J. Psychol.*, 1956, **10**, 13-18. Reprinted by permission of the author and the Univ. of Toronto Press.

24 hours a day, being released during that time only for meals or to go to the toilet. They wore cotton gloves and cylindrical cardboard cuffs which covered the hands and forearms, thus limiting tactual perception. Auditory perception was reduced by the partially sound-proof cubicle, by the U-shaped foam-rubber pillow in which the subject's head was placed, and by the continuous hum of the air-conditioning unit and other apparatus. During the entire experimental session, including meal and toilet periods, the subjects wore translucent plastic goggles which prevented pattern vision. The cubicle, painted a medium grey inside, was lighted by a shielded 60-watt lamp, so that as long as the subject kept his eyes open he was presented with a lighted, fairly homogeneous visual field, bounded nasally and temporally by the dark frames of the goggles. It was possible for the subjects to detect some texture in the plastic.

The observations which follow are taken from notes and recordings made during isolation, from recordings made while the observers were looking at the room immediately after the goggles were removed, and from diaries which were kept for several days after the isolation period.

OBSERVATIONS DURING ISOLATION

At first, although there was some impression of mistiness and depth, the visual field still seemed to have some surface qualities. By the third or fourth day, however, it became compellingly three-dimensional for one observer, and it seemed to him as if he were looking into a tunnel of fog.

All three observers reported hallucinatory activity after the first day. At first this tended to be "simple" in form (rows of dots, geometrical patterns, mosaics, etc.); later it became more "complex" (scenery, people, bizarre architecture, etc.). There was a considerable amount of movement in the hallucinations: landscapes might appear divided into strips which moved in opposite directions; parts of a scene, or entire scenes, might become inverted, and pivot slowly from side to side. At times this type of movement was unpleasant, and caused the observers to feel nausea. All three reported that their eyes became tired from trying to "focus" on the hallucinations. Particularly during the earlier stages of isolation, the "visual field" was often filled with a large number of identical small patterns or objects (such as geometrical forms, or plants, or animals); these were usually arranged in symmetrical rows.

OBSERVATIONS AFTER ISOLATION

The effects, which were observed both monocularly and binocularly, may conveniently be summarized under five headings: (1) Apparent movement independent of movement by the observer. There was a fluctuation, drifting, or swirling of objects and surfaces in the visual field. (2) Apparent movement associated with head or eye movements of the observer. The position of objects would appear to change when head or eye movements occurred. (3) Distortions of shape. (4) Accentuation of after-images and perceptual lag. (5) Effects on the perception of colour, and contrast effects.

(1) *Apparent Movement Independent of Movement by the Observer.* When the goggles were removed there was a great deal of random movement, unsteadiness, or drifting, which for the first few minutes seemed to involve almost all of the visual field.

Observer A. "My first glimpse of him [an experimenter] he was a little short joker, then he suddenly got tall, then he closed up again, then he sort of stabilized. . . . The room didn't look like a house on stilts, or a little short, fat house, it was going out and in, up and down like a crazy-house. The wall bulged towards me and went back."

Observer B. "The whole room is undulating, swirling. . . . You were going all over the fool place at first. The floor is still doing it. The wall is waving all over the place—a horrifying sight, as a matter of fact. . . . The centre of that curtain over there—it just swirls downward, undulates and waves inside. . . . I find it difficult to keep my eyes open for any length of time, the visual field is in such a state of chaos. . . . Everything will settle down for a moment, then it will start to go all over the place."

Observer C. These immediate effects were less marked with this observer, though he did report some "weaving" and "jumping about" of objects in the peripheral visual field.

After these initial gross effects there was some stabilization. The region which was fixated then seemed relatively still, though the area immediately surrounding it was still apt to drift and become distorted. Even the area fixated might undergo changes with prolonged inspection.

Observer A. "When I fixate here, that box behind you moves, and when I was fixating there, there was something wrong with this thing, which seemed to be swinging out. . . . There is a serious limit to what is in focus. I'm focusing on the mid-point of that rod, and there's a very small area of the rod which is clear. The rest of it is fluctuating all the time. . . . Have you ever looked at the bottom of a stream after you have dropped a stone in? A shallow stream, and you can look down through the circles going out? The centre is still and clear, but the rest is all ripply. Well, that's exactly the impression that I get. Wherever I fixate is the centre of the circle, and the rest of the stuff is behind these ripples." This observer continued to notice such distortions for several hours. Objects such as an ash tray or a watch appeared to expand or contract if he looked at them for any length of time. The apparatus used in tests which required prolonged fixation underwent changes. For example, the circular apperture in the Critical Fusion Frequency (CFF) apparatus changed its shape, and the four legs of a cross used as fixation point on a screen kept altering their relative lengths.

Observers B and C reported similar effects. Observer C found that, even 24 hours after coming out of the cubicle, objects or faces might expand and contract, bulge or writhe, if he looked at them for any length of time; only the region of fixation remained stable. Reading was difficult, since the portion of the page which was not directly fixated seemed to drift. The persistence of the effects in his case might be due to the fact that he found it impossible to sleep for 24 hours after emerging from the cubicle.

(2) *Apparent Movement Associated with Head or Eye Movements of the Observer.* A type of movement which was somewhat different, but no less striking, might be termed loss of "position constancy."

When the observer moved his head or eyes, it seemed to him as if objects in the visual field were moving. Typically, when he turned his eyes away from an object it appeared to move closer, while the object towards which his eyes were turned would retreat. In other words, an object seemed closer in peripheral vision than when it was directly fixated. When the observer approached or withdrew from objects in the visual field, it seemed as if the objects themselves were moving towards or away from him. This was one of the more lasting effects, occurring with sudden movements of the observer several hours after the isolation period.

Observer A. "Things just don't stay put. For instance, I'm fixating down there, and out of the corner of my eye I see that upright; but when I fixate the upright, it jumps back. . . . There's no position constancy, that's what it is. As I move, it moves. When I move back and forth like this, I can't orientate against anything. . . . It's most peculiar, I feel as if I'm in a swing. . . . If I turn quickly or move back, it's not me that moves, it's this thing that moves."

Observer B. "Those things shift position every time I shift my gaze. As I move my eyes to the left, things in the right periphery come at me. Every time I move, everything in the room swirls and moves."

Observer C noticed for hours afterwards that, if he rocked back and forth while looking at a wall, it would appear to move towards him as his head went forward and away from him when his head moved back.

(3) *Distortions of Shape.* Apart from the distortions in which movement was prominent, there was a tendency for straight edges or lines to appear curved, and for the region about the fixation point of flat surfaces to appear to bulge outwards. In addition, there were pronounced distortions of forms that occupied a large portion of the visual field. In some cases this seemed to be related to angular perspective, which appeared to be greatly exaggerated.

Observer A noticed that the curvature was most conspicuous in the case of those parts of vertical or horizontal lines or edges which were not directly fixated. As he ran his eyes along the line it would straighten out. When reading, about an hour after he had emerged, he found that the parts of the line which were not fixated seemed to curve upwards, but would fall into place when he fixated them. This observer noted that edges above and in the horizontal meridian appeared to be curving downwards, while those below the meridian seemed to curve upwards.

Observer B, glancing down at the floor-boards, observed that they seemed to sweep upwards from either side of the visual field into a mound or ridge which ran along the vertical meridian. When he fixated the midpoint between a pair of parallel vertical lines, the ends of the lines seemed to splay outwards. Horizontal lines above the horizontal meridian appeared to droop downwards at the ends.

Observer C reported effects similar to those of B. The curvature of vertical lines was particularly marked in his case, persisting for over 24 hours. Curvature appeared only after he had been fixating for some moments, and was greatest in the upper visual field.

(4) *After-images.* Observers A and C noticed pronounced negative after-images after looking at objects in the room and then at a blank wall. Both had difficulty with a CFF apparatus because of the after-images induced by the circular aperture. This had not occurred when they were tested before isolation.

Observer A reported a tendency for "perceptual lag" to occur when objects were moved across the visual field, part of the moving figure appearing to trail behind the rest. Thus, when a thin black line was rotated slowly against a dimly illuminated milk glass screen in a darkened room, the line seemed S-shaped because the ends "lagged" behind the centre part.

(5) *Colour and Contrast Effects.* Colours appeared bright, highly saturated or luminescent. Colour and brightness contrast was exaggerated, giving objects a glittering appearance. Black figures on a white background gave rise to subjective colours.

Observer A reported being disturbed by the brightness of some colours, and struck by the glistening appearance of objects. Surfaces gleamed as if they were wet. An experimenter's face appeared rosy and highly coloured.

Observer B noted that colours were dazzling, and was impressed by the wet, glistening appearance of the grain in a wooden surface. He reported that the experimenter's face appeared to be smeared with rouge. This tendency for people to appear rouged persisted for over 24 hours, as did the tendency for brightly coloured objects to seem luminous and highly saturated. A black square on a white background was surrounded by a blue and yellow iridescence.

Observer C reported that colour seemed brighter and more saturated than usual. Black figures on a white background were surrounded by blue and green patches. As in the case of the other observers, people appeared highly rouged.

Other Observations. All three observers were nauseated by the perceptual disturbances during the first few minutes after they emerged from isolation. Observer B, in fact, became so dizzy that he thought he was going to faint, and had to close his eyes. This nausea resembled that produced by hallucinations during the isolation period, but was more pronounced. It should also be noted that some of the swirling and undulation in the visual field after the isolation period was similar to that which occurred while the subject was hallucinating.

Finally, there is some evidence that hallucinatory activity persists for some time after the subject has emerged from isolation. Observer C still experienced hallucinations when he closed his eyes half an hour later. When the goggles were replaced, he experienced them with his eyes open.

COMMENT

Since these preliminary observations were made, we have been carrying out a more systematic study of these effects. Though the data are not yet fully analysed, they seem to bear out the observations which we have reported, and to elaborate them somewhat. We have found, for instance, as regards the curvature of surfaces, that the surface may appear *either* convex or concave, and that the two conditions may alternate in the same subject. This phenomenon may be related to changes in the apparent frontal-parallel plane, since measurements on recent subjects indicate that this is affected.

In addition, one of the causes of the apparent distortion of perspective is evidently a disturbance of size constancy. In an experimental situation in which a standard disc was presented 2 ft. in front of the subject and he was required to select a figure of the same size from a graduated row of discs 12 ft. in front of him, the experimental subjects consistently chose larger discs than did a comparable group of controls.

It is unlikely that the effects observed after isolation can be attributed merely to the forgetting of perceptual habits during the isolation period. They seem to resemble somewhat the effects reported after administration of certain drugs (such as mescal and lysergic acid) and after certain types of brain damage. When we consider as well the disturbances which occurred during isolation (e.g., vivid hallucinatory activity), it appears that exposing the subject to a monotonous sensory environment can cause disorganization of brain function similar to, and in some respects as great as, that produced by drugs or lesions.

That this is so is further indicated by changes in the subjects' EEGs during and after the isolation period. In eight subjects studied, slower frequencies appeared in the alpha band during isolation, and marked delta-wave activity developed. The EEG taken 3½ hours after the subject had emerged from the experimental conditions had still not returned to normal.

SUMMARY

Three observers were kept in a monotonous sensory environment for six days. On returning to a normal environment, they experienced the following perceptual disturbances: (1) there was fluctuation, drifting and swirling of objects and surfaces in the visual field; (2) the position of objects appeared to change with head or eye movements; (3) shapes, lines, and edges appeared distorted; (4) afterimages were accentuated; (5) colours seemed very bright and saturated, and there seemed to be an exaggeration of contrast phenomena.

REFERENCES

1. BEXTON, W. H., HERON, W., and SCOTT, T. H. Effects of decreased variation in the sensory environment. Canad. J. Psychol., 1954, 8, 70-76.
2. SCOTT, T. H. Unpublished doctor's thesis, McGill Univer., 1954.

SELECTION 24

....

The Theory of Adaptation-Level*

HARRY HELSON

PERCEPTION IS essentially concerned with the adjustment of the organism to the world about it and the stresses arising from within. Perceptual activities not only initiate and regulate homeostatic mechanisms but they also indicate how well adjustive mechanisms are working. The reflexive nature of perception enables the organism to know how well it is doing or at least to know whether its performance is satisfying or annoying. But recognition of the fact that perception is intimately concerned with vital activities is not in itself enough. The concept of adjustment, or what we may call behavioral homeostasis, must be formulated in such a way as to make it amenable to experimental control and quantitative evaluation. The concept of adaptation-level, conceived as a weighted mean function of all stimuli, present and active from the past, affecting the organism, makes possible a concrete approach to perceptual activities in the larger context of total organic functioning. Before proceeding with either a more detailed exposition of the theory or its applications to experimental and clinical phenomena, let us first consider some fundamental facts of adjustive behavior stressed in the formulation of the theory. They are as follows:

1. Bipolarity of Responses. In everyday responses individuals exhibit varying degrees of acceptance or rejection of objects, people,

* From *Psychiatric screening of flying personnel: perception and personality —a critique of recent experimental literature.* Randolph Field, Texas: Air University, USAF School of Aviation Medicine, Contract Number AF 33 (038)-13887, Project Number 21-0202-0007, Report Number 1; July, 1953, pp. v + 55. Pp. 35-42 reprinted by permission of the author and the USAF School of Aviation Medicine Headquarters.

or statements. The division of stimuli into good or bad, beautiful or ugly, loud or soft, pleasant or unpleasant, seems to be an expression of some primitive approach-avoidance type of behavior. The tendency to order stimuli by means of graded dichotomies seems to be natural for people of all ages and even for animals, as Razran (24) has pointed out. If the trouble is taken to require individuals to order a series of objects according to some criterion such as pleasant-unpleasant, it is usually found that in the transition from the positive (pleasant) stimuli to the negative (unpleasant) stimuli there is a stimulus or group of stimuli which is neutral or indifferent. The stimuli in this neutral, transitional zone represent the stimuli to which the organism is adapted so far as the quality or attribute in question is concerned. Various factors influence this neutral zone which the theory of adaptation-level attempts to evaluate. Once the level or position of the neutral zone is determined, it becomes possible to predict how stimuli will affect the organism and what type of response will be made to them.

2. *Adjustment to Changing Level.* If the level of stimulation is raised or lowered by changing all the stimuli, or by introducing an extreme stimulus into the field, or by changing the background against which stimuli are perceived, the adjustment of the organism changes correspondingly. We can say on the basis of numerous experiments that the level of adjustment of the organism more or less matches the level of stimulation. This characteristic of organic functioning is well known so far as certain sensory phenomena of adaptation are concerned, e.g., having good vision under widely different levels of illumination and finding water comfortable after the first shock of total immersion. Less well known are esthetic, social, and personal responses of various kinds which have been shown to be functions of the level of stimulation as when an esthetic object at the tail end of a beautiful series is judged ugly but is judged beautiful when at the head end of an ugly series!

3. *Position of the Neutral Category.* The stimulus which divides the positive from the negative stimuli is seldom, if ever, at the center or arithmetic mean of the series. If the stimuli are judged singly (i.e., without a comparison or background stimulus), the neutral or medium stimulus is generally below the mean of the group. Thus the stimulus judged "medium" (i.e., neither heavy nor light) in a series of weights ranging from 200 to 400 grams is about 250 grams, a value

well below the center of the series. This phenomenon of decentering to establish the balance point of the behavioral field seems at first sight to argue against adaptation or adjustment as the basic mechanism by which the organism responds to a series of stimuli. Upon closer consideration, however, the very fact of decentering is a strong argument for its adaptive nature, for by establishing its equilibrium point as *low* as possible, the organism does less work and is under less strain than if it neutralized extreme stimuli. The lag in adaptation-level represents conserving tendencies at work in the organism and may be regarded as the analogue in the individual to the resistance to change in group behavior long known as "social lag."

Decentering is not a purely perceptual or judgmental characteristic. It has been found and recognized in the sphere of motor development by Gesell (2), who calls it the "principle of functional asymmetry" and describes it as follows:

. . . man, in spite of his bilateral construction, does not face the world on a frontal plane of symmetry. He confronts it at an angle and he makes his escapes, also obliquely. He develops monolateral aptitudes and preferences in handedness, eyedness, footedness, and other forms of unidexterity. . . . The behavioral center of gravity always tends to shift to an eccentric position. Unidexterity of hand, foot or eye does not so much represent an absolute difference in skill as a predilection for stabilized psychomotor orientations.

These orientations are fundamentally postural sets; and they are asymmetric. Ideally reciprocal interweaving operates to preserve harmony and balance; but in actuality there is superadded ontogenetic deflection to insure the greater efficiency of functional asymmetry. (P. 307)

A number of phenomena which have stood as single, isolated facts may be better understood as phenomena of decentered adaptation-level. Space permits discussion of only two of them. The first concerns the tendency to overestimate "small" and to underestimate "large" values of stimuli. This tendency has cropped up in all sense modalities and in judgments involving considerable cognitive activity. It is the phenomenon long ago called central tendency by Hollingworth and negative time-order error in classical psychophysics. It is found in judging attributes of size, lightness, color, weight, loudness, pitch, and many other sensory attributes, and also in betting games, in estimating the number of dots in groups, in judgments of time intervals, and in various types of social judgments (cf. 8). But there are cases where *all* stimuli are over- or underestimated. This occurs when the adaptation level is far above or below the series stimuli because of the introduction of extreme stimuli into the field. Central tendency is therefore a special case found when the adaptation-level is not decentered too far.

4. Preponderant Stimuli. Within a field of stimuli are usually some stimuli which have a preponderant influence on adaptation-level because of their intensity, novelty, frequency, emotional connotation, or some other reason. Such stimuli have often been referred to as "anchoring stimuli." Examples of anchoring stimuli are found in auditory and visual backgrounds against which sounds and color are perceived; so also are the standards introduced for comparative purposes in the determination of differential thresholds or in judging esthetic objects. Objects which are purely imaginary may serve as "mental" standards and thus influence perception and judgment. The question arises as to the part played by such stimuli in the total adjustment of the organism. Are they the sole determiners of action or is their influence a function of the adaptation-level? If preponderant or anchoring stimuli were the sole determiners of behavior then the adaptation-level would be fixed simply by such stimuli with the result that they would be neutralized and would cease to be preponderant stimuli! Actually numerous experiments indicate that the adaptation-level is determined by all stimuli attended to in the field, by background stimuli, and by residuals from past experiences with similar stimuli, so that the effect of preponderant stimuli, while tending to raise or lower the level in their own direction, depends upon the way they are figured against the general level.

QUANTITATIVE FORMULATION OF THE CONCEPT OF ADAPTATION-LEVEL

We have already referred to the adaptation-level as the value of stimulus which elicits a neutral response when subjects judge stimuli in terms of qualitative or numerical rating scales. This is an operational definition. It specifies the adaptation-level, which is not directly observable, in quantitative terms as the value of stimulus eliciting the neutral response. Nonoperational definitions of adaptation-level may be given in terms of qualitative characteristics of stimuli which are readily identified. Thus stimuli perceived to be white, gray, or black are chromatically neutral, and so must be regarded as leaving the *color* receptors in equilibrium. Similarly, a verbal statement with which one neither agrees nor disagrees may represent his point of equilibrium with respect to the meaning universe represented by the statement, and propositions may be formulated which lie above (agree) or below (disagree) the level represented by this statement. In view of the shifts of adaptation-level with change in series stimuli, background stimuli, and past experiences with similar stimuli, we may regard any momentary adjustment of the organism as the pooled or weighted average of these three classes of stimuli. Quantitatively, the adaptation-level has been closely approximated in a wide variety of situations as a weighted log mean of series, background, and residual stimuli. More concretely,

$$\text{Log AL} = (k_1 \Sigma \log X_i/n + k_2 \log B + k_3 \log R)/(k_1 + k_2 + k_3)\,(1)$$

where X_i are series stimuli, B is the background stimulus, and R is the residual stimulus. Variation in any one of these factors will affect adaptation-level accordingly. Equation (1) may be employed in various experimental designs to evaluate the constants, k_1, k_2, and k_3, thus measuring the influence of series stimuli, background stimuli, and residuals from past experience in concrete situations (7, 17).

Factors or conditions which may affect adaptation-level and which must accordingly be weighted in its determination range from simple to complex. They include such obvious determinants of behavior as recency, frequency, intensity, nearness or remoteness, emotional effects, needs, and past experience. All factors in a situation are more or less important in determining the level of functioning and must be evaluated quantitatively in specific situations. The constants k_1, k_2, and k_3 in equation (1) can yield values showing the relative contributions of stimulus properties in the focus of response, the background stimuli, and the residuals from past experience. Examples of the use to which equation (1) may be put in the evaluation of factors affecting level are found in the differences revealed between vision in ordinary white light and in strongly chromatic illumination and their difference, in turn, from tactile sensitivity for lifted weights. In strongly chromatic illuminants the value of k_2 (the background weighting factor) was found to be 3.0 as against 1.0 for k_1 (the weighting factor for the stimuli on the backgrounds). Under these conditions background was most important in determining level. The residual factor played little or no role since the adaptation-level could be specified without the k_3 constant (6). However, judgments of lightness of gray papers on black and on white backgrounds *in white light* were found by Michels and Helson (17) to be strongly influenced by "stimuli more remote than those involved in the experiment . . . in the determination of the adaptation-level" (p. 364), as the weighting coefficient for the residual factor was 0.56, against 0.28 for the stimuli being judged, and 0.16 for the background factor. In lifted weight experiments it was found that the background stimulus was also much less important than the series stimuli in determining adaptation-level, the values of k_1 and k_2 being exactly reversed, from the values found for chromatic illumination, the former being 3.0 and the latter 1.0 (7). In these experiments residual factors were undoubtedly operative as individual differences in level appeared but were not evaluated because only adaptation-levels for group (averaged) data were of interest in the study. Other applications of the weighted log mean and other formulas to determine the relative importance of specific conditions in experimental situations will be found in Johnson (10), Philip (21), and Nash (19, 20).

The assumption that adaptation-level is the result of interaction among all factors in the situation confronting the organism is based upon considerable experimental evidence. Interaction is found in all sense modalities and is temporal as well as spatial since there are carry-over effects from stimulation after it has ceased (20). Interaction effects are not limited, however, to a single sense modality or to sensory phenomena alone (3, 25). Recently Werner and Wapner (31, 32) and their co-workers (33) have shown that visual perception of the vertical may be influenced by auditory, electrical, and accelerative and decelerative stimulation and by asymmetrical postural positions. Their work stresses the role of tonic impulses in visual space perception and the importance of inter-sensory interaction. The Werner-Wapner sensori-tonic theory seems to be limited to sensory interactions and is not stated in quantitative terms so as to yield quantitative inferences. Evaluation of the relative contributions of the senses which cooperate to maintain equilibrium (our adaptation-level) in some such manner as is suggested by our log mean formula would contribute significantly to an understanding of both the phenomena of sensory interaction and their central mechanisms (cf. 12, 13).

The factors which determine the level of organic functioning may be simple sensory stimuli with or without strong emotional accompaniments or complex social and cognitive stimuli having more or less meaning. An adequate theory should make no distinction between blindly, automatically acting forces and rational, cognitive factors. Both types of stimuli affect all levels of behavior. In the remaining portion of this section we shall show how the concept of adaptation-level may be fruitfully applied to the interpretation of both mechanical and meaningful sources of stimulation.

APPLICATIONS OF ADAPTATION-LEVEL THEORY
TO EXPERIMENTAL AND CLINICAL FINDINGS

That frequency, nearness, and spacing may operate as strongly in perception as in learning is shown by clinical as well as experimental evidence. Hastings et al. (5) report that the closeness of a traumatic event to the individual was a large factor in determining anxiety states. They point out "if he [a flier] were hit by a 20-mm. shell he would be more deeply affected than if he saw the man next to him hit, which would be worse than having someone hit in another part of the same ship, which would be worse than hearing of someone hit in his squadron, and so on to the point where it would mean essentially nothing to him to hear of someone being hit in a B-17 over Munda" (p. 132). Here a miss is not as good as a mile. Similarly, fliers differed in the amount of stress leading to anxiety symptoms. Crews joining the Eighth Air Force immediately found out that chances of survival were very slim. Some fliers requested removal from flying duties before actually making any flights. A second group did not break until after a few missions—usually by the fifth. A third group did not develop anxiety symptoms until around the twelfth to sixteenth mission. Here frequency of exposure to stress seemed to be the decisive factor in the breaking points of different individuals. Hastings et al. also describe cases showing marked individual differences as to when fliers exhibited anxiety symptoms, some having fear symptoms during flight, others not until after return from a mission.

Frequency and temporal factors play a role in the traumatizing effects of electro-convulsive shock. Stone (30) found a gradual lowering of maximal cognitive level with repeated (15 to 20) convulsive shocks. Worchel and Narciso (35) reported that a single electro-convulsive shock does not obliterate traces of material learned immediately prior to shock, but after 5 shocks in a period of 8 days the subjects were not able to learn a series of 10 nonsense syllables to criterion of one perfect repetition in 45 trials. Hence the effects of shock were cumulative. But it was also found that memory ability 5 to 9 days after the last shock was equal to that prior to the first shock, showing the effect was reversible. May there not be a limit to the number of shocks that can be given beyond which the effects are irreversible? We touch here upon questions of organic function which, at least in their physicochemical aspects, are best handled by physiologists. The theory of the general adaptation syndrome developed by Selye (28) stresses frequency, intensity, spacing, and other measurable characteristics of stimuli which affect functional level in much the same way as these factors are envisaged at the behavioral level in the theory of adaptation-level.

Animals, as well as humans, show evidence of the influence of spatiotemporal factors on adjustment. Fredericson (1) found greater traumatic effect in massed than in distributed confinements of dogs. Dogs confined 10 min. straight in a box gave from 680 to 1,822 yelps, whereas dogs confined for 1 min. and given 1 min. of freedom for a total of 10 min. gave from 21 to 916 yelps for the same total period of confinement. The averages for the two groups are even more striking: the massed group averaged 1,104 yelps per puppy, the spaced group averaged 347 yelps per puppy. A highly significant difference in the traumatizing effects of confinement was thus found.

In a study by Hartmann (4) distance between stimuli to be discriminated exercised an important influence on learning, but little or no notice has been taken of this fact because it fitted into no theoretical framework. Hartmann found that the rate of learning was adversely affected as the distance between the stimuli became larger or smaller than 45 cm., using distances of 15, 30, 45, and 60 cm. He concluded that there is an optimal *spatial* interval between all visual items that must be discriminated.

We have seen that spatiotemporal factors may importantly affect various psychological functions under both laboratory and everyday conditions, and we have shown how they may be evaluated when the factors are capable of quantitative determination. The theory of adaptation-level is not limited, however, to responses to physical stimuli. It is equally applicable to higher-level types of behavior in which social, personality, and meaning factors are the important determinants of behavior. It is our contention that when an experimental variable, be it an autochthonous or a functional variable, affects the level of organic functioning, its influence is easy to demonstrate. In the investigation of needs, values, motivations, past experiences, and cognitive factors in perception it is possible to apply the adaptation-level paradigm found useful with psychophysical data, provided suitable modifications are made for the different types of material employed. Our main concern, therefore, in the rest of this section will be to discuss applications of the theory to situations in which perception is influenced by residuals from past experience and by such autistic factors as needs, ego-involvement, and cognitive states.

The question as to whether or not past experience influences contemporary behavior, and, if it does, how it can do so has been a moot one for many years. It seems to be as easy to demonstrate that contiguity, frequency, reinforcement, reward, punishment, and need reduction do not (do) affect behavior as to show that they do (do not). Unless an experimental variable affects or taps the functional level of the organism it will not be effective in behavior. This may explain the contradictory results concerning the influence of various types of experience on contemporary behavior. A few repetitions of a stimulus may affect subsequent behavior if the adaptation-level is affected. Thus Johnson (10) found that a high (low) set of pitches influenced judgments of a low (high) set of pitches which immediately followed the first set, and he was able to demonstrate increasing influence from one to five pre-shift practice trials. The weighting factor for the practice effects changed from 0.36 for one practice trial to 0.65 for two, 0.96 for three, to 1.22 for five pre-shift trials. Johnson points out that his learning curves (changes in the category limens from practice to test trials) are only slightly similar to conventional learning curves. The usual learning curves deal with increments or decrements of performance, whereas here the center of the scale which the subjects were using was in question. Here patterning of practice effect, as revealed in the change of scale, was studied. Furthermore, as Johnson points out, the simple equation, similar to our equation (1), for determining the influence of pre-shift trials on the category threshold, represents the learning of abstract material of some degree of social significance since frames of reference are involved. This approach, he points out in agreement with the present writer, seems more pertinent to the learning of attitudes, social norms, concepts, and personality traits than the usual treatments of mazes and discrimination habits.

Results very similar to Johnson's were found by Nash (20) who

studied the effects of previous series stimuli upon judgments of succeeding stimuli. She also studied the relative importance of background and residual factors in perception. Nash found that the
stimulus judged medium in a series of weights ranging from 100 to
300 grams was 173 grams when judged initially, but when judged
terminally; that is, after having judged sets of 400 to 600, 350 to
500, and so on down to 100 to 300, the stimulus judged medium was
223 grams. The residual effect of the heavier, preceding sets manifested itself in a higher adaptation-level amounting to 50 grams
with corresponding changes in the perception of the 100 to 300
series. Displacement toward earlier levels of stimulation appeared
when the method of single stimuli was employed. When a 900-gram
background stimulus was introduced, it negated both the series and
residual effects to a great extent. Thus the stimulus judged medium
terminally by another group of subjects was 186 grams by method
of single stimuli but with the 900-gram background stimulus the
stimulus judged medium was 371 grams. The initial adaptation-level
for the 400-600 set was 419 grams by method of single stimuli and
453 grams with the 900-gram background stimulus. Hence the
background stimulus stabilized the adaptation-level so there was
little change from the heaviest (400-600) to the lightest (100-300)
set when the 900-gram background stimulus was always present.

An interesting finding in Nash's study concerns the visual paradoxical distance effect. Köhler and Wallach (15) found that stimuli
exposed somewhat farther from satiated areas suffered more displacement than stimuli exposed nearer such areas. Nash found that the
100-300 set of weights was more affected by a 900-gram background
stimulus than the 400-600 set. Conversely, in another set of observations, a 90-gram background stimulus affected the 400- to 600-gram
series more than it affected the 100- to 300-gram series. *This result
was found also when the 900 and the 90 background stimuli were
both presented with the two series of stimuli!* This effect follows from
equation (1) and, indeed, can be predicted from it since averaging
900 with the 100-300 set causes greater displacement of the obtained
adaptation-level than averaging 900 with the 400 to 600 series. The
same reasoning applies to the effect of the 90 background stimulus.
The paradoxical distance effect is thus found also with lifted weights.

An additional effect found with lifted weights should also be
found in visual satiation experiments. It is known that a background
stimulus repels stimuli near it in value to a greater extent than stim-

uli farther removed. Nash found that the 900-gram background stimulus repelled the heavier stimuli in each series from 400-600 down to 100-300 while the 90-gram background stimulus affected the lighter stimuli in each series. Hence there is a double "distance" effect: (1) the paradoxical distance effect stressed by Köhler and Wallach; and (2) the greater repellent effect of background stimuli on nearer stimuli *within* any given series. We would therefore predict an accordion-like displacement should be found in figural aftereffects if a series of vertical stripes is exposed as test figures near satiated areas. Since the formula for predicting judgments of individual stimuli with changing adaptation-level devised by the writer (8) fitted Nash's data very closely, we may conclude that this theory account for both the older paradoxical distance effect and the new effect discovered in Nash's data.

That the adaptation-level paradigm may be fruitfully employed in the study of needs and set is shown in an experiment by Postman and Crutchfield (23). Three variables were controlled in this study: (1) degree of stimulus-ambiguity or probability of food responses to different stimulus-objects; (2) degree of set for food responses discovered by forcing subjects to give varying numbers of food-responses prior to responding to the critical ambiguous stimulus-objects; and (3) intensity of hunger in terms of hours of food-deprivation and of subjective ratings. This design embodies the essentials of our adaptation-level paradigm of series stimuli, background stimuli, and residual factors. Each of the three factors was controlled and varied. The stimulus-words consisted of skeleton words with two letters missing which the subject could fill in to make a food or nonfood word, for example: PO—, which could be completed to make PORK or POND. Food words of varying probability (determined experimentally) were employed, with nonfood words randomly mixed in the lists. Set was varied by forcing subjects to give different numbers of food responses prior to the presentation of the critical (ambiguous) words. Five degrees of set and several intensities of hunger were tested. The results show that the word lists had different effectiveness in producing food responses so that, coupled with different intensities of set, they produced different numbers of food responses: 0 to 5 intensity of set gave a range of 14.92 to 14.98 food responses with low probability words, 15.38 to 16.30 food responses with medium probability words, and 18.61 to 19.80 food responses with high probability words. The intensity of need gave paradoxical results in that there was a decrease in the number of food responses with increase in hours of deprivation. Degree of hunger, they conclude, does not significantly influence the number of food responses.

Postman and Crutchfield's interpretation of their experiment is as follows: "Our argument is closely related to the concept of adaptation-level in sensory discrimination. The perceived value of a given stimulus-object depends upon the number and magnitudes of similar objects which have preceded it and which determine S's adaptation-level . . . the impact of a 'set'-inducing stimulus is similarly determined and depends upon the extent of S's prior orientation toward set-relevant objects" (pp. 211-212). As they recognize, the influence of set was much greater in this experiment than were the differential effects of hunger. They conclude that "There is no simple one-to-one relationship between intensity of need and the frequency of need-related responses. Need interacts in complex ways with . . . other major variables and the final result does not fit a simple formula of wish-fulfillment" (p. 215). This analysis, in terms of unitary language for motivational and nonmotivational factors, explains why experimental data regarding the effect of inner determinants on perception are conflicting. Until contemporary factors are balanced or evaluated against residual factors, conclusions cannot be drawn regarding either. The concept of pooling in adaptation-level theory provides a rationale for such evaluation.

That individual value systems or frames of reference affect perception and judgment was shown by Marks (16), who asked three groups of colored students to rate skin color and other characteristics of people whom they knew. Darker subjects rated others lighter than the lighter subjects did. "Each judge establishes his own reference scale and . . . this scale is independent of the subjects rated but not of the rater's past experience . . . each judge's rating scale tends to be egocentric, i.e., a subject is seen as darker or lighter than the rater and judgments are made accordingly." Marks adds that "The egocentricity of the reference scale of skin color judgments may well apply to judgments of any characteristic to which social value is attached" (pp. 374-375). In our terminology, the rater's own skin color furnishes the neutral point of lightness of skin color. He takes himself as "medium." However, as Marks points out, the very dark individual cannot see himself as neutral because the social environment insists on the "objective" facts so he compromises his tendency to put himself at the neutral point with the tendency to accept objective fact.

A study similar to Marks's study of skin color was made by Hinckley and Rethlingshafer (9) on judgments of height of college men. A group of 160 men was divided into short and tall subgroups, the former being 5 feet 8 inches and under, the latter 6 feet and above. Tall men judged heights as shorter than did the short men, the curve of height estimation for the former lying below the latter. Compared with "neutral" estimation, the short men overestimate and the tall men underestimate heights. The differences between the two groups were significant at the 1 percent level of confidence.

Can it be said that the tendency to over- or underestimate lightness of skin color or height is a fundamental personality trait? To assert this would be to confuse the rater's mode of perceiving and judging with a real trait—namely, his own skin color or height which, to be sure, vitally affects his perceptions. Klein (11) has argued from individual differences in estimating sizes of squares that fundamental traits of "sharpening" or "leveling" were in question. According to the theory of adaptation-level it should be possible to alter such judgments, including judgments of skin color and height, intimately as they are bound to one's own color and height, by exposing raters to people of predominantly light (or dark) color and short (or tall) height. Similarly, Klein's underestimators, by being subjected to small areas, might well be turned into overestimators when called upon to judge average-sized squares.

We have so far been concerned with phenomena of individual adjustments and adaptation-levels. It is not stretching the concept of adaptation-level too much to speak of social and cultural levels in view of the fact that there are indices of group behavior no less than of individual behavior. There are various ways in which we can approach the problem of group level. Two studies, concerned with verbal or meaningful materials, illustrate how products of groups may be interpreted in terms of adaptation-level theory. The first study, by Mosier (18), shows how the meanings of words may be quantified much after the fashion of sensory stimuli according to our paradigm. He suggests that the meaning of a word may be specified thus:

$$M = x + i + c \tag{2}$$

where M is the meaning of the word, x is that part of the meaning which is constant from person to person and context to context, i is the part that varies from person to person, and c is the part that varies from context to context. Since i and c often cannot be distinguished, the formula simplifies to:

$$M = x + v \qquad (3)$$

where v is a variable including individual and contextual variables. Subjects were asked to rate 296 words selected from Thorndike's word list and considered suitable for scaling along an unfavorable-neutral-favorable continuum. An 11-point rating scale was used in which 6 was neutral, 11 was most favorable, and 1 was most unfavorable. Subjects could assign 0 to a word which they did not understand or which they could not scale. From frequency distributions of the ratings and a modified Thurstone method of equal-appearing intervals, the words were scaled and measures of ambiguity were determined for each word. In Table I are given the distribution of responses, the median category, and the inter-quartile range (Q) of a selected number of words.

From such data as are given in Table I the status of a word along a favorable-unfavorable continuum can be determined in our culture and different words can be compared with each other. Mosier also studied the effect of adverbial modifiers on words and found that the effect of an intensive is to shift the meaning of the word away from the neutral point toward one of the extremes. This is an example of the change in level of meaning of words as a result of context. This article contains many more interesting findings which should

TABLE I. DISTRIBUTIONS OF RESPONSES TO WORDS, MEDIAN CATEGORY, AND Q VALUES (From Mosier, 120, p. 130)

Stimulus-Word	1	2	3	4	5	6	7	8	9	10	11	Md	Q
						Rating							
Disgusting	43	51	32	16	3							1.6	1.6
Unsatisfactory	14	39	47	31	17							2.5	1.8
Neutral				1	6	133	5		1			5.5	0.6
Normal	1			1		104	15	5	12	7	1	5.7	0.9
Desirable						3	9	29	57	43	8	8.6	1.6
Excellent							2	3	14	33	96	10.2	0.9

be of interest to the linguist, semanticist, and philosopher as well as to the psychologist. The possibilities for further research into social and cultural patterns by means of this technique are many and will not escape the discerning reader.

In a somewhat different vein is Philip's study (22) of the effect of general and specific labeling on judgmental scales. This study is also concerned with social and cultural factors, but in a different way from Mosier's study of the meanings of words. One hundred fifty lines of poetry from Shakespeare to the present were given to 198 students who had had from two to four courses in English. They were asked to rate the lines for melody on a scale from 1 to 10. Average melody was denoted by a rating of 5, surpassing beauty by 10, and anything below 5 was unpleasant. Three labeling conditions were used: (1) a line of poetry presented alone; (2) the line followed by the name of the author (specific labeling); and (3) the line followed by the name of the period of literature from which it was taken (general labeling). The average rating of the melody given by the group was taken as the measure of the melody of the line. The plotted results show that the curve for specific labeling (name of author appended) lies above, the curve for general labeling (name of period appended) lies below the nonlabeled curve. Specific labeling enhances, general labeling lowers the perceived melody of poetry. The effect of practice or repetition was to cause the ratings to approach an intermediate value which Philip interprets as an adaptation-level effect. While these findings are extremely interesting, they raise questions as to why there should be these differences in specific versus general labeling. One source might be in the prestige or halo surrounding the names of famous poets, making the poetry more acceptable, whereas the identification of a line of poetry with a period may have the effect of assimilating it to a group and thus lowering its value. This study suggests further work to determine more exactly possible sources of influence on esthetic perception and judgment.

Philip relates his findings to the Woodworth-Sells (34) atmosphere effect which concerns the influence of background upon thought processes. They point out that the atmosphere in syllogistic reasoning may be positive or negative, universal or particular, depending upon the nature of the premises. Whatever the premise is, it creates a sense of validity for the corresponding conclusion. A positive premise makes it easier to accept a positive conclusion and a universal premise predisposes toward a universal conclusion. Their analysis of the atmosphere effect in reasoning antedates our theory of adaptation-level and furnishes convincing evidence that cognitive processes, no less than perception and motivation, are subject to background and residual factors. The work of Sells (27) on reasoning furnishes considerable information about the role of set and "hypotheses" in perception and thinking and, taken in conjunction with the adaptation-level paradigm, opens up further fields of exploration in the cognitive processes.

How can adaptation-level theory envisage the total personality and its relations to the world? Perception is the gateway through which the organism receives its information and searches for new data and new ways and means in order to make its adjustments. But it is more than this, for the individual perceives himself as part of the world and his ego is part of the behavioral field, as Koffka (14) and Schilder (26) have pointed out. The normal individual is centered in the here-now and, while cognizant of past and future, he weights stimuli in accordance with their nearness, frequency, and intensity, but even more importantly, he weights objects according to their significance and value for him as a person. Psychotics show disturbances in normal weighting. In one type of disturbance, general paralysis, the patient is disoriented in space, and in another type of disturbance, schizophrenia, the patient may be spatially oriented but the here-now no longer has a normal feeling-tone and is unanchored (cf. Minkowski, quoted by Schilder, 26, p. 218).

Personality may thus be envisaged in general terms much as we have treated perception—namely, as a system in which the energies released by internal and external forces are somehow balanced. A similar point of view has been presented by Stagner (29). Objects and events and people, as well as internal states, are differentially weighted and assume significance accordingly. Overweighting of internal messages, of past or possible future happenings, of "things which can't be helped," of events far removed in space or time from the individual and about which he can do nothing except worry, distort his outlook. If this application of adaptation-level theory has any truth in it for personality, then it should be possible, within limits, to counterbalance factors which disturb the individual unduly by stressing others which may ameliorate or negate the disturbing elements.

REFERENCES

1. FREDERICSON, E. Distributed versus massed experience in a traumatic situation. *J. abnorm. social Psychol.*, 1950, **45**, 259-266.
2. GESELL, A. The ontogenesis of infant behavior. In L. Carmichael (Ed.), *Manual of child psychology.* New York: John Wiley and Sons, 1946, pp. 295-331.
3. GILBERT, G. M. Inter-sensory facilitation and inhibition. *J. Gen. Psychol.*, 1941, **24**, 381-407.
4. HARTMANN, G. W. Learning as a function of the spatial interval between discriminanda. *J. Genet. Psychol.*, 1936, **49**, 249-253.
5. HASTINGS, D. W., WRIGHT, D. G., and GLUECK, B. C. *Psychiatric experiences of the Eighth Air Force.* New York: Josiah Macy, Jr. Foundation, 1944, pp. 1-307.
6. HELSON, H. Fundamental problems in color vision. 1. The principle governing changes in hue, saturation, and lightness of non-selective samples in chromatic illumination. *J. exp. Psychol.*, 1938, **26**, 1-27.
7. HELSON, H. Adaptation-level as a frame of reference for prediction of psychophysical data. *Am. J. Psychol.*, 1947, **60**, 1-29.
8. HELSON, H. Adaptation-level as a basis for a quantitative theory of frames of reference. *Psychol. Rev.*, 1948, **55**, 297-313.
9. HINCKLEY, E. D., and RETHLINGSHAFER, D. Value judgments of heights of men by college students. *J. Psychol.*, 1951, **31**, 257-262.
10. JOHNSON, D. M. Learning function for a change in the scale of judgment. *J. exp. Psychol.*, 1949, **39**, 851-860.
11. KLEIN, G. S. The personal world through perception. In R. R. Blake and G. V. Ramsey (Eds.), *Perception: an approach to personality.* New York: Ronald, 1951, pp. 328-355.
12. KNOX, G. W. Investigations of flicker and fusion. II. The effect of the stimulus pattern on the CFF. *J. gen. Psychol.*, 1945, **33**, 131-137.
13. KNOX, G. W. Investigations of flicker and fusion. III. The effect of auditory stimulation on the visual CFF. *J. gen. Psychol.*, 1945, **33**, 139-143.
14. KOFFKA, K. *Principles of gestalt psychology.* New York: Harcourt, Brace and Co., 1935.
15. Köhler, W., and WALLACH, H. Figural after-effects. *Proc. Am. Philos. Soc.*, 1944, **88**, 269-357.
16. MARKS, E. S. Skin color judgments of negro college students. *J. abnorm. social Psychol.*, 1943, **38**, 370-376.
17. MICHELS, W. C., and HELSON, H. A reformulation of the Fechner law in terms of adaptation-level applied to rating-scale data. *Am. J. Psychol.*, 1949, **62**, 355-368.

18. Mosier, C. I. A psychometric study of meaning. *J. social Psychol.*, 1941, **13**, 123-140.

19. Nash, M. C. An experimental test of the Michels-Helson theory of judgment. *Am. J. Psychol.*, 1950, **63**, 214-220.

20. Nash, M. C. A quantitative study of effects of past experience on adaptation-level. Ph.D. dissertation, Bryn Mawr College, 1950.

21. Philip, B. R. The frame of reference concept. *Canad. J. Psychol.*, 1949, **3**, 73-79.

22. Philip, B. R. The effect of general and specific labelling on judgmental scales. *Canad. J. Psychol.*, 1951, **5**, 18-28.

23. Postman, L., and Crutchfield, R. S. The interaction of need, set, and stimulus-structure in a cognitive task. *Am. J. Psychol.*, 1952, **65**, 196-217.

24. Razran, G. Stimulus generalization of conditioned responses. *Psychol. Bull.*, 1949, **46**, 337-365.

25. Ryan, T. A. Interrelations of the sensory systems in perception. *Psychol. Bull.*, 1940, **37**, 659-698.

26. Schilder, P. *Mind: perception and thought in their constructive aspects*. New York: Columbia University Press, 1942.

27. Sells, S. B. The atmosphere effect: an experimental study of reasoning. *Arch. Psychol.*, 1936, **29**, 5-72.

28. Selye, H. Stress and the general adaptation syndrome. *Brit. Med. J.*, 1950, **1**, 1383 ff.

29. Stagner, R. Homeostasis as a unifying concept in personality theory. *Psychol. Rev.*, 1951, **58**, 5-17.

30. Stone, C. P. Losses and gains in cognitive functions as related to electro-convulsive shocks. *J. abnorm. social Psychol.*, 1947, **42**, 206-214.

31. Werner, H., and Wapner, S. Sensory-tonic field theory of perception. *J. Pers.*, 1949, **18**, 88-107.

32. Werner, H., and Wapner, S. Toward a general theory of perception. *Psychol. Rev.*, 1952, **59**, 324-338.

33. Werner, H., Wapner, S., and Chandler, K. A. Experiments on sensory-tonic field theory of perception. II. Effect of supported and unsupported tilt of body on the visual perception of verticality. *J. exp. Psychol.*, 1951, **42**, 346-350.

34. Woodworth, R. S., and Sells, S. B. An atmosphere effect in formal syllogistic reasoning. *J. exp. Psychol.*, 1935, **18**, 451-460.

35. Worchel, P., and Narciso, Jr., J. C. Electroshock convulsions and memory: the interval between learning and shock. *J. abnorm. social Psychol.*, 1950, **45**, 85-98.

....

Relational Determination in Perception*

Wolfgang Köhler

WHEN VISUAL OBJECTS, figures, dots, or lines have for some time occupied a given region of the field, other visual objects which are now shown in this region tend to be displaced or distorted. Phenomena of this kind are known as "figural after-effects." The objects which establish such effects are called "inspection (or I-) objects," and the objects which exhibit the effects, "test (or T-) objects" (10).

According to the definition of figural after-effects which has just been given, a T-object is affected only if it is located within or near the area in which the I-object has been shown. This area is defined in a retinal (or cortical) sense rather than in terms of "absolute" space. Suppose, for instance, that after the I-period the eyes of the subject turn to a new fixation mark. Under these conditions, an after-effect will be observed in the new direction if the retinal place of the T-object has the right relation to the retinal area previously occupied by the I-object. The T-object need not differ from the I-object. When inspected for some time, many visual objects change their own spatial characteristics. In a way, they then serve both as I- and as T-objects.

Most figural after-effects can be derived from the following principle: T-objects recede from areas in which I-objects have been shown, particularly from the regions in which the contours of these objects have been located. As a result, T-objects may be simply displaced. Figure 1 shows a combination of I- and T-objects in which this is the case. (Actually, the I-object alone is presented first, and is then replaced by the T-objects. The simultaneous presentation of

---

* From Jeffress, L. A. (Ed.), *Cerebral mechanisms in behavior—the Hixon symposium.* New York: John Wiley & Sons, Inc., 1951. Pp. 200-213 reprinted by permission of the author and publisher.

I- and T-objects in Figure 1 merely serves to show their spatial relation. The cross between the T-objects indicates the position of the fixation mark.) When, after an I-period of, say, one minute, the T-objects are presented, the one on the left side appears lower than its partner. The fact that the right T-object is not at all, or clearly less, affected demonstrates the localization of the effect.

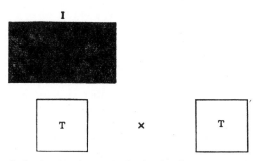

Fig. 1.   Typical stimulus figure. X is the fixation point, I the inspection figure, and T and T the test figures. (I is withdrawn before T is presented.)

Obviously, the left T-object may be shown above as well as below the area of the I-object; a T-object may also be shown on the left or on the right side of this area. In each case, it would appear displaced away from the I-object, if the second T-object were shown in a position which makes the displacement clear by comparison. Now it seems plausible to assume that inspection of an I-object alters the neural medium in which the process of this object occurs, and that a T-object is displaced because its process is affected by that alteration of the medium. But while inspection of a given object can cause only one pattern of alteration in the neural medium, we have just seen that this alteration may cause a number of different displacements, depending upon the location of the T-object in relation to the I-object. Consequently, we have to distinguish between the alteration of the medium as such and the various after-effects which may afterwards be demonstrated. These facts ought also to have different names. In previous reports the alteration of the medium has been called "satiation," and the term "figural after-effects" has been reserved for the changes which T-objects suffer when placed within or near satiated areas. These names will be used in the following discussion.

It will be seen immediately that, with certain spatial relations between I- and T-objects, the displacement of the latter must result in changes of distances and sizes. In Figure 2, for instance, which again shows I- and T-objects in one pattern, both the T-objects on the right side must recede from the I-areas in their immediate neighborhood, and thus their distance will be shortened. At the same time, both the T-objects on the left side must recede from the I-object between them, so that their distance grows. As a consequence, the four T-objects together will appear to form a trapezoid rather than a rectangle. The size of figural after-effects in general varies strongly from one individual to another; but most observers find the present example particularly convincing.*

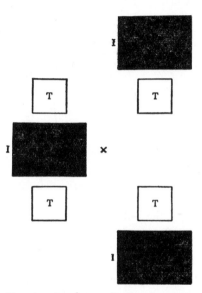

FIG. 2. Another stimulus pattern. (See Fig. 1 for explanation.)

While in the instance of Figure 2 it is empty distances which shrink or grow, in the following example (Figure 3) the size of an object is affected. After the I-period, the various parts of the T-circle on the left side recede from the outline of the I-circle, which constitutes a region of maximal satiation. Hence this T-circle must now be visually smaller than the objectively equal comparison object on the right side. This is actually the case. The effect can be measured by varying the size of the comparison object until it appears equal to the affected T-object. The distortion tends to be fairly conspicuous. The affected T-circle may lose more than 20 per cent of its area when the I-circle has been inspected for 45 seconds.

The displacement of T-objects in the neighborhood of satiated regions follows a rule which may at first appear to be paradoxical. Generally speaking, the displacement is maximal, not in the region

---

* At this point it should be mentioned that those who wish to experiment in this field ought to give sufficient attention to the quantitative spatial relations between I- and T-patterns, and also to the size of the distance between these patterns and the observer (see Köhler and Wallach, [ref. 10], pp. 297-303).

of maximal satiation, that is, when the T-object coincides with the I-object, but rather when the T-object is shown at a certain distance. Actually, this rule follows from the fact that T-objects recede from more into less satiated areas. Suppose that both the I- and the T-object are straight lines, and that these lines are parallel. Many observations prove that the I-object satiates not only the place in which it is located but to a degree also adjacent regions. If, how-

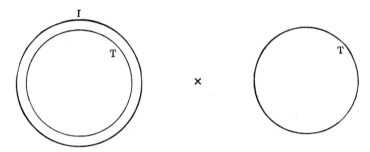

Fig. 3. Another stimulus pattern. (See Fig. 1 for explanation.)

ever, the I-object itself is bilaterally symmetrical, and if the medium can be regarded as homogeneous, the resulting pattern of satiation must be approximately symmetrical about the same axis. This applies, of course, to the case in which the I-object is a straight line. As a consequence, there are two positions of the T-line in which it cannot be displaced. First, it cannot be displaced when shown at a very great distance. For here its process must be virtually independent of changes in the medium, which the remote I-object has established. Second, there can be no displacement when the T-object coincides with the I-object. For, in this position, the T-line lies between two areas in which satiation has approximately the same pattern and the same intensity so that the object cannot move for reasons of symmetry.* It follows from this reasoning that major displacements of the T-line are possible only when this line is shown at some distance from the I-line, where satiation is less extended and less intense on one side of the T-line than it is on the other side. Naturally, displacements must again decrease when, at still greater distances, the T-line entirely emerges from the satiated area.

---

* For physicists I will add that under these circumstances the T-line is in a position of stable equilibrium.

Measurements of the displacement at varying distances from the I-line confirm this deduction. But there are further facts which can be derived from our argument. For instance, the T-line need not be parallel to the I-line. If the I- and the T-line form a small angle (see Figure 4),* one end of the T-line coincides with a point of the

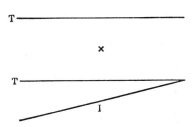

FIG. 4.   Another stimulus pattern. (See Fig. 1 for explanation.)

I-line, and can therefore not be displaced; but, from here towards its free end, its various parts have increasingly asymmetrical positions within the pattern of satiation, and must therefore be displaced by gradually growing amounts. As a result, the T-line must turn in space, away from the I-line. This is what actually occurs when the experiment is made. For the same reason, if the I-line consists of two straight lines which form an obtuse angle, the two halves of a straight T-line, which passes through the apex of this angle, must turn away from the two parts of the I-figure; in other words, the T-line must become a line bent in the direction opposite to that of the I-figure. That this really happens was first discovered by Verhoeff (13), and once more discovered by Gibson (5). Gibson also found that if an I- and a T-line intersect at a small angle, the T-line turns away from the I-line. Gibson, it is true, gave his excellent observations a different interpretation; but it can now no longer be doubted that these observations constitute figural after-effects in the sense in which Wallach and I are using this term. The same holds for Gibson's further discovery that, after prolonged inspection of a slightly curved line, a straight line in the same location and orientation appears curved in the opposite direction.

By choosing and combining I- and T-objects in one way or another, we can readily produce a great many further after-effects.

* The second (parallel) T-line is added as a neutral comparison object.

No more examples will be needed for our present purpose. I prefer to formulate some statements which refer to the nature of such effects in general.

1. Inspection of *any* visual objects gives rise to figural after-effects, provided that the objects are clearly segregated from their ground, and that the T-objects are shown in the right places.

2. It is the prolonged occurrence of the process of an I-object which, as such, establishes satiation and, if a T-object is afterwards shown, a figural after-effect.*

3. The locus of satiation is mainly cortical rather than retinal. For, after inspection of an I-object with one eye, a T-object seen with the corresponding region of the other eye also exhibits the after-effect.

In a more recent investigation, figural after-effects have served to answer an old theoretical question. It has been demonstrated that T-objects recede from the places of I-objects not only in the two dimensions of the frontal plane but also in the third dimension of visual space (9). In fact, all figural after-effects which are known to occur in the former case can also be observed in the dimension of depth. Moreover, the rules which they follow in the third dimension are identical with those which hold for the effects in the frontal plane. This applies also to the factor of localization. For instance, if with a given fixation mark a T-object is shown behind the place in which the I-object has been located, this T-object recedes to a greater distance; and if it is shown in front of that place it recedes from it toward the observer. (In both cases, the displacement is again greater at a certain distance from the place of the I-object than it is in its immediate neighborhood.) However, no effect is observed if, in retinal or cortical terms, the I- and the T-object lie in different directions. Such facts seem incompatible with theories, according to which the third dimension of visual space is merely

---

* A few remarks ought to be added to this statement. I do not wish to exclude the possibility that extra-visual factors influence the speed with which satiation develops. In fact, we have good evidence for assuming that, when attention is concentrated on an object, satiation in the area of this object is accelerated. Again, in referring to the prolonged occurrence of the process of an object, the statement does not imply more than that satiation grows with continued inspection. By using a technique of summation, Wallach and I have been able to show that low degrees of satiation develop when objects are shown only for fractions of a second. We are inclined to infer that virtually all perception of objects goes with a measure of satiation.

an artifact for which processes of learning are responsible. It will be remembered that, some time ago, Lashley and Russell reported findings of an entirely different kind which also contradict such theories (11).

There is only one difference between the figural after-effects in the frontal plane and those in the third dimension. For the most part, the latter tend to be more conspicuous than the former. We have never found a subject who failed to be impressed by the following observation. On a piece of white cardboard a number of thick black parallel lines are drawn in a vertical direction, and then the surface is given a curved shape, convex toward the observer, who fixates a mark in the middle of the pattern. When after a while this surface is replaced by a plane surface, with black lines and a fixation mark in strictly corresponding positions, this T-surface appears strikingly curved in the opposite sense. With an I-surface concave toward the observer, the T-plane assumes an equally pronounced convex appearance. At first, such observations may seem to be open to criticism because on a curved solid surface there will always be gradients of illumination which must give rise to common negative after-images. It might be argued that only the appearance of such negative after-images on the plane T-surface causes the impression of an opposite curvature. Actually, the same effect can be demonstrated when gradients of illumination are entirely absent. For this purpose, we have merely to prepare two plane but slightly disparate drawings which, when fused in a stereoscope or haploscope, again give a surface curved in the third dimension. It will be found that after inspection of such a surface a corresponding pattern in the plane appears curved in the opposite sense. Since in this experiment both drawings are objectively plane, it is easy to give them a uniform illumination, and thus to exclude any explanation in terms of gradients of illumination and their after-images.

Vision is not the only sense modality in which satiation and figural after-effects occur. When Gibson had discovered that after inspection of visual curves straight lines tangent to these curves were seen as curved in the opposite direction, he immediately made a similar experiment in kinesthesis. Blindfolded subjects were asked to move the fingers of one hand along a curved edge, and to repeat the movement a great many times. When afterwards the same hand followed a straight edge, this edge appeared curved in the opposite sense. It seems hardly plausible to assume that the nature of this phenomenon is essentially different from the curved-line effect in vision.

We have observed and measured another after-effect in kinesthesis (8). In vision, the distance between two paralled T-lines is increased when the subject has previously inspected a narrow rectangle which lies between them. On the other hand, if the same T-lines are shown inside the area of a wider I-rectangle, they recede from its edges, and their distance is decreased. Can the same effects be obtained in kinesthesis? We asked our subjects to move the fingers of one hand along the two edges of a long rectangle with the width 0.5 inch and the fingers of the other hand along the edges of a rectangle with the width 2.5 inches. The movement was repeated back and forth for half a minute. Afterwards the subjects were asked to move their fingers along the edges of two equal rectangles, the width of which was 1.5 inches. We expected that, if there is satiation in kinesthesis, and if it has the same effects here as it has in vision, the T-objects would not appear to have the same width. Rather, since the width of one would be increased, and that of the other decreased, the former would appear wider than the latter. Results confirmed this expectation. Moreover, if one of the T-objects was replaced by a scale, that is, an object the width of which varied by small and equal steps, our subjects were able to find a width on the scale which appeared equal to the width 1.5 inches felt with the other hand. Although individual differences as to the size of the phenomenon are again great, we have so far found no subject in whom the effect cannot be demonstrated. Our arrangement often gives very large distortions. For fifty college students we found an average of 43 per cent. After a satiation period of 30 seconds, the width 1.5 inches, presented on the side of the narrower satiation object, appeared equal to 2.15 inches on the scale which was given on the side of the wider satiation object.

In preliminary experiments we found that similar facts occur when objects are felt by passive touch rather than kinesthetically. On the whole, it now seems possible that any process which has a spatial structure is capable of satiating the medium in which it spreads. As a matter of fact, there is no reason why satiation should occur only in perception.

If the processes underlying object perception always establish satiation, any physiological theory of these processes must be a theory of satiation at the same time. It follows that in making assumptions about the facts which underlie object perception we must exclude such processes as cannot be responsible for satiation in our sense.

Present thinking about the functions of the human cortex is based on discoveries which were made in the early years of this century. According to these discoveries, interrelations between the periphery and the cortex are, in both directions, mediated by short-lived impulses which travel along individual nerve fibers. It is customary to assume that cortical function as such is essentially of the same type; in other words, that impulses which arrive in the cortex merely start further impulses in next neurons, and so forth. This assumption is not fundamentally altered by the thesis that neurons may be arranged in circular chains, and that impulses may travel around such closed circuits for considerable periods. At any rate, most neurophysiologists seem to be convinced that the physiology of the whole nervous system can be written in terms of nerve impulses.

I doubt whether the behavior of figural after-effects is compatible with this view, because it seems that in our experiments it cannot be nerve impulses per se which cause satiation. This statement is based on the following fact. Suppose that during the I-period we show a narrow black rectangle on a white ground, and that afterwards we present two T-objects, one within the area of the black object, the other just outside, the short distance of both from the edge of the I-object being the same. Under these circumstances, it will be found that the T-object within the area of the black I-object is more strongly affected than the T-object in the white environment.* To be sure, this T-object is also affected, as can readily be shown by comparing it with a third T-object which lies at a great distance. But the essential point is that within the area of the black I-object satiation is clearly maximal. On the assumption that satiation is caused by nerve impulses it would seem to follow that the frequency and density of nerve impulses are higher within the black object than they are at any point in the surrounding white. Can this conclusion be reconciled with present views about the behavior

---

* With a solid black object it is advisable to use one eye during the I-period, and to observe with the other eye during the test. In this fashion, observation of the figural after-effect will not be disturbed by after-images in the usual sense. The same procedure may be used in the situations to which Figures 1 and 2 refer.

of nerve impulses? Apparently, this is not the case. As a consequence, there appear to be only two ways in which satiation can be explained in physiological terms. Many will insist that the explanation be given in terms of nerve impulses. But this would imply a change in our mental picture of nerve impulses; for it has just been shown that the facts of satiation cannot be derived from the now prevailing picture. We shall later return to this point. As a second possibility, it may be assumed that nerve impulses as such are not responsible for satiation as investigated in our experiments. Then we must find another process by which it is actually caused. I propose now to discuss the latter alternative.

Obviously, if this alternative is to be seriously considered it must be applied to satiation in general. The way in which satiation develops within and around a white object on a black background does not essentially differ from that in which it develops within and around a black object on a white background. Satiation must therefore be given the same interpretation in both cases. Thus, on the premise that satiation in the region of a black object is not caused by nerve impulses, we shall have to assume that the same holds for satiation in the region of a white object.

By what other process could satiation be established? It appears that any speculation in this respect is restricted by conditions which are inherent in our experiments. According to our observations, *only* objects or patterns cause any demonstrable satiation. Hence, we must find a process which accompanies object or pattern vision rather than the perception of homogeneous surfaces. The assumption that such a process exists is supported by a fact which was first observed by Adrian (1). The alpha rhythm of the human brain is much more seriously disturbed by visual objects or patterns than it is by a bright homogeneous field. Adrian suggests that it is attention to which the alpha rhythm is so sensitive. But there remains the other possibility that, quite apart from this factor, the rhythm is strongly disturbed by a visual process which accompanies the perception of objects or patterns.*

From the point of view of stimulation, what is a visual object? It seems safe to say that, in terms of stimulation, an object is an area (or a volume) which differs from its environment either as a

---

* It is, of course, well known that the alpha rhythm may also be blocked by non-visual factors. I am here ignoring such evidence merely because it is not related to the present discussion.

whole or along its boundary. We see things of any kind only when a relation of inequality obtains between the stimulation in one area and that in another, surrounding, area. Thus it seems plausible to assume that the process which goes with object or pattern vision is a relationally determined process, and that satiation is established in regions in which this process takes place for some time. Relational determination is not a familiar term. I will therefore add that relationally determined processes are extremely common in physics. For instance, if temperatures differ in two parts of a system, a current of heat energy is established which tends to equalize the temperatures. The direction of the flow depends upon the direction of the difference, and in the absence of any difference there is no flow. Similarly, if a solution which contains certain molecules is surrounded by a second solution which contains these molecules in a different concentration, a current of diffusion will be observed, unless the solutions are separated by an impermeable barrier. The current flows as long as the concentrations differ. Thus, it is again a relation of inequality between the two parts of the system which maintains the process. Incidentally, our examples exhibit relational determination in more than one sense. As the currents of heat or diffusion spread, their distribution in space depends upon the shape of the boundary at which the parts of the systems are in contact. This shape is defined in terms of geometrical relations among parts rather than of merely local conditions, and the distribution of the flow adapts itself to such relations. Therefore, not only the flow as such is relationally determined, but the same holds also for its pattern in space.*

The examples given are by no means the only examples of relationally determined processes in physics. I need not mention further instances. In the present connection, it seems more important to remark that some such processes cause obstructions in the medium in which they occur, and that in this fashion after-effects are established when later further processes spread in the same medium.

---

* Relational determination of events must be distinguished from certain other facts. Not all instances in which two or more factors participate in causing an effect are, for this reason alone, instances of relational determination. For example, in synaptic transmission many cells are thrown into action only if more than one impulse arrives at their surfaces. A combination of several causes in this sense need not, of course, involve relational determination. In other words, to be relationally determined by two conditions is one thing, and summation of the effects of mutually independent causes is another thing.

Are any relationally determined processes likely to occur in the brain when objects or patterns are seen? Ten years ago, I suggested that the relationally determined process which underlies pattern vision is a direct electric current, and that such a current flows when conditions of excitation in one part of the visual cortex differ from those in an adjacent part.* An attempt was also made to explain how the electromotive forces originate which drive the current from one part to the other, and back again to the former. The explanation involved no hypothesis which is at odds with available knowledge of nerve impulses and their influence upon cortical tissue. Rather, those forces were derived from concepts which play a great role in present neurophysiological discussions. Nevertheless, this particular part of the theory need not now be described, because there may be various ways of deriving electromotive forces which would drive a direct current through the tissue. It seems that, whatever our choice may be, the distribution of the flow as such would always be about the same. It is this flow which we will now consider.

The flow would spread through the tissue as a volume conductor, which is to say that, in this connection, the brain must be regarded as a continuous medium to which principles of continuity physics apply.† In this respect, I merely emphasize a possibility which is implicit in present neurophysiology, even though its consequences have, until recently, not been explicitly considered. Surely, if the potentials of the alpha rhythm as well as those of "on" and "off" effects can spread through the skull, there is nothing in the brain to prevent such potentials from spreading through this medium as a continuum. As a result, it can hardly be a disturbing thesis that a steadier flow would do the same. In fact, the possibility that the brain is pervaded by field potentials was discussed by Gerard before I formulated the present theory (2). Later, he and Libet pointed out that functional interrelations in the frog's brain can best be interpreted from this point of view (3, 4, 12). Although the authors did not consider problems of perception, their views and mine may prove to be different versions of essentially the same conception.

---

* W. Köhler (6), pp. 212-215, 239-244, 351, and 370 f. See also W. Köhler (7), pp. 55-106. A more detailed account is given by W. Köhler and H. Wallach (10), pp. 322 ff.

† I am aware of the fact that physicists sometimes use the term "continuity physics" in a different sense, in which it is contrasted with "quantum physics."

In flowing through a continuum, a direct current assumes a distribution which, just as in our previous examples, is relationally determined by the shape of given boundaries. In object or pattern vision, the boundaries in question would be those between cortical areas in which retinal stimulation establishes different kinds or degrees of excitation. Wallach and I have indicated how the resulting distribution of the flow could be related to facts of space perception.* But in our present connection this particular question need not be raised. It will suffice if we consider a fact which concerns only the distribution of the current as such, and is quite independent of further theorizing. If excitation within a circumscribed cortical area differs from that in its environment, the resulting current must circle around the boundary at which the two areas are in contact. Moreover, unless the surrounded area is very large, the current must be denser in this area than it is in the environment in which it can spread widely. This is true whether or not local excitation is higher in the circumscribed area. Thus, if a black object is shown on a white background, the density of the flow must be maximal within the area of the black object, just as it is maximal within the area of a white object surrounded by black.

We can now turn to the problem of satiation. The present theory has no difficulty in solving this problem. Any direct currents which flow through the nervous system polarize the surfaces of cells, and also change their polarizability. Generally speaking, this effect, the so-called electrotonus, has the character of an obstruction. Further currents which afterwards flow through the same medium are weakened. At the same time, they suffer changes of their distribution in space. We are not introducing a special hypothesis if we assume that the currents of our theory are also electrotonically active, and that the resulting obstructions follow the same rules as hold for electrotonus in general. For instance, the degree to which the various parts of the medium are electrotonically affected is directly related to the density of the current in those parts. Now we know that the density of the currents postulated in our theory must be maximal within the area of a circumscribed object, still great in adjacent parts, and progressively lower at greater distances. Consequently, the intensity of the obstruction which the currents establish must exhibit the same distribution. But this is also the distribution of satiation as

---

* Reference 10, pp. 332 ff.

investigated in our experiments. Thus we are led to the conclusion that satiation is merely another expression for electrotonus. A more specific consideration of figural after-effects tends to confirm this conclusion. For example, the fact that satiation is more intense within the area of a black I-object than it is in its white environment now offers no problem. For, since in this case also the current must flow with greatest density through the restricted area of the object, its electrotonic action will again be maximal in this area. Quite apart from this special condition, how are the distortions to be explained which T-objects suffer in satiated areas? Obviously, if there are currents which go with I-objects, there must also be currents corresponding to T-objects. But the current of a T-object will be weakened and distorted, if the current of an I-object has previously pervaded the same region, and if its electrotonic effect still persists. To a degree, we can tell how the obstructions established by the currents of given I-objects must distort the currents of T-objects; and, if certain general premises are accepted, we can also compare such distortions with actually observed aftereffects. It seems at present that biophysical theory and psychological observation are in satisfactory agreement.

REFERENCES

1. ADRIAN, E. D., and MATTHEW, B. H. C. The Berger rhythm: Potential changes from the occipital lobes in man. *Brain*, 1934, **57**, 322-351.
2. GERARD, R. W. Factors controlling brain potentials. *Cold Spring Harbor Symposia*, 1936, **4**, 292-304.
3. GERARD, R. W. The interaction of neurones. *Ohio J. Sci.*, 1941, **41**, 160-172.
4. GERARD, R. W., and LIBET, B. The control of normal and "convulsive" brain potentials. *Amer. J. Psychiat.*, 1940, **96**, 1125-1153.
5. GIBSON, J. J. Adaptation, after-effect and contrast in the perception of curved lines. *J. exp. Psychol.*, 1933, **16**, 1-31.
6. KÖHLER, W. *The place of value in a world of facts.* New York: Liveright Publishing Corp., 1938.
7. KÖHLER, W. *Dynamics in psychology.* New York: Liveright Publishing Corp., 1940.
8. KÖHLER, W., and DINNERSTEIN, D. In *Miscel. Psychologica Albert Michotte.* Louvain, 1947.
9. KÖHLER, W., and EMERY, D. Figural after-effects in the third dimension of visual space. *Amer. J. Psychol.*, 1947, **60**, 159-202.

10. KÖHLER, W., and WALLACH, H. Figural after-effects, an investigation of visual processes. *Proc. Amer. Philos. Soc.*, 1944, **88**, 269-357.
11. LASHLEY, K. S., and RUSSELL, J. T. The mechanism of vision: XI. A preliminary test of innate organization. *J. Genet. Psychol.*, 1934, **45**, 136-144.
12. LIBET, B., and GERARD, W. Steady potential fields and neurone activity. *J. Neurophysiol.*, 1941, **4**, 438-455.
13. VERHOEFF, F. H. A theory of binocular perspective. *Amer. J. Physiol. Optics*, 1925, **6**, 416-448.

....

*Perceived Motion**

KURT KOFFKA

THE BEHAVIOURAL WORLD has been treated so far as though it were produced by unchanging stimulation, and contained, correspondingly, only objects at rest. This implicit assumption restricts our field of study to unique cases which are realized only under very special conditions. As a rule, moving objects are in our field; at this moment in my own field there is my pen which is moved across the page by my fingers; now a buzzing fly passes through my field of vision, and as soon as a visitor enters my office, he is never so rigidly calm as to produce an unchanging retinal image; but even if being alone I lean back in my chair and begin to think out the solution of a problem, my eyes are not kept steady but will change their line of regard from one object to another, thereby producing a change of the retinal patterns. In the first cases, real moving objects present in the field, the shift of the retinal pattern leads to behavioural motion of objects, whether I fixate a non-moving object or follow a moving one with my regard; in the second case, when my eyes roam over stationary objects, such a shift will *not* have this result. Although the two facts belong closely together, here we concentrate mainly on the first, even if we cannot entirely avoid referring to the second. Thus we turn now to the theory of perceived motion. It is a well-known fact that a paper on visual motion was the beginning of Gestalt psychology. Wertheimer (1912) utilized the results of his classical study to formulate briefly a number of new principles constitutive for every kind of psychological theory. Even though we have developed these principles in other fields and with the help of other facts, it might be tempting to introduce the discussion of our present topic with Wertheimer's paper and then follow the history of psychological progress in this field. I shall, how-

---

* From *Principles of Gestalt Psychology* by Kurt Koffka, copyright, 1935, by Harcourt, Brace and Co., Inc.

ever, choose a different mode of procedure and present facts and theories systematically according to all the knowledge now available, and shall in this attempt concentrate more on the later than on the earlier publications. The earlier ones are today fairly well known; they are, and they had to be, full of experiments which refuted theories accepted at the time they were written, but which today can be considered dead. Since I have treated the subject so often (1919, 1931), most explicitly in 1931 (an article which contains a great mass of detail which will be omitted here), a similar procedure would be mere repetition.

Wertheimer's paper and a number of publications which followed it dealt chiefly or exclusively with stroboscopic motion, i.e., the case where perceived motion is produced by stationary objects. Since it has been proved beyond a doubt (Wertheimer, Cermak and Koffka, Duncker 1929, Brown 1931, van der Waals and Roelofs 1933) that as far as psychophysical dynamics are concerned there is no difference between stroboscopic and "real" motion,[1] i.e., perceived motion produced by actually moving objects, it seems more adequate to begin with the latter case, which is the more usual.

A General Principle of the Theory of Perceived Motion. We begin with a very general statement formulated explicitly by Köhler (1933, p. 356). The physiological correlate of perceived motion[2] must be a real process of change within the total physiological process patterns. Supposing that the perceptual field were totally homogeneous except for one point moving through it, then the motion of this point would *not* lead to such a change as we have postulated, since in the totally homogeneous field it would be exposed to the *same* stresses everywhere, all positions being dynamically indistinguishable from each other. Under such conditions no motion would be perceived, and although this condition is unrealizable its discussion elucidates the significance of the conditions which are realized.[3] Our perceptual field is in this sense never entirely homogeneous. Even in complete darkness it has an above and below, right and left, near and far; and a point passing through it if it changes its

---

[1] This proof was once of great theoretical significance. We shall occasionally mention one or two points.

[2] Although we shall largely confine ourselves to visual motion, tactual and acoustic motion are essentially of the same kind (see my article 1931).

[3] Similarly Newton's first law of motion treats an unrealizable case and has nevertheless been of great significance.

distance from the fovea, apart from changing its position with regard to these three determinations, passes at the same time through regions of different functional properties. Inhomogeneity of the total field and a displacement of a point within such an inhomogeneous field are therefore two necessary conditions for the arousal of the psychophysical process of motion. For in an inhomogeneous field the motion of an object changes its dynamic condition, with regard to the total physiological process pattern. From this we can deduce that more inhomogeneous fields are more favourable for the arousal of perceived motion than less inhomogeneous ones, a deduction amply confirmed by facts. All movement thresholds are higher in relatively homogeneous fields than in inhomogeneous ones (see my article 1931, p. 1194 f.), and the apparent velocity of objects moving objectively with the same velocity is greater for those which move in inhomogeneous than for those which move in relatively homogeneous fields (Brown 1931, p. 218). These two facts are closely interrelated, as Brown (1931 b) has proved.

Our conclusion that perceived motion in the visual field presupposes displacement of objects relative to the rest of the field also fits the facts from which we started our discussion. If objects move in the geographical environment, then their retinal images are displaced with regard to other objects whether we fixate them or an object at rest, while movement of our eyes across stationary objects leaves their relation to the objects surrounding them intact. True enough, eye-movements also produce a shift of pattern on the retina, and therefore must have some effect of perceived motion, but this motion should not belong to the field objects. We shall see later that the perception of our eyes, or even of "ourselves," as moving is the result of this shift (Duncker).

Duncker's Experiments. Such a view of the origin of the perception of motion must lead to very definite experiments. The excellent work done by Duncker (1929) was entirely determined by it. Supposing the field is homogeneously dark and contains only two light objects, one of which is in objective motion while the other one is at rest. Then, if the velocity of the motion is not great, the chief determining factor will be the relative displacement of the two objects. This, according to our theory, must lead to perceived motion, but our theory does not permit us to deduce which of these objects will be the carrier of the motion, as long as their relative displacement and no other factor becomes effective. But our theoretical equipment contains other concepts which suggest a solution of this problem.

Systems of Reference. We fall back on our distinction of things and framework and our knowledge that the framework is more stable than the things within it. If we apply this to the case of motion we must deduce the following proposition: if one of the two field objects has the function of framework for the other, then it will be seen at rest and the other as moving no matter which of the two moves in reality. If on the other hand the two objects are both things, then under symmetrical conditions (fixation between them or freely wandering regard) they should both move in opposite directions.

Both these deductions were confirmed in Duncker's experiments. He also found, what Thelin had discovered before him, that fixation of one of the two equivalent objects tended to make it the carrier of motion, whether it moved objectively or not, a fact which he tentatively explains by the thing-framework, or figure-ground, distinction, the fixated point keeping its figure character, whereas non-fixated ones become part of the ground. Duncker's findings have been corroborated and amplified by an investigation of Oppenheimer's. Of her results I will only mention two: (1) the relative intensity of the objects plays a rôle, the stronger one tending to become the frame of reference for the weaker; therefore, *ceteris paribus,* the stronger one will be at rest, the weaker one in motion; (2) the shape of the objects determines the apparent motion in this way: if the relative displacement between the two objects occurs in such a manner that its direction coincides with one of the main directions of one object, but not with that of the other, the former will tend to be seen as moving further than the latter. The relative displacement does not, therefore, determine the motion carrier, but under these conditions it determines the *amount* of motion. This is an invariant, no matter whether one point is seen in motion, or both. As a matter of fact it was Duncker who introduced the concept of invariants (though he did not use the term), which has been so fruitful in our discussion of perceptual organization. The invariance of the amplitude of motion holds, if only two objects take part in it, whether they are equivalent to each other or whether one is the framework of the other. As soon as a third object enters, this invariance may no longer hold. If *a* is the framework of *b*, and *b* the framework of *c*, and objectively *b* is moved, then two different kinds of relative displacement take place; *b* changes its place in its own framework *a*, and *c* changes its place in its framework *b*. The sum of the two perceived motions resulting from these conditions will be greater than the perceived motion resulting if *b* is moved exactly as before but either object *a* or object *c* is removed. Duncker has discussed the possible relationships between a third object and the two other ones and has demonstrated experimentally that the effects on perceived motion depend upon the kind and degree of appurtenance between them. Plurality of frameworks, or systems of reference, has still another important effect, first recognized by Rubin (1927). His ingenious and elegant experiments were supplemented by Duncker. I shall discuss only a very simple case which is unique because of its familiarity. Continually we see wheels rolling over the ground, and perceive simultaneously two motions, a circular and a rectilinear translatory one. In reality each point of the wheel, with the exception of the centre, describes cycloids, whose shape is entirely different from that of the circle; the centre alone performs a pure translatory motion. But the points of the wheel have the centre as their point of reference, while the centre itself is referred to the general spatial framework, or, when the room is in darknss, to the observer himself. The double motion which is actually perceived is the result of this separation of systems of reference. If only one point of the wheel (not the centre) is visible during its rotation, then motion on a cycloidal curve is perceived. If the centre is added (Duncker) the phenomenon changes at once, different phenomena emerge, partly depending upon the velocity of the wheel motion, all of which have the common feature that the peripheral point describes a rotatory motion. If instead of adding the centre one adds a point on the same concentric circle as the first point, then, to judge from one of Rubin's experiments performed with a somewhat different motion pattern, one can see two such cycloidal motions. If one increases the number of such points, one soon reaches the normal wheel effect, i.e., one sees all points rotating round an invisible center, and at the same time a translatory motion.

Stroboscopic and Real Motion. Historically it is interesting that this theory of perceived motion was first developed for stroboscopic motion (Hartmann, Köhler 1923 a), and a special investigation was carried out by Scholz to prove it in this field. The fusion between the two successive processes must result from a force of attraction between them. The reality of this force was demonstrated by the fact that two stroboscopically exposed lines appear at a shorter distance from each other than two permanently exposed ones, and that the amount of contraction of their distance reaches its maximum when they are seen in optimal motion.

The problem of stroboscopic motion consists, according to this theory, in establishing the conditions under which fusion between the two (or more) separate excitations takes place, or when attraction, though not strong enough to result in fusion, affects the attracted processes sufficiently to displace them, with the phenomenal result that both or either are seen to move over part of the way (Wertheimer's dual and singular partial motion). Formulated in this way the problem of stroboscopic motion is no different from that of real motion, where processes separately started must fuse also. But because in real motion the spatial distance between the interacting processes is so small as to produce very strong forces of attraction so that other factors are small compared to them and therefore hard to demonstrate, such other factors play a much more important rôle in stroboscopic motion, where, owing to the greater distance between the processes, the forces are much weaker. Of such other factors I mention the temporal determinants, i.e., the exposure times and intervals, the intensities (or, better, the gradients between figures and background), the distance between the exposed objects, their size, and shape.

Von Schiller's Experiments. Von Schiller demonstrated that factors of organization determine the selection in potentially ambiguous patterns. Starting from a pattern like that of Fig. 1 he introduced all sorts of modifications by which he varied the distance, the quality and the shape of the exposed figures, and the pattern of the whole arrangement. He found the same laws operative for selection of stroboscopic motion that Wertheimer discovered for the organization of stationary forms. Thus he demonstrated the factors of proximity and equality, and showed at the same time that difference in brightness is more effective than difference in colour, a result which adds new weight to our finding that brightness differences have a stronger organizing power than mere colour differences. The factor of equality has, in these experiments, a very special aspect. Supposing in Fig. 1 the dots a_1 and d_2 to be dark blue, b_1 and c_2 light red. Then, if the motion follows the factor of equality, the blue point remains blue and the red red during the motion, whereas if stroboscopic motion were to occur in the counter-clockwise direction, the blue point would become red, the red one blue. This would involve a *change* of the total figure, and figures resist such changes. Therefore equality may produce a motion contrary to the factor of proximity, and this motion will be the stronger, the greater the number of aspects of equality (colour, brightness, size, and shape) that are employed. In extreme cases the direction may follow equality even when the lines of the cross intersect each other at an angle of 15°, so that the motion takes place through an angle of 75°, the

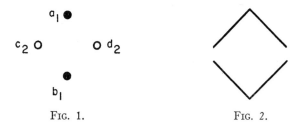

FIG. 1.   FIG. 2.

enormous superiority of the smaller angle being over-compensated by the equality factors. This resistance against change, together with the factor of the shortest path, results under proper conditions in tri-dimensional motion. If one exposes alternately the two forms of Fig. 2, then the motion most frequently perceived is that of a rotation round the horizontal axis of symmetry through the third dimension, less frequently a motion in the plane of the figure round a vertical axis, and quite rarely a down-up-down motion with distortion of the forms during the motion (Steinig, von Schiller). A last general law relates to the ensuing path; the tendency to make the total path (of all moving parts) as simple and well shaped as possible could be demonstrated in cases where this factor conflicted with equality factors.

....

On Constancy of Visual Speed*[,1]

Hans Wallach

When investigating the constancy of visual speed J. F. Brown[2] discovered what he called the transposition principle of velocity. In his account the constancy of visual speed and the principle of transposition occur as unrelated facts. This paper attempts to show that constancy of visual speed can be understood as a consequence of the transposition principle.

When objects which move with the same objective velocity are presented to the resting eye at different distances one perceives them as moving with approximately equal speed, although the displacements of their retinal images per unit of time vary in inverse proportion to the distance. This is what we call the constancy of visual speed. Its formal similarity to the constancy of size is obvious. Two identical objects presented at different but moderate distances from the eye have almost equal phenomenal sizes, although the linear extensions of the corresponding images are inversely proportional to the distances at which the two objects are presented to the eye. It seems plausible to assume that constancy of visual speed is simply a consequence of size constancy. One might argue that visual speed depends not on the length through which an image passes on the retina per unit of time but on the visual extension through which the object moves. Since the latter extension remains approximately constant even if its objective size is projected from different dis-

---

* From *Psychol. Rev.*, 1939, **46**, 541-552. Pp. 541-548 reprinted by permission of the author and publisher.

[1] The writer wishes to express his appreciation to Professor Wolfgang Köhler and also to Dr. Richard S. Crutchfield for their aid in preparation of this paper.

[2] J. F. Brown. Ueber gesehene Geschwindigkeiten. *Psychol. Forsch.*, 1927, **10**, 84-101. Also J. F. Brown, The visual perception of velocity. *Psychol. Forsch.*, 1931, **14**, 199-232.

tances and therefore with varying retinal size, the constancy of visual speed seems to follow without any further assumptions. This was indeed the reasoning which led J. F. Brown to his investigation of the constancy of speed. His actual observations, however, did not entirely confirm this view. While with moderate distances and under otherwise favorable conditions size constancy is almost absolute, constancy of speed proved to be considerably less perfect. When two objects moved at different distances from the eye, the objective velocity of the more distant object had to be distinctly greater, if the two phenomenal speeds were to appear as equal. Brown concluded that the constancy of speed cannot simply be deduced from the constancy of size. He therefore began a thorough investigation of "the factors that condition phenomenal velocity."

In his experiments Brown had his observers compare the speeds in two movement-fields which from experiment to experiment differed in various respects. Probably his most important finding is the transposition principle, which he established in experiments in which the two movement-fields differed only with respect to their size, being transposed in all their linear dimensions in a certain proportion. A movement-field consisted of an opening in a black cardboard screen and black dots of equal size moving through this opening on a white background. The dots were pasted on a roll of white paper running over two moving drums which were hidden by the screen. The drums were far enough apart so that only a flat surface was visible through the opening. The field in the opening was uniformly illuminated. The surface of the paper was smooth so that no cues of its motion could be obtained, except from the dots. The observer was to compare successively the speed with which the dots in two such movement-fields passed through their respective openings. In one of the fields the velocity was variable and could be stepped upwards or downwards under the direction of the observer until the speed in the two movement-fields appeared to be the same. Then the velocities were measured and their quotient was computed. The movement-fields were placed far enough apart so that only one could be seen at a time.

In one of these experiments, for instance, the movement-fields were transposed in a ratio 2 : 1, *i.e.* all the linear measures in one of the moving fields, namely the size of the opening, the diameter of the dots and their distance from one another, were twice as large as the same measures in the other moving field. After the objective velocities were so adjusted that the phenomenal speed in the two movement-fields was the same, the objective velocity in the larger field (A) was found to be almost twice as great as in the smaller field (B). Where V_A is the velocity in A and V_B the velocity in B when phenomenal equality is attained, $\dfrac{V_A}{V_B}$ was found to be 1.94 (average for 7 observers).[3] When the spatial transposition of the two movement-fields was 4 : 1, the speeds in the two fields were judged to be equal when the ratio of the objective velocities was 3.7 (average for 5 observers).[4] Thus the objective velocity in the 4 times larger field A was approximately 4 times as great as was that in the smaller field B, when visually both movements seemed to have the same speed. On the basis of these results Brown formulated the principle of velocity transposition: If a movement-field in a homogeneous surrounding field is transposed in its linear dimensions in a certain proportion, the stimulus velocity must be transposed in the same proportion in order that the phenomenal speed in both cases be identical.

The velocity ratios actually measured by Brown departed significantly from the figures called for by this principle, particularly when the difference in the dimensions of the two movement fields was still larger. When the transposition was in the proportion 10 : 1, the ratio of the velocities was 8.22 [5] (average for 4 observers; cf. below for additional results). Still these various departures from the theoretically expected values seem very small when we compare them with the enormous effects of the transposition phenomenon which were actually found. In the last mentioned case with a transposition of 10 : 1 where the departure from the expected value was 18 per cent, the actually measured effect of the transposition phenomenon was as high as 722 per cent.

In a quite similar way Brown had previously determined to what degree constancy of speed is actually realized. Two identical movement-fields were placed at different distances from the observer and the ratio of their velocities was varied until the speeds in the

[3] J. F. Brown. Ueber gesehene Geschwindigkeiten. *Psychol. Forsch.,* 1927, 10, 91, Table 5.
[4] *Ibid.,* p. 92, Table 8; also J. F. Brown, The visual perception of velocity. *Psychol. Forsch.,* 1931, 14, 216.
[5] J. F. Brown. The visual perception of velocity. *Psychol. Forsch.,* 1931, 14, 216.

two fields seemed to be equal. The movement in the more distant field was then 1.12, 1.15, and 1.21 times faster than the other, where the ratio of the distances from the observer was 1 : 3.3, 1 : 6.6 and 1 : 10 respectively.[6] Perfect constancy, of course, would have yielded in each case the ratio 1 instead of the listed quotients. Again, the actually found figures depart only little from the values to be expected for perfect constancy, when we compare them with the values which we should find if phenomenal speed were proportional to the velocities on the retina. On the other hand the departure from ideal constancy is here significantly larger than the departure which size constancy shows, a difference great enough to justify Brown's conclusion that constancy of speed cannot be deduced from size constancy.

We are thus facing an apparently paradoxical state of affairs. On the one hand we find a speed constancy of high degree, when speeds in movement-fields at different distances from the eye are compared; on the other hand the transposition experiments show that at a constant distance objective velocities may appear equal when one is as much as 8 times faster than the other. The fact that the reported transposition experiments were done under unnatural darkroom conditions affords no comfort. When Brown repeated the experiments with daylight illumination so that the continuity of the spatial framework was plainly given, he obtained for the same ratios of transposition, namely 2 : 1, 4 : 1 and 10 : 1, the velocity ratios 1.57, 2.71 and 6.17.[7] Even under these conditions of adequately structured visual field the transposition phenomenon remains striking.

In an intricate state of affairs like this the first thing to do is to examine closely the immediate stimulus situation. It is in the present case represented by the retinal images of the movement-fields. In a transposition experiment the retinal images of the two movement-fields bear to each other the same proportion as the objective movement-fields themselves, and the rates of the shifting dots on the retina are also proportional to the objective velocities. In the constancy experiment the situation is different in that here the movement-fields are presented at different distances from the eye, and the retinal images have different sizes, although they correspond to objectively identical fields. More specifically, their dimensions are

---

[6] *Ibid.*, 208, Table 1.
[7] *Ibid.*, 215, Table 7.

inversely proportional to the distances at which the corresponding movement-fields are presented. When, for instance, of two identical movement-fields, A is presented at 2 m. distance and B at 4 m. distance, the image of A is linearly twice as large as the image of B. Let us assume for the moment that constancy of speed is perfect, so that the speed in the fields A and B would seem to be the same when the objective velocities are equal. Since displacements in A and B produce retinal displacements which are twice as large in the case of A as they are in the case of B, phenomenal speeds are equal when the *retinal velocity in A is twice as great as that in B.* Let us now consider a case of the transposition phenomenon under the assumption that the principle of transposition also holds perfectly. If A' be a movement-field twice as large in all dimensions as B' and if both be presented at the same distance from the eye, the retinal image of A' is twice as large as that of B'. According to the transposition principle, the phenomenal speed in both fields is the same when the objective velocity in A' is twice as great as in B'. This being the case, *the velocity in the retinal image of field A' is also twice as great as is that in the retinal image of B'.* We thus find that the two different experimental situations yield essentially the same processes *on the retina.* The constellations of phenomenal equality in the constancy experiment on the one hand and in a transposition experiment on the other hand, both referred to the retina, are exactly alike. Thus, if we apply the principle of transposition *to the retinal images* of the two movement-fields in a constancy experiment, this principle leads to equality of phenomenal speed, *i.e.,* to just the fact which is commonly called constancy of speed. In this manner constancy of speed can be explained without any further hypothesis. Incidentally, in this explanation there is no reference to constancy of size. *The transposition principle alone, if applied to retinal images and retinal displacements, yields constancy of visual speed.*

In this connection, it may be useful to give the transposition principle another formulation. Velocity is usually measured as displacement per unit of time. We then may say: In movement-fields of identical shape and different dimensions the phenomenal speed is the same when the displacements per unit of time are equal fractions of the respective openings. Or simply: In transposed movement-fields, the perceived speeds are the same when the *relative* displacements are equal. Since in a transposition experiment the retinal images of the movement-fields have the same size proportions as the actually presented movement-fields, the principle applies directly to the retinal images. On the other hand, if in a constancy experiment the distance of a field A from the eye is half that of an identical field B, the retinal image of A is linearly twice as large as that of B. According to our principle, the two images will again yield the same phenomenal speed when the retinal displacements per unit of time cover equal fractions of their respective movement-fields on the retina. What does this mean in objective physical terms? The very problem of constancy of speed arises from the fact that the same physical displacement causes different retinal displacements, depending upon the objective distance of the movement-field. More concretely, the retinal displacements are inversely proportional to the distance of the field. But, as I just mentioned, the retinal image of the field itself is also linearly in inverse proportion to the distance. Consequently the retinal displacement per unit of time remains a constant fraction of the retinal movement-field when in objectively identical fields the same objective velocity is given at varying distances. Thus, from the point of view of the transposition principle, the condition for constant phenomenal speed is fulfilled precisely when objective circumstances are those of constancy of speed.

Actually, constancy of speed is not perfect. But the results of transposition experiments, too, fall somewhat short of exact proportionality as shown by the figures that have been quoted. In the case of the transposition phenomenon, Brown attributes the departures from the ideal values to defective homogeneity of the surrounding fields. Although as a rule the transposition experiments are performed under darkroom conditions, the illumination of the movement-fields themselves somewhat lightens the surroundings. That inhomogeneity of the surrounding fields reduces the transposition phenomenon is one of Brown's well-established results. He reports 3 series of transposition experiments under different conditions of illumination. We shall quote here only the results which he obtained with a transposition ratio of 10 : 1. They are representative for the trend in the 3 series. One experiment was made in daylight illumination, and gave the velocity ratio $\frac{V_A}{V_B}$ 6.17, where V_A refers to the 10 times larger field. Another experiment was done in a dark room, but the illumination of the movement-fields somewhat lightened the surroundings of the fields. This had a definite effect on the result, as Brown points out conclusively.[8] $\frac{V_A}{V_B}$ was here 6.83. In the third series the illumination of the movement-fields "was cut down considerably so that the surrounding fields approached homogeneity." The ratio here obtained was as high as 8.22. Indeed the departure from the ideal ratio (which would here be 10) is doubled when the observation is made with daylight illumination (6.17 as against 8.22). Brown was able to obtain a further decrease in proportionality. He covered the two cardboards in which the openings of the movement-fields were cut with a wallpaper which showed a regular geometric pattern. He then repeated the experiment, using an objective transposition ratio of 4 : 1, and of course daylight illumination. The resulting velocity ratio now was approximately 2, whereas the same pair of movement-fields gave a ratio of 2.7 when, again in daylight, a homogeneous black cardboard surrounded the movement-fields.[9]

This experiment clearly demonstrates the manner in which an inhomogeneous environment influences the velocity ratio. Such an environment disturbs the simple proportionality of the movement-fields. Phenomenal speeds are equal when the displacements per unit of time are the same in proportion to the dimensions of their respective fields. If both fields are surrounded by the same pattern, a common framework is introduced which will tend to equalize conditions and thus to reduce the influence of transposition. In the case of the ordinary daylight experiment the outer edge of the two equal cardboards is introduced as such a common framework.

---

[8] *Ibid.,* 216, discussion of curve *b.*
[9] *Ibid.,* 218.

SELECTION 28

∙∙

*Causality and Activity**

A. MICHOTTE

IN ORDER TO UNDERSTAND perception of causality, the first thing to do is to try to produce some characteristic perceptions of causation experimentally and to determine their conditions empirically. Naturally we started by examining the classical case of the collision of two bodies. From our first experiments we came to the conclusion, important from the theoretical as well as from the technical point of view, that the perception of causality is not necessarily connected with the use of "real," solid objects. One can produce perceived causation in a very convincing fashion, using forms reduced to objects without apparent thickness, in simple colored forms, even to images projected on a screen. This can be done even when the observers know perfectly well what is going on. This made experimentation easier, and permitted us to perform a great variety of experiments. In these there was systematic variation of the color, size, and form of the objects; the speed and the direction of their movements; the amplitude of their trajectories, and the temporal interval between "action" and "reaction"; etc.

It is possible to make the perception of causality appear or disappear at will, and to compare directly the cases in which it occurs with those in which it does not. As will be seen, the study of these cases makes it possible to detect the intervention of laws that are very close to those of the perception of form, and thus to join the perception of causality to previously known phenomena in this area. It also permits the categorical exclusion of any attempt to reduce this perception to a "projection" into things, to a result of the

---

* A slightly abridged translation by Michael Wertheimer of pp. 16-24 of Michotte, A., *La perception de la causalité* (*The perception of causality*). (2nd Ed.). Louvain, Belgium: Editions "Erasme," Publications Universitaires de Louvain, 1954. Translated and printed by permission of the author and Methuen and Co., publishers of the English edition, translated by T. R. Miles and E. Miles. London: Methuen, to appear.

efficacy of our internal activities, or to a secondary "interpretation" based on past experience and on acquired knowledge.

With these problems resolved, the task presented itself of "understanding" the phenomenon, making a theory for it, trying to find the particular conditions necessary for its production, and demonstrating definitely the elementary and primitive character of perceptions of causation.

For this purpose we have systematically utilized the method of *genetic analysis*. Essentially this consisted of discovering the stimulus conditions leading to perception of causality, simplifying them in various ways, and comparing the corresponding percepts with those given by the complete experiment. One can see how these percepts differ and how they resemble each other, and one can pursue in this way, step by step, the genesis of the perception of causation. It can be determined *what* it was, among the various conditions of stimulation, that induced the presence of these perceptual characteristics which originally seemed exclusively a property of the perceptions of causation.

In short, the aim of this analysis was to discover the related experiences involved in the perception of causation and eventually to find by this means the manifestations of simpler phenomena, even though these simpler phenomena are more or less modified in the sense of being occasionally unrecognizable by simple inspection in the full experience.

This method of analysis brings into the psychological domain of perception the methods used in all the comparative sciences, e.g., comparative anatomy. Just as the latter science tries to discover the "significance" of rudimentary organs and to relate them to completely developed organs by following the different stages of evolution, so in the domain of perception it is possible to follow the evolution of phenomena, and to recognize their homology under the apparently very different aspects that they can assume. Further, just as one arrives by this procedure at an "understanding" of a rudimentary organ and resolves the enigma it presents, so one can "understand" the nature of the perception.

Even if we are actually after the double aim sketched above, the experimental researches themselves are not necessarily distinct. Experiments intended to determine the conditions of the appearance of perception of causation are in general also those it is convenient to perform from the point of view of genetic analysis.

Two fundamental experiments are at the basis of this work; they involve the following procedures:

Exp. 1. The observer is placed at a distance of 1.50 meters from a screen with a slot in it 150 mm long and 5 mm high. Immediately behind this slit is a uniform white background on which two squares, 5 mm on each side, are visible. A red one is at the center of the slot; the other is black and is 40 mm to the left of the first. The black square object is referred to as A, and the red square object as B. The subject fixates object B. At a given moment, object A starts moving and travels towards object B at a speed of about 30 cm/sec. It stops at the moment it makes contact with B, while the latter now starts moving in turn and moves away from A, sometimes at the same speed and sometimes at a noticeably slower speed, e.g., at 6 or 10 cm/sec., the latter is preferable. It then stops, after having covered a distance of 2 cm or more, depending on the adopted speed.

A large number of experiments cited in this work will be described in terms of this one. When not otherwise indicated, the speeds of the two objects are the same.

The values of the speeds mentioned in connection with various experiments correspond to conditions we have actually used. However, there is nothing special about these exact values; that is to say, a margin of several cm/sec in no way affects the obtained results except in the case of very slow movements.

The result of this experiment is perfectly clear: the observers see object A push object B and *drive it, throw it forward, cast it, give it impulsion*. The perception is clear; it is *A that makes B proceed, that produces* its movement.

This experiment, as well as the following, has been done with a large number of subjects (several hundred of all ages), and all have given analogous descriptions, with the exception of one or two who, observing in an extremely analytical way, said they perceived two successive movements, simply coordinated in time. The same experiment has been repeated hundreds of times on certain subjects and their perception of causality remained intact.[1]

---

[1] It sometimes happens that the perception of causality does not appear on the first trial of the experiment, especially when it is performed with "new" subjects, unaccustomed to observation under the artificial conditions of the laboratory. These subjects do not, however, have the impression of a plain coordination of the two movements; instead they are "mixed up" and don't become aware of what is happening; their impression is chaotic and unor-

Exp. 2. Everything is set up in exactly the same way as for the preceding experiment except that object A continues its course without change in speed after having reached object B. The latter starts moving in turn, at the same speed as A, from the instant of contact. The two objects thus remain juxtaposed during their common movement and in combination constitute a two-colored rectangle, which traverses a distance of 3 or 4 cm before stopping.

Here one has the perception that object A *carries along* object B, that it *takes it with it,* that it *picks it up in flight,* or, under other conditions of speed and size of the objects, that it *pushes it forward.* The perception of causality is once again evident: it is *A that makes B move, which produces* B's displacement.

These are the two standard causality experiments; they are called, respectively, the launching effect and the carrying effect.[2]

In the case of both of these experiments, the production of the movement is thus directly experienced. There is no question whatever of an inference, nor of a "meaning" added to a perception of movement; in other words, the "given" is not a simple representation or a symbol of causality. Just as stroboscopic movement, psychologically speaking, is not the "symbol" of a movement, but *is* a phenomenal movement, so perceived causality *is* a phenomenal causality.

Indeed, a movement perceived at the cinema could evidently "stand for" the movement of a so-called "real" object, but this is a perceived movement which stands for another movement, in the same sense in which a form designed on a canvas can represent the

---

ganized. However, several trials suffice for the spontaneous establishment of a structuring in the direction of causality.

This delay in perceptual organization has no theoretical importance of any kind, for it is manifestly connected with the special conditions and unusual character of the experiment, and perhaps most of all, with the small size of the objects. Small size has a great influence on structural organization in cases of imperfect fixation. One can completely eliminate the delay by doing the experiment with stimuli projected on a screen which permits the presentation of stimulus objects of any dimension whatsoever. The perception of causation then appears at once.

[2] This term "effect" is used by physicists to designate certain particular facts, such as the Thompson effect, etc. It is used here in the same sense. As a matter of terminology it helps to avoid any misunderstanding and to make it clear that it is a matter of a phenomenal given *sui generis.* Thus we will speak of a separation effect in order to distinguish the specific perception of "separation" from the perception of simple movement which can correspond to an actual separation in the field, but without the objects being seen as related to one another.

form of a "real" object and, similarly causation perceived at the cinema "stands for" a "causal" influence of a "real" object on another "real" object. From the psychological point of view the experience in these experiments is of one phenomenal causality representing another.

The specific character of experienced causality is particularly well illuminated when one slightly modifies experiments 1 and 2 by introducing an interval of a fifth of a second or more between the two phases of the experiment (that is, between the moment object A joins object B and when B begins moving in turn, whether accompanied by A or not), and then directly compares the perceptions experienced with and without an interval.

The presence of the interval makes the perception of causality disappear totally; one sees A approach B, collide with it, and immobilize itself next to it, so that now they constitute a block, a two-colored rectangle. Then, one observes a new scene, independent of the preceding one: in the case of experiment 1, B separates itself from A and moves away from it; and in the case of experiment 2, the two-colored block simply starts moving as a block, as a "whole."

The result of the comparison is striking, and all observers agree that the perceptions are radically different. On the one hand, there are two intrinsically linked events, of which one "gives rise to" the other; and on the other hand, two sharply separate events which occur successively, and neither of which presents the slightest causal characteristics.

This last point deserves to be emphasized, for isolated phases could, a priori, correspond with various causal influences. The approach of A towards B could produce the impression that A is attracted by B; its stopping at the moment of contact could give the impression that B is an obstacle which hinders the continuation of A's movement; and the separation in the second phase, the impression that B is thrust forth by A; etc. In fact, nothing like this occurs; not only is there no perception of causality whatsoever, but not even the slightest tendency of a causal "interpretation."

On the other hand, isolated phases do not produce simple experiences of movement or displacements in space. They present the remarkable characteristics of "drawing nearer" and of separation. In addition, they have fundamentally and undeniably the quality of *activity*, which must be discussed.

This requires some explanation. The term "activity" actually is frequently used in psychological writing but unfortunately in different senses. As it is used here it is not a matter of a certain liveliness in the movement, nor of an impression of agitation, nor of an impression of tension and of excitation in the well-known sense of Wundt's theory. By speaking of activity in connection with the preceding experiments, we mean that one *sees the object act,* sees it *do something.* This is very different from the perception of a simple displacement, and even the most naive observers often make a distinction between the two in a clearcut manner.

Naturally it is difficult to fix the point at which perception of simple movement passes over into perception of activity, and one could discuss indefinitely the legitimacy of applying the term "activity" to such movements. This is an irrelevant question, for the essential fact is that observers spontaneously separate the cases, and further, the activity occurs with extremely marked differences. It is of secondary importance whether at the lower limit the difference is simply one of degree or one of quality.

In the experiments discussed here and at the speeds which we have employed,[3] perception is that A "goes toward B," that it *collides* with it, that it *strikes* it and unites itself with it; or else that B leaves A, that it *separates* from it, occasionally that it *flees* from it.[4]

As an alteration of conditions, A may be made to return to its point of departure immediately after reaching B while B remains immobile. This sequence is repeated regularly. Providing that speeds are appropriate, then the perception becomes that A *hits* B, *hammers* it, or *pounds* it. This is perceived as much more accentuated activity.

In the launching and carrying experiments, the perception of activity is still more salient, and finally approaches its maximum in the case of movements like creeping or swimming. These movements can be produced in a schematic form and under controllable conditions; the effect is surprisingly striking.

Thus activity is a phenomenal characteristic *sui generis.* This is

---

[3] This is important.

[4] Let us be clear that the perception of activity is obviously connected with the whole perceptual experience. The mobile and the immobile objects must be integrated into the same "whole." This occurs in the most "naive" observational attitude. On the other hand, an "analytical" attitude which results in the isolation of the mobile object necessarily makes the characteristic of activity disappear and substitutes the perception of a simple movement.

a most interesting fact, for if introspection on internal processes cannot bring any decisive evidence on this point of the various effects discussed here, it is evidently very different in the case of observations of external stimuli, where the experimental conditions can be modified systematically, and which are repeatable by any number of subjects.

The question is equally important from our particular point of view, for activity and causality are often confused by psychologists. It is truly a matter of two different conditions of appearance. The conditions which give rise to the perception of activity are simpler and in general easier to realize than those of causality. In fact, they are involved each time there is a perception of causality; this is why all cases of causality are also cases of activity, while the inverse is not true.

This distinction gives rise to certain difficulties. It might be supposed that if one perceives that an object "does something," this necessarily implies causation. It might be argued that from a phenomenal point of view even in the cases we have cited as examples of "activity" without causation there nonetheless exists a perceived cause and its effect.

Thus, in the collision example, it seems quite evident that the contact of the objects is an event distinct from the movement which brought them together and that it is the result of the movement. Must one not therefore consider the movement of A towards B as the cause of the collision? And yet observers refuse to admit that here they have a perception of causality comparable to that which is given them by the launching experiment. They are demonstrably incapable of answering when one asks them if there is cause and effect, and what is cause and what effect. The movement of A does not *produce* the collision, in the same sense as the collision produces the eventual movement of B.

The key to the enigma is provided by the following considerations. When one proceeds in an analytic and abstractive manner, as we have just been doing, one can rationally distinguish two successive events: the movement and the contact. But in reality there are not *two events;* there is but one which develops progressively. The collision is not limited to the fact of contact by the objects; it constitutes a *process,* of which the movement and the contact are both integral parts. This process evolves. It begins by an approach which, during its course, steadily ties the two objects more intimately together and, in its final stage, ends in their immediate union with a welding together. Perhaps at that moment there is a qualitative jump which is quite abrupt, but in any case, this union is simply the culmination, the ultimate phase of progressive changes which go on. The whole is *one* gradual development.[5]

Furthermore, when observers use expressions like "A gives a blow to B," they in no way intend to mean by this that it is the movement of A which gives a blow to B, for the "blow" manifestly includes the movement. Nor do they intend to mean that object A is the cause of the blow, which would be reduced to saying that it is the cause of its own movement. They simply want to indicate, as is easy to understand with a little thought, that object A executes the *operation of hitting*.[6]

This action belongs to object A; it is its "own way of being" at that moment; A is the sole executor of it. As for object B, it takes no active part whatever in the process, and its role is limited to serving as a point of reference for the process. Further, the operation is closed and complete; it demands no sequel and has none. The perception of causation could not arise under these conditions, for it requires the participation of object B in the process to carry out one of its phases.

---

[5] The unity of the process is still more apparent in the inverse case of the separation of objects, for it is evident that their dissociation could in no way be considered the cause of the subsequent movement, since it is quite distinct from this movement. The dissociation is only the aspect the movement takes on during its first stage.

[6] The expression "gives a blow" is in reality ambiguous. It could correspond, as in the present case, with merely exercising an activity, but it can also designate a case of causality, when the word "blow" is used in the sense of a deformation, of a wound, or even of pain induced by the collision. Here there is thus a clear distinction between the cause and the effect.

■■

The Physiological Control of Judgments of Duration: Evidence for a Chemical Clock[*][1]

HUDSON HOAGLAND

ONE'S ABILITY to estimate time correctly is often surprising. It is frequently possible to waken oneself within a few minutes of a time decided upon before going to sleep (5). Experiments involving the wakening of sleeping subjects and having them guess the time have shown an accuracy of ±15 minutes (3). These facts, along with our normal waking estimations of duration, call for a timing process of considerable accuracy.

It has been suggested that the pulse or the respiration may serve as a clock which becomes correlated with our conventional time scale, but evidence for this is unconvincing. For an experimental approach to this problem cf. Goudriaan (12).

In recent years investigators have shown that rhythmic fluctuations of electrical potential occur in groups of cells in respiratory centers of the nervous system. These fluctuations produce bursts of nerve impulses over efferent nerve fibers. The basic activity has been shown to be quite independent of afferent control (1, 2, 4). The relation of temperature to the rhythmic execution of creeping movements in poikilothermous animals, and of such rhythmic phenomena as the stridulations of crickets, earlier led Crozier and Stier (8) to suggest that the particular mechanism underlying each of these effects is of the nature of an irreversible chemical reaction in

---

* From the *J. gen. Psychol.*, 1932, **9**, 267-287. Pp. 267-274 reprinted by permission of the author and the publisher.

[1] The expenses of this work have been defrayed in part by a grant from the Permanent Science Fund of the American Academy of Arts and Sciences.

cells of the nervous system. The frequency of the emission of bursts of efferent impulses was assumed to be directly proportional to the velocity of the underlying reaction. It is interesting that similar suggestions were made by Crozier and Stier (8, 9) to account for rhythmic respiratory activity on the basis of the temperature analysis before direct discoveries of rhythmic fluctuation of electrical potentials within respiratory centers were made.

The multimodal frequency distribution curves of temperature characteristics found in the study of many biological processes (6, 7, 14) imply the existence of a limited number of catalytic substances involved in the control of rates of a wide variety of physiological mechanisms including the emission of repetitive discharges of impulses from nerve centers. The values of μ, the temperature characteristic or critical increment, for practically all known observations exhibit prominent modes at 8, 11, 12, 16, 18, 20, 22, 24, and 32 thousand calories. Specific catalytic substances have been assigned to a few of these magnitudes, such notably as 16,000 for iron catalysis in respiratory systems, 11,000 for hydroxyl ion catalysis, and 20,000 for hydrogen ion catalysis (cf. 14, p. 828, for summary).

The repetitive discharge of nerve impulses from the lateral-line receptors of fishes (13), and the effect of temperature on the frequency of these impulses considered in the light of the foregoing facts, suggested the possibility of investigating the estimation of duration as a function of temperature. If our judgments of time depend upon an underlying chemical "master reaction," in, let us say, cells of the brain, modification of the internal body temperature might be expected to alter judgments of time intervals in a way consistent with the Arrhenius equation and might yield a significant temperature characteristic. Such a finding might even imply a specifically catalyzed, irreversible chemical mechanism controlling the consciousness of duration.

My wife, having fallen ill with influenza, was used in the first of several experiments. Without, in any way, hinting to her the nature of the experiment, she was asked to count 60 seconds to herself at what she believed to be a rate of 1 per second. Simultaneously the actual duration of the count was observed with a stopwatch. The reciprocal of the number of actual seconds occupied by the count was taken as a direct measure of the rate of the physiological process underlying the count.

Table 1 shows data of this experiment taken over a period of 48

TABLE 1

Temperatures (°F) in Order of Recording	Actual Seconds per Counted Minute	Means
103.0	34, 37, 39, 40	37.5
102.0	35, 37, 37, 35, 37, 36	36.0
99.6	44, 45, 48	46.0
99.0	44, 50, 47, 46, 53	48.0
100.0	44, 43, 47, 42, 42	43.5
97.4	52, 52, 51, 52, 54	52.0

hours and covering a temperature range of 36.3°C to 39.5°C. The temperatures were taken by mouth with a clinical thermometer. Averages of at least five judgments were obtained at each of the experimental temperatures. The shaded circles of Figure 1 show the results plotted according to the Arrhenius equation,

$$\log_e \frac{k_1}{k_2} = \mu/R\ (1/T_2 - 1/T_1),$$

where k_1 and k_2 are proportional to the velocity constants of an irreversible chemical reaction at the respective absolute temperatures T_1 and T_2, R is the gas constant, and μ is the temperature characteristic.

The temperature range of only 3.2°C is too short to enable one to say with certainty that the Arrhenius equation adequately describes the data, but for the range used the essentially linear relation between log rate and $1/T$ is apparent. The value of $\mu = 24,000$ calories falls within one of the major modal groupings of temperature characteristics found for a variety of rhythmic processes investigated in poikilothermous animals (6, 7, cf. 14).

The two shaded squares of Figure 1 are obtained in the manner just described but from another subject, a colleague and a professional psychologist, also ill with influenza. If it is assumed that the Arrhenius equation describes the data, and the points are connected by a straight line, the slope is found to be essentially the same for both subjects, although the absolute values of the judgments by the two subjects differed.

To eliminate the influence of pathological factors which might be involved, a student, also naïve as to the nature of the experiment, agreed to submit himself to diathermy treatment. The equipment necessary for this experiment was made available through the kindness of Dr. Clifton T. Perkins of the Worcester State Hospital. The subject, insulated from heat loss by wrapping, was exposed to a high frequency alternating current until his temperature (by mouth) registered 38.8°C. Foged (10) states, on the basis of evidence obtained by the insertion of thermocouples in the cerebrospinal fluid of hospital patients, that the temperature of the nervous system in man is normally identical with the general internal body temperature. At each of several temperatures the subject of my experiment was asked to estimate intervals of one minute by the method already described. The triangles of Figure 1 show the results. The three higher temperatures give points which, when connected, yield $\mu =$ 24,000 calories. The first point obtained at the lowest temperature

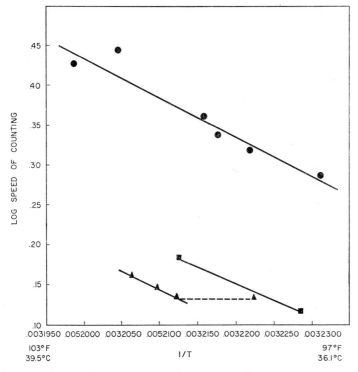

Fig. 1. Plot according to the Arrhenius equation of estimations of duration as a function of the internal body temperature. Three experiments of different subjects are indicated. For discussion see text.

is not on a line with the others of the plot. The subject was obviously nervous at the beginning of the experiment and his judgments
were at first quite erratic. Five to eight judgments were obtained
for each of the points.

After the completion of the foregoing experiments my attention
was called to a very interesting paper by François (11), from
Piéron's laboratory. He had been concerned with the effect of
temperature on estimations of duration and wished to determine a
value of the temperature coefficient, Q_{10}, for the time judgments.
He states that he was not concerned with theoretical considerations.
By methods about to be described he obtained Q_{10} values of 2.75 to
2.85. He points out that such values are of the order of magnitude
found for many physiological processes. The temperature coefficient,
Q_{10}, has been used extensively to describe effects of temperature
on various activities of organisms in attempts to interpret mechanisms underlying vital processes. Its value is, however, not constant over a given temperature range, its magnitude varying as
a function of temperature. It is without theoretical significance and
is valueless as an index of correlation of vital processes with physicochemical data. The temperature characteristic, μ, of the Arrhenius
equation does, however, furnish a theoretically meaningful basis for
such an analysis (6, 7, 8, 14).

François at first tested judgments of intervals in subjects as a
function of the normal diurnal rhythms of temperature fluctuation.
Temperature differences in his subjects, over nine- to ten-hour intervals, were sometimes as much as 0.8°C. The judgments were made
by having the subjects tap a telegraph key, operating a marker on a
kymograph drum, at rhythms requested by the experimenter. Mean
values of the cadences were obtained at each maximum and minimum
temperature. In another series of experiments the subjects were
asked to estimate metronome rhythms. Ten experiments on two subjects showed clearly a mean increase in the frequency of tapping the
key and an increase in the estimation of the cadence of the metronome with increased body temperature. The variability was large,
however. He next used short exposures to high frequency currents to
raise the temperatures of his subjects. In this way it was possible to
test the judgments at two temperatures, a degree apart, within half
an hour. With the diathermy technique much of the variability was
eliminated in the key-tapping procedure, although it remained
fairly high with the procedure in which the metronome was used.

Twenty-one experiments were made with three subjects using the former procedure. These experiments showed consistently an increase in the rhythm of tapping with an increase in body temperature, yielding the values of Q_{10} mentioned above. Very little correlation was found between the pulse rate and the judgments. In some experiments diathermy failed to increase the temperature but did increase the heart rate by as much as 20 per cent. Here, with the constant body temperature, the frequency of tapping was constant despite the increased pulse rate. The effect of diathermy treatment on the pulse was found to be very variable as compared to that on the rhythm of tapping.

Assuming that the Arrhenius equation describes these data, one may make a plot by connecting the mean high and low temperature-time judgment points by a straight line according to the equation. Figure 2 is such a plot in which the same large coordinates are used

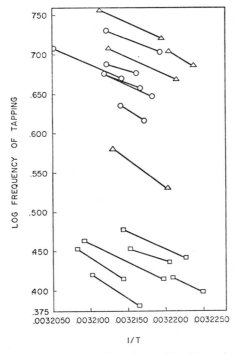

Fig. 2. Plot similar to Fig. 1 of data obtained by François (11) in which a different experimental procedure was employed from that used in obtaining the data of Fig. 1. For discussion see text.

as in Figure 1. The open circles, triangles, and squares represent three different subjects. Each of François' experiments involving the tapping of rhythms is represented by two points and their connecting line. Sixteen experiments on the three subjects are recorded in the figure. The slopes are seen to be surprisingly constant although the absolute rates, as determined by the ordinates, vary considerably, not only for different subjects but for different experiments with the same individual. The person indicated by the squares shows uniformly faster rhythms of tapping than either of the others but the effect of temperature on the rhythms is similar for all. The person indicated by triangles shows very large variation in his absolute judgments of time from day to day; it is as if his physiological clock were capable of fluctuations in speed over gross intervals of time. The unique nature of the clock is indicated, however, by the constancy of the effect of temperature as indicated by the uniform slopes of the lines.

Figure 3 shows a combined plot of the data of Figures 1 and 2. This plot was made by tracing each curve of Figures 1 and 2 in such a way that, while the same abscissas were used, the differences in the absolute values of the ordinates are eliminated. The ordinate scale is of the same size as that previously employed but the tracing paper was moved up or down and the points are brought together along the y axis to show the essential similarity of slopes of all the lines. The composite plot of Figure 3 yields a value of $\mu = 24,000$ calories.

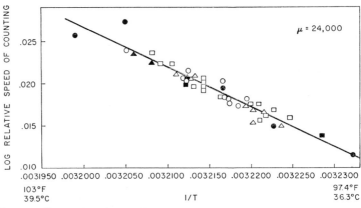

FIG. 3. Composite plot of data of Figs. 1 and 2 showing similarities of slopes (and hence μ values) for all of the experiments. For discussion see text.

These results are interesting since they imply the existence of a unitary chemical process probably irreversible in nature and perhaps catalyzed in a specific way. The fact that my results agree so well with those calculated from the data of François, of whose experiments I was unaware until after my calculations were completed, is worthy of note, especially since we employed different modes of evaluating the speed of judgments of time.

SUMMARY

1. Judgments of short durations vary with the internal body temperature.

2. The judgments of duration appear to be described by the Arrhenius equation for the short temperature range of $3.2°C$. A temperature characteristic of 24,000 calories is found for my own data and for those of François (11). These sets of data were taken independently and by the use of different experimental procedures.

3. The absolute judgments of time by the same subject may differ from day to day, but the effect of temperature on the time judgments is constant. It is suggested that judgments of short duration may depend immediately on the velocity of a particular continuous chemical reaction (clock) in the nervous system, probably irreversible in nature, and catalyzed in a particular manner corresponding to $\mu = 24,000$ calories.

REFERENCES

1. ADRIAN, E. D. Potential changes in the isolated nervous system of *Dytiscus marginalis. J. Physiol.*, 1931, **72**, 132-151.

2. ADRIAN, E. D., and BUYTENDIJK, F. Potential changes in the isolated brain stem of the goldfish. *J. Physiol.*, 1931, **71**, 121-135.

3. BORING, L. D., and BORING, E. G. Temporal judgments after sleep. In *Studies in psychology: Titchener commemorative volume.* Worcester, Mass.: Wilson, 1917, pp. 255-279.

4. BRONK, D. W., and FERGUSON, L. K. The nervous regulation of the respiratory movements of intercostal muscles. *Amer. J. Physiol. (Proc. Amer. Physiol. Soc.)*, 1933, **105**, 13.

5. BRUSH, E. N. Observations on the temporal judgment during sleep. *Amer. J. Psychol.*, 1930, **42**, 408-411.

6. CROZIER, W. J. On biological oxidations as a function of temperature. *J. Gen. Physiol.*, 1924-1925, **7**, 189-216.

7. CROZIER, W. J. The distribution of temperature characteristics for

biological processes; critical increments for heart rates. *J. Gen. Physiol.*, 1925-1926, **9**, 531-546.

8. CROZIER, W. J., and STIER, T. J. B. Critical thermal increments for rhythmic respiratory movements of insects. *J. Gen. Physiol.*, 1924-1925, **7**, 429-447.

9. CROZIER, W. J., and STIER, T. J. B. On the modification of temperature characteristics. *J. Gen. Physiol.*, 1925-1926, **9**, 547-559.

10. FOGED, J. La température du liquide céphalo-rachidien. *Acta psychiat. et neur.*, 1932, **7**, 125-133.

11. FRANÇOIS, M. Contribution à l'étude du sens du temps. La température interne, comme facteur de variation de l'appréciation subjective des durées. *Année psychol.*, 1927, **28**, 186-204.

12. GOUDRIAAN, J. C. Le rhythme psychique dans ses rapports avec les fréquences cardiaques et respiratoires. *Arch. néerl. de physiol.*, 1921, **6**, 77-110.

13. HOAGLAND, H. Quantitative analysis of responses from lateral-line nerves of fishes: II. *J. Gen. Physiol.*, 1932-1933, **16**, 715-731.

14. STIER, T. The rate of oxygen utilization by yeast as related to temperature. *J. Gen. Physiol.*, 1932-1933, **16**, 815-840.

Time Orientation and Social Class*

LAWRENCE L. LeSHAN

ONE OF THE MOST FRUITFUL AREAS of research in modern sociology has been the investigation of the various levels of social class in America. An extensive literature on this subject has arisen in the past ten years. Volumes such as Havighurst and Taba's *Adolescent Character and Personality* (7), Gardner and Davis' *Deep South* (4), and Warner, Meeker, and Eell's *Social Class in America* (10) have summed up some of the major studies.[1] Out of the vast amount of data collected, many of the important implications have been extracted and reported. However, in as rich and new a field as this, there are always new implications to be explored and tested.

This paper is an attempt to examine one of the possible differences between members of social classes in America. This variable might be termed "collective-ego-space-time" after Erickson (5). It concerns the perceived relationship of the individual and his goals in time. How far ahead is the time span with which the individual is concerned? What is the crucial time limit during which he will frustrate himself in order to attain a goal? Does he relate his behavior primarily to the far future, the immediate future, the present, or the past? Bateson has pointed out that this orientation seems to differ widely between Balinese culture and the culture of the (middle class) United States. There would be important implications in knowing if it differed in various classes within the United States itself.

---

* From *J. abnorm. soc. Psychol.*, 1952, **47**, 589-592. Reprinted by permission of the author and the publisher.

[1] Clear definitions of the various social classes may be found in any of the above-mentioned volumes. In the interest of space saving, these definitions are not included here.

THE HYPOTHESIS

The general hypothesis of this paper is that there are various temporal goal orientations in the various levels of social class. Very briefly, these temporal orientations may be described as follows:

1. In the lower-lower class, the orientation is one of quick sequences of tension and relief. One does not frustrate oneself for long periods or plan action with goals far in the future. The future generally is an indefinite, vague, diffuse region and its rewards and punishments are too uncertain to have much motivating value. In this social class, one eats when he is hungry; there are no regular meal hours and each member of the family takes food when he feels like it if food is available.

2. In the upper-lower, middle, and lower-upper classes, the orientation is one of much longer tension-relief sequences. As the individual grows older, he plans further and further into the future and acts on these plans. As an adult, he may start planning for retirement when he is in his twenties. In these classes, one eats at regular "clock" hours. One quickly learns to inhibit activity leading to the relief of a basic tension (food-getting behavior) until a watch shows that it is time to eat.

3. In the upper-upper class, the individual sees himself as part of a sequence of several or more generations, and the orientation is backward to the past. One eats at traditional hours and lives out the traditions set up in the past.

This hypothesis has been implied in many of the books and articles on social class. A few quotations may serve to demonstrate this.

. . . in a lower class family . . . the disciplinarian . . . is certain to believe that the way to make a child learn is to beat him. . . . It seems clear . . . that a child cannot be trained in this fashion to undergo the long periods of renunciation which the middle class ideal of socialization demands of him (2, p. 267).

Every individual in the upper class has a series of duties and privileges associated with . . . his direct lineal ancestors, symbols of the past (4, p. 84).

The greatest possible insult to an upper-upper class person is the defamation of his "original ancestor," the founder of his local line (4, p. 85).

Both upper-middle-class and lower-middle-class husbands and wives recognize the raising of a family as the primary function of their relationship, more important than the sexual enjoyment of their partners, their economic security, or their general physical comfort (4, p. 100).

EVIDENCES FROM CHILD-REARING PRACTICES

We would expect these various temporal orientations to be demonstrated in the techniques with which parents from these social classes train children. We would expect this for the double reason (*a*) that the parents themselves possess this orientation and (*b*) that we believe that children will, by and large, also have it when they mature. In studying training techniques as revealed in the various books and articles on social class, we find this expectation confirmed. In the third group (upper-upper) as postulated in this paper, we find training techniques such as: "What would your grandmother say?" or "Your grandfather would rather see you dead" (4, p. 98). In the second group (upper-middle, middle, and upper-lower), stress is on the future. Children are exhorted to do well in school, for example, by threats that they will not be able to get a good job, that they will not get a good spouse, or that they will not get into college (8). In the first group (lower-lower), training techniques are more in terms of immediate punishment and reward. Children are made to do (or stop doing) things by the threat that something will happen to them immediately if they do not obey (3, 4, 8). In this class, thumb-sucking and masturbation are stopped by threats of an immediate beating, physical punishment, or by physical restraint (3, p. 18). A reference to moral or developmental reasons for doing or not doing something is rarely if ever made.

In one lower-lower case studied (3, p. 44) a ten-year-old son has "found" some ice skates and brought them home. The father looks at them and says: "Now, listen, Johnny, I don't want you keepin' them if there's going to be any trouble with them."

This same case history of a lower-lower family was analyzed for the methods that the parents used to control the children. The interviewer became a close friend and confidant of the family and spent a great deal of time at their home. She observed very frequent attempts of the parents directly to make the child do, or not do, something. These can be broken down into categories as can be seen in Table 1. This table seems to indicate an orientation in the parents such as we have postulated, which one would suspect would be likely to produce a similar orientation in the children. Also of interest is the fact that 28 of the parental responses were unpredictable from the point of view of the child—as well as the point of view of the interviewer! As an example, we mention the following incident: The father had brought a three-year-old daughter some

TABLE 1. PARENTAL CONTROL METHODS IN A LOWER-LOWER CLASS
FAMILY, AN ANALYSIS OF THE ITEMS IN AN
UNPUBLISHED CASE STUDY (3)

Type of Control	Example	Number of Attempts Observed
1. Flat declarative statements	"Put down that bottle."	35
2. Immediate punishment or reward threatened	"You go back to bed or I'll beat you with this leather strap."	57
3. Reward or punishment to follow within 24 hours	(Taking a dirty toy from a child) "Wait until Tootsie comes home and we'll wash it and you can play with it."	7
4. Reward or punishment to follow within the week	(2 days before Xmas) "Santa Claus won't come if you're bad."	1
5. Reward or punishment after 1 week or at an indefinite time	"I'll never take you any place again."	1

candy cigarettes. The child pretended to smoke them, flicking off the ashes, etc. When she did this, the father took them away from her and spanked her for "putting on the dog."

Children of the lower-lower class soon learn that major changes in their lives often occur suddenly and unpredictably. The mother in the case history mentioned above describes the weaning of one child: "Yeah, one day she threw the bottle out of her crib and I gave it back to her and she didn't want it so I never gave it to her again" (3, p. 13). This is a far cry indeed from the careful, long-term weaning of the middle classes. With the lower-lower type of experience one might speculate that children would grow up not at all certain of the basic stability of the universe.[2]

Food, shelter, heat in the winter (and even personal safety) are also unpredictable. Food is present and eaten when father gets a pay check *if* he brings it home. There is never enough over a long period of time and one can never tell whether or not there will be food when he is next hungry.

[2] With such a frame of reference, planning for a distant future would not seem to be an intelligent procedure.

In the lower-lower group there seems to be a circular phenomenon at work. The parents' training is inconsistent because of their inability to work for long-range goals, and this prevents them from breaking out of the economic trap they are in. Economic pressures further decrease stability. Children who go through this training will also emerge unable to work for long-range goals and so on.

Other factors add to the inconsistency of training of children in the lower-lower class in relation to that of children in the middle and upper-upper classes. The lower-lower class child plays on the streets away from adult supervision. Here he is to a large degree at the mercy of his own impulses with reward or punishment following immediately on his actions. Rewards here may be in terms of motor activity, physical gratification, etc. The parents are at work or are usually unaware of what he is doing.

In the other social classes, the play situation tends to be quite different. Children play near the house or near the house of a neighbor and are, a large percentage of the time, under some adult supervision. Less often do both parents work and there is much more watching and controlling the children's play. Figuratively, they tend to play "in front of the house." The child has more training in controlling his own impulses because of the help in control he receives from older figures.

According to psychoanalytic theory, the individual must have a strong superego if he is to frustrate himself and renounce present pleasure for future gains. This is built up out of the child's image of the parents in his early years. It rewards him for self-control and punishes him for transgressions. In the second and third groups set up in this paper, the parents and families tend to remain constant for years at a time. In the first group, families are much more flexible: adults move in with other adults; children may be switched from one family to another for a while if this arrangement seems to be more convenient. Under this situation, it would be improbable that a strong and stable ego-ideal could be built up. There would be many shifting adults, all too inconsistent in their behavior for the child to build a model.

PROCEDURE

To test partially this time orientation hypothesis, the stories of 117 children of 8 to 10 years old were examined. These stories were told in response to the stimulus "Tell me a story." Seventy-four of the children were lower class and 43 were middle class. The groups were equated for age. The stories were examined in terms of the period of time covered by the action of the story. In line with the hypothesis, one might expect that the middle-class group would produce stories covering a longer time-period from beginning (the starting of action) to the end (final action) than would the lower-class group. This expectation was confirmed statistically (Table 2). A chi-square test indicated that the two groups were not from the same population insofar as this variable was concerned. There is a statistically significant difference between the length of time covered in stories told by children of these two social classes. If one accepts the hypothesis that in unstructured situations of this sort, individuals tend to project the world as they see it onto the stimulus, then our major hypothesis of different time orientations in different social classes is strengthened.

DISCUSSION

If our hypothesis of different time orientations for different social classes is valid, there are various implications which may be of importance, such as the need to think through again the problem of goals and methods in the public schools, and re-education in old age when a time span which includes planning for the future may lose its meaningfulness. It appears worth while to consider two such implications in a little more detail.

TABLE 2. LENGTH OF TIME COVERED BY ACTION OF STORIES TOLD BY 117 CHILDREN IN RESPONSE TO STIMULUS "TELL ME A STORY"

Class	Under 1 Hr.	1-12 Hrs.	12-24 Hrs.	1 Day- 7 Days	1-2 Wks.	2 Wks.- 1 Yr.	1 Yr. Plus
74 Lower-Class Children	44% (32)	32% (24)	5% (4)	8% (6)	5% (4)	4% (3)	1% (1)
43 Middle-Class Children	28% (12)	23% (10)	9% (4)	23% (10)	9% (4)	2% (1)	5% (2)
	$(df = 6)$				$(p = .001)$		

One of the trickiest problems in modern psychopathology has been the concept of the psychopath. Whether or not psychopaths exist, and if so what the symptoms and etiology are, has been discussed in a great many articles with no real agreement or even pragmatically useful results. The essence of the various definitions advanced seems to rest on two general symptoms: low frustration tolerance and marked hostility turned inward and/or outward. It may be of value to examine the psychopath category in terms of personal time orientation as discussed above. One might speculate that an individual raised in an environment where (a) reward and punishment generally follow immediately on action and (b) where these results are unpredictable a large part of the time, would have a low frustration tolerance. He would not have learned to act in terms of future reward and would, indeed, have learned the opposite since the future would be an unpredictable region and to work in terms of it would be nonsensical for him. Further, this orientation in a world that is primarily run on longer sequences might well produce conflicts, failures, and resulting hostility. This training factor has not, to the author's knowledge, been investigated and it may be that here lies one of the roots of psychopathy.

A further implication of the concept of personal time orientation is in the general area of the prevention of delinquency. A reform school will be neither a deterrent in the future nor a lesson from the past in an individual who has learned to respond only in terms of what is immediately present. It may well be that in order to control delinquency it will be necessary first to change the time orientations of the delinquents. At present, very little is known concerning the management of such learning and it would appear to be a fruitful subject for research.

CONCLUSION

The hypothesis that there are different personal time orientations in different social classes is advanced. Data are presented (a) from child-rearing practices in the various classes of American society and (b) from the greater time span of the action in stories told by middle-class children as compared with those told by lower-class children which tend to confirm this hypothesis. Some further implications of the hypothesis are discussed briefly.

REFERENCES

1. BATESON, G. Cultural determinants of personality. In J. McV. Hunt (Ed.), *Personality and the behavior disorders,* Vol. 2. New York: Ronald, 1944, pp. 714-735.
2. DAVIS, A., and DOLLARD, J. *Children of bondage.* Washington: American Council of Education, 1940.
3. DAVIS, A., and ERICKSON, M. An unpublished case study. The Committee on Human Development, Univer. of Chicago.

4. DAVIS, A., GARDNER, B. B., and GARDNER, M. R. *Deep South*. Chicago: Univer. of Chicago Press, 1941.
5. ERICKSON, H. Childhood and tradition in two American Indian tribes. In C. Kluckhohn and H. A. Murray (Eds.), *Personality*. New York: Knopf, 1949.
6. ERICKSON, MARTHA. Child rearing and social status. *Amer. J. Sociol.*, 1946, **52**, 3.
7. HAVIGHURST, R., and TABA, HILDA. *Adolescent character and personality*. New York: Wiley, 1949.
8. HOLINGSHEAD, A. B. *Elmtown's youth, the impact of social classes on adolescents*. New York: Wiley, 1949.
9. MOWRER, O. H., and ULLMAN, A. D. Time as a determinant in integrative learning. *Psychol. Rev.*, 1945, **52**, 61-90.
10. WARNER, L., MEEKER, MARCHIA, and EELLS, K. *Social class in America*. Chicago: Science Research Associates, 1949.

SELECTION 31

■■■

*Space Perception in the Chick**[*][†]

Eckhard H. Hess

Suppose we observe that members of a particular species of birds always sing the same song. Is the song of this species innate or is it learned through the young bird's imitation of its parents? Let us isolate some young of this species from the adults so that no opportunity for learning is allowed. Will the young sing the song of their species? If the species selected is the nightingale, we shall discover that the young birds do not sing in the same way that the adults normally do, showing that the song is ordinarily learned through imitation. If, on the other hand, we isolate young robins, we shall find that they still sing the song of their kind, indicating the existence of an innate ability.

Why does a duckling or a gosling tag along after its mother? Until recent years it was believed that the young of a species possessed an inborn capacity for following only their own parents. It has now been shown for many species that the young animal will become attached to other objects in place of the parent if those objects are present during a critical period shortly following its birth. A duckling may learn to follow a wooden decoy, a goose or even a human being if exposed to one of these objects instead of to its parent during this critical early period. Later it will follow that object in preference to its own mother.

Why is it important to know whether a certain behavior pattern is learned or innate? One reason is that once we have this information, we are well on our way to knowing under what circumstances the behavior can be changed. If it is learned, then we may alter the physical or psychological environment so that another behavior is

---

[*] From *Scientific American,* 1956, **195**, 71-80. Reprinted by permission of the author and the publisher.

[†] The drawings in this article were prepared for this volume by Dr. Hess.

learned in its place. If it is innate, we may not be able to modify the behavior unless we use the innate behavior pattern as a foundation upon which to build additional responses, so that the resulting composite behavior appears to be different.

Many psychologists believe that the ultimate aim of animal studies is to provide us with a better understanding of human behavior. Such an objective is not attained by generalizing from animal to human behavior—a practice of which comparative psychologists are commonly accused—although it is true that some hypotheses about man are occasionally suggested by the extension of behavioral trends observed in the progression from the lower to the higher animals. More likely, however, the understanding of human behavior is served through animal research in quite another fashion. That is to say, the animal laboratory is a testing ground for the evolution of techniques and the development of criteria which may ultimately be applied with ease and safety to humans.

If we can discover which of man's behaviors are learned and which are innate, we will know which ones may be readily changed and which can be modified, if at all, only within narrow limits. Such findings might explain why some experiences in an individual's early life affect his subsequent behavior whereas other early experiences apparently do not. We may learn how to create an environment in which desirable behaviors will be promoted and undesirable behaviors will be modified.

A further word should be said regarding innate and learned behavior. The simple fact that a behavior appears later than infancy does not necessarily mean that it is learned. It may represent the natural unfolding of innate processes occurring along with the individual's physiological development. We call this process maturation, and we may classify it as a special kind of innate behavior. Behavior which develops through maturation possesses, in all probability, the same resistance to modification that characterizes ordinary innate responses.

One problem which has for some decades been of interest to the comparative psychologist is the accurate localization of objects in space. When an organism first perceives the environment, can it accurately see where things are? A large number of experiments have been carried out on the development of pecking accuracy in chicks. The results, however, have been far from clear. Some investigators concluded that their experiments indicated a maturational process, others assumed that practice through trial and error led to this accuracy, and still others thought the entire process to be innately determined.

The experiments to be described were undertaken to ascertain whether a chick's visual perception of space—as measured through its accuracy in pecking at grain—depends upon learning or upon the maturation of an innate ability. One possible method for deciding this question would be to raise chicks to adulthood without permitting them the opportunity for normal visual experience and then expose them to a situation in which they might demonstrate their pecking ability. Prior to the experiment described here, experimenters who undertook this problem prevented young chicks from practicing the sensory-motor coordination involved in pecking by means of keeping them in dark enclosures or covering their heads with little hoods which masked their eyes but left their beaks free for eating. The results of these experiments were later laid open to question when it was suggested that in the absence of stimulation by light the eyes may fail to develop normally. Any inaccuracy in pecking might well have been the result of degeneration in the retina or the nerves.

To overcome this difficulty the author sought a method that would prevent normal visual experience and yet would not interfere with the normal physiological development of the eye. A solution to this problem was found in the technique of fitting the chicks' eyes with prismatic lenses which would displace the visual image to the right or to the left.

Suppose that a chick first sees the light of day wearing prisms which cause a displacement of the visual image seven degrees to the right. If the exact visual localization of objects in space is a totally learned ability, the chick's performance should be unaffected by the fact that it is wearing displacement prisms. When the chick sees a food object, it should start pecking but in a random fashion until, after trial and error, the object is eaten. Gradually, as sensory-motor associations are built up, the chick's accuracy should improve.

If, on the other hand, the chick is born with an innate ability to locate objects visually, the first pecks which such a chick directs toward objects seen through the displacement lenses should be about seven degrees to the right. Since the young chick starts its peck with its eyes about 25 to 30 millimeters away from the object, the actual displacement should be about 3 or 4 mm. with time and practice the chick might learn to correct for the displacement so that it would strike at objects seven degrees to the left of where they appeared to be. This, in fact, was the author's expectation.

In the actual experiment 28 Leghorn chicks were hatched in complete darkness and were immediately fitted with thin rubber hoods into which transparent plastic goggles had been inserted

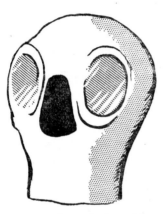

(Fig. 1). The hoods were placed over their heads quickly in such a subdued light that the animals had essentially no normal light experience. The goggles in the hoods of 10 of the chicks were flat pieces of plastic which produced no image displacement. These 10 were the control animals. Twelve of the chicks had hoods which were fitted with plastic prisms which displaced the whole visual field seven degrees to the right. Six of the animals wore lenses which caused a similar displacement of the visual field to the left.

Fig. 1. One of the rubber hoods fitted with flat prisms to displace the visual image.

All of the animals were returned to darkness for a period of about six hours so that they could become accustomed to the hoods. Then, when they were about one day old, all of the animals were tested for pecking accuracy. They were allowed to strike at small objects embedded in modeling clay. The targets were small brass nails, embedded so that they could not be dislodged by pecking. The modeling clay provided a simple means of recording the accuracy with which the chicks pecked at the nails. By photographing the dented clay after such a pecking session and then tracing the actual dispersion of pecks from a projected image of the negative, it was possible to get a clear picture of the accuracy or inaccuracy of the chicks as they were tested.

The pecks made by all of the chicks were scattered. There was, however, one fundamental difference in the performance of the control and experimental animals. In the control group the pecks were scattered about the target so that the target itself formed the center of the distribution (Fig. 2). For those chicks wearing lenses which

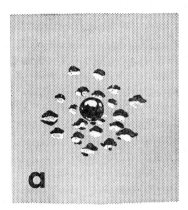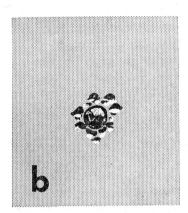

FIG. 2. Control chicks wearing hoods fitted with pieces of flat plastic were allowed to peck at a brass nail embedded in modeling clay. A chick one day old made the pattern at left; a chick four days old, the pattern at right. The patterns are centered on the nail.

displaced the visual field to the right, the pecks were similarly scattered, but they were centered about a point seven degrees to the right of the target. Similarly, the group whose lenses displaced their

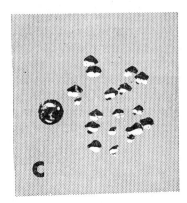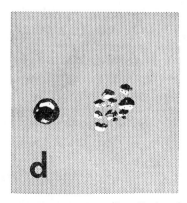

FIG. 3. Experimental chicks wore hoods fitted with prisms that displaced objects seven degrees to the right. A chick one day old made the pattern at left; a chick four days old, the pattern at right. The pecks are more tightly clustered but still displaced to right.

visual images to the left showed a scattering of pecks to the left of the target. Some pecks of chicks in all groups actually hit the target (Fig. 3).

Half of the control group and half of each of the two experimental groups were now placed in an enclosure in which grain had been loosely scattered on the floor. The other half of the three groups were placed in a box in which they had access to bowls of mash; accuracy in pecking was therefore not required. In the latter situation a chick which missed the grain at which it aimed would nevertheless hit other grains in the bowl almost every time it pecked. This was not true, of course, of those chicks which were pecking at individual grains scattered on the floor.

When the chicks were between three and four days old, they were tested again. The results showed a great increase in accuracy on the part of the control chicks: now their pecks clustered quite closely about the target. There was no detectable difference between the two subgroups of the control animals—those fed on scattered food and those fed on mash in bowls.

Among the animals wearing displacement prisms, improvement of a kind had also occurred. The pecks were clustered just as tightly as those of the controls, showing that increased accuracy had certainly been achieved. The centers of these clusters, however, were approximately 4 mm. to the right or to the left of the target, depending on which displacement glasses were worn by the experimental animal. Again there was very little difference in accuracy among the subgroups of experimental animals. But another difference was evident in the physical condition of the subgroups. Where the animals which had access to bowls of mash were as healthy as the control animals, the animals in the scattered grain situation were in poor physical condition and apparently would have died if they had been kept in the same situation. Two animals maintained in this situation died the following day.

We must conclude that the chick's visual apparatus for locating objects in space is innate and not learned. This conclusion is based on the fact that the chick wearing displacement prisms clustered its pecks about the spot where the object was seen. It did not simply peck at random until it struck the target.

Furthermore, the chick whose visual field was displaced appeared unable to learn through experience to correct its aim. Its only improvement was to increase the consistency of the distance by which it missed the target. Apparently the innate picture which the chick has of the location of objects in its visual world cannot be modified through learning if what is required is that the chick learn to perform a response which is antagonistic to its instinctive one.

The technique developed for the foregoing experiment seemed to offer an admirable opportunity for studying another aspect of bird vision—stereopsis, or binocular depth perception. The question to be answered was whether the bird possesses this capacity.

In man there is considerable overlap of the areas viewed by the two eyes. Since the pupils of the eyes are about two and a half inches apart, however, each eye gets a slightly different picture of the commonly shared view. In some way these two pictures are integrated in the brain so that objects viewed appear three-dimensional rather than flat.

In the chick, on the other hand, the eyes are at the sides of the head rather than at the front. Consequently, except for a relatively small area directly in front of the bird, the two eyes receive visual stimulation from different parts of the surroundings.

In man, optic fibers from each eye travel to both sides of the brain. In the bird this is not the case. The optic fibers from the chick's left eye presumably cross over completely to the right side of the brain and those from the right eye to the left side of the brain.

Essentially on the basis of these facts alone it was believed by some that the bird lacks binocular depth perception. In other words, it was thought that the bird's brain could not combine the two small overlapping images to produce an impression of depth or three-dimensionality. The bird's perception of depth and distance was believed to be entirely dependent upon monocular cues, *i.e.*, cues which can be utilized by one eye alone. One important monocular cue is received through the successive impressions of an object obtained by moving the head and viewing the object from various angles. Other monocular cues are the diminution of size with increased distance, the overlapping by nearer objects of more distant ones, and accommodation, or focus.

The author undertook the following experiment to determine whether the normal adult chicken uses binocular cues to localize objects in space. Rubber hoods were slipped over the heads of chickens six to eight weeks old. These hoods were fitted with prismatic lenses having their broad bases outward. If a man were to look through a similar, but larger, set of lenses, using binocular vision, objects would appear closer to him than they actually were. If he used his right eye alone, the object would appear to the left of its actual position. Similar results should be expected of chickens.

Of the six animals used, all pecked short at grains of mash placed before them. None struck the surface on which the grains rested. When the experimenter covered the right or the left eye of the chicken with masking tape, the bird struck the surface on which the grain rested but missed to the side away from the exposed eye. The conclusion to be drawn is that the normal adult chicken uses binocular cues to localize objects in space.

Later nine newly hatched chicks were outfitted with the same kind of prismatic lenses and were similarly tested. As with the adult chickens, the chicks struck in the direction of the grains but always short of them, thereby demonstrating that in the absence of any visual experience, binocular depth cues are still employed.

In the last of the three experiments on stereoscopic vision, nine chickens were raised to an age of two to three months with the opportunity of using only monocular vision. From the day of hatching they wore hoods, changed each day, which had openings for only one eye. In other words, on the first day they would wear a hood which would allow the use of only the right eye, on the second day a hood which exposed only the left eye, and so on. These hoods contained no lenses or prisms. The purpose of this procedure was simply to prevent experience with binocular vision, but at the same time to allow extensive use of both eyes. When these chickens were tested at the end of two or three months with binocular prisms having their broad bases outward, all nine animals pecked short of the grain. Apparently the lack of binocular experience did not prevent the appearance of binocular vision.

Summing up our results, we conclude that the naive chick as well as the experienced one possesses binocular depth perception. This innate organization for the perception of depth requires neither learning nor continued use for its presence in the adult animal.

....

Perception of Distance and
Space in the Open Air*

JAMES J. GIBSON

THE TRADITIONAL PSYCHOLOGICAL PROBLEM OF DEPTH PERCEPTION AND THE EMPHASIS ON OCULAR CUE

The Assumption of Binocular Basis of Depth Perception. If the pilot has to be able to judge tridimensional space in order to fly successfully, what is the sensory basis for the perception of such space? This question is, of course, the ancient problem of how we see a world which appears to extend away from us rather than a flat world, analogous to a picture, corresponding to the image formed on the retina of the eye. The accepted answer to this question—the answer given in the literature of aviation medicine and also by most of the textbooks in psychology and physiological optics—is that depth perception has its basis primarily in the existence of two eyes. The fact of binocular parallax, or stereoscopic vision, is commonly referred to as the main explanation of depth perception. It is usually stated that the binocular cue is supplemented by "monocular" cues for the perception of distance, but these are usually thought of as secondary. It is supposed that these latter signs or indicators of depth are not innate but are learned in the course of experience and therefore have little to do with the pilot's intrinsic or essential ability to see depth. These monocular cues are usually listed as including such factors as linear perspective, transposition of objects, shadows and shading, aerial perspective, and occasionally a few others. They

---

* From Gibson, J. J. (Ed.), *Motion picture testing and research.* AAF program, report #7, 1946. Pp. 181-195 reprinted by permission of the author and the Dept. of the Air Force.

The formulation and terminology have been somewhat revised in Gibson, J. J., *Perception of the visual world.* Cambridge, Mass.: Houghton-Mifflin, 1950; and the implied theory of perception has been made explicit in Gibson, J. J., Perception as a function of stimulation, in Koch, S. (Ed.), *Psychology: a study of a science,* Study I, Vol. I. New York: McGraw-Hill, 1958.

will be discussed in the next section. The question which arises here is whether the accepted emphasis on binocular vision is correct insofar as it concerns flying.

A good deal of evidence can be adduced to show that visual cues which are *not* dependent on the spatial separation of the two eyes are of much greater significance for the kind of distance perception which fliers need than has been realized in the past. The evidence will be listed in the following paragraphs.

THE PERCEPTION OF DISTANCE BY PERSONS WITH ONLY ONE EYE. There has been a sufficient number of monocular pilots who flew successfully to suggest that binocular vision is at least not absolutely essential for adequate flying performance. The most famous of these was Wiley Post, who was admittedly an excellent flier. If space can be judged successfully with the use of only one eye, then the monocular cues of the normal pilot with two eyes must also be capable of producing space perception. Probably the normal pilot has even better capacity for such perception because of the fact that each eye supplements the monocular vision of the other eye, quite apart from the binocular disparity of the two images, and because two eyes yield a wider field of vision than one eye alone. Training or experience may or may not be necessary for monocular space perception; the point is simply that the capacity is present.

THE PERCEPTION OF DEPTH IN PHOTOGRAPHS AND PICTURES. It is a familiar fact that depth perception can be produced artificially in the stereoscope, i.e. by presenting separately to each eye the picture which it alone would see in the corresponding real three-dimensional scene and superposing the two different pictures by prismatic lenses. The vivid perception of depth which results is taken to be a proof of the effectiveness of binocular or stereoscopic vision. What is less familiar is the fact that a striking depth effect can be seen if two *identical* photographs are substituted in the stereoscope for the two pictures taken from slightly different points of view. The depth effect in this case is frequently comparable to that obtained with genuine stereoscopic viewing. Similarly, if a single photograph of a three-dimensional scene is viewed in such a way as not to emphasize the flatness and the frame of the picture, the observer frequently gets as much effect as if he were looking through a stereoscope. As Schlosberg[1] and others have shown, the explanation is apparently

---

[1] Schlosberg, H., Stereoscopic depth from single pictures. *Amer. J. Psychol.*, 1941, **54**, 601-605.

that one sees depth in these single pictures because they are viewed through a lens which minimizes the surface quality of the picture and which hides its frame. This is the method by which stereoscopic photographs are viewed. The conclusion must be that a considerable part of the depth effect obtained with the stereoscope itself is not a genuine binocular effect at all but instead is dependent on the monocular stimuli for depth present in the single photographs but ordinarily inhibited by the circumstances under which they are viewed. These cues lose much of their effectiveness under the customary conditions for looking at photographs because they are contradicted by the cues which make the picture a flat rectangular surface. If the conclusion is valid for stereoscopic photographs it must also be valid for ordinary binocular seeing, i.e. it is implied that a considerable part of the depth effect in ordinary vision is not binocular but monocular in origin.

THE DIMINISHING OF THE BINOCULAR CUES WITH DISTANCE. It is a possibility that aerial distance perception at long range is mediated somewhat differently from distance perception at short range and that while binocular cues are important in the latter situation, they are less important in the former. It is likely that the depth effect produced by binocular parallax becomes ineffective beyond a certain distance from the observer. The eyes are about two and one-half inches apart. For objects in near space, this is enough to produce parallax; or otherwise stated, there will be a disparity between the images in the right and the left eye, which serves as one kind of stimulus for the perception of depth. But for objects in far space, the retinal disparity in the two eyes presumably becomes so minute as no longer to be an adequate stimulus for seeing depth and, for all practical purposes, the two eyes have identical images. At just what distance from the observer this occurs does not seem to be agreed upon; the range of stereoscopic vision is sometimes given as under a hundred feet and by others is estimated at a distance of as much as a thousand yards. All such estimates seem to be based on calculations rather than on empirical measurement of the effect of disparate retinal vision in real space. They assume that the just-noticeable retinal angle of disparity as determined with a stereoscopic apparatus is the determining factor for the maximum distance at which one can still see binocular depth in the open air. The actual range of stereoscopic vision, therefore, is not known. It is fairly certain, however, that the other binocular cue of the degree of convergence (with correlative accommodation) of the eyes has a fairly short range. At longer ranges, both convergence and accommodation disappear. They are, of course, essential for normal vision but as criteria of distance they are limited to what has been called room-sized space and are ineffective for the perception of aerial space. The only conclusion that can safely be drawn is that since the effectiveness of the binocular cues decreases with distance, the monocular cues are probably increasingly significant at large distances, and may even be the only cues available at such distances. Presumably it is this long-range distance perception which is important to fliers.

The evidence, above all, points to the conclusion that the visual stimuli for depth *not* dependent on the spatial separation of the two eyes—the so-called monocular cues—need to be taken into account in selecting and training fliers for effective space perception.

The Monocular Cues for Depth Perception. The list of accepted cues for the perception of depth has very largely remained unchanged since the discovery of the stereoscope. The non-binocular cues are sometimes called signs or indicators or criteria of depth to imply that they have not the same status of elementary sensations as has the fact of binocular retinal disparity. They are conventionally thought of as having to be interpreted rather than being sensed and they are assumed to be learned rather than innate. The list usually includes some or all of the following factors: *linear perspective* (such as converging railroad tracks), the *apparent size of objects of known size* (which decreases with distance from the observer), the *changes due to atmospheric conditions such as haze* (aerial perspective and blurring of outlines), *monocular parallax* (change of appearance with change of the observer's position), *interposition* (the superposing of near objects on far objects), *shadow patterns* (the light-and-shade relations yielding relief) and sometimes the *angular location of the object on the ground* (position of the object on the retinal dimension beginning with the observer and ending with the skyline). *Accommodation* is also sometimes given as a monocular cue for near depth. It is evident that all of these cues are not on the same explanatory level. Some of them will explain not how the distance of an object is visible but only how one object can be seen at a greater distance than another. For example, interposition and shadow patterns give the *relative* location of objects but do not produce the impression of a space which is continuous in the third dimension. Although all these cues have been described by many observers, they have in general not been experimentally isolated or systematically varied in relation to the perception of distance. They are described somewhat differently by different writers and have not been brought together into a consistent theory explaining how they can function. Nevertheless, if they are as significant for the perception of distance by fliers as seems likely, it is important that such a theory be formulated. If they are to be used as a basis for tests of the ability to judge distance or if they are to be described with sufficient exactness so that they can be used in training, they must be redefined. An attempt to define them and to formulate a theory will be made. Before doing so, however, it would be well to look into the question of the kind of space which they are required to explain.

The Kind of Distance Perception Required for Flying. When one describes the cues for the perception of distance in the terms above, the perception referred to is the distance of a particular object rather than the impression of continuous distance. Conceiving the problem in the traditional way, distance perception in general consists of the ability to judge the distances of a number of specific objects. This, however, is not the space in which the pilot flies. What he perceives is a continuous space. It is almost never a single distance which he needs to judge, but a dimension of distance. There is invariably beneath him a continuous terrain, and what he discriminates is the location of all points on this terrain rather than specific distances to given points. Objects on or above this terrain may be momentarily of great importance, it is true, but they are judged in terms of a continuum of distance or, in other words, a background of three-dimensional space.

Traditionally conceived tests for the perception of distance have concentrated on the problem of how well an observer can judge the relative distance of two objects, or how accurately he can equate the distance of two objects. But the judgments a flier makes are in terms of appropriate changes of speed and direction of flight in relation to the distance of the ground. Such distance judgments always involve the "here" position of the observer at one end of the distance to be judged. It might be suggested that the practical value of depth or distance perception is that it makes possible locomotion through a

continuous space which includes obstacles, and that both the obstacles and the locomotion itself involve the absolute distance from
here to there.

Tests for depth perception, therefore, should aim to set up a
kind of judgment similar to this. And the theory behind it should
be a theory of a continuous space with an underlying terrain in
which the observer is himself located and in which he can move.

THE STIMULUS VARIABLES FOR THE PERCEPTION OF DISTANCE AND CONTINUOUS SPACE IN THE OPEN AIR

The problem of three-dimensional vision, or distance perception,
is basically a problem of the perception of a *continuous surface*
which is seen to extend away from the observer. All spaces in which
we can live include at least one surface, the ground or terrain. If
there were no surface, there would be no visual world, strictly speaking. Whether we stand on it or fly over it, the ground is the basis of
visual space perception both literally and figuratively. It is obvious
enough that we could not stand or walk without the ground, but it
is equally true that a pilot cannot fly purposefully without the
ground and its horizon to guide and orient him. If by reason of fog
or darkness the ground is invisible, an instrument must be provided
to give him a substitute for it, an artificial horizon. The terrain, of
course, is not all there is to the visual world. Objects stand out
against the ground and they are usually what demand our attention.
But an array of objects by themselves does not make up visual
space; it is constituted instead by the ground or surface against
which these shapes and figures appear. The visual world consists of
object-surfaces on a background of an extended ground surface.
This is what is implied by the "figure-ground" distinction in perceptual psychology. If we ask how the distances of these objects are
seen and discriminated, it would be a mistake to disregard the surface
of the background which connects and lies behind them. This mistake has regularly been made in most theories of depth perception.
We need to explain not the "cues" or "indicators" to the distance
of specific objects but instead the dimension or sensory continuum
of distance, *as such*, which, once visible, determines how distant all
the objects within it are.

This view of the problem is in contrast to the classical formulation which asks how the retina of the eye can see a third dimension
in the sense of a theoretical line extending outward from the eye.

Points on this line at different distances must all be identical so far as the retina is concerned. Nevertheless we do see depth. How can this be? The solution to this dilemma is to recognize that visible distance does not consist of a line extending outward from the eye. The question to ask is not how do we see such a line but how do we see the substratum—the surface which extends away from us in the third dimension? The image of this surface is obviously *spread out* across the retina.

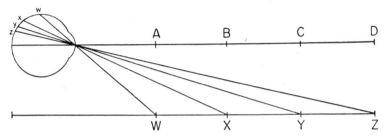

FIG. 1.   Two formulations of the Problem of Distance Perception.

Figure 1 illustrates the two formulations of the problem. The points A, B, C, and D cannot be discriminated by the retina. Distance along this line is a fact of geometry but not one of optics or of visual perception. But the points W, X, Y, and Z at corresponding distances can be discriminated by the retina. They represent the retinal image which corresponds to an extended substratum. It may be noted that the retinal points become progressively closer together as the distance increases.

If this view is correct, it is necessary to see a continuous surface in order to have an accurate sense of continuous distance. The sky may be a background but is not a surface. Distance appears to end at the skyline and the sky itself does not have a determinate distance. Single aircraft or clouds in the sky are of course objects having a surface, but since there is no background surface behind them, their distances ought in theory to be difficult to estimate, and in actual fact they are.

The stimulus variables which make possible the perception of such a continuous surface must necessarily consist of continuous differential stimulation on the retina. The retinal image of the surface must differ significantly at different points corresponding to those which are farther or nearer. There must, in other words, be retinal *gradients* of stimulation. The present use of the term "gradient" may be explained by the following illustration. It is sometimes stated that one of the monocular indicators for the perception of the distance of a point in space is its retinal location on the up-and-down dimension which begins with the lower margin of the visual field and ends with the horizon. Usually the lower margin of the visual field includes an image of the observer's feet and body—it always includes at least a faint marginal image of his cheeks and nose. The observer himself and the skyline are two points of reference on the retina and the distance of the object from the observer may thus be estimated on the basis of its visible up-and-down relationship to these two points of reference. Let us consider this statement. It is very doubtful if this retinal dimension should be thought of as a sensory variable *as such* for the perception of distance. It would be a stimulus only if there were differential stimulation yielding an extended *surface* in perception. The up-and-down location of a retinal point has a distance value only when it is located in relation to a gradient of retinal stimulation. The retinal limits of the skyline on the one extreme and the "bottom" of the field (the body) at the other are limits within which gradients of stimulation may lie, and, as we have already implied, a gradient of stimulation must exist if a continuous distance is to be perceived extending into the third dimension.

The sensory variables which underlie the perception of distance as defined above can now be described. The list will be found to differ considerably from the familiar list of cues for depth perception. The variables proposed are intended to be genuine dimensions of the stimuli affecting the retina, like the stimuli for color and brightness, and to differ from them chiefly in that the dimension is spread across the retina in the form of a gradient and that it is of a more complex order. To what extent they are learned or innate need not be discussed at this stage. They are all systematically related to the perception of a continuum of distance embodied in a substratum extending out to the horizon.

The Retinal Gradient of Texture. The difference between the perception of a surface, such as a flat wall, and the perception of an area without surface, such as the sky, has been investigated in the psychological laboratory. According to Metzger[2] and also Koffka[3]

---

[2] Metzger, W., Optische Untersuchungen am Ganzfeld. II. Zur Phänomenologie des homogenen Ganzfelds. *Psych. Forsch.*, 1930, **13**, 6-29.

[3] Koffka, K., *Principles of Gestalt Psychology.* New York: Harcourt-Brace, 1935, ch. 4.

the difference lies in the fact that the surface corresponds to a retinal image having minute irregularities, spots, or differences in stimulation from point to point, whereas the area without surface corresponds to a retinal image which is in effect completely homogeneous. The area is differentiated in the former situation and undifferentiated in the latter. The term which Metzger and Koffka use for this sensory quality is *microstructure*. When an area of the visual field has microstructure, a surface is visible at a determinate distance; when the area has no microstructure, nothing is seen but "film-color" and no determinate distance is visible.

It is possible to go a step farther and to point out that the retinal image may vary between extremely coarse and extremely fine differentiation. In order to include the extremes of this stimulus variable, it will here be called not microstructure but "texture." As a first approximation to a definition, it may be suggested that retinal texture is the size of the "spots" and of the gaps between them in a differentiated visual image.

Any surface, such as the ground, obviously possesses texture. If it extends away from the observer, the retinal texture becomes finer as the distance of the corresponding points of the surface becomes greater. Figure 1, already discussed, indicates the way in which the retinal image becomes more "dense" as one passes from point W to point Z. There will exist a continuous gradient of texture from coarse to fine with increasing distance of the surface. A retinal gradient of this sort is in fact an adequate stimulus for the perception of continuous distance whether or not it is produced by an actual surface extending into the third dimension. The effectiveness of this stimulus-variable may be illustrated by three examples. In Figure 2, there is a gradient of texture from coarse to fine running from the bottom to the top of the picture and, correspondingly, a continuous increase in the visible distance of the surface. In Figure 3 the same effect may be seen but with a texture of different character, i.e., a texture having elements of different shape and different mean size. The *gradients* in both pictures are, however, similar. It is an incidental fact that these texture-gradients were produced by photographing a ploughed field in the first illustration and a stubble field in the second; it is nevertheless true that the only effective stimulus for distance perception in the pictures is the variable of texture. Figure 4 may appear to be an even more convincing demonstration of the stimulus variable, since the gradient of texture was here constructed artificially. The line segments in this illustration were drawn increasingly smaller from the bottom to the top of the picture and so likewise were the vertical and horizontal spaces between them. The impression of a level terrain extending away from the observer is compelling.

It may be noted that the stimulus-correlate of distance in these

FIG. 2. Distance as Produced by a Natural Gradient of Texture. (From Gibson, J. J., *The perception of the visual world*. Boston: Houghton Mifflin Co., 1950. Reprinted by permission.)

Fig. 3.   Distance as Produced by a Different Natural Gradient of Texture.
(From Gibson, J. J., *The perception of the visual world*. Boston: Houghton
Mifflin Co., 1950. Reprinted by permission.)

illustrations is not the gross retinal size of the texture-elements but their *relative* size within the gradient. For example, the size of the line-segments in Figure 4, i.e. the elements of the texture, could

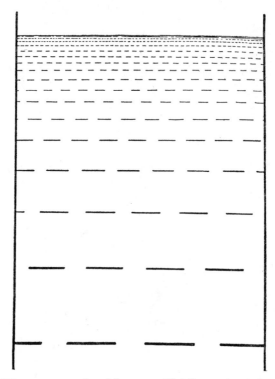

FIG. 4. Distance as produced by an artificially-constructed gradient of texture.

have been twice as large at the bottom of the picture and would then have been twice as large all the way up the picture to the horizon; the resulting impression of distance, would, however, have remained the same. This implies that in perceiving distance over real terrain, it is a matter of indifference to the observer whether the over-all texture of the terrain is made up of large or small elements—whether for example it is produced by sand, grass, brush, or trees.

It should also be noted that the line elements of Figure 4 were so drawn as not to fall one behind the other in straight lines converging to the horizon. This would have introduced the factor of linear perspective, which ought to be considered separately. The stimulus variable in that illustration was intended to be one of "pure" texture. The texture gradient is, however, a kind of perspective in the broad sense of that term and it is related to linear perspective inasmuch as in the case of both variables retinal size decreases with distance and vanishes at the horizon. All the retinal gradients to be described as stimulus variables for distance perception are analogous to perspective at least in respect to being extended on the surface of the retina. The variable just described, therefore, might well be given the name of *texture-perspective*.

The Retinal Gradient of Size-of-Similar-Objects. In almost every kind of terrain which the flier is likely to meet, and in most of the spaces of everyday life, objects are present in addition to the substratum itself. Commonly there are classes or types of similar objects scattered about or line up in the environment. Houses, fence posts, telegraph poles, fields, and even hills tend to be of similar physical size and shape, as do chairs, tables, and people. If there are more than a few of these similar objects in the visual field, there can exist a gradient of decreasing retinal size corresponding to their distance from the observer. The principle involved is the familiar one of size perspective. If more than one *homogeneous type* of object is present, there will be more than one gradient, and it may be assumed that different gradients may exist at the same time such as, for example, one for trees and another for houses. Gradients of size and gradients of texture are obviously analogous and the one merges into the other when the objects in the visual field become sufficiently numerous.

If the objects on a terrain are lined up in rows, or if extended objects like roads and fields having linear contours are present, the size perspective becomes linear perspective. This stimulus for distance is more familiar than the others, but it is merely a special case of the principle that retinal size decreases with distance until it vanishes, or becomes infinitesimal, on the horizon.

It should be pointed out that size perspective and linear perspective, when considered as retinal gradients, are stimulus-correlates of continuous physical distance. They are to be distinguished from the traditional "cue" for distance-perception of the apparent size of familiar objects, i.e., of objects whose real size is remembered from past experience. The comparison of an absolute retinal size and a remembered size and the inferring of the distance, assuming it to occur, is not an adequate explanation for the perception of a continuum of distance. The explanation proposed here does not assume the perceiving of absolute sizes as such but only the ability to react to a continuous gradient of retinal sizes.

The facts of texture perspective and size perspective as described refer to the *retinal image* of the terrain in two dimensions. The resulting *perception* of an extended terrain in three dimensions is characterized by objects and terrain features which do *not* shrink in size toward the horizon. Instead, they appear to maintain a substantially constant size and are perceived at a distance. The relation between this constancy of perceived size and the perception of distance will be discussed later.

The Retinal Gradient of Velocity During Movement of the Observer. A third stimulus variable for the perception of distance is one which is particularly applicable to the flying situation since it occurs during movement of the observer. It bears some relation to the cue of monocular motion parallax. When an observer moves, and particularly when he is flying or driving, the visual world is represented by images which also move across the retina of the eye. The simplest form of this retinal motion may be described by the statement that the image of the world expands radially outward on the retina as one moves straight forward. The expanding optical picture ahead as one drives a car is the most familiar example, and it has probably been noticed by nearly everyone. If, instead, one looks backward, the world (considered as a flat image) contracts inward on the retina as one moves away from it. The center of this expansion, the point from which it radiates, is that point toward which the observer is moving. There is a center of contraction at the opposite pole, i.e., the point he is moving away from. During ordinary locomotion, the center of expansion is on the horizon.

Now under such circumstances the retinal motion of the image corresponding to the terrain is subject to the principle of perspective. There exists, in other words, still another type which will be called retinal motion perspective. The *rate* of expansion of the image of any point or object is inversely proportional to the distance of that point or object from the observer. There is, in other words, a continuous gradient of the velocity of the ground as it "goes by"; the gradient begins with a maximum at the points of the terrain nearest the observer and ends with zero movement at the horizon. This rule holds no matter in what direction one looks. Such a gradient of velocities is capable of determining a continuum of distance and, within this dimension, the distance of any point or object is determinate from its retinal velocity.

When a retinal gradient of velocity exists in the way described, the perception which results is not that of a visual environment which moves but of a stationary world in which the observer himself moves. If the observer is not moving but is, let us say, sitting at a desk, it is nevertheless true that his head will move from time to time and that the image of his visual world moves on the retina. Optically speaking, the world is "alive" with retinal motion produced by only the ordinary slight displacements of the head and body, and the gradients of motion which result are ever present stimuli for the visible continuum of distance.

The description above leaves out of account a number of the characteristics of motion perspective, and makes no mention of several complicating factors. When the motion of the observer is not parallel to the terrain, as when a pilot lands an airplane, the formulation given must be modified. The effect of eye movements on motion perspective also needs to be considered. For the present purpose of listing the sensory bases for distance perception, the description above will suffice.

The Retinal Gradients Arising from Atmospheric Transmission of Light. The cue of aerial perspective as ordinarily described provides another kind of retinal gradient which is a continuous correlate of distance. The retinal image of a terrain stretching away to the horizon is constituted by light which at one extreme has passed through only a few feet of air and at the other extreme has passed through many miles of air. The character of the light stimulus varies with the amount of atmosphere through which it has been transmitted. The resulting color quality becomes less saturated and bluer with increasing atmospheric distance. The color is also described as being increasingly blurred or film-like in appearance with increasing lengths of aerial transmission, and the outlines within the image become less sharp. It is possible that these latter variations should be considered in relation to the texture variable.

The exact stimulus-variations involved have not been worked out in detail. They are effectively employed by painters but they have not been fully described in terms of physiological optics.

The Retinal Gradient of Binocular Disparity. A number of visual stimulus dimensions have just been defined which are concomitants of distance and which are presumably stimuli for the perception of space as the flier sees it. They are all based on gradients of stimulation in a single retina; that is to say, they do not depend on differences in stimulation between the two eyes. There is, in addition, however, the fact of binocular retinal disparity, or stereopsis, which has received most of the attention devoted to the problem of distance perception in the past. This variable can be defined, like the others, in terms of a gradient of stimulation, with only the addition of the fact that the stimulation referred to is a binocular rather than a monocular effect.

Assuming for the moment that the observer's eyes are fixated on the horizon, the retinal image of the terrain in the right eye will differ from that in the left eye. This difference at any given point is called retinal disparity, and is due to the different positions of the two eyes in relation to the terrain. Near points and objects on the terrain are displaced horizontally in the image of one eye relative to the other. This relative displacement decreases with increasing distance and becomes zero at the horizon itself. There is, in short, a gradient of disparity in the combined retinal field. It is, like the others already described, a vertical gradient, running up the field from the observer's body at one extreme to the horizon at the other. Any point on the terrain corresponds to a disparity which is inversely proportional to the distance of that point from the observer. It must be supposed that this variable is a stimulus-correlate of perceived distance.

This description holds true when the eyes are fixated on the horizon. If instead, the eyes are fixated on a near point, the disparity is zero at that point and reaches a maximum at the horizon. But this disparity is opposite in kind to that existing in the former situation; it is "uncrossed" rather than "crossed," or positive where the former was negative. The *gradient* of disparity with respect to its sign is therefore the same when the eyes are fixated on a near point as when they are fixated on a far point, or for that matter when they are fixated at any point. An increase in positive disparity being equivalent to a decrease in negative disparity, the gradient may run from minus to zero or from zero to plus and still be the same gradient. The stimulus which is concomitant with distance, therefore, is not simply disparity as such but disparity relative to a gradient which may lie anywhere on a scale of negative to positive.

The Relation of Other So-Called Cues for Depth to the Variables Above. All of the traditional cues for depth perception have been incorporated or reinterpreted in the variables listed, except for interception or superposition of contours and the distribution of shadows and shading. Interception is capable of determining the relative distance of two or more objects but, by its very nature, it is not a variable which can establish a continuum of distance. It has to do with the establishing of the figure-ground relationship and the relation of "behind" or "in front of" rather than with distance perception as such. The distribution of shadows produced by objects and the gradients of shading appearing on three-dimensional shapes are determiners of what is properly called relief or relative depth, but this is not the same thing as the sensory continuum of distance. They will not be discussed further, nor will any analysis be given of the retinal gradient associated with accommodation— a kind of "blur" gradient.

....

*Experiments in Perception**

WILLIAM H. ITTELSON AND FRANKLIN P. KILPATRICK

WHAT IS PERCEPTION? Why do we see what we see, feel what we feel, hear what we hear? We act in terms of what we perceive; our acts lead to new perceptions; these lead to new acts, and so on in the incredibly complex process that constitutes life. Clearly, then, an understanding of the process by which man becomes aware of himself and his world is basic to any adequate understanding of human behavior. But the problem of explaining how and why we perceive in the way we do is one of the most controversial fields in psychology. We shall describe here some recent experimental work which sheds new light on the problem and points the way to a new theory of perception.

The fact that we see a chair and are then able to go to the place at which we localize it and rest our bodies on a substantial object does not seem particularly amazing or difficult to explain—until we try to explain it. If we accept the prevailing current view that we can never be aware of the world as such, but only of the nervous impulses arising from the impingement of physical forces on sensory receptors, we immediately face the necessity of explaining the correspondence between what we perceive and whatever it is that is there.

An extremely logical, unbeatable—and scientifically useless—answer is simply to say there is no real world, that everything exists in the mind alone. Another approach is to postulate the existence of an external world, to grant that there is some general correspondence between that world and what we perceive and to seek some understandable and useful explanation of why that should be. Most of the prominent theories about perception have grown out of the latter approach. These theories generally agree that even though

---

* From *Scientific American*, 1952, **185**, 50-55. Reprinted by permission of the author and the publisher.

much of the correspondence may be due to learning, at some basic level there exists an absolute correspondence between what is "out there" and what is in the "mind." But there is a great deal of disagreement concerning the level at which such innately determined correspondence occurs. At one extreme are theorists who believe that the correspondence occurs at the level of simple sensations, such as color, brightness, weight, hardness, and so on, and that out of these sensations are compounded more complex awarenesses, such as the recognition of a pencil or a book. At the other extreme are Gestalt psychologists who feel that complex perceptions such as the form of an object are the result of an inherent relationship between the properties of the thing perceived and the properties of the brain. All these schools seem to agree, however, that there is some perceptual level at which exists absolute objectivity; that is, a one-to-one correspondence between experience and reality.

This belief is basic to current thinking in many fields. It underlies most theorizing concerning the nature of science, including Percy W. Bridgman's attempt to reach final scientific objectivity in the "observable operation." In psychology one is hard put to find an approach to human behavior which departs from this basic premise. But it leads to dichotomies such as organism *v.* environment, subjective *v.* objective. Stimuli or stimulus patterns are treated as though they exist apart from the perceiving organism. Psychologists seek to find mechanical relationships or interactions between the organism and an "objectively defined" environment. They often rule out purposes and values as not belonging in a strictly scientific psychology.

The experiments to be described here arose from a widespread and growing feeling that such dichotomies are false, and that in practice it is impossible to leave values and purposes out of consideration in scientific observation. The experiments were designed to re-examine some of the basic ideas from which these problems stem.

During the past few years Adelbert Ames, Jr., of the Institute for Associated Research in Hanover, N. H., has designed some new ways of studying visual perception. They have resulted in a new conception of the nature of knowing and of observation. This theory neither denies the existence of objects nor proposes that they exist in a given form independently, that is, apart from the perceiving organism. Instead, it suggests that the world each of us knows is a world created in large measure from our experience in dealing with the environment.

Let us illustrate this in specific terms through some of the demonstrations. In one of them the subject sits in a dark room in which he can see only two star points of light. Both are equidistant from the observer, but one is brighter than the other. If the observer closes one eye and keeps his head still, the brighter point of light looks nearer than the dimmer one. Such apparent differences are related not only to brightness but also to direction from the observer. If two points of light of equal brightness are situated near the floor, one about a foot above the other, the upper one will generally be perceived as farther away than the lower one; if they are near the ceiling, the lower one will appear farther away.

A somewhat more complex experiment uses two partly inflated balloons illuminated from a concealed source. The balloons are in fixed positions about one foot apart. Their relative sizes can be

Fig. 1. Figures are distorted when they are placed in a specially constructed room. The woman at left appears much smaller than the one at right because the mind "bets" that the opposite surfaces of the room are parallel.

varied by means of a lever control connected to a bellows, and another lever controls their relative brightness. When the size and brightness of both balloons are the same, an observer looking at them with one eye from 10 feet or more sees them as two glowing spheres at equal distances from him. If the brightnesses are left the same and the relative sizes are changed, the larger balloon appears to nearly all observers somewhat nearer. If the size lever is moved continuously, causing continuous variation in the relative size of the balloons, they appear to move dramatically back and forth through space, even when the observer watches with both eyes open. The result is similar when the sizes are kept equal and the relative brightness is varied.

With the same apparatus the effects of size and brightness may be combined so that they supplement or conflict with each other. When they supplement each other, the variation in apparent distance is much greater than when either size or brightness alone is varied. When conflict is introduced by varying size and brightness in opposition to each other, the relative change in distance is con-

FIG. 2. Heads are distorted by the same process. The head of the man at left appears to be much smaller than the head of the man at the right because the mind assumes that all the windows are the same height.

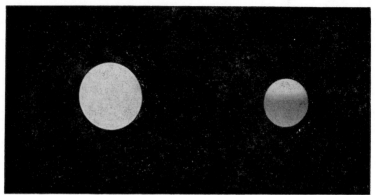

Fig. 3. Left balloon appears closer because it is larger and brighter than the balloon at the right. Both balloons, however, are at same distance.

Fig. 4. Balloons appear approximately equidistant when they are the same size. The qualities are manipulated with levers in the demonstration.

Fig. 5. Right balloon appears closer when it is larger and brighter. The demonstration shows that size and brightness are cues for distance.

siderably less than when they act in combination or alone. Most people, however, give more weight to relative size than they give to brightness in judging distance.

These phenomena cannot be explained by referring to "reality," because "reality" and perception do not correspond. They cannot be explained by reference to the pattern in the retina of the eye, because for any given retinal pattern there are an infinite number of brightness-size-distance combinations to which that pattern might be related. When faced with such a situation, in which an unlimited number of possibilities can be related to a given retinal pattern, the organism apparently calls upon its previous experiences and assumes that what has been most probable in the past is most probable in the immediate occasion. When presented with two star-points of different brightness, a person unconsciously "bets" or "assumes" that the two points, being similar, are probably identical (*i.e.,* of equal brightness), and therefore that the one which seems brighter must be nearer. Similarly the observed facts in the case of two star-points placed vertically one above the other suggest that when we look down we assume, on the basis of past experience, that objects in the lower part of the visual field are nearer than objects in the upper part; when we look up, we assume the opposite to be true. An analogous explanation can be made of the role of relative size as an indication of relative distance.

Why do the differences in distance seem so much greater when the relative size of two objects is varied continuously than when the size difference is fixed? This phenomenon, too, apparently is based on experience. It is a fairly common experience, though not usual, to find that two similar objects of different sizes are actually the same distance away from us. But it is rare indeed to see two stationary objects at the same distance, one growing larger and the other smaller; almost always in everyday life when we see two identical or nearly identical objects change relative size they are in motion in relation to each other. Hence under the experimental conditions we are much more likely to assume distance differences in the objects of changing size than in those of fixed size. In other words, apparently we make use of a weighted average of our past experience in interpreting what we see. It seems that the subject relates to the stimulus pattern a complex, probability-like integration of his past experience with such patterns. Were it not for such integrations, which have been labeled assumptions, the particular perceptual phenomenon would not occur. It follows from this that the resulting perceptions are not absolute revelations of "what is out there" but are in the nature of probabilities or predictions based on past experience. These predictions are not always reliable, as the demonstrations make clear.

Visual perception involves an impression not only of *where* an object is but of *what* it is. From the demonstrations already described we may guess that there is a very strong relationship between localization in space ("thereness") and the assignment of objective properties ("thatness"). This relationship can be demonstrated by a cube experiment.

Two solid white cubes are suspended on wires that are painted black so as to be invisible against a black background. One cube is about 3 feet from the observer and the other about 12 feet. The observer's head is in a headrest so positioned that the cubes are almost in line with each other but he can see both, the nearer cube being slightly to the right. A tiny metal shield is then placed a few inches in front of the left eye. It is just big enough to cut off the view of the far cube from the left eye. The result is that the near cube is seen with both eyes and the far cube with just the right eye. Under these conditions the observer can fix the position of the near cube very well, because he has available all the cues that come from the use of the two eyes. But in the case of the far cube seen with only one eye, localization is much more difficult and uncertain.

Now since the two cubes are almost in line visually, a slight movement of the head to the right will cause the inside vertical edges of the cubes to coincide. Such coincidence of edge is strongly related to an assumption of "togetherness." Hence when the subject moves his head in this way, the uncertainly located distant cube appears to have moved forward to a position even with the nearer cube. Under these conditions not only does the mislocated cube appear smaller, but it appears different in shape, that is, no longer cubical, even though the pattern cast by the cube on the retina of the eye has not changed at all.

The same point can be illustrated most dramatically by experiments in which the subject wears a pair of glasses fitted with so-called aniseikonic lenses, which are ground in such a way that they give images of different size and shape to the two retinas. This pro-

Fig. 6. Left cards appear closer than those at the center and right in each of the three rows in this picture. The illusion is revealed below.

Fig. 7. View of apparatus shows that right cards are closer in the rows at the center and right. Here the cues are size and the fact that the cards appear to overlap.

duces very marked distortions of any objects which the subject visualizes mainly through the use of two-eyed stereoscopic vision. In an ordinary environment there are generally enough one-eye cues, such as shadow, overlay, familiar objects of known size, and so on, to suppress the binocular cues and hold the visual world "in shape." But in an environment poor in one-eye cues the observer is forced to rely on binocular cues, and under these circumstances the distortion is enhanced for anyone wearing such glasses. It has been found that if an ordinary square room is lined with tree leaves, which reduce monocular cues to a minimum by covering the flat wall spaces, most observers looking through aniseikonic lenses perceive a great deal of distortion of the room and the leaves. To an observer looking at the room as a whole through certain glasses of this type the walls appear to slant inward from floor to ceiling, the ceiling seems much lower than it is and its leaves look very small. The floor, which is the object of interest in this particular analysis, appears to be much farther away than its true position, and the leaves covering it look huge. Now, if the observer wearing the same glasses looks at just the floor instead of the room in general, the floor changes markedly in appearance. It appears to be much nearer than before, and instead of being level it seems to rise from front to back at a pitch of about 45 degrees. The leaves, however, now look more nearly normal in size.

These perceptions can be explained in terms of the geometry of stereoscopic vision. The stimulus patterns on the retinas of the eyes are the geometric projections of an external surface. But identical projections may be produced by surfaces of different kinds. In this case a distant surface that is nearly horizontal, a closer surface that is slightly tipped and a very near surface that is sharply tipped all produce the same stereoscopic stimulus patterns. When the observer looks at the whole room, he "chooses" the nearly horizontal faraway floor surface as the focus of perception, probably because he cannot make a room out of the pattern if the floor is sharply tipped up. When he limits his gaze to the floor, he no longer needs to make a room of what he is looking at, and he sees the floor sharply tipped, perhaps because the leaves now appear more nearly the size he assumes them to be.

In the everyday environment outside the laboratory the wearing of these glasses produces similarly interesting illusions. For example, a large body of water such as a lake appears horizontal and farther away than its real position, but a large expanse of level lawn looks tipped and nearer than its real position. Presumably this happens because the observer brings to these occasions the assumptions, based on past experience, that the probability of a lake surface being other than horizontal is almost zero, while the probability of a grass surface being a slope is fairly high.

The most reasonable explanation of these visual phenomena seems to be that an observer unconsciously relates to the stimulus pattern some sort of weighted average of the past consequences of acting with respect to that pattern. The particular perception "chosen" is the one that has the best predictive value, on the basis of previous experience, for action in carrying out the purposes of the organism. From this one may make two rather crucial deductions: 1) an unfamiliar external configuration which yields the same retinal pattern as one the observer is accustomed to deal with will be perceived as the familiar configuration; 2) when the observer acts on his interpretation of the unfamiliar configuration and finds that he is wrong, his perception will change even though the retinal pattern is unchanged.

Let us illustrate with some actual demonstrations. If an observer in a dark room looks with one eye at two lines of light which are at the same distance and elevation but of different lengths, the longer line will look nearer than the shorter one. Apparently he assumes that the lines are identical and translates the difference in length into a difference in position. If the observer takes a wand with a luminous tip and tries to touch first one line and then the other, he will be unable to do so at first. After repeated practice, however, he can learn to touch the two lines quickly and accurately. At this point he no longer sees the lines as at different distances; they now look, as they are, the same distance from him. He originally assumed that the two lines were the same length because that seemed the best bet under the circumstances. After he had tested this assumption by purposive action, he shifted to the assumption, less probable in terms of past experience but still possible, that the lines were at the same distance but of different lengths. As his assumption changed, perception did also.

There is another experiment that demonstrates these points even more convincingly. It uses a distorted room in which the floor slopes up to the right of the observer, the rear wall recedes from right to left and the windows are of different sizes and trapezoidal in shape. When an observer looks at this room with one eye from a certain point, the room appears completely normal, as if the floor were level, the rear wall at right angles to the line of sight and the windows rectangular and of the same size. Presumably the observer chooses this particular appearance instead of some other because of

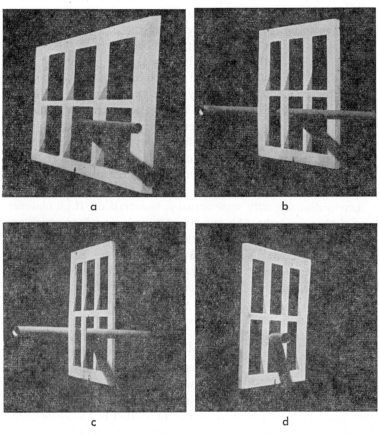

FIG. 8. Perception of moving objects was investigated with a rotating window. The window is a trapezoid painted to look like a normal rectangular window seen in perspective. When the trapezoid rotates, the assumption that it is rectangular causes a straight tube to do strange things. The sequence reads horizontally.

the assumptions he brings to the occasion. If he now takes a long stick and tries to touch the various parts of the room, he will be unsuccessful, even though he has gone into the situation knowing the true shape of the room. With practice, however, he becomes more and more successful in touching what he wants to touch with the stick. More important, he sees the room more and more in its true shape, even though the stimulus pattern on his retina has remained unchanged.

By means of a piece of apparatus called the "rotating trapezoidal window" it has been possible to extend the investigation to complex perceptual situations involving movement. This device consists of a trapezoidal surface with panes cut in it and shadows painted on it to give the appearance of a window. It is mounted on a rod connected to a motor so that it rotates at a slow constant speed in an upright position about its own axis. When an observer views the rotating surface with one eye from about 10 feet or more or with both eyes from about 25 feet or more, he sees not a rotating trapezoid but an oscillating rectangle. Its speed of movement and its shape appear to vary markedly as it turns. If a small cube is attached by a short rod to the upper part of the short side of the trapezoid, it seems to become detached, sail freely around the front of the trapezoid and attach itself again as the apparatus rotates.

All these experiments, and many more that have been made, suggest strongly that perception is never a sure thing, never an absolute revelation of "what is." Rather, what we see is a prediction— our own personal construction designed to give us the best possible bet for carrying out our purposes in action. We make these bets on the basis of our past experience. When we have a great deal of relevant and consistent experience to relate to stimulus patterns, the probability of success of our prediction (perception) as a guide to action is extremely high, and we tend to have a feeling of surety. When our experience is limited or inconsistent, the reverse holds true. According to the new theory of perception developed from the demonstrations we have described, perception is a functional affair based on action, experience and probability. The thing perceived is an inseparable part of the function of perceiving, which in turn includes all aspects of the total process of living. This view differs from the old rival theories: the thing perceived is neither just a figment of the mind nor an innately determined absolute revelation of a reality postulated to exist apart from the perceiving organism. Object and percept are part and parcel of the same thing.

This conclusion of course has far-reaching implications for many areas of study, for some assumption as to what perception is must underly any philosophy or comprehensive theory of psychology, of science or of knowledge in general. Although the particular investigations involved here are restricted to visual perception, this is only a vehicle which carries us into a basic inquiry of much wider significance.

....

Determinants of Apparent Visual Size with Distance Variant*

ALFRED H. HOLWAY AND EDWIN G. BORING

THE SIZE of the retinal image is a peripheral determinant of visual size. Presumably, if all other determinants were constant, perceived size would vary directly with the visual angle, which might even be used then as a measure of apparent size. It has been known for a long time, however—since Fechner[1] and Hering,[2] at any rate—that the visual angle does not provide a consistent measure of perceived size when the distance from O to the stimulus-object is varied. Martius' experiment[3] in 1889 demonstrated that the apparent size of objects may change scarcely at all when distance changes, and nowadays it is customary to use the term 'size constancy' as a reminder that, when perceived size is constant, the visual angle sometimes is not.[4]

Ordinarily, of course, size is not constant in spite of distance. Even the philosophers of the eighteenth century remarked that two parallel rows of trees appear to converge as one views the vista between the rows, and they attributed the convergence to the law of the visual angle and the underestimation of the greater distances.[5]

---

* From the *Amer. J. Psychol.*, 1941, **51**, 21-37. Pp. 21-27, 32-37 reprinted by permission of the author and the publisher.
[1] Fechner, G. T. *Elemente der Psychophysik*, II. 1860, 311-313.
[2] Hering, E. *Beiträge zur Physiologie*, I. 1861, 13-16.
[3] Martius, G. Ueber die scheinbare Grösse der Gegenstände und ihre Beziehung zur Grösse der Netzhautbilder. *Philos. Stud.*, 1889, **5**, 601-617.
[4] Cf. Koffka, K. *Principles of Gestalt Psychology*. 1935, 87-97, 235-240.
[5] Cf. Priestley, J. *The History and Present State of Discoveries Relating to Vision, Light and Colours*. 1772, 700-704; see also W. Porterfield, *A Treatise on the Eye*, 1759, II, 381-384.

To get things started toward a solution of this problem, Hillebrand [6] and others worked out the form of the curve that the walls of a short, narrow alley should have in order to appear equally separated at every distance; [7] these studies were factual in emphasis. Recently, Thouless [8] has conceived of the organism as regressing in perception from a proximal perceptual datum (the retinal image) toward a more remote one (the real object), so that actual perception can be regarded as a compromise between the proximal datum and objective constancy. Brunswik [9] has stressed this compromise in his concept of an intermediate perceptual object, the *Zwischengegenstand*, and his associate Holaday [10] has shown the properties of the *Zwischengegenstand* to depend upon a variety of perceptual data.

Size constancy is thus an hyperbole, except as the description of a limiting case. It is not a general rule. Only at times does the organism succeed in seeing an object with no change of size at all when distance is altered. On the other hand, these remarks apply with equal force to the *law of the visual angle,* the relation which prompted Fechner and Hering to make their original observations on the relation of size to distance. This law, too, is a special case. Let us scrutinize these cases.

Accommodated objects which subtend equal visual angles are equal in apparent size. That is the law of the visual angle. If the angle θ_s, subtended by a standard stimulus, is equal to the angle θ_c, subtended by a comparison stimulus, then

$$\tan \theta_c = \tan \theta_s \quad \dots\dots\dots\dots\dots\dots [A]$$

and

$$S_c = (D_c/D_s)S_s \quad \dots\dots\dots\dots\dots\dots [B]$$

where S_c is the linear size of the comparison object; S_s, the linear size of the standard; D_c, the distance from O to S_c; and D_s, the distance

---

[6] Hillebrand, F. Theorie der scheinbaren Grösse bei binocularen Sehen. *Denkschr. d. kais. Akad. d. Wiss. zu Wien,* math.-nat. Kl., 1902, **72**, 255-307.

[7] E.g., Blumenfeld, W. Untersuchungen über die scheinbare Grösse in Sehräume, *Zsch. f. Psychol.,* 1913, **65**, 241-404, who also gives an excellent history of this problem, 243-274.

[8] Thouless, R. H. Phenomenal regression to the real object. *Brit. J. Psychol.,* 1931, **21**, 339-359; 1931, **22**, 1-30.

[9] Brunswik, E. Die Zugänglichkeit von Gegenständen für die Wahrnehmung und deren quantitative Bestimmung. *Arch. f. d. ges. Psychol.,* 1933, **88**, 377-418.

[10] Holaday, B. E. Die Grössenkonstanz der Sehdinge bei Variation der inneren und äusseren Wahrnehmungsbedingungen. *Arch. f. d. ges. Psychol.,* 1933, **88**, 419-486.

from O to the standard S_s. The size of the comparison stmulus ($=$ apparent size of the standard) is equal to the size of the standard stimulus multiplied by the ratio of their respective distances.

The law of size constancy, on the other hand, states simply

$$S_c = S_s \dots\dots\dots\dots\dots\dots\dots\dots [C]$$

where S_c and S_s have the same meaning as in Equation [B]. Equation [C] expresses exactly the idea communicated to many investigators by the term *size constancy*. The size of the comparison stimulus is equal to the size of the standard, irrespective of their distances from O.[11]

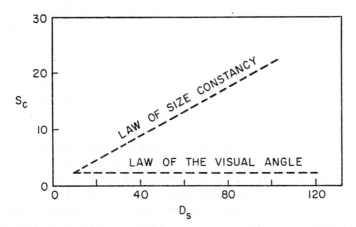

FIG. 1. LAWS OF VISUAL ANGLE AND OF SIZE CONSTANCY FOR OBJECTS OF ONE DEGREE. S_c is the diameter in inches of the comparison stimulus as equated in perceived size to the diameter of a standard stimulus (angle subtended $= 1°$). The comparison stimulus is at a constant distance (10 ft.) from O. The abscissa values are the distances in feet from O to the standard stimulus. The oblique broken line designates the locus of all data obeying the law of size constancy. The broken line parallel to the axis of abscissas is the locus of all points obeying the law of the visual angle.

Fig. 1 shows these two relations in the way in which they are presented later in the present paper. The standard and comparison stimuli are circular in outline, uniformly and equally illuminated as O sees them. The diameter of the standard stimulus subtends a constant visual angle ($\theta_s = 1°$). S_c is the size, in inches, of the comparison stimulus. D_c is

---

[11] For the more general mathematical implications of the principles of size constancy, see Boring, E. G. Size constancy and Emmert's law. *Amer. J. Psychol.*, 1940, **53**, 293-295.

constant at 10 ft. D_s is varied from 10 to 120 ft. The broken line drawn parallel to the axis of abscissas is the locus of all data which obey the law of the visual angle. The oblique line is the locus of values conforming to the law of size constancy.

If size constancy were a general rule, then the apparent size of the standard stimulus (*i.e.* the measured size of the comparison stimulus after the subjective equation is made) should be related to D_s by a function that is linear in form (slope $= \tan 1°$). If, on the other hand, the law of the visual angle were of general validity, then S_c should be constant, *i.e.* independent of distance. What actually happens is to be found for specific conditions. Systematically determined relations of this sort are wanted and wanting.[12] It must be kept in mind that the arrangement of the experiment is not in the usual form for testing size constancy, since the visual angle subtended by the standard stimulus is kept constant at 1°, so that the physical size of the standard stimulus must be increased proportionally to the distance. It is for this reason that size constancy is represented in the graphs by a straight line through the origin with slope equal to tan 1°, and the law of the visual angle is a horizontal line with slope equal to zero.

The present paper is a study of such functions, obtained under conditions in which distance is a common variant, as various effects of binocular regard, of accommodation, and of the visual frame of reference are successively eliminated. Functions relating the size of an adjusted stimulus to the distance from O to a standard stimulus subtending a constant visual angle ($\theta_s = 1°$) were studied under four different sets of conditions: (1) binocular regard, (2) monocular regard, (3) monocular regard through an artificial pupil, and (4) monocular regard through an artificial pupil and a long black reduction tunnel stretching from O to the standard stimulus, eliminating most of the visual frame of reference. The consequent data provide quantitative functions for a greater range of distances than has heretofore been available for such a variety of conditions.

PROCEDURE

The general plan of the experiment is sketched in Fig. 2. O sat in a chair at the intersection of two long darkened corridors where he had

---

[12] Koffka, *op. cit.*, 1935, 91, complained of the lack of complete data for this functional relation: "Although the first experiments of this kind were made in 1889 by Götz Martius, we have to the present day no complete knowledge of the quantitative relations, the range of distances over which the investigations have been carried out being rather limited."

an unobstructed view of a standard and a comparison stimulus. The comparison stimulus S_c, a uniformly illuminated circular light-image, was centered on a large white screen (8 x 8 ft.) by an ordinary projector. The screen stood at a constant distance (10 ft.) from O throughout the experiment. The image on this screen could be continuously varied in size by means of an iris diaphragm conjugate with the screen. The standard stimulus S_s was provided in a similar manner by another projector. The distance from the O to S_s, however, was not constant but was systematically varied by placing the screen at various fixed distances, ranging from 10 to 120 ft. The light images for these stimuli were formed by means of circular apertures cut in thin brass plates conjugate with the standard screen. At all distances, S_s subtended a constant angle (1°) at the eye of O. The intensity of the light (flux per unit area) from S_s was constant and equal to that from S_c. The intensities of the light from S_s and S_c at the eye of O were thus identical for all measurements.

E regulated the size of the comparison stimulus by varying the opening of the adjustable diaphragm conjugate with S_c until O signified that the standard and comparison stimuli were perceived as equal in size. O first fixated the standard stimulus (1°), then the comparison, looking back and forth until satisfied with the equation. E measured the diameter of S_c with a meter stick. No restriction was imposed upon O in regard to the length of time taken for the judgments.

All experiments were performed after midnight. Except for a few high lights, the corridors were dark. The brightest high lights were formed by light reflected from the waxed surface of the dark green tile on the floor of the corridor. Thus constellations of light images, not simply the primary images of the 'stimulus,' were located on the Os' retinas.

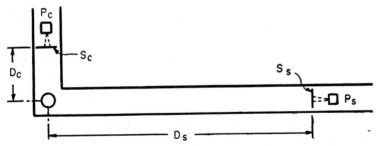

FIG. 2. PLAN VIEW OF THE CORRIDORS. S_c indicates the position of the comparison stimulus located at a constant distance ($D_c = 10$ ft.) from O. S_s at a distance D_s from O indicates one of the positions occupied by the standard stimulus. The standard stimulus always subtended a visual angle of 1°. Distance from O to the standard was varied from 10 to 120 ft. P_c and P_s indicate the positions of the projectors.

TABLE I. BINOCULAR OBSERVATION: APPARENT SIZE OF STANDARD
STIMULUS AS A FUNCTION OF ITS DISTANCE

D_s = distance (ft.) from O to standard stimulus. At all distances, standard stimulus subtended a constant visual angle of one degree. S_c = av. size (in.) of N settings of comparison stimulus, located at a distance of 10 ft. from O and equated in perceived size to standard stimulus. Intensity of light from the stimuli was constant at eye of O. m.v. = mean variation. O sat erect, facing the stimuli successively with direct binocular regard.

	E.G.B. (N = 20)		A.C.S. (N = 5)		A.H.H. (N = 10)		L.M.H. (N = 5)		M.J.Z. (N = 20)	
D_s	S_c	m.v.	S_c	m.v.	S_c	m.v.	S_c	m.v.	S_c	m.v.
10	2.2	0.21	2.2	0.19	2.2	0.19	2.2	0.14	2.4	0.18
20	4.6	0.44	4.8	0.40	4.7	0.32			4.5	0.45
30							7.0	0.44		
40	9.5	0.48			9.4	0.81			8.9	0.35
50			13.5	0.42			12.0	0.51		
60	11.5	0.71	13.2	0.60	15.0	0.71			13.7	0.48
70			15.9	0.39			15.5	0.62	16.4	0.75
80	15.8	0.70			17.6	0.37			19.8	0.36
90			17.1	0.55					19.9	1.08
100	18.7	1.13			24.0	0.93	23.0	0.93	25.3	0.93
120	20.6	1.07	25.5	0.66	24.5	1.02	25.2	1.16	28.4	1.75

Five Os were employed: A. C. S. Holway, L. M. Hurvich, M. J. Zigler, A. H. Holway, and E. G. Boring. E.G.B. and M.J.Z. served as Os for the first complete sets of measurements. For them, 20 measurements for size were made at every distance; 10 were made by increasing the size of S_c until O reported that the visual impression produced by it was equal in extent to that produced by S_s; 10 more were made by decreasing the size of S_c. The two procedures gave practically identical results, and for each distance the 20 measurements were averaged to obtain the desired measure of central tendency. A smaller number of results was secured from the other Os.

BINOCULAR OBSERVATION

The measurements for the binocular observations are shown in Table I. These data were obtained with binocular regard by altering the diameter of the comparison stimulus S_c, until it appeared equal to the standard stimulus (1°) in respect of perceived size, as the distance from O to the standard stimulus was varied from 10 to 120 ft.

The measurements for each O are also exhibited in Figs. 3-7. The coordinates are expressed in linear units. The ordinates give the size of the comparison stimulus (in.), the abscissas the distance (ft.) from O to the standard stimulus. Fig. 8 is the composite of the binocular data for all Os.

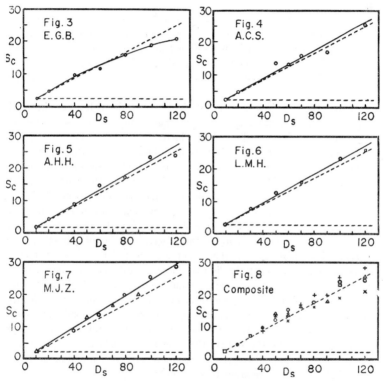

FIGS. 3-8. BINOCULAR OBSERVATION: APPARENT SIZE OF THE STANDARD STIMULUS AS A FUNCTION OF ITS DISTANCE. Figs. 3-7 show the apparent size of the standard stimulus as its distance from O is varied from 10 to 120 ft. Standard stimulus subtended a constant angle of 1° at eye of O. Circles are for first sitting; triangles and rectangles are for later sittings. For values of N, see Table I. The oblique broken line is the locus of all data obeying the law of size constancy. The broken horizontal line is the locus of all data conforming to the law of the visual angle. Fig. 8 is a composite of the data for all Os. Different symbols denote different Os.

The size of the comparison stimulus S_c in all instances increases with the distance of S_s from O. In other words, the apparent size $(= S_c)$ of a standard stimulus varies directly with the distance from O to the standard. The specific form assumed by the majority of these functions is surprising, since commonplace experience would lead one to expect diminishing returns for S_c at great distances. Except for the data of E.G.B., which exhibit a curvature that is concave toward the axis of the abscissas, the values of S_c are related to the distance of the standard stimulus by a linear function.

Much has been said concerning the likelihood of securing results intermediate between the limits of size constancy and the visual angle. The binocular data for most of our Os do not, however, lie within these limits, but *outside* of them. The most probable function is not only linear in form but it also has a slope greater than that demanded by the law of size-constancy.

At first thought, it seems as if we had here to do with a case in which apparent size is 'more than constant,' that is to say, a case where the apparent size of a receding object increases slightly while the retinal image diminishes greatly. It is quite possible, however, that there is in our equations a space error, such that S_c on O's left is seen a little smaller than an S_s of equal physical size on O's right, so that for subjective equation S_c has to be made a little too large. The discrepancy is of the order $1.12:1$, *i.e.* a value for binocular observation is about 1.12 times the corresponding theoretical value for size constancy. In two other similar experiments we have encountered this discrepancy in this direction once and failed to find it once. The chief argument for suggesting that a space error may be operative is that there is available no other sensible interpretation of why constancy should be 'exceeded.' It is our belief that this error—if indeed it be an error, for we have no other evidence than the foregoing—is not psychophysical but instrumental, like some mistake in the distance from O's head to the screen for the comparison stimulus. If such be the source, then the error would also apply to the other three functions discussed below, and a correction would be achieved by a slight clockwise rotation of the functions.

[The authors then repeated the observations under a series of conditions which progressively decreased the distance cues. First, the subjects made their judgments using only one eye and wearing a leather stop which completely covered the other. Then the judgments were made monocularly through an artificial pupil 1.8 mm in diameter held about 4 mm in front of the anterior corneal surface of the eye. In a final condition of monocular observation with artificial pupil, a tunnel of black cloth was constructed between the subject and the stimulus to eliminate light reflection from the corridor walls. There was some residual "haze" visible, but the amount

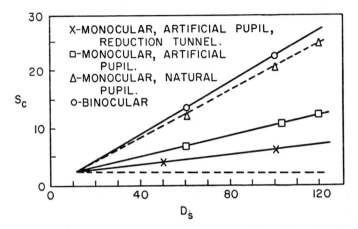

FIG. 9. DETERMINANTS OF APPARENT VISUAL SIZE WITH DISTANCE VARIANT. Apparent size as a function of distance for four sets of conditions. The figure is based on the averages of all the data obtained in the present experiment. The slope of the function relating apparent size to distance diminishes continuously as the mode of regarding the stimuli is altered from direct binocular observation to direct monocular observation, to monocular observation through a small artificial pupil, to monocular observation through the artificial pupil and a long black reduction tunnel. As the number of extraneous cues is diminished, the slope of the function approaches zero as a limit, i.e., it approaches the law of the visual angle.

of surrounding light was reduced. Figure 9 summarizes the results of these variations.]*

DISCUSSION

The net result of these experiments is exhibited in Fig. 9, which shows the functions for the various conditions brought into relation with each other as straight lines with different slopes. These functions summarize about 1,500 measurements altogether. Their slopes diminish regularly if the functions are considered in the order in which they have just been discussed. How are we to interpret such a relationship?

In 1911 Katz introduced into the psychology of perception the

---

* Editor's Abridgement.

concept of *reduction*.[13] The perceived phenomenon is a resultant of many determinants. Some one of them may be *primary* in the sense that it is essential to the perception although it may not play the principal role in determining the exact form or quality or amount of the perception. For instance, in the case of visual brightness, which Katz was considering, illumination of the perceived object is a primary factor, yet the phenomenal brightness is actually determined by many other factors that enter otherwise into the perception. If some of these additional determinants can be eliminated, then the perception can be reduced in the direction of the primary determinant. So Katz invented the "reduction screen," a screen with a hole in it so arranged that, when a colored surface is seen through the hole and all the circumstances of its relation to the surrounding field are excluded by the remainder of the screen, then the brightness, instead of remaining "constant" at the value proper for the perceived object, is "reduced" to a datum dependent almost entirely upon the actual retinal illumination.

In a similar manner we may regard the present series of conditions as representing successive reductions of the size perception. Let us list these conditions in order, adding as additional items the two theoretical limits of variation. Here the primary determinant is, of course, visual angle or retinal size. It is toward it that reduction is undertaken.

(*1*) *Size Constancy.* It is possible that size constancy represents one limit of variation, that perceptual organization, as Brunswik has suggested,[14] occurs in the interest of stabilizing the perceptual world. The organism utilizes, therefore, additional 'cues' which tend to keep the apparent size of an object constant when its visual angle varies with changing distance. According to this view, we should not expect to find an over-compensation, by which a receding object would increase in apparent size while its retinal image diminished.

(*2*) *Binocular Observation.* Free binocular observation presum-

[13] Katz, D. Die Erscheinungsweisen der Farben, *Zsch. f. Psychol.*, 1911, Ergbd. 7, esp. 36-39.

[14] Brunswik, E. Die Zugänglichkeit von Gegenständen für die Wahrnehmung und deren quantitative Bestimmung. *Arch. f. d. ges. Psychol.*, 1933, **88**, 377-418. See esp. the section on infendierte und intentional erreichte Wahrnehmungsgegenstände, pp. 378-387, and the section on Bestimmung des intentional erreichten Gegenstandes, pp. 387-411, which deals with der Grad der Dingkonstanz. The Helmholtzian conception of unbewusster Schluss seems by this route to be reentering the psychology of perception.

ably employs all the determinants available, and would thus be, as we find, the least reduced perception. It might therefore achieve size constancy or fall short. Our data, however, show over-compensation; the slope of the function for binocular observation exceeds the slope of the dotted line for size constancy in Fig. 9. This position of the line for binocular observation, as we have already noted, may merely indicate the existence of a space error in the experiment. If that assumption be correct, then the 'true' function for these data of binocular observation lies with the line for size constancy or below it.

(3) *Monocular Observation*. The stopping of vision from one eye is the first step in reduction of the perception. By it all binocular retinal conditions for the perception of distance are eliminated. It is obvious that the reduction of the perception from size constancy toward the law of the visual angle must depend upon the elimination of cues to distance, for the organism can compensate for diminution of retinal size with increase of distance only if cues to distance are available—only if it 'knows' how far away the object is and thus how much to compensate for distance. Reduction, therefore, must consist mainly in the removal of cues to distance.[15]

(4) *Artificial Pupil*. The use of an artificial pupil with monocular observation still further reduces the slope of the function (Fig. 9) and may thus be supposed to eliminate some more cues to the distance of the standard stimulus. Perhaps the stopping down of the pupil makes accommodation less effective and thus reduces its effectiveness as a differentia of distance.[16]

(5) *Reduction Tunnel*. Some faint illumination from the stimuli was visible by reflection from the surfaces of the corridor. The long black tunnel, 3 x 3 ft., was designed to eliminate these cues to distance and thus to reduce the perception entirely to retinal size. The result was not entirely successful. There was still a light haze visible within the tunnel which conceivably may have provided an indication of distance. At any rate the slope of the function was not re-

---

[15] Monocular observation also reduces apparent size because it reduces the total retinal illumination; cf. Holway and Boring. *Amer. J. Psychol.*, 1940, 53, 587-589. Since it affects both the standard and comparison stimuli, leaving their relation unchanged, it need not be considered here.

[16] The artificial pupil also reduces apparent size by reducing retinal illumination, but, like the reduction in monocular vision, it affects both the standard and comparison stimulus and can be ignored here.

duced to zero. Nevertheless, with the tunnel the perceptual field became much more homogeneous, and the slope of the function was greatly diminished.

(6) *Visual Angle.* Retinal size, as indicated by the visual angle, must be the limit of reduction and yield a function in which the slope is zero. For all that has been said by Gestalt psychologists against the validity of the law of the visual angle, it would nevertheless appear that, when no relevant datum other than retinal size is available, then the perception of size will after all vary solely with the visual angle. That statement is a tautology and must be true. Size constancy can be the law of size, therefore, only when determination is complex.

The following ratios show the relative slopes of the functions under discussion. To them are added the values for the theoretical laws of size constancy (1.00) and of visual angle (0). The "actual data" are the slopes as they occur in Fig. 9. The "adjusted data" are the slopes as they would be if we correct for a possible space error by rotating the functions clockwise through an angle of 10', so as to bring the line for binocular observation to where we think

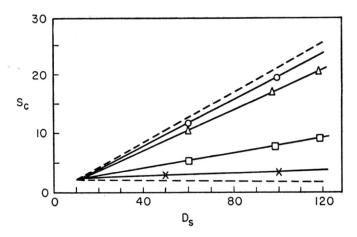

F‌ɪɢ. 10. DETERMINANTS OF APPARENT VISUAL SIZE WITH DISTANCE VARIANT. This figure is the same as Fig. 9, except that the four functions have been rotated clockwise through an angle of 10 min., in order to bring the function for binocular observation below the function for size constancy, as we think it would have to be, and as correction for a space error might require.

it should be, *i.e.* below the line for size constancy. These adjusted data are also plotted in Fig. 10.

	Size Constancy	Binoc. Obs.	Monoc. Obs.	Artif. Pupil	Red. Tunnel	Vis. Angle
Actual data	1.00	1.09	.98	.44	.22	0
Adjusted data	1.00	.93	.81	.30	.08	0

Our general conclusion from all these data is hardly more than a restatement of the obvious. The organism can perceive the size of an object as constant, even though its distance changes, provided the perception is complex enough to provide the essential differentiae. When the perception is reduced by the elimination of some of these determinants, the law of the variation of apparent size with distance approaches the law of variation of the remaining determinants. If the perception could be reduced to a single determinant— retinal size or any other—then apparent size would have to vary in accordance with the mode of variation of this sole remaining determinant. There is no alternative hypothesis.

SUMMARY

The apparent size of a standard stimulus subtending a visual angle of one degree was measured as the distance of the standard was varied from 10 to 120 ft. Functions relating apparent size to distance were obtained from 5 Os under four different sets of conditions: (1) direct binocular regard; (2) monocular regard; (3) monocular regard through a small artificial pupil; and (4) monocular regard through the artificial pupil and a long black reduction tunnel. For each of these conditions the most probable form of the function relating apparent size to distance was found to be linear.

These conditions, considered in the order in which they have been named, represent a serial reduction of the size perception. In binocular regard apparent size is the resultant of the interoperation of many determinants, which are successively reduced in number in the three remaining sets of conditions. This reduction is paralleled by a consistent change in the slope of the line that relates apparent size to distance. The limits of variation of this slope are—at least approximately—(1) the function for size as constant in spite of change of the perceived object's distance and (2) the function for size as proportional to the visual angle subtended by the perceived object. Binocular regard gave a function close to the function for size constancy. Reduction of the perception from binocular regard brought the function nearly, but not entirely, to the slope for apparent size as wholly dependent upon retinal size.

SELECTION 35

....

Reinforcement and Extinction
as Factors in Size Estimation* †

WILLIAM W. LAMBERT, RICHARD L. SOLOMON, AND
PETER D. WATSON

INTRODUCTION

IN RECENT EXPERIMENTS on the psychology of perceiving, there
has been a noticeable tendency to emphasize determinants which
might be classed as motivational in character. The work of Sanford
(6, 7) involving the relationship between drive states and 'autistic
perceiving,' and the extension of this work by Murphy and his collaborators (3, 5, 8), and by McClelland and Atkinson (4), illustrate this trend. More closely related to the present problem is the
work of Bruner, Postman, and their collaborators (1, 2) dealing
with the 'selection' and 'accentuation' of perceived objects relative
to the 'value systems' of an individual. Two of their experiments
in particular illustrate the operation of the conceptualized value
dimension. Bruner and Postman (2) found that circles of the same
diameter, embossed with (1) a high-valued social symbol, and (2)
a low-valued social symbol, were judged to be larger than circles
embossed with (3) a neutral symbol. This might indicate that 'perceptual accentuation' is a U-shaped function of a value dimension
varying from −1 to +1, with a minimum of accentuation at 'neu-
trality.' Bruner and Goodman (1) have shown that poor children
tend to overestimate the size of coins more than rich children do.

* From the *J. exp. Psychol.*, 1949, **39**, 637-641. Reprinted by permission of
the authors and the publisher.

This problem has been further studied in Lambert, W. W., and Lambert,
E. C. Some indirect effects of reward on children's size estimations. *J. abnorm.
soc. Psychol.*, 1953, **48**, 507-514.

† This research was facilitated by the Laboratory of Social Relations, Harvard University. The authors wish to thank Miss Winifred Lydon, Director
of the Harvard Veteran's Nursery School, and Major Gertrude Atkinson, of
the Salvation Army Nursery School, Boston, for their indispensable help and
cooperation in carrying out this study.

These experimenters stated: "The reasonable assumption was made that poor children have a greater subjective need for money than rich ones." (1, p. 39) They further asserted that "the greater the value of the coin, the greater is the deviation of *apparent* size from *actual* size." (1, p. 38)

The multitude of influences correlated with being rich or poor makes it difficult to analyze the specific determinants of size overestimation. It was thought that some light could be shed on this problem by experimentally controlling the life history of children with respect to an initially neutral object. Specifically, we wished to associate a relatively neutral poker chip[1] with candy reward and later extinguish this association by removal of reward and to measure the effects of such procedures on the estimated size of the poker chip. Our hypothesis was that 'value,' as defined by changes in apparent size, is a function of both reinforcement and extinction procedures.

SUBJECTS AND PROCEDURE

In the first study, 32 children from the Harvard Nursery School (ages three to five) were divided into 22 experimental subjects and 10 control subjects. In the second study, 22 children of comparable age from a Salvation Army Nursery School provided 15 experimental subjects and 7 control subjects.

The experimental subjects were individually introduced to a token-reward situation where they turned a crank 18 turns in order to receive a white poker chip which, when put into a slot, led to the automatic delivery of a piece of candy. The control subjects were introduced into the same situation, but candy came directly after work, *without* the mediation of a poker chip. In the first study, both groups worked (and were rewarded) once a day for 10 days; in the second study, the subjects worked (and were rewarded) *five* times a day for 10 days.

Size estimates of the white poker chip token were made by the subjects (1) prior to the experiment; (2) after 10 days of reward; (3) after extinction had occurred (11th day); and (4) after reward had been reinstated (12th day).

Measurements were taken with the equipment designed and used by Bruner and Goodman (1). This equipment was composed of a rectangular wooden box (9 × 9 × 18 in.) with a 5-in. square ground-glass screen in the center of the front panel, and a control knob at the lower right-

---

[1] Only one of our children knew what a poker chip was. It was called a circle in our experiment.

hand corner. At the center of the ground-glass screen the subject was presented with a circular patch of light (16.2 app. ft. cdls.) the diameter of which was under the control of the knob. The light source was a 60-watt incandescent light shining through an iris diaphragm which could be varied (in terms of the visible light patch) from ⅛ to 2 in. As Bruner and Goodman reported: "The circle was not truly round, containing the familiar nine-elliptoid sides found in the Bausch and Lomb iris diaphragm. It was so close, however, that subjects had no difficulty making the subjective equations required of them." (1, p. 37)

The subjects stood in front of the apparatus with the light patch at or slightly below eye level, and about 12 to 18 in. away. The token, pasted on a 5-in. square gray cardboard, was held by the experimenters so that it was parallel to the circular patch. About 7 in. separated the centers of the two objects to be compared.

The judgment problem was presented to the children of both groups as a game. Each child made his estimates alone. Two judgments starting from the open and two starting from the closed position of the iris were obtained from each child at each measurement session; these judgments were made in an order which was counter-balanced for direction of turning of the control knob. The children were not informed of their success in approximating the actual size of the poker chip.

On the 11th day—after 10 days of rewarded trials—extinction was instituted. The children of both groups worked, but no candy was forthcoming. They worked until they met the arbitrary criterion of extinction: three min. during which they did not turn the handle of the work machine. The size estimates were made immediately after the subject had met the extinction criterion.

On the 12th day the subjects were reintroduced to the reward sequence, and the work brought candy to the control group and token plus candy to the experimental group. Size estimates were made immediately after this 12th session.

RESULTS

The results for both nursery schools were combined and they are shown graphically in Fig. 1. The four size estimation sessions are distributed on the x-axis; the mean estimate of the token size in terms of percent of actual size is shown on the y-axis. The actual size is indicated by the horizontal line parallel to the x-axis. The means for the experimental group are connected by the solid lines, and the means for the control group are connected by the dotted lines. The connecting lines are meant to increase legibility; they do not imply a continuous function of any sort.

It would appear that the control group showed no significant changes with experience. The experimental group, however, showed a rise in the apparent size of the token after ten days of using the token to obtain reward. The estimates dropped to the level of the beginning estimates following the extinction procedure in which the token no longer led to candy reward. The estimates went back in the direction of over-estimation when reward was reinstated on the 12th day.

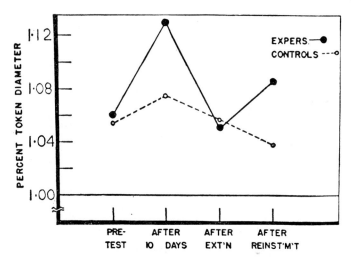

Fɪɢ. 1. Effects of the experimental conditions upon children's estimates of the diameter of a token when these estimates are taken as percents of the true diameter.

The mean size estimates in arbitrary units of the comparison-stimulus diameter are given in Table I, together with the corresponding percent of the actual token diameter, for each of the four points in our experiment. The results for our two studies are combined, since there were no appreciable differences between the 10-reinforcement and the 50-reinforcement experiments.

Analyses of variance[2] were performed on the data which are summarized in Table I. The following differences are of interest: (1) In the experimental group, the estimated size of the token after 10

---

[2] These analyses are uncorrected for the correlation between successive sets of estimates. They are thus conservative.

TABLE I. THE ALTERATION OF SIZE ESTIMATION WITH
EXPERIENCE IN THE EXPERIMENTAL SITUATION

Experimental Group

	Mean Estimated Size*	σ_m	Percent Actual Size
Pretest	66.8	1.2	1.06
After 10 days	70.9	1.1	1.13
After extinction	66.3	1.3	1.05
After reinstatement	68.5	1.8	1.09

Control Group

	Mean Estimated Size*	σ_m	Percent Actual Size
Pretest	66.4	1.5	1.05
After 10 days	67.7	1.2	1.07
After extinction	66.6	1.2	1.06
After reinstatement	65.4	1.4	1.04

* Actual size of poker chip is 63.0 in arbitrary units of diameter. The error of measurement of diameter by experimenter is ±0.2 units.

days of reinforcement was significantly greater than at the pretest. This difference is reliable at the one percent level of confidence. (2) In the experimental group, the size estimates after extinction were significantly smaller than they were after the 10 days of reinforcement. This difference is reliable at the one percent level of confidence. (3) In the experimental group the rise in estimated size following reinstatement of reward is significant at the one percent level of confidence. (4) In the control group, none of the four mean estimates is significantly different from any other. (5) The mean estimates for the experimental and control groups after ten days of reinforcement are significantly different from one another with a reliability between the one and five percent levels of confidence. (6) The mean estimates for the experimental and control groups after reinstatement of reward are not significantly different from one another even though a marked trend seems evident.

DISCUSSION

Several alternative theoretical interpretations for our results could be made. Since experiments are in progress to study further the factors involved, these possibilities will merely be listed at this time. These views are not mutually exclusive, but overlap, as do so many formulations in this field.

1. The estimation changes in the experimental group may be compatible with a generalized pattern of behavior which we could call the 'cookie effect.' That is, the effect may be peculiar to our culture where, for example, a 'bigger cookie is *better* than a little one.' 'Bigness' and 'value,' or 'bigness' and 'goodness,' may be acquired equivalencies for our children, particularly at the ages of the subjects used here. Experiments have been planned which may provide evidence on whether this phenomenon is 'culture bound' or not.

2. These results may provide a measure reflecting some of the secondary reinforcing characteristics taken on by the token during the reinforced trials. These characteristics become lost when reinforcement is not maintained, as during extinction, but are restored when reward is reinstated. This formulation, if further bulwarked with evidence, could serve to integrate perceptual distortion phenomena with learning theory and possibly provide a valuable indirect measure of secondary reinforcement.

3. It is possible that the size enhancement phenomenon can provide us with inferences about perceptual processes as envisioned by Bruner and his collaborators (1, 2). They hypothesize: "The greater the social value of an object, the more will it be susceptible to organization by behavioral determinants." (1, p. 36) In its learning aspects, however, over-estimation of size may reflect either 'expectancy' or 'hypothesis' formation (and decay) or it may, as stated above, reflect learned 'needs' which operate in the workings of this conceptualized perceptual process. The actual mechanism which produces overestimation following reinforcement is, however, entirely obscure at the present stage of our research.

In view of the fact that relatively 'neutral' poker chips were used in the experiment, our data cannot be legitimately compared with the coin size data of Bruner and Goodman (1). In addition, our two nursery school groups do not fulfill the criteria of distinct economic class differences. In no sense can we call one group 'rich children' and the other group 'poor children.'

It is interesting to note the possibility that effects such as those discussed here depend on a 'difficult' or 'ambiguous' judgment situation. Probably, the more ambiguous the stimulus situation, the more strongly can reinforcement and motivational factors operate in determining size judgments.

4. It is interesting to note that, following extinction procedures, the estimates of the experimental group do not increase above the original level, when the chip was 'neutral.' This could mean that the U-shaped function postulated to relate accentuation and value does not apply here. Or it could mean that extinction removes positive value without producing negative value. Perhaps extinction by punishment is necessary for producing negativity and an increase in size estimates at the negative end of the U-shaped function.

SUMMARY

We have described the results of an experiment which was designed to investigate the effects of reinforcement and extinction on size estimation. It was found that the establishment of a token reward sequence results in relative overestimation of the token size. Extinction of the sequence removes this overestimation tendency to a great extent. The results are thought to have relevance for both learning and perception theory.

REFERENCES

1. Bruner, J. S., and Goodman, C. C. Value and need as organizing factors in perception. *J. abnorm. soc. Psychol.*, 1947, **42**, 33-44.
2. Bruner, J. S., and Postman, L. Symbolic value as an organizing factor in perception. *J. soc. Psychol.*, 1948, **27**, 203-208.
3. Levine, R., Chein, I., and Murphy, G. The relation of the intensity of a need to the amount of perceptual distortion: a preliminary report. *J. Psychol.*, 1942, **13**, 283-293.
4. McClelland, D. C., and Atkinson, J. W. The projective expression of needs: I. The effect of different intensities of hunger drive on perception. *J. Psychol.*, 1948, **25**, 205-222.
5. Proshansky, H., and Murphy, G. The effects of reward and punishment on perception. *J. Psychol.*, 1942, **13**, 295-305.
6. Sanford, R. N. The effect of abstinence from food upon imaginal processes; a preliminary experiment. *J. Psychol.*, 1936, **2**, 129-136.
7. Sanford, R. N. The effect of abstinence from food upon imaginal processes; a further experiment. *J. Psychol.*, 1937, **3**, 145-159.
8. Schafer, R., and Murphy, G. The role of autism in a visual figure-ground relationship. *J. exp. Psychol.*, 1943, **32**, 335-343.

The Localization of Actual Sources of Sound*

S. S. STEVENS AND EDWIN B. NEWMAN

QUANTITATIVE INFORMATION relative to the ability of an O to localize actual sources of sound in free space is prerequisite to the formulation of an adequate theory of localization. The acquisition of such information depends upon the possibility of generating pure tones for a wide range of frequencies and of presenting them to an O in such a way that no reflected waves reach the ears. The present study attempts to satisfy these two conditions.

ANTECEDENTS

The earliest systematic investigations of localization were conducted by what might be called the 'sound-cage school.' Their results were limited by the fact that, owing to the absence of electrical generating apparatus, they were forced for the most part to use clicks and noises as stimuli. Another limiting factor was their custom of experimenting in closed rooms whose walls were not sound-absorbent. In spite of these drawbacks, certain facts were established.[1] Os are able (1) to locate noises better than tones and (2) to distinguish right from left. However, they tend (3) to confuse the location of sounds lying in the median plane and (4) to locate sounds at the sides with the least accuracy. The greater inaccuracy of localization at the sides is exactly what one would expect on the basis of recent measurements[2] of the variation of the difference in loudness at the two ears of a speech-source rotated in a horizontal plane around the head. Throughout an angle of about 70° on either side the difference in loudness at the two ears remains virtually constant. In the face of this constancy it is obvious that within the 70°-angle there could be no intensive cues for exact localization. An area of in-

*From Amer. J. Psychol., 1936, 48, 297-306. Reprinted by permission of the authors and the publisher.

[1] Pierce, A. H. Studies in Auditory and Visual Space Perception. 1901, 52.

[2] Steinberg, J. C., and Snow, W. B. Physical factors in auditory perspective. Bell System Tech. J., 1934, 13, 247-260.

exact localization at the sides is also indicated as the effect of the differ-ence of phase at the two ears,[3] when the stimulus is a tone of low fre-quency.

From the sound-cage attention turned to the matter of the presentation of sounds which differ at the two ears in respect of intensity, phase, time of arrival, or a combination of these factors. In this way there arose the 'dichotic school,' whose problem it was to determine the relative merits of the intensity-theory, the phase-theory, and the time-theory.[4] Each of the differential factors—intensity, phase and time—influences localiza-tion, each has been nominated by one or more experimenters as the most important factor in localization, and each has also been reduced in theory to one of the others. The facts established by this school are (1) that localization is towards the side of greatest intensity, (2) that in the case of low tones lateral localization can be got by advancing the phase at one ear, and (3) that localization is towards the side of the sound which leads in time. Presumably phase-difference is but a special case of time-difference[5] so that in reality there are just two factors available as cues for the localization of pure tones. A final answer as to the rôle of these two factors could not be given, however, since it has not been known to what extent actual sounds can be localized.

A novel attack on the problem of localization, only recently initiated, is the investigation of auditory perspective: the stereophonic effect of multiple sources of sound.[6] Sounds picked up in one room by three micro-phones spaced several feet apart and broadcast through three correspond-ingly placed loud speakers in another room can be localized with consider-able accuracy. The localization is what would be expected on the basis of the intensive difference at the ears of the O as calculated from meas-urements[7] of the effect of the sound-shadow cast by the head. Up to the present time, however, such studies have dealt only with complex sounds.

---

[3] Stewart, G. W. Phase relations in the acoustic shadows of rigid sphere. *Phys. Rev.,* 1914, 4, 252-258; Hartley, R. V. L. Function of phase difference in binaural localization of pure tones. *Ibid.,* 1919, 13, 373-385.

[4] Trimble, O. C. The theory of sound localization: A restatement. *Psychol. Rev.,* 1928, 35, 515-523.

[5] von Hornbostel, E. M., and Wertheimer, M. Über die Wahrnehmung der Schallrichtung. *Sitzber. d. preuss. Akad. d. Wissensch.,* 1920, 388-396; E. G. Boring, Auditory theory with special reference to intensity, volume, and local-ization, *Amer. J. Psychol.,* 1926, 37, 157-188.

[6] Fletcher, H., et al. Auditory perspective: A symposium. *Bell System Tech. J.,* 1934, 13, 239-310. The essential facts of perspective with two-channel trans-mission were demonstrated in the Harvard Psychological Laboratory in 1929; cf. unpublished affidavit by M. Upton and W. D. Turner.

[7] Sivian, L. J., and White, S. D. Minimal audible sound fields. *J. Acous. Soc. Amer.,* 1933, 4, 288-321.

APPARATUS

The present experiments were conducted entirely in the open air. In order to avoid possible reflecting surfaces a tall swivel chair was erected on top of a ventilator which rises 9 ft. above the roof of the new Biological Laboratories at Harvard University. O was thus placed in a position where there were no vertical reflecting surfaces on any side of him, and the nearest horizontal surface on the side toward the source of the sound was approximately 12 ft. below him. At the present time this procedure appears to be the only practicable means of avoiding errors due to the reflection of sound.

The source of the sound was mounted on the end of a 12-ft. arm attached to the pedestal of the chair. When properly counterbalanced, it could be moved noiselessly in a complete circle in a horizontal plane on the level of O's ears.

For the larger portion of the experiments a small 4-in. magnetic speaker, mounted in a 12-in. baffle, served to generate the tones. Only in the case of the lowest frequency (60 cycles) was it necessary to use a large Western Electric type-560 cone speaker in order to obtain sufficient power. This speaker was mounted on the same arm at a distance at 6 ft. from O.

A beat-frequency oscillator, which could be adjusted to the desired frequency, supplied ample power to the loud speaker. The voltage was adjusted by means of a 7000-ohm potentiometer, while a further shunting resistance was used to turn the tone on and off without producing clicks. The elimination of clicks in the loud speaker is, indeed, an important consideration. The tones were made reasonably pure by the use of suitable filters: tones of 2200 cycles and above passed through a high-pass section with a cut-off frequency of 2500 cycles; tones 3000 cycles and below passed through suitable low-pass sections which reduced the partials other than the fundamental by at least 30 db. The 60-cycle voltage was obtained directly from the lighting circuit. Two check experiments with unfiltered power at frequencies of 400 and 1000 cycles showed that slightly more accurate localizations could be expected with these less pure tones.

Comparative results for two noises were obtained by the use of a click and a hiss. The click was produced by applying 45 volts from a battery to the loud speaker for a brief instant. It was heard by O as a single sharp click which possessed the high frequency characteristic of the speaker. The hiss was produced by blowing air through a small brass tube, the end of which had been cut and pinched. The brass tube was attached to the end of the swinging arm and was blown through a long rubber tube by E. The sound produced contained a perceptible high-pitched whistle with a frequency of about 7000 cycles. The remaining energy was probably distributed over a wide band of frequencies.

The sensation level of the tones used in this experiment was determined approximately by comparison of the voltages used with threshold voltages determined under comparable conditions in a soundproof and sound-deadened room. Comparison of the sensation levels thus determined with standard audibility curves shows that tones of the middle range from 400 to 4000 cycles had a loudness level of 50 to 60 db. Tones in the extreme ranges, although they were of moderately high intensity, reached a loudness level of about 30 db.

The apparent intensity of the tones was reduced in the experimental situation by the presence of a constant background of sound consisting of distant traffic noises. The level of this noise was determined by a comparison of the thresholds obtained in the soundproof room with those obtained on the roof. The masking effect is measured by the rise in threshold for the various tones. The average rise in threshold for five frequencies between 400 and 7000 cycles, the region in which the effect was greatest, was 28.0 db.

PROCEDURE

In the present experiment each of the two authors acted alternately as O and E. The tones were presented at certain definite positions in the horizontal plane of the O's head. The O's task was to name the position of the source of sound in this plane. We found in some preliminary experiments conducted in the spring of 1933 that reversals of right and left practically never occurred. Therefore, in the main series of observations which were made during the summer of 1934, the sounds were presented at 13 different positions on the right side of the O. These positions were spaced 15° apart from 0° directly in front to 180° directly behind. Ten observations were made at each position by each O.

The O tried, of course, to distinguish sounds in front from sounds behind, but his success, as will be shown later, depended upon what sound was being used. Since front-back reversals were frequent, we decided that the fairest measure of localizability could be obtained only if such reversals were not counted as errors. Therefore, the size of the error in the localization of a given sound was obtained by taking the difference between the reported position and either the actual position or the corresponding position in the other quadrant, depending upon which was the smaller. Thus, when the source was at 0° the localization was considered correct if it were either 0° or 180°; if the source was at 30°, both 30° and 150° were considered correct responses. This procedure is equivalent to the assumption that dichotic differences of phase or intensity provide a basis for lateral localization alone.

LOCALIZATION AS A FUNCTION
OF FREQUENCY

The average of the errors made by both Os at each of the frequencies used is shown in Fig. 1. The errors, computed by the

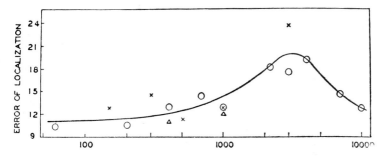

FIG. 1.   Dependence of localization on frequency. The ordinate represents the average of the errors in degrees made by both Os. The crosses are for the shorter series of judgments made in 1933. The circles represent the results obtained in 1934. The triangles represent the results obtained with unfiltered tones. Note the critical region at about 3,000 cycles.

method described above, are relatively constant at low frequencies, but become larger as the frequency approaches 3000 cycles. This change accords with the general findings of the 'dichotic school.' However, above 4000 cycles localization improves again and is fully as accurate at 10,000 as at 1000 cycles. This result, as far as we know, has not been anticipated by previous experimenters. In fact, it has been suggested [8] on several occasions that high tones can not be localized at all—for no better reason, it would seem, than that no one had really tried to localize high tones.

The explanation of the shape of the curve in Fig. 1 must concern us. The inexact localization of tones between 2000 and 4000 cycles is precisely what we should expect from a consideration of the effects of the two localizing factors, difference in phase and in intensity. Owing to the size and shape of the head, there are certain theoretical limits to the possible effectiveness of each of these factors. The limits are shown graphically in Fig. 2. It is well established that differential phase is most effective in determining the localization of low tones, and that above about 600 cycles its effec-

---

[8] Halverson, H. M. The upper limit of auditory localization. *Amer. J. Psychol.*, 1927, **38**, 97-106, esp. p. 97.

tiveness decreases with increasing frequency. In Fig. 2 are shown the results (dotted line) obtained by Halverson[9] for the maximal lateral shift in localization obtainable with 180° phase-difference as a function of frequency and also the results to be expected theoreti-

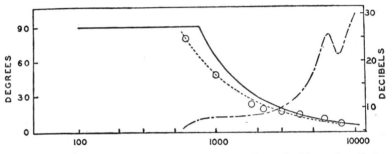

FIG. 2.   Absence of phase-effect at high frequencies and of intensity-effect at low frequencies. The solid curve represents theoretically the maximum angle by which a tone can be displaced by 180° change in phase. The circles on the dotted curve are the obtained maxima of displacement (Halverson). The dot-dash curve represents the observed difference in intensity at the two ears of tones originating at the side of the observer (Sivian and White).

cally. The theoretical curve (solid line) is a first approximation and was obtained by considering the difference in the distance a sound-wave would have to travel to reach the two ears. If the radius of the head is taken as 8.75 cm. the difference in distance is given by

$$d = 8.75 \ (\sin \theta + \theta).$$

Since our method of treating front-back reversals reduces the problem to a consideration of the phase-effect within a single quadrant, we should not expect confusions to arise until the frequency is so high that two or more positions within a quadrant would give rise to the same phase-difference at the ears of the O. The frequency at which this first occurs is that whose wave-length is equal to the maximum value of d, or 1520 cycles.

   Fig. 2 also shows the difference in intensity at the two ears for tones of different frequency originating at the side of the O (dot-dash line). This curve is due to Steinberg and Snow[10] and shows that the difference at the two ears tends to increase with frequency,

[9] Halverson, *loc. cit.*
[10] Steinberg and Snow, *loc. cit.*

as one would expect in view of the sharper sound-shadows obtained with high frequencies.

It is obvious from Fig. 2 that at low frequencies the phase-effect is ample to account for localization, and that at high frequencies the intensity-effect is sufficiently marked to afford good cues. Furthermore, in the region of 3000 cycles neither phase nor intensity is available as a differential cue. Hence the sharp maximum in the curve in Fig. 1 at about this frequency. In general, then, we can conclude that at low frequencies the localization of pure tones is made on the basis of phase-differences, at high frequencies it is made on the basis of intensitive differences, and that in a region near 3000 cycles localization is poor, because of the absence of both types of differences.

Additional reason for believing that differences in intensity alone are operative at high frequencies is afforded by the fact that at about 2800 cycles the action currents in the auditory nerve cease to be synchronized with the stimulus.[11] This fact suggests that although below 2800 cycles phase-differences might well be effective since they could be transmitted as such to the brain, whereas above 2800 cycles any discrimination in terms of the phase-effect should be impossible. On the other hand, Halverson's results show at this frequency no sharp break which could be associated with a breakdown of synchronization. However, Halverson reports that marked changes of intensity occurred as the phase of the high-frequency tones was altered. It may be that his results were due to changes in intensity rather than phase.

LOCALIZATION AS A FUNCTION OF POSITION

Since the work of Bloch[12] in 1893, it has been generally recognized without serious contradiction, that the localization of sounds in the horizontal plane is most accurate in the region directly in front or behind the O.

The average results for the fourteen main series of our experiment are shown in the following table.

---

[11] Davis, H., Forbes, A., and Derbyshire, A. J. The recovery period of the auditory nerve and its significance for the theory of hearing. *Science*, 1933, **78**, 552.

[12] Bloch, E. Das binaurale Hören. *Zsch. f. Augenheilkunde*, 1893, **24**, 25-86.

Position in degrees from median plane	0°	15°	30°	45°	60°	75°	90°
Average error in degrees	4.6°	13.0°	15.6°	16.3°	16.2°	15.6°	16.0°

The values for 60° and 75° are weighted means. The weights were assigned in proportion as the errors due to reversals exceeded those expected on the basis of a normal distribution of errors. In order to determine these values the mean average deviation of the distribution was used: it is 15.8°. Using this value the number of reversals to be expected when the stimulus was at a given position could be determined from a table of the probability integral. The 'weighted mean' is thus a mean which includes those errors of localization in the other quadrant which would be expected as errors and which considers the remaining errors in the other quadrant as true reversals.

The results for individual frequencies show considerable variability because of the limited number of cases involved in each average. With the exception, however, of the three critical frequencies, 2200, 3000, and 4000 cycles, they are in substantial agreement with the table presented above.

Since localization at low frequencies is based on the phase-effect, we should expect the errors of localization to be inversely proportional to the rate of change of phase-difference as a function of azimuth, or equal to $k/(\cos \theta + 1)$. The errors made by N at low frequencies agree fairly well with this expectation, but those made by S are too large at the 15° and 30° positions. We have reason to suspect a systematic error at these positions.

In general, the shape of the function relating errors and position is what might be expected upon theoretical grounds.[13] The fact that the function is essentially the same at the very high frequencies, however, requires explanation. The greater effectiveness of differential intensity near the median plane is not, as early investigators supposed, an example of Weber's Law. On the contrary, the effect can be predicted from the way in which the relative intensity at the two ears depends upon the azimuth of the sound. Both the theoretical values of Hartley and Fry[14] and the experimental deter-

---

[13] Stewart and Hartley, *loc. cit.*

[14] Hartley, R. V. L., and Fry, T. C. The binaural localization of pure tones. *Phys. Rev.*, 1921, **18**, 431-442.

minations of thresholds by Sivian and White[15] indicate that a relatively large displacement of the source is necessary at the side of the O to produce a given change of intensity. It is to be expected, therefore, that localization would be best near the median plane and poorest at the extreme lateral positions.

Somewhat more striking in our experiments was the ability of the O to distinguish between front and back. The relative frequency of reversals has been taken as a measure of front-back discrimination. In Fig. 3 are presented the average results of both Os plotted

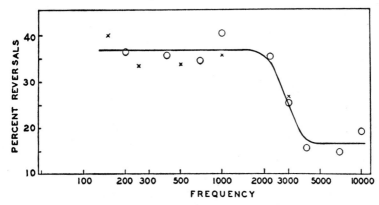

FIG. 3.   Percentage reversals of the front-back quadrants. The crosses are for the data obtained in 1933, the circles for 1934. The critical region is at about 3,000 cycles; cf. Fig. 1.

against frequency. The individual curves agreed closely in form with the average curve. One function (for N) was displaced upward and slightly to the left of the other (for S).

It is apparent at once that the total range of frequencies is divided into two distinct regions separated by a narrow critical range at about 3000 cycles. For tones below 2000 cycles, where localization is based on phase-differences, discrimination between the front and back quadrants is only a little better than chance. Above 4000 cycles the number of reversals is but one-third of those expected by chance. Taken in connection with the other data presented in this paper, these results offer striking confirmation of the double mechanism (differential phase and intensity) involved in normal localization. The ability of the O to distinguish front from back in the case

[15] Sivian and White. *loc. cit.*

of tones of high frequency is very largely a function of the difference in intensity between sounds in front and behind.

A number of checks were made in order to demonstrate the validity of this hypothesis. A continuous tone of high frequency, when swung about the O decreased very markedly in loudness from front to back. A number of tests were made in which intensity was varied from trial to trial in chance order; and the percentage of reversals, for six series at 3000 to 7000 cycles, was found to increase from 18.6% with the usual procedure to 47% with this test procedure. It appears that the O had formed a subjective standard of intensity in the main series after a very few trials. After this the tones in back "seemed weak" while those in front were loud and close. Sound-shadows from the pinna are probably sufficient to account for this effect.

LOCALIZATION AS A FUNCTION OF COMPLEXITY

The experimental series in which the click and the hiss were used confirm the fact that complex sounds are more easily localized than pure tones. The localization of the hiss in particular was very definite, almost as definite as though one were looking at the source! The average of the errors of localization was only 8.0° for the click and 5.6° for the hiss. Thus it may be remarked that the fact that the click was much better localized than any of the pure tones shows the importance of eliminating all of the clicks and extraneous noises which are present if the onset of a pure tone is too abrupt. In the case of the hiss neither O was aware of any intensive or qualitative difference at the different positions during the test series; but careful observation afterwards revealed noticeable differences of both kinds. When in front the hiss was more *shh* and less *sss* and was louder than when behind. The qualitative differences were due, of course, to the differential effect of the shadow of the head upon the frequencies composing the hiss.

In view of findings of the present experiment relative to the ease with which high tones can be localized, it is not surprising that noises with high-frequency components are very easily localized. Noises in general have both high and low frequencies present. The low frequencies provide sufficient phase-differences and the high frequencies sufficient intensitive differences for localization. The two types of cue render each other mutual support, and the result is an accuracy of localization greater than that obtainable with pure tones.

CONCLUSIONS

(1) The ability to localize tones varies markedly with frequency. It is approximately constant below 1000 cycles, drops rapidly to a minimum between 2000 and 4000 cycles, and rises again to its former level at higher frequencies. See Fig. 1.

(2) The error of localization is smallest for tones located near the median plane and increases as the tone is moved toward the side of the O. The relation between the azimuth of the tone and the error of localization is approximately the same for both high and low frequencies.

(3) The confusion of positions lying in the quadrant in front of the O with those in the quadrant behind him is very frequent. Below 3000 cycles the frequency of such reversals was about that which should be given by chance. Above 3000 cycles it was only about one third of the chance value.

(4) Noises (a click and a hiss) were localized more readily than any of the tones. Differences of quality and intensity were discernible between different positions of the noises.

(5) All of the above facts are consistent with the hypothesis that the localization of low tones is made on the basis of phase-differences at the two ears, and that the localization of high tones is made on the basis of intensitive differences. There is a band of intermediate frequencies near 3000 cycles in which neither phase nor intensity is very effective and in which localization is poorest.

SELECTION 37

....

On Sound Localization*

HANS WALLACH

THE TWO FACTORS governing sound localization which have been seriously discussed in recent years are time difference and intensity difference. Both are supposed to have the same effect: they determine the lateral angle of a given sound to the one side or the other. With increasing time difference the perceived sound is located more and more to the side where the stimulation occurs first, and with increasing difference of intensity, the sound is said to appear further and further toward the side of the stronger stimulation.

These so-called primary cues for sound localization convey merely the angular distance of the given sound from the median plane or, more conveniently, from the axis of the ears. This angle from the aural axis we shall call the lateral angle. In the horizontal plane the primary cues derived from sound in a certain direction consequently determine a *pair* of possible directions. One of them might be perceived as well as the other. And indeed in the laboratory one frequently finds reversals of sound direction between front and back resulting from this ambiguity.

Sound localization, however, is not a problem confined to a plane. We do distinguish different elevations of the source of sound. Here the primary cues serve to determine not only two but a multitude of equivalent sound directions. If, for instance, a sound direction is given which lies on the right, entirely to the side, not in the axis of the ears but 45° above the horizontal plane, the primary factors will indicate nothing but that the sound is on the right side about 45° away from the aural axis. Consequently it might be heard, for instance, in the horizontal plane 45° to the side as well as in the actually given elevated direction. Moreover, all directions of 45° angular distance from the right pole of the aural axis are equivalent in that respect. If any one of them is actually given, any one of

* From the *J. Acoust. Soc. Amer.*, 1939, **10**, 270-274. Reprinted by permission of the author and the publisher.

them could be perceived. Taken together they form a geometrical locus which has the shape of a cone.

So we have to look for another factor which could help to complete localization. It must be determined which of all the directions rendered possible by the primary factors is actually given, and consequently which is the proper one to be perceived. There is one thing we can say about this new factor: It ought to be of such a nature that it can work together with those which determine the lateral angle. In the various experiments done in the field of sound localization it should have occurred now and then that, by some chance, the factors determining the lateral angle were present, but the factor to be discovered was lacking. If they functioned independently of each other, now and then a ring-shaped region of possible sound directions as determined by the known factors should have been perceived as such. Yet it has never happened, which seems to indicate that the two groups of factors, the known ones which convey the lateral angle, and the ones to be sought, work intimately together and are perhaps even of the same nature. There seems to be only one solution of our problem which is in accordance with this consideration: One obtains the cues for a number of lateral angles for the same sound direction by turning one's head while the sound is being given. Geometrically, a sequence of lateral angles obtained in this manner completely determines a given direction, as shown in the next paragraph, and the experiments to be reported indicate that the perception of sound direction actually works on this principle.

We shall confine the following geometrical considerations to idealized head movements where the head revolves around a constant axis so that the ear axis shifts in one plane. If this constant axis is vertical, and the given sound direction horizontal, the lateral angle of the sound changes by the same amount as that by which the ear axis, in a given head movement, changes its position in space. This is different when the locus of the sound is elevated. In the limiting case where it is vertically above the observer (i.e., in the direction of the axis of the head movement) the sound direction remains rectangular to the ear axis for all positions of the head, and the lateral angle does not change at all. If the sound direction is obliquely elevated the lateral angle is altered by the head movement, but the change of the lateral angle is smaller than the corresponding change of the position of the ear axis. Where ψ stands for the lateral angle and β for the angular displacement of the ear axis, $d\psi/d\beta$ decreases with increasing elevation of the sound direction. It has the value 1 when the sound source is located in the equatorial plane of the head movement, and the value 0 when the angle of elevation is 90°. Two directions of the same elevation, one in front and the other in the rear, will undergo opposite changes of lateral angle for one given head movement. When the head is being turned to the right, a source of sound in front will approach the left pole of the ear axis; a source of sound in the rear will approach the right pole. There remains still an ambiguity in the determination of the direction, namely, on which side of the equatorial plane of the head movement the direction is located. Obviously, two directions in symmetrical positions with respect to the equatorial plane yield the same sequence of lateral angles. For discrimination between these two equivalent directions another head movement around a different axis is required. The excursion of this second movement can be comparatively small because it has only to yield this discrimination and does not have to furnish data for an established direction; thus a slight deviation of the shift of the ear axis from its plane should be sufficient. Since a natural head movement never consists in a revolution around a constant axis, the case is well provided for.

According to our analysis, the direction of the source of sound is given by a sequence of lateral angles procured by a movement of the head while the sound is heard. If this is actually so, we should be able to achieve an experience of a certain sound direction by presenting during a head movement the proper sequence of lateral angles by any means whatsoever. It has been shown above that every lateral angle can be represented by a great number of single directions, every one of which is equivalent in that respect. So it should be possible to present during a head movement a sequence of lateral angles representing a certain sound direction without presenting the sound direction itself. Such a synthetic production of a sound direction would prove that sound localization really works on the principle we have outlined.

When the observer turns his head about the vertical axis, the direction of a sound vertically above is characterized in such a way that the lateral angle remains 90° for any position of the head. In order to produce this essential condition we have only to provide that during such a head movement the sound always stays at a right angle to the aural axis. Actually, the sound may be presented in the horizontal plane; if, in keeping with the head movement, it shifts in the horizontal plane so that it is at any moment in a median position, the observer will hear the sound straight above his head.

The apparatus we used for this and similar experiments yielded shifts of the actually given sound which were directed by the head movement itself. Twenty loudspeakers were arranged in an arc around the observer. His head was attached to a switch, in which a contact spring slid over a series of contact points when he turned his head. Each of these contact points was connected to one of the loudspeakers so that, while the spring slid over the contact points, the loudspeakers were successively brought into action by the speaker current, which passed the switch without interruption.

In the above-mentioned experiment, the angular distance of the loudspeakers equaled those of the contact points so that the displacement of the sound was equal to the displacement of the head. The observer's head was attached to the switch in such a way that the loudspeaker in the median position was connected. Thus during a head movement each loudspeaker was connected at the moment when it was in the median position. When the speaker current was turned on and the observer moved his head, he heard the sound vertically above. The image of the sound retained this position after the movement of the head had stopped. The experiment was successful with all observers who were able to localize sounds above under ordinary circumstances (10 out of 17).

If other sound directions are to be produced synthetically, the ratio between the angular distances of the loudspeakers and the distances of the contact points has to be changed. Where ϑ stands for the elevation of the direction above the equatorial plane of the head movement and β, as above, stands for the angular displacement of the ear axis, the lateral angle ψ, i.e., the angular distance of the sound direction to be produced from the ear axis, can be computed for any given position of the head by the formula $\sin (90° - \psi) = \sin \beta \cdot \cos \vartheta$. This formula can be simplified by replacing the two sine functions by the values of the angles themselves. Within a limited yet practical range the resulting error is subliminal. Through this simplification the lateral angle becomes a constant fraction of the angle β $(90° - \psi = \beta \cdot \cos \vartheta)$. The angular distance of two loudspeakers α can be computed from the formula $\alpha = \beta -$

$(90° — ψ)$ which, combined with the simplified formula for the lateral angle reads $α = β \cdot (1 - \cos \vartheta)$. It will be seen at once that this expression becomes $α = 0°$ when $\vartheta = 0°$; $α = β$ when $\vartheta = 90°$ (sound image directly overhead); $α = 2β$ when $\vartheta = 180°$ (sound image opposite the loudspeakers). In order to compute the angular distance of two adjacent loudspeakers one has to substitute for $β$ the value $3°$, i.e., the angular distance of the contact points on the switch. If, for instance, a sound direction $60°$ above the loudspeakers is to be produced, the distances of the loudspeakers from each other are $1½°$ ($\cos 60° = 0.5$). Table I gives the experimental

TABLE I

60°	78°	120°
64°	80°	130°
61°	75°	122°
60°	75°	122°
55°	75°	119°
50°	70°	118°
48°		115°
43°		114°

results obtained with this set-up. The numbers in the top row are the theoretically expected values of angles of elevation in three different experiments, the directions which the observers were expected to perceive. Below are the actually heard directions as indicated by the observers either by pointing toward the sound image or by estimating the elevation of its position. The meaning of $120°$ (third column) is that the synthetically produced direction is $120°$ away from the loudspeaker arc, i.e., $60°$ above the horizontal in the rear when the loudspeakers are in front of the observer.

Both the formula for the lateral angle and the formula from which $α$ is computed, contain the angle ϑ as a cosine function. This means that the values of $ψ$ and $α$, respectively, change only insignificantly for changes of ϑ between $0°$ and $30°$. Consequently, sound directions near the equatorial plane of the head movement are poorly defined. This has not much bearing on sound localization under natural conditions because, as it has been pointed out, natural head movements do not consist of revolutions about a stable axis. In the experiments, however, the head must be turned precisely about a single stable axis, and directions near the equatorial plane cannot be produced successfully. Therefore a tilting movement of the head from side to side was used for the production of sound directions of smaller elevations. The whole set-up was shifted about the ear axis by 90°. The shaft of the switch, now horizontal, was attached to the back of the head, and the loudspeaker arc extended above the observer from the left to the right. Table II gives

TABLE II

Obs.	30°	20°
A	35° front	19° front
B	33° back	15° back
B	22° back	13° back
C	22° front	17½° back
D	35° back	27½° back
E	43½° back	37½° back
F	30° front	16° back
G	46° front	31° front

the experimental results for the directions $\vartheta = 60°$ and $\vartheta = 70°$. The set-up was so arranged that these directions lay, respectively, 30° and 20° above the horizontal. The two directions were chosen so close together in order to find out whether they can be distinguished from each other. The data show that this holds true. Despite conspicuous deviations from the expected values there is no reversal between the angles indicated by each observer. It has been pointed out above that there are two directions characterized by the same sequence of lateral angles when the head is turned about a single axis. They lie in symmetrical positions with respect to the equatorial plane of the head movement. For the tilting movement of the head this plane is vertical, extending from the left to the right. Accordingly, we may expect the synthetically produced direction to appear in front *or* in the rear, and this is true as indicated in the table. The same ambiguity in the stimulus situation exists here, as in the experiments described above in which the head was turned, but there it happened only once that the observer perceived the sound below. There seems to be a strong preference to localize above the horizontal plane.

To have the loudspeakers placed in the equatorial plane of the head movement is only one among many possible arrangements for the synthetic production of sound directions. Any set-up which provides the proper presentation of the characteristic sequence of lateral angles is equally suitable. In one experiment, for instance, the loudspeakers were arranged in the horizontal plane in front of the observer while the head was tilted from side to side.[1] This set-up was arranged to produce a direction of 30° elevation above the horizontal plane. The results obtained were the best secured in any experiment (31°, 30°, 29°, 27½°, 24°, 22°). The sound image was always in front, and the observers were allowed to describe its location in visual terms.

It was not the aim of the experiments to gather data on the accuracy with which sound directions can be synthetically produced. We wished merely to obtain confirmation of the theory and to this extent the results seem to be convincing. However, the change of lateral angle with respect to a head movement is not the only factor which furnishes information about the position of the sound source in the dimension of the median plane. One can readily discriminate between front and back without a head movement, and for some sorts of sound a crude discrimination of different elevations is possible with resting head. The factor in question has not been closely studied yet, but it seems evident that it is effected by the selective sound shadow of the pinnae. In every case of a successful synthetic production the pinna factor is overcome by the cues procured by the head movement, for here the perceived direction is quite different from the direction from which the sound actually arrives at the head.

On the other hand, the pinna factor may account for an occasional failure in the synthetic production experiments. To be sure, most of the failures which occurred can be accounted for by an inability to perceive sound directions of high elevation. In most cases, observers who fail to perceive a synthetically produced direction of high elevation are also unable to localize a sound which is objectively presented in that direction. Approximately two out of five inexperienced observers have this difficulty. But there is still another case. In the experiment in which a direction of 60° eleva-

---

[1] For this type of set-up α can be computed from the simplified formula $\alpha = \beta \cdot \cos \vartheta$. When the observer tilts his head to the right, the sound shifts in the horizontal plane to the left, and vice versa.

tion above the loudspeaker arc was to be synthetically produced, observers failed who had been successful in other experiments with directions of high elevation. Here interference of the pinna factor is apparently indicated.

Synthetic production experiments in which the direction to be perceived is horizontal were always successful. In one case the observer had to tilt his head from side to side and the loudspeaker arc extended above the observer from the left to the right. The distances of the loudspeakers were such that the sound remained in the median position when the head was properly tilted, and so the sound image appeared in the direction of the axis of the head movement, i.e., horizontally in front or behind. In an experiment with head movement about a vertical axis, designed to produce a sound image behind the observer, the loudspeaker arc was in front, and the distance of two adjacent loudspeakers, as computed from our formula by substituting for ϑ the value 180°, was 6°. This experiment was performed with a great number of observers, and never failed. Here the discrepancy between the direction perceived and the position of the actual sound source was maximal, and cues obtained from the pinna factor disagreed most strongly with the ones from the head movement. Under ordinary circumstances, discrimination between front and back on the basis of the pinna factor alone, i.e., without head movement, is quite reliable. The fact that this factor is invariably overcome in the synthetic production experiment indicates quite clearly its subordinate role.

The Role of Head Movements in Sound Localization*,[1]

HANS WALLACH

IN A PREVIOUS PAPER[2] the writer has demonstrated that a distinct localization of sound exists for directions which do not fall into the horizontal plane but lie above or below at varying elevations, in other words that a discrimination of directions with respect to above and below and front and back is possible as well as discrimination with respect to right and left which has been studied for many years. It was found that only a head movement during the presentation of the sound affords an adequate discrimination of sound direction in the dimension of above and below and thus makes localization complete. This is probably the reason why sound localization with respect to above and below has not been demonstrated in the laboratory at an earlier time. The paper referred to gives an analysis of the manner in which a complete perception of a sound direction is achieved with the help of a head movement. The binaural cues on which sound localization is primarily based do not suffice to characterize a sound direction completely. Yet, during a head movement the binaural cues as produced by the sound direction are altered, and the particular form of this change can in each case strictly determine the given sound direction. This is thoroughly

* From The role of head movements and vestibular and visual cues in sound localization, *J. exp. Psychol.*, 1940, **27**, 339-368. Pp. 339-346 reprinted by permission of the author and the publisher.

[1] The writer wishes to express his gratitude to Prof. W. Koehler and to Dr. Mary Henle for their help in preparing this manuscript.

[2] Ueber die Wahrnehmung der Schallrichtung. *Psychol. Forsch.*, 22, pp. 238-266 (I). A short English report on the same work has been published in the *J. Acoust. Soc. Amer.*, 1939, pp. 270-74 (II). The two papers will be referred to as I and II respectively. In the present paper the writer has attempted to present the material in such a way that it can be understood without knowledge of the previous papers. While paper II lacks theoretical discussion it may be useful for a quick reference to previous experimental results.

discussed in the article mentioned. Experiments are reported in which perceived sound directions were synthetically produced in accordance with the head movement principle, which was thus verified. It is obvious that the change which the primary factors undergo due to the head movement can characterize a sound direction only if the exact kinematic properties of the particular head movement are taken into account. Two sets of sensory data enter into the perceptual process of localization, (1) the changing binaural cues and (2) the data representing the changing position of the head. It is the latter with which this paper is concerned. The manner in which they are secured is the object of this investigation.

THE ROLE OF HEAD MOVEMENT IN AUDITORY LOCALIZATION

It has been shown that the binaural cues for sound localization, time difference and difference of intensity, convey the angular distance of the given sound direction from the axis of the ears. Thus, they only determine how far from the median plane, on the left or on the right side, the given source of sound is located. Whether it lies in front or in the rear, above or below the horizontal plane, remains undetermined, and the same is true of the amount of its elevation. The angular distance of the given sound direction from the aural axis which is actually determined by the binaural cues has been called the lateral angle (ψ), and it is treated in this paper as if it were a directly given sensory datum.[3] This lateral angle can be counted from either pole of the aural axis. If it is 90°, the sound direction lies in the median plane of the head. It follows that *the binaural cues determine merely a range of directions, any of which would, if actually presented, produce the same binaural stimulation.* It is significant that such a range of possible directions for a given sound is never perceived. We hear a sound that appears for the most part in one definite direction. It has been shown that this is due to head movements during the perception of the sound. A motion of the head will, in most cases, alter the position of the aural axis and at the same time change the angle between the latter and

---

[3] This is the terminology employed in paper II. In paper I, the term lateral angle refers to the complement of the angle ψ and is called φ. φ is thus the angular distance of the sound direction from the median plane and was chosen to represent the lateral angle for historical reasons. The motive for changing to ψ was the greater ease with which the angle ψ can be visualized.

the given sound direction. It will be seen shortly that this change of the lateral angle can define the direction of the source of sound; and actually the perception of the proper direction is achieved through a head movement affording such a change of the lateral angle.

In order to show that the change of the lateral angle with the head movement can define a direction, we shall consider a number of particular cases. We shall at first assume that the head is turned about a vertical axis, so that the displacement of the aural axis occurs in the horizontal plane. If the given direction lies in the same plane, the angle between this direction and the aural axis (the lateral angle) changes by the amount of the displacement of the aural axis. This is obviously no longer true when the given direction is not in the horizontal plane, but is above or below. While in the case of the horizontal direction the lateral angle is measured within the horizontal plane, in the case of an elevated direction the angle between this direction and the aural axis extends in an oblique plane. It can easily be seen that this angle is affected to a lesser degree by a shift of the aural axis in the horizontal plane than is the lateral angle in the case of a horizontal direction. If the reader finds himself unable to visualize these spatial relations, the following consideration will lead to the same conclusion.

Take the case in which the direction is exactly vertical. The direction then exactly coincides with the axis of the head movements, and the displacement of the aural axis will not alter the lateral angle at all. It remains 90° throughout the head movement. This is the extreme case. For all other directions the lateral angle will be changed by a displacement of the aural axis. A direction may be given 60° above the horizontal plane, and, before the head movement starts, exactly in front. At this stage, the lateral angle amounts to 90°. When a movement of the head by 90° brings the direction in the lateral position, the lateral angle will amount to 60°, the aural axis still lying in the horizontal plane with the direction 60° above it. A 90° shift of the aural axis thus brings about a 30° change of the lateral angle. For a horizontal direction, on the other hand, a like displacement brings about a 90° change of the lateral angle, as we have seen, while for the vertical direction the lateral angle does not change at all. These three cases are sufficient to suggest what can be learned directly from a visualization of the spatial relations, namely, that the amount by which the lateral angle changes varies with the elevation of the direction. For a given head movement this change is maximal when the direction lies within the horizontal plane, and decreases as the direction approaches the vertical.

Thus the angular distance of the direction from the horizontal plane (angle of elevation) varies with the rate of change of the lateral angle and is determined by it. For a given lateral angle, there are however in most cases four directions, which have the same angular distance from the horizontal plane: in front and in back, above and below. Of these, the two in front are distinguished from the two in back by another feature of the change of lateral angle, the direction, viz., the sign, of the change. When the head is turned to the left a direction in front will shift toward the right side of the head. For the same head movement, a direction in back will shift toward the left side of the head. That is to say, for a direction in front the lateral angle decreases toward the right, for a direction in back it decreases toward the left, and the two directions may thus be distinguished, although both may have the same elevation, and consequently the lateral angle will change for both at the same rate. Only one ambiguity remains: two directions in symmetrical position with respect to the horizontal plane, one above and the other below, are so far not distinguished.

These considerations concerning the rate and the direction of the change of lateral angle are independent of the particular spatial orientation of the head movement. The angle of elevation does not, of course, refer to the horizontal plane as such, but to the plane in which the aural axis is displaced by the head movement, which in the particular case we chose coincided with the horizontal plane. Our considerations apply as well to such a case as a movement about a horizontal axis, that is, a tilting of the head from side to side. Here the aural axis shifts in a vertical plane, the 'angle of elevation' extends toward the front or the rear, and above and below now play the same rôle as front and back did in the case in which the head was turned. They are distinguished from one another through the direction of the change which the lateral angle undergoes due to the tilting motion.

When, upon a movement of the head about a vertical axis, two directions remain which are both consistent with the given change of lateral angle, one above and the other below the horizontal plane, a subsequent tilting of the head, or any motion which contains the tilting as a component, can distinguish between the two possibilities. In fact, natural head movements are rarely accurate revolutions about a constant axis; they must rather be described as revolutions with varying axis. This does not interfere with the qualification of the head movement for procuring a change of lateral angle which can determine a sound direction to the extent indicated above. But the displacement of the axis which occurs during the head movement probably suffices to remove the ambiguity which would result from an accurate revolution about a constant axis.

We have found a number of different movements of the head to be effective in sound localization. The most frequent natural head movement is a turning of the head upon which a tilting to the side is gradually superimposed as the motion approaches the end of the excursion. In the synthetic production of sound directions which were previously reported, a revolution about a vertical axis, in which all components of tilting to the side had to be strictly excluded, was successfully used. In another group of these experiments the head movement was even more artificial; it consisted of a tilting of the head from side to side. With such unnatural movements most accurate localizations were achieved. We are probably justified in saying that any movement of the head which involves an angular displacement of the aural axis can be effective in sound localization. That a head movement which does not involve such a displacement of the aural axis must be ineffective is evident. No change of lateral angle can result from it. Such a head movement is a revolution about a horizontal axis extending from the left to the right, as it occurs in a straight nodding. It is, of course, also ineffective as a component in a kinematically more complicated natural head movement. Briefly, any head movement may be effective to the extent to which it contains as a component a revolution about an axis which lies in the median plane of the head.

The manner in which sound directions can be synthetically produced has been thoroughly discussed in a previous paper; thus only a general outline will be presented in the following.

In experiments on synthetic production, the binaural stimulation which a given objective sound direction would have produced is brought about without actual presentation of this sound direction. We have seen that for a given position of the head the binaural stimulation which is produced by a given sound corresponds to quite a number of directions. All directions which have the same lateral angle produce the same binaural stimulation. Thus, so far as binaural cues are concerned, any one of these directions can be substituted for any other one. Where the lateral angle of a given direction changes in a characteristic way during a head movement, this direction can be replaced by a series of other directions which together present the same changing lateral angle. For every position through which the aural axis passes the lateral angle can be ascertained, and an equivalent direction can be substituted for the given direction. In practice one need not even consider an infinite number of such positions because a differential threshold exists in discrimination of the lateral position of a sound. Of two positions of the head for which the lateral angle is merely subliminally different, only one need be taken into account. We find it sufficient to consider separate positions which are as much as 3° apart. For the synthetical production of a certain sound direction, a definite head movement must be selected. Separate positions through which the aural axis passes during this head movement are chosen 3° apart from each other, and for each of these positions the lateral angle of the direction which is to be produced is ascertained. Thereupon, for each of these positions a direction can be selected among those which have the specific lateral angle ascertained for this position. In this way a series of directions is obtained which are equivalent to the direction which is to be produced, if each is presented at the moment when the head in its movement passes through the position to which it belongs. For the presentation of each of these different directions at the proper moment, the head of the observer is attached to a switch with 20 contact points. Each of these contact points is connected with a loudspeaker. In a particular experiment the switch permits only that movement of the head which is chosen in planning the experiment. It is always a revolution about a constant axis lying in the median plane of the head. During such a movement a contact spring slides over the contact points one after another, thus connecting each loudspeaker in turn. With every 3° displacement of the aural axis the center of another contact point is passed. The position of head and aural axis at the moment when the center of each contact point is passed can easily be ascertained, and the corresponding loudspeaker is placed in the direction which has previously been chosen to present the proper lateral angle for this particular phase of the head movement. When all the loudspeakers are arranged in this manner, the apparatus achieves precisely what is necessary for the synthetic production of the sound direction. While the head is moved, directions are presented which are equivalent to the direction to be produced. Together they present the same sequence of lateral angles which the synthetic sound direction would bring forth if it were actually given. In such experiments the physically given sound directions differ widely from the synthetic directions which are perceived.

In previously reported experiments the twenty loudspeakers which presented the sound were arranged in front of the observer, while the synthetic direction was, for instance, in back of or above the observer's head. In another experimental arrangement the observer perceived a sound directly in front, while all the actually presented directions lay above his head, distributed from left to right. Localization functioning on a basis other than the head movement principle should lead to the perception of sound in the directions actually presented or in their general neighborhood. If nevertheless the synthetic direction is perceived, one can be sure that it is solely on the basis of the head movement principle.

SELECTION 39

■■

Toward a General Theory of Perception[*,1]

HEINZ WERNER AND SEYMOUR WAPNER

THIS PAPER OUTLINES a stage in the development of a general
theory of perception. Underlying this development are certain notions concerning the place of theory in psychology. There is a growing conviction among psychologists that theory does not function
simply as a rigid frame into which facts are to be fitted. On the
contrary, theory construction is a continual process of dynamic
interrelationship between scientific thought and empirical research.[2]
Once constructs have evolved, the next step is to test them in the
laboratory by setting up hypotheses. But this is by far not the
whole story: A theory is sterile, and, so to speak, dies of old age,
if the facts which support the theoretical considerations do not have
the effect of generating new hypotheses which in themselves lead
to further research and subsequent reformulation of theory.

Our attempts toward the development of a perceptual theory are
admittedly at an early stage; our constructs are somewhat crude, the
experimental situations rather elementary.

GENERAL AIM OF SENSORY-TONIC FIELD THEORY: MAIN CONSTRUCTS

Perceptual theory of today cannot limit itself to the interpretation
of traditional psychophysical facts, it must do more; it must deal
with facts which have been unearthed by clinical and social psychologists. In other words, it must develop basic constructs which
tie together sensory, conative and cognitive factors.

* From the *Psychol. Rev.*, 1952, **59**, 324-338. Reprinted by permission of the
authors and the publisher.
[1] The experimental work referred to is supported by a research grant from
the National Institute of Mental Health, of the National Institutes of Health,
Public Health Service.
[2] Closely related to this position are the views presented by Marquis in his
presidential address to the APA (3).

In a different way it may be stated that a general perceptual theory must account for the projective nature of perception. By this we do not mean only the facts of clinical psychology concerned with so-called projective techniques, but the assumption is that any perception is essentially "projective," i.e., cognitive and conative organismic states (needs, motivation, thought) are an intricate part of perception.

This notion of the "projective" nature of perception poses one difficulty. This difficulty is concerned with the question of how two essentially alien elements such as emotion, motivation, etc., on the one side, and visual or tactual processes, etc., on the other side, can influence each other or even fuse. This problem we have called the paradox of interaction.

Let us suppose that it is true, as Bruner and others have tried to demonstrate, that the size of a coin is seen as bigger when it is highly valued. How can we understand that two factors, such as the visual factor of size and the personal factor of need, interact?

The logical solution of such a paradox must lie in the conception that these factors are only seemingly, but not actually, alien to one another.

For traditional psychology, which has dichotomized functions such as emotions, motor activity, and sensory functions into separate entities, this paradox is insurmountable. Modern organismic theory is not troubled by this difficulty because, at least speculatively, such a dichotomy does not exist. A bare statement, however, to the effect that we are dealing with a total organism, no matter how refined such a statement may be, is unsatisfactory. To be satisfactory such theory must be developed around constructs which are amenable to experimental manipulation. This we are trying to do. Before going into a discussion of some experimental work, we shall briefly state some of these constructs.

We have tentatively named our theoretical approach the sensory-tonic field theory of perception. It is an organismic theory and its essential tenet is that organismic states are part and parcel of perception. We have used the term "sensory-tonic" advisedly. This notion aims to overcome the paradox of interaction between sensory events and events such as motor activity, drives, and other characteristics of organismic states.

Just because visual objects send out stimuli which affect our visual apparatus, the conclusion is not warranted that the perceptual process is purely sensory. Numerous physiologists, Sherrington, Magnus, Stein, Metzger etc., have shown that sensory stimulation has an effect on muscular tonus (8, p. 94 f.). Accordingly, we maintain that any stimulation whether it comes through extero-, proprio- or intero-ceptors is sensory-tonic in nature. Tonus, in traditional terms, refers to somato- as well as viscero-tonic tension.

The perceptual properties of an object are a function of the way in which the stimuli coming from that object will affect the existing sensory-tonic state of the organism. Instead of talking, as traditional psychology does, about a visual object stimulating the retina and other visual areas, we talk about a stimulus object always arousing sensory-tonic events, i.e., events which involve the total organism.

A consequence of this sort of conceptualization is the notion of equivalence of functions with respect to sensory-tonic states. Since any neuro-psychological entity is neither sensory nor motor but a dynamic process prior to both, it may be affected in a similar way by stimulation through the receptors, as well as by direct stimulation of the muscles. Thus perception may be affected equivalently by various kinds of sensory stimulation and direct muscular changes. Some evidence for this will be given later.

It may be stated further that the sensory-tonic theory is a field theory. This means that there is a field constituted of two parts: body (psychophysical) and object (psychophysical). The perceptual properties of an object depend on the way in which stimuli from a physical object affect the organism and on the subsequent specific and active manner in which the organism reacts to it.

What will happen will depend on the relation between stimulus-object and existing sensory-tonic state of the organism. Principally, the stimuli may or may not interfere with the present organismic state. If the stimuli interfere, or are incommensurate with the organismic state, there emerges a tendency in the organism to change its state in the direction toward establishment of equilibrium between body and object.

We believe that the perceived properties of the object are a mirror of these dynamic relations between the object stimuli and ensuing body activity.

To summarize, we are using a number of concepts such as sensory-tonic state, functional equivalence, object-body relationship in a field, and tendencies toward equilibrium. We hope that these concepts will become clearer by a concrete discussion of experimental work.

FUNCTIONAL EQUIVALENCE: EQUILIBRATION:
STUDIES OF VERTICALITY

As stated above, our ultimate goal is the development of a theory, general enough to account for the many facets of perception including its status as a factor in personality dynamics. This goal can be approached only in a stepwise fashion. Other investigators have started at a rather high level of complexity; we feel, however, that it is necessary to begin with experimental situations which, on the one hand, are concise, simple and manageable, and on the other, paradigmatic of the relationships on a higher level of complexity.

Many of our experiments deal with the perception of the vertical. We have chosen the vertical for investigation because it represents a simple case where a perceptual property (verticality) can be studied as dependent on organismic states, or better, on the relation between the object stimulating the organism and the organism reacting to the stimulation.

One of the assumptions of the sensory-tonic theory is that with respect to the total perceptual process there is a functional equivalence between sensory and muscular factors. If that assumption is sound, we should expect that stimulation through the sense organs, such as the ear, and direct stimulation of the muscles, by electrical means, at least under certain circumstances, should produce analogous results in perception. This we have demonstrated. In one of our situations, the S had the task of adjusting a rod in a darkroom so that it appeared vertical to him. The position at which a physical line is seen vertical is referred to from now on as "apparent vertical." In these experiments the physical position of the apparent vertical differed under various conditions. For instance, under electrical stimulation of the right neck muscle it was tilted more to the left (6). Auditory stimulation functions in an analogous way, i.e., one-sided application shifts the position of apparent vertical opposite to the side to which the auditory stimulus is applied (6). Furthermore, related results are obtained under conditions of body tilt (11) and rotation around the vertical axis of the body (7). When the body is tilted slightly to one side, the position of the apparent vertical, again, is tilted to the other side.[3] It will be noted that the

[3] Some readers might erroneously interpret this statement to be in contradiction to that given in a preliminary exposition of the theory (8, p. 99). In these previous statements the displacement was discussed in terms of the perception of a plumb line (i.e., of a rod when set a true vertical); this dis-

effect is due to stimuli which do not come from the object; these stimuli are called "extraneous" stimuli.[4]

To understand more clearly these relationships we may ask the question, what is the vertical? We believe that one cannot conceive of a vertical line as existing in a relatively isolated space independent of the body; the singular quality of verticality, as we see it, is due to a particular dynamic relation between the position of a line and the organismic state.

We have tried to understand this relationship through the development of the construct of equilibrium, a construct widely used in biological dynamics. Our general view is that the organism tends to establish a steady state or body equilibrium. If the organism is subjected to stimuli, one of two relationships may be present: (1) The stimuli may not interfere with the present organismic state. By this we mean that the object is, so to speak, in balance with the existing body equilibrium. (2) The stimuli may be disturbing to the body equibrial state. Under these conditions there is a tendency to re-establish the balance. One of the several ways of re-establishing the balance is by changing the position of the object. To be more specific, when the body is erect, a perpendicular rod will be perceived as vertical because, as we believe, its stimuli do not disturb the existing body equilibrium. If, however, the body equilibrium should change, such a perpendicular rod will be incommensurate with the equilibrial state and therefore no longer seen as vertical. Now, the rod has to be shifted into an objectively tilted position in order to be in balance with the newly established body equilibrium, i.e., to be seen as vertical. In summary, if the body is tilted, or ex-

---

placement was inferred from the adjustment of the rod to the apparent vertical. In contradistinction, the statements made here and elsewhere (5, 6, 7, 9, 10, 11) are in terms of the position of apparent vertical, i.e., the position of a rod when adjusted by the *S* to the vertical. As one can easily see, the perceived displacement of a perpendicular rod (plumb line) under given extraneous stimulation is opposite to that of the position of the apparent vertical. That is to say, if the position of apparent vertical is left of perpendicular, the perpendicular is perceived displaced to the right. It might be added that this change in the verbalization of the results is not coincidental but reflects rather a change in theoretical thinking forced by evidence. The emphasis has shifted from the question of how the perpendicular is perceived to the question of what is apparent verticality and what is its objective spatial position under various conditions.

[4] The effects of extraneous stimulation and postural tilts have been studied not only with respect to the visually perceived apparent vertical, but also with respect to kinaesthetically experienced vertical. The same effects have been observed (5).

traneous stimulation (auditory, etc.) is applied to one side, our assumption is that this induces a change in the body equilibrial state; because of this shift of body equilibrium, the line has to be shifted in order to appear vertical. This expectation, as mentioned before, is verified in the experiments.

In order to understand the dynamics underlying shifts of the position of apparent vertical due to extraneous stimulation, we may turn to neuropathological cases with instability of body balance. Patients with an injury to the cerebellum provide the best examples. In these patients, tilt of the body results frequently in falling to the side of the tilt. Similarly if these patients are stimulated asymmetrically by light or auditory stimuli (extraneous stimuli), there is also a tendency to fall to the side at which the stimulus is applied. The reason for this lack of balance is that the increase in muscular tonus due to tilt or stimulation is not properly counteracted with an increase in tonus to the other side. From this clinical picture we learn two things: first, that body tonus is changed asymmetrically through sensory stimulation in a similar way as it is through muscular action, secondly, that asymmetric stimulation needs counteractive forces to bring about a new steady state. Applying this information to our situations, a hypothetical dynamic schema can be constructed which is presented in Fig. 1. This schema is based on the assumption that extraneous stimulation increases the neuromuscular tonus to one side (primary force) and counteractive or balancing forces are brought forth in order to establish a new stable dynamic equilibrium. Such a new equilibrial state under tilt, or stimulation to the left, and tilt, or stimulation to the right, is represented in the figure.

The steps which led to this schema are summarized as follows:

(1) It is assumed that a line perceived as vertical is in a position undisturbing to the body equilibrium, or in other words, is in a position in tune with the body equilibrium.

(2) It is assumed that the existing body equilibrial state is change in a specific manner under conditions of extraneous stimulation. Under extraneous stimulation counteractive forces come into play on the side opposite the stimulation to balance its effects. This has the consequence that a new body equilibrial state emerges. For the sake of simplicity we may characterize the equilibrial state by an axis. Thus we depict the new body equilibrial state in terms

of rotation of the equilibrial axis toward the side of the counteractive or balancing force.

(3) The body equilibrial state, with its equilibrial axis is indicated by the position of the apparent vertical. The emergence of the new equilibrial state is indicated by the shift of the apparent vertical; it is a fact that the apparent vertical is tilted to the side of the counteractive force, or in terms of our representation of the body equilibrial state, rotated in the same direction as the equilibrial axis.

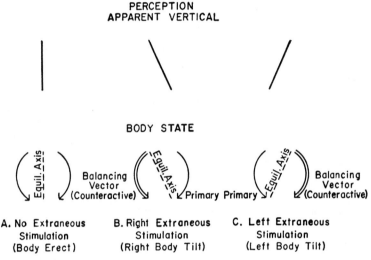

FIG. 1.   Positions of apparent vertical corresponding to three body equilibrial states.

This diagram conveys what is meant by the statement that verticality is that position of a line which is in tune with the existing body equilibrium.

This hypothetical schema has been a valuable aid in our thinking and experimental planning. First of all, it has been productive because it has led to a number of new experimental facts. Secondly, it has helped to bring together seemingly unrelated facts such as individual equilibrial states, so-called figural adaptation, the relation between perception and motor activity, the problem of "straight ahead" or the median plane, and problems of configuration. Illustrations of these problems will now be discussed briefly.

The first of these facts to be mentioned is that of very consistent individual differences which concern the way a subject adjusts a line to the position of apparent verticality when sitting erect. For the majority of subjects the apparent vertical has a position rotated to the left; for others it has a position rotated to the right. According to our schema the consistent individual differences would mean that each individual has a characteristic steady state, or individual body equilibrium.

The next problem to be discussed has a bearing on so-called "figural adaptation" (10).

Up to now we have dealt principally with the results on extraneous stimulation and their interpretation. Two points have been made: (1) Shifts in body equilibrial state occur due to extraneous stimulation; (2) the shift of the position of apparent vertical is an indicator of the shift in body equilibrial state.

It should be noted that extraneous stimulation is considered to influence the body equilibrial state irrespective of the presence or absence of objects. With the introduction of an object, a new dynamic factor emerges. This factor we have identified as "object-body equilibration trend." We believe that some of the instances of "figural adaptation" discovered by Gibson and his co-workers are an expression of object-body equilibration trends (10).

Gibson and others have shown that if one views a slightly tilted line, it will appear progressively less tilted during the course of inspection, until it finally appears vertical. This so-called adaptation effect can be accounted for by the tendency of the organism toward equilibration as follows: When the body is erect, a tilted line interferes with the existing body equilibrium; subsequently, a shift in the body equilibrium is induced so that it is now more in tune with the line. We infer the nature of this shirt from the results on extraneous stimulation in the following way: (1) We make the assumption that in general there is an invariant relation between position of apparent vertical and equilibrial state. (2) Given an equilibrial state induced by extraneous stimulation to the left such as that depicted in Fig. 1C a line appears perpendicular when tilted objectively to the right. (3) From the two foregoing statements we make the deduction: If a line is objectively tilted to the right but in the course of inspection becomes vertical, this happens because the equilibrial state has shifted correspondingly, namely to that depicted in Fig. 1C. Similarly, if a line tilted to the left is seen perpendicular after some time, the equilibrial state, during that time, has shifted to the equilibrial state depicted in Fig. 1B.

To repeat, we draw this inference from an assumption which is in keeping with the general principles underlying sensory-tonic theory. That is to say, there is an invariable correspondence between the position X of a line perceived as perpendicular and a particular equilibrial state Y: If we know that under induced equilibrial state Y, a line is seen as perpendicular when in position X, then, if a line in position X is seen as perpendicular, the equilibrial state Y is inferred.

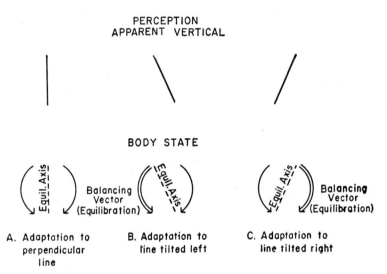

FIG. 2.   Figural adaptation: Three kinds of object-body equilibration.

The reader should keep in mind that in relating the body equilibrial states under extraneous stimulation and under "figural adaptation," we are dealing in our schema with formal relationships among balancing vectors irrespective of where they came from. In one case, the balancing vector is a function of counteraction to the effects of extraneous stimulation (body balance); in the other case, the balancing vector is a function of the disbalancing effect of object stimulation (body-object balance). Thus, in Fig. 2, which in all formal aspects is identical with Fig. 1, we have identified the nature of the balancing vectors for the case of figural adaptation.

In sum, adaptation to the vertical is here interpreted as an object-body equilibration trend.[5] Under perfect adaptation a tilted line no longer disturbs the equilibrium because the new equilibrial state is in tune with the tilted line. The perceptual effect is that the line now appears vertical.

Since, in most of our experiments on the vertical, we have introduced tilted objects (lines) we have to expect figural adaptation to occur. In some of these experiments, for instance, the subject has the task of adjusting to the vertical a rod which is initially tilted. In half of the trials the rod is initially tilted to the left; in the other half of the trials it is tilted to the right. We find that the subject adapts himself to the initial tilt, with the consequence that the apparent vertical is always closer to the tilted position from which the rod was started.

INTERACTION STUDIES

The principal results on the effects of extraneous stimulation, body tilt, etc., around which our discussion has centered may now be presented in a unified way. The direction of the influencing factors may be described by vectors. Vectors are introduced into our hypothetical schema to indicate the direction and magnitude of the shift of the equilibrial state (equilibrial axis). These vectors are depicted in conformity with the results obtained under the various test conditions. The present state of our investigation does not warrant specification of the magnitude of the vectors.[6] The influencing factors and their vectors are summarized in Table 1. There, "+" means a right vector or a tendency to shift the equilibrial axis and the position of the apparent vertical to the right of the perpendicular, and "−" means a left vector or a tendency to shift the equilibrial axis and the position of the apparent vertical to the left of the perpendicular. It can be seen from the table that there is functional equivalence of extraneous stimulation left, body tilt left, and starting position right; similarly, of extraneous stimulation right, body tilt right, and starting position left. Individual equilibrium, as noted previously, has predominantly a left vector.

---

[5] Below (p. 505) the problem of object-body equilibration trends is treated in a broader framework. There the basic assumption underlying object-body equilibration trends is identified as "the principal of minimal disturbance."

[6] In general, in the discussion which follows, the vectors are treated as being of the same magnitude with the exception of the vector for the body tilt factor. We have clear evidence that this vector has a greater magnitude than those of the other factors involved in these experiments.

TABLE 1. FACTORS INFLUENCING VERTICALITY

Exper. Conditions		Vectors	
		$\rightarrow$ $+$	$\leftarrow$ $-$
Extraneous Stimulation	Left	$+$	
	Right		$-$
Body Tilt	Left	$+$	
	Right		$-$
Starting Position (Adaptation)	Left		$-$
	Right	$+$	
Individual Equilibrium			$-$

We have designed a series of experiments to test our theoretical formulations. They are in the form of interaction studies. The principal feature of these numerous experiments consists in the analysis of the varying effects dependent on the simultaneous operation of several or all of these factors. The notion of functional equivalence leads to the expectation that the effect of a combination of two or more functionally equivalent factors is the summative resultant of the vectors involved.

As an illustration, the results of one of these interaction studies will be presented. In this study there was simultaneous operation of the following factors: body tilt, electrical stimulation, starting position, and individual equilibrium. If our notion of functional equivalence of these factors is correct, then, disregarding their magnitude, we are to expect that in each case the perceptual result should be a summative effect of all the vectors present in a particular experimental situation. Therefore, if the various vectors involved have the same direction, the equilibrial axis and thus the position of the apparent vertical should show a greater shift to that side than where the vectors are not of the same direction (Table 2). The

TABLE 2. INTERACTIVE EFFECTS: INDIVIDUAL EQUILIBRIUM, STARTING POSITION, EXTRANEOUS ELECTRICAL STIMULATION, BODY TILT

	Combination of Vectors						Mean Adjustment of Rod	
Indiv. Equil.	Starting Position		Elect. Stimul.		Body Tilt = 15°		Men	Women
	Left	Right	Left	Right	Left	Right		
← −	← −	→ +	→ +	← −	→ +	← −	(N = 20)	(N = 20)
−	−			−		−	−7.4	−7.7
−	−		+			−	−5.1	−5.2
−		+		−		−	−5.8	−6.0
−		+	+			−	−4.4	−4.2
−	−			−	+		+3.5	+2.4
−	−		+		+		+5.0	+3.6
−		+		−	+		+3.6	+2.8
−		+	+	+	+		+6.1	+4.2

most extreme differences are expected if all the vectors in one situation are to one side and all the vectors in the other situation are to the other side. The signs on the left side of the table indicate the vector direction: "−" to the left and "+" to the right. On the right side the empirical findings are presented; analogously the signs attached to the numbers indicate whether apparent vertical is tilted to the left (−) or to the right (+) of perpendicular. The numbers indicate the degrees of deviation of apparent vertical from objective vertical.

The table shows clearly that where all vectors are "−", the apparent vertical is tilted most to the left (−7.4° for men; −7.7° for women), and where the majority of vectors are "+" the apparent vertical is tilted most to the right (6.1° for men; 4.2° for women). Since we know from previous experiments where the variables have been studied singly that body tilt has an effect significantly more potent than the other variables, the table has to be examined separately for right and left body tilts. Within each body tilt the results closely follow the expectation: For right body tilt, with minus vectors for electric stimulation and starting position, the apparent vertical is tilted most to the left (−7.4° for men; −7.7° for women): where these factors have plus vectors, the apparent vertical is least to the left (−4.4° for men; −4.2° for women). Where these two factors have opposite vectorial signs, the shifts of the apparent vertical are intermediate. Analogous relationships hold for left body tilt.

In the results of the numerous interaction studies in which combinations of these and other variables have been studied in our laboratory, the predictions are verified to a surprisingly high degree. These interaction studies, of which the one described above is representative, provide the best evidence we possess at present for the adequacy of some of our basic theoretical constructs.

ANOTHER DIMENSION OF SPACE: THE MEDIAN PLANE

Further evidence of the usefulness of the constructs discussed is their applicability to another dimension of space, *viz.*, that of the median sagittal plane which may be defined as that position in space which is experienced as "straight ahead."

Experiments have been conducted which demonstrate the effect of extraneous stimulation on the apparent median plane. The task for the S was to indicate a point straight ahead of him in the fronto-parallel plane. This position was explained to the S as a straight-forward projection of the point of S's nose on the fronto-parallel plane. Analogous to the experimentation of verticality, the task was carried out under conditions of asymmetrically applied extraneous light stimulation. The stimulation was provided by specially built goggles with light bulbs inserted within each of the two eye pieces.[7] It was found that there is a significant difference in effect of right and left eye stimulation. Stimulation to the right shifts the apparent median plane more to the left and vice versa. As one can readily see,

---

[7] It may be mentioned that this effect is similar to that of a Ganzfeld possessing a brightness gradient.

extraneous stimulation operates analogously for the median plane and the vertical. The dynamic mechanism hypothesized for the effects of extraneous stimulation on verticality may therefore be applied to the interpretation of these median plane effects.

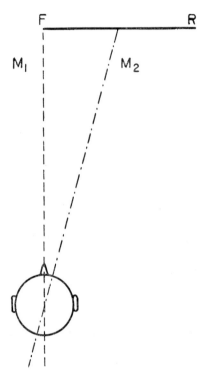

Quite another kind of effect on apparent median plane was brought out by the following experiments suggested by Roelofs' (8, p. 96) observations.[8] A homogeneously luminescent upright rectangle presented in a dark room had to be adjusted by S in such a way that either the left edge or the right edge was in the apparent median plane. This means that when the left edge is fixated, the figure extends entirely to the right of fixation line (asymmetrical object position right); and when the right edge is fixated, the figure extends to the left (asymmetrical object position left). There is a significant difference in apparent median plane depending on which edge is fixated. When the left edge is fixated the apparent median plane is shifted to the right, *viz.*, toward the center of the rectangle; and when the right edge is fixated the apparent median plane is shifted to the left, *viz.*, toward the center of the rectangle. An illustration is given in Fig. 3. In subsequent experiments it has been found that

Fig. 3. Diagrammatic representation of shift in apparent median plane under asymmetrical object position. (View from above) Asymmetrical position of rectangle, R, to the right is depicted here. Apparent median plane shifts from position M_1, toward the center of the rectangle, M_2. This has the perceptual effect that the rectangle is seen displaced to the left.

---

[8] The reader will note that the tentative explanation given for the results of Roelofs' experiment in a previous paper (8) has been abandoned and replaced in consequence of new facts discovered during our own experimentation.

these effects do not depend on homogeneous illumination of the figure. When a contour rectangle rather than a solid one is used, the described effects are the same.

These effects can be interpreted as analogous to the figural adaptation effects discussed above for the vertical dimension of space. As one will remember, adaptation to the vertical was interpreted as an equilibration trend. A tilted line initiates a change in the equilibrial state of such a nature that the objectively tilted line and the body equilibrial state become in "tune" with one another. Consequently, the objectively tilted line appears vertical. Applying this reasoning to the shift of the apparent median plane, the following interpretation can be made. The observed shift of the apparent median plane toward the center of the figure is interpreted as a tendency of the organism toward "symmetrization." That is to say, "symmetrization" is an expression of the tendency of the organism to change its equilibrial state in such a way that the stimuli coming from the object will make for minimal disturbance of the organism. Thus, in our interpretation, "verticalization" (adaptation of a tilted line to the vertical) and "symmetrization" (adaptation of an asymmetrical figure to an apparent symmetrical position) are considered here as two manifestations of the principle of minimal disturbance.[9]

FIGURAL AND GROUND STIMULI

If one scans the many experimental results of our studies, one is struck by a systematic difference between the effects of so-called extraneous stimulation and those of stimuli coming from objects. In direction, these effects are opposite to each other. For instance, extraneous stimulation to the left side of the body has the effect of tilting the position of the apparent vertical to the right side. On the other hand, stimuli from a line tilted left has the effect of tilting the apparent vertical toward the left.

Similar relations hold for the median plane. Extraneous stimulation to the left shifts the apparent median plane to the right. On the other hand, asymmetrical object position left of fixation shifts the apparent median plane left. In other words, in these experiments

---

[9] The terms "minimal disturbance" and "in tune with," as used in describing the dynamic happenings when an organism is faced with object-stimuli, represents a basic assumption behind our conception of what we have called the "field." This assumption and its implications for the field theory will be made more explicit in a future publication.

on the median plane we are dealing with two kinds of asymmetrical visual stimulation, the one affecting the body *qua* "flux," the other affecting the body *qua* "configurated flux," or as an object out in space. The organism deals with these two kinds of stimuli in ways which show up in diametrically opposed end-effects.

These effects may be summarized by the utilization of "plus" and "minus" vectors which have been introduced above. Table 3 summarizes these differences by vectors which are operationally defined in terms of the effect of the various types of stimulation.

TABLE 3. OPPOSITE EFFECTS OF TWO KINDS OF STIMULI:
OBJECT STIMULI AND EXTRANEOUS (GROUND) STIMULI

Direction of Application	Kind of Stimulation	Vectors*	
		Vertical	Median Plane
LEFT	Extraneous Stimulation	+	+
	Stimuli from Object	−	−
RIGHT	Extraneous Stimulation	−	−
	Stimuli from Object	+	+

* For the vertical, a plus vector means that the stimulation results in a clockwise angular displacement of the apparent vertical in the fronto-parallel plane (around the anterior-posterior horizontal axis of the body). For the median plane, a plus vector means a clockwise angular displacement of the apparent median plane around the vertical axis of the body. Analogously, the displacements in the counterclockwise direction are indicated by minus vectors.

These differences in effects of the two types of stimuli prepare the way for a new kind of behavioral analysis, that of the behavior of the organism depending on whether the adjustment occurs with reference to objects or with reference to stimuli not experienced as objects. "Objects" are defined for the subject through certain characteristics. Outstanding among these characteristics are: (1) definite location in space, and (2) contour. In contrast there are stimuli which lack contour, and definite location in space. These stimuli, previously called extraneous, can be thus considered as ground stimuli.

Object stimulation presupposes articulation between object and body. The organism copes with object stimuli in terms of equilibration tendencies affecting the relation between both. Ground stimuli do not have object properties. Thus, object-body equilibration tendencies are absent. Ground stimuli affect the organismic state irrespective of the presence or absence of objects. For instance, if extraneous stimulation is asymmetrically applied, counterbalancing forces come into play resulting in a new body equilibrial state. The changes in perception of objects come about because of organismic changes which as such occur whether the object is present or not. We may express this difference in another way by referring to homeostasis. The effects of ground stimuli pertain to internal homeostasis; the effects of object stimuli refer to homeostasis of the field comprised of object and body. This analysis, we hope, will eventually provide the basis for an organismic conception of the difference between figure and background which Gestalt psychologists have analyzed mainly in phenomenological terms.

VICARIOUSNESS

The notion of dynamic equivalence of sensory and muscular factors leads to a related construct, that of vicariousness of functions. By vicariousness is meant that available energy, i.e., sensory-tonic energy, may be released through different channels. It is postulated that the available sensory-tonic energy may, for instance, be released either through muscular-tonic activity of movement, or through perceptual activity.

Several studies may be mentioned which suggest such vicarious relationships between body action and perception.

One of these investigations deals with the perception of autokinetic motion under conditions of various degrees of body activity (1). The underlying hypothesis of this experiment was that if sensory-tonic energy is blocked from being released through bodily-motor channels it should find expression in heightened perceptual motion. Contrariwise, if this energy is released through greater motor activity, the degree of perceptual motion should be reduced. Observations of a fixed pin point of light in the darkroom were made under three conditions: (1) Immobilization, (2) control, and (3) increased motor activity.

Immobilization was achieved by strapping S into a chair for a period of 10 minutes preceding and during the test trials. Under control conditions, the S sat at ease, and under conditions of increased activity, the S had to move his arms continually while making the observations.

The principal measure was the time taken before autokinetic motion was reported. As predicted, the time taken to perceive motion was shortest for the immobilization condition, next for the control condition, and longest for observations under heightened body activity. Further results were obtained for another criterion, duration of autokinetic motion, leading to the same conclusion.

Another experiment dealing with vicariousness was reported by Korchin, Meltzoff, and Singer at the Chicago meetings (1951) of the American Psychological Association (2). Following the same hypothesis, these investigators inhibited motor activity preceding the presentation of a Rorschach card. Under these conditions, the number of movement responses were more numerous than under conditions where motor activity was not inhibited.

Another experiment—conducted at Clark—shows a similar relationship of vicariousness. Subjects were required to report what they saw when line drawings such as a train, baseball player, etc., were presented tachistoscopically. Before the pictures were exposed, the experimental group had to press vigorously against a push-board. After pushing against the board, the S stood still and looked at the exposed picture. The reports of the experimental group were compared with those of a control group which made observations without preceding muscular tension. The number of movement responses reported by the experimental group was significantly smaller than that reported by the control group.

The problem of vicariousness also has bearing on some experiments which were undertaken for the purpose of relating individual directional preferences in walking and individual differences in the perception of verticality. Preliminary investigations suggest that individuals are consistent in the direction of walking while blindfolded and also behave consistently in adjusting a luminescent rod to apparent vertical in the dark. Without going into further details, the concept of vicariousness suggested the hypothesis that there is an inverse relation between walking direction and angular displacement of the apparent vertical. In keeping with this hypothesis it has been found that for right-walkers the position of apparent vertical is angularly displaced more to the left than for left-walkers (9).[10]

One will easily recognize the relation between the concept of vicariousness and that of energy transformation as it appears in psychoanalysis. We are in the process of studying differences in the way such channelizing of energy occurs typically in individuals. The possibility remains, then, that a concept such as energy transformation may become amenable to rigid experimental test.

CONFIGURATION AND PERCEPTUAL DYNAMICS

Up to now we have dealt with the relation between objects and organismic states by utilizing simple spatial properties of objects such as verticality. It is one of our goals to deal with more complex properties of perceptual objects, in traditional terms called configurational characteristics, such as the difference between a triangle and a square, and a triangle and a circle etc. or more complex figures.

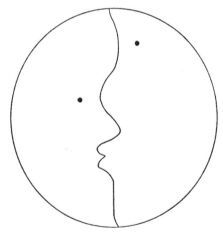

FIG. 4.   Ambiguous form. Adapted from Schafer and Murphy (4).

As one knows, Gestalt psychology has made tremendous contributions in this area. However, for the most part, Gestalt psychology handled the problem of configuration in terms of structure rather than dynamics. The problems of Gestalt psychology were mainly those of part and whole, reorganization, and formal laws of or-

---

[10] These very tentative results need further verification. One of the difficulties we are now attempting to overcome is that of obtaining a large enough field which is level and relatively noiseless.

ganization such as autochthonous laws. Wherever the problem of perceptual dynamics was treated, it was either in terms of phenomeno-logical analysis or in terms of electro-physiological or electro-chemical models. We are beginning to attack the problem of configuration in terms of object-organism relations.

In order to clarify the problem we may start with a discussion of an ambiguous figure (Fig. 4). This figure may be seen as a face looking toward the left, or as a face looking toward the right. Here we are dealing with changes in formal organization, but moreover, with differences in "visual dynamics." In terms of pure description it may be stated that in the one case there is a dynamic quality to the left, and in the other, to the right. While it is one thing to state one's introspections, it is quite another thing to demonstrate dynamic differences of this sort experimentally.

This problem of visual dynamics can be attacked experimentally by utilizing figural displacements in the median plane which have been described above.

Working in a darkroom, a luminescent rectangle is placed so that its right edge is in the objective median plane, i.e., so that this edge is objectively directly in front of S. On opening his eyes the S sees the edge not in the median plane but to the right of it (see previous section on median plane). If we now ask him to put this edge in such a position that it appears to be directly in front of him, he moves it to the left of the objective median plane. We describe this result by saying that his apparent median plane, or his medial equilibrial axis, has shifted to the left.

If we now substitute a right profile of a face with the nose in the objective median plane and ask the S to bring the nose of the face into S's median plane, we find again that the apparent median plane, or medial equilibrial axis, has shifted. A similar change takes place with an arrowhead-like triangle where the apex is to the right. The crucial result is that the two triangular forms (face and triangle) are seen more to the right and, therefore, have to be shifted significantly more to the left than the rectangle (see Fig. 5).

This experimental finding is important because it demonstrates, and also gives us some understanding of, what has been referred to as "visual dynamics." We mentioned before that when people look at a right profile of a face, they experience a vectorial dynamic quality, or a directional force, so to speak, to one side. In this experiment, we believe we have demonstrated that visual dynamics is behaviorally measurable. We think we have also shown that the nature of this dynamics consists in organismic effects, i.e., in particular, in effects on equilibration tendencies of the organism.

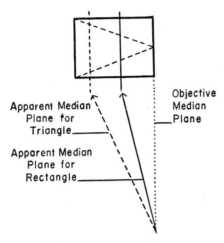

FIG. 5. Diagrammatic shift of apparent median plane to the left for rectangular and triangular form (face). It will be noted that the figures are seen as correspondingly displaced to the right, the triangle more than the rectangle.

Here we are at the threshold of understanding those dynamic characteristics of perception which have been variously called "demand qualities," "physiognomic qualities," etc. At the moment it cannot be stated what the object-body relations are which give a chair the qualities of "sitting tone" or "invitingness," but we feel that the nature of these qualities is principally not different from the dynamic qualities just described for simple configurations.

In conclusion we should like to point to a further goal of our experimentation. This goal is concerned with motivational factors in perception; here we shall be concerned not only with somato-tonic activity but with viscero-tonic activity as well. The step does not seem too large to us from the demonstration of dynamics of configurations as just described to the understanding of mechanisms underlying the effect of conative factors on perception. The shifts in perceptual space discussed here have absorbed our interest because they are paradigms of "projective" perception on an elementary level and tell us something about the object-organism relationships that, in our way of thinking, underlie perception in general.

REFERENCES

1. GOLDMAN, A. E. The effect of motor activity on the autokinetic phenomenon. Paper presented at the 1952 meetings of the EPA.
2. KORCHIN, S. J., MELTZOFF, J., and SINGER, J. L. Motor inhibition and Rorschach movement responses. Paper presented at the 1951 meetings of the APA. *Amer. Psychol.*, 1951, **6**, 344.
3. MARQUIS, D. G. Research planning at the frontiers of science. *Amer. Psychol.*, 1948, **3**, 430-438.
4. SCHAFER, R., and MURPHY, G. The role of autism in a visual figure-ground relationship. *J. exp. Psychol.*, 1943, **32**, 335-343.
5. WAPNER, S., and WERNER, H. Experiments on sensory-tonic field theory of perception: V. Effect of body status on the kinesthetic perception of verticality. (To be published.)
6. ———, and CHANDLER, K. A. Experiments on sensory-tonic field theory of perception: I. Effect of extraneous stimulation on the visual perception of verticality. *J. exp. Psychol.*, 1951, **42**, 341-345.
7. ———, and MORANT, R. B. Experiments on sensory-tonic field theory of perception: III. Effect of body rotation on the visual perception of verticality. *J. exp. Psychol.*, 1951, **42**, 351-357.
8. WERNER, H., and WAPNER, S. Sensory-tonic field theory of perception. *J. Pers.*, 1949, **18**, 88-107.
9. ———. Perception and body motion. Paper presented at the 1951 meetings of the APA. *Amer. Psychol.*, 1951, **6**, 287.
10. ———. Experiments on sensory-tonic field theory of perception: IV. Effect of initial position of a rod on apparent verticality. *J. exp. Psychol.*, 1952, **43**, 68-74.
11. ———, and CHANDLER, K. A. Experiments on sensory-tonic field theory of perception: II. Effect of supported and unsupported tilt of the body on visual perception of verticality. *J. exp. Psychol.*, 1951, **42**, 346-350.

....

The Nature and Importance of Individual Differences in Perception*

HERMAN A. WITKIN

PROBLEM AND METHODS

THE ABILITY to establish the upright as quickly, effectively, and accurately as we ordinarily do is based upon the stable and compelling representation of the upright in our surroundings and upon our possession of adequate sensory equipment for its detection. First, the direction of gravity, which corresponds to the true upright, is readily apprehended through the continuous postural adjustments made to this force. Second, the visual environment has the character of a framework, whose main outlines represent the true vertical and horizontal; and this also provides a ready basis for establishing the upright. The co-operation between these two sets of factors is ordinarily very intimate, resulting in a unified impression of the upright; and, furthermore, since the visual and gravitational uprights coincide in direction, the outcome is the same whichever determinant is used as the main basis of perception. This perceptual process is of great and continuous importance to the person, since it involves his body directly and enters constantly into his adjustments to objects in the environment. These and other characteristics to be discussed later make it especially useful in the study of personal factors in perception.

To investigate individual differences in manner of establishing the upright, three standardized test situations were developed. Use was made of knowledge obtained in earlier studies, in which the

* From *J. Pers.,* 1949, **18**, 145-170. Pp. 146-158, reprinted by permission of the author and the publisher.

The original paper has also been published in Bruner, J. S., and Krech, D. (Eds.), *Perception and personality, a symposium.* Durham, N. C.: Duke Univ. Press, 1950.

roles of various structural characteristics of the situations and of the main sensory determinants involved had been carefully worked out.[2] Attention was also given to the following considerations:

(1) Under ordinary conditions, as noted, the visually and posturally indicated uprights coincide in direction, so that judgment of the upright on the basis of one or the other, or both, leads to exactly the same result. Hence, even if people do differ in manner or extent of dependence on one or the other standard, such differences cannot ordinarily be detected. To detect them, it is necessary to separate these standards experimentally. This was done in the first two test situations described below by tilting the visual framework while the gravitational upright remained unaltered. In the third test situation the separation was accomplished by altering the direction of the gravitational force acting on the body while the visual framework remained upright. With both types of change

---

[2] Before a perceptual situation is applied to the study of personal determinants of perception, it must be carefully investigated, in order to establish the roles of other types of variables that influence performance in it. Unless the effects of these variables, and in particular their contributions to individual differences in performance, are known and controlled, it is not possible to presume that differences among subjects reflect differences in the operations of personal factors. Such an advance understanding of the perceptual situation is especially necessary, since perceptual processes are typically quite "sensitive" in that they are readily affected by slight changes in the conditions under which they are produced. Thus, it is not unusual for a slight modification in the instructions used in defining the subject's task to lead to important changes in results.

It may be noted here too that often even well-known and long-used perceptual techniques cannot simply be taken over as they are for use in the study of personal factors in perception. To make them reliable and valid instruments for testing the perception of individuals, or differences among individuals, they typically require very considerable development and adaptation.

The three tests discussed here are described in greater detail in: The nature and measurement of individual differences in space orientation. *J. Pers.* 1950, **19**, 1-15. The earlier experimental work with the situations used in these three tests is described in the following reports: Witkin, H. A. Perception of body position and of the position of the visual field. *Psychol. Monogr.*, 1949, **63**, No. 7, (Whole No. 302); Witkin, H. A., and Asch, S. E. Studies in space orientation. IV. Further experiments on perception of the upright with displaced visual fields. *J. exp. Psychol.*, 1948, **38**, 762-782; Witkin, H. A. Perception of the upright when the force acting on the body is changed. *J. exp. Psychol.*, 1950, **40**, 93-106; Witkin, H. A. Further studies of perception of the upright when the force acting on the body is changed. *J. exp. Psychol.*, 1952, **43**, 9-20. Later studies are discussed in: Witkin, H. A., et al. *Personality through Perception.* New York: Harper, 1954.

adherence to the visual framework results in a different location of the perceived upright than does adherence to the posturally experienced gravitational upright; and this permits evaluation of the extent of an individual's dependence on each factor.

(2) The task of determining the direction of the upright presents itself in the following different, though not necessarily separate, ways. (a) The direction of the field as a whole must be determined —for example, whether the cockpit of a plane, in a fogbank which obliterates the earth below, is level. (b) The direction of an object within the field must be determined—for example, whether a picture on the wall of a room is straight. (c) The position of the individual's body in relation to the upright must be determined—for example, whether it is erect or tilted at a given moment. These tasks are represented in the three tests described below—(a and c) in the first and third tests, (b) in the second test. These tests together present the person with essentially all conditions under which orientation toward the upright may be required.

(3) In order to evaluate a given person's perception in various situations, or to determine even small differences among people in a given situation, it is desirable that the subject's perception be expressed in quantitative terms. The alternative procedure of simply obtaining from the subject a report of his impressions would make such evaluation and comparison extremely difficult. To translate the subject's perception into a quantitative result, each of these tests required some *measurable* action from him: he was called on to make changes in the position of the visual framework, or of his own body, or of another object in space. The assumption was made, of course, that the action in these circumstances corresponded directly with the subject's perception of position, and that differences in action reflected differences in perception.

THE PERCEPTUAL TESTS

1. The Tilting-room-tilting-chair Test. This test evaluates the individual's perception of the position of his body, and of the whole surrounding field, in relation to the upright. The apparatus used consists of a small room within which is a chair. Each may be tilted to left or right, by any amount, either by the experimenter or by the subject seated in the chair. Since room and chair are provided with independent driving mechanisms, they may be tilted alone or together, to the same side or opposite sides, at the same speed or different speeds. The subject, seated in the chair, cannot see outside the room in which he is contained, so that his judgments of the upright must be based on whatever information he can obtain from his own body and from the visual field of the experimental room. The test procedure consists of tilting the room and chair to set positions, and then requiring the subject to adjust one or the other to the upright—the room on some trials, his chair on other trials. The positions to which room and chair are brought may be measured to the nearest degree, so that the results are expressed in quantitative terms.

The standard test consists of four parts. (a) Series 1: Room and chair are initially tilted to the same side (room at $56°$ and chair at $22°$), and the task is to adjust the room to the upright. (b) Series 2: Room and chair are initially tilted to opposite sides (room at $56°$ and chair at $22°$), and again the room must be adjusted to the upright. (c) Series 3a: Room and chair are initially tilted to the same side (room at $35°$ and chair at $22°$), but now the chair must be brought to the upright. (d) Series 3b: Room and chair are initially tilted to opposite sides (room at $35°$ and chair at $22°$), and again the chair is brought to the upright. Four trials are given in Series 1 and 2, and three in Series 3a and 3b. Series 1 and 2 both involve adjustment of the room, and Series 3a and 3b adjustment of the chair.

2. *The Rod-and-frame Test.* This test evaluates the individual's perception of the position of an item in a field. The apparatus used consists, first of all, of a luminous square frame, pivoted at its center so that it may be tilted to left and right. Pivoted at the same center, but moving independently of the frame, is a luminous rod. Since the test is conducted in a completely darkened room, all the subject can see is the frame and the rod. These are presented in tilted positions, and the subject is required to adjust the rod to the true upright while the frame remains in its initially tilted position. As a further variable, the subject's body is upright during some trials, tilted during others. It is, of course, much more difficult to make use of one's body in judging the position of a distant line when the body is tilted than when it is erect. In this test, therefore, it is possible to determine the extent to which the subject is able to make use of postural experiences in overcoming the influence of

the frame, both at times when it is easy to use these experiences and at times when it is difficult.

Three series, each consisting of eight trials, comprise the standard test. (a) Series 1: The subject is tilted to one side (at 28° left or 28° right) and the frame is tilted to the same side (at 28° left or 28° right). The rod is to be adjusted to the upright from an initial tilt of 28° (at times to the same side as the frame, at other times to the opposite side). (b) Series 2: Body and frame are tilted to opposite sides (both at 28°). (c) Series 3: The body is erect and the frame is tilted to left or right (at 28°).

3. The Rotating-room Test. This test evaluates the subject's perception of the position of his body and of his surroundings when the direction of the force acting on his body has been changed. In the two previous tests the procedure followed was that of tilting the field and tilting the body. Whereas tilting the field does fundamentally change the direction of the visual upright, tilting the body does not at all change the direction of the gravitational upright. Though more difficult than with body upright, it is still possible when the body is tilted to detect the direction of gravity through the bodily sensations arising from postural adjustment to this pull. The rotating-room test, however, by actually altering the direction of the force acting on the body, changes the postural factors in a more fundamental way. To alter the force on the body, an outward-acting centrifugal force, produced by rotating the subject, is added to the downward pull of gravity, yielding a resultant with a direction intermediate between the two forces.

The apparatus employed consists of a small, fully enclosed room, mounted on a carriage that is driven about a circular track. This room may be tilted from side to side, and contains a chair that may also be tilted to one side or the other. The rotation of the whole unit and the tilting of room and chair are controlled by the experimenter from the outer laboratory.

The standard test consists of two parts, in each of which four trials are given: (a) Series 1: Room and chair remain in their initial objectively upright positions, and the subject's task is to make the room straight if it appears tilted to him. (b) Series 2: Again room and chair remain in their initial objectively upright positions, and now the subject's task is to make his chair straight if he perceives himself as tilted.

THE NATURE OF INDIVIDUAL DIFFERENCES
IN MODE OF ORIENTATION

Studies with the situations used in these three tests have established the general principles governing orientation toward the upright. The following discussion will be limited, however, to those findings that are related to the problem of individual differences in perception.

Though presenting a variety of conditions, the three test situations have an important feature in common: they all involve a conflict between the main (visual and postural) determinants of the perceived upright. Therefore each presents the problem of integrating these conflicting sensory experiences and arriving at a unified perceptual impression. The results clearly show that in all the test situations subjects differed markedly in how they resolved the conflict and consequently in how they perceived the situation. Specifically, they differed with regard to the relative emphasis assigned to visual impressions and to bodily experiences in the final integration. Whatever the outcome, a given way of perceiving the situation represented in almost all cases an automatic and spontaneous experience for the person. Thus in the tilting-room-tilting-chair test, with the structure of the situation identical for all subjects, the room (tilted at 56°) immediately *looked* straight to some, *looked* mildly tilted to others, and *looked* very much tilted to still others. The same kinds of differences were found in the way the subjects perceived their own body position. These findings indicate that even a fairly well-structured situation will not be perceived in the same way by everyone. The discovery of such differences, of course, is dependent on the use of appropriate experimental procedures.

The nature and extent of the observed differences in perception may be illustrated with some specific results for each of the three tests. First to be considered is the tilting-room-tilting-chair test, and in particular that part of the test in which the subject was required to adjust the room to the upright (Series 1 and 2). Most often in this situation subjects tended to "go along with the field," so that the perceived upright was shifted toward the vertical of the tilted room. Some subjects simply identified the true upright with the vertical of the room, perceiving the room at the outset as fully erect at its initial 56° tilt. Others located it somewhere between the vertical of the room and the vertical indicated by experiences of body position, and moved the room from its initial tilt to some position closer to the true vertical. Still others, few in number, were successful in bringing the room to the true upright, indicating that they judged the upright independently of the field and in accordance with the position of the body. In Series 2, for example, where room and body were both initially tilted to opposite sides and the task was to straighten the room from its 56° tilt, the average scores (representing the objective tilt of the room when it was judged to be upright) were 22.9° for men and 28.1° for women. Examples of extreme performance were found at both ends of the range. One subject, a man, succeeded in bringing the room to within an average of 2.5° of the upright in the four trials of this series; another subject, a woman, perceived the room as upright at its initial 56° tilt on all four trials.

Equally striking differences were obtained in that part of the test where the subject's perception of the position of his own body was evaluated (Series 3a and 3b). When required to straighten the body, with the room tilted, most subjects moved it in the direction of the tilt of the room, indicating that they based their judgments not only on how the body felt, but also on how it looked—i.e., whether or not it was aligned with the surrounding field. (The average amount of tilt of the subject's body when it was judged to be upright was 8.2° for men and 10.3° for women.) Most subjects moved the body to some position intermediate between the vertical of the tilted room and the true upright. Others succeeded in bringing it to the true upright, regardless of the position of the room, basing their judgments entirely on bodily sensations. Still others, at the opposite extreme, moved the body into alignment with the tilted room, indicating that the visual basis of judgment alone was being used, to the neglect of bodily sensations. This visual mode of orientation is dramatically illustrated in the following result. In Series 3a, where room and chair were tilted to the same side, some subjects reported the body as tilted to the side *opposite* to its actual tilt. With the chair at 22° left and the room at 35° left, for example, such individuals judged themselves to be tilted *right* and requested that they be moved to the *left* to become straight. When the chair was brought to a position of near-alignment with the tilted field, they judged themselves to be upright. This obviously illustrates the use of a purely visual basis for perception of position. Experiments have established that contradictory postural sensations are actually suppressed under the influence of these strong visual impressions, even when large objective tilts of the body are involved. Most of the subjects who judged their body position on such an extreme visual basis proceeded in a confident and untroubled manner. A few, however, experienced great difficulty. When the body was moved into full alignment with the field, so that it looked upright, it began to *feel* tilted. When it was moved back to eliminate this felt tilt, the lack of alignment with the field made it *look* tilted. Prolonged back-and-forth movement usually failed in such cases to locate a position in which the subject could both feel and see himself as upright.

Turning to the results for the rod-and-frame tests, one again finds a very wide range of performances under all the conditions used. In this situation, where an objectively upright rod is surrounded by a tilted frame in the absence of any other visual field, the rod appears, to almost everyone, to be tilted in the opposite direction to the frame. Accordingly, when asked to adjust the rod to the upright, most subjects displaced it from the upright in the direction of the tilt of the frame. The mean amounts by which the rod was displaced in the two series where the body was tilted (Series 1 and 2) were 16.7° and 18.3° for women, and 12.5° and 14.5° for men. In Series 3, where the body was erect and therefore more useful in estimating the upright, the mean amount of displacement of the rod was 12.1° for women and 7.4° for men. In general, then, the tilted frame exerted a marked influence on the perceived position of the rod, especially when the body was tilted. When individual performances are considered, however, it is found that people differed very markedly in the extent to which they were affected by the frame. Some subjects were able to escape the influence of the frame, both with body erect and with body tilted, and succeeded in bringing the rod to within a few degrees of the true upright. The ability to perceive the rod independently of the field, or to deal with the presented visual situation analytically, undoubtedly reflects the effective use of body experiences as a basis for perception. Other subjects—and these constituted the largest group—"went along with" the frame to various extents, bringing the rod to a position that represented some degree of compromise between the vertical of the tilted field and the vertical indicated by the body. For a third group, perception of the rod continued to be based almost exclusively on its relation to the frame. In such cases the tilted frame itself was usually perceived as fully upright, so that straightening the rod became a simple matter of aligning it with the frame. Among subjects whose perception depended upon the frame in this extreme fashion, a very striking phenomenon was observed. At times, in the absence of any actual movement, the subject would suddenly experience a perceptual shift in the axes of the frame, so that its topmost side would be perceived as its left side, for example—that is, parallel to the left wall of the unseen outer room. When perception of the frame showed this kind of lability, alignment of the rod with the shifted axes of course led to exceedingly large errors in estimation of the upright. Surprisingly, these shifts occurred even when the subject's body was upright. When this happened the subject might report that the rod was upright (and therefore presumably aligned with his erect body) when it formed a 62° angle with his body.

In most cases of extreme adherence to the frame, the subject actually perceived it as properly upright, or nearly so, and his judgments were made quickly and confidently. In some other instances, however, adherence to the frame resulted from a stated inability to make use of the body in judging the position of the rod, so that the frame became the only usable standard for judgment. Subjects in these cases reported that they could not resurrect the axes of the unseen outer room, or that space had "taken on the shape of the frame," or that they could not tell which way their bodies were oriented, and so on. Judgments of the rod under these conditions were made with great difficulty and in very troubled fashion.

Subjects whose perception of the rod tended to be based mainly on its relation to the prevailing field sometimes gave very paradoxical performances. To illustrate: A subject would report that the frame, which was at a 28° angle, was tilted, but that the rod, which was actually aligned with it, was perfectly upright. The subject often failed to notice the obvious contradiction in his report. Although this seems to be a rather stupid kind of error, it is clearly due to a particular kind of perception, rather than to any intellectual difficulty. The rod, being within the field of the frame, is perceived entirely in relation to this field. The frame, on the other hand, is perceived on the basis of its relation to the body. There are thus two perceptual systems involved; and the trouble in such cases is that these are kept separated. This separation undoubtedly has adaptive value; for such people the effect of the field upon their perception of the rod is so compelling that any effort to involve the body in the judgment would present too great a difficulty. This was found to be true when the contradiction in their reports was pointed out and they were encouraged to reconsider their judgments. Their subsequent attempts to integrate their strong visual impressions with more remote bodily experiences almost always proved unsuccessful, and they fell back on their earlier procedure of aligning the rod with the frame. The overlooking of so obvious a contradiction in experience, the resistance offered to recognizing it when it was forced on their attention, and the adaptive consequences of operating in this fashion, all suggest that we are dealing here with an instance of repression in perception. Many other examples of similarly "stupid" errors were found in this work, all lending themselves to the same interpretation.

The range of quantitative results in adjustment of the rod to which these differing modes of perception led may be illustrated with the data for Series 3, where the body was erect. One subject, a male, succeeded in adjusting the rod to within an average of less than 1° of the upright in the eight trials of the series. At the opposite extreme another subject, a female, made errors averaging 40.1° in these eight trials (even though she was sitting erect and therefore had the opportunity of simply aligning the rod with her body). On some of the trials this subject experienced perceptual shifts of the frame.

Considering finally the results for the rotating-room test, great variability among subjects is again found, again depending on differences in manner of integrating visual and postural impressions. With the force on the body forming a 43.7° angle with the true upright, most subjects tilted both room and body in a direction opposite to the direction of this force, when required to make them upright. This alteration of the postural determinant of position thus led to a shift in the perceived positions of both body and field, though the shift did not correspond in magnitude to the change in the force.

Examination of individual performances shows that people were affected quite differently in their perception by the change in the force acting on their bodies. In almost all cases subjects felt tilted, to various degrees, while seated in the upright chair during rotation. Many also perceived the upright room as tilted, again to various degrees. When asked to adjust themselves to the upright, some subjects, at one extreme of the performance range, moved themselves to positions approximately at right angles to the force and thus compensated for it in full. These subjects moved the room to an equally marked extent; for them the force experienced by their bodies was the main determinant in perceiving both body and field position. At the opposite extreme were subjects for whom the room continued to appear fully upright throughout rotation and who therefore did not need to move it at all. In this area of the distribution there were even instances in which its alignment with the field caused the body itself to be perceived as fully upright throughout rotation. This manner of perception reflected a complete disregard of the intense lateral tug on the body. It is clear that under the same field conditions and with a force of the same magnitude and direction acting on their bodies, people differ markedly in their perception.

CONSISTENCY AND STABILITY OF THE INDIVIDUAL'S MODE OF PERCEPTION

Some results will now be presented which indicate that a given mode of perception represents a pervasive and deep-seated characteristic of the individual.

Consistency of Perception. Up to this point the differences in perception found in each part of the three orientation tests have been described. The next question for consideration relates to the *consistency* of a given person's mode of perception in different parts of a given test and in the different tests. To answer this question correlations have been computed [3] among the basic parts of each test and among the three tests. In view of the existence of important sex differences in performance in these tests (to be considered later), results for men and women have been treated separately. The correlations are presented in Table I. For both men and women, the values are sufficiently high to indicate that the manner of a person's orientation toward the upright is fairly consistent, whether the specific task involves perception of the position of a part of a field, of the field as a whole, or of one's own body. More specifically, a tendency to rely mainly on the visual framework or mainly on bodily experiences represents a fairly general characteristic of the individual's orientation.

Stability of Perception. The next question to be considered is whether a given mode of perception is a transient feature of the

---

[3] When it was necessary to obtain a single score for several different parts of a test, standard scores for each part were computed and an average of these taken.

TABLE I. INTERCORRELATIONS AMONG BASIC PARTS OF EACH
ORIENTATION TEST AND AMONG THE THREE TESTS

Test Situation	Men (N = 46)	Women (N = 45)
1. Tilting-room-tilting-chair test: Room-adj. (Series 1 + 2) *vs.* chair-adj. (Series 3a + 3b)	.60*	.42
2. Rod-and-frame test: Body-tilted (Series 1 + 2) *vs.* body-erect (Series 3)	.70	.66
3. Rotating-room test: Room-adj. Series *vs.* chair-adj. Series	.58	.62
4. Tilting-room-tilting-chair test *vs.* rod-and-frame test	.64	.52
5. Tilting-room-tilting-chair test *vs.* rotating-room test	−.51**	−.63
6. Rod-and-frame test *vs.* rotating-room test	−.25	−.18

* Values of .38 or higher are significant at the 1 per cent level of confidence, and those of .29 or higher at the 5 per cent level.

** The negative correlations between the rotating-room test and the other two tests occur because, in the former, "going along with" the visual field results in little or no displacement of body and room from the upright, whereas in the latter it results in larger displacements of body, room, and rod.

person or whether it tends to characterize him over an extended period of time. An answer was provided by a study in which a group of subjects was retested in the tilting-room-tilting-chair situation and in the rod-and-frame situation after a period of more than a year. The test-retest correlations for the two situations, respectively, were .85 and .88 for men and .86 and .87 for women. These values are very high, especially for the types of test used, and indicate marked stability in the individual's perception, as far as orientation toward the upright is concerned.

∙∙

Effects of the Gestalt Revolution: The Cornell Symposium on Perception*,1

Julian E. Hochberg

"Structuralism" and the Gestalt Revolution. Before the turn of the century, the psychology of sensation and perception enjoyed in "structuralism" a relatively unified approach. New data and interests soon forced the system apart at the seams; as to perception, the most important criticisms came from the Gestaltists. One main purpose of this symposium was to consider what areas of agreement could be found three decades after the introduction of *Gestalt-theorie*. Discussion centered around two areas of research: perceptual change (or learning), and the perception of "events." Let us review briefly what made these areas important to Gestalt theory.

The "Constancy Hypothesis" and "Event Perception." Structuralism tended to assume that: ". . . things look as they do because the proximal stimuli are what they are" (16, p. 80), and that ". . . the result of a local stimulation is constant . . . that all

---

* From the *Psychol. Rev.,* 1957, **64**, 73-84. Reprinted by permission of the author and the publisher.

1 Participants were: Egon Brunswik, University of California; James Drever, University of Edinburgh; James J. Gibson, Cornell University; Fritz Heider, University of Kansas; Julian Hochberg, Cornell University; Gunnar Johansson, University of Stockholm; George Klein, New York University; Ivo Kohler, University of Innsbruck; Robert B. MacLeod, Cornell University; Wolfgang Metzger, University of Munster; T. A. Ryan, Cornell University; Hans Wallach, Swarthmore College.
This symposium, held in June, 1954, was made possible by a National Science Foundation Grant. No attempt was made to preserve either the specific order of discussion, or the identity of the source of each opinion, though I have in a few instances inserted names of contributors. Since such reworking tends to take the responsibility out of the hands of the other participants, I have endeavored to return it to them by circulating copies of the report for their comments, addenda, and post-mortem alterations, and to take account of their replies, where length permitted.

locally stimulated excitations run their course without regard to other excitations" (16, pp. 96 f.)—the "Constancy Hypothesis." Any failure of this relationship was explained in terms of previous associations: ". . . things do not look as they ought to on the ground of pure perceived stimulation, and they differ from such an expectation by looking more like . . . the things with which we have real dealings. . . . in dealing with things we acquire experience about them, and this experience enters our whole perception" (16, pp. 84 f.).

It is easy to embarrass the Constancy Hypothesis. We can obtain the same responses to different stimuli or different responses to the same stimuli, as in the phenomena of object constancy, the geometrical illusions, etc. (16). Auditory stimuli affect visual experience, and vice versa (24); forms appear identical when stimulating totally diverse elements,[2] yet are rendered unrecognizable without changing the elements (16). The Gestaltists held that the theoretical error lay in the choice of too-small units of analysis; this was to be avoided by a "naive" phenomenology as opposed to formalized analytic introspection. Moreover, the "elements" are not independent, and the "laws" of their interaction were to be understood in terms of a new and unorthodox view of the underlying molar cerebral processes.

The phi phenomenon is a good example here. The (illusory) apparent motion can be made as completely convincing as real motion; the explanation of perceived real motion as the tying together by association of successive sensations of position becomes questionable. The apparent motion is a unitary experience, and Wertheimer started the Gestalt search for "brain models" by postulating an equally unitary cortical process. Perhaps more important, when Korte (18) investigated the dependence of the phi phenomenon upon brightness, separation, etc., a new form of psychophysics began to emerge, in which the experience was a full *event*, rather than a fragmentary "sensation," and in which *the stimulus variables manipulated were not necessarily ones which seemed intuitively similar to, or attributively responsible for, the quality of the response.* In general, Gestaltists hoped to restore stimulus-response correlations by treating entire configurations as the stimuli, and entire

---

[2] A recent experiment by Wallach and Austin (2) makes it necessary to qualify this statement, however, since it now appears that there is at least some dependence of form recognition on retinal locus of original presentation.

phenomenal events as the responses; in the process, the simple associational formulae of perceptional learning were discarded. Note
that the Gestalt theorists were *not* nativists in the traditional sense.
They did not deny that learning affects perception. They denied
only that all departures from the Constancy Hypothesis are to be
explained in terms of past associations.

ADAPTATION TO THE DISTURBANCE
OF STIMULATION: PERCEPTUAL RELEARNING

Up-Down Inversion. The effects of natural visual disturbances
(long-term cataracts, etc.) have been reviewed (11), and contribute
to a modern version of the old nativist-empiricist controversy; despite the recognized importance of the Stratton experiment (27),
however, few experiments have been performed with humans (6,
27). In Erismann's laboratory, different kinds of protracted disturbance are under investigation, and Ivo Kohler's (cf. 17) findings
are striking and important.

Let us survey the course of adaptation to visual disturbance, especially in inversion (in which up becomes down and vice versa).

Stage 1. When disturbing spectacles are first put on, the world
seems strange in various ways: faces look unfamiliar, walking people seem mechanical (the up-and-down component, normally not
"seen," becomes apparent), brightness contrast seems greater, colors
more saturated. As head and eyes move, the normally stationary
world swings about. The unfamiliarity of faces eventually wears off;
in later stages, one can recognize features, etc., but even to the last,
expressions cannot be discerned. The subject is almost incapaci-
tated, with his motor actions appropriate at best to a world which
appears upside down.

Stage 2. The subject can negotiate streets, can "fence" with the
experimenter, etc. However, we cannot accept such task performance
as the operational index of perception, or perceptual response (cf.
23), without residuum: *despite such effective motor performance,
the world remains phenomenally inverted!* Perceptuo-motor adjustment, and phenomenal adaptation, run separate (but related)
courses, and we cannot safely equate the two. Phenomenal inverted-
ness first disappears for objects connected with the subject's body-
system, or with clear indications of gravity. An object grasped, a
plumb line, a face with a cigarette between its lips, with smoke ascending from the tip—these are seen as upright for a short time.

The relationship between the phenomenal upright, obtained through "adaptation" to an inverted stimulus, and the original phenomenal upright is by no means clear. Kohler reported that if a subject is shown two faces, one upside down (so that its retinal image is now, through the inverting spectacle, that which would without the spectacles have occurred from a face right side up) alongside an upright (and hence retinally inverted) face with a smoking cigarette between the lips, now *both* appear "upright"— *but in different ways and in opposite directions!* Kohler plans to adapt only *one* eye to inverting prisms, to permit further investigation of this question.

Stage 3. About a month later, the perceived world is almost continuously congruent with geography and independent head movements, even while the subject performs complicated behavior (bicycling, etc.). A specific familiar object (e.g., a given house) will appear unfamiliar when first viewed through the spectacles, even after other objects (e.g., other houses) have achieved familiarity through adaptation (Stage 3). Objects familiarized only through the spectacles become unfamiliar when the spectacles are removed. Transfer is restricted both for visual and motor adaptation, and the process is not in any sense a learning to "invert the whole stimulus field."

Stage 4. If the spectacles are now removed, *the world appears inverted with normal stimulation.*

Form Distortions. Adaptation to visual inversion may *not* be generalized, but adaptation to other disturbances may be. Wedge-deforming prisms contract one side of the field horizontally and expand it vertically, as compared with the other; phenomenal adaptation eventually occurs and, with spectacles removed, the reverse form distortion appears as an aftereffect. Two classes of distortion effects appear: (*a*) general throughout the field, such as the *curvature* of lines; (*b*) conditional upon direction of gaze, such as the *angles* at which lines join.

Adaptation to width distortions (measured by rotation of an additional prism to eliminate phenomenal distortion) was slowest and weakest. Then came adaptation for curves, then for angles (at the right stage a subject will correctly see a square as *right-angled, but with curved sides*—an example of the inconsistency apparently permissible in the docile geometry of the visual field),[3] with adaptation to distortions of movement fastest and strongest.

Tentatively, therefore, it appears that adaptation may be faster when apparent differences between disturbed and familiar conditions are greater. Thus, adaptation is faster to up-down inversion than to right-left reversal, perhaps because our environment shows more bilateral symmetry around a vertical than a horizontal axis: gravity is a universal, whereas there are few comparable universals in a left-right sense.

Adaptation to Color-Fringes (Half Spectra). When viewed through prisms, each achromatic contour bears a fringe of color—a red-yellow half-spectrum to the left, blue to the right. This effect, also, is *general,* since the fringes appear everywhere in the field, independent of eye position. It is also *differential* in that, for any contour, the fringe is red-yellow on one side, and blue on the other.

After about a month, adaptation is complete: no more color-fringes are seen! *When the spectacles are removed, every contour in the field now appears surrounded by a reversed color fringe, i.e., blue on the side to which the red-yellow previously appeared, and vice versa.* If each eye adapts separately to opposite prismatic color fringes, each eye displays (in rivalry) its own aftereffect. These data appear innocent enough, but are actually quite resistant to a satisfactory yet detailed explanation.

Split-Field Chromatic Disturbances. The differential effects were more strikingly isolated as follows. With the left half of each spectacle lens blue and the right half yellow, white objects at first appear blue when viewed to the left, and yellow when viewed to the right. The usual desaturation appears if the eyes are fixed to one side but, obviously, as soon as they move to the other side, the complementary color appears. The astonishing fact is that, after protracted adaptation, eventual disappearance of all chroma occurs despite eye movement, in which the light at the fovea is at one time blue, at the next, yellow, and color is seen in neither case. With spectacles removed, *the aftereffect is also conditional upon eye position: with the eyes left, the world appears yellow; with the eyes*

---

[3] However, we cannot be sure from Kohler's report that this necessarily involves any visual inconsistency; if, as was not ascertained, the subject sees the square as being on an appropriately curved surface (Ryan), no inconsistency remains.

right, blue! Thus, both effects are tied to, and therefore phenomenally independent of, eye movement.

Discussion of the Adaptation to Disturbed Stimulation. Traditionally, for each sensation one could isolate one stimulus, and vice versa; perceptions entailed past associations, "unnoticed sensations," and "unconscious inference." The study of perception was possible only because, despite such associations, the underlying sensations remained tied to the stimulus and were rigorously investigable by the psychophysical methods. After Gestalt (and other) emphasis on the indistinguishability of sensation and perception, at least three extreme alternatives remained open:

1. To reconnect stimulus and percept by discovering the physiological mechanisms responsible for the (presumably) "organizational" lack of correspondence (cf. 16, 30); this has not, thus far, proved very fruitful.

2. To re-analyze the stimulus field in order to determine what aspects or "higher order variables," if any, *are* in correspondence with perceptual response (cf. Gibson, 9). This treats *perception* psychophysically as previously only *sensation* was investigated, and seeks to restore a new version of the Constancy Hypothesis.

3. To treat all stimulus-response relations as previously *perception* was investigated, i.e., as so determined by the organism's past experience with an unreliable environment that only the loosest, most statistical connection between proximal stimulus and perceptual response can be expected. Kohler's experiments constitute the greatest systematic change of relationship between stimulus and experience as yet reported, and are well suited for examination of this issue.

Brunswik's approach comes closest to the third position: the correspondence between the response and the physical (distal) stimulus must be imperfect. This ambiguity, supposedly inherent in the equivocal relationship between distal stimuli and the proximal stimuli (the *cues*) to which the organism can respond, means that each cue has only a limited probability of being "correct." Thus, an *ecological sampling* reveals that the correlation is less than 0.6 between the cue of vertical position and the distal stimulus distance, and less than 0.4 between the cue of "space filling" (number of distinguishable intervening steps) and actual distance. An adjusted organism therefore must use many cues, weighting each according to its relative frequency (ecological validity) by some process of probability learning, of which Brunswik postulates two varieties: (a) *distribution learning,* and (b) *correlation learning.* Distribution learning (e.g., that hanging objects are rare) is very general, and, with enough reversals of cases, a "revolution" in such expectancies will occur. Correlation learning grasps concomitance, the reliability of any cue as a correlate of the object. Perception is, to Brunswik, a reasoning-like ("ratiomorphic") process, much faster to respond than is reasoning, but slower to change what has been learned; it is a speeded up, conservative, stereotyping, reasoning-like function (3).

The distributional perceptual learning provisions which are at the heart of this viewpoint may *in principle* accommodate Kohler's general findings, but they do not begin to explain the very singular specific data reported. Despite the apparent ease of the first Gestalt attack on the empiricist position, it is extremely difficult to refute any general "explanation" couched in terms of past experience. Consequently, we must *specify* the relationship between past and present stimuli and percepts, or we have "explained" little more by invoking "past experience" than by invoking "human nature." A more specific attempt to account for the conditional effects through "conditioning" to the eye movements—or, more accurately, through extinction of previously conditioned responses (Drever),—did not seem very fruitful, although it may be possible to do more justice to findings with the greater number of assignable variables in the Hullian repertoire.

Metzger proposed as a Gestalt theoretical explanatory principle that *aspects of the visual world tend to become independent of behavior,* classing Kohler's results with the various perceptual constancies of size, motion, etc. (and explaining why reversed binocular disparity never adapted, since no added stability re the individual's behavior would thus be gained). However, this fails to explain adaptation to the half-spectra, in which the viewer's activity is hard to denote, and these phenomena seem at once the most general and the most puzzling. This proposal also leaves unexplained the fact that many aspects of the disturbance fail to reach complete adaptation, e.g., curvature adaptation appears asymptotic at about one-third. Metzger suggested that the "stresses" toward straightening are not strong enough to overcome completely the curvature of the actual stimulus; however, as Wallach pointed out, if the "internal stresses" of "organization" are insufficient to straighten an extreme curvature, adaptation should go farther with weaker prisms; yet Kohler reported that after prisms of a given strength caused an asymptotic degree of distortion-adaptation, prisms of double that strength cause adaptation to start again, with a new asymptote, still short of complete correction.

Why not, Gibson asked, from a position he had previously taken on the problem of curved line adaptation (8), suppose that *the physical norm tends to become the phenomenal neutral point?* Such norms must still be defined,[4] but the consensus appeared to be, at this point, that a process of "partialing out" norms does seem to be a general principle during adaptation: what is *always* present becomes "unnecessary" to perceive. The blue half-spectrum to the right is always present, and so becomes the chromatic norm, and white light, the previous norm, will appear yellow. The problems affecting the previous formulations seem less troublesome from this point of view, but before its utility can be evaluated, much more explication is necessary.

Before we essay any conclusions, however, let us turn to the second general problem, that of *event perception.*

EVENT PERCEPTION

Recent advances have been made in three divergent salients—events involving the motion of several parts (Johansson, 15; Michotte, 22; Duncker, 5); the perception of social events (Heider and Simmel, 12); the kinetic depth effect, i.e., the depth perception consequent to sequential proximal stimulation from a rotating distal stimulus (Wallach and O'Connell, 29; Metzger, 20).

The General Problem. We know that one can see motion when there is none on the retina. Johansson's series of studies (15) permit some fairly definite psychophysical relationships to be laid down for the perception of motion.

---

[4] Such norms need not be defined simply by statistical analysis of the distal stimulus. The straight line among curved lines, the rectangle among acute and obtuse angles, etc., are norms in other than a frequency sense: they are neutral points in "opposition series" (cf. 8), which run, say, from concave to the left to concave to the right, from obtuse to acute, etc. These are norms in a logical rather than an actuarial sense; a mathematical analysis of the visual world around us will be simpler, as Kohler puts it, if our reference tools are straight lines and right angles than if they are curves or obtuse or acute angles, so that the straight line and right angle would be analytic norms even if they never occurred in experience.

A horizontal row of four lights simultaneously moving up and down with the same phase appears as one entity in motion. With two pairs of lights 180° out of phase, "common fate" acts as a first, primitive law: those moving at the same time in the same direction appear as parts of one object. With more complex phase relations, those elements with the least phase difference form a group. Three-dimensional arrangements appear if they preserve a constant spatial distance between the elements in relative motion, picking out a constant shape in motion (cf. Metzger, 20, 21). When we depart from parallel harmonic motions to such motions at angles to each other ("Lissajous combinations"), the situation changes. With two moving lights having perpendicular paths, the same frequency, and phases such that they come to the point common to the two paths at the same time, they appear to move toward and away from each other *along the sloping line joining their extreme positions*. In addition, there appears a slight motion of the whole system in the perpendicular direction. If two points move in opposite directions with the same frequency in circular paths which, touching at one point, approach each other, they fuse, and then retreat on a horizontal line; simultaneously, the path along which they travel moves up and down. In short, *the physical motion which is present in the stimulus appears to have disappeared without any trace in perception, while a movement is perceived which appears to have no simple counterpart in the stimulus*. However, the perceived motions *do* correspond to component vectors into which the stimulus motions may be analyzed: ". . . the phenomenon can fittingly be described as motions relative to two different coordinate systems, one fixed, and the other moving, in accordance with the principles for relative motion" (15, p. 97).

Thus, one can "extract" a given component from a complex motion and obtain the predicted "remainder." For example, a simple straight-line harmonic motion may be analyzed into two harmonic motions of lower amplitude and a 45° phase difference. Consequently, if one point is given an harmonic motion, and a second point is given the motion of one of its two components, the relative motion should be that of the remaining component; and in fact this is what is seen. One point moves back and forth, and the other moves back and forth with respect to it, like a planet rotating around its sun (in fact, although this *can* be seen as motion in a flat plane, many subjects see it in three dimensions, as an orbital motion).

In general, a "figural hierarchy" of motion is perceived: first, a static background; next, and in reference to this, the common motion; and highest, the components of motion relative to the common motion. If we have one point *a* moving in a circular path, and the other *b* in a vertical path, point *a* appears to move toward and away from *b* in a horizontal path, while both *a* and *b* move up and down. With *b* removed, *a* is seen to move in a circle; with *a* removed, *b* is seen to move vertically. If we repeat the procedure, but with the vertical path of *b* shorter than the diameter of *a*'s circular path, both points *a* and *b* move vertically together, with *a* describing an ellipse, and the vertical component of *a*'s motion has lost the length of travel "used up" by *b*'s motion. In general, of two motions which are the same in other respects, the motion which has the shorter path or, more generally, the *lower velocity,* will determine the magnitude of motion of the combined system. It is this combined motion which forms the frame of reference within which the remaining motions occur. If two or more simultaneous motions or components of motion, equal in magnitude and direction, are analyzable within the stimulus motion, these will be seen as a single motion.

In general, Johansson states his findings as follows: In every case, if we abstract the motion components common to all of the moving points (as a special case, the common motion may reduce to zero), the remaining components become the relative motion of the parts, while the common motion becomes the motion of the whole relative to the stationary background. It is therefore always the shortest excursion which will determine the common motion.

Motion and Three-Dimensional Space: The Kinetic Depth Effect. In many of Johansson's experiments, the percept was three-dimensional, even though both proximal and distal stimuli were two-dimensional.

Just as we can study the psychophysical relationships in apparent motion without *necessary* concern with ontogenetic or historical antecedents, so can the emergence of depth as an aspect of event perception be studied in its own right. In fact, specific knowledge concerning perceptual learning begins to emerge from such study, to replace gross appeals to empiricism.

Particularly informative here are the investigations of the "kinetic depth effect" (29). Wallach was originally concerned with depth perception without the "primary" depth cues (binocular disparity, etc.). In an at least partially empiristic view, one originally had "depth" experience only where there were such "cues" (making the case of monocular individuals awkward to explain); in terms of the "spontaneous organization" of *Gestalt-theorie*, we are just lucky, phylogenetically speaking. However, as one walks around in the world of objects, the proximal stimuli projected by distal objects are pretty much those which would be cast by the axial rotation of those objects, and the rotation of most of the objects around us will yield three-dimensional experience even when viewed monocularly. Can subjects (monocular or otherwise) "learn" from this kinetic effect, while in motion, the three-dimensional nature of a given object? (Remember also the importance of motion in the "relearning" of space in Kohler's findings.)

Wire patterns were chosen whose projections evoked two-dimensional responses; these gave way to three-dimensional responses when the wire forms were rotated. After this experience with a given form, it would tend in the future to appear three-dimensional, even when stationary. (This is not simply *knowledge* that the given form is projected by a three-dimensional object, since it displays unexpected and involuntary perspective reversal: what was near now looks far, with appropriate consequent size and shape "distortions.") Wallach terms this a *memory*, rather than *learning*, since only a specific "trace" is involved, and this is a long way from the creation of "trace complexes," with high generality of function— e.g., size constancy, which cannot be referred to any single memory trace.

But *why* should the rotation of a form bring its projected shadow perceptually into three dimensions?

The stationary two-dimensional projection of *any* given object is ambiguous in that there is an exceedingly large number of three-dimensional objects which will produce that projection. The *transformations* undergone by the projections as the objects rotate are unique, at least for many objects—but only if certain restrictive assumptions are made, e.g., that the projecting object must be a rigid form, etc. It is easy to say to this that, with the exception of animate creatures, most objects in our environment *are* rigid, and that this is simply a matter of distribution learning, in Brunswik's sense. However, we do not yet have any estimate of the ecological distribution of rigidity; moreover, Johansson finds with complex motions that rigidity is *not* always what is seen, even if the distal stimulus is really rigid (15).

Ambiguity (between distal and proximal stimuli) therefore must remain, but each successive momentary projection of the rotating object must, as Wallach points out, bring new information about it, and decrease the number of forms it may have and still give rise to the specific projection series. This does not immediately solve the problem of a working psychophysical correspondence, since any finite decrease of an infinite number of alternatives cannot do much toward specificity. However, if we note with Gibson that the transformation *sequence* undergone by the projection becomes *one* piece of information in the case of the usually "correct" perception of the distal stimulus, and that this requires less information to be specified than would that of describing each stage in the sequence separately—and if, as this writer has suggested elsewhere (13), that perceptual response will tend to occur which is the most economical of information—then a form of specificity returns to the stimulus-percept relationship. We must deal not with unique relationships between distal stimulus, proximal stimulus, and response, but with relationships of varying probabilities. In Brunswik's terms, ecological validity and reliability may frequently be quite low. However, for most *normal* situations only one ecologically probable distal stimulus can yield the given proximal stimulus—*if we choose adequate higher-order variables of stimulation for our analysis.* Between proximal stimulus and perceptual response, then, there may be or may not be ambiguity of relationship. Where ambiguity is low, there is no problem for psychophysics; where ambiguity is high, a more probabilistic psychophysical correspondence may be in order.

A psychophysics without a punctate Constancy Hypothesis, and which employs relatively large units of analysis and tolerates probability statements of psychophysical relationship, permits the study of events of much wider scope than those we have been considering. The study of what may be termed the psychophysics of perceived causation, by Michotte (22), is only one step up the ladder from the event perceptions of motion and depth toward the study of the perception of self and others (7, 19, 25, 23). There is no intrinsic reason why such a "global psychophysics," to use MacLeod's term, cannot be applied to the study of any phenomena in which discriminal responses are obtainable. The utility of such research, of course, awaits empirical findings.

The Perception of Social Events. A start has been made in Heider's pioneer researches on the "social perception" of moving geometrical figures (cf. 12). We have seen that perceived motion might be more closely determined by change of brightness than by actual motion; here, the Constancy Hypothesis suffers some further interdimensional fracturing: objective motion may serve as stimulus not for perceived motion, but for perceived purpose, life or animation. Under Kohler's disturbed visual conditions, animate actions became mechanical motions; contrariwise, motion configurations may give rise to the perception of action and purpose, rather than of mechanical motion (15).

Heider's "animated cartoon" had a large triangle, a small triangle, and a small circle engage in some charmingly social peregrinations through the familiar "apparent motion" of stroboscopic presentation. Naive observers describing what they had just seen differed as to content, but agreed as to the actions in many portions of the film. Is this film only a projective technique, only a focal point around which individual antecedent experiences determine the response? If so, can at least gross similarities of experience be assumed or established? Answers can only be obtained by psychophysical research. However, we can appeal to certain at least peripherally relevant considerations.

Klein reported that when Heider's film is shown to psychotic patients (paranoid), the contents differ from those reported by normals, but the actions seen are the same. Despite the probably very great differences from individual to individual, certain stimulus variables seem important; many of us who watched Heider's film felt that, in general, uniform motion was not a compelling stimulus for perceived action, depending more upon context for its animate qualities than did nonuniform motion. Johansson reported that rows of lights moving with simple phase relations (say 180°) were described by subjects in terms of some moving mechanism; with more complex phase relations (say 90°), the motion was that of a wave, snake, etc.; with still more complex phase relations (say 45°, 135°, and 45° between the lights), almost always living motion. Tentatively, then, perhaps nonrigid, nonuniform motion is conducive to the perception of action.

SUMMARY AND CONCLUSIONS

Empiricism-Nativism. Empiricist and nativist "explanations" were essayed quite frequently throughout the discussion, and proved equally unedifying. What one participant considered stimulus-determined (and probably innate) another considered at least partially "learned" (e.g., compare 14 and 28). One suspects that the issues of this traditional controversy have been reduced to specific questions of conditions and mechanisms which have to be settled by detailed investigation. Perhaps this is due to the fact that (at least with humans) it appears possible to find an empiricist "explanation" for almost any perceptual phenomenon; however, without concrete knowledge about perceptual learning, such general accounts are quite useless, if well-nigh invulnerable.

The Minimum Principle. The most generally acceptable summing up of Kohler's results was as follows: Two kinds of association between distal and/or proximal stimuli (including tactual-kinesthetic feedback stimulation) in our visual environment, can be at least roughly distinguished, namely invariable relations ($r \cong 1.0$) and contingent relations ($r < 1.0$). Where an invariable relationship occurs, instead of repeating it in each perceptual response, it becomes "partialled out" as norm, framework, or neutral point. As Kohler finally put it, it is as though the mathematical description of the world made by the organism takes the simplest possible form.

In Johansson's motion studies, those components in a complex moving stimulus which are common to all members of a group are "partialled out" and form a single framework in relation to which the residual motions appear. Such unification achieves an "informational" economy since, for any given stimulus, the percept entailing the least number of changes is obtained. Objectively changing color or brightness tends to be perceived as appropriate changes in the motion of objects of unchanging color or brightness.[5] In general,

---

[5] Johansson finds that if the brightness of two motionless spots is varied with the same frequency, but 180° out of phase, the perceptual response quickly stabilizes as "a light of constant brightness moving back and forth behind the two windows." With a colored filter behind one window, a moving *white* light of constant intensity is perceived to move with no alteration, and the *window* is seen as colored. If color changes synchronize with the intensity changes, a light seems to travel back and forth behind the two windows, which are changing colors as though a bicolored curtain were being raised and lowered. That is, it seems preferable to see two such separate

wherever a response in terms of a single unchanging distal stimulus moving in depth would be more "economical" than one in terms of continually changing relationships in two dimensions, subjects will tend to report the three-dimensional alternative. Wallach has shown that this kinetic stimulus for depth can endow even motionless projections of the distal stimulus with perceived depth, so that it seems likely that we have here one of the building-blocks by which perceptual space is achieved or modified by perceptual learning.

With respect to the perception of social events, little is yet known aside from the demonstration by Heider (and incidental observations by Michotte) that psychophysical study of such higher-order variables of stimulation seems both possible and fruitful. Heider feels that we cannot talk about those motions which are perceived as actions except in terms of short, readily remembered concepts, and that the simplest action will determine the perceptual response (cf. Brunswik's "ratiomorphism"); thus, those motions most difficult to describe in simple mechanical terms appear most readily as actions.

Residual Effects of the Gestalt Revolution. After the elimination of those principles upon which agreement could not be reached, several important points remain.

1. It is frequently useful to admit subjects' statements as to what they see ("naive" phenomenal reports) as at least contributory evidence about the percept (e.g., consider the separate courses taken by perceptuo-motor adaptation and phenomenal adaptation to visual disturbance). We cannot identify percept with perceptuo-motor manifestations, despite recent trends to do so. This is not an epistemological issue, but simply one of methodology.

2. Attention should be focused on higher-order variables of stimulation. The attempt to return to the restricted (and once presumably physiologically identifiable) "atomistic" units of pre-Gestalt days seems hopeless. Whatever measurable aspects of stimulation over space and time may be extracted and brought into correspondence with abstractable dimensions of response now constitute fair game for the investigator of perception.

---

motion events rather than a single one which involves both motion and color changes. This appears to be quite general. Changes of stimulation which are objectively changes along other dimensions—brightness, color, etc.—tend to be ascribed to changes in the dimension of spatial motion.

3. Of all of the positive Gestalt formulations which sought to replace the Constancy Hypothesis, the principle of "simplicity" or "maximum homogeneity" has proved most general. It seems as quantifiable in terms of the objective stimulus as most of the others, and more so than some, such as the "law" of *Prägnanz*. Since existing physiological models fail to explicate the "laws" of sensory cortical organization to any useful extent, the necessity for predicting response from stimulus characteristics has become progressively more urgent. The precise form of the statement and the unequivocality of the minimum principle varied with the discussants but, in one form or another, it was held by all present. What to me is its most promising approximation to date—the formulation that, other things equal, that perceptual response to a simulus will be obtained which requires the least amount of information to specify (1, 13)—obtained agreement among Heider, Gibson, Kohler, Metzger, Johansson, and myself. Some differences existed as to whether or not this tendency is itself likely to be learned, or how precisely it should be formalized; at its simplest, it could be described as a "laziness of the perceptual imagination" (cf. Wheeler's "law of least action," etc.).

Several areas stand out as important for future investigation.

1. The problem of perceptual learning remains very poorly understood or formulated, and yet is an extremely critical area (cf. 10).

2. The perception of space, depth, and distance is frequently treated in the textbooks as a solved problem. Despite the fact that some restricted areas of precise and applicable knowledge exist, however, the basic problems in this area are completely *unsolved,* and we must launch a fresh attack on what is historically one of the oldest of the systematic problems of psychology.

3. The perception of physical and social events is an area of great promise not only for the field of perception but for potential application within and without psychology. However, it must be confessed that—aside from a very few pioneer studies in event perception, facial expression of emotions, the so-called "physiognomic perceptions," and some specific esthetic and artistic investigations (e.g. 4, 12, 25)—we know little more about the general area than that fruitful research seems possible.

4. The study of the results of prolonged visual disturbance is critically important in the understanding of the perceptual process.

5. The *minimum principle* (the "principle," in the traditional

sense, which met with most general agreement) requires more concrete and self-conscious research tests, to determine precise applicability and limits, and to avoid what Wallach and Johansson see as a potential unwarranted elevation to a metaphysical dictum.

REFERENCES

1. ATTNEAVE, F. Some informational aspects of visual perception. *Psychol. Rev.*, 1954, **61**, 183-198.
2. AUSTIN, P., and WALLACH, H. The effect of past experience on the reversal of ambiguous figures. *Amer. Psychologist*, 1953, **8**, 314. (Abstract)
3. BRUNSWIK, E. "Ratiomorphic" models of perception and thinking. In *Proc. 14th Internat. Congress Psychol.*, Amsterdam, North Holland, 1955. Pp. 108-110.
4. BRUNSWIK, E., and REITER, L. Eindruckscharaktere schematisierter Gesichter. *Z. Psychol.*, 1937, **142**, 67-134.
5. DUNCKER, K. Uber induzierte Bewegung. *Psychol. Forsch.*, 1929, **12**, 180-259.
6. EWERT, P. H. A study of the effect of inverted retinal stimulation upon spatially coordinated behavior. *Genet. Psychol. Monogr.*, 1930, **7**, 177-363.
7. GAGE, N. L. Accuracy of social perception and effectiveness in interpersonal relationships. *J. Pers.*, 1953, **22**, 128-141.
8. GIBSON, J. J. Adaptation with negative after-effect. *Psychol. Rev.*, 1937, **44**, 222-244.
9. GIBSON, J. J. *The perception of the visual world.* Boston: Houghton Mifflin, 1950.
10. GIBSON, J. J., and GIBSON, E. J. Perceptual learning—differentiation or enrichment? *Psychol. Rev.*, 1955, **62**, 32-41.
11. HEBB, D. O. *The organization of behavior.* New York: Wiley, 1949.
12. HEIDER, F., and SIMMEL, M. An experimental study of apparent behavior. *Amer. J. Psychol.*, 1944, **57**, 243-259.
13. HOCHBERG, J., and McALISTER, E. A quantitative approach to figural "goodness." *J. exp. Psychol.*, 1953, **46**, 361-364.
14. HOCHBERG, J. E., and BECK, J. Apparent spatial arrangement and perceived brightness. *J. exp. Psychol.*, 1954, **47**, 263-266.
15. JOHANSSON, G. *Configurations in event perception.* Uppsala: Almquist & Wiksell, 1950.
16. KOFFKA, K. *Principles of Gestalt psychology.* New York: Harcourt Brace, 1935.
17. KOHLER, I. Uber Aufbau und Wandlungen der Wahrnehmungswelt. *Oesterr. Akad. Wiss. Philos.-Histor. Kl.; Sitz.-Ber.*, 1951, **227**, 1-118.

542   Julian E. Hochberg

18. KORTE, A. Kinematoskopische Untersuchungen. *Z. Psychol.*, 1915, **79**, 193-296.
19. MACLEOD, R. B. The place of phenomenological analysis in social psychological theory. In J. H. Rohrer & M. Sherif (Eds.), *Social psychology at the crossroads*. New York: Harper, 1951.
20. METZGER, W. Tiefenerscheinungen in optischen Bewegungsfeldern. *Psychol. Forsch.*, 1935, **20**, 195-260.
21. METZGER, W. *Gesetze des Sehens*. Frankfurt: Kramer, 1953.
22. MICHOTTE, A. *La perception de la causalité*. Louvain: Inst. Sup. de Philosophie, 1946.
23. POSTMAN, L. Experimental analysis of motivational factors in perception. In *Current theory and research in motivation*. Lincoln: Univer. of Nebraska Press, 1952.
24. RYAN, T. A. Interrelations of the sensory systems in perception. *Psychol. Bull.*, 1940, **37**, 659-698.
25. SCHLOSBERG, H. The description of facial expressions in terms of two dimensions. *J. exp. Psychol.*, 1952, **44**, 229-237.
26. SNYDER, F. W., and PRONKO, N. H. *Vision with spatial inversion*. Wichita: Univer. of Wichita Press, 1952.
27. STRATTON, G. M. Vision without inversion of the retinal image. *Psychol. Rev.*, 1897, **4**, 341-360; 463-481.
28. WALLACH, H. Brightness constancy and the nature of achromatic colors. *J. exp. Psychol.*, 1948, **38**, 310-324.
29. WALLACH, H., and O'CONNELL, D. N. The kinetic depth effect. *J. exp. Psychol.*, 1953, **45**, 205-217.
30. WERTHEIMER, M. Untersuchungen zur Lehre von der Gestalt II. *Psychol. Forsch.*, 1923, **4**, 301-350.

PART FOUR

Imagery and Fantasy

SELECTION 42

●●

An Experimental Study of Imagination*

CHEVES WEST PERKY

A COMPARISON OF PERCEPTION WITH
THE IMAGE OF IMAGINATION

THE OBJECT of our first experiments was to build up a perceptual consciousness under conditions which should seem to the observer to be those of the formation of an imaginative consciousness. A visual stimulus was presented, gradually and with increasing definiteness, while the observer was asked to imagine the object whose color and form were thus given in perception. Hence by 'image of imagination' we here mean, not the elementary image-process that is co-ordinate with sensation, but such an image arises in a mind of the visual type at the command, e.g., 'Shut your eyes and think of an orange.'

The Cornell Laboratory possesses a dark room, 5 x 6.5 m., which is set longwise to the middle of a light, gray-tinted room of considerably larger size. The dividing wall contains, at its centre, a window of 1 x 1.5 m., which is filled with a sheet of ground glass, and which may be closed on the light-room side by two swinging shutters that can be made to stand at any angle. For the purposes of the present experiment, a black cardboard screen, with a central opening of 36 x 36 cm., was placed in the dark room immediately behind the ground glass. Facing the glass, in the dark room, was a projection lantern, whose arc-lamp was replaced as occasion required by various types and powers of incandescent lamp. The light room is profusely supplied with incandescent lamps; and after some preliminary trials with daylight, we decided to use this artificial light throughout the experiments.

Our first problem was to determine the color-limen for the various stimuli that we intended to employ, and we succeeded in making this determination for a certain red, orange, deep yellow, light yellow, green and blue. The observer sat, in the light room, at a

---

* From the *Amer. J. Psychol.*, 1910, **21**, 422-452. Pp. 428-433 reprinted by permission of the publisher.

distance of about 8 m. from the ground-glass window. It was the task of the experimenter to vary the luminosity of the lamp in the lantern, the screens of ground and colored glass, colored and colorless gelatine, and white tissue paper, necessary to reduce the light from the lantern, the distance of the lantern from the window and from these various media, and (on the other side of the ground-glass window) the illumination of the observation room, in such a way that the open square should appear just noticeably colored, without there being any such glow or shine upon the glass as could suggest the presence of a source of light behind it. After a great deal of empirical testing, this end was attained, with a satisfactoriness and a precision that we ourselves—discouraged by repeated failures —had at last not dared to expect. Serial determinations of the limen of hue were obtained from Professor Titchener and the writer; a number of less systematic observations were made by Professor Bentley. The apparatus, we may repeat, was clumsy and empirical; but it worked (apart from errors of manipulation, to which we later refer) with admirable sureness and delicacy. We were especially on the watch for changes of tint; but we were able to eliminate them, positively for ourselves, and at least so far that they escaped notice for all of our observers.

The limen was thus determined as a diffused flush of color over the open square. The next step was to shape this flush into the representation of some object of perception. We prepared a set of black cloth-covered screens, in which were cut the forms of certain familiar objects; the forms were thus represented by holes in the screens. The edges of the forms were softened in outline by layers of fine black gauze, which projected successively farther and farther into the holes. The screens themselves were hung upon a rigid cross-line, along which they could be silently shifted in or out of their place behind the open square. A solid screen was used, to fill the square, while the stimulus-screens were in motion. When this solid screen was removed, the colored light shone through the reducing and diffusing media and the stimulus-screen, and the faintly colored and hazily outlined form lay upon or rather within the background of neutral gray.

The stimuli were presented in a definite order: a tomato (red), a book (blue), a banana (deep yellow), an orange (orange), a leaf (green), a lemon (light yellow). The adoption of a fixed procedure was necessary, since the apparatus required the services of three experimenters, and confusion might easily arise. One experimenter had charge of the lantern-lights, colored and ground glasses, colored and colorless gelatines, and tissues. A second ran the stimulus-screens into place, gave them a very slight, slow motion during their exposure (in imitation of the oscillations of a 'subjective' image), and replaced them on signal by the solid screen. A third sat in the light room, with the observer, to give instructions, take down introspective reports, and signal to the experimenters in the dark room for the appearance or removal of a particular stimulus. The electrical signal apparatus was arranged on the floor, under the desk at which this third experimenter sat; as the wires were concealed, and the experimenter's hands were free, the connection with the dark room was, unless mistakes of manipulation occurred, not suspected by any observer.

The experimenter who was in charge of the lantern had an exact table of the changes required to raise the color-stimulus from a definitely subliminal to a moderately supraliminal value. This table was based upon the serial results obtained from the observers mentioned above. When the signal for a particular stimulus was given, the color-stimulus was exposed, step by step, as the table prescribed, and in a tempo that had been standardized by practice. That the observer, in reporting an image, really perceived the stimulus, at any rate in the great majority of cases, seems to us to be proved by the fact that in only one single instance, throughout the entire series of successful experiments, did an observer report an image before the stimulus was (1) supraliminal for the cooperating experimenter and (2) of such objective intensity that its perceptibility might be expected from the results of the preliminary control experiments. It may, of course, be objected that this proof is not demonstrative: the experimenter may have been suggestible, and the position of the limen may vary considerably from observer to observer. At the end of the enquiry we accordingly took control observations from several of our graduate observers; and we found (3) that, when the arrangement of the experiment was explained to them, so that they were in the position of the co-operating experimenter in the actual experiments, they invariably recognized the appearance of the stimulus at or before the point at which they had previously reported an image of imagination.

Care was needed that no sound should come from the dark room; that the forms should oscillate or flicker into view very gradually;

and that no shimmer of light should show between the edges of the screens as the stimuli passed in and out. The first of the sources of error was easily avoided; mistakes in manipulation occasionally occurred, however, and were, naturally, fatal to the success of the experiment with the observer in question. They will be noted in detail in what follows. We discovered no other source of error in the experiments.

A white fixation-mark was placed on the ground glass window at the centre of the open square. The work was done, as we have intimated, in the evening and by artificial light; all preparations were carefully made beforehand, so that the observer supposed that he and the (third) experimenter were the only persons present in the laboratory at the time of observation. Instruction was made as simple as possible; the observer was merely told to fixate the white point, and to hold this fixation while he 'imagined' a colored object, —"for instance, a tomato." He was then to describe his 'image,' if any image took shape. As soon as the description was begun, the attention of the observer was distracted from the window by some indifferent question ('What was that, once more?' or 'Quite clear, did you say?' or something of the kind), and at the same moment the experimenter signalled to the dark room for the turning out of the lantern-lamp or the swinging into place of the solid black screen.

No blank experiments were introduced, as we feared that their introduction would reveal the actually perceptual character of the induced 'image.'

Experiment I. Partly in order to rehearse the technique of the experiment, partly in order to see what would happen with wholly unsophisticated observers, our first observations were taken from three children; two girls of 13 and 14, and a boy of 10. The elder girl took the perceptions, as a matter of course, for images of imagination. The younger girl was excited and pleased by the 'images,' but had no suspicion of their perceptual character; she was astonished and chagrined when informed, the next day, of the arrangement and object of the experiment. The boy caught a flash of light (due to faulty manipulation in the dark room) early in the course of the experiment, and jumped to the conclusion that he was seeing 'shadows' cast somehow upon the screen.

Experiment II. Full sets of observations were obtained from a group of 27 observers, of whom 19 were sophomores in the university, and 8 were graduate students engaged in advanced work in the laboratory. Only 3 of these 8, however, were familiar with their furniture of images, and had worked experimentally on the topic of imagery.

Three of the undergraduate observers were ruled out, early in the experiment, by an error of technique, which was at once pounced upon and reported. The remaining 24, men and women alike, invariably mistook the perceptual for the imaginative consciousness. At the end of the series, after all the introspections had been recorded, the observer was asked whether he was 'quite sure that he had imagined all these things.' The question almost always aroused surprise, and at times indignation. Yet when asked, further, if he had ever had such images before, he would usually reply that 'he could not remember that he had; but then, he had never tried.'

It is unnecessary to quote the introspections in detail. The following remarks are taken each from the report of a different observer.

"It seems strange; because you see so many colors, and know that they are in your mind; and yet they look like shadows." "I can spread it [the color] over if I want to." "It is a pure memory, with a little effort I could move it to the wall." "It is just like seeing things in the dark; I had it in my mind." "It is just as imagination makes it." "I can get blue better, because I have been working with a blue square lately." "I can get it steadily so long as I keep my mind absolutely on it." "I can get the shading on it as I think of it; at first I think it flat, as if painted." "I can see the veining of the leaf and all." "The banana is up on end; I must have been thinking of it growing." "It is more distinct than I usually do [than the images I usually have]; but I have never tried much." "I got it; that was grand." "I am imagining it all; it's all imagination." "Feels as if I was making them up in my mind." "I get thinking of it, and it turns up."

Several times an observer remarked, towards the end of the series, that his images were something like after-images, and that he felt he could move them by moving his eyes; here, no doubt, the slight oscillation and fluctuation of the stimulus were in play. One graduate observer apologized for her 'poor imagination,' and said she could get forms but not colors; as a matter of fact, she failed to see the color of the stimulus even when it was increased very considerably beyond the ordinary supraliminal point; the forms she regarded as imaginative. Another graduate observer, who had had long experience in the laboratory and had worked to some extent, with imagery, showed, both by the time of appearance of the image and by its characteristics (shape, position, size), that he was incorporating the perception in it, while he nevertheless supplied a context of pure imagery: the tomato was seen painted on a can, the book was a particular book whose title could be read, the lemon was lying on a table, the leaf was a pressed leaf with red markings on it. All the observers noted that the banana was on end, and not as they had been supposing they thought of it; yet the circumstance aroused no suspicion. Some saw an elm leaf when they had been trying for a maple leaf. The observers not infrequently volunteered the statement that they could continue to hold the image after closing the eyes.

There is, then, no ambiguity about the results. The experiment is, however, open to the objection that the observations were made, for the most part, by unpractised observers.

Experiment III. To meet this objection, we repeated the experiment, after a year's interval, with five graduate students: K, S, T (men), and C and V (women). All had had practice, and T and V unusually extended practice, in the observation of images.

S was for some time confused: at first he thought the figures imaginary; then he speculated whether they might not be after-images of some sort, or akin to after-images. Finally, after the appearance of the fourth form, he remarked: "It seems like a perception, though the attention is more active than in perception; yet I feel sure that it is there, and that I did not make it; it is more permanent and distinct than an image." The permanence and distinctness were, unluckily, due to faulty technique; the signal to put out the light failed to carry its message, and the stimulus was left showing at rest.

T thought that the 'image' was rather more like an after-image than the images he was accustomed to get in daylight; but he was emphatic that it was not a perception. K, too, insisted that the figures were imaginative.

C took the perception for an image of imagination until a mistake of technique (with the fourth form) revealed its real nature. V added many imaginary details, such as 'printing' on the book, but was sure that the figures were "all imagination, of course"; "quite like those I get in the daytime—perhaps more normal"; "more strain than in a perception" (*cf.* *S*'s active attention); "could feel it formed in my mind—came right out of me"; "if I hadn't known I was imagining, should have thought it real."

The results thus confirm those of the previous experiments. And the net outcome of the work is, we think, positive and important enough to justify the time and labor spent upon its preliminaries. We find, in brief, that a visual perception of distinctly supraliminal value may, and under our conditions does, pass—even with specially trained observers—for an image of imagination. We are at a disadvantage in not being able to express our stimuli in quantitative terms. This much may, however, be said: at the conclusion of the experiments, a demonstration of the colored forms was made to a number of students in the psychological department, and to some psychologically competent visitors. Every one of these observers showed great surprise; most of them 'would, of course, take our word' for the facts, but could hardly credit them; a few remained entirely incredulous—'we asked them to believe too much.' These attitudes are sufficient warrant for the normally supraliminal character of the stimuli employed.

....

Cultural Factors in the Structuralization of Perception*

A. Irving Hallowell

BELIEF AND PERCEPTION

I SHALL ATTEMPT TO DEMONSTRATE, by reference to the Northern Ojibwa how entities that have *no* tangible or material existence may become perceptual objects in the actual experience of individuals. That is to say, the reality of what to outsiders are only symbolically mediated and concretely elaborated images may receive perceptual support through the experiences of individuals for whom such entities are reified in an established system of traditional beliefs. Under these conditions it is even predictable, I think, that some persons will not only report perceptual experiences involving such entities, but will *act* as if they belonged in the category of tangible or material objects.

From a descriptive point of view the belief system of the Northern Ojibwa includes several different classes of non-human "spiritual" entities, i.e., orders of sentient beings that are not classed as *Anicinabek* (men-Indians). It will be unnecessary to describe these in detail here since the major point I wish to make is that the Ojibwa themselves distinguish between these orders of being with respect to the manner in which they become manifest to *Anicinabek*. Their most characteristic manifestation is in dreams and the generic term *pawaganak* may be translated as "dream visitors." Furthermore, *pawaganak* become closely associated with an individual in so far as they function as his guardian spirits. He obtains these guardian spirits in the dreams of his puberty fast and he does not expect these particular *pawaganak* to manifest themselves to him in any other way. In short, the Ojibwa does not *expect* to perceive

---

* From Rohrer, J. H., and Sherif, M. (Eds.) *Social psychology at the crossroads.* New York: Harper, 1951. Pp. 178-190 reprinted by permission of the author and the publisher.

them under the same circumstances as the objects and events of daily life. By cultural definition *pawaganak* are "perceivable" only in the "inner world" of dreams. But if a man is a conjurer, he may call some of his guardian spirits to his conjuring tent where they become audible to other persons. Consequently, it is particularly interesting to note that there is one reified being, the High God, who never becomes the guardian spirit of an individual, nor appears as a "dream visitor," nor becomes an object of perception even in the conjuring tent. The existence of this being is a matter of faith. By cultural definition the High God is not a perceptible object in any context. If any Indian reported that he had seen or heard *kadabendjiget,* his veracity would be challenged, or he might be thought "crazy."

Now in addition to these types of spiritual beings, there is another category of special interest. The Ojibwa believe in the existence of certain animals of exceptionally large size, despite the fact that animals of this type are seldom seen. Among others, there are Big Turtles, Big Snakes, Big Frogs, and Thunder Birds. Although these large animals are classed by the Ojibwa with the other fauna of their habitat, in only one or two cases are there actual species of animals of the same family that differ markedly in size. One example would be the Turtles. In this case, there exists one species of large turtle—along with smaller ones that are called the "younger brothers" of *mikinak.* Considered as a class, therefore, the "big" animals are "mythical" animals from our point of view. What is of special interest, even if confusing to us, is that there is a "mythical" *mikinak,* too. I call attention to this because it is likewise paradoxical that the faunal counterpart of this "mythical" turtle is very rare and seldom *seen* whereas the reified *mikinak* has been *heard* by everyone. For along with other *pawaganak* he speaks, and even sings, in the conjuring tent.[1] In this conjuring rite a small structure is built which conceals the conjurer. He has the power to invoke the *pawaganak* who happens to be among his guardian spirits. They manifest themselves audibly to the Indians who sit on the ground, outside the tent. These *pawaganak* talk and sing like human beings and the dogma is that it is not the conjurer's voice that you hear. From the standpoint of perceptual experience, therefore, the con-

---

[1] For further information see Hallowell, A. I. *The Role of Conjuring in Saulteaux Society, Publications, Phila. Anthropological Society,* Vol. 2. University of Pennsylvania Press, 1942.

juring rite is a device whereby spiritual entities become reified through sound as the sensory medium. Since *mikinak* always has something to say in a conjuring performance, he becomes a familiar figure to everyone. On the other hand, his actual faunal counterpart is scarcely ever seen.

As I have already pointed out, Thunder Birds, Great Snakes, and Great Frogs have no faunal counterparts. But since they are classified with the fauna of the region in the conceptual scheme of the Ojibwa, it follows, logically enough, that these animals *may* be heard, seen, or some other evidence of their "actual" existence be perceived by any one, even though rarely. Rarity of observation is irrelevant to the conviction that animals of this category actually exist.

Among the large animals, Thunder Birds are familiar to everyone because thunder is their cry. They are put in the avian category, moreover, for a very good reason. Their cries are only heard from late spring until early fall, so it is said that they belong in the same class with the Summer Birds who migrate north at this time and leave the country before winter sets in. As a matter of fact, I once compared the meteorological facts on record regarding the occurrence of thunder with the facts on bird migration to this region and there is an almost perfect correlation.[2] So the reification of Thunder Birds like the Great Turtle of the conjuring tent is actually supported by auditory experience, but in a different context. On the other hand, although Thunder Birds may appear to an individual in dreams, they are *rarely* seen. Some years ago there was a man who claimed to have seen *pinesi* (a Thunder Bird) "with his own eyes" when he was about twelve years old. During a severe thunderstorm, he ran out of his tent and there on the rocks lay a strange bird. He ran back to get his parents but when they arrived, the bird had disappeared. He was sure it was *pinesi* but his elders were skeptical because it is almost unheard of to *see* a Thunder Bird. Sometime later the veracity of the boy's experience was clinched when a man who had dreamed of *pinesi* verified the boy's description.

In the case of Big Snakes, Big Frogs, and certain other animals of the same category who are believed to be terrestrial in habitat, it is thought that there are relatively few of them about. And since

---

[2] Cf. Hallowell, A. I. Some Empirical Aspects of Northern Saulteaux Religion. *Amer. Anth.*, 1934, **36**, 389-404.

they are never sought out, like other animals, it is not expected that they will be frequently observed. But there is always the possibility that these animals, or their tracks, may be seen in the most literal sense.

Thus Maman, the best hunter of the Little Grand Rapids Band, a man of high intelligence, and vivid imagination as judged both from common sense observation and his Rorschach record,[3] told me he saw one of the Great Snakes when he was hunting moose up a small creek that runs into Family Lake. He was so surprised, he said, that he did not shoot. The creature was moving into the water. He saw the head, which looked something like that of a deer, but without horns. The snake was white around the chin. I asked him about the diameter of the body. "It was as big around as that" he said, pointing to a stove pipe. He said he saw as much of the snake as the diagonal distance across the cabin in which we were sitting at the time, which was about 15-16 feet. The Great Snake moved in a straight path, not this way and that, as the smaller snakes do. I also have another eye-witness account of a Great Snake seen by my informant Chief Berens and his two sons when they were on a hunting trip. Both these accounts document the fact that culturally reified images may, under given conditions, become directive factors in the perceptions of the individual. But these cultural constituents of perception may have much deeper implications than these relatively simple instances demonstrate. For in any given situation they may also evoke deep-seated attitudes and emotions that precipitate action. Cognitive and motivational factors become inextricably linked. Great Frogs, for instance, are greatly feared, so that no one wishes to meet one. On one occasion when four Indians were crossing Lake Winnipeg in a canoe and landed on an island where they expected to spend the night, one of them discovered what he interpreted as tracks of a Great Frog. His companions examined the tracks and agreed. All of these men became stricken with fear so although night was approaching and they had a considerable distance to paddle, nevertheless, they felt compelled to leave the island at once.

What I should like to stress in this example is the fact that all of these men were excellent hunters and were accustomed to differentiate the tracks of the various animals that inhabit this region. Yet

---

[3] He had an extraordinary number of M's; not only more than any other subject, but excellent in quality.

all of them agreed that the marks they saw indicated traces of a Great Frog. Hence the significant thing to be noted is the depth of the affect associated with the conceptualization of Great Frogs. Once this was touched off, it was impossible for any of them to examine the tracks on the beach in the *unemotional* way the tracks of the ordinary fur-bearing animal or a moose or deer would be inspected. And then fear, in turn, made it inevitable that they should leave the island with the greatest haste, since the whole perceptual situation became meaningfully structured in terms of flight. The psychological field in which these Indians were behaving, although culturally constituted, was much more complex than the accounts I have cited in the case of the Great Snakes. Furthermore, the conduct of these men would be completely *unintelligible,* if viewed or analyzed in terms of the "objective" situation alone. Their belief in and attitude toward Great Frogs alone give it meaning and explain their overt conduct.[4] It is a concrete exemplification of the general assertion of MacLeod that: "Purely fictitious objects, events and relationships can be just as truly determinants of our behavior as are those which are anchored in physical reality."[5]

As a final example, I wish to discuss another case in which I happen to have a more detailed personal account of the experience of an Indian who "met" and took flight from a cannibal giant—a *Windigo*. A belief in such monsters is an integral part of Northern Ojibwa culture. There are two categories of *Windigowak*. The first comprises actual persons who have turned into cannibals. In this discussion, I am not concerned with *Windigowak* of this class. The second category consists of mythical cannibal giants who may be found roaming the country, especially in the spring, avid for human flesh. They are conceptualized as horrible in appearance, they have hearts of ice and every time they call out they get taller so that to hear the

---

[4] Donald W. MacKinnon in his chapter on Motivation, Boring, E. G., Langfeld, H. S., and Weld, H. D. *Introduction to Psyc.* New York: 1939, p. 159, stresses the need for distinguishing the physical situation, i.e., the environment "considered as having independent real existence" from the psychological field, viz., "the situation as it exists psychologically for the individual." "The psychological field," he goes on to say, "is not to be equated merely to what is consciously perceived or known but rather to everything that at the moment determines the behavior of an individual." In the case described there was no "fearful object" in the situation, objectively viewed; the source of the fear was in the *psychological field.*

[5] MacLeod, Robert B. The Phenomenological Approach to Social Psychology. *Psychol. Rev.,* 1947, **54**, 205.

shouts of a *windigo* is enough to make one shudder with fear. Only a few such shouts and he is taller than the towering spruce which are so characteristic a feature of the landscape.

Both categories of *windigowak* are the focus of a considerable number of anecdotes. For just as it was considered necessary to kill actual persons who had turned into cannibals, there are parallel anecdotes which relate the heroic battles between human beings and monster mythical cannibals. Besides anecdotes of this sort there are those told in the first person by individuals who have heard the blood-curdling shouts of a *windigo* in the bush, or by those who have seen the tracks of such a creature. The following anecdote of this class is of particular interest with reference to the total structuralization and functioning of perception since Adam Big Mouth became convinced that a *windigo* was close by, although he never saw him, and only toward the end of the anecdote is there any reference to a shout. The circumstances under which an objectively innocuous situation became perceived as an extremely dangerous one can best be conveyed in Adam's own words:

Once in the spring of the year, I was hunting muskrats. The lake was still frozen, only the river was open, but there was lots of ice along the shore. When it began to get dark I put ashore and made a fire close to the water edge to cook my supper. While I was sitting there I *heard* someone passing across the river. I could *hear* the branches cracking. I went to my canoe and jumped in. I paddled as hard as I could to get away from the *noise*. Where the river got a little wider I came to a point that has lots of poplars growing on it. I was paddling quite a distance from the shore when I came opposite to this point. Just then *I heard a sound* as if something was passing through the air. A big stick had been thrown out at me but it did not strike me. I kept on going and paddled towards the other side again. But he went back and headed me off in that direction. This was in the spring of the year when the nights are not so long. He kept after me all night. I was scared to go ashore. Towards morning I reached a place where there is a high rock. I camped there and when it was light I went to set a bear trap. Later that day I came back to the river again. I started out again in my canoe. Late in the evening, after the sun had set, there was a place where I had to portage my canoe over to a lake. I left my canoe and went to see whether the lake was open. There were some open places so I went back to get my canoe. Then I *heard* him again. I carried my canoe over to the lake—it was a big one—and paddled off as fast as I could. When I got to the other end of the lake it was almost daylight. I did not *hear* him while I was traveling. I went ashore and made a fire. After this I *heard* something again. I was scared. "How am I going to get away from him," I thought. I decided to make for the other side of an island in the lake. I was sitting by my canoe and I *heard* him coming closer. I was mad now. He had chased me long enough. I said to myself, "The number of my days has been given me already!" So I picked up my axe and my gun and went in the direction of the *sounds I had heard*. As soon as I got closer to him he made a break for it. I could *hear* him crashing through the trees. Between the shore and the island there was a place where the water was not frozen. He was headed in this direction. I kept after him. I could *hear* him on the weak ice. Then he fell in and I *heard* a terrific yell. I turned back then and I can't say whether he managed to get out or not. I killed some ducks and went back to my canoe. I was getting pretty weak by this time so I made for a camp I thought was close by. But the people had left. I found out later that they had *heard* him and were so scared that they moved away.

In the foregoing anecdote there are thirteen references to *hearing* the *windigo*. Auditory stimuli alone appear to have been the chief *physical* source of the subject's interpretation of the initial presence of a *windigo* and all his *subsequent* overt behavior. In principle, therefore, there is some analogy to a linguistic situation although, in speech sounds, there is a very high order of patterning. But in principle a succession of sounds is heard which, although they are physical stimuli, become significant to the perceiver because they also convey a conventional *meaning*. This meaning is only understood because the perceiver has undergone a learning process which makes the meaning intelligible. And intelligibility in linguistically conveyed meanings always involves concepts. Analogously, the sounds heard by Adam "meant" *windigo* to him. But this was only possible because cannibal monsters were among the traditionally reified concepts and imagery of his culture. Furthermore, just as a word or a sentence may induce an affective response, or immediately define a situation as dangerous and thus call forth appropriate conduct, such was the case here. Once the situation became perceptually structuralized in this way, subsequent sounds likewise became meaningful in terms of the same pattern. I should also like to stress the fact that, at the time, a premise for action became established in terms of which Adam's behavior becomes thoroughly intelligible. It is important to recognize this because we see exemplified in this case, too, the integral relation between perception and action that is characteristic of all organisms. In actual life situations, perceptual responses never occur in a behavioral vacuum. Considered in cross-cultural perspective I think we may say that, in addition to enabling man to adapt himself to a world of physical objects and events, like other animals, perception in our species enables human beings to adjust to a realm of culturally constituted objects as psychologically "real" as other orders of phenomena. Consequently, motivation and appropriate conduct must be judged with reference to a culturally constituted order of reality. Adam's behavior, therefore, was highly appropriate in his own frame of reference.

But there is another side to this coin which may, at first, seem paradoxical. Perception in man may be said to have acquired an overlaid *social* function. For is it not true, that in the light of the foregoing material, perception serves such a function to the extent that it is one of the chief psychological means whereby belief in reified images and concepts as integral parts of a cultural order of reality, are *substantiated* in the experience of individuals? It is through the activity of the same sensory modalities that always have been considered sufficiently reliable in bringing us into contact with the "reality" of the outer world that the "reality" of objects that have their roots in man's inner world are reinforced.

PERSONALITY FACTORS AND PERCEPTION

Part of the psychological interest of Adam Big Mouth's experience with a *windigo* lies in the fact that he himself was responsible for the perceptual structuralization of *this particular situation*. Another Indian in the same objective situation and belonging to the same cultural group may, or may not, have perceived a *windigo*. Consequently, it is inaccurate and misleading, I believe, to speak of cultural *determinism* in such a case. It is for this reason that I have deliberately referred to culturally constituted factors in perception, when speaking of individuals. This leads to a more general question. While given a belief in giant cannibals, it may be predicted that *some* Ojibwa Indians will report perceptual experiences which offer tangible evidence for the actual existence of *windigowak,* are there not selective factors that determine which particular individuals have these experiences under given conditions? I am sure that everyone agrees that there are such factors even though it may be difficult to identify them and to demonstrate their relevance in a given instance. Let us call them idiosyncratic or personal determinants.

Is there any evidence for the operation of such determinants in the case of Adam Big Mouth? I think that there is some evidence, although I do not have sufficient details to push it too far. (1) Adam's father was a very powerful medicine man. (2) He was also one of those who was reported to have *killed* mythical cannibals. (3) Adam was the man who told me more anecdotes about cannibals than anyone else. (4) When he was a small boy Adam had also seen a *windigo* a short distance from where his family was camping. He reported this to his father. (5) Adam's Rorschach record is characterized by the fact that out of a total of thirteen responses he gave a whole answer to each card. This was always his first answer and he responded with considerable rapidity. Furthermore, in this immediate interpretation of each successive blot as a whole Adam was almost unique in my series. And when I add that his wholes were not particularly good ones, I believe that the relevance of his Rorschach performance to his responses in the situation narrated is even more fully evident. His rapid but not too accurate structuralization of an ambiguous situation gave free play to the influence of traditional belief as well as personal determinants.

Although Adam was a conjurer and medicine man too, he did not enjoy the reputation of his father. One might guess that all this indicates that Adam wished to be like his father and to have his power but he had never succeeded in his inner striving for identification. I also suspect that the anecdote I have narrated might be psychologically interpreted to mean that although Adam unconsciously wished to be able to face a *windigo* and kill it as his father had done, he was not quite up to it. He did not have the courage of his father. Nevertheless, he managed to escape from the *windigo* alive. At first he was terrified; ultimately he regained his courage for he says: "I was mad now. He had chased me long enough." So at that point he starts off in the direction of the *windigo* and the *windigo* becomes pursued and falls through the ice! In the end, Adam became a kind of hero to himself, which satisfied an inner need. From the personal angle, therefore, it matters little whether his account is strictly accurate. It is quite possible that he may have elaborated it as time went on. But taken at its face value, his experience not only illustrates cultural factors in the structuralization of perception but, at the same time, personal needs as directive factors in perception.

Another case that illustrates the integral functioning of cultural and idiosyncratic variables has quite a different setting than the one just described. It will serve to demonstrate the importance of directive factors in perception in the area of interpersonal relations among a nonliterate people. On the face of it the facts look very simple. An old man named Kiwetin (North Wind) told me that a married woman who was his neighbor was using sorcery against him. He had been sick and Catherine, he said, was back of it.

From a cultural point of view, therefore, we have a belief in sorcery to consider and the general attitudes it engenders among a people who are convinced of its reality. On the personal side we have to ask: Why did Kiwetin think that Catherine was responsible? Was it simply because she had the reputation of being a witch or were there selective factors of a more idiosyncratic nature rooted in the psychodynamics of his personality? Since I do not have all the necessary facts in this case, including any personal impressions of Catherine, whom I never met, my main purpose in discussing it at all is to use it as a sort of paradigm. I want to call attention to some of the possibilities that the investigation of the role of perception in interpersonal relations affords in a primitive society.

A belief in sorcery, of course, is based on the assumption that human individuals may possess, and exercise at will, malevolent powers against other individuals. Such a belief is found in many human societies. Among the Ojibwa there are certain provincial features that must also be understood. (1) Typically, men rather than women are thought to possess powers of sorcery. If women have magic power they use it principally to protect themselves and their children. (2) Power that can be used malevolently comes from the same sources of power that can be used benevolently, such as curing people who are ill. These sources are the *pawaganak*, already referred to. They are a man's guardian spirits. They confer certain powers upon him and stand ready to do his bidding. (3) Since such powers are acquired in a lonely vigil at puberty, no one can tell how much power another individual has, or whether it enables him to do evil or not. (4) Sorcery, by cultural definition is always practiced covertly. No one ever admits he possesses evil power, or that he has acted malevolently, except under circumstances I need not go into here. The only really tangible evidence of the practice of sorcery is that in some cases of illness, believed to be due to malevolent action of this kind, a special kind of doctor removes an object from the body of the patient—a piece of hair, a quill, a sharp piece of bone.

Among the Ojibwa there are certain obvious psychological consequences of a belief in sorcery. Men in particular are wary of one another; they cannot fully trust each other. For sorcery is always a potential threat to the central value of these people—*pimadaziwin*— Life, in the sense of longevity and freedom from illness and misfortune. Interpersonal relations are affectively toned by suspicions that may arise from the manner, tone, facial expression, gestures, attitudes, and conduct of persons with whom an individual is associated in daily life. There is always a latent anxiety that can be easily aroused because sorcery is believed to exist and may threaten *pimadaziwin*. If I fall ill my anxiety increases, because someone may have bewitched me. In consequence I am highly motivated to reflect upon the whole matter, my purpose being to discover *who* it might be. To arrive at a satisfactory answer I have to have some evidence on the basis of which I can make a judgment. So I appeal to the "evidence of my senses." Where else, indeed, could I turn?

The chief point I want to emphasize is the important psychological fact that the Ojibwa have to pick out sorcerers for themselves. With reference to our central topic we may ask: What kind of perceptual evidence becomes important in the identification of a particular sorcerer? And what kind of directive factors influence perception? The situation would be quite different, of course, in a society where there was a cultural definition of the traits of sorcerers or even where ordeals of a public nature were customary so that an accused individual could be put to some test. Where ordeals exist, everyone can see for himself whether an accused sorcerer passes the test or fails. But among the Ojibwa sorcery itself is not only covert. If I am sick I may privately make up my mind who is responsible and take whatever measures I see fit. If I have any power myself, I may sorcerize my enemy covertly in turn. This is the essence of the situation. So it is easy to see how in this sort of socio-psychological field it is inevitable that projective mechanisms will operate with the utmost freedom. There are culturally constituted barriers to any kind of reality testing.

Returning now to the particular case I mentioned, there are several facts to be noted which seem to me to have special importance. In the first place, Catherine, although I never saw her, was, from all accounts, an unusual woman. She was even notorious. She was large in size, terrifically dynamic for an Indian woman, and she had had many husbands. Besides this, many Indians were convinced that she had a knowledge of sorcery which, in itself, made her unusual.

Kiwetin at the time of which I speak was a widower, living by himself. I had gone to see him because he had once been active in the *Midewiwin* whose major function was curative. He was a medicine man reputed to have considerable power. How did Kiwetin arrive at the conclusion that *Catherine* was using sorcery against him? In the first place he had been sick. Since he did not respond at once to the medicine used, his suspicions became aroused. Someone must be using malevolent power against him. But why Catherine? What struck me so forcibly when Kiwetin told me his story was the kind of evidence he regarded as decisive. It was the woman's *outward display of amiability and kindness toward him* that made him think she had malevolent intentions. She smiled pleasantly at him. But he knew this was put on. "It was only on her face, not in her mind," he said. She also had invited him into her house to have something to eat. But he always refused. She might put something in his food. The selection of outward amiability as evidence of covert malevolence in this instance is not unique. I have heard the same thing in one or two other cases. On one occasion when I heard a rumor that one old man was a very wicked sorcerer, I naïvely said, "But he is such a nice old man." "That's just it," my informant said, "That's why you have to watch him." I do not wish to create the impression that outward amiability among the Ojibwa is *institutionalized* as indicative of malevolent intentions. This is far from being the case. What is interesting is the fact that what might be supposed to be a universal expression of positive attitudes in interpersonal relations may be perceived as having a completely negative meaning. How far it would be possible to institutionalize a negative appraisal of *all* expressions of kindness and amiability in any culture is a nice question. In the case of Catherine, I may add, I think there is good reason to believe that, in reality, there was no actual malevolence involved.

This leads us to a consideration of directive factors of a purely idiosyncratic nature that may have been responsible for Kiwetin's "choice" of a witch. What finally clinched the whole matter for Kiwetin was the fact that, in a dream, one of his *pawagan* informed him that Catherine was responsible for his illness. This suggests that unconscious as well as conscious forces were operating in the same direction. This fact is of importance because, as I pointed out in the beginning, men, rather than women, are the chief manipulators of malevolent power. So why choose a woman? My hypothesis would be that Kiwetin's choice of Catherine was involved with his basic psychosexual adjustment. His interpretation of the whole situation was a projection on his part which served as an effective personal defense against Catherine, whom he could not help seeing and being aware of constantly since she was his neighbor. At the conscious level, therefore, he made use of a belief well-entrenched in his culture, backed up, of course, by the "evidence of his senses," to build up a rationalization that enabled him to avoid her and condemn her. Unconsciously, I have no doubt, he was fearful of women and Catherine in particular, while at the same time he was attracted to her.

In this case, therefore, we find perception linked to complex personal needs which influence it selectively. At the same time we see another instance in which perception served a social function in so far as it helped to corroborate the belief that witches, even if unusual, existed. Faced with the same personal problem, in some other culture, Kiwetin would have had to make use of some other means of rationalization. Defense mechanisms and perception are universal processes in human adjustment. Culturally available means are local and variable. But in the whole adjustment process the central role which perception plays is evident. Perception is made the basis of judgment, decision, action. Abstractly stated, this is an old axiom in psychology. A case such as the foregoing suggests that the kind of judgments made, the nature of the decisions arrived at, and the consequences in terms of motivation and conduct are related to both cultural and idiosyncratic variables. Consequently, the dynamics of perception are not entirely clear if we do not approach the whole problem in a fashion that enables us to take account of non-sensory as well as sensory determinants.

An inclusive approach such as is now being more systematically pursued than formerly, and which stresses functional factors, is directly relevant to a deeper understanding of the role of cultural factors in the structuralization of perception and even necessary for the explanation of concrete behavior in cross-cultural perspective.

....

The Projective Expression of Needs. II. The Effect of Different Intensities of the Hunger Drive on Thematic Apperception[*][1]

JOHN W. ATKINSON AND DAVID C. MCCLELLAND

THE FIRST EXPERIMENT in this series (7) attempted to measure the effects of different intensities of the hunger drive on perception for which the objective determinants had been reduced to a minimum. Its purpose was to seek any principles which might govern the relationship between need intensity and its expression in perception. The results provided clues as to how perceptual material should be interpreted to diagnose the strength of a drive such as hunger.

But most so-called projective methods do not deal with perceptual material unless, like the Rorschach, they are concerned more with the formal than the contentual aspects of phantasy. Therefore, the next step is to see whether the findings with perceptual material apply to a projective method more nearly like those ordinarily employed—the Thematic Apperception Test, for example. Several previous attempts have been made to measure the effect on imaginative productions of specific experimentally induced conditions (2, 5, 11), but none has dealt with the problem very extensively or attempted to control the amount of the variable, the effect of which is to be measured.

In the present experiment the intensity of the hunger drive was

* From the *J. exp. Psychol.*, 1948, **38**, 643-658. Reprinted by permission of the authors and the publisher.

[1] This project was made possible by a grant from the Office of Naval Research. The authors are grateful for this aid and particularly for the cooperation of Captain C. W. Schilling, formerly director of the Medical Research Laboratory, U. S. Naval Submarine Base, New London, Conn., and his staff.

controlled as in the previous experiment by depriving the subjects of food for one hour, four hours, and 16 hours. They then wrote out short stories about pictures drawn mostly from Murray's Thematic Apperception Test (referred to hereafter as the TAT). This design permitted the direct comparison of contentual aspects of the stories told under the influence of three degrees of intensity of the hunger drive.

PROCEDURE

The Ss were drawn from Naval personnel attending the submarine training school at the U. S. Navy Submarine Base at New London, Conn., obtained as previously described (7). Food deprivation was also controlled as before. In fact, some of the Ss used in the previous experiment participated in this experiment after concluding the tests of perception. In all there were 44, 22, and 37 Ss in the one, four, and 16 hour deprivation groups respectively who took the entire test and whose records were analyzed. 30 more Ss had to be discarded because they did not meet the experimental hunger conditions or because their stories were too incomplete to work with. Of the 103 Ss whose stories were analyzed, 22 had to be discarded for most of the results reported in the paper because they did not see two of the pictures.

The pictures used are described in Table I with the code letter used to identify them. They were chosen to suggest all types of situations relating

TABLE I. DESCRIPTION OF PICTURES, GIVING CODE LETTER AND SOURCE

A. Four 'bums' resting (TAT 9 BM in 1943 edition)
B. 'Beachcomber' (TAT earlier edition, cf. 10, p. 542)
C. 'Father' talking to 'son' (TAT 7 BM)
D. Woman looking into room (TAT 5)
E. Restaurant balcony scene—man and woman looking out window, table in foreground (Meier-Seashore Art Judgment Test picture No. 84)
F. Older man in black hat, younger blond man, piece of raw meat with knife beside it (especially designed for this experiment—three picture elements in color not joined together in a single scene)
G. Man standing under lamp (TAT 20)
I. Men in tavern or coffee shop talking (especially designed for this experiment)

to hunger—satiation (A), deprivation (B), invitation to eat (D), place of eating (E), food (F) etc. Slides were made of all these pictures (except F) and were visibly projected under conditions described elsewhere (7). F was projected by reflection. There were two orders of presentation as follows: pictures A B C D E F G I and D A F B E G I (picture C was dropped as it gave no food responses). As stated above, 22 subjects did not see pictures G and I, but their results are included in the analysis of characteristics of various pictures. Most of the Ss saw the pictures in the second order but 13 in the one hour group and 15 in the 16 hour group saw them in the first order.

The procedure is best described from the instructions given the subjects after they had entered the room in groups of 7-15 and taken seats facing the screen.

"Please fill out the information blank on the top of your answer sheet [which asked simply for name, rank, dates of birth and induction].

"This is a test of your creative imagination. Six pictures will be projected on the screen. You will have twenty seconds to look at the picture and then five minutes to write what you think about it. Notice that on each of the six pages on your answer sheet corresponding to the six pictures to be shown, the same four questions are asked. Try to spend about one minute answering each question. I'll help you keep track of the time so that you can answer all four questions for each picture. I'll tell you when to go on to the next question. You'll have time to go back and finish up before the next picture is shown.

"Obviously there are no right or wrong answers, so you may feel free to make up any kind of a story about the picture that you choose. The more vivid and dramatic the better. I would suggest writing as fast but as legibly as you can, in order to make your story about the picture as vivid and detailed and imaginative as you can. Remember this is a test of creative imagination. Do not merely describe the picture. Anyone can do that. Make up a story about it. The four questions will guide your thinking so that you may cover all the ground in the time required.

"You may start writing as soon as you like after the picture is projected. The lights will be turned on after twenty seconds. Don't wait more than 15 seconds to start or you won't have time to do a complete job. The four questions are:

1. What is happening? Who are the persons?
2. What has led up to this situation? That is, what has happened in the past?
3. What is being thought? What is wanted? By whom?
4. What will happen? What will be done?

"These questions cover the whole plot of the story pretty well. If you need more room for any question use the back of the paper. Make the stories as interesting as you can. Work as fast as you can—feel free to make up any kind of story at all. Be as imaginative as you are able to be. Does every one understand the directions? No questions will be answered after we once start. Also please do not say anything when the pictures are shown."

Special instructions were necessary to introduce picture F which was made up of three disconnected parts. The following comment was therefore made just before it was shown in the third or sixth position.

"This picture is a little different. There will be a number of disconnected pictures, persons or objects that you can fit into a story. On the basis of what you see in this next picture, work out a story including what you see and anything else you might want to bring into it. Be imaginative."

In choosing the materials and in following the procedure just outlined every attempt was made to follow previous practices so far as possible in order to eliminate results peculiar to a different technique. For instance, the four questions spaced apart on the record sheets are those ordinarily raised at the beginning of a TAT session (10, p. 532). They were repeated here to remind the *S*s of the various aspects of a story which were wanted and to facilitate the scoring of the records.

Scoring the records proved to be the major difficulty in obtaining results, as seems always to be the case with the experimental use of projective methods. There are any number of solutions to the difficulty which have been proposed (4, 9, 12), but there is no standard method of scoring which could be adopted. This is particularly unfortunate because the results obtained by one method of scoring cannot be compared with those from any other method. Since there was no adequate methodological basis for choosing a system, one was finally worked out for use here which was based in part on Murray's need analysis, in part on the customary analysis of a behavior sequence (need, instrumental act, goal response), and in part on results obtained in the first experiment in the series.

More than 50 stories were read and considered before any category of analysis was formulated. The effort was to construct categories which could be identified by the *S*'s actual words with a minimum of inference on the part of the judge. The categories finally used follow with a brief description of each:

F I   *Food related imagery.* Any reference to anything having to do with food or eating. This is the criterion for further analysis. It indicates that food is at least incidental to the story being told. All stories not checked in this category were not analyzed any further.

F th *Food thema*. Food getting or food enjoying activity is the central plot of the story. Someone goes to the store to buy meat for supper. A family is getting ready to eat, etc.

D th *Food deprivation thema*. Deprivation of food is the central plot of the story. The deprivation story dwells on the threatening situation, the shortage (the black market), the down and out person on the verge of starvation etc.[2] Instrumental acts are aimed at removing the deprivation. In food stories there may be difficulties in getting food but unless they constitute the primary theme or emphasis of the story, they were not scored D th (but were scored D).

O th *Other themas*. All themas not classified as F or D, i.e. food was not central to their plot.

N *Need food*. Someone in the story wants food (as actually stated, not inferred). This category includes most food themas and also all cases where someone wants food but the central thema of the story is about something else. The need must be stated and is not inferred from instrumental food-getting activity.

D *Food deprivation*. Any shortage, scarcity, blocking by external agent etc. leading to food deprivation, temporary or permanent. This includes all Deprivation Thema stories and also all other cases of food deprivation whether food is central to the plot or not.

I, f or d, +, —, or o. *Instrumental activity* aimed at getting food (I f) or at removing deprivation (I d) which is successful (+), unsuccessful (—) or of unknown outcome (o). Someone in the story must do something either to get food (I f) or to overcome the deprivation such as the black market (I d).

G *Goal activity* (terminal behavior). Someone is eating, will eat immediately after the action or has just finished eating. Mealtime words such as lunch and dinner were scored G.

H, i, s or p. *Hostility*, either instrumental (i), subjective (s), or pressive (p). In the first instance, aggression (stealing, violent action) is used as the instrumental activity to get food or overcome the deprivation. In the second, one or more characters in the stories feels angry or aggressive, but doesn't do anything about it. In the third, there is a hostile or aggressive press (either actual or imagined), usually the source of the deprivation. If someone stole food (H i) and was met with defensive hostility, this was not

---

[2] There were scoring difficulties with picture B because many Ss wrote severe deprivation stories for it (shipwreck, airplane crash etc.) but it was hard to decide whether food deprivation was primary. A general rule of thumb was finally established that it would be scored D th if only *one* other need beside food was mentioned (e.g., water or rest). If two or more other needs were mentioned it was scored D but not D th.

scored H p. This category contains only easily identifiable hostility and aggression.

A, s or g.   *Anxiety* over survival (s) (fear of death or starving) or over guilt (g) as when food has been stolen, black market purchases made, etc.

P   *Phantasy.* Someone wishing for or dreaming about getting food. This does not include the ordinary thoughts or intents that precede action.

WF   *Wish fulfillment.* The person in need of food is satisfied by chance, an act of fate, a handout, etc. but not by his own efforts.

S   *Substitution.* Some other need is satisfied at the end of the story in place of the blocked or partly blocked need for food. This does not include satisfactions from overcoming food deprivation.

F p *Friendly press.* Someone in the story is invited to eat or helped to get food.

This system of categories was designed to cover the major aspects of a behavior sequence involving food—to wit, the motivating state, the kind of situation (deprivation or food-seeking), the instrumental activities (active or passive wish fulfillment, real or unreal, hostile or problem solving) and the goal response activity (amount of eating enjoyment of food). Its utility can perhaps best be illustrated by its application to three typical sample stories. All of the following occurred in response to picture F in the 16 hour deprivation group.

Story 1. "The persons are a man from the black market and an honest citizen of a small Southern town. The citizen hasn't had any meat for a couple of weeks and the man from the black market knows it. The man from the black market thinks he can sell the meat for twice what it is worth. The citizen doesn't want to buy from the black market but he is wanting the meat. The citizen doesn't buy the meat and reports it to the police."

There is food related imagery (F I). The central thema is clearly the need of the 'honest citizen' for the meat (F th) which he wants (N). Deprivation (D) is stated in the words 'hasn't had any meat for a couple of weeks.' The instrumental acts do not get food (I f−) but do get rid of at least part of the reason for the shortage—the black marketer (I d+). There is also some substitute satisfaction (S) implied for doing the right thing ('doesn't want to buy . . . reports it to the police').

Story 2. "The man in black is a detective and he is studying the meat to see if he can get a clue to the black marketer who is the man in grey. There has been a shortage of meat and also a large cost when available. The detective thinks he can catch the crook—he wants a clue. The detective will investigate anything that arouses his suspicion and he will catch the crook."

This story has the necessary food related imagery (F) but it is clearly about the shortage of meat and is therefore a deprivation story (D th). No food need is stated and the action is simple. He catches the crook (I d+).

Many of the stories were more complicated than these which have been chosen to illustrate some of the essential differences in the classification categories. Story 3 illustrates some of the difficulties in scoring that occurred.

Story 3. "The man on the top was a preacher in a Catholic Church and the younger man a member of his parish. It being Friday, all Catholics should sustain (sic) from eating any flesh of any animal. Upon visiting the member's home and discovering that they are having meat to eat he is shocked. The pastor will tell the younger man his fault, and how he is not a good Catholic. The man will outwardly say he's sorry, but he will do it again because he wants what he wants when he wants it."

This is a food thema story which involves actual eating (G) as well as the need for food (N). There is interference on the part of the priest (D) but the response is successful in overcoming it (I d+). The problem here lies partly in deciding that this is not centrally concerned with a threatened deprivation (a decision based mostly on the actual eating as compared with absence of real deprivation) and partly in deciding that the priest's intervention is deprivation and not hostile press (a decision based on the absence of actual aggression). Most classification problems were of this sort and usually they could be resolved on some such basis as these.

To arrive at the final scores, one E (JWA) first classified all the stories. The other E (DCM) then classified independently all the stories in response to picture F (which accounted for nearly half the food stories given). A running tally showed there was agreement on about 75-80 percent of the classifications. However, most of the disagreements came in the hostility category in trying to decide whether it was i, s, or p. In the main categories (F I, N, G, etc.) there was disagreement in less than five percent of the cases. Then the two judges decided together which of two classifications a response should receive. During discussion the hazier definitions were clarified so that there was ready agreement on practically all classifications, once the definitions were fully understood by both judges in the same way. Finally the same procedure was adopted with the remainder of the stories. In general only the most obvious points were scored—that is, there had to be actual words that supported each tally. The scores should therefore be considered as conservative estimates of the most obvious trends. The judges knew to which group the Ss belonged, but could not have easily influenced the results as they had no clear-cut expectations as to how the results would come out.

RESULTS

The major results of the experiment are presented in Tables II (for the situation) and III (for the reactions) in terms of the per-

TABLE II. NUMBER AND PERCENTAGE OF Ss SHOWING VARIOUS KINDS OF SITUATIONAL STORY CHARACTERISTICS AT LEAST ONCE IN THE TOTAL TEST OF SEVEN PICTURES

Chi-square = 3.8 and 6.6 at the 5 percent and 1 percent levels of significance.

Characteristic	1 Hour Deprivation N = 38		4 Hour Deprivation N = 21		16 Hour Deprivation N = 22		Chi-Square of Differences		
	N	%	N	%	N	%	1-4 hr.	4-16 hr.	1-16 hr.
Food imagery	35	92.1	18	85.7	20	90.9			
Food central	25	65.8	13	61.9	20	90.9		3.52 *	4.69
F thema	19	50.0	13	61.9	13	59.1			
D thema	7	18.4	3	14.3	11	50.0		6.24	6.62
Block **	2	5.3	1	4.8	2	9.1			
Need food	21	55.3	18	85.7	18	81.8	5.60		4.32
F deprivation	19	50.0	11	52.4	18	81.8		4.24	5.97

* Yates's correction used.

** Blocks do not include Ss who blocked on more than half the picture and hence were voided.

centage of the subjects in each deprviation group showing a given characteristic at least once in the seven stories told. This method of tabulating the data is somewhat insensitive, as it does not count the times beyond the first that a characteristic appears. Other methods were tried, such as the number of times a characteristic appeared out of the total possible number of times, but they yielded such small percentages that, although the results were the same, the major trends in the data were more difficult to see. Furthermore the differences among the groups obtained by the method used in Tables II and III, when compared with mean scores wherever there were enough cases to calculate a mean, were the same as obtained by the use of mean scores when the total number of appearances of a characteristic were taken into account.[3]

Table II, which summarizes the data on the statement of the situation, shows that there is no overall increase in food imagery as hunger increases. Since this is a case where the percentages are high and therefore possibly insensitive to small differences, the mean number of times food imagery appeared in the seven pictures for each of the three groups was also calculated. The means for the one hour, four hour and 16 hour groups were respectively: 2.32, $\sigma_m = .20$; 2.29, $\sigma_m = .28$; and 2.23, $\sigma_m = .28$. The differences are slight and insignificant. When, however, the relevance of food to the central plot of the story is considered, a very different picture appears. Here there is a decided increase in the number of times the plot revolves around food as hunger increases. Further analysis[4] reveals that the increase lies in the food-deprivation plots and not in the food getting plots. This last point is confirmed by the increase in food deprivation whether central or not which appears in the last line of the table. In general, these differences appear only between the one and four hour groups and the 16 hour group. The only difference of any significance between the one hour and the four hour groups was in the number of times the need for food was expressed.

Table III continues the comparison for some of the reactions of the characters in the stories to a behavior sequence involving food. The differences which are significant or fairly large are checked by means of chi-square. As hunger increases, there is an increase in instrumental activity which is focussed not on food getting but on removing the source of deprivation of food. On the other hand, there is a marked decrease in goal activity (eating) and in press actively promoting goal activity (invitations to eating). None of the other differences is reliable, though several are in an understandable di-

---

[3] A rough check on the stability of these percentages was made by dividing the 38 Ss in the 1 hour group into two groups of 19 Ss and correlating the frequencies obtained by the two groups for each of 21 categories. The product moment correlation was .89 (uncorrected) which indicates a fair degree of reliability of the data as far as results on groups of around 20 Ss are concerned. This also provides some check on the ability of the judges to classify the characteristics consistently.

[4] Note that the sum of the percentages of the two sub-categories is usually more than the percentage in the overall category. This is because the overall category includes those Ss who show *either* F th *or* D th, while some may show *both*, a fact which appears separately in the subclassifications.

TABLE III. Number and Percentage of *S*s Showing Various Kinds of Reactions in Their Stories at Least Once in the Total Test of Seven Pictures

Characteristic	1 Hour Deprivation N = 38		4 Hour Deprivation N = 21		16 Hour Deprivation N = 22		Chi-Square of Differences		
	N	%	*N*	%	*N*	%	1-4 hr.	4-16 hr.	1-16 hr.
Instrumental									
Activity	23	60.5	14	66.7	20	90.9		2.83*	6.33
f+	12	31.6	10	47.6	9	40.9	1.49		
d+	5	13.2	2	9.5	12	54.6		10.89	11.75
f− or d−	5	13.2	5	23.8	8	36.4			3.08
fo or do	7	18.4	4	19.1	4	18.2			
Goal activity	28	73.7	13	61.9	8	36.4	.89	2.81	8.09
Hostility	17	44.7	12	57.1	11	50.0			
Instr.	8	21.1	6	28.6	7	31.8			
Subj.	5	13.2	4	19.1	2	9.1			
Press	6	15.8	5	23.8	3	13.6			
Friendly									
Press	9	23.7	7	33.3	0	0.0		6.56*	4.39*
Wish phantasy	11	29.0	4	19.1	4	18.2			
Wish fulfillment	8	21.1	4	19.1	4	18.2			
Anxiety									
Guilt	8	21.1	3	14.3	4	18.2			
Survival	5	13.2	3	14.3	7	31.8			1.99*
Substitution	2	5.3	3	14.3	2	9.1			

Chi-square = 3.8 and 6.6 at 5 percent and 1 percent levels of significance.
* Yates's correction used.

rection (e.g., increase in anxiety over survival, increase in instrumental hostility as a means of getting food, decrease in phantasies just wishing for food, etc.).

Some of the major results are presented graphically in Fig. 1, which shows, first, the failure of food imagery to increase; second, the complementary shift from goal to instrumental activity; and third, the flatness of the food getting thema curve as compared with the sharp increase between four and 16 hours deprivation for the

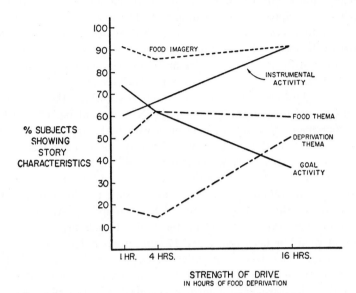

Fig. 1. Percentage of *S*s showing selected food related story characteristics as a function of increasing hunger.

deprivation thema curve which is characteristic of all deprivation related measures (D th, D, I d+, f−, or d−).

On the basis of these shifts a scoring method was devised for summarizing each person's standing in relation to his projected need for

TABLE IV. MEAN NEED FOOD (NF) SCORES OF THE THREE DEPRIVATION GROUPS WITH ESTIMATED RELIABILITIES OF THE DIFFERENCES AMONG THEM

Hours Food Deprivation	Mean NF Score	σ_m	Difference and Probability of its Occurring by Chance with			
			4 hr.	P	16 hr.	P
1 hour	.74	.36	.83	<.10	3.31	<.01
4 hour	1.57	.52	—	—	2.48	<.01
16 hour	4.05	.66	—	—	—	—

food. The following categories were scored +1: D th, N, D, and I f— or d—. I d+ was scored +2 (because of the size of its chi-square) and G and F p were scored —1. A characteristic was scored each time it appeared in the total test. The resulting total will be referred to as the *Need Food score* (NF Score). Table IV summarizes the mean NF scores for the three deprivation groups. As far as means are concerned, the one and four hour groups are significantly lower on the NF scale than the 16 hour group. A more interesting question is whether the group from which the *S*s came could be correctly identified from the NF score alone. Obviously the four hour group overlaps so much with both other groups that the members of this group cannot be very successfully identified from their NF scores. However if the 60 subjects in the one and 16 hour groups were thrown together and sorted out with those scoring one or less in the one hour group, those scoring two in neither, and those scoring three or more in the 16 hour group, 65 percent of the *S*s would be correctly placed on the basis of their projections, 18 percent would be unclassified, and 17 percent would be wrongly classified ('false positives or negatives'). Of course, it is possible to eliminate the wrong classifications by changing the criteria, but only by greatly increasing the number unclassified. For example, none of the *S*s in the 16 hour group had a minus NF score while nine out of the 38, or 24 percent of the one hour group had minus scores. It can therefore be said with certainty (within the limits of this sample) that anyone receiving a minus NF score is not in a state of hunger, i.e., he has not been deprived of food for as long as 16 hours. On the other hand, it can be said almost with as much certainty (there is one exception) that anyone scoring five or more (as 10, or 46 percent, of the 16 hour group did) has not eaten recently (within the last one to two hours).

Table V presents a breakdown of scores for some of the main categories on five of the pictures for which data were available on the larger number of *S*s.[5] Also for the sake of simplicity only the percentages of *S*s showing a characteristic in the one hour and 16 hour groups are presented. Several facts immediately emerge from these data. In the first place, the pictures differ widely in the extent to which they evoke food related stories. By far the most successful picture in this respect was F, which was constructed especially for

---

[5] The results on pictures G and I show identical trends but the frequencies are so small it was decided not to include them in the table.

TABLE V. PERCENTAGE OF ALL THE Ss IN THE ONE HOUR DEPRIVATION
GROUP (N = 44) AND IN THE 16 HOUR GROUP (N = 37) SHOWING
SELECTED CHARACTERISTICS FOR DIFFERENT PICTURES

	F I	N	D	I	I d	G	Fp	Mean NF Score
Picture A (Four 'bums' resting)								
1 hour	50.0	6.8	2.3	9.1	2.3	27.3	0.0	−.14
16 hour	35.1	10.8	8.1	5.4	0.0	18.9	0.0	.03
Picture B ('Beachcomber')								
1 hour	27.3	15.0	18.2	11.4	5.4	4.6	0.0	.45
16 hour	32.4	21.6	32.4	24.3	16.2	2.7	0.0	1.03
Picture D (Woman looking into room)								
1 hour	13.6	2.3	0.0	2.3	0.0	6.8	0.0	−.11
16 hour	18.9	5.4	0.0	10.8	0.0	8.1	10.8	−.16
Picture E (Restaurant balcony scene)								
1 hour	22.7	2.3	0.0	2.3	0.0	18.2	2.3	−.21
16 hour	13.5	2.7	0.0	5.4	0.0	10.8	0.0	−.08
Picture F (Two men and piece of meat)								
1 hour	81.8	36.4	27.3	43.2	2.3	27.3	18.2	.39
16 hour	83.8	54.1	40.5	64.9	21.6	10.8	2.7	1.62
Chi-square		2.6		3.8	5.8*	3.4	3.4*	

* Yates's correction used.

this test. It was unique in two respects. It was the only picture that
had food in it—i.e., a piece of meat—and it was the only picture
which was 'unstructured'—i.e., which was not a single scene, but
three isolated picture elements which had to be combined into a plot.
There was no other picture which approached it in any category
except perhaps picture B in the D category.

In the second place, the data do not reveal any very great differences among the pictures in their sensitivity to changes in the hunger drive. For example, the increase in the D category from the one to the 16 hour group is about 13 percent for picture F and about 14 percent for picture B. The decrease in the G category for picture F is about 16 percent and for picture A about nine percent. The best pictures should be those which give enough food-related responses to be scored and which give the largest differential for different degrees of hunger. The size of the differential does not seem to vary markedly with the food-evoking capacity of the picture or with the nature of the picture, though obviously some pictures fail to evoke a certain characteristic at all. The rule seems to be that if a picture evokes a characteristic moderately frequently (in at least 15-20 percent of the Ss), it will discriminate the two groups regardless of its other properties. It should be noted, however, that though this holds true for the size of the differential it does not hold true for its reliability. Only the differences for picture F approach statistical significance.

Furthermore there is an interesting exception to the rule. Picture E and picture A are both suggestive of satiation or at the very least of meal times (supper and lunch). The 16 hour group reacted to both pictures by producing less overall food imagery than the one hour deprivation group. If the data on F I for pictures A and E are combined so that the percentage of Ss who produced F I on either picture is recorded, the difference approaches significance (chi-square = 3.50). This suggests that with pictures implying goal activity there is a blockage of the normal food associations for hungry Ss, a fact which is clearly in line with the decrease in their production of goal responses (G). The difference probably did not appear in picture F because the piece of meat was supposed to be fitted into the plot which almost required that food imagery be used by all Ss.

The final fact to be gathered from Table V is that all the pictures except D showed a shift in mean NF score in the correct direction (more positive for the hungrier group). The discriminative power of the various pictures as reflected by the critical ratios of the differences was as follows: first, picture F (C. R. = 4.50); second, picture B (C. R. = 1.81); third, picture E (C. R. = 1.63); and fourth, picture A (C. R. = 1.00). Picture D showed small and insignificant, if consistent reversals in most categories and in NF score. It is difficult to draw any general conclusion from this except that, since it was the least food related of the five pictures, a certain minimal relation between a picture and the need it is supposed to reflect is absolutely necessary before it will accurately reflect that need.

DISCUSSION

The Apperceptive Expression of a Need. The present experiment makes some important contributions to the central problem of this series of papers—namely, how a need expresses itself in perception and apperception. It has collected the first real data showing how thematic apperception stories are related to a known condition of the subjects. Murray (9) in his list of the ways in which story inter-pretations can be validated does not mention the technique used here. He is chiefly concerned with how an interpretation can be checked against biographical data, against the results of different tests, or against future behavior. Here the approach has been to discover *how* a need expresses itself so that the judge will have some actual basis for making or improving his interpretations of thematic stories.

Of course, judges have always used, consciously, or unconsciously certain clues for deciding whether or not a story or a series of stories indicated the presence of a need. The present results suggest that some of these clues may have been misleading. For instance, it has commonly been assumed (cf. 3, p. 189) that phantasies serve the function of partially gratifying unfulfilled desires. One might there-fore expect that hungry subjects would project more food objects which could serve to gratify an unfulfilled wish for food. The present data clearly indicate that this assumption (which Murray also makes —10, p. 260) is wrong, at least so far as these data are concerned. Or again, on the basis of Bellak's finding (1) that criticism increases aggressive words in such stories, one might suppose that hunger would increase the overall number of food related words and images, but it does not.[6] There must be many other such clues that clinicians use in making their interpretations, but not many of them have been made explicit. Since the only check on whether the clues used are correct is the checking of the total impression against some other source of knowledge, it is extremely difficult to improve the basis of such judgments because it is almost impossible to know what

---

[6] There is the possibility, of course, that the method of scoring used here—presence of food imagery in a story—is less sensitive than the method used by Bellak of counting every need-related word.

factors formed the total impression and to vary them systematically as they are validated against an outside criterion.

The present method promises better results. It can now be stated with some certainty that a person trying to diagnose hunger from thematic stories should look for: (1) food deprivation, both as the central plot of the story and as a secondary characteristic; (2) instrumental activities which successfully overcome the source of food deprivation but which often do not get the person food; (3) statements implying hunger or a need for food in the characters; (4) a fewer than normal number of references to goal activity such as eating, to friendly press such as an invitation to eat; and (5) a decreased responsiveness in terms of food imagery to pictures strongly implying satiation or the recent termination of eating.

These are the primary characteristics of 'hungry' stories. There are some secondary ones which are not as well established. For instance, the judge should not expect an increase in successful food getting activity, but he might look for an increase in anxiety over survival, and a decrease in thinking about food at an unreal level (wish phantasy or fulfillment).

It has been shown how these clues can be combined into a composite numerical score which gives a pretty good indication for most of the Ss of how long they have been without food. Naturally it is hoped that this procedure will have a much wider significance than could be attached to the determination of hunger from Ss' stories. It would be much simpler to ask the Ss when they last ate! The results become of major importance only if changes occur in the same way in the same categories of response with other experimentally induced needs—particularly psychogenic ones. Other experiments in the series tackle this problem.

Theoretical Considerations. The data also shed some light on the nature of the processes involved in thematic apperception. The first point of theoretical interest is that the results are much the same as those obtained in the first experiment (7) on the effect of hunger on perception. Perception and apperception apparently respond to a need in much the same way. The chief difference lies in the greater freedom of the apperceptive processes to show a variety of changes under the conditions of the experiment. For instance, the first experiment showed an increase with hunger in the perception of objects instrumental to eating. The second experiment elaborates this finding by showing that instrumental activities as well as objects are concerned but the activities are not so much connected with food getting as with eliminating deprivation. One might even argue that the Ss in the first experiment saw plates rather than oranges, not because the plates were instrumental, but because they were empty. That is, the increase in perception of food-related objects rather than actual food may have signified not instrumentality but the deprivation so characteristic of the 'hungry' stories.

Or again, in the first experiment, the Ss failed to perceive an increased number of food objects, but in the second experiment, the more sensitive apperceptive processes reflected an actual significant *decrease* in goal activity. Also, perception did not clearly differentiate the four hour from the 16 hour deprivation group. Apperception did, though it did not reflect many significant changes between the one and four hour groups.[7]

Even if it is granted that apperception is merely reacting more sensitively than perception but according to the same underlying process, the problem remains as to what the process is and why it functions in this particular way. Cattell suggests (3, p. 180) that there are three processes involved in what is ordinarily called 'projection.' The first, 'naive inference from limited personal experience,' could be illustrated in the present experiment by the Ss' 'naively' inferring that people in the pictures have been deprived of food because they have been. The second, 'unconscious, immediate, or true projection,'[8] can probably not occur as a defense mechanism against such a non-ego-involving drive as hunger, but a case could be made for the fact that the hungry Ss' tendency to attribute the hunger motive to others in the pictures objectifies the need so that it can be handled more effectively. The third, 'projection of press required by emotional state,'[8] is illustrated perhaps by the refusal of the Ss to give goal activity responses to situations normally evoking them. That is, since they feel hungry, they see the world as a place with less food in it which 'explains' how they feel.

The data indicate that a number of such processes occur and the writers feel that there is little to be gained by trying to label certain

---

[7] The curious increase in the estimated numbers of neutral objects in the first experiment has not been checked here by analyzing the stories for characteristics unrelated to food. It is planned to do this in the future.

[8] The distinction between this and the third process is essentially the same as Murray makes (8) between supplementary and complementary apperceptive projection

processes projection and others something else. It is all behavior and should be treated like any other behavioral attempt at adjustment by the organism. That is, perception and apperception are determined like any other behavior is—partly by the state of the S (including needs and drives), partly by his past experience, and partly by the objective situation. The major difference between this and any other situation is that the objective cues have been reduced or nearly eliminated so that the behavior must be determined mostly by needs and past experience.[9]

The view that the cognitive and perceptual processes involved here do not function essentially differently from any behavioral attempts at adjustment is supported by Knapp's (6) and Allport and Postman's (1) similar conclusions from studies of rumor and by the nature of the changes that actually occurred here. That is, in general it is to the obvious advantage of the organism to concern itself more and more with instrumental rather than goal activity as the need increases. It is also useful to emphasize the problem (deprivation) and ways of overcoming it (I d+). Perhaps the only surprising element in the situation is that this mobilization at the imaginative level of the resources of the organism toward solving or handling the problem of food deprivation goes on apparently very largely without the S's knowledge or conscious intent.

Secondary Implications. The data bear on several problems that have been raised insistently by previous research in this field. For instance, what is the effect of recent experiences on the validity of projective tests such as the TAT? As Coleman says, "the TAT should not be subject to such day-to-day fluctuations" (5, p. 257). Both he and Bellak (2) conclude that it is not—at least not at any very fundamental level. The present data do not support this conclusion entirely. If, for instance, an S takes a TAT at 11 A.M. in the morning and he has missed his breakfast (a situation comparable to the 16 hour deprivation group), there is much greater likelihood

<hr>

[9] The difference between this and the situations in which Freud described projection is that he was dealing with cases in which the need was so strong as to render ordinary objective determinants relatively unimportant. In phantasy situations the objective determinants are rendered unimportant by the experimenter so that behavior can be more completely reflective of needs. The end result is often the same except that the Freudian projection will only occur in cases of such extreme need that the ordinary objective determinants of an interpretation are overridden.

of his telling a general deprivation story to picture A (the 'beach-comber' from an early TAT edition) than if he takes the TAT shortly after lunch. This does not mean, of course, that the basic picture of the man's personality structure will be altered. There may be alteration only in the manifest and not in the latent content, as in Freud's dream analyses. But it does suggest caution at least to the extent of finding out what significant things have happened to a person in the last few hours or even days before administration of a projective test.

What kinds of pictures are most effective in eliciting the needs of the S? Here again there have been several studies (12, 13) most of which conclude that they should be vague and contain characters with whom the person can identify. The basis for choosing these characteristics has not been any demonstrated discriminative power of such pictures but rather the quality of the stories they produce. So far as any conclusion can be drawn from the few pictures used here, it would seem that the projection pictures should contain objects or situations related to the need one is interested in meas-uring. This is to insure a sufficient frequency of responses related to the need under consideration to get differential reflections of it. To be more explicit, the pictures should contain goal objects in an un-structured relationship to a person with whom the S can identify. In this connection, the technique of presenting three or more elements which the S must weave into a story seems particularly promising. They should also present situations suggestive of terminal or goal activity and of deprivation or blockage of instrumental activity. The present set of TAT pictures is particularly deficient in the first char-acteristic. That is they do not contain goal objects around which themes can be woven, but present instead situations which may be so ambiguous that like picture D in the present series they fail to evoke much of any response (and hence no differential response) related to the needs which the experimenter is interested in measur-ing. These points, it must be emphasized, are merely suggestions which arise from a very limited number of pictures under the influence of a simple physiological drive, and yield no firm factual support for wide generalization. However, they have seemed worth making, since this is one of the first attempts which has been made to determine the effectiveness of pictures in terms of their actual discriminating power for the need being measured.

SUMMARY

A group of 81 men, applicants for admission to Naval submarine training school, wrote out brief stories in response to seven projected pictures, 38 after one hour, 21 after four hours, and 22 after 16 hours of food deprivation. Results from 22 more men who wrote stories in response to five of the seven pictures were used in the analysis of the comparative merit of the pictures in eliciting responses reflecting hunger. The stories were analyzed by two judges independently for 23 characteristics relating to the hunger drive. The following conclusions appear justified:

1. The judges were able to agree in categorizing story content in a large percentage of cases. The correlation between the categories for two groups of 19 Ss under the same condition was .89, indicating a considerable degree of stability for group percentages in various categories.

2. As hunger increased, there was no overall increase in the percentage of Ss showing food imagery or food themas, but there was a decided increase in the percentage showing food deprivation themas, characters expressing a need for food, and activity successful in overcoming deprivation, but not always instrumental in getting food. On the other hand, as hunger increased, there was a decided decrease in the amount of goal activity (eating) and in friendly press, favorable to eating.

3. A composite need food score was devised by scoring +2, +1 or −1 all instances in each record of categories which showed reliable increases or decreases for the groups as hunger increased. The mean need food score differentiated reliably the three deprivation groups with little overlap in score between the one and 16 hour deprivation groups.

4. No outstanding differences in sensitivity to reflecting hunger was discovered for the various pictures used provided the picture was enough related to hunger to produce a sufficient number of food-related responses to show a differential. The most successful picture in differentiating the three food deprivation groups was one containing a goal object (food) in a completely unstructured relationship to a young man with whom the Ss could identify.

The application of these findings to the clues used in interpretation of Thematic Apperception Test records is discussed. It is suggested in particular that the amount of need deprivation and of instrumental activity present in stories is a better index of the strength of a need than is the amount of goal activity. If the results are confirmed at more complex need levels, it should be possible to obtain a single score measuring need strength which would combine the shifts occurring in story content as the strength of the need increases.

Consideration of the theoretical implications of these results indicates that it is desirable to treat apperceptive behavior as functioning like any other type of behavior rather than to attempt to fit it under the limited principles governing Freudian or defensive projection which appears to be a special case.

REFERENCES

1. ALLPORT, G., and POSTMAN, L. *The psychology of rumor*. New York: Holt, 1947.
2. BELLAK, L. The concept of projection. *Psychiatry*, 1944, **7**, 353-370.
3. CATTELL, R. B. Projection and the design of projective tests of personality. *Char. & Pers.*, 1944, **12**, 177-194.
4. CLARK, R. M. A method of administering and evaluating the Thematic Apperception Test in group situations. *Genet. Psych. Monogr.*, 1944, **30**, 3-55.
5. COLEMAN, W. The Thematic Apperception Test. I. Effect of recent experience. II. Some quantitative observations. *J. clin. Psych.*, 1947, **3**, 257-264.
6. KNAPP, R. H. Experiments in serial reproduction and related aspects of the psychology of rumor. Unpublished Ph.D. thesis, Harvard University, 1948.
7. MCCLELLAND, D. C., and ATKINSON, J. A. The projective expression of needs. I. The effect of different intensities of the hunger drive on perception. *J. Psychol.*, 1948, **25**, 205-222.
8. MURRAY, H. A. The effect of fear upon estimates of the maliciousness of other personalities. *J. soc. Psychol.*, 1933, **4**, 310-329.
9. MURRAY, H. A. Techniques for a systematic investigation of fantasy. *J. Psychol.*, 1937, **3**, 115-143.
10. MURRAY, H. A. *Explorations in personality*. New York: Oxford Univ. Press, 1938.
11. RODNICK, E. H., and KLEBANOFF, S. G. Projective reactions to induced frustration as a measure of social adjustment. *Psychol. Bull.*, 1942, **39**, 489.
12. SARGENT, H. Projective methods, their origins, theory and application to personality research. *Psychol. Bull.*, 1945, **42**, 257-293.
13. SYMONDS, P. M. Criteria for the selection of pictures for the investigation of adolescent fantasies. *J. abnorm. soc. Psych.*, 1939, **34**, 271-274.

....

PART FIVE

Recognition and Identification of Figures

SELECTION 45

••

Frequency of Usage as a Determinant of Recognition Thresholds for Words[*][1]

RICHARD L. SOLOMON AND LEO POSTMAN

THE TACHISTOSCOPIC PRESENTATION of words has been used in attempts to detect the role of personality variables in perception. In general, the procedure has been to present printed words, drawn from various relevant "meaning" classes, for very short periods of exposure; the S's task is to identify the words. Recognition thresholds are determined by increasing either the duration of exposure or the intensity of illumination. These thresholds have been considered to be an index of perceptual sensitivity or ease of recognition for the stimuli. The thresholds have also been interpreted as measures of the amount of "stimulus material" necessary for elicitation of the correct response.

The results of such experiments have lent some support to the view that personality variables may be significant determiners of perceptual sensitivity to visually presented verbal stimuli. The demonstrable effects of such factors are not large in absolute terms but often appear to be internally consistent and statistically reliable. Evidence has been presented for the selective effects of personal values and needs on perceptual sensitivity as measured in the tachistoscopic situation (6, 7, 11, 12, 16). It has also been suggested that words which may arouse anxiety because of their emotional connotations have significantly higher thresholds than neutral words (8). There

* From the *J. exp. Psychol.*, 1952, **43**, 195-201. Reprinted by permission of the authors and the publisher.

[1] Parts of this research were supported by the Laboratory of Social Relations, Harvard University. Other parts were carried out at the University of California.

is, however, some evidence that anxiety arousing stimuli may have lower thresholds than words to which S is indifferent (2, 5).

It is important to ask to what extent the apparent effects of complex personality factors reduce to the operation of basic psychological variables of wider generality. In a related series of experiments (3, 12, 13, 14) an attempt has been made to explore systematically some of the variables whose contribution must be taken into account in analyzing the effect of personality factors on recognition thresholds. Since the tachistoscopic studies of word recognition involve the presentation of verbal stimuli and the elicitation of verbal responses, these experiments concentrated on variables which have been shown to be extremely important in the psychology of *verbal learning*. Specifically, they have considered the effects of frequency and recency on the probability of occurrence of verbal responses in the presence of tachistoscopically exposed verbal stimuli. Howes and Solomon (3) have shown that when word length, word structure, and practice effects are roughly controlled or held constant, a very powerful correlate of the visual recognition thresholds for words is the *relative frequency* with which a word is used in the English language. Using the Thorndike-Lorge word counts (15) as an index of relative frequency of occurrence, these Es found that visual duration thresholds for tachistoscopically presented word stimuli seem to approximate a linear, inverse function of the logarithm of frequency of usage. The correlations between the thresholds and relative frequency of occurrence of words were found to range from .60 to .90, dependent upon the attendant experimental conditions.

The variable of word frequency had not been taken into account in previous experiments relating recognition thresholds to such factors as personal value (11). Solomon and Howes (14) showed that a very considerable amount of the variance attributed to personal value could be accounted for in terms of the frequency variable. Postman and Schneider (12) confirmed these findings. The question is still open whether the residual effects of value, interest, and so forth, can be reduced to individual Ss' deviations from the frequency of word usage in the general population.

Howes and Solomon (4) applied a similar critical analysis to McGinnies' evidence for "perceptual defense" against taboo words (8). His taboo words had a low frequency of occurrence in the English language when compared to his neutral words, and higher thresholds for taboo words should, therefore, be expected on the basis of relative frequency of usage. McGinnies (9), in rebuttal, argued that the Thorndike-Lorge word counts are derived from literature, not verbal usage in everyday living, and so are not representative. This point is, however, quite inappropriate when it is realized that tachistoscopic presentation of words is very much like a reading situation; and, if laws of stimulus generalization are at all valid, frequency of occurrence of words *in literature* may be expected to predict visual duration thresholds for word stimuli at least as well as will some index of actual verbal response frequency in conversation. This problem remains to be explored.

In addition to the studies which have related frequency of usage to visual recognition thresholds, an experiment of Postman and Solomon (13) has shown that, when relative word frequencies are equated, the *recency* of word usage is significantly correlated with duration thresholds for verbal stimuli. Other things being equal, the more recently a word has been exposed to *S*, the lower will be the recognition threshold for that word stimulus. The variables of frequency and recency are not, of course, entirely independent. The more often a word occurs relative to all other words, the more likely it is to have occurred more recently than other words, either in literature read by the *S* or in words uttered by the *S*.

There is one fundamental weakness in the studies which have demonstrated the importance of frequency and recency in the determination of recognition thresholds for words. The index of frequency of word usage which these studies employed—the Thorndike-Lorge word counts—is a *population index* and allows us to estimate in only very rough ways the relative frequency of word usage for individual *S*s. This method, of course, represents a lack of adequate control over the word frequency variable. In all probability, the relationship between the relative frequency of word usage and recognition thresholds has been underestimated owing to this imprecision. Experimental control of relative word frequencies will make a more precise statement of the relationship possible. Once this frequency variable has been experimentally controlled and its effect on recognition thresholds measured, we shall have an important baseline for the evaluation of emotional, valuative, and need-related variables.

With this point in mind, and with a view to the inadequacy of previous indices of word frequency, two experiments were carried out. In both these experiments, relative frequency of word usage was "built in" experimentally and then related to the recognition thresholds for the words.

PROCEDURE

Experiment 1. Five undergraduates at Harvard University participated in this experiment. The *S*s were misled as to the purpose of the experi-

ment. When S entered the experimental room, he was given the following instruction:

> This is an experiment concerning the effectiveness of repetition in
> learning to pronounce strange words correctly. It has a direct bearing
> on the problem of reading words in a foreign language, as compared to
> hearing the words spoken. In addition, we are interested in knowing
> whether the relative effectiveness of the two kinds of learning methods
> depends on general reading ability.
>
> We are going to give you a deck of cards. On each card is printed a
> strange word. We would like you to look at each card carefully and
> then pronounce the word in the way it would be pronounced if it were
> a word in the English language. Proceed steadily from card to card,
> turning over each one after you have finished with it. Go right through
> the deck and then stop unless you have serious doubts about your
> pronunciations.

TABLE 1. STIMULUS WORDS USED IN THE EXPERIMENTS

Core-Words		Filler-Words	
JANDARA	IKTITAF	KADIRGA	UDIBNON
AFWORBU	SARICIK	ADAFNAW	DILIKLI
BIWOJNI	ZABULON	BORULCE	MECBURI
NANSOMA	CIVADRA	NIJARON	OLMADIK
ENANWAL	LOKANTA	ENSHIMI	BOZULMA
		INKULAM	AMARIJA
		TAVHANE	FEVKANI

The E then handed S a pack of 100 cards. The pack consisted of a
series of pronounceable nonsense words, seven letters each, typed in
capitals across the middle of each card. The 100 cards contained 24 different nonsense words, repeated with varying frequencies. There were
two words replicated 25 times, two words replicated 10 times, two words
replicated five times, two words replicated 2 times, and 14 words appearing only once.

The pack of 100 cards was shuffled thoroughly before S went through
it, card by card, reading and pronouncing each nonsense word. The nonsense words, selected from a Turkish-English dictionary, are presented
in Table 1.

The first ten words of the list were the *core-words;* they were used
later, in the tachistoscopic presentation. The other 14 words were "padding" to the deck, and they appeared one time each in the deck of cards.
Each of the *core-words* was varied in its frequency of appearance in the

pack from *S* to *S*, in such a way that a latin-square experimental design was completed.

This design was used in order to try to control for inherent differences among words in memorability and structural variations. Thus, each of the five *S*s was exposed to the same 24 words (ten core-words plus 14 padding words), but each *S* received different frequencies of exposure to the different core-words. Two core-words were used at each frequency, in order to replicate for words per se.

After the *S*s had read the 100 cards, they were given an irrelevant task in order to cover up the purpose of the experiment. *S*s were handed a book and given the following instructions:

Now, we would like you to read the passage marked off in this book. We want you to read as clearly and distinctly as possible without faltering, in order that we may get a general index of your reading ability.

The *S* then read a page from a section on ethics in a randomly chosen textbook in philosophy. After this, *E* ushered *S* into another room for the tachistoscopic phase of the experiment and read these instructions:

We are going to present to you, one at a time, some words. If you look in the eye-piece in this box, you will be able to see two lines. The words we will show you will appear directly between those lines. Each word will be presented to you for very short intervals of time, and at first you will not be able to tell what the words are. However, after each presentation we would like you to make a guess as to what the word was. Each word will be presented to you several times until you have correctly recognized it. I will say "Ready" before each exposure of the word, and I will tell you when you have correctly recognized the word and when a new word is going to be presented to you.

The words used in the tachistoscopic procedure contained the core-words of the pack of cards. These words were "buried," in random sequence, among 20 other words in the list of words for tachistoscopic presentation. These 20 words contained ten English words, varying in frequency over a large range in the Thorndike-Lorge counts, plus ten pronounceable nonsense words that previously had never been exposed to *S*. Thus, the total number of words to be exposed was 30. They were (a) the ten core-words; (b) English words (*welfare, surmise, testify, titular, example, promise, machete, venture, deserve, balance*); and (c) nonsense words never exposed before (*afsanaf eksimek, peyapey, awnahdi, bilogos, akliyat, pisirik, nobetiki, levahik, fedakar*). In addition to these 30 words, four practice words were given at the start of the tachistoscopic session (*Harvard, teacher, university, professor*). The words in the tachistoscope were typed in the same capitals used on the cards of the deck described above. The ascending method of limits was used to determine the duration threshold (to the nearest .01 sec.) for зach of the 30 words. The duration threshold was defined as the flash duration just necessary for correct recognition. For details of apparatus and procedure, the reader is referred to previous experiments (3, 11).

Experiment II. The purpose and design of the second experiment were similar to those of the first experiment with the following exceptions: (a) The second experiment was run as a group experiment. (b) The Ss —30 undergraduate and graduate students at the University of California —were instructed to pronounce the words subvocally after E had read them. (c) Because this was a group experiment, there was, of course, no possibility of counterbalancing the words, and, therefore, different frequencies were assigned to different words arbitrarily. This procedure confounded frequencies and whatever effects stemmed from word structure. (d) Tachistoscopic exposure was by means of a projector equipped with a shutter which was set at a constant exposure duration of .01 sec. Each word was exposed 18 times with the illumination intensity increasing from exposure to exposure by an amount equivalent to a change of 2.5 v. (e) The number of trials required for the first correct recognition of the exposed word was used as a measure of the recognition threshold.

RESULTS

Experiment I. The average duration thresholds, in seconds, for all *core-words* are given in Table 2 and plotted in Fig. 1. The control words to which Ss had not been previously exposed, are listed as having a frequency of zero. Clearly, thresholds vary inversely with frequency of prior usage. Before evaluating the differences among the thresholds, we must take account of practice effects. The core-words were scattered through the tachistoscopic list randomly, but the same order of presentation was given to each S. In order to adjust for practice effects, the list was divided into thirds, and separate standard scores were computed for each third of the list. The standard scores for the three thirds were then comparable to each other, and further analysis could then be made on the assumption that practice effects could not differentially affect thresholds for different core-words. The average standard scores for words with different frequencies of usage are listed in Table 2.

An analysis of variance was performed on the standardized threshold data (for core-words only). The main experimental variable—frequency—was found to be a significant source of variance ($F = 4.75$, $df = 4$ and 25, $p < .01$). Differences among sets of words fell short of significance ($F = 1.51$, $df = 4$ and 25). Finally, individual differences among Ss were significant ($F = 23.44$, $df = 4$ and 25, $p < .01$).

TABLE 2. AVERAGE RECOGNITION THRESHOLDS FOR CORE-WORDS OF
DIFFERENT FREQUENCIES

Core-Word Frequency	Experiment I		Experiment II	
	Av. Threshold (sec.)	Av. Standard Score	Av. Threshold (no. trials)	Av. Standard Score
0	.96	+.52	12.80	+1.02
1	.40	+.16	7.88	−0.24
2	.27	+.29	6.95	−0.48
5	.26	−.02	9.63	+0.09
10	.20	−.27	7.25	−0.44
25	.12	−.48	5.92	−0.77

Experiment II. The average duration thresholds, in number of trials required for recognition, are listed in Table 2 and presented graphically in Fig. 1. Table 2 also shows the average duration thresh-

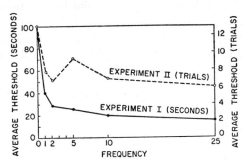

FIG. 1. Average recognition thresholds for core-words of different frequencies.

olds in standard score form. Analysis of variance again showed frequency to be a highly significant source of variance ($F = 45.60$, $df = 5$ and 145, $p < .01$). In the case of Exp. II, individual differences among Ss were not significant ($F = .32$).

Although the general trend of the thresholds as a function of frequency is the same as in Exp. I, the reversal between words having two and five presentations must be noted. It will be remembered that in Exp. II the core-words could not be counterbalanced among the various frequencies. It is probable that the particular structural characteristics of the words given two and five presentations out-weigh the differential effect of frequency. When the Thorndike-Lorge word counts are used, the structural characteristics of partic-ular words probably obscure the effects of frequency in a similar manner. In the absence of control for word structure, the general resemblance of the curves obtained in Exp. I and II is striking evi-dence for the importance of frequency of usage as a determiner of recognition thresholds.

DISCUSSION

The data presented in Fig. 1 indicate quite clearly that visual recognition thresholds for words are a negatively accelerated decay function of frequency of prior exposure to a given word. In the previ-ous work of Howes and Solomon (3), using the Thorndike-Lorge count as a word-frequency estimate, recognition thresholds have appeared to be an inverse linear function of the logarithm of fre-quency of word usage. A logarithmic transformation is not, how-ever, appropriate to the present data. Whereas Howes and Solomon never had occasion to assign a frequency of zero to any English words, there is a true zero frequency point in the present function. The logarithm of zero frequency is relatively meaningless for our purposes without some sort of correction. The shape of the func-tions in Fig. 1, moreover, does not yield a linear plot when trans-formed logarithmically.

It is interesting to note, however, that the mean thresholds for fre-quencies of word usage varying from 1 to 25 (omitting the zero fre-quency) do yield a very good fit to an inverse linear logarithmic function. Therefore, there is some reason to suspect that, when a word has been exercised at least once, or has been encountered at least once, its recog-nition threshold will be roughly an inverse function of log frequency of prior exposure or usage.

The results shown in Fig. 1 provide a theoretical bridge between learning theory and perception theory. Let us assume that, by dif-ferentially exercising pronounceable nonsense words in this experi-ment, we have established associations of differential strength be-tween the visually presented verbal stimulus and the response of reading or saying the word.[2] The strength of this association is meas-

---

[2] For purposes of the present analysis it probably makes very little differ-ence whether we think of these associations in terms of S-R connections or S-S patterns (hypotheses).

₄red by the duration or intensity of the stimulus exposure necessary for a correct verbal report.

Given a population of associations, the one which has been exercised most frequently will have the greatest probability of being elicited relative to other, like associations. How will this fact influence S's responses in a tachistoscopic situation? When a stimulus pattern is presented at short durations or at low illumination intensities, only fragments of the total word stimulus are "effective." Such a stimulus fragment may be considered to represent a point on the generalization dimension of stimulus patterns capable of eliciting the correct verbal response. A given stimulus fragment may, of course, be located on several generalization dimensions, each involving a different word. Which verbal response will be given depends on the relative strengths of association which have been established, through generalization, between the particular stimulus fragment and the different response words. If the visually presented stimulus word has had a greater frequency of prior usage than any of the competing response words, a correct response is highly probable.

Words of lower prior exercise frequency will be interfered with by words of higher exercise frequency. This interference will manifest itself in the tendency for S's "guesses" to be high frequency words. If the actual stimulus word is a low frequency word, effective stimulus fragments will elicit erroneous "guesses" until the amount of effective stimulation becomes great enough on successive exposures to reduce the number of competing word responses. One may describe the increase in effective stimulation as limiting the range of competing "hypotheses" (1, 10) or one may speak of a restriction of stimulus generalization. In this connection it is interesting to point to the parallel between overt intrusions in retroaction and proaction experiments and wrong pre-recognition responses in the tachistoscopic situation. In both cases, a strong competing response temporarily replaces the correct response.

Frequency or prior occurrence used as an independent variable contains two aspects: (a) frequency of prior stimulation; and (b) frequency of prior response. When the Thorndike-Lorge word counts are used as a frequency index, these two aspects of environmental history are confused. Such is also the case in the experiments reported in this paper. When the pronounceable nonsense words were exposed to the Ss, and they were asked to read them, either aloud or subvocally, a frequency index was being established into which the effects of exposure and response enter to unknown degrees. At present, we do not know whether frequency of prior *exposure* or frequency of prior *responses* is the more important determinant of visual duration thresholds to words. A series of experiments aimed at this problem would have considerable bearing on the relative strengths and weaknesses of cognitive learning theory as compared with S-R learning theory in handling the facts of word-recognition experiments.

Our experiments point to frequency of prior usage as an important determinant of recognition thresholds but leave open the question of the process mediating the effect of frequency. The interaction of motivational factors with frequency has just begun to be explored (12, 14). Frequency of one type of sequence need not be equivalent to another type. The functions shown in Fig. 1 were obtained with verbal sequences which had no important motivational consequences for the Ss. To what degree consequences of a high motivational nature will alter these functions is a question to be answered experimentally.

One final methodological note. Using operations typical of perception experiments (determination of thresholds), we have attacked our problem in terms of concepts derived from verbal learning. The phenomena of word recognition can play a strategic role in the rapprochement of theories of perception and verbal learning. The fact that many perceptual experiments concerned with nonverbal stimuli use verbal reports as their basic data makes it highly desirable to explore further the relations between the laws of verbal behavior and the laws of perception.

SUMMARY

This experiment was concerned with the relationship between tachistoscopic recognition thresholds for words and frequency of prior usage of the words.

Pronounceable nonsense words were used as stimuli. Frequency of usage was controlled experimentally by requiring Ss to read and pronounce different nonsense words with frequencies ranging from 1 to 25. Later, Ss' tachistoscopic recognition thresholds for these words were determined as well as for control words which had zero frequency of prior usage. Recognition thresholds were found to vary inversely with frequency of prior usage.

The discussion stresses the close relationship between Ss' responses in a tachistoscopic recognition situation and responses measured in experiments on verbal learning. Frequency of past usage is a determiner of response strength in both types of situation. The importance of controlling such variables as frequency of usage in experiments relating perceptual sensitivity to personality variables is pointed out.

REFERENCES

1. BRUNER, J. S. Personality dynamics and the process of perceiving. In R. R. Blake and G. V. Ramsey (Eds.), *Perception: an approach to personality.* New York: Ronald Press, 1951.
2. BRUNER, J. S., and POSTMAN, L. Emotional selectivity in perception and reaction. *J. Pers.,* 1947, **16,** 69-77.
3. HOWES, D. H., and SOLOMON, R. L. Visual duration threshold as a function of word probability. *J. exp. Psychol.,* 1951, **41,** 401-410.
4. HOWES, D. H., and SOLOMON, R. L. A note on McGinnies' "Emotionality and perceptual defense." *Psychol. Rev.,* 1950, **57,** 229-234.
5. MCCLEARY, R. A., and LAZARUS, R. S. Autonomic discrimination without awareness: an interim report. *J. Pers.,* 1949, **18,** 171-179.
6. MCCLELLAND, D. C., and ATKINSON, J. W. The projective expression of needs: I. The effect of different intensities of the hunger drive on perception. *J. Psychol.,* 1948, **25,** 205-222.
7. MCCLELLAND, D. C., and LIBERMAN, A. M. The effect of need for achievement on recognition of need-related words. *J. Pers.,* 1949, **18,** 236-251.
8. MCGINNIES, E. M. Emotionality and perceptual defense. *Psychol. Rev.,* 1949, **56,** 244-251.
9. MCGINNIES, E. M. Discussion of Howes' and Solomon's note on "Emotionality and perceptual defense." *Psychol. Rev.,* 1950, **57,** 235-240.
10. POSTMAN, L. Toward a general theory of cognition. In J. H. Rohrer and M. Sherif (Eds.), *Social psychology at the crossroads.* New York: Harper, 1951.
11. POSTMAN, L., BRUNER, J. S., and MCGINNIES, E. M. Personal values as selective factors in perception. *J. abnorm. soc. Psychol.,* 1948, **43,** 142-154.
12. POSTMAN, L., and SCHNEIDER, B. H. Personal values, visual recognition and recall. *Psychol. Rev.,* 1951, **58,** 271-284.
13. POSTMAN, L., and SOLOMON, R. L. Perceptual sensitivity to completed and incompleted tasks. *J. Pers.,* 1950, **18,** 347-357.
14. SOLOMON, R. L., and HOWES, D. H. Word frequency, personal values and visual duration thresholds. *Psychol. Rev.,* 1951, **58,** 256-270.
15. THORNDIKE, E. L., and LORGE, I. *The teacher's word book of 30,000 words.* New York: Teachers Col., Columbia Univer., 1944.
16. VANDERPLAS, J. M., and BLAKE, R. R. Selective sensitization in auditory perception. *J. Pers.,* 1949, **18,** 252-266.

SELECTION 46

••

An Experimental Distinction between Perceptual Process and Verbal Response[*,1]

ULRIC NEISSER

DATA FROM PERCEPTUAL EXPERIMENTS are necessarily behavioral. We may be interested in what the subject sees, but we can only record what he says or does. This situation gives rise to a number of theoretical problems. Some of these problems concern the very subject matter of the field of perception. Thus, while Graham (1) suggests that perceptual experiments are essentially concerned with certain types of responses or behavior functions, Osgood (5, p. 194) discusses "awareness, as . . . indexed by verbal or other modes of response."

Broad differences in approach are not the only consequences of the mediated character of perceptual data. More concrete issues are affected. For example, we know that duration thresholds for tachistoscopically presented words are a function of language frequencies (2); but we do not know whether the more frequent words are more readily *seen* or *said*. A related problem concerns the duration thresholds of words with emotional connotations (4).

The present experiment is intended to demonstrate that the effect of preparatory set in tachistoscopic experiments is to facilitate seeing rather than saying the words presented. That is, a set does not raise the probabilities of the critical responses generally, but only under restricted stimulus conditions; namely, when the expected words are shown.

* From the *J. exp. Psychol.*, 1954, **47**, 399-402. Reprinted by permission of the author and the publisher.

[1] This research was supported in part by the United States Air Force under Contract No. AF18(600)-322, monitored by the Human Factors Operations Research Laboratories, Air Research and Development Command, Bolling Air Force Base, Washington, D. C. The writer is particularly indebted to Dr. George A. Miller for his advice and counsel during the course of the study and the writing of the report.

If the demonstration is valid, it suggests a corresponding interpretation of the other tachistoscopic studies. For example, the effect of language frequency may then also be supposed to be at the stimulus end of the process. On the other hand, these data are not presented as evidence relevant to the fundamental problem of perception and response. Indeed, even a discussion of the possibility of such evidence is beyond the scope of this paper. At best, demonstrations like the one presented here may be useful in some future clarification of the issue.

The demonstration depends upon the use of homonyms: words that are spelled differently yet are pronounced alike. A set is induced for one member of a homonym pair, and the consequent decrease in threshold for that member is compared with the decrease for the second member. The same verbal response (within the limits of experimental measurement) is employed in reporting either word of the pair. Therefore, recognition of the second member will be facilitated if the set has operated directly on response probabilities, but will not be facilitated if the set affects perceptual processes.

METHOD

Subjects. The Ss were 12 male undergraduates at the Massachusetts Institute of Technology, naive with respect to the purpose of the experiment. Each had been accustomed to tachistoscopic testing during a preliminary session. No word was shown in the preliminary session which was to be used in the main experiment.

TABLE 1. WORDS USED IN THE EXPERIMENT

IA	IB	IIA	IIB	IIIA	IIIB
no	know	threw	through	corps	core
rain	reign	phrase	frays	one	won
paste	paced	seed	cede	scene	seen
whirled	world	ruff	rough	wail	whale
colonel	kernel	aloud	allowed	metal	mettle

Apparatus. Word recognition thresholds were measured with an electronically timed mirror tachistoscope. This instrument was built by Dr. J. Volkmann of Mt. Holyoke College, who generously permitted its use in the M.I.T. laboratories. In design, it closely resembles the tachistoscope recently described by Kupperian and Golin (3). The timing circuit[2]

---

[2] Designed by Dr. E. Davis.

allowed variation of the exposure duration in 17 steps from 60 to 290 msec. Under the illumination conditions employed, no S recognized any stimulus word at the shortest exposure time, while failures of recognition at the longest exposure occurred only three times.

The customary modified method of limits was used in the determination of thresholds. Measurements on each S were made from an individual base line—one of the 17 exposure speeds—which had been determined during the preliminary session. Each word was successively exposed at increasing exposure times above this base line until it was correctly recognized. Guessing was encouraged. Since the purpose of the experiment was the comparison of different classes of words for each S individually, accurate exposure times were not required. Only the ordinal number (1-17) of the threshold exposure was recorded, and only ordinal statistics are employed in evaluating the results.

Stimulus Materials. The words used as stimulus materials are shown in Table 1. They were arbitrarily divided into three groups of five homonym pairs each, as indicated.

Procedure. Each S was instructed that he would be given 1 min. to study a card on which a list of ten words was typed. He was told that some of these words would appear among the words to be displayed in the tachistoscope, and that he should keep the list in mind as well as possible since this might help him to see or guess the words in tachistoscopic presentation.

The words shown to each S were chosen from the experimental mate-

TABLE 2. EXPERIMENTAL DESIGN

Subject Number	Words Presented on Preliminary List	Words Tested Tachistoscopically
1	IA, IIA	IA, IIB, IIIA
2	IB, IIB	IA, IIB, IIIA
3	IA, IIA	IB, IIA, IIIB
4	IB, IIB	IB, IIA, IIIB
5	IA, IIIA	IA, IIIB, IIA
6	IB, IIIB	IA, IIIB, IIA
7	IA, IIIA	IB, IIIA, IIB
8	IB, IIIB	IB, IIIA, IIB
9	IIA, IIIA	IIA, IIIB, IA
10	IIB, IIIB	IIA, IIIB, IA
11	IIA, IIIA	IIB, IIIA, IB
12	IIB, IIIB	IIB, IIIA, IB

rials in the manner indicated in Table 2. The order of the words was determined separately for each S from a table of random numbers.

After S had studied the card for 1 min., it was taken from him and the tachistoscopic test was begun. Thresholds were determined successively for 17 words, in the manner described above. The first two words were irrelevant practice items. The remaining 15 were drawn from the experimental materials according to Table 2. The order in which the words were tested was determined individually for each S from a table of random numbers.

The design of the experiment, as outlined in Table 2, provides certain controls. Each S was tested on three classes of words: (a) five words from the list he had been shown; (b) five words that were homonyms of the list words not directly tested; (c) five words that were new to him. These three classes will be referred to as set words, homonyms, and controls respectively. Every word in the experiment appeared equally often (twice) in each of the three classes. The words of Group IA, for example, were set words for Ss No. 1 and 5, homonyms for Ss No. 2 and 6, and control words for Ss No. 9 and 10.

RESULTS

It was not possible to make meaningful comparisons between the tachistoscopic test scores of the several Ss, because a different base line was employed for each S, as explained above.

In order to study differences among individual words, the data for each S were analyzed to find his median threshold. Each of the words on which he had been tested was then classified as falling either above, below, or at this median. This analysis revealed substantial differences in the perceptibility of the different words. Seven of the 30 words in Table 1 were never recognized more quickly than the median by any S; these were *phrase, scene, wail, metal, cede, core, mettle*. Five words were never slower than the median; these were *ruff, one, kernel, allowed, whale*. These differences are not related to the main variable of the experiment (set), since each word appeared equally often in each of the three experimental classes. To the extent that the differences among words are significant, they are probably due to differences in structural characteristics and in frequency of use.

Data from each S were analyzed to determine how many of each class of words were recognized faster than, slower than, or at his median recognition threshold. The results are totaled in Table 3.

Table 3 shows that set words tend to be recognized more quickly than average, while homonyms and controls behave substantially alike in being slower than average. Although these results appear clear-cut, it is impossible to test their statistical reliability, since the 180 entries in Table 3 are not independent. There are 6 different entries based on each word, and 15 based on each S.

TABLE 3. COMPARISON OF EXPERIMENTAL CONDITIONS

Recognition Speed	Set Words	Homonyms	Controls	Total
Slower than median	15	32	29	76
Faster than median	29	16	17	62
(At median)	(16)	(12)	(14)	(42)

Note.—The figures represent the total number of cases (all Ss and words) in the given categories.

The reliability of the results was therefore estimated by comparisons based on independent samples, in this case the 12 Ss. It was first necessary to determine for each S whether he saw homonyms more quickly than controls or the reverse, and to make similar determinations for the two other crucial pairings (homonyms vs. set words, set words vs. controls). Such determinations for a given S were made by finding the direction of the cross product in the appropriate fourfold table: a table with one entry for each homonym or control (say) recognized with a speed above or below the median threshold for the S.

A comparison based on these determinations revealed no significant differences between homonyms and controls. Five Ss were faster on homonymns and 4 on controls, while 3 were equally fast on each. Set words, however, were consistently superior to both other classes. Nine of 11 Ss recognized set words more readily than controls (one showing no difference), while 11 of 12 Ss recognized set words faster than homonyms. Simple sign tests indicate that the probabilities of obtaining results deviating from the chance 50% by at least the given amounts are .065 for 9/11 and .006 for 11/12. These probabilities are based on the null hypothesis that every S is equally likely to recognize either class of words more readily; both tails of the binomial distribution are thus used.

Thus the superiority of set words to both homonyms and controls is reasonably reliable, while there is no discernible difference between homonyms and controls. This substantiates the hypothesis that the set does not merely raise the probabilies of certain verbal responses, but rather facilitates the perception of specific visual paterns.

SUMMARY

Twelve Ss were given a list of ten words to study for 1 min. Tachistoscopic duration thresholds were secured on five words from this list, five words which were homonyms of items on the list, and five control words. A balanced design was used. The results indicate that the preliminary presentation facilitated the recognition of specific items on the list, but in no way facilitated the recognition of their homonyms. Since the same verbal response is employed in reporting a homonym as in reporting the word itself, it appears that the effect of a set of this type is to facilitate recognition processes without generally facilitating the corresponding verbal responses. This conclusion may be related to certain recurrent problems in the interpretation of perceptual data.

REFERENCES

1. GRAHAM, C. H. Visual perception. In S. S. Stevens (Ed.), *Handbook of experimental psychology*. New York: Wiley, 1951, pp. 868-920.
2. HOWES, D. H., and SOLOMON, R. L. Visual duration threshold as a function of word-probability. *J. exp. Psychol.*, 1951, **41**, 401-410.
3. KUPPERIAN, J. E., and GOLIN, E. An electronic tachistoscope. *Amer. J. Psychol.*, 1951, **64**, 274-276.
4. McGINNIES, E. Emotionality and perceptual defense. *Psychol. Rev.*, 1949, **56**, 244-251.
5. OSGOOD, C. E. *Method and theory in experimental psychology.* New York: Oxford Univ. Press, 1953.

SELECTION 47

....

Accuracy of Recognition with Alternatives Before and After the Stimulus*,1

Douglas H. Lawrence and George R. Coles

It has been clearly demonstrated that a subject's accuracy in recognizing tachistoscopically presented stimuli improves when he is told in advance that the object will be one of a limited number of alternatives. There is no common agreement, however, concerning the manner in which this restriction of alternatives facilitates the recognition process. Some investigators speak of "tuning the organism," of "selective sensitization," and of like influences with the seeming implication that the presentation of alternatives modifies S's perception of the stimulus. If the term perception is limited to the actual activity occurring *during the interval of stimulus presentation,* these terms suggest that S's knowledge of what can be expected results in his accentuating those characteristics of the stimulus that are relevant to distinguishing between the alternatives and suppressing those characteristics that are irrelevant to this discrimination. This possibility is strongly suggested by the work of Yokoyama (1) and Chapman (2). Such modification of the perceptual process is to be distinguished from changes that might occur in the memory trace or in the availability of responses as the result of the presentation of alternatives. The present study attempts to evaluate the relative contributions to the accuracy of recognition of these three possibilities: perceptual modification, memory trace modification, and availability of response.

* From the *J. exp. Psychol.,* 1954, **47**, 208-214. Reprinted by permission of the authors and the publisher.

1 This experiment is one in a series of studies of problem solving being done under Project NR 150-104 and supported by Contract Nonr 225(02) between Stanford University and the Office of Naval Research. Work on the contract is under the general direction of Dr. Donald W. Taylor. Permission is granted for reproduction, translation, publication, use, and disposal of this article in whole or in part by or for the United States Government.

If the major facilitative effect of alternatives is due to the fact that they modify the actual perception during the stimulus presentation, then it follows that this facilitative effect should occur only when the alternatives are given prior to the stimulus, and that it should disappear when the same alternatives are not presented until after the stimulus exposure. Selective perception can operate only when the organism is "set" for the stimulus. If this expected differential effect between alternatives presented before and after a stimulus fails to occur, it rules against the perceptual modification hypothesis.

It would still be possible to argue, however, that two different processes are involved. When the alternatives are presented prior to the stimulus the perception is actually modified, but when presented after the stimulus they facilitate recognition by operating on the memory trace. This two-factor hypothesis can be tested if additional assumptions are made about the relationship between the perception and its memory trace. It seems reasonable to assume that the perception is a "richer," more adequate representation of the stimulus object than is the memory trace. The trace will contain fewer of the stimulus aspects than the perception, or else contain them in a distorted form.

If this assumption is justified, then discrete alternatives should tend to be equally effective when presented before or after the stimulus, but similar alternatives should have a differential effect under the two conditions. By discrete alternatives is meant those that lead the subject to expect possible perceptual experiences that have little overlap in attributes or characteristics such as color, form, or the like. With such alternatives even a "poor" trace should contain sufficient aspects of the initial perception to permit a discrimination between alternatives. Thus there would be relatively little decrement in the accuracy of recognition when such alternatives are presented after the stimulus rather than before. With similar alternatives, however, there should be a differential effect. By similar alternatives is meant those that lead S to expect possible perceptual experiences that overlap in many characteristics and are differentiated on only a relatively few. If such alternatives are presented prior to the stimulus, it is still possible for S to accentuate the discriminating characteristics while suppressing the overlapping ones. When presented after the stimulus, however, it is to be expected, on a probability basis, that many of these discriminating characteristics will have dropped out or have been distorted in the trace so that the accuracy of recognition will decrease. Thus in terms of the two-factor hypothesis there should be a measurable interaction between the type of alternative used and whether the alternatives are presented before or after the stimulus.

METHOD

Subjects and Materials. Sixty undergraduates, divided approximately equally between men and women, were used as Ss. The stimuli consisted of 50 black-white pictures of familiar objects cut from magazines. In most instances the background of the picture was homogeneous but in a few it contained shadows, landscapes, and the like. The tachistoscope consisted of an opaque projector with a calibrated camera shutter mounted in front of the lens.

The pictures were divided randomly into five sets of ten pictures each. For each picture two sets of alternatives were constructed, each consisting of the names of four objects including the correct name for the object shown. The first set consisted of discrete alternatives (DA) and the second of similar alternatives (SA). The alternatives were constructed in the following rough manner. The four names in the DA set selected by the Es and two judges were names which denoted perceptually discrete objects; i.e., the objects denoted had very little similarity in terms of form, pattern of light and dark areas, and like characteristics when viewed tachistoscopically. In constructing the SA the Es were aided by four judges who viewed the pictures tachistoscopically and then listed a series of objects that would appear similar to the picture exposed. The assumption was made that if the stimulus object suggested these alternatives with about equal frequency, they, in turn, when presented to S would suggest quite similar perceptual objects. Care was taken in constructing both sets of alternatives to have the correct names for the 50 pictures appear with equal frequency in each of the four possible positions of the set.

Conditions. The 60 Ss were divided randomly into three groups of 20 each. The first group (AB) was given the set of four alternatives just before viewing the picture, the second group (AF) was given the set of four alternatives immediately following the presentation of the picture, and the third group (AN) viewed the pictures but was not given any alternatives.

The reason for including the AN group in the present design was to demonstrate that the sets of alternatives used actually did facilitate the identification of the stimuli. Unless it can be shown that the AB and AF groups are superior to the AN group, it can be argued that Ss were not using the alternatives to any extent, that they were relying on recall memory for the identification, and that consequently there would be no reason to expect a differential effect between alternatives presented before and those presented following the stimuli.

Procedure. The Ss were seated at a table 14 ft. from the screen and directly in front of it. A fluorescent overhead light directly in back of them was left on to facilitate the marking of the scoring sheets, to reduce the contrasts in the picture so as to increase the difficulty of identification, and to reduce any possible effect of after-images. The procedure for Group AB was to project the set of four alternatives on the screen for 30 sec., remove them, and immediately afterwards to expose the picture. As soon as each S had marked his paper, the next set of alternatives was presented. In the case of Group AF, the picture was exposed and immediately afterwards the alternatives were presented for 30 sec. Only the pictures were exposed for Group AN, but they were spaced at the same average intervals as for the other two groups. All Ss were instructed in the appropriate procedure and then shown a demonstration picture tachistoscopically. In addition, the AB and AF groups were shown a demonstration set of alternatives.

Experimental Design. The experimental design is shown in Table 1. Five different exposure times were used, 1/50, 1/25, 1/10, 1/5, and 1/2 sec.

TABLE 1. EXPERIMENTAL DESIGN

Subgroups	Exposure Time in Seconds				
	.02	.04	.10	.20	.50
	SA & DA	SA & DA	SA & DA	SA & DA	SA & DA
I	A_1	B_3	C_5	D_2	E_4
II	B_2	C_4	D_1	E_3	A_5
III	C_3	D_5	E_2	A_4	B_1
IV	D_4	E_1	A_3	B_5	C_2
V	E_5	A_2	B_4	C_1	D_3

The capital letters in the table represent the five different subsets of ten stimuli each that were used. Five of these pictures in each subset were presented with SA and five with DA alternatives. The numbers in the table represent the trials or order of presentation of the stimulus subsets and time intervals. Five Ss were assigned at random to the five sequences represented by the rows. This design was replicated four times for each group of 20 Ss. In two of these replications the five stimuli in a subset having SA alternatives in the present table had DA alternatives, and the five having DA had SA. This difference between replications was ignored in the analysis of the data. In the case of the 20 Ss in Group AN, of course, the SA versus DA was a dummy contrast.

Scoring. The two groups with alternatives were given scoring sheets on which they checked a number from 1 to 4 depending on which one of the numbered alternatives shown them they thought identified the object. Group AN wrote in the name of the object. These Ss were instructed always to write in some object even though it involved guessing. The answers of this group were scored correct if, in the opinion of two judges, the name clearly indicated the object even though it was not the specific alternative presented to the other groups. Because of the difference in scoring, no generalizable conclusions can be reached about the relative superiority of recall and recognition memory. Nonetheless, if the AB and the AF groups are superior to the AN group, it supports the contention that in this experiment at least the presence of alternatives actually facilitated the identification of the stimuli.

RESULTS

The accuracy of each of the three groups, as measured in terms of the percentage of pictures correctly identified at each exposure time, is shown in Fig. 1, the uncorrected data in the left panel and the same data corrected for chance in the right. The correction for chance was made by scoring each S in the two groups with alternatives on the basis of the number of correct minus one-third the number wrong. This correction is based on the assumption that all the errors made were equally distributed between the four alternatives.

The curves indicate increasing accuracy for all groups with increasing exposure time. Both Group AB and Group AF appear superior to Group AN in this specific situation, but there is no apparent difference between Groups AB and AF. Thus while the sets of four alternatives seem to improve the accuracy of recognition, it apparently makes no difference whether they are given before or after the presentation of the stimulus.

The first statistical check on the data was made to determine if the presence of alternatives before the stimulus significantly increased the accuracy of identification over what would be expected from pure recall alone. For this purpose each S in Group AB was given two scores, the number of SA and the number of DA correctly identified. Each *S* in Group AN was given a score which was one-half the total number correctly identified. The two averages of the AB group were then compared with the average of the AN group by means of *t* tests. In each instance Group AB was superior beyond the .01 level of significance. These tests were then repeated after the scores in Group AB had been corrected for guessing. Again both tests indicated that the latter group was superior to Group AN beyond the .01 level of significance. These results clearly indicate that both the DA and SA used in this experiment improved the accuracy of identification to a greater extent than could be accounted for on the hypothesis of more accurate guessing because of the restriction in alternatives. Thus the evidence suggests that the stimuli and the alternatives used in this experiment are appropriate for a test of the hypothesis that there should be an interaction effect between the type of alternative used and whether the alternatives are presented before or after the stimulus.

The contrast of the DA and SA groups in Fig. 1 indicates that the former permit a more rapid improvement in recognition with increasing exposure time than do the latter, but that this difference tends to be independent of whether the alternatives come before or

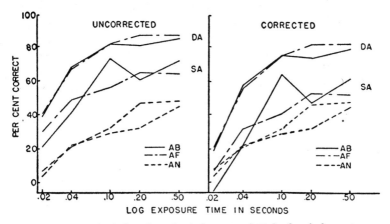

FIG. 1. Each point is based on the judgments of 20 *Ss*, five judgments per *S*. The symbols DA and SA stand for discrete alternatives and similar alternatives, and the symbols AB, AF, and AN, respectively, indicate groups with the alternatives presented before and after the stimulus and a group with no alternatives presented. The two AN curves represent a dummy contrast between the DA and SA.

after the stimulus. It is true that the curves in Fig. 1 suggest that there might be a difference between Groups AB and AF on the similar alternatives, especially at the .1-sec. exposure. But it should be noted that equally large variations are found in the dummy contrast between the two AN groups which experimentally were treated exactly alike.

The statistical significance of these comparisons is confirmed by the analysis of variance presented in Table 2. This analysis compares Groups AB and AF on the basis of uncorrected scores only. This analysis emphasizes four main points: (a) according to Bartlett's test for homogeneity of variances, the three interactions involving individuals are not significantly different; (b) this same test indicates that the remaining interactions between experimental variables are homogeneous; (c) of the experimental variables, only the SA versus the DA and the various time intervals significantly influenced the accuracy of recognition whereas neither the different stimulus sets nor the successive trials showed such an influence; and (d) there is no evidence of a differential influence between alternatives given before and those given after the stimulus or of an interaction between this variable and the type of alternative employed.

One further analysis of the data was made to check on the basis of the superiority of the DA over the SA. It is possible that the DA were so chosen that only two of the three incorrect alternatives were used. If this were so, it could mean that the difference between the DA and the SA was not due to a differential facilitative effect on identification. Instead it could mean that the superiority of the DA was the result of more accurate guessing due to this greater restriction of alternatives. As a rough check on this possibility, the 18 pictures were selected on which the total errors for the combined AB and AF groups were five or more on the DA and five or more on the SA. Using the distribution of errors between the three wrong alternatives, two measures of uncertainty (3) were computed for each picture, one for the DA set and one for the SA set. This measure has the value of 1.58 when the errors are equally distributed between the three wrong alternatives, and decreases as the distribution becomes unequal. The weighted average of these 18 uncertainty measures for the DA was 1.18 and for the SA it was 1.32. In each instance the average value indicates some discrepancy from perfect equality of distribution, but it is doubtful if these discrepancies are much larger than would be expected by chance for such

Table 2. Analysis of Variance of Uncorrected Scores for
Groups AB and AF

Source	df	Variance
1. Alt. before vs. after	1	0.25
2. Discrete vs. similar alt.	1	86.49*
3. Time	4	69.29*
4. Stimulus sets	4	2.58
5. Trials	4	3.93
6. Subgroups	4	2.12
7. Confounded interactions		
a. (3 × 4 × 5 × 6)	8	1.73
b. 1 × (3 × 4 × 5 × 6)	8	0.39
c. 2 × (3 × 4 × 5 × 6)	8	1.07
d. 1 × 2 × (3 × 4 × 5 × 6)	8	0.48
8. Unconfounded interactions		
a. 1 × 2	1	0.36
b. 1 × 3	4	1.78
c. 1 × 4	4	0.77
d. 1 × 5	4	1.03
e. 1 × 6	4	0.81
f. 2 × 3	4	0.55
g. 2 × 4	4	1.37
h. 2 × 5	4	3.50
i. 2 × 6	4	4.08
j. 1 × 2 × 3	4	1.59
k. 1 × 2 × 4	4	0.31
l. 1 × 2 × 5	4	0.33
m. 1 × 2 × 6	4	1.73
9. Individuals treated alike	30	1.67
a. 2 × 9	30	0.94
b. 9 × conditions	120	0.87
c. 2 × 9 × conditions	120	0.82

* Beyond the .01 level of significance.

small samples of errors. Similarly, while the mean of the DA is somewhat smaller than that of the SA, only 12 of the 18 comparisons showed a difference in this direction while the remainder showed it in the opposite direction. Thus while the evidence is very tentative, it suggests that the errors tended to be distributed evenly between the three incorrect alternatives and that there was no real difference between the DA and the SA in this respect.

DISCUSSION

The fact that alternatives presented both before and after the stimulus facilitate the recognition of tachistoscopically presented stimuli to an equal extent is clearly contrary to any hypothesis implying that perception is modified during the interval of stimulus presentation. Thus when the alternatives are said to "tune" or "set" the organism for "selective perception," it cannot be taken to mean that the reception of the stimulus complex is different from what it would be if those alternatives had not been presented. Rather it must be interpreted as meaning that the facilitative effect of alternatives probably results from their interaction with the memory trace. It is conceivable that even when the alternatives are presented prior to the stimulus, their actual influence is checked until after the reception of the stimulus event, especially with tachistoscopic exposures. An alternative to this emphasis on the memory trace is that the influence of alternatives is primarily on the response variables in the sense of making available or facilitating the occurrence of responses that otherwise would not be made.

These latter two hypotheses are made more plausible by the finding that there is no measurable interaction between the type of alternative used and whether the alternatives are presented before or after the stimulus. If taken at its face value, this clearly rules out the possibility that alternatives presented before the stimulus modify the perceptual process but those presented afterwards operate upon the memory trace. It should be emphasized that the stimuli and alternatives employed in this experiment appear to be quite appropriate for a test of this interaction hypothesis. The initial statistical analysis indicated that in Group AB both the DA and the SA facilitated identification to a greater extent than could be accounted for on the assumption that only recall memory was involved and that the greater accuracy was due to improved guessing as the result of a restriction in alternatives. The analysis in terms of uncertainty measures also tended to rule out this possible explanation of the superiority of the DA over the SA. Consequently, if there were a real interaction between type of alternative and whether they were present before or after the stimulus in this experiment, the sets of alternatives used were sensitive enough to measure it. Despite this, no evidence of such an interaction effect was found.

The generality of these findings is restricted by the present experimental design. It is possible that an increase in the number of alternatives beyond four, an increase in the time interval between the alternatives and the stimulus presentation, or even a more sensitive index of what is perceived would show a differential in favor of the alternatives presented prior to the stimulus. It should be noted, however, that even the present emphasis on the role of the memory trace would predict a differential in favor of alternatives presented prior to the stimulus when the temporal interval between the stimulus and alternatives is lengthened. With the prior alternatives, there is little reason to anticipate that they will be forgotten over relatively long intervals. Consequently, their full influence on the memory image can take effect immediately after the presentation of the stimulus. With alternatives presented after the stimulus, their influence on the trace cannot take place until after the delay interval. During this interval, however, there should be a progressive forgetting of the trace. In such circumstances it is to be expected that alternatives presented after the stimulus would be less effective than those presented prior to the stimulus. It is only when the interval is very brief, as in the present study, that strict equality would obtain. A similar argument applies to an increase in the number of alternatives. Increasing the alternatives implies that the number of discriminating characteristics between them become more restricted, and thus are more likely to be lost in the trace. With these further implications in mind an even stronger argument can be made for the parsimony of the present hypothesis that the alternatives facilitate the recognition process by operating on the memory trace or the responses rather than by modifying the perception itself.

SUMMARY

Sixty Ss, divided into three groups of 20 each, were shown tachistoscopically presented pictures at various exposure intervals and asked to identify them. The control group had no alternatives presented to it, whereas the two experimental groups each had a set of four alternatives specified for each stimulus. One experimental group had the alternatives presented before the stimulus exposure and the other group following the exposure. The alternatives were of two types: (a) SA, or very similar alternatives all suggesting perceptually similar objects, and (*b*) DA, or discrete alternatives all suggesting perceptually different objects. The results and the interpretations made were as follows:

1. The two groups with alternatives were superior to the control group without alternatives in accuracy of recognition even when allowance was made for guessing.

2. Alternatives before and after the stimulus facilitated recognition to an equal extent.

3. The facilitative effect of DA was consistently greater than that of the SA at all exposure times, but there was no evidence of an interaction effect between the type of alternative and when it was presented in relation to the stimulus exposure.

4. These results tend to rule out the hypothesis that the facilitative effect of alternatives results from an actual modification of perception and support the hypothesis that they operate either on the memory trace or response aspects of the recognition process.

REFERENCES

1. BORING, E. G. Attribute and sensation. *Amer. J. Psychol.*, 1924, **35,** 301-304.
2. CHAPMAN, D. W. Relative effects of determinate and indeterminate *Aufgaben. Amer. J. Psychol.*, 1932, **44,** 163-174.
3. NEWMAN, E. B. Computational methods useful in analyzing series of binary data. *Amer. J. Psychol.*, 1951, **64,** 252-262.

SELECTION 48

....

Personality Dynamics and Auditory Perceptual Recognition*,†

RICHARD S. LAZARUS, CHARLES W. ERIKSEN, AND
CHARLES P. FONDA

THERE HAVE BEEN many recent experiments which have studied the relationships between perceptual behavior and need states. The study which we are reporting here is basically personality-centered. This means that we have used perceptual behavior as a means of studying personality dynamics.

An extensive bibliography dealing with the correlations between needs and values and perceptual recognition thresholds for need-related stimuli has accumulated. A few examples of experiments in this area may be noted (1, 2, 5, 6, 7, 8, 9). Along with these experiments has come a great deal of controversial discussion concerning the nature of the relationships. Many of the articles in this area have been concerned with the nature of the perceptual process itself. In this paper we are not concerned with the controversial issues concerning the definition of perception. Regardless of the types of mechanisms and processes which may be involved, we believe that the obtained correlations afford an excellent opportunity to study personality dynamics. Clinical psychologists and personality theorists have always had as a main objective the analysis of the motive systems of the individual and the ways in which he deals with them. That defense mechanisms manifest themselves through such psycho-

* From *J. Pers.,* 1951, **19**, 471-482. Reprinted by permission of the authors and the publisher.

† The authors are grateful for the co-operation of the Veterans Administration, the staff of the V. A. Mental Hygiene Clinic, Baltimore, Maryland, and particularly to Dr. Edward L. Slockbower, Chief Psychologist of this clinic. The conclusions and opinions expressed in this article are those of the authors and do not necessarily reflect the views of the Veterans Administration.

Much of the data was collected by Gordon T. Heistad, whose efforts on behalf of this study are also appreciated.

logical processes as learning and retention has not been subject to argument. We have begun again to believe that perceptual behavior may also reflect such dynamic processes.

Let us consider some of the ways in which perceptual behavior may be used to study personality dynamics. The extent to which perceptions are accurate should give clues as to the strength of the relevant needs as well as the "reality contact" of the individual. For example, the extent to which the individual fails to recognize what other people agree is there may be analogous to the personality concept of "ego strength." A strong ego can, presumably, perceive even those things which threaten it. The type of effect upon perception, sensitization, or defense may indicate the acceptability of the need for the individual as well as something about the form of the ego defense mechanism involved. Experiments by Eriksen (2, 3) and McClelland and Liberman (6) constitute a start in this direction.

The present study is a part of a project which has been organized to study personality mechanisms through perceptual behavior. We believe that with our present state of knowledge, the highest priority should be given to determining the extent of these relationships between personality variables measured by clinical instruments and perceptual behavior. Particular consideration should be given to the identification of the various personality variables that may be involved in either inhibiting or accentuating the perception of emotionally threatening material.

In this report we are concerned with the expression of sexual and aggressive needs on a sentence completion test and the auditory recognition of sexual and aggressive material. We have predicted that needs revolving around sex or aggression which are freely expressed in the sentence completion situation will produce relatively high recognition accuracy. Those which are inhibited or repressed will be associated with relatively low recognition accuracy. Moreover, we hypothesized that intellectualizing patients (determined by case history and psychiatric evaluation) would show higher accuracy for threatening material than the repressing type of patient.[1]

---

[1] A brief explanation should be offered concerning the words "intellectualizer" and "represser." By an intellectualizing patient we mean one who talks readily about emotional matters. He freely verbalizes hostility or sexuality, or tends to ruminate about these matters, at least on a superficial level. Repressers, on the other hand, are patients who avoid contact with such emotional material. They are apt to block in the presence of sexual or aggressive stimuli.

In other words, type of ego defense should determine to some extent whether threatening stimuli will or will not be accurately perceived when the conditions producing ambiguity are present.

PROCEDURE

In designing the present study we used auditory rather than visual perceptual recognition. We believed that it offered an ideal medium for producing perceptual effects because of the prominent role of speech in our normal communication and in the learning of responses to anxiety-producing stimuli. Moreover, speech and sound are somewhat ambiguous because of their temporal nature. Once presented they can only be referred to by memory. Vanderplas and Blake (9) have also used this medium in an experiment similar to to one performed by Postman, Bruner, and McGinnies (8).

Stimulus Materials. A recording on wire was made of 48 sentences.[2] The intelligibility of the sentences was controlled in a manner similar to that used in the Harvard Psycho-Acoustic Laboratories. The sentences were presented at a constant speech intensity against a white noise background. By preliminary experimentation a speech-to-noise ratio was established which produced an over-all intelligibility of about 50 per cent. This means that the average subject could hear and report correctly about half of the words in the recording. After each sentence was played the recording was stopped while the subjects wrote down what they had heard. Subjects were encouraged to guess if they were not sure, and to fill in the gaps in what they wrote.

The first three sentences on the record were practice items. Fifteen of the sentences expressed sexual ideas, 15 contained aggressive implications, and 15 were relatively neutral. Within the sexual and hostility categories of sentences there was an equal representation of expression of guilt and inadequacy, and feelings which were expressed toward such objects as mother, father, and peers. In order to prevent systematic bias the categories and subcategories of con-

---

If a patient was diagnosed obsessive-compulsive neurosis, he was placed in the intellectualizing group. Conversion hysterics were classified as repressers. In all other cases, e.g., anxiety state, the case record and psychiatric judgments were screened for differentiating information based upon the above criteria. While we do not believe such a classification technique is without error, it does provide us with a reasonably clear differentiation on the basis of defense mechanism.

[2] The assistance of Wendell R. Garner in arranging the sound system for the wire recording is sincerely acknowledged.

tent were systematically randomized throughout the test. There will be reasonable agreement that the sentences we have chosen will communicate with some of the most important sources of anxiety among psychoneurotic patients. In a preliminary experiment such as this, we believed that the use of broad categories such as sexual, aggressive and neutral, although heterogeneous within themselves, would be most useful in testing the relationships in question.

The diagnostic information was obtained from the use of a sentence completion test of our own construction. The items varied in character from highly structured ones like "Henry was sexually attracted to ———," to more ambiguous cases such as, "His mother ———." We attempted to select some completion items to give the subjects an opportunity to interpret them spontaneously in hostile or sexual terms. Other items were designed to confront the subject with an idea which required a sexual or aggressive interpretation so that we could observe how he dealt with it. The sentence completion test was timed in order to observe differential reaction times to specific items, or blocking as a characteristic response.

Subjects and Procedure. The subjects were 35 literate psychoneurotic patients at the Veterans Administration Mental Hygiene Clinic in Baltimore. Random selection of the cases resulted in a variety of diagnoses, the most prominent of which were obsessive-compulsive neurosis, hysteria, and anxiety state. In order to maintain their co-operation at the highest possible level, the testing was conducted as part of the routine diagnostic procedure of the clinic. Appointments were arranged for each patient by his therapist. The actual testing was done in two sessions. At the first meeting the auditory recognition test was administered in small groups. At the second session the sentence completion test was individually administered.

Scoring. On the auditory recognition test two types of scoring were used. The number of words correctly perceived by the subject (omitting prepositions and conjunctions) in the three content areas was obtained. In addition the record was evaluated for the sentence meaning correctly perceived. This was a more subjective technique which provided three possible values for each sentence: perfect recognition was given a value of two; correct recognition of the main idea even though the words used might be wrong was given a value of one; failure to get the essential elements of the idea was given a value of zero. Table I presents the reliability of this scoring method obtained for two scorers working independently.

TABLE I. SCORING RELIABILITY FOR THE AUDITORY PERCEPTION AND THE SENTENCE COMPLETION TEST

	Auditory Perception (Sense-Perceived)		
	Sexual Sentences	Hostile Sentences	Neutral Sentences
Perfect agreement	94.2%	97.5%	93.3%
Number of items	120	120	120
	Sentence Completion		
	Sexual Sentences	Hostile Sentences	Neutral Sentences
Perfect agreement	83.0%	82.0%	
Number of items	293	135	172

In scoring the sentence completion test we desired to measure two kinds of responses to each of the content areas. Some patients were profuse in their interpretations of aggressive material, and gave spontaneously a great many hostility responses. At the other extreme, some subjects failed to respond at all with hostile associations. Even when forced into it they avoided the hostile implications as much as possible. For example, one of the completion items was, "He hated ———." A subject freely expressing hostility would complete this item with a statement like, "He hated successful people." On the other hand, such responses as the following were not infrequent: "He hated to be caught in the rain without his umbrella." By counting up the number of times the subject responded with an aggressive completion, and by weighting the answer one if it were weak, and two if it were strong, a score was obtained which reflected the subject's readiness to express hostility. A high score meant that the subject gave many such responses. If the subject showed blocking behavior—abnormally long response time, or verbal comments which suggested emotional upset, this was treated as a failure to give a positive answer in this category. The same method of scoring was employed in the sexual category. The results of reliability checks based upon independent scoring may also be found in Table I.

RESULTS

This section contains only the bare data of the experiment. Our first concern is the relation between auditory perceptual recognition of sexual and hostile statements and the clinical evaluation of the corresponding areas on the sentence completion test. We have used three measures of auditory perception. Besides scoring the sentences in terms of the number of words correctly reproduced, and on the basis of sense perceived, we have adjusted the sense perceived scores for differences in "general perceptual acuity" among the subjects. This adjustment amounts to subtracting each subject's score on the neutral sentences from his scores on the sexual and hostility ones.[3] In Table II these three perceptual measures in sex and hostility are correlated with their corresponding areas on the sentence completion test.

TABLE II. THE PRODUCT MOMENT CORRELATIONS BETWEEN
SCORES ON THE SENTENCE COMPLETION TEST AND THE
AUDITORY PERCEPTION MEASURE

	Words Correct	Sense Perceived	Adjusted Sense Perceived
Sex	.60	.74	.64
Hostility	.46	.57	.51

Evaluated via Fisher's z transformation, r's of .43 and .58 are significant at the .01 and the .001 levels, respectively.

Regardless of which of the three measures of perceptual recognition is used, the correlations are high. All are significant beyond the .01 level. The relationships are highest for the uncorrected sense-perceived scores and lowest when the atomistic word count scoring is used.

---

[3] This adjustment technique was used in preference to partial correlation. The best estimate of an individual's perceptual acuity in this situation is his own performance on the neutral material. Empirical evidence for the validity of this technique is shown by zero correlations between the adjusted sex and hostility scores and the neutral scores.

In order correctly to evaluate these correlations it was necessary to determine the intercorrelations of sex and hostility scores within the sentence completion test, within the perceptual test, and between the two tests. Table III shows these intercorrelations when the sense-perceived scoring is used, and Table IV when the adjusted sense-perceived score is used. It will be noticed that the interrelationships among the different measures tend to be quite high, even when the latter scoring method is used. In only two instances do the correlations lack significance at the .05 level.

TABLE III. THE INTERCORRELATIONS OF SENTENCE COMPLETION TEST SCORES AND SENSE PERCEIVED SCORES FOR AUDITORY PERCEPTION

		Sentence Completion		Auditory Perception		
		Sex	Hostility	Sex	Hostility	Neutral
Sentence Completion	Sex		.521	.737	.574	.477
	Hostility			.387	.565	.151
Auditory Perception	Sex				.785	.691
	Hostility					.669

Evaluated via Fisher's z transformation, r's of .336 and .430 are significant at the .05 and the .01 levels respectively.

There is the possibility that differences in perceptual accuracy for the sexual and hostility material could be accounted for in terms of different response preferences among the patients. In other words patients whose incorrect guesses on the auditory recognition test were frequently sexual in nature should on a probability basis obtain a higher accuracy on sexual sentences.

To test this possibility a count was made for each patient of the number of times he wrote incorrect sexual or hostile interpretations of the sentences. This gave us a score which represented his response frequency in these two areas. The correlations between these frequency scores and the sense-perceived scores (accuracy) were .161 for hostility and .014 for sex.

TABLE IV. THE INTERCORRELATIONS OF SENTENCE COMPLETION TEST
SCORES AND THE ADJUSTED* SENSE PERCEIVED SCORES FOR
AUDITORY PERCEPTION

		Sentence Completion		Auditory Perception		
		Sex	Hostility	Sex	Hostility	Neutral
Sentence Completion	Sex		.521	.643	.310	.477
	Hostility			.410	.514	.151
Auditory Perception	Sex				.609	.125
	Hostility					−.088

Evaluated via Fisher's z transformation, r's of .336 and .430 are significant at the .05 and the .01 levels, respectively.
   * See text.

We will consider in the discussion section the implications of these correlations. For the present we want to point out that the partial correlation coefficient between sex scores on the sentence completion test and the adjusted sense-perceived score for sex on the perceptual test is .55, with hostility scores on the two tests held constant. The corresponding partial correlation for hostility is .45.

Our second concern was the effect of defense mechanism upon perceptual accuracy. We were able from case history and therapeutic interview data to classify 25 of our subjects into intellectualizers and repressers. The superficial verbal insights and the verbal preoccupation with problems that characterize the intellectual defense led us to predict that this kind of individual would show high perceptual accuracy for the threatening material and ready verbalization of sexual and aggressive concepts. On the other hand repressers are notable for their blocking and inability to deal with threatening material. As a consequence their perceptual accuracy should be low and their sentence completion verbalizations minimal. In Table V a comparison between these two groups is made.

The comparison on the perceptual recognition test is in terms of the adjusted sense-perceived scores. Scores greater than zero indicate that need-related material was perceived better than neutral material. On the sentence completion test high scores indicate less blocking and a greater readiness to verbalize sexual or hostility material.

TABLE V. COMPARISON OF INTELLECTUALIZERS AND REPRESSERS ON PERCEPTUAL RECOGNITION AND SENTENCE COMPLETION TEST

	Repressers (N = 12)		Intellectualizers (N = 13)		
	Mean	S.D.	Mean	S.D.	t
Auditory Perceptual Recognition					
Sex*	−.25	1.18	+1.60	1.48	3.32
Hostility*	−1.10	1.32	+.30	1.25	2.67
Neutral	5.27	1.59	6.17	1.59	1.36
Sentence Completion Test					
Sex	6.20	1.39	9.10	4.52	2.02
Hostility	5.50	1.70	8.00	4.31	1.77

For a one-tailed test, t values of 1.71 and 2.50 are significant at the .05 and the .01 levels, respectively.

* Using adjusted sense-perceived scores (that is, subtracting neutral score from score on critical material—sex and hostility respectively; if less critical material was correctly perceived than neutral, score would be minus).

In accordance with our expectations the intellectualizers show significantly better accuracy in the perception of threatening material. Their performance on the sentence completion test also shows more ready expression in the sexual and hostility areas. But here we must also note the differences in variability. Comparison of the variability of the two groups on the sentence completion test gives an F ratio of 6.46 for hostility and 10.45 for sex. These ratios are significant beyond the .01 and the .001 levels, respectively.

Although the intellectualizers showed greater accuracy in recognition of threatening material, there was *no* tendency on their part to give incorrect sexual or aggressive responses more frequently than the repressers. For the intellectualizers the mean response frequency score for sex was 2.42 and for hostility 3.40. The corresponding means for the repressers were 2.35 and 3.15. The t tests of these mean differences between the intellectualizing and repressing patients did not approach significance at the .20 level.

DISCUSSION

How do these results bear upon the questions we asked in undertaking this experiment? Our first concern was whether correlations would be found between the data from the sentence completion test and auditory recognition scores. As indicated in Table II all of the correlations are quite high. Significant relationships are seen not only when the perceptual records are scored in terms of the sense perceived, but also, to a lesser extent, when a simple word count is used. The lower relationship for the word count scoring was to be expected since the words in the sentences were everyday words. Most of them could be perceived without communicating the threatening ideas in the sentences. An explanation of these results in terms of simple word frequency does not therefore seem to us to be fully appropriate.

There are a few questions we must ask concerning the basis of the correlations between scores on the sentence completion test and scores in the corresponding content areas on the perceptual recognition test. In the first place, can these correlations be understood in terms of such variables as degree of motivation, degree of contact with the environment, and intellectual functioning? For example, does an unco-operative attitude produce low scores on both tests, and vice versa? This possibility appears very unlikely because the correlations are scarcely affected when the sense-perceived scores are adjusted for perceptual performance in the neutral material. This adjustment holds constant individual differences in auditory perceptual acuity and intelligence as well as other irrelevant variables.

A second question concerns the intercorrelations which were found between sexual and aggressive scores on the sentence completion test, within the perceptual recognition test, and between these two tests. These intercorrelations may be accounted for in two ways. First, disturbance in sexual and hostility areas may tend to go together in our culture. Secondly, and somewhat implied by the first, a given individual may have a generalized method of responding to any emotionally threatening material. It is not necessary in any one case for disturbance which occurs to hostility material to be found also with sexual content. But when it does, the same defense appears to be used for both areas. The high partial correlations which were obtained when the contributions of either sex or hostility scores, respectively, are held constant, indicate that the specific meaning of the material is also important.

Something of the nature of this general way of responding can be seen in the analysis of patients diagnosed as intellectualizers on the one hand and repressers on the other. The data from this aspect of the study support our contention and the frequently noted clinical assumption that a general mechanism of ego defense may be employed by an individual when confronted with threat.[4] The intellectualizers perceive more of the threatening material than do the repressers when neutral scores are held constant. Therefore it is possible to observe the defense mechanisms of patients in action by measuring their perceptual accuracy.

Some perceptual theorists (4) may prefer to describe these relationships as measuring common response preferences in the two test situations. They might suggest that the repressers do not have sexual and aggressive words or ideas as easily available as do the intellectualizers. This kind of analysis appears to lead to an overemphasis on such concepts as frequency and recency of ideas and words as determiners of the readiness to respond.

We have no doubt that in many of the experiments that have related values to perceptual recognition the positive correlations can be explained in terms of response frequency. In fact Howes and Solomon (4) and Lazarus and McCleary (5) have presented this kind of evidence. This explanation, however, is superficial. It does not account for the individual differences in response frequency. In personality-centered research this is a most important problem. Why do certain individuals acquire response preferences in one area and not in another?

In addition to the criticism of superficiality, our data suggest some serious limitations to the generality of response frequency as an explanatory concept. You will recall that there was no relationship between response frequency of sexual and aggressive ideas and recognition accuracy for them. The difference between our findings

---

[4] It is possible that the differential accuracy in recognition between the repressers and the intellectualizers may be interpreted as indicating different amounts of threat rather than the effects of different defensive mechanisms. This, however, appears rather unlikely to us.

and those of the above studies may lie in the threatening nature of our stimulus material for psychiatric patients. In any case, it would appear difficult to account for our patients' differential perceptual accuracy on the basis of a simple response frequency concept.

Whatever the concepts we may use to identify the perceptual process we have studied, it is apparent that accuracy of perceptual recognition and clinical diagnostic data are highly related. The behavior in the two situations depends upon both the content of the stimulus material and, for any individual, a characteristic way of responding to threatening stimuli.

Brief mention might be made of a preliminary study which was reported at the APA, September, 1950. The auditory recognition test which we have described here was administered to seven psychotic patients with varied diagnoses at Sheppard-Pratt Psychiatric Hospital in Baltimore. Psychiatrists who knew the patients were able to make fairly accurate independent predictions concerning the kind of performance the patient would give on the recognition of sexual and hostility material.

SUMMARY

This experiment has studied the relationships between performance on a sentence completion test and auditory perceptual recognition of sexual, aggressive, and neutral sentences. A wire recording was used consisting of 48 sentences masked with white noise so that recognition was about 50 per cent accurate. Our sample was composed of 35 Veterans Administration psychiatric outpatients. The following results were obtained:

1. High positive correlations were obtained between performance on the sentence completion test and perceptual accuracy for both the sexual and hostility areas. Accuracy was found to be unrelated to response frequencies in these areas.

2. Two basic reactions to threatening stimuli were found: (a) high perceptual accuracy and ready verbalization; and (b) low perceptual accuracy and minimal verbalization with blocking. Individuals were found to be consistent in their use of either of these basic reactions. For example, if an individual was threatened by both sexual and hostile material the same perceptual mechanism was used in dealing with both.

3. Patients with intellectualizing mechanisms perceived threatening material with significantly greater accuracy than those with

repressing mechanisms. There was no difference in response frequency. The classification of intellectualizers and repressers was based upon case history and therapeutic interview data. It was made independently of the experimental data.

REFERENCES

1. BRUNER, J., and POSTMAN, L. Emotional selectivity in perception and reaction. *J. Pers.*, 1947, **16**, 69-77.
2. ERIKSEN, C. W. Perceptual defense as a function of unacceptable needs. *J. abnorm. soc. Psychol.*, 1951, **46**, 557-564.
3. ERIKSEN, C. W. Some implications for TAT interpretation arising from need and perception experiments. *J. Pers.*, 1951, **19**, 282-288.
4. HOWES, D. H., and SOLOMON, R. L. A note on McGinnies' "Emotionality and perceptual defense." *Psychol. Rev.*, 1950, **57**, 229-234.
5. LAZARUS, R. S., and MCCLEARY, R. A. Autonomic discrimination without awareness: An experiment on subception. *Psychol. Rev.*, 1951, **58**, 113-122.
6. MCCLELLAND, D. C., and LIBERMAN, A. M. The effect of need for achievement on recognition of need-related words. *J. Pers.*, 1949, **18**, 236-251.
7. MCGINNIES, E. Emotionality and perceptual defense. *Psychol. Rev.*, 1949, **56**, 244-251.
8. POSTMAN, L., BRUNER, J., and MCGINNIES, E. Personal values as selective factors in perception. *J. abnorm. soc. Psychol.*, 1948, **43**, 142-154.
9. VANDERPLAS, J. M., and BLAKE, R. R. Selective sensitization in auditory perception. *J. Pers.*, 1949, **18**, 252-256.

••

Is There a Mechanism of Perceptual Defense?*

LEO POSTMAN, WANDA C. BRONSON, AND
GEORGE L. GROPPER

SEVERAL INVESTIGATORS have reported higher thresholds of perceptual recognition for negatively valued or taboo materials than for neutral or positively valued materials (2, 3, 6, 8, 11, 14, 17). *Perceptual defense,* an unconscious mechanism of resistance to recognition of threatening stimuli, has frequently been invoked to explain the differences in speed of recognition. Is such a concept necessary?

Whatever its face validity, it is uneconomical to consider perceptual defense as a special mechanism of *perception* as long as the experimental findings can be subsumed under more general principles. Such reanalysis would deny neither the importance of motivational factors in perception nor their relevance to personality theory. The aim is to formulate the determinants of perceptual behavior at the highest level of generality possible. Many determinants are equally applicable to meaningless and meaningful, need-relevant, and neutral materials. The contributions of specific motivational variables must be evaluated against a base line specified in terms of such general determinants.

A principle of perceptual defense was first considered by Bruner and Postman (2, 11) in explanation of high thresholds for negatively valued and emotionally charged words. The individual tends to ward off the recognition of threatening and inimical stimuli as long as possible within the constraints of the stimulus situation. Although this statement is descriptively true for some situations, it is now clear that the original formulation of the principle of perceptual defense was inadequate because (*a*) it did not specify the

*From the *J. abnorm. soc. Psychol.,* 1953, **48**, 215-224. Reprinted by permission of the authors and the publisher.

mechanisms producing the raised thresholds and (*b*) it failed to consider explanation of the observed facts in terms of more general determinants of perceptual recognition. In a later theoretical statement (9) one of us suggested, for example, that apparently defensive thresholds may be due to the competition of alternative recognition responses (perceptual hypotheses). Interference by competing responses is, of course, a general principle not restricted to emotionally charged materials.

Perceptual defense, as a *special perceptual mechanism,* was affirmed and elaborated in a study by McGinnies (6). In his experiment, McGinnies compared recognition thresholds for emotionally toned taboo words and neutral words. Without exception, thresholds were higher for emotional words than for neutral words. In addition, the Ss' GSR's were measured during the period preceding recognition in an attempt to obtain evidence for systematic reaction to the stimulus words prior to correct verbal report. GSR's prior to recognition of the critical words were found to be significantly greater than those preceding recognition of the neutral words. Finally, Ss' incorrect guesses suggested a tendency actively to avoid recognition of the emotionally toned words. McGinnies considered these findings as strong evidence for the operation of perceptual defense and went on to speculate concerning the neurological mechanisms mediating the unconscious defensive activity.

McGinnies' study precipitated severe criticisms of perceptual defense as an unwarranted *ad hoc* assumption. These criticisms, advanced by Howes and Solomon (4), directly lead to new and critical questions which must be answered experimentally in order to clarify the status of perceptual defense. There are, in the opinion of Howes and Solomon, two more plausible, and simpler, reasons for McGinnies' results. First and foremost, the taboo words used by McGinnies are, according to the Thorndike-Lorge word count (16), much less familiar words than the neutral words with which they were compared. On the basis of the known general relationship between word familiarity and recognition speed (5, 13), lower thresholds for the neutral words are to be expected regardless of differences in emotionality. Second, Howes and Solomon consider it very probable that McGinnies' Ss tended to withhold overt reports of the socially unacceptable words until they were completely sure of having recognized them correctly. McGinnies, however, has defended his original interpretation (7, 8). He is not convinced that the lower thresholds for neutral words can be ascribed to their greater familiarity. The correlation between familiarity and speed of recognition "does not constitute other than circumstantial evidence for the assumption that the higher thresholds of the taboo words were determined by their alleged infrequency of occurrence. If . . . the elevated duration thresholds for these words were a function of their affective connotation, the net regression effect would be the same" (7, p. 237). We can decide between the alternative explanations only by comparing thresholds for neutral and taboo words which have been equated for familiarity.

There is no substantial evidence, according to McGinnies, that *S*s do, in fact, withhold their verbal reports of taboo stimulus words. As a positive indication against the hypothesis of selective verbal report, he presents the finding that recognition thresholds for *neutral* words are raised when these words are exposed immediately following the perception of taboo words (8). These results, he argues, constitute indirect evidence for perceptual defense since the avoidance reaction appears to generalize to temporally adjacent neutral words which the *S* ordinarily has no reluctance to report. We do not believe that these findings represent cogent evidence for perceptual defense or dispose of the problem of selective report. Perceptual defense has been alleged to be an avoidance reaction specific to threatening stimuli and must be demonstrated *as such* before it is appropriate to assert its generalization to neutral stimuli. By the same token, one would not speak of the generalization of a conditioned response before the presence of such a response was established. It is clear that we must attack the problem of selective verbal report directly in order to gauge its contribution to relative thresholds for neutral and taboo words.

Finally, McGinnies feels that the systematic differences between prerecognition responses to neutral and emotional words constitute further evidence for perceptual defense (cf. also 11). He classified the prerecognition responses into four categories: (*a*) *structurally similar,* i.e., words resembling the stimulus words in letter structure; (*b*) *structurally unlike;* (*c*) *nonsense,* i.e., words without dictionary meaning; and (*d*) *part,* i.e., disconnected groups of letters. Proportionately more similar and part responses were given to the neutral words, and proportionately more unlike and nonsense responses to the critical words. McGinnies interprets the greater frequency of unlike and nonsense hypotheses as "tactics apparently designed to delay accurate recognition of the stimulus word" (6, p. 250). Such responses, he argues, represent distortions by which S can avoid seeing the dangerous stimulus. It is difficult to insist on this interpretation because exactly the opposite findings could be equally well reconciled with the hypothesis of perceptual defense. If there were more structurally similar and part responses to the charged words, one could argue that perceptual defense delays final correct organization of the word even though the conditions are adequate for recognition of component parts of the stimulus. Structurally similar and part hypotheses could with great facility be labeled compromises between the impact of the stimulus and S's "resistance to its recognition"! The process of perceptual defense has not been sufficiently specified to make the reported differences in prerecognition responses relevant to its demonstration. Such differences can equally well be ascribed to the uncontrolled variations in the familiarity of the words.

Other recent experiments which have been offered in support of perceptual defense are beset by similar difficulties. Rosenstock (14) compared recognition thresholds for neutral and affectively charged sentences and found the latter subject to perceptual "repression." The only control of familiarity consisted of matching the second clauses of critical and neutral sentences in terms of the "number of meaning units." Clearly *number* of words, syllables, etc. does not provide an estimate of the familiarity of a sentence or part of a sentence. Whether and to what extent the thresholds for the two types of sentences were a function of differential emotional content must remain indeterminate. Eriksen's findings (3) concerning recognition thresholds for neutral and need-relevant pictures are equally difficult to interpret. When need-relevant pictures are recognized more slowly than neutral pictures we cannot speak of defense (or of relative amounts of defense in the case of different pictures) unless and until we have shown that both sets of stimuli have been equated in terms of structural characteristics and familiarity.[1] It should be noted that both Rosenstock and Eriksen instructed their Ss to expect unusual stimuli in order to decrease the likelihood of selective verbal report. The effects of such instructions can be fully eval-

---

[1] These criticisms do not affect the validity of differences among groups of Ss exposed to the same sets of materials. The interpretation of these differences as reflecting various degrees of *defense* is, however, questioned.

uated, however, only by comparison with the effects of other instructions.

The problems raised by these experiments have important general implications. They bring us squarely up against the question whether what appears to be perceptual defense can be reduced to the operation of determinants which are not specifically emotional. The controversy can be resolved only by direct experimental confrontation of the alternative explanations. If the difference between thresholds for emotional and neutral words can be varied at will by manipulating factors other than the emotional significance of the stimulus words, the status of perceptual defense will be rendered highly doubtful.

METHOD

Major variables. This experiment represents an extension and modification of McGinnies' study on perceptual defense. In the light of the criticisms advanced against McGinnies' findings and interpretations, the effects of two variables on recognition thresholds for neutral and taboo words were investigated: (*a*) the relative familiarity of the two classes of stimuli and (*b*) conditions affecting Ss' set and readiness to give verbal reports of taboo words. The hypothesis was tested that it was the failure to take these variables into account which was largely responsible for the threshold differences observed by McGinnies. It follows from this hypothesis that the difference between thresholds can be increased or decreased in predictable ways by proper manipulation of the variables of familiarity and set.

The factor of familiarity. Control of familiarity was achieved by the following procedure. Like McGinnies, we used seven taboo words and eleven neutral words. The taboo words were the same as those used by McGinnies. Each of the taboo words was matched in familiarity with a neutral control word by means of the Thorndike-Lorge semantic count (16). The remaining four neutral words had frequencies of usage corresponding to the average frequency of the taboo words. Two of the taboo words, which do not appear in the Thorndike-Lorge semantic count, were matched with control words having a frequency of one (i.e., one in 4½ million words) according to the semantic count.[2] The list of stimulus words and their frequency values appear in Table 1.

The question may be raised whether equating of familiarity in terms of the Thorndike-Lorge word count is appropriate. This count is based

---

[2] Such an estimate is appropriate in view of the probability (discussed below) that the frequency of taboo words is systematically underestimated by the Thorndike-Lorge count.

TABLE 1. LIST OF STIMULUS WORDS. WORDS ARE LISTED IN THE
ORDER OF PRESENTATION. TABOO WORDS ARE IN ITALICS

Word	Frequency Value*	Word	Frequency Value*
lotus	10	*kotex*	1**
capon	10	mixer	1
raped	13	terse	4
lathe	11	*penis*	1**
belly	47	hilly	10
noted	45	knack	13
cleat	1	*filth*	4
whore	4	clove	4
tiara	4	*bitch*	4
	Av. taboo	10.6	
	Av. neutral	10.3	

* Frequency of occurrence in $4\frac{1}{2}$ million words according to the Thorndike-Lorge semantic count.
** Estimated frequency.

on the frequency with which words appear in a broad sample of literary sources. Taboo words probably appear less frequently in written English than they do in conversation, and hence the word count may systematically underestimate their frequency of usage. It should be remembered, however, that the tachistoscopic presentation of words (used by both McGinnies and ourselves) creates essentially a *reading* situation for the Ss. An estimate of frequency based on usage in reading material is, therefore, reasonable. On the other hand, it is not known to what extent visual duration thresholds are influenced by the frequency of spoken as well as written usage. The possibility must be acknowledged, therefore, that we have underestimated the familiarity of the taboo words. Such an error would not, however, vitiate the test of the experimental hypothesis. According to McGinnies, the difference between thresholds for neutral and taboo words is due to a defensive reaction and is not primarily determined by their relative familiarity. Thresholds for taboo words should be *higher* even if the control of familiarity is short of perfect. Application of the familiarity hypothesis, on the other hand, would predict *lower* thresholds for taboo words if their frequency had been systematically underestimated, or *equal* thresholds if the estimate were correct.

The factor of selective verbal report. If Ss deliberately withhold their reports of taboo words, the thresholds for such words would appear to be unduly high. The possibility that *Ss*' reports are deliberately suppressed or falsified exists in every perceptual experiment and can never be completely discarded. In the case of recognition of taboo words, this problem may be critical since *Ss* have to give verbal responses which they have presumably been taught to avoid. It is futile to argue after the fact whether or not there was such deliberate suppression or falsification. We can, however, attempt to manipulate explicitly the conditions which we believe contribute to *Ss*' readiness to report faithfully what they perceive. The resulting changes in perceptual response can then provide us with an estimate of the amount of variance attributable to *Ss*' readiness to report.

In this experiment, manipulation of *Ss*' readiness to report taboo words was attempted in two ways: (*a*) by preliminary instructions and (*b*) by varying the *S-E* relationship.

Four different sets of instructions were used. The *Uninformed Group* was given the usual instructions for tachistoscopic recognition, without any indication that taboo words would be included among the stimuli:

> This is an experiment on visual perception. We want to find out how well you can recognize words that are presented for short periods of time. When I say "Ready," fixate your eyes on this screen. About one second later a word will be flashed for a brief period of time and will appear on the screen. As soon as the word has been flashed on, write down everything you saw or thought you saw, including single letters, on the record sheet.

The *Informed Group* was given the same general instructions, with the following additional statement informing them of the presence of taboo words among the stimuli:

> Some of the words which will be shown are of the kind not commonly used in polite society, especially in the presence of members of the opposite sex. Remember, some, not all, of the words that we will show are of this type.

The instructions given to the *Facilitation Group* were designed to discourage *Ss* from withholding reports of taboo words. These *Ss* were given the same instructions as the Informed Group with the following additional statement:

> It has been found that some people find it difficult to recognize such words when they are presented for brief periods of time and are anxious about reporting them when they have seen them. In general, difficulties in seeing and reporting such words are a sign of emotional trouble. Some types of patients show this difficulty to a severe degree.

Finally, the *Inhibition Group* was given instructions designed to maximize the tendency to withhold reports of taboo words. These *S*s were given the same instructions as the Informed Group but with this additional statement:

> It has been found that some people find it difficult to recognize such words when they are presented for brief periods of time and are anxious about reporting them when they have seen them. In general, difficulties in seeing and reporting such words are a sign of good mental adjustment. Most normal people show this kind of reaction to some extent, particularly people who are socially successful.

To the extent that these different instructions were effective in manipulating *S*s' set and readiness to report taboo words, we would expect the measured thresholds for taboo words to be (*a*) lower for the Informed Group than the Uninformed Group, and (*b*) lower for the Facilitation Group than the Informed Group, since the former is both informed about the presence of taboo words *and* encouraged to report them. It would be difficult to predict exactly where the Inhibition Group should fall since it has the advantage of expecting the appearance of taboo words but is discouraged from reporting them. In any event, the thresholds of the Inhibition Group for taboo words should be higher than those of the Facilitation Group.

An additional experimental treatment was introduced in a further attempt to manipulate *S*s' readiness to report. Most of the taboo words are of a kind that one would be particularly reluctant to use in the presence of the opposite sex. Deliberate withholding of taboo words might be expected to occur more often in the presence of an *E* of the opposite sex than in the presence of an *E* of the same sex. Two *E*s—one male and one female—were, therefore, used in the experiment. Under each of the four major experimental conditions, each *E* tested two groups of *S*s, one group of males and one group of females. There were, therefore, 16 different experimental subgroups. Each of the subgroups consisted of 6 *S*s, giving a total of 96 *S*s.

Subjects. The *S*s were undergraduate students at the University of California who had volunteered for the experiment. They were assigned to the various experimental conditions at random. The *S*s did not know the purpose of the experiment.[3]

Apparatus and procedure. The stimulus words, typed in capital letters, were shown on 2 × 2 lantern slides. The slides were exposed on a ground-glass screen from a projector equipped with photographic shutter. The

---

[3] Members of the Facilitation Group and Inhibition Group were, of course, disabused concerning the instructions at the end of the experimental session but admonished not to discuss the experiment with others.

speed of exposure was held constant at .01 sec. The threshold was approached by increasing the brightness of the exposure flash in even steps. Each successive exposure represented an increase of 1.3 volts. Each slide was exposed 18 times, which was sufficient in virtually all cases for correct recognition of the word. The Ss were tested in groups of three. They wrote their responses on prearranged record sheets, using a separate sheet for each word.

RESULTS

Analysis of Recognition Thresholds. The number of exposures required for correct recognition of a word was used as a measure of the threshold. As usual, Ss' tachistoscopic acuity varied widely. In

TABLE 2. SUMMARY OF ANALYSIS OF VARIANCE OF
RECOGNITION THRESHOLDS

Source	df	Sum of Squares	Mean Sum of Squares	F	p
Stimulus Words	1	598.55	598.55	98.12	<.01
Sex of Ss	1	1.17	1.17	—	—
Sex of E	1	0.42	0.42	—	—
Conditions	3	4.31	1.44	—	—
Stimulus Words × Conditions	3	48.67	16.22	2.66	.05
Stimulus Words × Sex of Ss	1	30.88	30.88	5.06	.01-.05
Stimulus Words × Sex of E	1	2.76	2.76	—	—
Conditions × Sex of Ss	3	6.22	2.07	—	—
Conditions × Sex of E	3	4.06	1.35	—	—
Sex of E × Sex of Ss	1	2.30	2.30	—	—
Stimulus Words × Conditions × Sex of Ss	3	20.03	6.67	1.09	—
Stimulus Words × Conditions × Sex of E	3	62.23	20.74	3.40	.01-.05
Stimulus Words × Sex of E × Sex of Ss	1	17.58	17.58	2.88	—
Conditions × Sex of E × Sex of Ss	3	14.28	4.76	—	—
Pooled Error*	163	994.62	6.10		
Total	191	1808.08			

* Individual differences among Ss treated alike and the third-order interaction, which were not significant, were included in the error term.

order to make the relative thresholds for neutral and emotional words independent of S's acuity level, each S's threshold measures were converted into standard scores. All tabulations and comparisons will be presented in terms of standard scores. Table 2 presents the summary of an analysis of variance performed on the transformed threshold data. We shall refer to the results of this analysis throughout our discussion of the experimental results.

Average Thresholds for Neutral and Emotional Words. Table 3 shows the average recognition thresholds for neutral and emotional words for the four major experimental groups and for all groups combined. Under all conditions, the thresholds for taboo words are *lower* than the thresholds for neutral control words. This difference is highly significant. Clearly, there is no evidence here for perceptual defense. Taboo words are recognized sooner than neutral words, probably because of a systematic underestimation of the familiarity of the taboo words. When neutral words no longer have the advantage of greater familiarity, the raised thresholds for taboo words disappear. In fact, the *direction* of the difference in recognition thresholds has been changed by manipulation of the familiarity variable.[4]

The Effects of Preparatory Instructions. As Table 3 and Fig. 1 show, the observed relative thresholds for neutral and emotional words vary with the instructions given at the beginning of the experiment. The interaction, Conditions × Stimulus Words, is statistically significant. The Uninformed Group has higher relative thresh-

TABLE 3. AVERAGE RECOGNITION THRESHOLDS (STANDARD SCORES) FOR
TABOO AND NEUTRAL WORDS UNDER THE DIFFERENT
EXPERIMENTAL CONDITIONS

Group	Taboo Words	Neutral Words
Uninformed	−.11	.10
Informed	−.22	.14
Facilitation	−.29	.20
Inhibition	−.20	.14
All Groups	−.20	.14

olds for taboo words than any of the groups that had been forewarned about the nature of the stimuli. We may assume that the warning to expect taboo words produced a preparatory set which

[4] Our attention has just been called to a recent communication by McGinnies and Adornetto in the news letter *Cognitive Processes* (compiled by the Department of Psychology, University of Alabama). They report an experiment in which a group of normals and a group of schizophrenics were tested with taboo words (the same as used previously) and neutral words equated for familiarity. They still find higher thresholds for taboo words although the difference is considerably smaller than in McGinnies' original study. For the normal *S*s the difference now is only 8.2 milliseconds as compared with the previously reported difference of 45 milliseconds. The remaining discrepancy between this result and ours may be due, of course, to the different neutral words used. At best, then, the raised thresholds are a "now-you-see-it-now-you-don't" phenomenon once the familiarity factor has been equated.

facilitated recognition of such words. In addition, however, the variations among the forewarned groups suggest that the instructions affected Ss' readiness to report taboo words once they had been recognized. The Facilitation Group, which had been explicitly discouraged from withholding reports of taboo words, has the lowest relative thresholds for such words. This group probably had lower criteria of certainty for reporting emotional words than any other group. The Inhibition Group, which was encouraged to hesitate about reporting taboo words, has higher relative thresholds for emotional words than the Facilitation Group. The results for the Inhibition Group are virtually identical with those in the Informed Group. In the absence of any explicit statement concerning speed

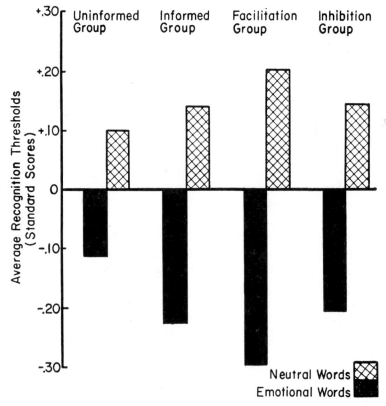

FIG. 1.   Averaged recognition thresholds for taboo and neutral words under the different experimental conditions.

of reporting, the Ss in the Informed Group may have adopted the same cautious criteria for verbal report as did the Ss in the Inhibition Group. It appears, then, that preparatory set and selective verbal report contribute to the observed threshold differences.

Sex Differences. Male Ss recognize taboo words more readily than female Ss (Table 4). This difference is significant. The thresholds of both men and women Ss are, however, equally affected by the nature of the preliminary instructions: the interaction, Conditions × Stimulus Words × Sex of Ss, is not significant.

Experimental-Subject Relationship. Table 4 fails to reveal any tendency for slower recognition of emotional words in the presence of an E of the opposite sex than in the presence of an E of the same sex. If anything, the opposite seems to be the case. The interaction, Stimulus Words × Sex of E × Sex of Ss, is, however, not significant.

TABLE 4. AVERAGE RECOGNITION THRESHOLDS (STANDARD SCORES) FOR TABOO AND NEUTRAL WORDS, GROUPED BY SEX OF E AND SEX OF Ss

Sex of E	Male Ss		Female Ss	
	Taboo Words	Neutral Words	Taboo Words	Neutral Words
Male	−.22	.16	−.22	.15
Female	−.28	.20	−.10	.08
Av.	−.25	.18	−.16	.12

Other Interactions. As Table 2 shows, there is only one other interaction which approaches significance: Stimulus Words × Conditions × Sex of E. Inspection of the data indicates that the female E obtained larger systematic threshold differences from condition to condition than did the male E. All Ss, male and female, tended to conform more to the instructions in the presence of the female E. We do not know, of course, whether this result is a function of the particular Es in this experiment or whether it has wider generality. In any event, this finding confirms the view that the reporting situation may have significant effects on the observed recognition thresholds.

Prerecognition Responses. As we pointed out above, we do not

consider the classification of prerecognition responses used by Mc-
Ginnies crucial to the demonstration of perceptual defense. It is of
interest to point out, however, that we were unable to duplicate his
findings concerning the differential distributions of prerecognition
responses for emotional and neutral words. Table 5 shows the percentages of prerecognition responses for the two types of words
falling into the various content categories used by McGinnies. In
order to make our findings as comparable as possible with his, Table
5 presents only the findings for our Uninformed Group, which was
given the same type of instructions as were his *Ss*. (The distributions of prerecognition responses are, however, substantially the
same for all our groups.) Clearly, there is no systematic difference
between neutral and emotional words with respect to the distributions of prerecognition responses. Our neutral words were, of course,
different from those used by McGinnies. With familiarity held constant, the differences in prerecognition responses, like the raised
thresholds, are absent.

TABLE 5. PERCENTAGES OF PRERECOGNITION RESPONSES FALLING INTO
VARIOUS CONTENT CATEGORIES

Type of Response	Taboo Words	Neutral Words
Similar	18.30	19.96
Part	67.12	64.73
Unlike	3.05	2.32
Nonsense	11.52	12.98

DISCUSSION

Familiarity, Motivation, and Recognition Thresholds. In McGinnies' study, the observed differences in recognition thresholds for
neutral and emotional words could be ascribed either to differences
in familiarity or to the operation of perceptual defense. In our experiment, we have attempted to "untie" these two factors. With
familiarity controlled, there is no indication of perceptual defense.
In fact, the emotional words have lower thresholds, probably because of an underestimation of their familiarity.

One may object at this point that the effects of familiarity and
perceptual defense are not mutually exclusive. Is it not possible

that the relative thresholds for the taboo words would have been even lower had it not been for the operation of perceptual defense? If the familiarity of the emotional words has, in fact, been underestimated, this error may obscure the effects of perceptual defense. In advancing such an argument, one would deprive the concept of perceptual defense of most of its substance. One would concede its effectiveness to be so small as to be counteracted by an error in the estimate of familiarity. In any event, the invocation of an hypothetical effect which is obscured by the operation of a known variable would carry little conviction.

We are emphatically not arguing here that recognition thresholds are completely determined by the sheer frequency with which the subject has been exposed to, and/or has used, the stimulus words. Frequency is a major parameter of whatever processes produce variations in perceptual readiness, whether they be S-R connections, "hypotheses," or what have you. There is some evidence that motivational factors interact with frequency of occurrence to determine readiness for perceptual recognition of words (10, 12, 13). It appears, however, that the taboo characteristics of the words used in this experiment do not produce effects which interact significantly with familiarity. In any event, whatever evidence *is* found for the effectiveness of motivational determinants does not call for a proliferation of special perceptual mechanisms, but is most economically analyzed in the framework of a general theory of perception which provides for the conceptualization of motivational variables (1, 9).[5]

Selective Verbal Report and Recognition Thresholds. The significant variations in thresholds produced by differences in instructions can be interpreted in two alternative ways. We may assume that preliminary information concerning the presence of taboo words (*a*) aroused perceptual expectancies which facilitated recognition of such words (cf. 12, 15, 18), and (*b*) influenced Ss' readiness to report such words. Such an interpretation appears to be in agreement with the general trend of the experimental results. An alternative formulation might assert that the nature of the instructions influenced the degree of perceptual defense. The variations in thresholds produced by instructions may be regarded as evidence of different strengths of "resistance" to the recognition of taboo words. We reject this alternative explanation for the following reasons. First, since

---

[5] McGinnies' recent attempt (8) to translate defense into S-R reinforcement terms represents a move in this direction.

perceptual defense has not been demonstrated in terms of the over-all trends in thresholds, it would be inappropriate to speak of variations in degree of defensive response induced by instructions. Furthermore, and this is the theoretically more important consideration, the processes described by such terms as "defense" or "repression" surely are not to be conceived as subject to significant manipulation by means of preparatory instructions! If they were so manipulable, such defenses or repressions would, indeed, be very different from those described by personality theorists. We prefer, therefore, to think of the instructions as producing variations in Ss' set and selective verbal reports.

Attempts to control Ss' set may, of course, fail. Our manipulation of the E-S relationship did not produce consistent results. (It is possible that this procedure would have been more effective if Ss had been required to report their responses orally rather than to write them down.) Whatever trends did appear, e.g., the tendency toward greater conformity with instructions in the presence of the female E, emphasize the need to consider the influence of *situational* variables on perceptual thresholds.

Sex Differences. The fact that women had significantly higher relative thresholds for emotional words than men is again open to alternative interpretations. "Sex difference" is not a unitary psychological variable. We can only guess as to the characteristics of male and female Ss which result in the threshold differences. Consistently with our general argument, we may assume that female Ss are (a) less familiar than the male Ss with the taboo words used in this experiment, and (b) are less ready to report these words, i.e., may require a somewhat higher level of certainty for reporting.

One may, on the other hand, assert that female Ss are more prone to perceptual defense than are male Ss. Again, we would object to such an explanation because it is inconsistent with the major experimental results. We see, moreover, no cogent theoretical reasons for postulating the type of personality differences between male and female Ss which such an interpretation would require.

The Status of Perceptual Defense. We conclude that the experimental findings to date have failed to lend support to the concept of perceptual defense. The results have been either indeterminate or can be explained in terms of more general principles. It may, of course, be argued that stimuli such as those used by McGinnies and ourselves are not appropriate for testing the hypothesis of perceptual defense. Such may or may not be the case; the possibility of future positive evidence cannot, of course, be excluded. At the present, however, perceptual defense has, at best, the status of an unconfirmed hypothesis.

SUMMARY

The concept of *perceptual defense* has been used to explain raised recognition thresholds for emotional stimuli as compared with neutral stimuli. The invocation of such a principle would, however, appear unnecessary if the facts can be subsumed under more general principles of perceptual behavior. This experiment was designed to answer the question whether there is any evidence for perceptual defense in word recognition when the factors of familiarity, set, and selective verbal report are taken into account.

A series composed of taboo words and neutral words was presented tachistoscopically for recognition. The familiarity of the two types of words was equated as closely as possible by means of the Thorndike-Lorge word count. Four different sets of instructions were used. The Uninformed Group was not given any indication that taboo words would be included among the stimuli. The Informed Group was explicitly warned to expect taboo words. The Facilitation Group was given instructions designed to discourage Ss from withholding reports of emotionally charged words. Finally, the instructions given to the Inhibition Group were intended to maximize Ss' hesitation about the reporting of taboo words. Two different Es, one male and one female, conducted the experiment. Under each of the four major experimental conditions, each E tested both a group of male Ss and a group of female Ss.

Analysis of the recognition thresholds yielded the following results:

1. Under all conditions of the experiment, the thresholds for taboo words were somewhat *lower* than the thresholds for neutral words. The difference in thresholds is probably due to a systematic underestimation of the familiarity of the taboo words.

2. The relative thresholds for neutral and emotional words varied significantly with the nature of the preliminary instructions. The Uninformed Group had higher relative thresholds for taboo words than any of the groups forewarned to expect taboo words. The Facilitation Group had the lowest relative thresholds for such words. The results for the Inhibition Group are almost identical with those for the Informed Group. These findings indicate that set

and selective verbal report contribute to the observed threshold differences.

3. Women have higher relative thresholds for taboo words than do men. It is possible that women are less familiar with these words than are men and/or that women are more prone to selective verbal report.

4. Relative thresholds for taboo words are not significantly different in the presence of an E of the opposite sex than they are in the presence of an E of the same sex. There is, however, a significant tendency for all Ss to conform to instructions more fully in the presence of the female E. The E-S relationship has demonstrable effects on the observed threshold differences.

The experimental results thus fail to provide any support for a mechanism of perceptual defense. The discussion stresses the inadequacy of *ad hoc* mechanisms for the analysis of motivational factors in perception. The effects of such factors are most economically treated in the framework of a general theory of perception.

REFERENCES

1. BRUNER, J. S. Personality dynamics and the process of perceiving. In R. R. Blake and G. V. Ramsey (Eds.), *Perception: an approach to personality.* New York: Ronald, 1951.
2. BRUNER, J. S., and POSTMAN, L. Emotional selectivity in perception and reaction. *J. Pers.,* 1947, **16,** 69-77.
3. ERIKSEN, C. W. Perceptual defense as a function of unacceptable needs. *J. abnorm. soc. Psychol.,* 1951, **46,** 557-564.
4. HOWES, D. H., and SOLOMON, R. L. A note on McGinnies' "Emotionality and perceptual defense." *Psychol. Rev.,* 1950, **57,** 229-234.
5. HOWES, D. H., and SOLOMON, R. L. Visual duration thresholds as a function of word probability. *J. exp. Psychol.,* 1951, **41,** 401-410.
6. McGINNIES, E. Emotionality and perceptual defense. *Psychol. Rev.,* 1949, **56,** 244-251.
7. McGINNIES, E. Discussion of Howes' and Solomon's note on "Emotionality and perceptual defense." *Psychol. Rev.,* 1950, **57,** 235-240.
8. McGINNIES, E., and SHERMAN, H. Generalization of perceptual defense. *J. abnorm. soc. Psychol.,* 1952, **47,** 81-85.
9. POSTMAN, L. Toward a general theory of cognition. In J. H. Rohrer and M. Sherif (Eds.), *Social psychology at the crossroads.* New York: Harper, 1951.
10. POSTMAN, L., and BROWN, D. R. The perceptual consequences of success and failure. *J. abnorm. soc. Psychol.,* 1952, **47,** 213-222.

11. POSTMAN, L., BRUNER, J. S., and McGINNIES, E. M. Personal values as selective factors in perception. *J. abnorm. soc. Psychol.*, 1946, **43**, 142-154.
12. POSTMAN, L., and LEYTHAM, G. Perceptual selectivity and ambivalence of stimuli. *J. Pers.*, 1951, **19**, 390-405.
13. POSTMAN, L., and SCHNEIDER, B. H. Personal values, visual recognition and recall. *Psychol. Rev.*, 1951, **58**, 271-284.
14. ROSENSTOCK, I. M. Perceptual aspects of repression. *J. abnorm. soc. Psychol.*, 1951, **46**, 304-315.
15. SIIPOLA, E. M. A group study of some effects of preparatory set. In J. J. Gibson (Ed.), Studies in psychology from Smith College. *Psychol. Monogr.*, 1935, **46**, No. 6 (Whole No. 210), 27-38.
16. THORNDIKE, E. L., and LORGE, I. *The teacher's word book of 30,000 words.* New York: Teachers College, Columbia Univer., 1944.
17. VANDERPLAS, J. M., and BLAKE, R. R. Selective sensitization in auditory perception. *J. Pers.*, 1949, **18**, 252-266.
18. ZANGWILL, O. L. A study of the significance of attitude in recognition. *Brit. J. Psychol.*, 1937, **28**, 12-17.

SELECTION 50

....

On the Perception of Incongruity: A Paradigm*

JEROME S. BRUNER AND LEO POSTMAN

THE PRINCIPAL CONCERN of this paper is with the perceptual events which occur when perceptual expectancies fail of confirmation —the problem of incongruity. Incongruity represents a crucial problem for a theory of perception because, by its very nature, its perception represents a violation of expectation. An unexpected concatenation of events, a conspicuous mismatching, an unlikely pairing of cause and effect—all of these have in common a violation of normal expectancy. Yet incongruities are perceived. Through a process of trial-and-check, to borrow a phrase from Professor Woodworth (8), the organism operates to discover whether any given expectancy will "pay off." It is either a very sick organism, an overly motivated one, or one deprived of the opportunity to "try-and-check" which will not give up an expectancy in the face of a contradicting environment.

It would be our contention, nonetheless, that for as long as possible and by whatever means available, the organism will ward off the perception of the unexpected, those things which do not fit his prevailing set. Our assumption, and it is hardly extravagant, is simply that most people come to depend upon a certain constancy in their environment and, save under special conditions, attempt to ward off variations from this state of affairs: "Thar ain't no such animal," the hayseed is reputed to have said on seeing his first giraffe.

---

* From the *J. Pers.*, 1949, **18**, 206-223. Pp. 208-223, reprinted by permission of the authors and the publisher.

The original paper has also been published in Bruner, J. S., and Krech, D. (Eds.), *Perception and personality, a symposium.* Durham, N. C.: Duke University Press, 1950.

Turning now to the specific study to be reported, our aim was to observe the behavior of intact, normal organisms faced with incongruous situations. How are such situations coped with perceptually? What is seen and under what conditions? We shall not be concerned with factors making for differences among individuals in their "tolerance for incongruity." Such studies are now being planned. It is essential first to examine *how* incongruity is dealt with, what repertory of responses is available to the organism in incongruous situations.

THE EXPERIMENT

Twenty-eight subjects, students at Harvard and Radcliffe, were shown successively by tachistoscopic exposure five different playing cards. From one to four of these cards were incongruous—color and suit were reversed. Order of presentation of normal and incongruous cards was randomized. The normal and "trick" cards used were the following.

TABLE I. ORDERS OF PRESENTATION

Order	Card 1	Card 2	Card 3	Card 4	Card 5
Isolated "trick"					
1	4H (B)	5H	7S	AH	5S
2	7S	5H	4H (B)	AH	5S
3	5S	AH	7S	5H	3H (B)
Isolated "normal"					
4	5H	2S (R)	AD (B)	3H (B)	6S (R)
5	6S (R)	3H (B)	7S	6C (R)	2S (R)
6	4H (B)	6C (R)	2S (R)	3H (B)	5H
Mixed					
7	2S (R)	4H (B)	AH	7S	6S (R)
8	5S	2S (R)	4H (B)	6S (R)	AH
9	4H (B)	7S	AH	6S (R)	3H (B)
10	5H	2S (R)	5S	6S (R)	4H (B)
11	5S	AH	6S (R)	4H (B)	5H
12	2S (R)	5H	7S	AH	4H (B)
13	7S	3H (B)	6S (R)	AH	5S
14	3H (B)	5H	6S (R)	7S	AH

Normal cards (printed in their proper color): five of hearts, ace of hearts, five of spades, seven of spades.

Trick cards (printed with color reversed): three of hearts (black), four of hearts (black), two of spades (red), six of spades (red), ace of diamonds (black), six of clubs (red).

Fourteen orders of presentation were worked out, and two subjects were presented the cards in each of these orders. There were three types of stimulus series: (1) a single trick card embedded in a series of four normal cards; (2) a single normal card embedded in a series of four trick cards; (3) mixed series in which trick and normal cards were in the ratio of 3 : 2 or 2 : 3. A summary of the orders of presentation appears in Table I. The reader will note that the average number value of the trick cards is slightly under 4 (3.94) and slightly over 4 for the normal cards (4.35)—a flaw which operates slightly against the recognition of normal cards since lower value cards are probably more easily recognized.

Each card was presented successively until correct recognition occurred, three times each at 10 ms., 30 ms., 50 ms., 70 ms., 100 ms., 150 ms., 200 ms., 250 ms., 300 ms., 400 ms., 450 ms., 500 ms., and then in steps of 100 ms. to 1000 ms. If at 1000 ms. recognition did not occur, the next card was presented. In determining thresholds, correct recognition was defined as two successive correct responses. At each exposure, the subject was asked to report everything he saw or thought he saw.

The cards were mounted on medium gray cardboard and were shown in a Dodge-Gerbrands tachistoscope. The pre-exposure field was of the same gray color and consistency as the exposure field save that it contained no playing card. The light in the tachistoscope was provided by two G. E. daylight fluorescent tubes.

A word about the color of the incongruous cards is in order. Our efforts to have them printed by a playing card company were in vain. We therefore used poster paints to alter the colors of the cards. We had difficulty matching the red of a playing card, our best match being a slightly muddier and less yellow red than that of a regular card. Because of this, all red cards—trick and normal alike —were painted over in this color.

RESULTS

Thresholds. Perhaps the most central finding is that the recognition threshold for the incongruous playing cards (those with suit and color reversed) is significantly higher than the threshold for normal cards. While normal cards on the average were recognized correctly—here defined as a correct response followed by a second correct response—at 28 milliseconds, the incongruous cards required 114 milliseconds. The difference, representing a fourfold increase in threshold, is highly significant statistically, t being 3.76 (confidence level $<.01$).

The threshold data, expressed as the cumulative percentage of stimuli correctly recognized as a function of increasing exposure time, are presented in Figure 1. The curves, generally, are parallel.

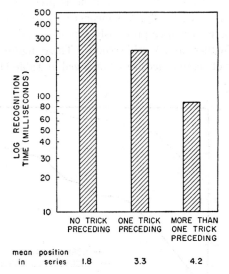

Fig. 1. Cumulative percentage of normal and incongruous playing cards correctly recognized as a function of increasing exposure time.

The reader will note that even at the longest exposure used, 1000 ms., only 89.7 per cent of the incongruous cards had been correctly recognized, while 100 per cent of the normal cards had been recognized by 350 milliseconds.

Our design was such that we might test the hypothesis that the more experience a subject had had in the past with incongruity, the less difficulty would he have in recognizing incongruity of a related nature. Indeed, this is tantamount to saying that when one has experienced an incongruity often enough, it ceases to violate expectancy and hence ceases to be incongruous. Experience with an incongruity is effective in so far as it modifies the set of the subject to prepare him for incongruity. To take an example, the threshold recognition time for incongruous cards presented before the subject has had anything else in the tachistoscope—normal or incongruous— is 360 milliseconds. If he has had experience in the recognition of one or more *normal* cards before being presented an incongruous stimulus, the threshold rises slightly but insignificantly to 420 milliseconds. Prior experience with normal cards does not lead to better recognition performance with incongruous cards (Table II). If, however, an observer has had to recognize *one* incongruous card, the threshold for the next trick card he is presented drops to 230 milliseconds. And if, finally, the incongruous card comes after experience with two or three previously exposed trick cards, threshold drops still further to 84 milliseconds. These figures, along with relevant tests of significance are summarized in Table III and plotted in Figure 2.

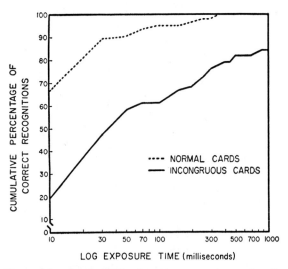

FIG. 2.   Recognition thresholds for incongruous cards as a function of past experience with such cards.

The point immediately arises as to how much the decrease in threshold noted above is due to sheer number of trials in the tachistoscope (skill practice) and how much to the heightened expectancy

TABLE II. THE EFFECT OF PREVIOUS EXPERIENCE WITH NORMAL CARDS
UPON THE FIRST RECOGNITION OF INCONGRUOUS CARDS

Previous Practice with Normal Cards	Mean Recognition Time	Number of Threshold Determinations	Mean Serial Position of First Incongruous Card
None	360 ms.	14	1
One or more normal cards.	420 ms.	14	2.6

$$t = .38$$
$$P = .68$$

TABLE III. THE EFFECT OF PREVIOUS EXPERIENCE WITH INCONGRUOUS
CARDS ON THE RECOGNITION OF SUBSEQUENT INCONGRUOUS CARDS

Nature of Previous Practice with Incongruous Cards	Mean Recognition Time	Threshold Number of Determinations	Mean Serial Position of Incongruous Cards
None	390 ms.	28	1.8
One card	230 ms.	22	3.3
Two or more cards	84 ms.	20	4.2

Tests of significance:

None vs. one.................. $t = 1.42, P = .16$
None vs. two or more........ $t = 3.20, P = .001$
One vs. two or more......... $t = 1.72, P = .08$

of incongruity. Unfortunately our data are confounded in a complicated way here, and we shall have to depend upon rather broad inferences. We cannot partial out the differential effect of serial position of a card, whether first or third or fifth in the series independently of the kinds of experience the subject had before being presented any given card. Because of the nature of our design, such a procedure would leave us with groups differing in number and in the difficulty of cards presented. What evidence we have points, however, to the importance of previous experience with incongruity quite apart from skill practice. We have remarked already that previous tachistoscopic experience with normal cards serves to raise slightly the threshold for incongruous cards. Sheer skill practice cannot, then, be solely or even largely responsible for decreasing the threshold for incongruous cards.

Reactions to Incongruity. We may ask properly at this point why the recognition threshold for incongruous stimuli was four times as high as the threshold for normal cards. The answer, it appears from an analysis of the data, lies in the manner in which subjects dealt with or coped with incongruity per se.

Generally speaking, there appear to be four kinds of reaction to rapidly presented incongruities. The first of these we have called the *dominance* reaction. It consists, essentially, of a "perceptual denial" of the incongruous elements in the stimulus pattern. Faced with a red six of spades, for example, a subject may report with considerable assurance, "the six of spades" or "the six of hearts," depending upon whether he is color or form bound (*vide infra*). In the one case the form dominates and the color is assimilated to it; in the other the stimulus color dominates and form is assimilated to it. In both instances the perceptual resultant conforms with past expectations about the "normal" nature of playing cards.

A second technique of dealing with incongruous stimuli we have called *compromise.* In the language of Egon Brunswik (2), it is the perception of a *Zwischengegenstand* or compromise object which composes the potential conflict between two or more perceptual intentions. Three examples of color compromise: (a) the red six of spades is reported as either the purple six of hearts or the purple six of spades; (b) the black four of hearts is reported as a "grayish" four of spades; (c) the red six of clubs is seen as "the six of clubs illuminated by red light."

A third reaction may be called *disruption.* A subject fails to achieve a perceptual organization at the level of coherence normally attained by him at a given exposure level. Disruption usually follows upon a period in which the subject has failed to resolve the stimulus in terms of his available perceptual expectations. He has failed to confirm any of his repertory of expectancies. Its expression tends to be somewhat bizarre: "I don't know what the hell it is now, not even for sure whether it's a playing card," said one frustrated subject after an exposure well above his normal threshold.

Finally, there is *recognition* of incongruity, the fourth, and viewed from the experimenter's chair, most successful reaction. It too is marked by some interesting psychological by-products, of which more in the proper place.

Consider now each of these four reactions, the forms they take, and the way in which they differentiate responses to normal and trick cards.

DOMINANCE REACTIONS

A first datum is that 27 out of our 28 subjects showed dominance responses to the trick cards in their records, some considerably more than others. Strictly speaking, there is often no determinate way of discovering dominance reactions to a *normal* card. A correct response may be a dominance response—either dominance of color or dominance of form. A few instances of discernible dominance reactions to the normal cards were observed in the case of erroneous perceptions. There were, for example, instances in which a red normal card was seen as black and form was assimilated to match the black color. One subject saw the red five of hearts as the black five of spades for 8 out of the 25 exposures required for full recognition; another saw the red ace of hearts as the black ace of clubs for 3 out of 15 trials required for recognition. In sum, then, 7 per cent of the subjects showed dominance responses to the normal cards—attempting to rectify an incongruity imposed on themselves by seeing our imperfect red cards as black—while 96 per cent of the subjects showed dominance reactions to the incongruous cards.

The nature of the dominance reactions to the trick cards is easily described. First, such reactions occurred with equal frequency to trick black and trick red cards. Two options were available: either the subject could organize the field in terms of suit, e.g., hearts seen as red regardless of their stimulus color; or the field could be organized in terms of color, e.g., a red card seen as a heart or diamond regardless of its true suit.

It must be said, with whatever bearing it may have for Rorschach theory, that subjects showed a marked preference for one or another of the dominance options. Assuming that a fifty-fifty distribution of form- and color-dominant responses would be expected by chance, we tested for form and color types among our subjects. Of the 27 subjects showing dominance responses, 19 showed preferences for form or color in excess of chance at the .05 level or better; the remaining 8 being equally prone to both kinds of response.

To sum up, dominance reactions to trick cards were almost universal among our subjects. An incongruous stimulus was rendered congruent with expectancy by the operation of either form or color dominance. Only a small fraction of the responses to the normal cards was of this type; and where such responses occurred, they were always elicited by incongruities imposed by the subject through a failure to perceive correctly one of the attributes of the normal cards—e.g., perceiving a red card as black.

COMPROMISE REACTIONS

As we have already noted, a compromise perception is one in which the resultant perception embodies elements of both the expected attribute and the attribute provided by stimulation. Compromise reactions are, of course, limited to certain types of stimulus situations where a "perceptual middle ground" exists between the expectancy and the stimulus contradicting the expectancy. Our situation was one such. The subjects often perceived color in such a way as to make it more in keeping with, or to bring it nearer to, normal expectation about what colors go with what suits. Perhaps the best way to illustrate the point is to list the different colors reported when subjects were presented with red spade and club cards.

Brown	Black on reddish card
Black and red mixed	Olive drab
Black with red edges	Grayish red
Black in red light	Looks reddish, then blackens
Purple	Blackish brown
Black but redness somewhere	Blurred reddish
Rusty color	Near black but not quite
Rusty black	Black in yellow light
Lighter than black, blacker than red	

Several questions arise at once. To what extent can the color compromise reactions be attributed to the action time required for the development of red? To what extent is compromise color due to the fact that our cards were not precisely "playing card" red in color? Answers to these questions can be provided in two ways.

First, the *normal* red cards (hearts and diamonds) were colored in precisely the same manner as the incongruous red cards (trick spades and clubs). This being the case, we would expect (if action time or off-color alone accounted for compromise) that there would be no difference between normal and trick red cards. There is, however, a striking difference. In reacting to trick red cards, 50 per cent of the subjects showed compromise responses; only 15 per cent showed such responses to the normal red cards. It should be noted, moreover, that if action time were a major factor, the normal cards, recognized on the whole at briefer durations, should have been more susceptible of compromise.

We have also checked on the *frequency* of compromise responses per card for those cards which elicited any compromise responses at all. When compromise responses do occur, will there be a difference in their frequency for normal and incongruous cards? Using percentages of exposures on which compromises occurred, weighted by total number of trials to recognition, we find that the percentage of compromises elicited by incongruous cards averages 63 per cent of the exposures preceding correct recognition. On the other hand, those normal cards which produced compromise responses did so on the average in only 32 per cent of the prerecognition exposures.

In sum, then, it seems highly unlikely that either "off-coloredness" or action-time alone accounted for these interesting responses. The question remains, of course, as to whether these two considerations *facilitated* the appearance of compromise. Although we lack publishable evidence on the point at this time, it seems to us on the basis of our own direct observations of briefly presented colors that both are important. Color, briefly presented, is subjectively more labile; one is somewhat less subjectively certain about its hue, and saturation is less. Given the decreased stability of the color in our briefly presented cards, it is not surprising that the normal expectation should readily lead to compromise. And when, moreover, the card falls somewhat short of "playing card redness," the tendency toward partial assimilation may become even greater.

Compromise reactions to black cards were considerably rarer than such reactions to the red cards. When they did occur, they were always given to trick black cards, never to normal ones. Only 11 per cent of the subjects showed such responses. Where they did appear, they constituted a weighted proportion of only 12 per cent of the prerecognition trials. The quality of the compromise responses to black trick cards was not strikingly different from that already reported for red cards.

> Grayish tinged with red
> Black with reddish gray background
> Dark red
> First black, then red, then black

Why so few compromise responses to the black cards? Several highly conjectural answers are worth examining. The first, and perhaps the most likely, has to do with the greater phenomenal stability of black at rapid exposure. There is, to be sure, a certain graying effect if the black is figural on white, which probably has to do with the poorly defined boundaries of such a figure at brief exposure. But the gray does not have the same quality of lability or instability of the chromatic card when presented for a brief duration (e.g., 10-50 ms.).

What, precisely, is involved in perceptual compromise? The most parsimonious assumption, we think, is that we are dealing with a special case of color assimilation, viz., assimilation to expectancy. The effect has been noted before, although it may not have been called "compromise." For example, Duncker (3) reports that a green felt leaf in hidden red illumination maintains its greenness *better* than an identically colored felt donkey in the same illumination. It is apparent from his subjects' color matches that *neither* stimulus object maintained green *perfectly*, but that the leaf did so *more* than the donkey. The color wheel used as the variable stimulus for matching contained green, orange, and white sectors. The green sector for the leaf was 60 degrees, for the donkey, 39 degrees. Like us, Duncker was dealing in his experiment with the problem of "expectancy color"—i.e., that leaves are green—and as in our case his subjects were compromising between an expected color (leaf green) and a given color (the resultant of leaf green in hidden red illumination). Very probably other experimenters, to name Grace Heider (5) and Fuchs as but two examples, obtained color compromises at least in part dependent upon their subjects' expectations about the color of the objects being partially obscured by a differently colored episcotister.

DISRUPTION

Disruption is a gross failure of the subject to organize the perceptual field at a level of efficiency usually associated with a given viewing condition. Let us say that for *normal* cards the subject is able to perceive the color, suit, and number at from 20 to 50 milliseconds. The same subject, faced with an *incongruous* card at 50 milliseconds may just begin reporting with some degree of confidence and only partial accuracy on the number and suit and color of the card before him. This may go on for several exposures as duration is increased, let us say, to 100 milliseconds—well above his normal threshold range. At this point, the subject "loses confidence," becomes perceptually confused. Said our most extremely disrupted subject at 300 milliseconds in response to a red spade card:

I can't make the suit out, whatever it is. It didn't even look like a card that time. I don't know what color it is now or whether it's a spade or heart. I'm not even sure now what a spade looks like! My God!

Disruption was not frequent in terms of the number of exposures on which it appeared. But it did occur in 16 of our 28 subjects in response to trick cards. Among these 16 subjects and for those cards on which disruption occurred at all, it occurred on the average in 4 per cent of their prerecognition responses (percentages weighted by number of trials preceding recognition). Disruption typically occurred after the subject had "tried out" his available hypotheses and failed to come to a satisfactory recognition. In Woodworth's terms (8), the trial-and-check procedure had failed to yield a stable percept.

The kinds of disruption varied from subject to subject and even from card to card. In analyzing disorganized reactions, one can find any one or any combination of five disruptive effects. One might

Color disruption................	4 Ss
Form disruption.................	10 Ss
Form-color disruption...........	3 Ss
Number* disruption.............	2 Ss
"Corner"** disruption...........	3 Ss

well expect that disruption would be selective, affecting those attributes of the stimulus with which the subject was having maximum difficulty. Indeed, the figures above point to such selectivity—form and color being the primary loci of incongruity. Having exhausted his resources in trying unsuccessfully to perceive the incongruous pairing of form and color, the subject might indeed be expected to end in the plight characterized by the typical remark:

"I'll be damned if I know now whether it's red or what!"

---

* Number disruption is a loss of perceptual certainty about the number of symbols on the card.

** Corner disruption refers to confusion about what is in the corner of the card, e.g., reports that the pip in the corner is "wrong" or displaced or that the number in the corner seems out of place.

But what of number disruption? How to account for it? Only two subjects, to be sure, seemed to show disruptive uncertainty about the number of pips present—in both cases after they had already perceived number correctly. In these instances one had the impression that the subjects had, so to speak, displaced their uncertainty upon an attribute of the stimulus which was not causing the real "perceptual trouble." Indeed, an additional exploratory experiment has indicated that in an extremely difficult incongruity situation such "displaced" disruptions are more common than in the present experiment. In that experiment a series of normal cards had interspersed at random among them two rather fantastic cards procured from a magic supply house: a card containing eleven diamonds but labeled in the corner with the notation for the fifteen of diamonds; the other was made up in the same way but was in the suit of spades and bore the notation of the fourteen of spades. In response to both cards subjects not infrequently ran the gamut of displacement: first being uncertain, properly, about the number, then suit, then color, then (though not frequently) about the size of the card.

Tempting though it might be to relate proneness to disruption to such concepts as Frenkel-Brunswik's tolerance for ambiguity (4) or the concept of frustration tolerance (7), we do not at this time have any information which would warrant such an essay. One can, however, point to the phenomenon as a consequence of the "frustration" attendant upon failure to confirm a series of perceptual hypotheses. In this sense, the frustration is predominantly a perceptual matter (although some subjects grew irritated at their inability to "get" the stimulus).

A final word disposes of the frequency of disruption responses to the normal cards. There were none.

RECOGNITION

In the perception of the incongruous stimuli, the recognition process is temporarily thwarted and exhibits characteristics which are generally not observable in the recognition of more conventional stimuli.

One specific way in which the recognition process is affected by the thwarting of well-established expectations is the emergence of a "sense of wrongness." The subject may either, even while "dominance" and "compromise" responses are continuing, suddenly or gradually begin to report that there is something wrong with the stimulus without being able to specify what it is that is wrong. It is not infrequent after such a report to witness the onset of perceptual disruption. But at the same time, such a "sense of wrongness" may also turn out to be a prelude to veridical recognition, for it often has the effect of making the subject change his hypotheses or give up his previous expectation about the nature of the stimulus.

Occasionally, as in 6 of our 28 subjects, the sense of wrongness may become focused upon a rather tangential, but, in point of fact, correct aspect of the incongruous stimuli and in so doing lead to a successful unmasking. These six subjects, prior to correct recognition, all reported that the position of the pips on the card was "wrong." All these responses were given either to spades printed in red or hearts printed in black at a time when the subject was calling the black hearts "spades" or the red spades "hearts."

What's the matter with the symbols now? They look reversed or something. (6SR)

The spades are turned the wrong way, I think. (4HB)

For those who do not have playing cards before them or who cannot remember the position of heart and spade pips, the former are printed with the point down in the top tier of pips and with the points up in the bottom, while spades are up-pointed in the top tier, down-pointed in the bottom.

Four of the six subjects who focused on this odd, and usually overlooked, positional arrangement of pips on a card finally achieved recognition. Two of the subjects failed to recognize their cards correctly in spite of unmasking this tell-tale feature.

Perhaps the greatest single barrier to the recognition of incongruous stimuli is the tendency for perceptual hypotheses to fixate after receiving a minimum of confirmation. As we have noted, some of our subjects persisted up to 1000 milliseconds in giving dominance responses to incongruous stimuli. Once there had occurred in these cases a partial confirmation of the hypothesis that the card in the tachistoscope was a black club or a black spade, it seemed that nothing could change the subject's report. One subject gave 24 successive black color-dominant responses to the black three of hearts, another 44 of them (both calling it the three of spades). Another persisted for 16 trials in calling it a red three of hearts. There were six instances in which subjects persisted in a color or form dominance response for over 50 exposures up to 1000 milliseconds, finally failing to recognize the card correctly.

Such fixation tendencies are, one might say, the chief block to perceptual learning. In another article on the effects of stress on perception (6), we pointed out that perceptual recklessness often resulted when a subject had to work under difficulties—the formation and fixation of "premature" and incorrect perceptual hypotheses. It would appear, indeed, that working in incongruous situations where partial confirmation of expectancy can occur (the form of a spade is not so different from that of a heart, even if the colors are) has the same effect of inducing premature fixation.

As for correct recognition of incongruity following an unsuccessful period of trial-and-check, we have irreverently come to call the response of some of our subjects the "My God!" reaction. For, to borrow a phrase from a distinguished literary critic, what occurs can well be characterized as "the shock of recognition."

One could, we suppose, liken the process of correct recognition to Köhler's description of insight. Indeed, it has some of the characteristics of sudden solution following unsuccessful attempts to master a situation. When a subject says: "Good Lord, what have I been saying? That's a *red* six of spades," there is no question about the sudden phenomenal emergence of the new perception.

Our reluctance in likening the phenomena to Köhler's description of insight is the suspicion that there is more to the matter than "sudden emergence." The uncertainty that sometimes comes before, the "sense of wrongness," the disruptions—all these point to the gradual weakening of previous hypotheses before "sudden reorganization" can occur. Indeed, to match cases of "sudden phenomenal emergence," one sometimes finds a very gradual and almost timed approach to the correct recognition of incongruous object color. A subject viewing a red spade may start by reporting a red tint which gradually becomes redder on succeeding trials until he finally asserts that the card is a red spade.

Unfortunately, we have no light to throw on this particular variant of the "continuity-noncontinuity" sequence in perceptual reorganization.

CONCLUSIONS

Our major conclusion is simply a reaffirmation of the general statement that perceptual organization is powerfully determined by expectations built upon past commerce with the environment. When such expectations are violated by the environment, the perceiver's behavior can be described as resistance to the recognition of the unexpected or incongruous. The resistance manifests itself in subtle and complex but nevertheless distinguishable perceptual responses. Among the perceptual processes which implement this resistance are (1) the dominance of one principle of organization which prevents the appearance of incongruity and (2) a form of "partial assimilation to expectancy" which we have called compromise. When these responses fail and when correct recognition does not occur, what results may best be described as perceptual disruption. Correct recognition itself results when inappropriate expectancies are discarded after failure of confirmation.

REFERENCES

1. BRUNER, J. S. Perceptual theory and the Rorschach test. *J. Pers.*, 1948, **17**, 157-168.
2. BRUNSWIK, E. *Wahrnehmung und Gegenstandswelt*. Vienna: Deuticke, 1934.
3. DUNCKER, K. The influence of past experience upon perceptual properties. *Amer. J. Psychol.*, 1939, **52**, 255-265.
4. FRENKEL-BRUNSWIK, E. Intolerance of ambiguity as an emotional and perceptual personality variable. *J. Pers.*, 1949, **18**, 108-143.
5. HEIDER, G. New studies in transparency, form and color. *Psychol. Forsch.*, 1932, **17**, 13-55.
6. POSTMAN, L., and BRUNER, J. S. Perception under stress. *Psychol. Rev.*, 1948, **55**, 314-323.
7. ROSENZWEIG, S. Frustration theory. In J. McV. Hunt, *Personality and the behavior disorders*. New York: Ronald, 1944.
8. WOODWORTH, R. S. Reenforcement of perception. *Amer. J. Psychol.*, 1947, **60**, 119-124.

SELECTION 51

....

Intolerance of Ambiguity as an Emotional and Perceptual Personality Variable*

ELSE FRENKEL-BRUNSWIK

FROM EMOTIONAL AMBIVALENCE TO COGNITIVE AM-
BIGUITY. PERSONALITY-CENTERING IN THE PRES-
ENT APPROACH

THE APPROACH USED in the present paper is to discuss problems which were originally developed and perfected in the clinical and social fields; they are reformulated and broadened here to absorb certain fitting elements of recent perceptual thought. It is this that we mean when we say that our approach is personality-centered rather than perception-centered.

The prime concern is to bring together a variety of aspects in order to study the generality or lack of generality of the personality patterns involved, that is, the readiness to spread from one area of manifestation to another. Can basic formal attitudes such as subjectivety, rigidity, fear of ambivalence and of ambiguity, etc., be taken as unified traits of the organism, or are we to find a more differential distribution, varying from one area to another?

A second advantage offered by the carrying of personality problems into perception is that tendencies which in the social and emotional fields are manifested in a vague fashion are rendered more clearly accessible to experimental verification.

It is hoped that by discussion of the same formal principles in all three, the motivational, social, and perceptual contexts, greater

---

* From the *J. Pers.,* 1949, **18**, 108-143. Pp. 112-132 reprinted by permission of the author and the publisher.

The original paper has also been published in Bruner, J. S., and Krech, D. (Eds.), *Perception and personality, a symposium.* Durham, N. C.: Duke University Press, 1950.

conceptual clarity can be achieved than through a discussion of any of those channels alone. To the richness of motivational concepts clarity will be added by nailing them down on the more objective and precise perceptual level. As will be seen, differentiations lost or obscured in the globality of the motivational approach can be reestablished in this manner; on the other hand, problems in perception will gain in significance and fruitfulness if questions in personality and social psychology are allowed to help in the choice of problems. The gain is far from being restricted to the conceptual level. Important empirical relations are revealed along with clarification, throwing further light on the first-mentioned problem of the generality vs. specificity of behavior as well as on problems concerning the interrelation of the levels of personality.

A third advantage is what may be called the reduction of social bias. By the shift of emphasis from the emotional to the perceptual area, certain preconceived notions which only too readily slip into the investigation of social and clinical issues can be greatly reduced and controversial issues delineated and at least indirectly decided on a more nearly neutral platform.

The last-named two advantages are, of course, contingent upon the first point in that any shifting of problems to other areas is valid only to the extent to which the mechanisms involved throughout these areas or levels tend to be similar within the same individuals. Only a beginning will be made in this paper toward answering this problem in an empirical manner. The major emphasis will lie on the following two points: (1) on a development of the underlying reasoning from previous evidence based on the writer's own work as well as on sources from the literature; and (2) on a showing of possible ways of attacking the problem experimentally. Experimental evidence as cited below, although scattered or preliminary and by no means conclusive thus far, partly points in the direction of the generality of the personality traits mentioned, partly is suggestive of compensatory relations which may make for the simultaneous presence of opposite tendencies.

The topic to serve as a medium through which this procedure will be followed is given by what seems to this writer one of the basic variables in both the emotional and the cognitive orientation of a person toward life and what she has suggested be labeled "tolerance vs. intolerance of ambiguity" (10, 11, 12).

The material evidence is based primarily on a project conducted at the Institute of Child Welfare of the University of California[1] and dealing with rigid adherence vs. disinclination to ethnic prejudice in children, and the motivational and cognitive correlates of these social attitudes. This study has involved, to date, the construction of a series of scales for the direct and indirect measurement of prejudice[2] and for the assessment of factors suspected to be related. Data have been collected from 1500 public school children, eleven to sixteen years old, in several samples. With 120 of these subjects, representing the extremes of prejudice and of freedom from prejudice, more intensive studies were conducted in terms of individual interviews and projective tests. Furthermore, the parents of the children interviewed were visited and likewise interviewed. Approximately forty of the intensively studied children were further submitted to some of the experiments in perception proper and in memory which are to be described below.[3] An advance report of some aspects of this project has been given by the present writer not long ago (11, 12). Those of her collaborators who worked on the aspects discussed here will be mentioned in the proper context later in this paper.

The line of argument will now be outlined in somewhat greater detail. Starting from the observation that some of her subjects were able to tolerate emotional ambiguities better than others, the writer became involved in the question of whether this attitude of intolerance of more complex, conflicting, or otherwise open structures extends beyond the emotional and social areas to further include perceptual and cognitive aspects proper.

The importance of individual differences in the insistence on unqualified assertions was first brought to the attention of the writer in a study on mechanisms of self-deception conducted at the University of Vienna before the war (7). The greater the definiteness and lack of shading, that is, the greater the intolerance of ambiguity, in the self-description of favorable traits, the less were such assertions as a rule verified in the judgment of close acquaintances.

---

[1] The writer is indebted to Dr. Harold E. Jones, the director of the Institute, for giving her the opportunity to carry out this project as well as for suggestions regarding its execution.

[2] This was done in collaboration with Murray E. Jarvik and Milton Rokeach.

[3] While the project on social discrimination in children referred to here has some features in common with the project on adults referred to under (1), it is distinguished from the latter, among other things, by the use of experiments and a greater emphasis on cognitive factors in general.

The background of the problem of ambiguity thus becomes related to the vast fund of knowledge supplied by psychoanalysis in connection with the development of the concept of "ambivalence," as defined by the coexistence, in the same individual, of love- and of hate-cathexis toward the same object. The existence of ambivalence in a person and the further fact of this person's ability to face his or her ambivalences toward others must be considered an important personality variable. As in other areas of personality, psychoanalytic statements referring to content, such as attitude toward parents, repression of certain id-tendencies, etc., are perhaps difficult of access to experimental verification. Here, however, we are dealing with experimentation concerning formal factors, such as intolerance of ambiguity, or rigidity, and the question of whether or not these attitudinal variables are restricted to the emotional area.

From here, a first step toward a more cognitively slanted reformulation is achieved by shifting to the problem of the recognition, by one and the same individual, of any actual coexistence of positive and negative features in the same object, e.g., in parents or other "in-groups." Ability to recognize such coexistences in all likelihood constitutes another important, emotional-cognitive, personality variable, which is not to be confused with emotional ambivalence in the original sense of the word. At the end of a scale defined by this ability stand those with a tendency to resort to black-white solutions, to arrive at premature closure as to valuative aspects, often at the neglect of reality, and to seek for unqualified and unambiguous over-all acceptance and rejection of other people. The maintenance of such solutions requires the shutting out of aspects of reality which represent a possible threat to these solutions. It is this problem of "reality-adequacy" vs. "reality-inadequacy" which injects a distinctly cognitive element into the broader sphere of the problem of ambivalence.

Our material gives evidence of individual differences both in emotional ambivalence and the readiness to face it, and in the more cognitive recognition of traits of conflicting value in others. Since the clinical aspects of the problems involved have been discussed in greater detail elsewhere (11, 10, 1), they will be presented here in a summary fashion only.

Some individuals are more apt to see positive as well as negative features in their parents and can accept feelings of love and hate toward the same persons without too much anxiety or conflict. Others seem compelled to dramatize their image of the parents in seeing them either as altogether good or as altogether bad. The following question suggests itself in this context: Is this second attitude an intolerance of an existing underlying ambivalence, or is it merely absence of ambivalence? Why do we doubt that a thoroughly positive description of the parents with denial of any negative features or discrepancies as given to us by some of the children is not a true representation of the children's feelings? On what basis are we entitled to claim that the individual has repressed the negative side of an ambivalence out of some hypothetical intolerance of ambiguities and complexities?

We list here only a few of the facts which were used as the basis of such an inference. First, the description of the parents in the second type of cases is often stereotypical and exaggerated, indicating a use of clichés rather than an expression of genuine feelings. The range of responses in such cases is rather narrow and without the variations commonly found in the description of real people. Only the more palpable, crude, and concrete aspects are being mentioned. Thus we find a preponderance of references to physical and other external characteristics rather than mention of more essential and abstract aspects of the parents' personalities. Furthermore, a child relating only positive feelings while talking directly about his or her parents may at the same time reveal a negative attitude on manifestations which are more indirect. For instance, he may omit his parents from the list of people he wants to take to a desert island. Or, when describing parents in general rather than his own, e.g., in his responses to parental figures on the Thematic Apperception Test, he may stress the coercive and punitive aspects of parents. It is data of this and other kinds which induce us to state that the children concerned split the positive and negative side of their feeling and attitudes rather than become aware of their coexistence.

Both the exaggerated concreteness and the stereotypy of the descriptions can serve as diagnostic indices of dynamic states. The above considerations concerning the diagnosis of the "real" emotional state are a further demonstration of the greater conceptual power of the depth-psychological approach. The latter rests upon the inclusion of minimal cues as well as on material of an indirect type such as projective techniques. For a more detailed discussion of the relationship of the underlying genotypical or conceptually more derived level to the manifest or phenotypical level of personality as relevant in this context, see Frenkel-Brunswik (8, 9).

Synopsis of a variety of data suggests that the attempt to master aggression toward parental figures who are experienced as too threatening and powerful are among the important determinants of the tendency rigidly to avoid ambiguity of any sort.[4] The requested submission and obedience to parental authority is only one of the many external, rigid, and superficial rules which such a child learns. Dominance-submission, cleanliness-dirtiness, badness-goodness, virtue-vice, masculinity-femininity are some of the other dichotomies customarily upheld in the homes of such children. The absoluteness of each of these differences is considered natural and eternal, excluding any possibility of individuals trespassing from the one side to the other. There is rigid adherence to these clearly delineated norms even if this implies restrictions and disadvantages for the own group. Thus, not only boys but also girls exhibiting the need for dichotomizing subscribe to restrictions for women rather than expose themselves to more flexible but at the same time more uncertain norms.

In line with this, in the type of home just referred to, discipline is experienced by the children significantly more often as threatening, traumatic, overwhelming, and unintelligible, as contrasted with an intelligent, non-ego-destructive type of discipline in the home with the more flexible atmosphere. Actually, in the home with rigid [5] orientation the discipline is more often based upon the expectation of a quick learning of external, rigid, superficial rules beyond the comprehension of the child.[6] Family relationships are based on roles clearly defined in terms of dominance and submission. Some of the children live in a situation comparable to permanent physical danger which leaves no time for finer discriminations and for attempts to get a fuller understanding of the factors involved but in which quick

---

[4] For a discussion of attitudes toward authority and the resulting patterns of life, see also Fromm (13).

[5] Few concepts in recent personality psychology have been used with such a variety of connotations as that of rigidity. Unless otherwise specified, the term "rigid" refers in this paper to the various kinds of intolerance of ambiguity discussed.

[6] Most recently, the relationship between frustration and rigidity was experimentally demonstrated by Christie (5). In a task similar to that by Rokeach as described below (see also 20) subjects exposed to a frustrating situation given by an unsolvable reasoning problem persisted, more often than a nonfrustrated control group, in a set maladaptive to the task.

action leading to tangible and concrete results is the only appropriate behavior.[7] It is of course true that no child can fully master his environment. Global, diffuse, concrete, undifferentiated types of reaction have thus been described by Werner (24) and others as characteristic of the child in general. It depends on the atmosphere of the home and the more specific expectations regarding the child's behavior, however, whether such reactions become fixated or whether progress toward higher developmental stages is being encouraged. For the latter course a reduction of fear and a tolerance toward weakness in the child are necessary.

Further factors contributing to the rigidification of personality in children are the stress on stereotyped behavior, an expectancy of self-negating submission, and the inducement to repress nonacceptable tendencies. As a result we find a break and conflict between the different layers of personality which contrast sharply with the greater fluidity of transition and intercommunication between the different personality strata of the child in the permissive home. Repression and externalization of instinctual tendencies reduce their manageability and the possibility of their control by the individual, since it is now the external world to which the feared qualities of the unconscious are being ascribed.

Data on the parents of the children in the rigid, intolerant group reveal that it is their feeling of social and economic marginality in relation to the group to which they aspire from which ensues the desperate clinging to external and rigid rules. These parents report significantly more often their own parents as foreign born, indicating perhaps that they still see themselves entangled in the process of assimilation. They well may be furthering everything which they deem advantageous and repressing everything which they deem detrimental to this goal. Obviously, the less secure they are in their feeling of belonging the more they will insist on maintenance of the cultural norms in themselves and in their children. It is this rigid adherence to norm which furnishes the key to an understanding of all the various avoidances of ambiguities listed in this paper.

In order to reduce conflict and anxiety and to maintain stereotyped patterns, certain aspects of experience have to be kept out of awareness. Assumptions once made, no matter how faulty and out of keeping with reality because of a neglect of relevant aspects, are

---

[7] For the relationship between frustration and rigidity, see especially Rosenzweig (21).

repeated over and over again and not corrected in the face of new evidence.

The spontaneous interview statements of children in the rigidly intolerant group show a tendency toward polarization similar to the one referred to above. Often this is done in moralistic terms avoiding any qualification or expression of conflicting feeelings. The evidence from both direct and indirect material thus suggests that children who tend to make unambiguous statements, either of total acceptance or of total rejection, seem to be aware of only one of two aspects coexisting within their dynamic, attitudinal make-up. A static superstructure appears to be superimposed upon a most conflict-ridden understructure, with resulting major discrepancies and stresses between the two levels. In this state of affairs the conflicting tendencies are isolated from each other and expressed only alternatively through different types of media, each of them representing a different layer of the total personality.

The fact that the tendency toward emotional dichotomizing in inter-personal relationships is related to dichotomizing in the social field is not a surprising one. In analyzing, say, the aspects contained in racial prejudice, one is first reminded of the more general dichotomy of ingroup vs. outgroup in its more rigid form that precludes the possibility of crosspassing. A further feature is that the criterion for the distinction is usually an external one, such as color or place in the social hierarchy. Moreover, the distinction tends to become a totalitarian one in that all of the "good" characteristics are ascribed to those of the ingroup and all of the "bad" ones to the outgroup. There is, finally, the introduction of a double standard of values as a further type of dichotomy. (For an analysis of the various dimensions of ethnocentrism, see 17, 1.)

In order to maintain the rigid and moralistically tainted distinctions just mentioned, one and the same trait—e.g., erudition or aggressive orientation toward success—is considered objectionable in the outgroup yet definitely desirable in the ingroup. There is little awareness of the ambivalent or ambiguous quality which these traits acquire by this double-assessment. Both ingroup and outgroup are thus characterized by a Gestalt which has great "pregnance" (is highly clear-cut), as was noted above for such concepts as that of masculinity and femininity. These Gestalten are "closed" and cannot be modified by new experiences, which are immediately viewed from the standpoint of the old set and classified in the same way as the previous ones. Such tendencies as premature closure, jumping to generalizations on the basis of certain specific and external aspects, carrying over old sets, and the like, will become evident in the cognitive and perceptual reactions as they are evident in the emotional and social spheres. "Speed and strength of closure" turned out to be one of the major factors in Thurstone's analysis of perception (22). The question which is up for discussion in this paper is whether or not to see *Gestalten* which are too "good" in the sense of the principle of *Prägnanz* is an even more generalized type of reaction, although the seeing of relatively circumscribed and closed *Gestalten* may be at the price of not being able to perceive the broader over-all connections.

One must add that a great variety of perceptual and cognitive processes may be considered as formal approaches to reality which may be very revealing of a person's style of life. The establishment of the relationship of these formal aspects to content is an important task of psychology. The question may be raised as to what are the consistencies, and positive correlations, and what are the compensations in terms of behavior. It is such problems which led to the experiments discussed subsequently in this paper.

Concentrating on tolerance of ambiguity, the question takes the form as to whether those incapable of conflicting emotions—or of conflicting value judgments—are generally incapable of seeing things in two or more different ways. It is at this point that a well worked-over area of psychological research is again being approached. This is the area covered by the concept of perceptual ambiguity (*Gestalt-mehrdeutigkeit*) as originally defined by Benussi (2) and as further developed in the well-known work of Rubin on figure-ground reversals and in the studies of the Gestalt psychologists proper (see Koffka, 16). In its own right, this problem of cognitive ambiguity is of very broad scope. In its more recent ramifications it includes the problems posed by the fact that ambiguity of cognitive responses must be seen as a reflection of the uncertainties existing in the environment itself, thus opening up the field of "probability" as a new area of psychological research (see Egon Brunswik, 4).

Academic research on ambiguity and on probability adjustment has discovered a number of important principles by which cognitive responses are linked to characteristics of stimulus-configurations and stimulus-combinations in the environment, such as to the relative size of the figure vs. ground area, or the relative frequency of reward on the two sides of a rat maze, respectively. In turn, problems of personality patterns with respect to ambiguity such as those outlined in some of the preceding paragraphs were as a rule by-passed; in the typical case, individual differences in ambiguity reactions are rarely mentioned.

In the type of study with which the present paper concerns itself, this procedure is reversed. There is no more than a passing interest in the external conditions of ambiguity, basic in perception psychology. The entire development of the problem is under the aspect of personality. Issuing from this latter aspect, excursions are made into perception psychology, adapting some stock experiments or taking them as cues for new experiments but always subordinating them to patterns of personality differences as the basic problem, with an eye to developing them eventually as diagnostic tools or tests.

This personality-centered rather than perception-centered approach may be linked to certain further developments within psychoanalysis proper. An example of the occasional parallels between motivational and perceptual processes drawn in the psychoanalytic literature which at the same time is related to our own problem can be found in Fenichel's discussion of the compulsive character (6). After an examination of the general dynamics of this syndrome Fenichel describes the need for being systematic and for clinging to definite systems as it occurs in the compulsive. This need, often manifested in the tendency to "type" and to classify in categories, is seen as protection against surprise and fear of drive impulses. Deviations from symmetry are not tolerated but are experienced as deviations from general norms, especially moral. Compare this depth-psychological explanation of the tendency toward symmetry with the one given by Gestalt psychology in terms of dynamic factors in the brain field and you have a further illustration of the difference between the personality-centered and the perception-centered approach.

The clinically well-known mechanism of isolation found in the compulsive character can, according to Fenichel, lead to an inhibition to see "Gestalten" and to a perception of a sum of elements instead. Related to this is said to be the preoccupation with small, insignificant detail which often is found to be taken as a symbol for more important aspects of objects. In psychoanalysis, assumptions of this kind are as a rule not based upon actual experiments in perception or cognition. In some cases such experiments can be easily undertaken, however. In fact, the experiments referred to below bear decidedly upon the topics just described.

In order to investigate empirically how far basic personality trends, found in the emotional and social sphere, such as ambivalence, are apt to spread beyond this area to include perceptual and cognitive aspects, it was decided to combine the personality studies of the children in our project on ethnic prejudice referred to above not only with an ascertainment of their social beliefs but also with an investigation of their perceptual reactions. To quote from the theoretical considerations in an advance report of 1945, the writer had been led "to expect prejudice to be associated with perceptual rigidity, inability to change set, and tendencies to primitive and rigid structuring of ambiguous perceptual fields. Well-tested experimental approaches are available for these variables. It only remains to use them in connection with susceptibility to prejudice" [8] (see also 11).

At first the problem was approached in a more summary fashion. Such traits as "intolerance of ambiguity," "distortion of reality," and "rigidity" were defined in a general manner, and each child was rated, without knowledge of his prejudice score, on the basis of a synopsis of the available clinical material. The same group which manifested extreme racial prejudice received on the average high ratings on these traits also.

Furthermore, children with a tendency to dichotomize in the social field on the basis of external characteristics—i.e., the ethnically prejudiced children—at the same time tend to subscribe to statements included in a personality inventory and expressly designed to reveal a dichotomizing attitude, a rejection of the different, or an avoidance of ambiguities in general. Examples of the statements used are:

People can be divided into two distinct classes: the weak and the strong.

Teachers should tell children what to do and not try to find out what the children want.

Only people who are like myself have a right to be happy.

---

[8] The report from which this passage is quoted has been written for the Research Department of the American Jewish Committee which sponsored the first two years of the project on social discrimination in children mentioned above.

Girls should learn only things that are useful around the house.

Refugees should be thrown out of this country so that their jobs can be given to veterans.

There is only one right way to do anything.

To this more general evidence of the relationship between emotional-social ambivalence and its repression, on the one hand, and tolerance of cognitive ambiguity, on the other, we now add a brief description of some relevant experiments, some of them still in a highly tentative state.

DIFFERENTIAL DISTORTION OF REALITY IN AN EXPERIMENT ON MEMORY

First a memory experiment will be discussed in which there is still some emotional and social involvement. Among other things, it will bring out closeness of opposites, a point which has been stressed above as an important characteristic of the personality-centered approach.

The task was the recall of a story. It was carried out in 1946 as a group experiment with forty-two children of the 6th, 7th, and 8th grades to whom a number of tests developed in our above mentioned project had been given. In this case, no selection of subjects was made in terms of their standing on the prejudice scale, so that the sample includes extremes as well as subjects of intermediate attitude. The writer is indebted to Mr. Murray E. Jarvik and Mr. Donald T. Campbell for their participation in the construction of the experiment, and to Mr. Leonard Gordon for his assistance in evaluating the material.

The "story"—actually a somewhat broadened milieu characterization—deals with the pupils of a school and their attitudes toward newcomers. In an introductory paragraph one short sentence each is devoted to examples of the boys in the school, labeling them by first names and giving one or two facts about each of them relating either to their individual habits or achievements—such as playing the violin or having been on a radio quiz—or to their fathers' occupation, economic status, religious affiliation or ethnic and racial group membership. Of the eleven children thus introduced one is a Negro and one is Jewish. The major part of the story starts out by listing three of the boys as newcomers to the school. It then proceeds to give short generalized sketches of the behavior of a number of the old-timers toward the newcomers in terms of aggressiveness vs. protectiveness in the fighting that develops against the newcomers. The story ends with a description of the somewhat futile efforts of the newcomers to defend themselves. The entire material covers one and one-half double-spaced typewritten pages. With its many participants it is deliberately somewhat confusing. To render accuracy even more difficult, it was read to the children only once. After a short interval they were asked to reproduce it in writing.

In the context of the present paper we may conceive of the story as a piece of reality and ask ourselves what changes this reality undergoes in the memory of the children, especially also in the direction of an elimination of ambiguities and other complexities.

As was to be expected, children scoring relatively high on prejudice mentioned the Negro boy significantly more often in an unfavorable context, with or without explicitly referring to his being a Negro, than did the less prejudiced. The negative characteristics ascribed to him were subjective elaborations on the part of the subjects concerned since the story itself says no more about him than that his "father was a Negro and worked in a hotel."

The negativistic tendency in the distortion of story content on the part of the prejudiced children is not limited to the description of this particular boy with his minority status. The prejudiced children tend generally to recall a higher ratio of undesirable over desirable characteristics. This result is in line with the general overemphasis on negative, hostile, and catastrophic features found in the clinical data, the interviews, and the Thematic Apperception Test stories of the highly ethnocentric subjects.

It is further to be noted that in those scoring low on ethnic prejudice, the ratio of undesirable to desirable features recalled is closer to the ratio in the story itself. In short, low-scorers stuck closer to the "truth," in this respect at least, than did high-scorers. Over and beyond the hostility mentioned above, the distortions of the high-scorers tend not only to be more frequent but also to be of a cruder nature. All this is revealed by the fact that 43 per cent of the high-scoring children, as contrasted with only 8 per cent of the low-scorers, recalled exclusively that part of the story which deals with the fighting without mentioning any of the other themes (statistical significance is at the 1 per cent level of confidence). It may be added that evidence from the interviews likewise points toward the relatively great attraction which fighting has for this group of children. In the recall of the prejudiced children the story gets generally more simplified and less diverse. Often a unified attitude of aggressiveness is assumed toward the newcomer, with the only theme, fighting, sharply focused on this group alone. It is in these extreme cases that the rooting of negativistic reality distortion in the tendency to avoid emotional ambivalence becomes most convincingly evident. The low-scoring children, on the other hand, tend to refer more often to the individual differences between the children, sometimes with an explicit emphasis on the content of the first paragraph of the story which states that there are many kinds of children in this school.

The differential recall in the two groups of children is especially manifested in their answers to three more specific questions asked after they had written down their recall of the story as a whole. The last of these three questions called for a description of "the old-timer who stuck up for the newcomers." Of all those failing to answer one, but no more than one, of the three questions, the percentage of high-scorers who omitted the last question was significantly higher than that of low-scorers. On the other hand, a significantly higher percentage of low-scorers omitted answering the second question which asked for the description of "the stoolpigeon," a boy with some undesirable characteristics.

Although the ratio of positive to negative characteristics mentioned by the low-scorers is closer to the one in the story, their emphasis on positive and nurturant aspects leads them sometimes to omissions. Gross distortions of the kind often found in the prejudiced group remain rare in their case, however. The fact that low-scorers on the whole approximate more correctly the actual configuration of stimuli will also be seen in the results of the perceptual experiments to be discussed below.

There are, further, still more general differences in the dealing with the story material which are of interest in this connection. The tendency to stray from the content of the story is in the high-scoring children combined with a tendency faithfully to remember certain single phrases and details. Some of the children in this group may show predominance of either the first or the second type of reaction. As in the Thematic Apperception Test, some will show a restricted approach concentrating on description of details of picture or story; others will go off altogether, telling stories which show almost no relation to the material presented. Thus there is either a clinging to the presentation with little freedom and distance, i.e., a stimulus-boundness in the sense of Goldstein (15), or a neglect of the stimulus altogether in favor of purely subjective fantasies. It is in this manner that a rigid, cautious, segmentary approach goes with one that is disintegrated and chaotic, sometimes one and the same child manifesting both patterns in alternation or in all kinds of bizarre combinations. As does negativism and distortion in general, both these patterns help avoidance of uncertainty, one of them by fixation to, the other by tearing loose from, the given realities.

EXPERIMENTS ON PERCEPTUAL AMBIGUITY

We now turn to a group of experiments in perception proper. These are quite free from emotional and social content and are designed to help investigate whether or not such characteristics as intolerance of ambiguities are generalized. If such intolerance should turn out to be a formal characteristic of the organism independent of content, experiments on perceptual ambiguity could be used as diagnostic tools. We begin with preliminary experiments which showed a certain trend in the direction suggested in a relatively small number of subjects, although statistical signifrcance was as a rule not scrutinized. This trend then was corroborated in further, somewhat modified experiments using more adequate numbers of subjects. In most cases the subjects were children in our project mentioned above who had scored extremely high or extremely low on ethnic prejudice. Unless otherwise specified, all the experiments discussed in this section were conducted between 1946 and 1948.

So long as experiments in perception dealt primarily with universal trends, the description of the sociological characteristics of the sample was comparatively irrelevant, or at least it seemed to be so. In entering the field of individual differences, however, the sociological attributes of the sample become decisive. Our own sample consisted mainly of a lower middle-class group in an area restricted by covenant. In samples of this kind the rigid extreme is apt to be strongly preoccupied with the maintenance of his or her middle-class status and of the social distance from the ethnic minority groups and from the unskilled workers living near by. The experiments on ambiguity reported in this section were to a large extent conducted with such extreme individuals within our sample; because of their tenuous social position, greater over-all rigidity is found here than in samples belonging to other classes or exhibiting a higher educational level.

Against the general objection which may be raised to the effect that intolerance of ambiguity is nothing but lack of intelligence, the following may be said. First, the correlations between absence of ethnic prejudice, on the one hand, and intelligence, on the other, are generally low. Second, there is no reason why rigidity could not be considered a malfunctioning of intelligence, although it would seem to be a rather specific aspect of intelligence that may be involved.

In the first of the preliminary experiments a disk-shaped reversible figure-ground pattern was presented to a total of 14 subjects. It was expected that prejudiced subjects would display a smaller number of spontaneous shifts, that reaction time in shifting would be longer, and that there would be a tendency to settle on one of the possible solutions. The answer to this may throw some light on the question as to whether subjects who exhibit rigidity in the emotional and social field are generally less likely to shift back and forth between alternative interpretations of an ambiguous perceptual configuration. The results of this experiment so far are not conclusive.

In another tentative experiment,[9] first the picture of a dog was shown, followed by a number of pictures representing transitional stages leading finally to the picture of a cat. At every stage the subjects were asked to identify the object on the given card. In spite of the fact that the cards were not too well drawn for the purpose, distinct trends became evident. The prejudiced group

---

[9] The use of gradual transitions between objects of different kind occurred to the writer in reading Goldstein's (14, p. 309) description of certain schizophrenic patients who insisted on assigning "individual words" to each in a series of shades of green. Although the schizophrenics differ from the ethnically prejudiced in the degree of reality disturbance, the two seem to have in common a tendency to absolutize, or to absorb at one end of the scale, or to discard entirely differences which others will be able to integrate into a continuum of gradual steps. Relatively unstable stimuli representing intermediate stages between more clearcut configurations have been common in experiments on the perception and memory-distortion of form for some time. For suggestions regarding one of the experiments reported here the writer is indebted to Dr. Warner Brown.

Drawings representing transitions between objects more drastically different from one another than those mentioned above, such as between a tree and a house, seem to be more suitable for our purpose.

tended to hold on longer to the first object and to respond more slowly to the changing stimuli. There was greater reluctance to give up the original object about which one had felt relatively certain and a tendency not to see what did not harmonize with the first set as well as a shying away from transitional solutions. Once this perseveration was broken, there seemed to be in this group either a spell of haphazard guessing or a blocking by the uncertainties inherent in the situation. It may well turn out upon further evidence that intolerance of perceptual ambiguity is related to a broader psychological disturbance of which prejudice—itself often a deviation from the prevalent code, especially in school—is but another manifestation.

Turning again to less specific situations, figural aftereffects of what is, or has temporarily become, the "familiar" seems to show generally a relatively strong resistance to change in this group. It is as if any stimulus—or what seems to be "the" stimulus in the person's interpretation—is playing the role of an authority to which the subject feels compelled to submit. Situations which seem to be lacking in firmness are apparently as strange, bewildering, and disturbing to the prejudiced as would be a leader lacking in absolute determination. With internal conflict being as disturbing as it is in this group, there apparently develops a tendency to deny external ambiguity as long as such denial can be maintained. Underlying anxiety issuing from confusion of one's social identity and from other conflicts is apparently so great that it hampers individuals in this group in facing even the purely cognitive types of ambiguity. The mechanism discussed is somewhat related to what Postman, Bruner, and McGinnies (18) have called "perceptual defenses." A desperate effort is made to shut out uncertainties the prejudiced individual is unable to face, thus narrowing what Tolman (23) has called the "cognitive map" to rigidly defined tracks. Persons with less severe underlying confusions, on the other hand, may be able to afford facing ambiguities openly, although this may mean an at least temporary facing of conflicts and anxieties as well. In this case the total pattern is that of a broader integration of reality without shutting off parts of it, and thus a more flexible adaptation to varying circumstances.

In a further experiment in which one after another in a progressive series of hues was to be named, the writer gained the tentative impression that prejudiced subjects again perseverate longer than the unprejudiced, in this case with a given color-term, conceive of fewer and cruder steps along the scale, or tend toward one-dimensional rather than more complex systems of classification.

Another experiment, conducted recently along the general line of the one with the cat-dog pictures just mentioned, is one by Mr. Norman Livson and Mrs. Florine Berkowitz Livson. Numbers were used rather than objects, thus reducing the possibility of involvement with content. Two statistically significant differences were found (both at the 1 per cent level of confidence) for a total of forty-two of the children in our social discrimination project. One is the relatively slow recognition of numbers emerging from indistinctness, the other the relatively slow recognition of numbers changing from other numbers, by the ethnocentric group. Again, there was a prolonged clinging to the first impression, even though faulty, on the part of the prejudiced.

Rokeach (20) investigated a problem of rigidity related to ambiguity. He used a gestalt-psychological thinking problem involving the manipulation of three jars. A mental set was first established by presenting the subjects with a series of problems which could be solved only by a relatively long and complex method. The subjects were then presented with further problems which could be solved either by maintaining the original set or by using a more advantageous direct and simple method. A measure of rigidity was derived from the number of cases in which the established set was maintained and thus an inability demonstrated to restructure the field and to perceive the direct solution. The results presented by Rokeach indicate clearly that the children scoring extremely high on ethnic prejudice solve the new problems more rigidly than those extremely low on prejudice. Over and above the measure of rigidity, based on maladaptive perseveration, Rokeach utilized the amount of scratch paper used as an aid in solving the problems as a measure for concreteness of thinking. Those high on prejudice were found to use more scratch paper than those low on prejudice. A spatial problem also devised by Rokeach, calling for the finding of a shorter path on a map after a set for a longer route had been established, has further borne out the greater rigidity of the ethnically prejudiced.

The fact that the sample of children from our project on social discrimination who were used as subjects in the experiments of Rokeach had been studied with respect to a variety of personality characteristics made it possible to interrelate different measures of rigidity. Thus the rigidity scores derived from the simple arithmetic problems just referred to tend to correlate with over-all clinical ratings of children's rigidity based on their attitudes toward parents, sex roles, self, moral values, etc., as revealed in our clinical interviews.[10] Similarly, significant correlations were found between rigidity scores gained by Rokeach and the total score on the personality inventory. This personality inventory had been designed to measure dichotomizing in emotional and social attitudes. It consists of a series of statements referring to attitudes toward authority, aggression, weakness, etc. A few statements from this inventory have been quoted above.

As mentioned earlier, intolerance of ambiguity must further be related to a reluctance to think in terms of probabilities and a preference to escape into whatever seems definite and therefore safe. Murray E. Jarvik adapted a technique developed by Egon Brunswik in a probability discrimination experiment with rats in which food rewards had been distributed with differing relative frequencies on the two sides of a simple T-maze (3). Jarvik presented a long series of pictures of white and Negro children to our ethnically prejudiced and unprejudiced children, asking them to state in each case whether they were dull or bright looking. After each response, the supposedly correct answer was given by the experimenter. For half of the children 75 per cent of the whites and 25 per cent of the Negroes were designated as "bright," and the rest as "dull," and vice versa for the other half of the children. A preliminary inspection of the data shows that the children extremely low on prejudice caught on to this probability learning situation more readily than those high on ethnocentrism; the latter tended to persist in their preconceptions, being less able to absorb the general trend of the information given.

Some of the traits mentioned in this section may be more fully ascertained by the use of such projective tests as the Rorschach, especially when the slant of interpretation given to these tests by Rapaport (19) is applied. Aside from a certain advantage of setting up specific experiments for specific variables, perceptual experiments of the kind described ordinarily offer a "reality" more clearly delineated, whereas projective techniques are purposely being kept

---

[10] The evaluation of these interviews was undertaken by Miss Joan Havel in collaboration with the present writer.

vague in a greater variety of directions. Since we were in the present context more interested in the handling and mastery of a well-circumscribed reality, and less in projections as such, the experiments listed have an edge over projective tests for our particular purpose.

Though the over-all trend of the data discussed in this section seems to indicate a certain generality, within the individuals concerned, of the approach to reality which we have subsumed under the term "intolerance of ambiguity," a much wider array of both techniques and population samples would be necessary to establish this generality with an adequate degree of definiteness. It must further be kept in mind that, as is being pointed out elsewhere in this paper, compensation of rigidity by—often exaggerated—flexibility is probably as much present as is positive correlation between different aspects of rigidity.

Detailed inspection of case studies which include both clinical data and data from experiments on such cognitive topics as perception, memory, and problem solving show consistencies as well as apparent inconsistencies in this respect. For instance, there are perhaps some exceptional cases of children who are extremely high on the prejudice scale but manifest only an average amount of mental rigidity. The discussion of such inconsistencies would easily fill another paper. We shall give here only some indication of the complexity of the facts involved. In one of the inconsistent cases of the kind just described a boy's ethnic prejudice turned out to stem mainly from a marked physical marginality. His mother was loving and permissive, and her method of child training fitted better to the boy's relative mental flexibility than to his high prejudice. On the other hand, a girl who was most articulate in proclaiming a liberal ideology and who at the same time displayed more mental rigidity than is common in the unprejudiced turned out to be a member of a family which, though clinging in a dogmatic and militant way to a liberal ideology, did so with a great deal of inexorability and a lack of willingness to arbitrate with, or to accept, those who thought differently.

REFERENCES

1. ADORNO, T. W., FRENKEL-BRUNSWIK, E., LEVINSON, D. J., and SAN-
FORD, R. N. *The authoritarian personality.* New York: Harper, 1949.

2. BENUSSI, V. Zur Psychologie des Gestalterfassens. In A. Meinong (Ed.), *Untersuchungen zur Gegenstandstheorie und Psychologie.* Leipzig. 1904.

3. BRUNSWIK, E. Probability as a determiner of rat behavior. *J. exp. Psychol.,* 1939, **25**, 175-197.

4. BRUNSWIK, E. Organismic achievement and environment probability. (From: Brunswik, Hull, Lewin, *Symposium on psychology and scientific method.* University of Chicago, 1941.) *Psychol. Rev.,* 1943, **50**, 255-272.

5. CHRISTIE, J. R. The effects of frustration upon rigidity in problem solution. Doctoral dissertation, Univ. of Calif., 1949.

6. FENICHEL, O. *Psychoanalytic theory of neurosis.* New York: Norton, 1945.

7. FRENKEL-BRUNSWIK, E. Mechanisms of self-deception. *J. soc. Psychol.* (S.P.S.S.I. Bulletin), 1939, **10**, 409-420.

8. FRENKEL-BRUNSWIK, E. Psychoanalysis and personality research. (In G. W. Allport (Ed.), *Symposium on psychoanalysis by analyzed experimental psychologists.*) *J. abnorm. soc. Psychol.,* 1940, **35**,. 176-197.

9. FRENKEL-BRUNSWIK, E. Motivation and behavior. *Genet. Psychol. Monogr.* 1942, **26**, 121-265.

10. FRENKEL-BRUNSWIK, E. Dynamic and cognitive categorization of qualitative material: I. General problems and the thematic apperception test, II: Interviews of the ethnically prejudiced. *J. Psychol.,* 1948, **25**, 253-260, 261-277.

11. FRENKEL-BRUNSWIK, E. A study of prejudice in children. *Human Relations,* 1948, **1**, 295-306.

12. FRENKEL-BRUNSWIK, E. Tolerance toward ambiguity as a personality variable. (Abstract.) *Amer. Psychologist,* 1948, **3**, 268.

13. FROMM, E. *Escape from freedom.* New York: Farrar and Rinehart, 1941.

14. GOLDSTEIN, K. The significance of psychological research in schizophrenia. In S. S. Tomkins (Ed.), *Contemporary psychopathology.* Harvard Univ. Press, 1943, 302-318.

15. GOLDSTEIN, K., and SCHEERER, M. Abstract and concrete behavior. *Psychol. Monogr.,* 1941, **53**, No. 239.

16. KOFFKA, K. *Principles of gestalt psychology.* New York: Harcourt Brace, 1935.

17. LEVINSON, D. J. An approach to the theory and measurement of ethnocentric ideology. *J. Psychol.,* 1949, **28**, 19-39.

18. POSTMAN, L., BRUNER, J. S., and McGINNIES, E. Personal values as selective factors in perception. *J. abnorm. soc. Psychol.,* 1948, **43**, 142-154.

19. RAPAPORT, D., SCHAFER, R., and GILL, M. *Manual of diagnostic psychological testing:* II. Personality and ideational content. New York: Macy Foundation, 1946.

20. ROKEACH, M. Generalized mental rigidity as a factor in ethnocentrism. *J. abnorm. soc. Psychol.,* 1943, **48,** 259-278.

21. ROSENZWEIG, S. A dynamic interpretation of psychotherapy oriented towards research. In S. S. Tomkins (Ed.), *Contemporary psychopathology.* Harvard Univ. Press, 1943, 235-243.

22. THURSTONE, L. L. *A factorial study of perception.* Univ. of Chicago Press, 1944.

23. TOLMAN, E. C. Cognitive maps in rats and men. *Psychol. Rev.,* 1948, **55,** 189-208.

24. WERNER, H. *Comparative psychology of mental development.* First translation, 1940. Revised edition, Chicago: Follett, 1948.

....

On Perceptual Readiness[*,1]

JEROME S. BRUNER

ABOUT TEN YEARS AGO I was party to the publication of an innocent enough paper entitled "Value and Need as Organizing Factors in Perception." It was concerned with what at that time was the rather obscure problem of how extra-stimulus factors influenced perception, a subject then of interest to only a small band of us— Gardner Murphy, Nevitt Sanford, Muzafer Sherif, and a few others. Obviously, Professor Boring is quite right about the mischievousness of the *Zeitgeist*, for the appearance of this paper seemed to coincide with all sorts of spirit-like rumblings within the world of psychology that were soon to erupt in a most unspirit-like torrent of research on this very topic—perhaps three hundred research reports and theoretical explications in the ten years since then. F. H. Allport (1) and M. D. Vernon (81) have each recently had a fresh look at the field, sorting out the findings and evaluating the theoretical positions, and they have done superb service. Their labors free me to pursue a more relaxed course. What I should like to do in this paper is to set forth what seem to me to be the outlines of an approach to perception congruent with this body of new (and often contradictory) findings and to sketch out what appear to me to be the persistent problems still outstanding.

ON THE NATURE OF PERCEPTION

Perception involves an act of categorization. Put in terms of the antecedent and subsequent conditions from which we make our inferences, we stimulate an organism with some appropriate input and he responds by referring the input to some class of things or

* From the *Psychol. Rev.*, 1957, **64**, 123-152. Reprinted by permission of the author and the publisher.
[1] The present paper was prepared with the invaluable assistance of Mr. Michael Wallach. I also benefited from the comments of Professors W. C. H. Prentice, Karl Pribram, and M. E. Bitterman, and from various associates at Princeton University, Kansas University, and the University of Michigan, where versions of this paper were presented.

events. "That is an orange," he states, or he presses a lever that he has been "tuned" to press when the object that he "perceives" is an orange. On the basis of certain defining or criterial attributes in the input, what are usually called cues although they should be called clues (35), there is a selective placing of the input in one category of identity rather than another. The category need not be elaborate: "a sound," "a touch," "a pain," are also examples of categorized inputs. The use of cues in inferring the categorial identity of a perceived object, most recently treated by Bruner, Goodnow, and Austin (9) and by Binder (4), is as much a feature of perception as the sensory stuff from which percepts are made. What is interesting about the nature of the inference from cue to identity in perception is that it is in no sense different from other kinds of categorial inferences based on defining attributes. "That thing is round and nubbly in texture and orange in color and of such-and-such size —therefore an orange; let me now test its other properties to be sure." In terms of process, this course of events is no different from the more abstract task of looking at a number, determining that it is divisible only by itself and unity, and thereupon categorizing it in the class of prime numbers. So at the outset, it is evident that one of the principal characteristics of perceiving is a characteristic of cognition generally. There is no reason to assume that the laws governing inferences of this kind are discontinuous as one moves from perceptual to more conceptual activities. In no sense need the process be conscious or deliberate. A theory of perception, we assert, needs a mechanism capable of inference and categorizing as much as one is needed in a theory of cognition.

Let it be plain that no claim is being made for the utter indistinguishability of perceptual and more conceptual inferences. In the first place, the former appear to be notably less docile or reversible than the latter. I may know that the Ames distorted room that looks so rectangular is indeed distorted, but unless conflicting cues are put into the situation, as in experiments to be discussed later, the room still looks rectangular. So too with such compelling illusions as the Müller-Lyer: in spite of knowledge to the contrary, the line with the extended arrowheads looks longer than the equal-length one with those inclined inward. But these differences, interesting in themselves, must not lead us to overlook the common feature of inference underlying so much of cognitive activity.

Is what we have said a denial of the classic doctrine of sense-data? Surely, one may argue (and Hebb [36] has done so effectively) that there must be certain forms of primitive organization within the perceptual field that make possible the differential use of cues in identity categorizing. Both logically and psychologically, the point is evident. Yet it seems to me foolish and unnecessary to assume that the sensory "stuff" on which higher order categorizations are based is, if you will, of a different sensory order than more evolved identities with which our perceptual world is normally peopled. To argue otherwise is to be forced into the contradictions of Locke's distinction between primary and secondary qualities in perception. The rather bold assumption that we shall make at the outset is that all perceptual experience is necessarily the end product of a categorization process.

And this for two reasons. The first is that all perception is generic in the sense that whatever is perceived is placed in and achieves its "meaning" from a class of percepts with which it is grouped. To be sure, in each thing we encounter, there is an aspect of uniqueness, but the uniqueness inheres in deviation from the class to which an object is "assigned." Analytically, let it be noted, one may make a distinction, as Gestalt theorists have, between a pure stimulus process and the interaction of that stimulus process with an appropriate memory trace—the latter presumably resulting in a percept that has an identity. If indeed there is a "pure stimulus process," it is doubtful indeed that it is ever represented in perception bereft of identity characteristics. The phenomenon of a completely unplaceable object or event or "sensation"—even unplaceable with respect to modality—is sufficiently far from experience to be uncanny. Categorization of an object or event—placing it or giving it identity— can be likened to what in set theory is the placement of an element from a universe in a subset of that universe of items on the basis of such ordered dimensional pairs, triples, or n-tuples as man-woman, mesomorph-endomorph-ectomorph, or height to nearest inch. In short, when one specifies something more than that an element or object belongs to a universe, and that it belongs in a subset of the universe, one has categorized the element or object. The categorization can be as intersecting as "this is a quartz crystal goblet fashioned in Denmark," or as simple as "this is a glassy thing." So long as an operation assigns an input to a subset, it is an act of categorization.

More serious, although it is "only a logical issue," is the question of how one could communicate or make public the presence of a nongeneric or completely unique perceptual experience. Neither language nor the tuning that one could give an organism to direct any other form of overt response could provide an account, save in generic or categorial terms. If perceptual experience is ever had raw, i.e., free of categorial identity, it is doomed to be a gem serene, locked in the silence of private experience.

Various writers, among them Gibson (26), Wallach (83), and Pratt (66), have proposed that we make a sharp distinction between the class of perceptual phenomena that have to do with the identity or object-meaning of things and the attributive or sensory world from which we derive our cues for inferring identities. Gibson, like Titchener (78) before him, urges a distinction between the visual field and the visual world, the former the world of attributive sense impressions, the latter of objects and things and events. Pratt urges that motivation and set and past experience may affect the things of the visual world but not the stuff of the visual field. And Wallach too reflects this ancient tradition of his Gestalt forebears by urging the distinction between a stimulus process pure and the stimulus process interacting with a memory trace of past experience with which it has made a neural contact on the basis of similarity. The former is the stuff of perception; the latter the finished percept. From shirtsleeves to shirtsleeves in three generations: we are back with the founding and founded content of the pre-Gestalt Gestalters. If one is to study the visual field freed of the things of the visual world, it becomes necessary—as Wallach implies—to free oneself of the stimulus error: dealing with a percept not as an object or as a thing with identity, but as a magnitude or a brightness or a hue or a shape to be matched against a variable test patch.

If we have implied that categorizing is often a "silent" or unconscious process, that we do not experience a going-from-no-identity to an arrival-at-identity, but that the first hallmark of *any* perception is some form of identity, this does not free us of the responsibility of inquiring into the origin of categories. Certainly, Hebb (36) is correct in asserting like Immanuel Kant, that certain primitive unities or identities within perception must be innate or autochthonous and not learned. The primitive capacity to categorize "things" from "background" is very likely one such, and so too the capacity to distinguish events in one modality from those in others —although the phenomena of synesthesia would suggest that this is not so complete a juncture as it might seem; e.g., von Hornbostel (39). The sound of a buzz saw does rise and fall phenomenally as one switches room illumination on and off. The full repertory of innate categories—a favorite topic for philosophical debate in the 19th century—is a topic on which perhaps too much ink and too little empirical effort have been spilled. Motion, causation, intention, identity, equivalence, time, and space, it may be persuasively argued, are categories that must have some primitive counterpart in the neonate. And it may well be, as Piaget (65) implies, that certain primitive capacities to categorize in particular ways depend upon the existence of still more primitive ones. To identify something as having "caused" something else requires, first, the existence of an identity category such that the two things involved each may conserve identity in the process of "cause" producing "effect." Primitive or unlearned categories—a matter of much concern to such students of instinctive behavior as Lashley (51) and Tinbergen (77) —remain to be explicated. In what follows, we shall rather cavalierly take them for granted. As to the development of more elaborated categories in terms of which objects are placed or identified, it involves the process of learning how to isolate, weigh, and use criterial attribute values, or cues for grouping objects in equivalence classes. It is only as mysterious, but no more so, than the learning of any differential discrimination, and we shall have occasion to revisit the problem later.

A second feature of perception, beyond its seemingly categorial and inferential nature, is that it can be described as varyingly veridical. This is what has classically been called the "representative function" of perception: what is perceived is somehow a representation of the external world—a metaphysical hodgepodge of a statement but one which we somehow manage to understand in spite of its confusion. We have long since given up simulacral theories of representation. What we generally mean when we speak of representation or veridicality is that perception is predictive in varying degrees. That is to say, the object that we *see* can also be *felt* and *smelled* and there will somehow be a match or a congruity between what we see, feel, and smell. Or, to paraphrase a younger Bertrand Russell, what we see will turn out to be the same thing should we take a "closer look" at it. Or, in still different terms, the categorial placement of the object leads to appropriate consequences in terms of later behavior directed toward the perceived object: it appears as an apple, and indeed it keeps the doctor away if consumed once a day.

Let it be said that philosophers, and notably the pragmatist C. S. Peirce, have been urging such a view for more years than psychologists have taken their urgings seriously. The meaning of a proposition, as Peirce noted in his famous essay on the pragmatic theory of meaning (63), is the set of hypothetical statements one can make about attributes or consequences related to that proposition. "Let us ask what we mean by calling a thing *hard*. Evidently, that it will not be scratched by many other substances" (White [84]). The meaning of a thing, thus, is the placement of an object in a network of hypothetical inference concerning its other observable properties, its effects, and so on.

All of this suggests, does it not, that veridicality is not so much a matter of representation as it is a matter of what I shall call "model building." In learning to perceive, we are learning the relations that exist between the properties of objects and events that we encounter, learning appropriate categories and category systems, *learning to predict and to check what goes with what*. A simple example illustrates the point. I present for tachistoscopic recognition two nonsense words, one a 0-order approximation to English constructed according to Shannon's rules, the other a 4-order approximation: YRULPZOC and VERNALIT. At 500 milliseconds of exposure, one perceives correctly and in their proper place about 48 per cent of the letters in 0-order words, and about 93 per cent of the letters in 4-order words. In terms of the amount of information transmitted by these letter arrays, i.e., correcting them for redundancy, the subject is actually receiving the same informational input. The difference in reportable perception is a function of the fact that the individual has learned the transitional probability model of what goes with what in English writing. We say that perception in one case is more "veridical" than in the other—the difference between 93 per cent correct as contrasted with 48 per cent. What we mean is that the model of English with which the individual is working corresponds to the actual events that occur in English, and that if the stimulus input does not conform to the model, the resulting perception will be less veridical. Now let us drop the image of the model and adopt a more sensible terminology. Perceiving accurately under substandard conditions consists in being able to refer stimulus inputs to appropriate coding systems; where the information is fragmentary, one reads the missing properties of the stimulus input from the code to which part of the input has been referred. If the coding system applied does not match the input, what we read off from the coding system will lead to error and nonveridical perception. I would propose that perceptual learning consists not of making finer and finer discriminations as the Gibsons (27) would have us believe, but that it consists rather in the learning of appropriate modes of coding the environment in terms of its object character, connectedness, or redundancy, and then in allocating stimulus inputs to appropriate categorial coding systems.

The reader will properly ask, as Prentice (67) has, whether the notion of perceptual representation set forth here is appropriate to anything other than situations where the nature of the percept is not "clear"—perceptual representation under peripheral viewing conditions, in tachistoscopes, under extreme fatigue. If I am given a very good look at an object, under full illumination and with all the viewing time necessary, and end by calling it an orange, is this a different process from one in which the same object is flashed for a millisecond or two on the periphery of my retina with poor illumination? In the first and quite rare case the cues permitting the identification of the object are superabundant and the inferential mechanism operates with high probability relationships between cues and identities. In the latter, it is less so. The difference is of degree. What I am trying to say is that under *any* conditions of perception, what is achieved by the perceiver is the categorization of an object or sensory event in terms of more *or* less abundant and reliable cues. Representation consists of knowing how to utilize cues with reference to a system of categories. It also depends upon the creation of a system of categories-in-relationship that fit the nature of the world in which the person must live. In fine, adequate perceptual representation involves the learning of appropriate categories, the learning of cues useful in placing objects appropriately in such systems of categories, and the learning of what objects are likely to occur in the environment, a matter to which we will turn later.

We have neglected one important feature of perceptual representation in our discussion: representation in perception of the space-time-intensity conditions of the external world. Perceptual magnitudes correspond in some degree to the metrical properties of the physical world that we infer from the nature of our perception. That is to say, when one line *looks* longer than another, it is likely to *be* longer as measured by the ruler. There are constant errors and sampling errors in such sensory representation, but on the whole there is enough isomorphism between perceiving without aids (psychology) and perceiving with aids (physics) to make the matter perennially interesting.

Is this form of representation subject to the kinds of considerations we have been passing in review? Does it depend upon categorizing activities and upon the construction of an adequate system of categories against which stimulus inputs can be matched? There is probably one condition where perceptual acts are relatively free of such influences, and that is in the task of discriminating simultaneously presented stimuli as alike or different—provided we do not count the "tuning of the organism" that leads one to base his judgment on one rather than another feature of the two stimuli. Ask the person to deal with one stimulus at a time, to array it in terms of some magnitude scale, and immediately one is back in the familiar territory of inferential categorizing. Prentice, in his able defense of formalism in the study of perception (67), seems to assume that there is a special status attached to perceptual research that limits the set of the observer to simple binary decisions of "like" and "different" or "present" and "absent," and to research that also provides the subject with optimal stimulus conditions, and Graham (31) has recently expressed the credo that no perceptual laws will be proper or pure laws unless we reduce perceptual experimentation to the kinds of operations used in the method of constant stimuli.

There was at one time a justification for such a claim on the grounds that such is the best strategy for getting at the sensory-physiological processes that underlie perception. As we shall see in a later section, current work in neuro-physiology brings this contention into serious doubt. In any case, the point must be made that many of the most interesting phenomena in sensory perception are precisely those that have been uncovered by departing from the rigid purism of the method of constants. I have in mind such pioneering studies as those of Stevens on sensory scales, where the organism is treated as an instrument whose sensory categorizations and scalar orderings are the specific object of study (74). Add to this the advances made by Helson on adaptation level (37) and by Volkmann on the anchoring of sensory scales (82)—both using the "sloppy" method of single stimuli—and one realizes that the nature of representation in perception of magnitudes is very much subject to categorizing processes, and to perceptual readiness as this is affected by subjective estimates of the likelihood of occurrence of sensory events of different magnitudes. Indeed, Helson's law of adaptation level states that the subjective magnitude of a singly presented stimulus depends upon the weighted geometric mean of the series of stimuli that the subject has worked with, and the ingenious experiments of Donald Brown (7) have indicated that this adaptation level is influenced only by those stimuli that the subject considers to be within the category of objects being considered. Ask the subject to move a weight from one side of the table to the other with the excuse that it is cluttering up the table, and the weight does not serve as an anchor to the series, although it will show a discernible effect if it is directly included in the series being judged. In short, the category systems that are utilized in arraying magnitudes are also affected by the requirement of matching one's model of the world to the actual events that are occurring—even if the categories be no more complicated than "heavy," "medium," and "light."

The recent work of Stevens (75) on "the direct estimation of sensory magnitudes" highlights the manner in which veridicality in sensory judgment depends upon the prior learning of an adequate category set in terms of which sensory input may be ordered. Subjects are presented a standard tone of 1000 cps at 80 db. sound-pressure-level and are told that the value of this loudness is 10. Nine variable loudnesses all of the 1000 cps are then presented, varying 70 db. on either side of the standard, each one at a time being paired with the standard. "If the standard is called 10, what would you call the variable? Use whatever numbers seem to you appropriate—fractions, decimals, or whole numbers." If one then compares the categorial judgments made with the sound pressure level of the various tones presented, using a log-log plot (log of the magnitude estimation against log of sound-pressure-level), the resulting function is a straight line, described by the empirical formula

$$L = kI^{0.3},$$

where L is loudness and I intensity. In short, categorial sorting of sensory magnitudes provides one with a mapping or representation of physical intensity. There are, to be sure, many problems connected with such a procedure, but the point remains: the magnitude categories in terms of which we scale sensory events represent a good fit to the physical characteristics of the world. Call this "veridicality" if you wish—although I do not see what is gained thereby; yet whatever one calls it, one must not lose sight of the fact that the judgments made are predictive of other features of the sensory inputs. Given the empirical conversion formula, one can predict from categorial judgment to physical meter readings.

To summarize, we have proposed that perception is a process of categorization in which organisms move inferentially from cues to categorial identity and that in many cases, as Helmholtz long ago suggested, the process is a silent one. If you will, the inference is often an "unconscious" one. Moreover, the results of such categorizations are representational in nature: they represent with varying degrees of predictive veridicality the nature of the physical world in which the organism operates. By predictive veridicality I mean simply that perceptual categorization of an object or event permits one to "go beyond" the properties of the object or event perceived to a prediction of other properties of the object not yet tested. The more adequate the category systems constructed for coding environmental events in this way, the greater the predictive veridicality that results.

Doubtless, the reader will think of any number of examples of perceptual phenomena not covered by the simple picture we have drawn. Yet a great many of the classic phenomena are covered— psychophysical judgment, constancy, perceptual identification, perceptual learning, and so on. This will become clearer in the following sections. What must now be dealt with are the phenomena having to do with selectivity: attention, set, and the like.

CUE UTILIZATION AND CATEGORY ACCESSIBILITY

A fruitful way of thinking of the nature of perceptual readiness is in terms of the accessibility of categories for use in coding or identifying environmental events. Accessibility is a heuristic concept, and it may be defined in terms of a set of measures. Conceive of a person who is perceptually ready to encounter a certain object, an apple let us say. *How* he happens to be in this state we shall consider later. We measure the accessibility of the category "apples" by the amount of stimulus input of a certain pattern necessary to evoke the perceptual response "there is an apple," or some other standardized response. We can state the "minimum" input required for such categorization by having our observer operate with two response categories, "yes" and "no," with the likelihood of occurrence of apples and nonapples at 50:50, or by using any other definition of "maximum readiness" that one wishes to employ. The greater the accessibility of a category, (a) the less the input necessary for categorization to occur in terms of this category, (b) the wider the range of input characteristics that will be "accepted" as fitting the category in question, (c) the more likely that categories that provide a better or equally good fit for the input will be masked. To put it in more ordinary language: apples will be more easily and swiftly recognized, a wider range of things will be identified or mis-identified as apples, and in consequence the correct or best fitting identity of these other inputs will be masked. This is what is intended by accessibility.

Obviously, categories are not isolated. One has a category "apples," to be sure, but it is imbedded by past learning in a network of categories: "An apple a day keeps the doctor away" is one such category system. So too, are "apples are fruits" and other placements of an object in a general classification scheme. Predictive systems are of the same order: e.g., "The apple will rot if not refrigerated." We have spoken of these systems before as the "meaning" of an object. We mention them again here to indicate that though we speak analytically of separate or isolated categories as being accessible to inputs, it is quite obvious that category systems vary in accessibility as a whole.

It follows from what has just been said that the most appropriate pattern of readiness at any given moment would be that one which would lead on the average to the most "veridical" guess about the nature of the world around one at the moment—best guess here being construed, of course, as a response in the absence of the necessary stimulus input. And it follows from this that the most ready perceiver would then have the best chances of estimating situations most adequately and planning accordingly. It is in this general sense that the ready perceiver who can proceed with fairly minimal inputs is also in a position to use his cognitive readiness not only for perceiving what is before him but in foreseeing what is likely to be before him. We shall return to this point shortly.

We must turn now to the question of cue utilization, the "strategies" in terms of which inferences are made (by the nervous system, of course) from cue to category and thence to other cues. I prefer to use the term strategy for several reasons. Perceiving, since it involves inference, rests upon a decision process, as Brunswik (17), Tanner and Swets (76) and others have pointed out. Even in the simplest threshold-measurement test, the subject has the task of deciding whether what he is seeing or hearing is noise only or signal-plus-noise. Given a set of cues, however presented, my nervous system must "decide" whether the thing is an airplane or a sea gull, a red or a green, or what not.

There appears, moreover, to be a sequence of such decisions involved in categorizing an object or event. A common-sense example will make this clear. I look across to the mantelpiece opposite my desk and see a rectangular object lying on it. If I continue this pursuit, subsequent decisions are to be made: is it the block of plastic I purchased for some apparatus or is it a book? In the dim light it can be either. I remember that the plastic is downstairs in one of the experimental rooms: the object "is" a book now, and I search for further cues on its dark red surface. I see what I think is some gold: it is a McGraw-Hill book, probably G. A. Miller's *Language and Communication* that I had been using late this afternoon. If you will, the process is a "bracketing" one, a gradual narrowing of the category placement of the object.

Let us attempt to analyze the various stages in such a decision sequence.

a. Primitive Categorization. Before any more elaborate inferential activity can occur, there must be a first, "silent" process that results in the perceptual isolation of an object or an event with certain characteristic qualities. Whether this is an innate process or one depending upon the prior construction of a cell-assembly, in the manner of Hebb (36), need not concern us. What is required simply is that an environmental event has been perceptually isolated and that the event is marked by certain spatio-temporal-qualitative characteristics. The event may have no more "meaning" than that it is an "object," a "sound," or a "movement."

b. Cue Search. In highly practiced cases or in cases of high cue-category probability linkage, a second process of more precise placement based on additional cues may be equally silent or "unconscious." An object is seen with phenomenal immediacy as a "book" or an "ash tray." In such instances there is usually a good fit between the specifications of a category and the nature of the cues impinging on the organism—although "fit" and "probability of linkage" may stand in a vicarious relation to each other. Where the fit to accessible categories is not precise, or when the linkage between cue and category is low in probability in the past experience of the organism, the conscious experience of cue searching occurs. "What is that thing?" Here, one is scanning the environment for data in order to find cues that permit a more precise placement of the object. Under these circumstances, the organism is "open" to maximum stimulation, in a manner described below.

c. Confirmation Check. When a tentative categorization has occurred, following cue search, cue search changes. The "openness" to stimulation decreases sharply in the sense that now, a tentative placement of identity having occurred, the search is narrowed for additional confirmatory cues to check this placement. It is this feature of perceptual identification that Woodworth (85) in his paper on the "Reenforcement of Perception" speaks of as "trial-and-check." We shall speak of a selective gating process coming into operation in this stage, having the effect of reducing the effective input of stimulation not relevant to the confirmatory process.

d. Confirmation Completion. The last stage in the process of perceptual identification is a completion, marked by termination of cue searching. It is characteristic of this state that openness to additional cues is drastically reduced, and incongruent cues are either normalized or "gated out." Experiments on the perception of incongruity (14), error (69), and the like (15), suggest that once an object has been categorized in a high-probability, good-fit category, the threshold for recognizing cues contrary to this categorization increases by almost an order of magnitude.

The question of fit between cue and category specification brings us to the key problem of the nature of categories. By a category we mean a rule for classing objects as equivalent. The rule specifies the following about the instances that are to be comprised in the category.

a. The properties or *criterial attribute values* required of an instance to be coded in a given class.

b. The manner in which such attribute values are to be com-

bined in making an inference from properties to category membership: whether conjunctively (e.g., a_i and b_i), relationally (e.g., a_i
bears a certain *relation* to b_i), or disjunctively (e.g., a_i or b_i).

    c. The weight assigned various properties in making an inference
from properties to category membership.

    d. The acceptance limits within which properties must fall to be
criterial. That is to say, from what range of attribute values may
$a_i, b_i \ldots k_i$ be drawn.

When we speak of rules, again it should be made clear that "conscious rules" are not intended. These are the rules that govern the
operation of a categorizing mechanism.

The likelihood that a sensory input will be categorized in terms
of a given category is not only a matter of fit between sensory input
and category specifications. It depends also on the accessibility of a
category. To put the matter in an oversimplified way, given a
sensory input with equally good fit to two nonoverlapping categories, the more accessible of the two categories would "capture"
the input. It is in this sense that mention was earlier made about
the vicarious relationship between fit and accessibility.

We have already noted that the accessibility of categories reflects
the learned probabilities of occurrence of events in the person's
world. The more frequently in a given context instances of a given
category occur, the greater the accessibility of the category. Operationally, this means that less stimulus input will be required for the
instance or event to be categorized in terms of a frequently used
category. In general, the type of probability we are referring to is
not absolute probability of occurrence, where each event that occurs is independent of each other. Such independence is rare in the
environment. Rather, the principal form of probability learning affecting category accessibility is the learning of contingent or transitional probabilities—the redundant structure of the environment.
That either the absolute or the contingent probability of events
makes a crucial difference in determining ease of perceptual identification is readily supported by research findings: in the former case
by ·studies like those of Howes (40) and Solomon and Postman
(72), and in the latter by the work of Miller, Heise, and Lichten
(62) and Miller, Bruner, and Postman (61).

But the organism to operate adequately must not only be ready for likely events in the environment, the better to represent them, and in order to perceive them quickly and without undue cognitive strain: it must also be able to search out unlikely objects and events essential to its maintenance and the pursuit of its enterprises. If I am walking the streets of a strange city and find myself hungry, I must be able to look for restaurants regardless of their likelihood of occurrence in the environment where I now find myself. In short, the accessibility of categories I employ for identifying the objects of the world around me must not only reflect the environmental probabilities of objects that fit these categories, but also reflect the search requirements imposed by my needs, my ongoing activities, my defenses, etc. And for effective search behavior to occur, the pattern of perceptual readiness during search must be realistic: tempered by what one is likely to find in one's perceptual world at that time and at that place as well as by what one seeks to find.

Let me summarize our considerations about the general properties of perception with a few propositions. The first is that *perception is a decision process*. Whatever the nature of the task set, the perceiver or his nervous system decides that a thing perceived is one thing and not another. A line is longer or shorter than a standard, a particular object is a snake and not a fallen branch, the incomplete word L*VE in the context MEN L*VE WOMEN is the word LOVE and not LIVE.

The second proposition is that *the decision process involves the utilization of discriminatory cues,* as do all decision processes. That is to say, the properties of stimulus inputs make it possible to sort these inputs into categories of best fit.

Thirdly, *the cue utilization process involves the operation of inference*. Going from cue to an inference of identity is probably the most ubiquitous and primitive cognitive activity. The utilization of inference presupposes the learning of environmental probabilities and invariances relating cues to cues, and cues to behavioral consequences. Cue utilization involves various stages: a primitive step of isolating an object or event from the flux of environmental stimulation, stages of cue searching where the task is to find cues that can be fitted to available category specifications, a tentative categorization with more search for confirming cues, and final categorization, when cue searching is severely reduced.

Fourth, *a category may be regarded as a set of specifications* regarding what events will be grouped as equivalent—rules respecting the nature of criterial cues required, the manner of their combining, their inferential weight, and the acceptance limits of their variability.

Fifth, *categories vary in terms of their accessibility,* the readiness with which a stimulus input with given properties will be coded or identified in terms of a category. The relative accessibility of categories and systems of categories seems to depend upon two factors: the expectancies of the person with regard to the likelihood of events to be encountered in the environment; and the search requirements imposed on the organism by his needs and his ongoing enterprises. To use the functionalist's language, perceptual readiness or accessibility serves two functions: *to minimize the surprise value of the environment* by matching category accessibility to the probabilities of events in the world about one, and *to maximize the attainment- of sought-after objects and events.*

Veridical perception, so our sixth proposition would run, *consists of the coding of stimulus inputs in appropriate categories* such that one may go from cue to categorial identification, and thence to the correct inference or prediction of other properties of the object so categorized. Thus, veridical perception requires the learning of categories and category systems appropriate to the events and objects with which the person has commerce in the physical world. When we speak of the representative function of perception, we speak of the adequacy of the categorizing system of the individual in permitting him to infer the nature of events and to go beyond them to the correct prediction of other events.

Seventh, *under less than optimal conditions, perception will be veridical in the degree to which the accessibility of categorizing systems reflects the likelihood of occurrence of the events that the person will encounter.* Where accessibility of categories reflects environmental probabilities, the organism is in the position of requiring less stimulus input, less redundancy of cues for the appropriate categorization of objects. In like vein, nonveridical perception will be systematic rather than random in its error insofar as it reflects the inappropriate readiness of the perceiver. The more inappropriate the readiness, the greater the input or redundancy of cues required for appropriate categorization to occur—where "appropriate" means that an input is coded in the category that yields more adequate subsequent predictions.

MECHANISMS MEDIATING PERCEPTUAL READINESS

Having considered some of the most general characteristics of perceiving, particularly as these relate to the phenomena of perceptual readiness, we must turn next to a consideration of the kinds of mechanisms that mediate such phenomena. Four general types of mechanisms will be proposed: *grouping and integration, access ordering, match-mismatch signaling,* and *gating.* They will be described in such a form that they may be considered as prototypes of neural mechanisms and, where possible, neurophysiological counterparts will be described briefly. Six years ago, Edward Tolman (79) proposed that the time was perhaps ripe for reconsidering the neural substrate of perception. Perhaps he was right, or perhaps even now the enterprise is somewhat premature. Yet, the body of perceptual data available makes it worth while to consider the kinds of mechanisms that will be required to deal with them. To use Hebb's engaging metaphor, it is worth while to build a bridge between neurophysiology and psychology provided we are anchored at both ends, even if the middle of the bridge is very shaky.

Grouping and Integration. It is with the neural basis of the categorizing process that Hebb's *Organization of Behavior* (36) is principally concerned. Little is served by recapitulating his proposals here, for the reader will be familiar with the concise account in Chapters 4 and 5 of that book, where the concepts of cell assembly and phase sequence are set forth with a clarity that permits one to distinguish what is neurophysiological fact and what speculation. In essence, Hebb's account attempts to provide an anatomical-physiological theory of how it is that we distinguish classes of events in the environment, and how we come to recognize new events as exemplars of the once established classes. The theory seeks also to provide a mechanism for integration of sorting activity over time: the formation of phase sequences for the conservation of superordinate classes of events and superordinate sequences. Basically, it is an associational or an "enrichment" theory of perception at the neural level, requiring that established neural associations facilitate perception of events that have gone together before. The expectancies, the centrally induced facilitations that occur prior to the sensory process for which they are appropriate, are learned expectancies based on the existence of frequency integrators. These frequency integrators may be neuroanatomical in the form of synaptic knobs, or they may be any process that has the effect of making activity in one locus of the brain increase or decrease the likelihood of activity in another. To be sure, Hebb's theory depends upon some broad assumptions about convergence of firing from area 17 outward, about synchronization of impulses, and about the manner in which reverberatory circuits can carry organization until the much slower process of anatomical change can take place. But this is minor in comparison with the stimulation provided by facing squarely the question of how the known facts of categorization and superordination in perception *could* be represented in the light of present knowledge.

While it is difficult indeed to propose a plausible neural mediator to account for category formation and the development of elaborated categorial systems (e.g., our knowledge of the relations between classes of events in the physical world which we manipulate in everyday life), it is less difficult to specify what such mechanisms must account for in perceptual behavior.

At the level of the individual category or cell assembly, the phenomena of object identity must be accounted for. Moreover, identity conservation or object constancy requires explanation in terms common with the explanation of identity. Experiments by Piaget (65) suggest that the capacity to maintain the phenomenal identity of an object undergoing change is the hard-won result of maturation-and-learning. In connection with the later discussion of gating processes, we shall have occasion to consider the manner in which, at different stages in clue utilization, the required fit between an input and a cell assembly changes.

Where integration is concerned, there must be a process capable of conserving a record of the likely transitions and contingencies of the environment. The moment-to-moment programming of perceptual readiness depends upon such integrations. In short, the relation between classes of events is conserved in such a way as to be subject to change by learning. Several things can be guessed about integration processes. It is unlikely that it is a simple autocorrelation device. Clearly, the conceptions of transitional probabilities that are established in dealing with sequences of events show biases that no self-respecting autocorrelation computer would be likely to operate with. One of these is a strong and early tendency to treat events as nonindependent of each other over time. In the absence of evidence, or even in the presence of contrary evidence, humans—as their behavior has been observed in choice tasks, e.g., Estes (23), Goodnow

(29)—treat random sequences of events as though they were governed by dependent probabilities. The spate of research on two-choice decision behavior has made us quite sharply aware of this characteristic of cognitive functioning. The typical pattern is the gambler's fallacy or, more properly, the negative recency effect. Given two equiprobable events whose occurrences are random, the repetition of one event progressively leads to the expectancy of the other. As in the elegant experiments of Jarvik (44) and Goodnow (29), the probability that a person will predict one of two events increases directly as a function of the number of repetitions of the other event. Such behavior persists over thousands of opportunities for testing, and it appears under a variety of testing conditions (9).

The second feature of sequential probability integration mechanisms is that, in establishing a conception of the probability with which events will occur, the typical human subject will bias his estimate in terms of desired or feared outcomes. As in the experiments of Marks (60) on children and of Irwin (41) on adults, the subjectively estimated probability of strongly desired events will be higher per previous encountered occurrence than the estimated likelihood of less desired events. Quite clearly, then, the establishment of estimates depends upon more than frequency integrations biased by assumptions of nonindependence. The "something more" is a motivational or personality process, and we shall have more to say about it in considering phenomena of so-called "perceptual sensitization" and "perceptual defense."

Access Ordering. The term "accessibility" has been used in preceding pages to denote the ease or speed with which a given stimulus input is coded in terms of a given category under varying conditions of instruction, past learning, motivation, etc. It has been suggested, moreover, that two general sets of conditions affect accessibility: subjective probability estimates of the likelihood of a given event, and certain kinds of search sets induced by needs and by a variety of other factors.

Let us consider a few relevant facts about perception. The first of these is that the threshold of recognition for stimuli presented by visual, auditory, or other means is not only a function of the time, intensity, or "fittingness" of the stimulus input, but also varies massively as a function of the number of alternatives for which the perceiver is set. The size of the expected array, to say it another way, increases the identification threshold for any item in the array. Typical examples of this general finding are contained in papers by Miller, Heise, and Lichten (62) and by Bruner, Miller, and Zimmerman (10). The actual shape of the function need not concern us, save that it is quite clear that it is not what one would expect from a simple binary system with a fixed channel capacity. What we are saying holds, of course, only for the case where the perceiver has learned that all the items in the expected array are (a) equiprobable and (b) independent, one of the other, in order of appearance.

The first hunch we may propose, then, about access-ordering mechanisms is that degree of accessibility of coding categories to stimulus inputs is related to regulation of the number of preactivated cell assemblies that are operative at the time of input. In an earlier paper (8), discussing factors that strengthen an hypothesis in the sense of making it more easily confirmable, I proposed that one of the major determinants of such strength was monopoly: where one and only one hypothesis is operative with no competing alternatives, it tends to be more readily confirmable. It is the same general point that is being made here. Accessibility, then, must have something to do with the resolution of competing alternatives.

As between two arrays of expected alternatives, each of the same size, we may distinguish between them in terms of the bias that exists in terms of expected likelihood of occurrence of each alternative. If one could characterize the expected alternatives in terms of probability values, one could conceive of the array ranging in values from a figure approaching 1.0 at one extreme, to another approaching 0.0 at the other. The findings with respect to perceptual readiness for the alternatives represented in such an array are well known. For a constant-sized array, the greater the estimated likelihood of occurrence of an alternative, the more readily will the alternative be perceived or identified. This is known to be true for large arrays, such as the ensemble of known words in the English language, whose likelihood may be roughly judged by their frequency of occurrence in printed English (e.g., 40). It is not altogether clear that it is the case for arrays of expected alternatives that are within the so-called span of attention—i.e., less than seven or eight alternatives. That the principle holds for middling arrays of about 20 items has been shown by Solomon and Postman (72).

What is particularly interesting about change of accessibility, under conditions where estimates of the likelihood of occurrence of alternatives become biased, is that the biasing can be produced either by a gradual learning process akin to probability learning *or* by instruction. Thus, Bitterman and Kniffin (5), investigating recognition thresholds for taboo and neutral words, show that as the experiment progresses, there is a gradual lowering of threshold for the taboo words as the subject comes to expect their occurrence. Bruner and Postman (14) have similarly shown that repeated presentation of stimulus materials containing very low-probability incongruities leads to a marked decrease in threshold time required for recognizing the incongruous features. At the same time, both Cowen and Beier (20) and Postman and Crutchfield (70) have shown that if a subject is forewarned that taboo words are going to be presented, his threshold for them will tend to be lower than for neutral words, whereas it will be higher if no instruction is given. In short, preactivation of cell assemblies—assuming for a moment that *degree of preactivation* is the mechanism that represents subjective estimates of likelihood of occurrence of an event—such preactivation can be produced by gradual learning or quantally by instruction. Moreover, biasing may be produced by the nature of the situation in which the perceiver is operating. A recent study by Bruner and Minturn (11) illustrates the point. Subjects are presented at brief exposure a broken capital B with a small separation between the vertical and the curved component of the letter so that it may be perceived as a B or as a 13. The manner in which it is reported is determined by whether the subject has previously been presented with letters or with numbers to recognize. In short, expectancy of one or the other context preactivates a related array of categories or cell-assemblies, not just a single, isolated one.

What the neural correlates of access ordering will look like is anybody's guess. Lashley (52) has remarked that, for all our searching, we have not located a specific memory trace—either in the form of a reverberatory circuit, a definite change in fiber size as proposed by J. Z. Young (88) and Eccles (21), a synaptic knob—in the manner of Lorente de No (57) or in any known form. To be sure, Penfield (64) has activated memories by punctate electrical stimulation of the cortex, but this is a long remove from a definition of the neural properties of the trace. For the time being, one does better to deal in terms of the formal properties that a trace system must exhibit than to rest one's psychological model on any neurophysiological or anatomical conception of the memory trace.

And, quite clearly, one of the formal properties of a trace system is that its elements vary in accessibility to stimulus input with the kinds of conditions we have considered. It is instructive to note that when a theory of traces lacks this feature, it ceases to be useful in dealing with the wide range of perceptual categorizing phenomena of which we now have knowledge. Gestalt theory is a case in point. According to Köhler's view (48), a stimulus process "finds" its appropriate memory trace, resulting in identification of the stimulus process, on the basis of distinctive similarity between stimulus process and memory trace. The theory has been criticized, justly I think, for failing to specify the nature of this similarity save by saying that it is a neural isomorph of phenomenal similarity. But since similarity may be highly selective—two objects may be alike in color but differ in dozens of other respects—there is obviously some *tertium quid* that determines the basis of similarity. More serious still is the inability of such a theory to deal with the increased likelihood of categorization in terms of particular traces as a function of changes in search set or subjective likelihood estimates. The Bruner-Minturn results would require that, as between two traces with which a stimulus process may make contact, each equally "similar" to the stimulus, the stimulus process will make contact with the one having a higher probability of being matched by environmental events. This is interesting, but it is far from the spirit of Gestalt theory.

Match-Mismatch Processes. One may readily conceive of and, indeed, build an apparatus that will accept or reject inputs on the basis of whether or not they fulfill certain specifications. Selfridge (71) has constructed a machine to read letters, Fry (24) has one that will discriminate various phonemes, and Uttley (80) has constructed one that, like Tinbergen's graylay geese, will recognize the flying silhouette of a predator hawk. All such machines have in common that they require a match between a stimulus input and various specifications required by the sorting mechanism of the machine.

In the examples just given, there is no consequence generated by whether a given input fulfills the specifications required by the identifying machine. It fits or it doesn't fit. But now let us build in two other features. The first is that the machine emit a signal to indicate how closely any given input comes to fulfilling the specifications required: either by indicating how many attributes the object has in common with the specifications, or by indicating how far off the mark on any given attribute dimension a given input is. The second is that the machine do something on the basis of these signals: to increase sensitivity if an object is within a given distance of specifications for a closer look, or to decrease it if the object is further than a certain amount from specifications, or to stop registering further if the input fits.

In short, one can imagine a nervous system that emits all-or-none match-mismatch signals or graded match-mismatch signals, and one can also imagine that these signals could then feed into an effector system to regulate activity relevant to continuing search behavior for a fitting object, or to regulate other forms of activity. MacKay (59) has recently proposed such a model.

We must return for a moment to an earlier discussion. In the discussion of cue utilization, a distinction was made between three phases of "openness" in cue search. The first was one in which a given input was being scanned for its properties so as to place it in one of a relatively large set of possible alternative categories. Here one would register on as many features of an object as possible. In a second stage, the input has been tentatively placed, and the search is limited to confirming or infirming criterial cues. Finally, with more definite placement, cue search is suspended and deviations from specification may even be "normalized." It is for the regulation of such patterns of search or cue utilization that some mechanism such as match-mismatch signaling is postulated.

Let it be said that while match-mismatch signaling-effector systems are readily conceivable and readily constructed, there is no knowledge available as to how a system like the nervous system might effect such a process. That there is feedback all over the system is quite apparent from its detailed anatomy, and this is the process out of which a large-scale system such as we have described would be constructed.

Gating Processes. The picture thus far presented is of a conceptual nervous system with a massive afferent intake that manages somehow to sort inputs into appropriate assemblies of varying accessibility. It seems unlikely that this is the nature of the nervous system, that there should be no gating or monitoring of stimulus input short of what occurs at higher centers. It is with this more peripheral form of screening of inputs that we shall now be concerned.

It has long been known that the concept of the "adequate stimulus" could not simply be defined as a change in enviromental energy sufficient to stimulate a receptor. For quite evidently, a stimulus could be peripherally adequate in this sense and not be "centrally" adequate at all, either in eliciting electrical activity in the cortex or in producing a verbal report of a change in experience by the subject. Indeed, the very nature of such complex receptor surfaces as the retina argues against such a simple notion of "adequate stimulus." For the reactivity of even a retinal cell at the fovea seems to be "gated" by the state of stimulation of neighboring cells. Thus, if cells A, B, and C lie next each other in that order in a row, stimulation of B suppresses the sensitivity of C. If A now be stimulated, B is suppressed and C is released or heightened in sensitivity. So even at the level of the first synapse of a sensory system, there is mediation *outward* or gating from internuncial to receptor cells that programs the nature of the input that can come into the sensory system. And to be sure, there are many phenomena in perception itself that speak for this same kind of gating. When we are fixated upon the vase in the Rubin reversible figure, the background recedes, is less surfacy, and in general seems to provide a generally less centrally adequate form of sensory input. So too with the studies of Yokoyama (87) and Chapman (19) where subjects, set to report on one of several attributes of briefly presented stimuli, accomplished their selective task with a loss of ability to discriminate on the attributes for which they had not been set. We shall propose that such phenomena are very likely mediated by a gating process which "filters" input before ever it reaches the cortex.

There is now a growing body of neurophysiological evidence that part of this screening process is relegated to peripheral levels of the nervous system—even as far out as the second synapse of specialized sensory systems. In an earlier paper I used the rather fanciful phrase that "perception acts sometimes as a welcoming committee and sometimes as a screening committee." It now appears that both these committees are closer to the entrance port than previously conceived.

Consider first the evidence of Kuffler and Hunt (50) on so simple a "reflex" as the stretch reflex of the biceps femoris muscle of the cat in an isolated spinal nerve-muscle preparation. Recall a little anatomy first. Muscle tissue contains special cells called spindles that are receptors in function, discharging with contraction or stretch of the muscle in which they are imbedded. The muscle itself is innervated by an efferent nerve trunk emerging from the ventral horn of the spinal cord and, in turn, an afferent nerve travels to the dorsal root of the spinal cord. According to the classical law of Bell and Magendie, the ventral root of the spinal cord carries efferent-motor impulses down to the muscles, while the dorsal root carries sensory impulses up to the cord. Now, it has been known for a long time that the presumed efferent nerve going to muscles carries fibers of large and of small diameter. A quarter-century ago Eccles and Sherrington showed that the ventral nerve branch supplying the biceps femoris of the cat shows a "striking division of the fibers into two diameter groups" (49), one group centering around 5μ in diameter, the other around 15 or 16μ. The large fibers are, of course, fast conductors, the small ones slow. Leksell (55) has shown that stimulation of the slow-conducting smaller fibers did not cause detectable contractions or propagated muscle impulses. When the larger and fast-conducting fibers are stimulated, the usual motor-unit twitch occurred. Kuffler and Hunt (50) state that, in the lumbosacral outflow, about $2/3$ of the fibers are of the large-diameter, fast-conduction type; the other third are of the small type that in mammalia are "ineffective in directly setting up significant muscular contraction." There has been much speculation about what these fibers are there for, and the answer is now fairly clear. It is revolutionary in its implications and brings deeply into question both the classical Bell-Magendie law and the simplistic notion of the reflex arc on which so much of American learning theory is based.

It is this. The small fibers of the presumably motor trunk go to the spindle cells and the activity in these fibers serves to modulate or gate the receptivity of these specialized sensory endings. For example, if the small-diameter fibers are firing into the muscle spindle it may speed up the amount of firing from this cell into the afferent nerve that is produced by a given amount of stretch tension on the muscle. We need not go into detail here. It suffices to note that the state of presumed motor discharge does not simply innervate the muscle; it also regulates the amount and kind of kinesthetic sensory discharge that the sensory cells in the muscle will send back to the central nervous system. Instead of thinking of a stimulus-response reflex arc, it becomes necessary even at this peripheral level to think of the efferent portion of the arc acting back on sensory receptors to change the nature of the stimulus that can get through.

Two additional pieces of evidence on gating mechanisms at higher levels of integration may be cited. Where vision is concerned, Granit (32) has recently shown that pupillary changes produced by the ciliary muscle of the eye create changes in the pattern of firing of the retina: changes in muscular state working its way back through the nervous system into the visual system and back outward to the retina. There is also evidence of gating working from the visual system backward in the opposite direction: during binocular rivalry, the nondominant eye shows a less sensitive pupillary reflex than the dominant eye.

Finally, we may cite the recent evidence of Hernandez-Péon, Scherrer, and Jouvet (38) working in Magoun's laboratory, work confirmed by analogous findings of Galambos, Sheatz, and Vernier (28) at the Walter Reed Hospital. If one stimulates the cat with auditory clicks, it is possible to record an evoked spike potential from the cochlear nucleus. Repetition of the clicks leads to a gradual diminution of the evoked potential, as if the organism were adapting. It is quite extraordinary that such adaptation should be registered as far out peripherally as the cochlear nucleus, which is, after all, only the second synapse of the VIIIth nerve. Now, if the clicks are previously used as conditioned stimuli signaling shock, the diminution of the evoked potential no longer occurs upon repetition of the clicks. Evidence that the response from the brain is not being produced by the muscular activity produced by the click as a conditioned stimulus is provided by the fact that the same kind of effects is obtained from cats with temporarily induced muscular paralysis. Further, if one take a cat whose cochlear nucleus is still firing upon click stimulation and introduce a mouse into its visual field, the clicks no longer evoke a spike potential. A fish odor or a shock to the paw has the same effect of inhibiting spike potentials at the cochlear nucleus, if these distracting stimuli occur concurrently with the click. "Distraction" or "shifting of attention" appears to work its way outward to the cochlear nucleus.[2]

---

[2] Since the above was written, evidence has been presented by Galambos indicating that efferently controlled inhibition operates as far out to the periphery as the hair cells of the organ of Corti and fibers carrying such inhibitory impulses have been traced as far centrally as the superior olivary nucleus—not very far, but a start.

Perhaps the foregoing account has been needlessly detailed on the side of neurophysiology. Yet, the interesting implications of the findings for perceptual theory make such an excursion worth while. That the nervous system accomplishes something like gating is quite clear, even without the neurophysiological evidence. The data of behavior are full of examples, and the phenomena of attention require some such mechanism to be explained. Indeed, it is quite clear that the nervous system must be capable of more selective gating than physiology has yet been able to discover. That is to say, there must be a filter somewhere in the cat's nervous system that will "pass" the squeak of the mouse in the Hernandez-Péon experiment but not the cough of the experimenter. And it is to this problem that we turn now.

I would propose that one of the mechanisms operative in regulating search behavior is some sort of gating or filtering system. In the preceding section, it was proposed that the "openness" of the first stage of cue utilization, the "selectivity" of the second stage, and the "closedness" of the third stage were probably regulated by a match-mismatch mechanism. What may be proposed here is that the degree of "openness" or "closedness" to sensory input during different phases of cue utilization is likely effected by the kind of gating processes we have been considering. How these work in intimate detail is far from known, yet the work of the last years in neurophysiology suggests that we are drawing closer to an answer.

Having considered some general properties of perception and some possible mechanisms underlying these, we turn now to some selected problems in perception better to explore the implications of what has thus far been proposed.

ON FAILURE OF READINESS

From the foregoing discussion, it is clear that veridical perception under viewing or listening conditions that are less than ideal depends upon a state of perceptual readiness that matches the probability of occurrence of events in the world of the perceiver. This is true, of course, only in a statistical sense. What is most likely to occur is not necessarily what will occur, and the perceiver whose readiness is well matched to the likelihoods of his environment may be duped. In Farquhar's handsome seventeenth-century phrase: "I cou'd be mighty foolish, and fancy myself mighty witty; reason still keeps its Throne—but it nods a little, that's all." The only assurance against the nodding of reason or probability, under the circumstances, is the maintenance of a flexibility of readiness: an ability to permit one's hypotheses about what it is that is to be perceptually encountered to be easily infirmed by sensory input. But this is a topic for later.

There appear to be two antidotes to nonveridical perception, two ways of overcoming inappropriate perceptual readinesses. The one is a re-education of the misperceiver's expectancies concerning the events he is to encounter. The other is the "constant close look." If the re-education succeeds in producing a better match between internal expectancies and external event-probabilities, the danger of misperception under hurried or substandard conditions of perceiving is lessened. But the matter of re-educating perceptual expectancies is complex. For where consequences are grave, expectancy concerning what may be encountered does not change easily, even with continued opportunity to test the environment. In this concluding section we shall consider some of the factors that contribute to states of perceptual "unreadiness" that either fail to match the likelihood of environmental events or fail to reflect the requirements of adjustment or both.

Before turning to this task, a word is in order about the "constant close look" as an antidote to inappropriate perceptual readiness. There is for every category of objects that has been established in the organism a stimulus input of sufficient duration and cue redundancy such that, if the stimulus input fits the specifications of the category, it will eventually be correctly perceived as an exemplar of that category. With enough time and enough testing of defining cues, such "best fit" perceiving can be accomplished for most but not all classes of environmental events with which the person has contact. There are some objects whose cues to identity are sufficiently equivocal so that no such resolution can be achieved, and these are mostly in the sphere of so-called interpersonal perception: perceiving the states of other people, their characteristics, intentions, etc., on the basis of external signs. And since this is the domain where misperception can have the most chronic if not the most acute consequences, it is doubtful whether a therapeutic regimen of "close looking" will aid the misperceiver much in dealing with more complex cue patterns. But the greatest difficulty rests in the fact that the cost of close looks is generally too high under the conditions of speed, risk, and limited capacity imposed upon organisms by their environment or their constitutions. The ability to use minimal cues quickly in categorizing the events of the environment is what gives the organism its lead time in adjusting to events. Pause and close inspection inevitably cut down on this precious interval for adjustment.

Inappropriate Categories. Perhaps the most primitive form of perceptual unreadiness for dealing with a particular environment is the case in which the perceiver has a set of categories that are inappropriate for adequate prediction of his environment. A frequently cited example of such a case is Bartlett's account (3) of the African visitors in London who perceived the London bobbies as especially friendly because they frequently raised their right hand, palm forward, to the approaching traffic. The cue-category inference was, of course, incorrect, and they should have identified the cue as a signal for stopping traffic. The example, however, is not particularly interesting because it is a transient phenomenon, soon corrected by instruction.

A more interesting example, because it is far less tractable, is provided by second-language learning and the learning of a new phonemic system. Why is it, we may ask, that a person can learn the structure of a new language, its form classes, morphemes, lexemes, and so on, but still retain a "foreign accent" which he cannot, after a while, distinguish from the speech flow of native speakers around him? And why is it that a person learning a new language can follow the speech of a person with his own kind of foreign accent more readily than he can follow a native speaker? The answer lies, I think, in the phenomenon of postcategorization sensory gating: once an utterance has been "understood" or decoded in appropriate categories, on the basis of some of the diacritica of the speech flow, the remaining features are assimilated or normalized or screened out. The phonemic categories that are used, moreover, are modifications of those in the first language of the speaker. Normalization is in the direction of these first-language phonemic categories. It is only by a special effort that, after having achieved adequate comprehension of the second language, one can remain sensorially "open" enough to register on the deviation between his own phonemic pattern and that of native speakers. And since there is common categorization of the "meaning" of utterances by the native speaker and the fluent foreigner, there is no built-in incentive for the foreigner to maintain a cognitively strainful regimen of attending further to speech sounds.

Lenneberg (56) has recently shown the difficulties involved in learning new modes of categorizing such continua as chromatic colors. He taught subjects various nonsense languages, explaining to them that the words were Hopi names for colors and that their task was to learn what colors they stood for. His stimulus materials were graded Munsell colors going in a circle from *brown*, through *green*, through *blue*, through *pink*, and then back to *brown*. A standardizing group was used to find the frequency distribution of color naming over the circle when the English color names mentioned above were used. Experimental groups, six in number, were then run, each being exposed to the use of the nonsense color names "as these are used by the Hopi." Then they were tested on their usage of the names. A first group was taught the nonsense words with exact correspondence to the usage found for the standardizing group on *brown*, *blue*, *green*, and *pink*. The other groups were given distorted usage training— distorted from English usage. The distortions were both in the slopes of the frequency of usage and in the points on the color continua where the highest usage frequencies fell. That is to say, the mode of a distribution in some cases would fall at a color which in English had no specific name, or fall between two English categories.

The principal results of the experiment are these. If the reference and probability relationship is the same for a nonsense language as it is for English, relearning is very rapid. The slightest deviation from this correspondence increases difficulty of learning quite markedly. It is disturbing either to shift the center of the categories on the color continuum or to change the shape of the frequency-of-calling functions, even when these are made *more* determinative (i.e., rectilinear) than they normally are. A shift in the shape of the frequency-of-calling functions is more disruptive than a shift in placement on the color continuum. What is quite striking is that a highly determinative frequency-of-calling function can be learned much more rapidly than one in which there is a gradual transition in color naming from one color to another on the color continuum.

Now, I suspect that the difficulty in learning a set of neighboring categories with a state of equivocality prevailing in the area between the "typical instances" of each category comes precisely from the tendency to normalize in the direction of the center of one category or the other. If there is a sharp transition between one color category and another, this tendency aids learning. If the transition is gradual, it hinders it. For it is noteworthy, as in the experiment of Bruner, Postman, and Rodrigues (16) that equivocal colors are readily subject to assimilation in the direction of expected value.

It is perhaps in the realm of social perception, where the problem of validating one's categorizations is severe, that one finds the most striking effects of inappropriate category systems. What is meant here by validation is the testing of the predictions inherent in a categorization. If, on the basis of a few cues of personal appearance, for example, one categorizes another person as dishonest, it is extremely difficult in most cases to check for the other cues that one would predict might be associated with instances of this category. There is either a delay or an absence of opportunity for additional cue checking. Moreover, there is also the likelihood, since cues themselves are so equivocal in such a case, that available equivocal signs will be distorted in such a manner as to confirm the first impression. It is much as in the experiments of Asch (2) and of Haire and Grunes (33) on the formation of first impressions, where later cues encountered are cognitively transformed so as to support the first impression. The reticence of the man we categorize as dishonest is seen as "caginess"; the "honest" man's reticence is seen as "integrity" and "good judgment."

It is perhaps because of this difficulty of infirming such categorial judgments that an inappropriate category system can be so hard to change. The slum boy who rises to the top in science can change his categories for coding the events of the physical world quite readily. He has much more difficulty in altering the socially related category system with which he codes the phenomena of the social world around him.

Inappropriate Accessibility Ordering. Perhaps the most noticeable "perceptual unreadiness" comes from interference with good probability learning by wishes and fears. I have in mind the kind of distorted expectancies that arise when the desirability or undesirability of events distorts the learning of their probability of occurrence. The experiments of Marks (60) and of Irwin (41), cited earlier, are simplified examples of the way in which desired outcomes increase estimates of their likelihood of occurrence. Certain more persistent general personality tendencies also operate in this sphere. It is indeed the case that some people are readier to expect and therefore quicker to perceive the least desirable event among an array of expected events, and others the most desired. This is quite clearly a learned adjustment to the events one is likely to encounter, even if it may be supported by temperamental characteristics. How such learning occurs, and why it is so resistant to correction by exposure to environmental events, are hardly clear. But one matter that becomes increasingly clear is that before we can know much about how appropriate and inappropriate perceptual readiness is produced, we shall have to know much more about how organisms learn the probabilistic structure of their environments. This is a point that Brunswik has made for some years (17), and it is one that is now being taken seriously by such students of probability learning as Bush and Mosteller (18), Bruner, Goodnow, and Austin (9), Estes (23), Galanter and Gerstenhaber (25), Hake and Hyman (34), Edwards (22), and others.

There is another important feature of learning that affects perceptual readiness. It has to do with the range of alternatives for which organisms learn to be set perceptually. Put the matter this way. It is a matter of common observation that some people are characteristically tuned for a narrow range of alternatives in the situations in which they find themselves. If the environment is banal in the sense of containing only high probability events and sequences or, more properly, events and sequences that are strongly expected, then the individual will do well and perceive with a minimum of pause for close looking. But should the environment contain unexpected events, unusual sequences, then the result will be a marked slowdown in identification and categorizing. Cue search must begin again. We speak of such people as "rigid" or "stuck." George Klein's work (46) on shifting category judgments suggests that, in general, people who are not able to shift categorization under gradually changing conditions of stimulation tend also to show what he describes as "overcontrol" on other cognitive and motivational tasks. At the other extreme is specialization upon diversity, and how such specialization is learned is equally puzzling. I can perhaps best illustrate the phenomenon by a commonly observed pattern found in subjects in tachistoscopic experiments. There are subjects who show rather high thresholds of identification generally, and who seem to be "weighing" the stimulus in terms of a wide array of interpretive categories. Jenkin (45) has recently described such perception as "rationalized," the subject describing what he sees as "like a so-and-so" rather than, as in the "projective" response, reporting it "as a so-and-so." It is as if the former type of response involved a greater cue searching of stimulus inputs for a fit to a wide range of things that it "could be." It is also very likely that premature sensory gating occurs in individuals with a tendency to be set for a minimum array of alternatives, leading them into error. The topic is one that bears closer investigation. To anyone who has had much experience in observing subjects in tachistoscopic work, it seems intuitively evident that there are large and individual differences possibly worth examining here.

We come finally to the vexing problem of "perceptual defense"—the manner in which organisms utilize their perceptual readiness to ward off events that are threatening but about which there is nothing they can do. There has been foolish and some bitter ink spilled over this topic, mostly because of a misunderstanding. The notion of perceptual defense does not require a little homuncular ego, sitting behind a Judas-eye, capable of ruling out any input that is potentially disruptive—as even so able a critic as F. H. Allport (1) seems to think. Any preset filtering device can do all that is required.

Let me begin with the general proposition that failure to perceive is most often not a *lack* of perceiving but a matter of *interference* with perceiving. Whence the interference? I would propose that the interference comes from categorizations in highly accessible categories that serve to block alternative categorizations in less accessible categories. As a highly speculative suggestion, the mechanism that seems most likely to mediate such interference is probably the broadening of category acceptance limits when a high state of readiness to perceive prevails; or, in the language of the preceding section, the range of inputs that will produce a match signal for a category increases in such a way that more accessible categories are likely to "capture" poor-fitting sensory inputs. We have already considered some evidence for increase in acceptance limits under high readiness conditions: the tendency to see a red four of clubs as either a four of diamonds or a four of clubs, with color-suit relationship rectified (14), the difficulty of spotting reversed letters imbedded in the middle of a word (69), and so on.

Let us examine some experimental evidence on the role of interference in perceptual failure. Wyatt and Campbell (86) have shown that if a subject develops a wrong hypothesis about the nature of what is being presented to him for perception at suboptimal conditions, the perception of the object in terms of its conventional identity is slowed down. This observation has been repeated in other studies as well. Postman and Bruner (68), for example, have shown that if a subject is put under pressure by the experimenter and given to believe that he is operating below standard, then he will develop premature hypotheses that interfere with correct perception of the word stimuli being presented to him. The authors refer to "perceptual recklessness" as characterizing the stressed subjects in contrast to those who operated under normal experimental conditions. It may well be, just in passing, that stress has not only the specific effect of leading to premature, interfering hypotheses but that it disrupts the normal operation of match-mismatch signaling systems in the nervous system. Unpublished studies from our own laboratory carried out by Bruner, Postman, and John (15) have shown the manner in which subjects misperceive low-probability contingencies in terms of higher probability categories. For example, a subject in the experimental group is shown tachistoscopically a picture of a discus thrower, wound up and ready to throw. In his balancing arm and placed across the front of him is a large bass viol. A control subject is shown the same picture, the exact space filled by the mass viol now being occupied by the crouching figure of a track official with his back to the camera. The brightness, shading, and area of the viol and the official are almost identical. Subjects begin by identifying the first flash of the picture as an athlete with a shadow across him. The subjects faced with the incongruous picture then go on with reasonable hypotheses—including the hypothesis of a crouching human figure, "probably an official," as one subject put it—and in the process of running through the gamut of likely hypotheses, correct perception is interfered with. It will not surprise you if I report that the threshold for the incongruous stimulus picture is markedly higher than that for the more conventional one.

Hypotheses and states of readiness may interfere with correct perception in yet another way: by creating a shifting "noise" background that masks the cues that might be used for identifying an environmental event. At the common-sense level this can best be illustrated by reference to perceptual-motor learning where kinesthetic cues are of importance. In teaching a person how to cast a fly, it is necessary for him to guide his forward delivery by feeling the gentle pressure release that occurs when the line reaches the end of its uncurving on the backcast. If your flycasting pupil is too eager to spot this cue, he will be rather tense, and his own muscular tension will mask the gentle pressure release that he must use as a signal.

A good instance is provided by the experiment of Goodnow and Pettigrew (30) at Harvard. It is concerned with the ability of subjects to perceive a regularity in a sequence of events—a very simple regularity, like the alternation left-right-left-right. . . . The experiment is done on a conventional two-armed bandit, the subject having the task of betting on whether a light will appear on the left or on the right. The task is simple. A subject is first given some pretraining, in one of four pretraining groups. One is given pretraining by learning a simple alternation pattern of payoff, another is trained to find the payoff all on one side (not easy for all subjects), a third is trained to find the pattern LLRLLR . . . , and a final group is given no pretraining. Following the pretraining and without pause, all subjects are given a series of 60 choices in which the payoff is randomly arranged, the two sides totaling out to 50 : 50. Immediately following this random phase, and again without pause, the payoffs now go into a stage of simple alternation, LRLR. . . . How long does it take the subject to perceive the regularity of the final temporal pattern? The speed of discovery depends, it turns out, upon the kinds of behavioral hypotheses a subject develops during the phase of random payoff. If he develops any regularity of response—like win-stay-lose-shift or win-shift-lose-stay—then he will quickly spot the new pattern. Pretraining on a constant one-side payoff or on single alternation both produce such regularity, and both forms of pretraining produce equally good results—the subject requiring but eight or nine exposures to the pattern introduced after the random phase to begin responding without error. No pretraining, or pretraining on the pattern LLRLLR . . . , does not produce the regularity of response required. Instead, the subject works on odd and constantly shifting hypotheses during the random period. When the single-alternation regularity is introduced, the result is a marked reduction in ability to spot the new pattern—some subjects failing to discover the pattern in 200 trials. What we are dealing with here is interference—hypotheses and responses serve to mask the regularity of events in the environment. In order for an environmental regularity to be perceived, there has to be a certain amount of steadiness in the hypotheses being employed and in the response pattern that is controlled by it. Short of this, masking and clumsy perceptual performance results.

Now what has all this to do with "perceptual defense"? The concept was introduced some years ago by Postman and myself as a description of the phenomenon of failure to perceive and/or report material known by independent test to be regarded as inimical by the subject. It was proposed (13) that there was a hierarchy of thresholds, and that an incoming stimulus could be responded to without its reaching the level of reportable experience—as in the McGinnies (58) and Lazarus and McCleary (54) studies, where autonomic response followed presentation of a potentially traumatic stimulus without the subjects being able to give a report of the nature of the stimulus. The study of Bricker and Chapanis (6) threw further light on the concept of a hierarchy of thresholds by demonstrating that, though subjects could not report spontaneously on the identity of the shock syllables used by Lazarus and McCleary, they could guess them well in excess of chance if given a restricted choice regarding what word had been presented. I would like to propose two additional factors that might lead to a failure of perception of emotionally negative material.

It is conceivable that the estimates of probability of occurrence of disvalued events are, in some individuals, reduced—essentially the obverse of what was observed in the experiments of Marks (60) and Irwin (41), where probability estimates were inflated by desirability. If accessibility is decreased by such disvaluation, then a cognitive counterpart of what is clinically called "repression" can be posited. It is known, however, that not everyone shows this tendency to be unready for objects and events that are anxiety-arousing. Others seem to *inflate* their estimate of the likelihood of occurrence of inimical events. Certainly one finds clinical evidence for such a pattern among anxiety neurotics. In an early paper, Postman and Bruner (68) described two types of performance with respect to known anxiety-producing stimuli, defense and vigilance, the former a heightened threshold of identification for such stimuli, the latter a lowered threshold. In a carefully designed experiment contrasting the performance of clinically diagnosed "intellectualizers" and "repressors," Lazarus, Eriksen, and Fonda (53) have shown that the former group indeed are faster in recognizing negatively charged material than they are in recognizing neutral material, while the latter show the reverse tendency. Again, I find it necessary to revert to a point made earlier. I do not think that we are going to get much further ahead in understanding hyper- and hyporeadiness for encountering anxiety-evoking stimuli short of doing studies of the learning of environmental probabilities for sequences containing noxious and beneficial events.

One additional mechanism may be operative in lowering or generally in altering readiness to perceive material that in some way may be threatening. I hesitate to speak of it in detail, since it is of such a speculative order, and do so only because some experiments suggest themselves. It is this. Conceivably, categories for classes of objects that are pain-arousing are set up with narrow acceptance limits for stimulus inputs related to them. That is to say, what we speak of as "repression" may be the establishment of very narrow category limits that prevent the evocation of match signals for inputs that do not fit category specifications very precisely. I am mindful that as far as autonomic reactivity is concerned potentially traumatic stimuli work in quite the reverse direction. If anything, a wide range of objects, appropriate and inappropriate, arouse autonomic reactions, without leading to verbalizable report concerning the categorial identity of the eliciting objects. Yet it is conceivable that with respect to one kind of threshold (autonomic) the acceptance limits are broad, and with respect to another (reportable awareness) very narrow. I think it would be worth while in any case to investigate the acceptance limits of inimical stimulus inputs by altering the characteristics of objects so that, in essence, one gets a generalization gradient for recognition. My guess is that the gradient will be much steeper for anxiety-arousing stimuli than for neutral ones. All that remains is to do the experiment.

Finally, it may also be the case that category accessibility reflects the instrumental relevance of the environmental events they represent. There is evidence that the recognition threshold for noxious objects about which one can do something is lower than normal, whereas for ones about which nothing instrumental can be done, the threshold is higher. That is to say, words that signal a shock that can be avoided show lowered thresholds, words signaling unavoidable shock show a threshold rise. One may well speculate whether the instrumental relevance of objects is not a controlling factor in guiding the kind of search behavior that affects category accessibility.

The problem needs much more thorough investigation than it has received.

We have touched on various conditions that might lead a person to be inappropriately set for the events he must perceive easily and quickly in his environment. Many other studies could be mentioned. But the intention has not been to review the rather sprawling literature in the field, but to propose some possible mechanism affecting readiness so that research might be given a clearer theoretical direction.

CONCLUSIONS

We have been concerned in these pages with a general view of perception that depends upon the construction of a set of organized categories in terms of which stimulus inputs may be sorted, given identity, and given more elaborated, connotative meaning. Veridical perception, it has been urged, depends upon the construction of such category systems, categories built upon the inference of identity from cues or signs. Identity, in fine, represents the range of inferences about properties, uses, and consequences that can be predicted from the presence of certain criterial cues.

Perceptual readiness refers to the relative accessibility of categories to afferent stimulus inputs. The more accessible a category, the less the stimulus input required for it to be sorted in terms of the category, given a degree of match between the characteristics of the input and the specifications of the category. In rough form, there appear to be two general determinants of category accessibility. One of them is the likelihood of occurrence of events learned by the person in the course of dealing with the world of objects and events and the redundant sequences in which these are imbedded. If you will, the person builds a model of the likelihood of events, a form of probability learning only now beginning to be understood. Again in rough terms, one can think of this activity as achieving a minimization of surprise for the organism. A second determinant of accessibility is the requirements of search dictated by need states and the need to carry out habitual enterprises such as walking, reading, or whatever it is that makes up the round of daily, habitual life.

Failure to achieve a state of perceptual readiness that matches the probability of events in one's world can be dealt with in one of two ways: either by the relearning of categories and expectancies, or by constant close inspection of events and objects. Where the latter alternative must be used, an organism is put in the position of losing his lead time for adjusting quickly and smoothly to events under varying conditions of time pressure, risk, and limited capacity. Readiness in the sense that we are using it is not a luxury, but a necessity for smooth adjustment.

The processes involved in "sorting" sensory inputs to appropriate categories involve cue utilization, varying from sensorially "open" cue searching under relative uncertainty, to selective search for confirming cues under partial certainty, to sensory "gating" and distortion when an input has been categorized beyond a certain level of certainty.

Four kinds of mechanisms are proposed to deal with known phenomena of perceptual categorizing and differential perceptual readiness: *grouping and integration, access ordering, match-mismatch signal utilization,* and *gating.* The psychological evidence leading one to infer such processes was examined and possible neurological analogues were considered. The processes are conceived of as mediators of categorizing and its forms of connectivity, the phenomena of differential threshold levels for various environmental events, the guidance of cue search behavior, and lastly, the phenomena of sensory inhibition and "filtering."

Finally, we have considered some of the ways in which failure of perceptual readiness comes about—first, through a failure to learn appropriate categories for sorting the environment and for following its sequences, and second, through a process of interference whereby more accessible categories with wide acceptance limits serve to mask or prevent the use of less accessible categories for the coding of stimulus inputs. The concept of "perceptual defense" may be reexamined in the light of these notions.

In conclusion, it seems appropriate to say that the ten years of the so-called New Look in perception research seem to be coming to a close with much empirical work accomplished—a great deal of it demonstrational, to be sure, but with a promise of a second ten years in which hypotheses will be more rigorously formulated and, conceivably, neural mechanisms postulated, if not discovered. The prospects are anything but discouraging.

REFERENCES

1. ALLPORT, F. H. *Theories of perception and the concept of structure.* New York: Wiley, 1955.
2. ASCH, S. E. *Social psychology.* New York: Prentice-Hall, 1952.
3. BARTLETT, F. C. *Remembering.* Cambridge, England: Cambridge Univer. Press, 1932.
4. BINDER, A. A statistical model for the process of visual recognition. *Psychol. Rev.,* 1955, **62**, 119-129.
5. BITTERMAN, M. E., and KNIFFIN, C. W. Manifest anxiety and "perceptual defense." *J. abnorm. soc. Psychol.,* 1953, **48**, 248-252.
6. BRICKER, P. D., and CHAPANIS, A. Do incorrectly perceived tachistoscopic stimuli convey some information? *Psychol. Rev.,* 1953, **60**, 181-188.
7. BROWN, D. R. Stimulus similarity and the anchoring of subjective scales. *Amer. J. Psychol.,* 1953, **66**, 199-214.
8. BRUNER, J. S. Personality dynamics and the process of perceiving. In R. R. Blake and G. V. Ramsey (Eds.), *Perception: an approach to personality.* New York: Ronald, 1951, pp. 121-147.
9. BRUNER, J. S., GOODNOW, J. J., and AUSTIN, G. A. *A study of thinking.* New York: Wiley, 1956.
10. BRUNER, J. S., MILLER, G. A., and ZIMMERMAN, C. Discriminative skill and discriminative matching in perceptual recognition. *J. exp. Psychol.,* 1955, **49**, 187-192.
11. BRUNER, J. S., and MINTURN, A. L. Perceptual identification and perceptual organization. *J. gen. Psychol.,* 1955, **53**, 21-28.
12. BRUNER, J. S., and POSTMAN, L. Emotional selectivity in perception and reaction. *J. Pers.,* 1947, **16**, 69-77.
13. BRUNER, J. S., and POSTMAN, L. Perception, cognition, and behavior. *J. Pers.,* 1949, **18**, 14-31.
14. BRUNER, J. S., and POSTMAN, L. On the perception of incongruity: a paradigm. *J. Pers.,* 1949, **18**, 206-223.
15. BRUNER, J. S., POSTMAN, L., and JOHN, W. Normalization of incongruity. Research memorandum. Cognition Project, Harvard Univer., 1949.
16. BRUNER, J. S., POSTMAN, L., and RODRIGUES, J. Expectation and the perception of color. *Amer. J. Psychol.,* 1951, **64**, 216-227.
17. BRUNSWIK, E. *Systematic and representative design of psychological experiments.* Berkeley: Univer. of California Press, 1949.
18. BUSH, R. R., and MOSTELLER, C. F. *Stochastic models for learning.* New York: Wiley, 1955.
19. CHAPMAN, D. W. Relative effects of determinate and indeterminate Aufgaben. *Amer. J. Psychol.,* 1932, **44**, 163-174.

20. Cowen, E. L., and Beier, E. G. The influence of "threat expectancy" on perception. *J. Pers.*, 1951, **19**, 85-94.
21. Eccles, J. C. *The neurophysiological basis of mind.* Oxford: Oxford Univer. Press, 1953.
22. Edwards, W. The theory of decision making. *Psychol. Bull.*, 1954, **51**, 380-417.
23. Estes, W. K. Individual behavior in uncertain situations: an interpretation in terms of statistical association theory. In R. M. Thrall, C. H. Coombs, and R. L. Davis (Eds.), *Decision processes.* New York: Wiley, 1954; pp. 127-137.
24. Fry, D. P., and Denes, P. Mechanical speech recognition. In W. Jackson (Ed.), *Communication theory.* New York: Academic Press, 1953.
25. Galanter, E., and Gerstenhaber, M. On thought: extrinsic theory of insight. *Amer. Psychologist*, 1955, **10**, 465.
26. Gibson, J. J. *The perception of the visual world.* Boston: Houghton Mifflin, 1950.
27. Gibson, J. J., and Gibson, E. J. Perceptual learning: differentiation or enrichment? *Psychol. Rev.*, 1955, **62**, 32-41.
28. Galambos, R., Sheatz, G., and Vernier, V. G. Electrophysiological correlates of a conditioned response in cats. *Science*, 1956, **123**, 376-377.
29. Goodnow, J. J. Determinants of choice-distribution in two-choice situations. *Amer. J. Psychol.*, 1955, **68**, 106-116.
30. Goodnow, J. J., and Pettigrew, T. E. Some difficulties in learning a simple pattern of events. Paper presented at annual meeting of the East. Psychol. Ass., Atlantic City, March, 1956.
31. Graham, C. H. Perception and behavior. Presidential address to the East. Psychol. Ass., Atlantic City, March, 1956.
32. Granit, R. *Receptors and sensory perception.* New Haven: Yale Univer. Press, 1955.
33. Haire, M., and Grunes, W. F. Perceptual defenses: processes protecting an organized perception of another personality. *Hum. Relat.*, 1950, **3**, 403-412.
34. Hake, H. W., and Hyman, R. Perception of the statistical structure of a random series of binary symbols. *J. exp. Psychol.*, 1953, **45**, 64-74.
35. Harper, R. S., and Boring, E. G. Cues. *Amer. J. Psychol.*, 1948, **61**, 119-123.
36. Hebb, D. O. *The organization of behavior.* New York: Wiley, 1949.
37. Helson, H. Adaptation-level as a basis for a quantitative theory of frames of reference. *Psychol. Rev.*, 1948, **55**, 297-313.
38. Hernandez-Péon, R., Scherrer, R. H., and Jouvet, M. Modification

of electric activity in the cochlear nucleus during "attention" in unanesthetized cats. *Science*, 1956, **123**, 331-332.

39. HORNBOSTEL, E. M. VON. Unity of the senses. *Psyche*, 1926, **7**, 83-89.
40. HOWES, D. On the interpretation of word frequency as a variable affecting speed of recognition. *J. exp. Psychol.*, 1954, **48**, 106-112.
41. IRWIN, F. W. Stated expectations as functions of probability and desirability of outcomes. *J. Pers.*, 1953, **21**, 329-335.
42. ITTLESON, W. H. *The Ames demonstrations in perception.* Princeton, N. J.: Princeton Univer. Press, 1952.
43. JARRETT, J. Strategies in risk-taking situations. Unpublished doctors dissertation, Harvard Univer. Library, 1951.
44. JARVIK, M. E. Probability learning and a negative recency effect in the serial anticipation of alternative symbols. *J. exp. Psychol.*, 1951, **41**, 291-297.
45. JENKIN, N. Two types of perceptual experience. *J. clin. Psychol.*, 1956, **12**, 44-49.
46. KLEIN, G. S. The personal world through perception. In R. R. Blake and G. V. Ramsey (Eds.), *Perception: an approach to personality.* New York: Ronald, 1951, pp. 328-355.
47. KOHLER, I. Rehabituation in perception. Published separately in three parts, in German, in *Die Pyramide*, 1953, Heft 5, 6, and 7 (Austria). Translated by Henry Gleitman and edited by J. J. Gibson. Privately circulated by the editor.
48. KÖHLER, W. *Dynamics in psychology.* New York: Liveright, 1940.
49. KUFFLER, S. W., HUNT, C. C., and QUILLIAN, J. P. Function of medullated small-nerve fibers in mammalian ventral roots: efferent muscle spindle innervation. *J. Neurophysiol.*, 1951, **14**, 29-54.
50. KUFFLER, S. W., and HUNT, C. C. The mammalian small nerve fibers: a system for efferent nervous regulation of muscle spindle discharge. *Proc. Assoc. Res. Nerv. Ment. Dis.*, 1952, Vol. 30.
51. LASHLEY, K. S. Experimental analysis of instinctive behavior. *Psychol. Rev.*, 1938, **45**, 445-471.
52. LASHLEY, K. S. In search of the engram. *Symp. Soc. Exp. Biol.*, 1950, **4**, 454-482.
53. LAZARUS, R. S., ERIKSEN, C. W., and FONDA, C. P. Personality dynamics and auditory perceptual recognition. *J. Pers.*, 1951, **19**, 471-482.
54. LAZARUS, R. S., and MCCLEARY, R. A. Autonomic discrimination without awareness: a study of subception. *Psychol. Rev.*, 1951, **58**, 113-122.
55. LEKSELL, L. The action potential and excitatory effects of the small ventral root fibers to skeletal muscles. *Acta Physiol. Scand.*, 1945, **10**, Suppl. 31.

56. LENNEBERG, E. H. An empirical investigation into the relationship between language and cognition. Unpublished doctoral dissertation, Harvard Univer. Library, 1956.

57. LORENTE DE NO, R. Transmission of impulses through cranial motor nuclei. *J. Neurophysiol.*, 1939, **2**, 402-464.

58. McGINNIES, E. Emotionality and perceptual defense. *Psychol. Rev.*, 1949, **56**, 244-251.

59. MACKAY, D. M. Toward an information-flow model of human behavior. *Brit. J. Psychol.*, 1956, **47**, 30-43.

60. MARKS, R. W. The effect of probability, desirability, and "privilege" on the state of expectations of children. *J. Pers.*, 1951, **19**, 332-351.

61. MILLER, G. A., BRUNER, J. S., and POSTMAN, L. Familiarity of letter sequences and tachistoscopic identification. *J. gen. Psychol.*, 1954, **50**, 129-139.

62. MILLER, G. A., HEISE, G. A., and LICHTEN, W. The intelligibility of speech as a function of the context of the test materials. *J. exp. Psychol.*, 1951, **41**, 329-335.

63. PEIRCE, C. S. How to make our ideas clear. *Popular Sci. Mon.*, 1878, **12**, 286-302.

64. PENFIELD, W. Memory mechanisms. *Arch. Neurol. & Psychiat.*, 1952, **67**, 178-191.

65. PIAGET, J. *Play, dreams, and imitation in childhood.* New York: Norton, 1951.

66. PRATT, C. C. The role of past experience in visual perception. *J. Psychol.*, 1950, **30**, 85-107.

67. PRENTICE, W. C. H. Paper read at the Symposium on Conceptual Trends in Psychology, at Amer. Psychol. Ass., New York, September, 1954.

68. POSTMAN, L., and BRUNER, J. S. Perception under stress. *Psychol. Rev.*, 1948, **55**, 314-323.

69. POSTMAN, L., BRUNER, J. S., and WALK, R. D. The perception of error. *Brit. J. Psychol.*, 1951, **42**, 1-10.

70. POSTMAN, L., and CRUTCHFIELD, R. S. The interaction of need, set, and stimulus structure in a cognitive task. *Amer. J. Psychol.*, 1952, **65**, 196-217.

71. SELFRIDGE, O. Pattern recognition and learning. Memorandum of Lincoln Laboratory, Massachusetts Institute of Technology, 1955.

72. SOLOMON, R. L., and POSTMAN, L. Frequency of usage as a determinant of recognition thresholds for words. *J. exp. Psychol.*, 1952, **43**, 195-201.

73. SMITH, J. W., and KLEIN, G. S. Cognitive control in serial behavior patterns. Dittoed manuscript, available from author, 1951.

74. STEVENS, S. S. Chapter I in S. S. Stevens (Ed.), *Handbook of experimental psychology*. New York: Wiley, 1951.

75. STEVENS, S. S. The direct estimation of sensory magnitudes—loudness. *Amer. J. Psychol.*, 1956, **69**, 1-25.

76. TANNER, W. P., JR., and SWETS, J. A. A decision-making theory of human detection. *Psychol. Rev.*, 1954, **61**, 401-409.

77. TINBERGEN, N. *The study of instinct*. Oxford: Oxford Univer. Press, 1951.

78. TITCHENER, E. B. *A beginner's psychology*. New York: Macmillan, 1916.

79. TOLMAN, E. C. Discussion. *J. Pers.*, 1949, **18**, 48-50.

80. UTTLEY, A. M. *The conditional probability of signals in the nervous system*. Radar Research Establ., British Ministry of Supply, Feb., 1955.

81. VERNON, M. D. *A further study of visual perception*. Cambridge, England: Cambridge Univer. Press, 1952.

82. VOLKMANN, J. In M. Sherif and J. H. Rohrer (Eds.), *Social psychology at the crossroads*. New York: Harpers, 1951.

83. WALLACH, H. Some considerations concerning the relation between perception and cognition. *J. Pers.*, 1949, **18**, 6-13.

84. WHITE, M. *The age of analysis*. New York: New American Library, 1955.

85. WOODWORTH, R. S. Reenforcement of perception. *Amer. J. Psychol.*, 1947, **60**, 119-124.

86. WYATT, D. F., and CAMPBELL, D. T. On the liability of stereotype or hypothesis. *J. abnorm. soc. Psychol.*, 1951, **46**, 496-500.

87. YOKOYAMA, J. Reported in E. G. Boring, *A history of experimental psychology*. (2nd Ed.) New York: Appleton-Century, 1954.

88. YOUNG, J. Z. *Doubt and certainty in science*. Oxford: Oxford Univer. Press, 1951.

Index*